FIFTY
YEARS
of GREAT
WRITING

SPORTS ILLUSTRATED

1954 - 2004

EDITED BY ROB FLEDER

SPORTS ILLUSTRATED BOOKS

I

THE
PLAYERS

The Boxer and The Blonde

BY FRANK DEFORD

This is the story of Billy Conn, the pride of Pittsburgh and the light-heavyweight champion of the world, who won the girl he loved but lost the best fight ever.

THE BOXER AND THE BLONDE ARE TOGETHER, DOWNSTAIRS in the club cellar. At some point, club cellars went out, and they became family rooms instead. This is, however, very definitely a club cellar. Why, the grandchildren of the boxer and the blonde could sleep soundly upstairs, clear through the big Christmas party they gave, when everybody came and stayed late and loud down here. The boxer and the blonde are sitting next to each other, laughing about the old times, about when they fell hopelessly in love almost half a century ago in New Jersey, at the beach. *Down the Jersey Shore* is the way everyone in Pennsylvania says it. This club cellar is in Pittsburgh.

The boxer is going on 67, except in *The Ring* record book, where he is going on 68. But he has all his marbles; and he has his looks (except for the fighter's mashed nose); and he has the blonde; and they have the same house, the one with the club cellar, that they bought in the summer of 1941. A great deal of this is about that bright ripe summer, the last one before the forlorn simplicity of a Depression was buried in the thick-braided rubble of blood and Spam. What a fight the boxer had that June! It might have been the best in the history of the ring. Certainly, it was the most dramatic, alltime, any way you look at it. The boxer lost, though. Probably he would have won, except for the blonde—whom he loved so much, and wanted so much to make proud of him. And later, it was the blonde's old man, the boxer's father-in-law (if you can believe this), who cost him a rematch for the heavyweight championship of the world. Those were some kind of times.

The boxer and the blonde laugh again, together, remembering how they fell in love. "Actually, you sort of forced me into it," she says.

"I did you a favor," he snaps back, smirking at his comeback. After a couple of belts, he has been known to confess that although he fought 21 times against world champions, he has never yet won a decision over the blonde—never yet, as they say in boxing, *outpointed* her. But you can sure see why he keeps on trying. He still has his looks? Hey, you should see her. The blonde is past 60 now, and she's still cute as a button. Not merely beautiful, you understand, but schoolgirl cute, just like she was when the boxer first flirted with her down the Jersey shore. There is a picture of them on the wall. Pictures cover the walls of the club cellar. This particular picture was featured in a magazine, the boxer and the blonde running, hand in hand, out of the surf. Never in your life did you see two better-looking kids. She was Miss Ocean City, and Alfred Lunt called him "a Celtic god," and Hollywood had a part for him that Errol Flynn himself wound up with after the boxer said no thanks and went back to Pittsburgh.

The other pictures on the walls of the club cellar are mostly of fighters. Posed. Weighing in. Toe-to-toe. Bandaged. And ex-fighters. Mostly in Las Vegas, it seems, the poor bastards. And celebrities. Sinatra, Hope, Bishop Sheen. Politicians. Various Kennedys. Mayor Daley. President Reagan. Vice President Bush. More fighters. Joe Louis, whom the boxer loved so much, is in a lot of the pictures, but the largest single photograph belongs to Harry Greb, the Pittsburgh Windmill, the middleweight champeen, the only man ever to beat Gene Tunney. When the boxer's mother died that summer of '41, one of the things that mattered most then was to get her the closest possible plot in Calvary Cemetery to where Harry Greb already lay in peace.

But then, down on the far wall, around the corner from Greb, behind the bar, there's another big photograph, and it's altogether different from the others, because this one is a horizontal. Boxing pictures are either square, like the ring itself, or vertical, the fighter standing tall, fists cocked high. If you see a horizontal, it's almost surely not a boxing photograph but, more than likely, a team picture, all the players spread out in rows. And sure enough, the photograph on the far wall is of the 1917 New York Giants, winners of the National League pennant, and there in the middle of the back row, with a cocky grin hung on his face, is Greenfield Jimmy Smith. The story really starts with him. He was the one who introduced the boxer and the blonde down the Jersey shore.

The book on Greenfield Jimmy Smith as a ballplayer was good mouth, no hit

(.219 lifetime). His major talent earned him another nickname up in the bigs, Serpent Tongue. Muggsy McGraw, the Giants' manager, kept Smith around pretty much as a bench jockey. But after the Giants lost to the White Sox in the '17 Series, four games to two, McGraw traded him. That broke Smith's heart. He loved McGraw. They were both tough cookies.

"Ah, rub it with a brick," Greenfield Jimmy would say whenever anybody complained of an injury. He was just a little guy, maybe 5' 9", a banty rooster, but one time he went over to the Dodger dugout and yelled, "All right, you so-and-sos, I'll fight you one at a time or in groups of five." Not a single Dodger took up the offer.

Greenfield Jimmy's grandchildren remember a day in Jimmy's 60s, when he took them out for a drive. A truck got behind him coming up Forbes Avenue and sat on his tail, and Greenfield Jimmy slowed down. The truck driver rested on his horn until finally the grandfather pulled his car over and got out. Livid, the big truck driver came over and started hollering down at the little old guy. Softly, Greenfield Jimmy cut in, "Oh, I'm so sorry, but my neighbor over there saw the whole thing."

"What neighbor?" the big truck driver asked, twisting his head to catch a glimpse of this witness. That was his mistake. As soon as he turned to the side, Greenfield Jimmy reared back and popped him flush on the chin. The old man wasn't anything but a banjo hitter on the diamond, but he could sure slug off it.

Greenfield Jimmy played in the bigs as late as '22, but by then the 18th Amendment was the law of the land, and he was discovering that his playing baseball was getting in the way of a more lucrative new career, which was providing alcoholic beverages to those who desired them, notwithstanding their legal unavailability. Sometimes, as decades later he confided to his grandchildren, he would even carry the hooch about in the big trunks that held the team's uniforms and equipment.

Back in Pittsburgh, where he hailed from—the Greenfield section, as you might imagine—Greenfield Jimmy Smith became a man of substance and power. He consorted with everybody, priests and pugs and politicians alike. He ran some speakeasies and, ultimately, The Bachelor's Club, which was the classiest joint in town—a "city club," so-called, as opposed to the numerous neighborhood clubs, which would let in anybody with a couple of bucks annual dues and the particularly correct European heritage. But The Bachelor's Club was a plush place, and some of Pittsburgh's finest made a great deal of walking-around money by overlooking its existence. Even after repeal, The Bachelor's Club offered games of chance for those so inclined. It helped that, like so much of the Steel City constabulary, Greenfield Jimmy Smith was Irish.

The Bachelor's Club was located in the East Liberty section of Pittsburgh—or

'Sliberty, as it's pronounced in the slurred argot of the community. In a city of neighborhoods, before automobiles begat suburbs, 'Sliberty was known as a very busy place; people came to shop there. For action, though, it was probably not the match of Oakland, a couple of miles away. Most neighborhoods in Pittsburgh were parochial, with a single ethnic legacy, but Oakland had more of a mix and stronger outside influences as well, inasmuch as it embraced the University of Pittsburgh and Forbes Field (where the Pirates played), and the Duquesne Gardens, which has got to be the only boxing arena that was ever set right across the street from a cathedral, which, in this particular case, was St. Paul's.

The Gardens was an old converted carbarn—which, once upon a time, was a place where streetcars were kept when they were sleeping. Pittsburgh was strictly a streetcar town. That was how everybody got to the steel mills. Only in Pittsburgh, nobody ever said "carbarn." They said "coreborn." In Pittsburgh, even now, they don't knew how to correctly pronounce any of the vowels and several of the consonants. Even more than the a's, they mess up the o's. A cawledge, for example, is what Pitt is; a dawler is legal tender; and, at that time, the most popular bawxer at the Duquesne Gardens was a skinny Irish contender from 'Sliberty named Billy Cawn, which, despite the way everybody said it, was, curiously, spelled Conn.

Greenfield Jimmy took a real liking to the kid. They had a lot in common. Somebody asked Conn once if he had learned to fight in the streets; no, he replied, it was a long time before be got to the streets from the alleys. Early in '39, after 50 fights around Pittsburgh and West Virginia and two in San Francisco, Conn finally got a shot in New York. "Uncle" Mike Jacobs, the promoter, brought him to Gotham in order to get beat up by a popular Italian fighter, a bellhop out of San Francisco named Freddie Apostoli. Only it was Conn who beat Apostoli in 10, and then, in a rematch a month later, with 19,000 fans packed to the rafters of the old Madison Square Garden on Eighth Avenue, he beat Apostoli in a 15-round bloodbath. As much as possible, then, the idea was to match the ethnic groups, so after Conn had beat the Italian twice, Uncle Mike sent him up against a Jew named Solly Krieger. And when the Irisher beat Krieger in 12, he was signed to fight Melio Bettina for the world light-heavyweight title the following July.

Suddenly, Conn was the hottest thing in the ring. "Matinee-idol looks," they all said, curly-haired, quick with a quip, full of fun, free, white and (almost) 21. Money was burning a hole in his pocket, and the dames were chasing him. Right at the time, he took up with an older woman, a divorcée, and remember, this was back in the days when divorcée meant Look Out. He left her for a couple of days and came to Greenfield Jimmy's summer place down the Jersey shore in a Cadillac driven by a chauffeur.

Billy Conn was the cat's meow, and Smith was anxious for his wife and kids to meet him, too. Greenfield Jimmy wasn't just a provider, you understand, but also a great family man, and, they said, he never missed Mass. He thought it was really swell when Billy volunteered to take Mary Louise, his little daughter, out to dinner that evening. She was only 15, and for her to be able to go over to Somers Point and have a meal out with Sweet William, the Flower of the Monongahela, would sure be something she could tell the other girls back at Our Lady of Mercy Academy.

How would Greenfield Jimmy ever know that before the evening was over, Billy Conn would turn to the pretty little 15-year-old kid and say right out, "I'm going to marry you."

Mary Louise managed to stammer back, "You're crazy." She remembered what her father had advised her—that all prizefighters were punchy—only it surprised her that one so young and good-looking could be that way. Only, of course, he wasn't punchy. He had just fallen for the kid doll like a ton of bricks.

So now you see: It is Billy Conn who is the boxer in the club cellar and Mary Louise who is the blonde. By the time Greenfield Jimmy Smith (who prided himself on knowing everything) found out what was going on right under his nose, it was too late.

The Conn house is in the Squirrel Hill district. It has long been mostly a Jewish area, but the house was a good bargain at $17,500 when Billy bought it 44 years ago, and he wanted to stay in the city. Billy is a city guy, a Pittsburgh guy. Billy says, "Pittsburgh is the town you can't wait to leave, and the town you can't wait to get back to." They loved him in Gotham, and they brought him to Tinseltown to play the title role in *The Pittsburgh Kid*, and later he spent a couple of years in Vegas, working the Stardust's lounge as a greeter, like Joe Louis at the Dunes down the Strip. His son Timmy remembers the time a high roller gave the boxer $9,000, just for standing around and being Billy Conn. But soon the boxer grew tired of that act and came back to the house in Squirrel Hill where, in the vernacular, he "loafs with" old pals. Like Joey Diven, who was recognized as the World's Greatest Street Fighter.

Pittsburgh may be a metropolitan area of better than two million souls, but it still has the sense of a small town. "Everybody's closely knitted," Diven explains. "A guy hits a guy in 'Sliberty, everybody knows about it right away, all over." Or it's like this: One time the boxer was trying to get a patronage job with the county for a guy he loafs with. But everybody was onto the guy's act. "Billy," the politician said, "I'd like to help you. I really would. But everybody knows, he just don't ever come to work."

Conn considered that fact. "Look at it this way," he said at last. "Do you want *him* around?" The guy got the job.

Pittsburgh, of course, like everyplace else, has changed . . . only more so. The mills are closed, the skies are clear and Rand McNally has decreed that it is the very best place to live in the United States. Oakland is just another cawledge town; the warm saloons of Forbes Avenue have become fast-food "outlets." Where Forbes Field once stood is Pitt's Graduate School of Business, and in place of Duquesne Gardens is an apartment house.

It was so different when Conn was growing up. Then it was the best of capitalism, it was the worst of capitalism. The steel came in after the Civil War—Bessemer and his blasts—and then came the immigrants to do the hard, dirty work of making ore into endless rolls of metal. Then the skies were so black with smoke that the office workers had to change their white shirts by lunchtime, and the streetlights seldom went off during the day, emitting an eerie glow that turned downtown Pittsburgh into a stygian nightmare. At the time Conn was a kid, taking up space at Sacred Heart School, H.L. Mencken wrote of Pittsburgh that it was "so dreadfully hideous, so intolerably bleak and forlorn that it reduced the whole aspiration of a man to a macabre and depressing joke."

The people coughed and wheezed, and those who eschewed the respiratory nostrums advertised daily in the newspapers would, instead, repair to the taprooms of Pittsburgh, there to try and cut the grime and soot that had collected in their dusty throats. The Steel City was also known as "the wettest spot in the United States," and even at seven in the morning the bars would be packed three-deep, as the night-shift workers headed home in the gloom of another graying dawn, pausing to toss down the favored local boilermaker—a shot of Imperial whiskey chased by an Iron City beer. An Iron and an Imp.

And then another. Can't expect someone to fly on one wing.

Conn's father, Billy Sr., was such a man. He toiled at Westinghouse for 40 years. Eventually, Billy would come to call his old man Westinghouse instead of Dad. But even in the worst of the Depression, Billy Sr. kept his job as a steam fitter, and he was proud of it, and one day he took his oldest boy down to the plant, and he pointed to it and said, "Here's where you're gonna work, son."

Billy Jr. was aghast. "That scared the s--- out of me," he says. Shortly thereafter he began to apprentice as a prizefighter, and when he got to New York and began to charm the press, he could honestly boast that his greatest achievement in life was never having worked a day.

The mills meant work, but it was a cruel living, and even so recently as the time when Conn was growing up, two-thirds of the work force in Pittsburgh was foreign-born. "People think you gotta be nuts to be a fighter," he says now.

Well?

"Yeah, they're right. I was nuts. But it beats working in those mills."

The immigrants shipped in from Europe to work in the mills mostly stayed with their own—the Galway Irish on the North Side, the Italians in the Bloomfield section, the Poles and Balkans on the South Side, the Irish in 'Sliberty, the Germans on Troy Hill. Harry Greb was German, but his mother was Irish, which mattered at the gate. Promoters liked Irishers. A good little lightweight named Harry Pitler, Jewish boy, brother of Jake Pitler, who would play for the Pirates and later become a Brooklyn Dodger coach, took the Irish handle of Johnny Ray to fight under. Jawnie Ray, one of Erin's own.

Everybody fought some in Pittsburgh. It was a regular activity, like dancing or drinking. It wasn't just that the men were tough and the skies were mean; it was also a way of representing your parish or your people. It wasn't just that Mr. Art Rooney, promoter, or Mr. Jake Mintz, matchmaker, would pit an Irishman against a Jew or a Pole vs. an Italian, or bring in a colored boy the white crowds could root against at Duquesne Gardens. No, it was every mother's son scuffling, on the streets or at the bar rail. It was a way of life. It was also cheap entertainment.

Greenfield Jimmy Smith, as we know, enjoyed fighting all his life. So did Billy Conn Sr., Westinghouse. Nearing 50, he was arrested and fined a five-spot for street fighting only a few weeks before his son fought for the heavyweight title. Just for kicks, Westinghouse used to fight Billy all the time. When Westinghouse came to New York to watch his boy in the ring one time, Billy told the press, "My old man is a fighting mick. Give him a day or two here, and he'll find some guys to slug it out with."

Billy fought even more with his younger brother Jackie, who was an absolutely terrific street fighter. One time Jimmy Cannon wrote that "if the ring in Madison Square Garden were made of cobblestones," it would be Jackie Conn, not Billy, who would be the champion of the world. A night or so after Cannon's tribute appeared in the paper, Jackie came strolling into Toots Shor's. He was dressed to the nines, as usual. Jackie fancied himself a fashion plate, and he regularly rifled his brother's wardrobe. So Jackie took a prominent seat at the bar, and he was sitting there, accepting compliments and what have you from the other patrons, when a stranger came over to him and asked if he were Jackie Conn, the street-fighting champion of the world.

Jackie puffed up and replied that indeed he was, whereupon, the stranger coldcocked him, sending Jackie clattering to the floor of Toots Shor's Saloon. "Now I'm the champion," the guy said.

Still, everybody says that Joey Diven was the best street fighter who ever lived. There are stories that he would, for amusement, take on and beat up the entire Pitt football team. Joey is a decade younger than Billy, in his 50s now, working as an assistant to the Allegheny County commissioner. He is a big, red-faced Irishman. That's unusual because most ace street fighters are little guys. Does Billy Martin come to mind? Big guys grow up figuring nobody will challenge them, so they don't learn how to fight. Big guys break up fights. Little guys are the ones who learn to fight because they figure they had better. Billy always told his three sons, "Don't fight on the streets, because you'll only find out who's good when it's too late."

But Joey Diven was good and big. So first the other Irish pretenders in the neighborhood—the champion of this street or that bar—would come by to find him at the Oakland Cafe, where he loafed, and when he was done beating all those comers, the champs from the other neighborhoods would come over and insult him, so as to get into an interethnic fight.

Insults were automatic. People routinely referred to one another, face-to-face, with the racial epithets we find so offensive today. For fighting, it was the dagos and the Polacks, the micks and the jigs, and so forth. Sticks and stones. Before a fight with Gus Dorazio, when Dorazio was carrying on at the weigh-in about what color trunks he would wear, Conn cut the argument short by snapping, "Listen, dago, all you're going to need is a catcher's mitt and a chest protector." It was late in Conn's career before be took to using a mouthpiece, because, like his hero Greb, he got a kick out of insulting the people he fought.

On the street, stereotypes prevailed all the more. Usually that meant that everybody (your own group included) was dim-witted, everybody else practiced poor hygiene, everybody else's women were trash, and everybody but the Jews drank too much and had the most fun. Were the Irish the best fighters? Joey Diven says, "Ah, they just stayed drunk more and stayed louder about it."

One time Joey Diven was working as a doorman over at the AOH on Oakland Avenue. The AOH is the Ancient Order of Hibernians. You needed a card to get into the place, which was located on the third door, or, as Joey explains it, "Up 28 steps if you accidentally fell down them." This particular night, a guy showed up, but he didn't have a card, so Joey told him to take off. "Come on, let me in, I'm Irish," the guy said. Joey said no card, no admittance, and when the guy persisted, Joey threw him down the steps.

Pretty soon there was a knock on the door again. Joey opened it. Same guy. Same thing; no card. "Come on, let me in, I'm Irish." Joey threw him down the steps again.

A few more minutes and another knock. And get this: It was the same guy. What did Joey do? He ushered him in, and said, "You're right. You must be Irish."

What made Joey Diven such a good street fighter was that he held no illusions. Poor Jackie Conn (who is dead now) was different. He thought he could be as good as his brother in the prize ring. Jackie was on the undercard a night in '39 when Billy defended against Gus Lesnevich, but the kid brother lost a four-rounder. The failure ate him up so, he came apart afterward in the locker room. Just before Billy went off to fight Lesnevich, he had to soothe Jackie and make sure the brother would be taken to the hospital and sedated. Diven was different. "Ah, I didn't ever have the killer instinct like Billy in the ring," he says. "You see, even though Billy's such a God-fearing man, he could be ruthless in the ring. That's why Billy was so good."

Still, Joey will razz Billy good. For example, he says that Conn always was a rotten drinker—"Three drinks, and he's talking about the Blessed Mother or Thomas Aquinas." He also kids Conn that, when he travels, he still sleeps with all his valuables tucked into his pillowcase. Once when they were staying together in Las Vegas, Billy got up in the middle of the night to take a leak, and Joey was awakened by the sound of change rattling in the pillowcase. Billy was taking his nickels and dimes with him to the bathroom.

"Hey, Billy," Joey said. "You didn't have to take the pillow to the toilet. There's nobody here."

Conn stopped. "*You're* here," he said,

Joey had a lot of fun with Billy. They had a lot of fun street-fighting. It wasn't ever vicious. In those days, nobody ever drew guns or knives or even clubs. Nobody was loco with drugs. You could do all the same stuff Billy did in the ring—gouging and biting and that type of thing, plus the friendly name-calling—all the things that made up what used to be known as a *fair fight*. "No booting, though," says Joey.

"And it never took more than four or five minutes. Somebody would get in one good shot, and that would wear you out pretty quick, and after that there'd be a lot of mauling and rassling, and then it was history." It wasn't at all like in the movies, where the fights go on forever no matter how many times people got clobbered. "As soon as a guy said he'd had enough, that was it. No more," Joey says. That was the code. "Then you'd go back into the joint together and buy each other a drink, maybe even end up getting fractured together." An Iron and an Imp, twice. Do this again for both or us. One more time.

That was the sort of environment young Billy grew up in in 'Sliberty—scrapping with everyone in the neighborhood, running errands for the bootleggers over on Station Street, filching pastries from the bakery wagon to put a little something extra on the family table. There were four younger brothers and sisters. To help make ends meet, Billy's father didn't altogether shy away from the bootleggers; the authorities estimated there were 10,000 stills in the Pittsburgh area during Prohibition. Westinghouse sometimes brewed beer in the family bathtub. For Mrs. Conn, the former Marguerite McFarland, the most devout of Catholic women, this made it nearly impossible to ensure that cleanliness would take its assigned runner-up spot to godliness. "Be patient, woman, the beer'll be ready in a few days," Westinghouse would chide his wife as she fretted over her dirty-necked tykes.

Billy adored his mother. He was the one who named her Maggie, and he called her that as he grew older. He always gives nicknames to the people he loves the most. Maggie had come over in steerage from County Cork when she was a young girl, and she never did lose all of her brogue. She grew plump, but with her magnificent skin and blue eyes in a beautiful face framed by black hair, she was a colleen to the day she died. She lavished all that she could upon her oldest, and she was not frightened when he told her he wanted to be a boxer. She knew how hard it was in the mills, and when Westinghouse gave the boy gloves one Christmas, Maggie made him some fine, Celtic-green trunks.

Billy Conn leans back in his chair in the club cellar and takes a deep drag on his cigarette, and this is what he says: "Your mother should be your best friend."

Maggie's boy did have one other talent besides boxing and loafing, and that was art. He could draw, and it he were growing up in Pittsburgh today, when Irish boys stay in school and don't lace on gloves, no doubt he would become an artist or a draftsman of some sort. But he never pursued drawing, never even played team sports. His children—Timmy, Billy, Susan and Mike—all had to learn games from their granddad, Greenfield Jimmy, and they still like to laugh at their old man, the former champion of the world, because he throws like a girl.

He stayed two years in the eighth grade at Sacred Heart before one of the sisters suggested that he give up his seat to someone who might use it to greater advantage. He departed school then, but it didn't matter because already, as he puts it, "I was going to cawledge at Jawnie Ray's." That was in 'Sliberty. Ray had retired from fighting, but he ran a gym so he could keep himself in bootleg whiskey. It came in milk bottles and cost 15 cents a pint.

The first time Billy ventured into the gym, Ray was amazed at how tiny and smooth the boy's face was. And Billy couldn't have weighed more than 80, maybe 85, pounds. But Jawnie let him audition in the ring, and he saw the instincts and the courage right off. So he let Billy work around the gym, tidying the place up, fetching him his booze, earning the occasional chance to spar.

One day a bunch of older neighborhood toughs confronted Billy as he came back to the gym toting a pint of moonshine. "What are you, a messenger boy for the rummy?" one of them said, and they jostled and taunted Billy. He pulled himself up as tall as he could, and he hollered back, "You bums! Someday, I'm gonna be a champeen!"

They laughed, and he went on inside and gave Ray the moonshine. Billy came to call him Moonie for his addiction, and Moonie called him Junior. "All right now, Junior," Moonie would say, swilling the rotgut, "keep your hands up and punch straight." This was the shell defense Jawnie Ray taught. "Moonie was quiet, but he was a Michelangelo as a teacher. Hell, I didn't know he drank until one day I saw him sober. You know how it is—no Jews drink. I get the one who does. Only I tell you one thing, Jawnie Ray knew more about bawxing drunk than anybody else did sober."

Conn stayed with Ray in the gym three years but never was allowed to engage in an official fight. That was because Ray didn't believe in amateur fisticuffs. If you were going to chance being hit in the kisser, then you should make a dawler off it. Also, what could you learn from some amateur? During one period in the late '30s and early '40s, the Pittsburgh area gave the world five champions, and Conn got to practice against a lot of talent in the gym. When Joe Louis came to town to fight Hans Birkie, Conn made a buck holding the spit box for the Brown Bomber. It was the first time he ever saw the man with whom he would be linked forever in boxing history.

Finally, when he was 17 years aid, Ray drove him down to Fairmount, W.Va., where he went four rounds against an experienced 24-year-old named Dick Woodwer. There were probably 300 fans at the armory, and Woodwer outpointed the novice. Conn's share was $2.50.

Ray gave him four bits. "Hey, Moon, what is this?" Billy said. "I get two and a half."

"We gotta eat," Ray said.

"Yeah, but how come we're both eating out of my share?"

"You were the one who lost," said Ray.

They never had a contract, but no other man ever managed Billy Conn. He even told the mob to back off when it tried to muscle in.

In the beginning, Ray had Billy fighting somebody somewhere every two weeks or so. Fairmount, Charleston, Wheeling, Johnstown. It was nickel hamburgers, 15-cent moonshine and 16-cents-a-gallon gas that kept them going. "You tell kids that nowadays, they're sure you ran into too many of Joe Louis's blows," Billy says. And nowadays it's not just the prices that are different. A prospect is brought along against handpicked roundheels on Sunday afternoon TV. After 10 bouts everybody gets to fight for the championship of something or other. Conn was barely out of West Virginia after 10 fights, and even after 14 he was hardly .500; then he had to win or draw 13 in a row before he was allowed a 10-rounder. It was against Honeyboy Jones.

But he was learning. Always, he learned. Even when he fought for championships, he seldom won any of the early rounds. "They don't matter," he says. They counted, but they didn't matter, because that was the time you picked up the other guy's style. And Ray put him in against everybody, every style.

Near the end of 1936, when Conn was still only 18, Ray threw the boy in against the older Fritzie Zivic. "He put an awful face on me," Billy says, and he still honors Zivic, a Pittsburgh guy, by calling him the dirtiest fighter he ever met. But Billy outpointed Zivic and moved out of the welterweights.

A few months later, he won his 23rd in a row over a red-haired black powerhouse named Oscar Rankins, who knocked Billy down in the eighth with such a stiff blow that, says Conn, "I didn't know I'd won till I read it the next day in the paper." Years later, when Joe Louis heard that Conn had fought Rankins, he said to Billy, "The people who managed you must not have liked you very much. Nobody would let me fight that sonuvabitch."

Conn's favorite photograph in the club cellar is a wire photo of himself bandaged and stitched after he won the rematch with Freddie Apostoli. The headline reads: IF THIS IS THE WINNER, WHAT DOES THE LOSER LOOK LIKE? Conn howls at that, and to this day he speaks with greatest affection about the fighters who did him the most damage.

Damn, it was fun. After he beat Zivic and made big money, $2,180, Conn bought himself a brand new Chevy for $600. When he whipped Bettina for the title, he said, "Gee, I'm champion. Now I can eat regular." Then he went back home to Pittsburgh and out to 'Sliberty. "I hadn't been around the corner for a long time," he says. But now he made a point of going back, and he found the guys who had ridiculed him when he had just been starting out, running errands for Jawnie Ray. They were loafing in a bar. "Remember the messenger boy you laughed at?" he asked, and they nodded, cowering. Billy brought his hands up fast, and they ducked away, but all he did was lay a lot of big bills on the hardwood. "Well, all right," Billy said, "stay drunk a long time on the light-heavyweight champeen of the world."

He bought Maggie anything she wanted. He gave her champagne, the real stuff. She loved champagne. He bought presents for his younger brothers and sisters, and for the dames he found and who found him. He was even interviewed by a New York fashion editor on the subject of how a woman should be turned out.

"I guess these women's fashions are O.K.," Conn declared. "That is, except those dizzy hats and the shoes some of them wear. . . . I wouldn't wear a boxing glove for a hat, but some girls do. . . . Plaid dresses are pips. I think plaid looks swell on any woman, and I like any color as long as it's red. . . . Some evening dresses are pretty nice, it they're lacy and frilly and with swoopy skirts. But most girls look too much like China dolls when they're dressed in evening dresses. But what the hell! They're going to dress up the slightest chance you give 'em. And I'm for giving them every chance."

"We're just a bunch of plain, ordinary bums having a good time," Jawnie Ray explained. He and Billy would scream at each other and carry on constantly. "I'm glad we ain't got a contract, you dumb mick sonuvabitch," Jawnie would holler, "because maybe I'll get lucky and somebody even dumber than you will steal you from me." "Yeah, you rummy Jew bastard," Billy would coo back. It was like that, right to the end. The last time Billy saw him, Jawnie was at death's door in the hospital, and Joey Diven and Billy were visiting him.

"C'mon, you guys, sneak me outta here for some drinks," Jawnie Ray pleaded from the hospital bed.

"Moonie," Billy replied, "the only way you're gettin' outta this place is with a tag tied on your big toe."

Sometimes Westinghouse joined the traveling party, too, and on one occasion, coming back from Erie, he and Jawnie Ray got into a first-class fight. As Conn described it in a contemporary account, "My old man swung. Jawnie swung. When it was finished, Pop had a broken nose and Jawnie had lost a tooth. That made them pals."

Yes, sir, it was a barrelful of monkeys. They all loved to throw water on one another, too, and to play practical jokes with the telephone and whatnot. Eventually, when Jackie had grown up enough to come on board, it made it even more fun because then Billy had a partner to scuffle with. Billy would always go after Jackie when he caught him wearing his clothes. One time Billy was voted Best Dressed Sportsman of the Year, so that must have made Jackie the Second-Best-Dressed Sportsman of the Year.

The day before Conn defended his crown in Forbes Field against Bettina in September of '39, Billy found out that Jackie had been joyriding with his pals in Billy's new black Cadillac, so he put out a $300 bounty on his brother, and when he caught up with him he thrashed him bare-knuckled in the garage. "O.K., get it over," Jackie said when he had positively had enough, and he laid out his chin for Billy to paste him square on it. Billy popped him a right, and Jackie was sliding down the wall clear across the garage when Jawnie Ray and Uncle Mike Jacobs and the cops burst in, all of them in disbelief that Billy would get into a fraternal dustup right before a championship fight. They were much relieved to discover that the blood all over Billy was only Jackie's.

Billy wiped himself clean and outpointed Bettina in 15. He was the toast of Pittsburgh and the world, as well. The New York *Daily News* rhapsodized: "The Irishman is indeed a beauteous boxer who could probably collect coinage by joining the ballet league if he chose to flee the egg-eared and flattened-nose fraternity." When Conn fought in New York, Owney McManus, who ran a saloon in Pittsburgh, would charter trains, and hundreds of the Irish faithful would follow Conn to Gotham—the Ham and Cabbage Special, they called it—and loaf on Broadway, even it it meant that maybe when they went back to the mills in Pittsburgh they'd be handed a DCM.

A DCM is a Don't Come Monday, the pink slip.

When Conn fought in Oakland, at the Gardens, the streetcars would disgorge fans from all over the Steel City. Pittsburgh's streetcar lines were almost all laid out east-west, except for one, which ran north from the mills along the river. It was called the Flying Fraction because it was number 77/54—a combination of two east-west lines, the 77 and the 54—and it went right past both the Gardens and Forbes Field. Three rides to a quarter, and if you were getting off for the fights you got a transfer anyhow and sold it for a nickel to the people waiting, so they could save 3 cents on their ride home.

Photos of Conn went up in all the bars where those of Greb and Zivic were to be seen, and in a lot of other places where the Irish wanted strictly their own hero. And now that Billy had grown into a light heavyweight and had beaten all of them, it seemed like the only one left for him to fight was the heavyweight champion, the Brown Bomber himself. There wasn't anybody Irish in the country who wasn't looking forward to that. And by this point, there probably wasn't anybody Irish in Pittsburgh who hadn't seen Billy Conn fight, except for Mary Louise Smith.

"I've never seen a prizefight in my life," she said just the other day. Mary Louise just never cared very much for Billy's business, even when he was earning a living at it.

"You didn't miss anything," Billy replied.

But even if she hadn't seen him work, she was in love with him. She had fallen in love with the boxer. He gave her a nickname, too: Matt—for the way her hair became matted on her brow when she went swimming down the Jersey shore. She was still only a kid, still at Our Lady of Mercy, but she had become even more beautiful than she had been at that first dinner, and the sheltered life Greenfield Jimmy had imposed upon her was backfiring some. Billy had the lure of forbidden fruit. "I was mature for my age," Mary Louise says, "something of a spitfire. And I guess you'd have to say that when my father didn't want me to see Billy, I turned out to be a good prevaricator, too." She sighs. "Billy just appealed to me so."

"Ah, I told her a lot of lies," he says.

They would sneak off, mostly for dinners, usually at out-of-town roadhouses, hideaways where they could be alone, intimate in their fashion, staring into each other's blue eyes. It was so very innocent. He was always in training, and she was too young to drink, and kisses are what they shared. That and their song, *A Pretty Girl Is Like a Melody*. Well, Billy made it their song, and he would request it from the big band on Saturdays when they would get all gussied up and go dancing downtown at the William Penn Hotel, which was the fanciest spot in Pittsburgh. And he was the champion of the world, and she was the prettiest girl, dressed *all lacy and frilly and with swoopy skirts.*

Even if Greenfield Jimmy didn't know the half of it, he could sense that it was getting out of hand. Mary Louise played Jo in *Little Women* at Our Lady of Mercy, and he liked that; he wanted her to be an actress, to be something, to move up. He liked Billy, he really did, and he thought he was as good a boxer as he had ever seen, but he didn't want his daughter, his firstborn, marrying a pug. So Greenfield Jimmy sent Mary Louise to Philadelphia, to a classy, cloistered college called Rosemont, and he told the mother superior never to let his daughter see the likes of Mister Billy Conn.

So Billy had to be content sending letters and presents. When he came into Philly for a fight he had 20 ringside tickets delivered to Rosemont so that Mary Louise could bring her friends. The mother superior wouldn't let any of the young ladies go, though, and when Billy climbed into the ring and looked down and saw the empty seats, he was crestfallen. His opponent that night was Gus Dorazio, and despite Billy's lipping off at the weigh-in, Billy was even slower than usual to warm up, and the fight went eight rounds before Billy won on a KO.

Greenfield Jimmy was pleased to learn about these events and that Mary Louise was going out with nice young men from the Main Line, who went to St. Joseph's and Villanova, who called for her properly and addressed her as Mary Louise, and not anything common like Matt. Greenfield Jimmy sent her off to Nassau for spring vacation with a bunch of her girlfriends, demure young ladies all.

As for Billy, he went into the heavies, going after Louis. "We're in this racket to make money," Jawnie Ray said. Billy had some now. He rented Maggie and the family a house on Fifth Avenue, an address that means as much in Pittsburgh as it does in New York. One of the Mellons had a mansion on Fifth with 65 rooms and 11 baths. "The days of no money are over, Maggie," Billy told his mother. She said fine, but she didn't know anybody on Fifth Avenue. Couldn't he find something in 'Sliberty? "Bring your friends over every day," Billy told her.

Maggie was 40 that summer, a young woman with a son who was a renowned champion of the world. But she began to feel a little poorly and went for some tests. The results were not good. Not at all. So now, even it Billy Conn was a champion, what did it mean? Of the two women he loved, one he almost never got to hold, and now the other was dying of cancer,

CONN'S FIRST fight against a heavyweight was with Bob Pastor in September of 1940. Pastor irritated him. "I hit him low one time," Billy recalls. "All right, all right. But he just kept on bitching. So now, I'm *really* gonna hit him low. You know, you were supposed to do everything to win." He knocked Pastor out in 13, then he outpointed Al McCoy in 10 and Lee Savold in 12, even after Savold busted his nose in the eighth.

All too often now, though, Conn wasn't himself. He couldn't get to see Mary Louise, and worse, Maggie was becoming sicker and weaker, and almost every cent he made in the ring went to pay for the treatment and the doctors and the round-the-clock nurses he ordered. "His mother's illness has Billy near crazy at times," Jawnie Ray explained after one especially lackluster bout. Between fights Billy would head back to Pittsburgh and slip up to see Maggie, and, against doctor's orders, he would bring her champagne, the best, and the two of them would sit there on an afternoon, best friends, and get quietly smashed together. They were the happiest moments Maggie had left.

June 18, 1941 was the night set for the Louis fight at the Polo Grounds, and Uncle Mike Jacobs began to beat the biggest drums for Conn, even as Louis kept trooping the land, beating up on what became known as the Bums-of-the-Mouth. Incredibly, 27,000 people—most of them coming off the Flying Fraction—showed up at Forbes Field to watch Conn's final tune-up in May, against a nobody named Buddy Knox.

Everywhere the world was swirling, and that seemed to make even everyday events larger and better and more full of ardor. Even if Americans didn't know what lay ahead, even if they told themselves it couldn't happen here, that foreign wars wouldn't engage us, there may have been deeper and truer instincts that inspired and drove them as the year of 1941 rushed on. It was the last summer that a boy hit .400. It was the only summer that anyone hit safely in 56 straight games. A great beast named Whirlaway, whipped by Eddie Arcaro, the little genius they called Banana Nose, ran a Derby so fast that the record would stand for more than 20 years, and he finished up with the Triple Crown in June. That was when the Irishman and the Brown Bomber were poised to do battle in what might have been the most wonderful heavyweight fight there ever was. And all this as the Nazis began their move toward Russia and Yamamoto was okaying the attack on Pearl Harbor.

The pace was quickening. Mary Louise was as impetuous now as the boy she loved. It couldn't go on this way anymore. On May 28, a couple of days after he beat Knox, Billy drove her to Brookville, way north out of Pittsburgh, and took out a marriage license. DiMaggio got a triple, in Washington, at Griffith Stadium, to raise his streak to 13. Mary Louise was 18 now, and Greenfield Jimmy couldn't change her plans any more than he could her heart, but she and Billy were good Catholic kids, and they wanted to be married in the Church, and that meant the banns had to be posted.

So Greenfield Jimmy heard, and he fulminated, "I'm just trying to raise a decent family, and I know where these boxers end up." He said he would punch Billy's lights out, and Westinghouse said he would rattle Greenfield Jimmy's cage first. Greenfield Jimmy went directly to the rectory where the bishop lived in

Pittsburgh. He banged on the door and said there had better not be any priest anywhere in Pennsylvania who would marry his flesh and blood to the pug.

It worked, too. The next Saturday, Billy left his training camp and went to a nearby parish named St. Philomena's. He and Mary Louise had someone who had promised to marry them at the altar at 9:30 a.m., and an excited crowd had gathered. But the priests wouldn't buck Greenfield Jimmy, and, after a couple of hours of bickering, somebody came out and told the people there wouldn't be any June wedding this day.

Billy went back to prepare to fight the heavyweight champion. DiMaggio got three singles against the Brownies that afternoon.

The next time Billy left camp, a few days before the bout, he flew to Pittsburgh to see his mother. He probably didn't realize how close to the end she was, because she kept the news from him. "Listen, I've got to live a little longer," Maggie told everyone else in the family. "I can't worry Billy."

He couldn't bring her champagne this time. Instead, he brought her a beautiful diamond bracelet, and he gave it to her. "Maggie," he said, "this is for you." She was so sick, so weak, so in pain that she could barely work up a smile, but she thanked him the best she could. And then she pushed it back.

"Oh, it's so beautiful, Billy," she said. "But don't give it to me. Give it to Mary Louise." And Maggie told him then that he was to marry her, no matter what Greenfield Jimmy said, because he was her boy and a good boy and as good as any boy, and because he loved Mary Louise more than anyone else in the world.

Billy nodded. He kept his hand wrapped around the bracelet. He couldn't stay much longer. Just these few minutes had tired Maggie so. He kissed her and got ready to leave. "Maggie," Billy said, "I gotta go now, but the next time you see me, I'll be the heavyweight champion of the world."

Maggie smiled one more time. "No, son," she said, "the next time I see you will be in Paradise."

Tuesday, the 17th, the day before the fight, DiMaggio made it an even 30 in a row, going 1 for 4 against the Chisox across the river in the Bronx. That night, Billy slept hardly at all. And he always slept. Sometimes he would even lie down in the locker room while the undercard bouts were being fought and doze right off just minutes before he had to go into the ring. But this whole night he barely got 40 winks. And he wasn't even worrying about getting in the ring with Joe Louis. He was worrying about Maggie and Matt.

At the weigh-in the next morning Louis, who had trained down because of Conn's speed, came in at 199½. Conn tipped 169. That made Uncle Mike a bit nervous. It was already 17–5 for the champion in the betting, and this weight spread was making the bout look like homicide. Uncle Mike announced Conn's weight at a more cosmetic 174.

Conn went back to his hotel to rest, but the Ham and Cabbage Special had just got in, and all the fans, wearing leprechaun hats and carrying paper shamrocks and clay pipes, came over to see him, and when a bunch of them barged right into his room, Billy went outside and loafed with them.

Finally, Jawnie got him back to his room, but who should come storming in, wearing a zoot suit and smoking a big cigar, but Jackie. Naturally, he and Billy started wrestling each other all over the suite, driving the trainer, Freddie Fierro, nuts. People can get hurt wrestling. At last Fierro was able to separate them, but Billy still couldn't sleep, so he looked in on Jackie and saw him snoring with his mouth open. He called down to room service, ordered a seltzer bottle and squirted it right into Jackie's mouth. You can bet that woke Jackie up.

Jackie chased Billy into the hall. Billy was laughing, and he wasn't wearing anything but his shorts. That was how Billy spent the day getting ready for the Brown Bomber. Just a few miles away, at the Stadium, DiMaggio went 1 for 3 to stretch it to 31.

Back in Pittsburgh the Pirates had scheduled one of their few night games for this evening, June 18. They knew everybody wanted to stay home to listen to the fight on the radio, so the Pirates announced that when the fight began, the game would be suspended and the radio broadcast would go out over the P.A. Baseball came to a halt. Most of America did. Maybe the only person not listening was Maggie. She was so sick the doctors wouldn't let her.

Billy crossed himself when he climbed into the ring that night.

And then the Pirates stopped, and America stopped, and the fight began, Louis's 18th defense, his seventh in seven months.

Conn started slower than even he was accustomed to. Louis, the slugger, was the one who moved better. Conn ducked a long right so awkwardly that he slipped and fell to one knee. The second round was worse, Louis pummeling Conn's body, trying to wear the smaller man down. He had 30 pounds on him, after all. Unless you knew the first rounds didn't matter, it was a rout. This month's bum.

In his corner, Conn sat down, spit and said, "All right, Moon, here we go." He came out faster, bicycled for a while, feinted with a left and drove home a hard right. By the end of the round he was grinning at the champ, and he winked to Jawnie Ray when he returned to the corner. The spectators were up on their feet, especially the ones who had bet Conn.

The fourth was even more of a revelation, for now Conn chose to slug a little with the slugger, and he came away the better for the exchange. When the bell rang, he was flat-out laughing as he came back to his corner. "This is a cinch," he told Jawnie.

But Louis got back on track in the fifth, and the fight went his way for the next two rounds as blood flowed from a nasty cut over the challenger's right eye. At Forbes Field in Pittsburgh the crowd grew still, and relatives and friends listening downstairs from where Maggie lay worried that Billy's downfall was near.

But Conn regained command in the eighth, moving back and away from Louis's left, then ripping into the body or the head. The ninth was all the more Conn, and he grew cocky again. "Joe, I got you," he popped off as he flicked a good one square on the champ's mouth, and then, as Billy strode back to his corner at the bell, he said, "Joe, you're in a fight tonight."

"I know it," Louis replied, confused and clearly troubled now.

The 10th was something of a lull for Conn, but it was a strategic respite. During the 11th, Conn worked Louis high and low, hurt the champ, building to the crescendo of the 12th, when the New York *Herald Tribune* reported in the casual racial vernacular of the time that Conn "rained left hooks on Joe's dusky face." He was a clear winner in this round, which put him up 7–5 on one card and 7-4-1 on another; the third was 6–6. To cap off his best round, Conn scored with a crushing left that would have done in any man who didn't outweigh him by 30 pounds. And it certainly rattled the crown of the world's heavyweight champion. The crowd was going berserk. Even Maggie was given the report that her Billy was on the verge of taking the title.

Only later would Conn realize the irony of striking that last great blow. "I miss that, I beat him," he says. It was that simple. He was nine minutes from victory, and now he couldn't wait. "He wanted to finish the thing as Irishmen love to," the *Herald Tribune* wrote.

Louis was stumped in his corner. Jack Blackburn, his trainer, shook his head and rubbed him hard. "Chappie," he said, using his nickname for the champ, "You're *losing*. You gotta knock him out." Louis didn't have to be told. Everyone understood. Everyone in the Polo Grounds. Everyone listening through the magic of radio. Everyone. There was bedlam. It was wonderful. Men had been slugging it out for eons, and there had been 220 years of prizefighting, and there would yet be Marciano and the two Sugar Rays and Ali, but this was it. This was the best it had ever been and ever would be, the 12th and 13th rounds of Louis and Conn on a warm night in New York just before the world went to hell. The people were standing and cheering for Conn, but it was really for the sport and for the moment and for themselves that they cheered. They could be a part of it, and every now and then, for an instant, that is it, and it can't ever get any better. This was such a time in the history of games.

Only Billy Conn could see clearly—the trouble was, what he saw was different from what everybody else saw. What he saw was himself walking with Mary Louise on the Boardwalk at Atlantic City, down the shore, and they were the handsomest couple who ever lived, and people were staring, and he could hear what they were saying. What they were saying was: "There goes Billy Conn with his bride. He just beat Joe Louis." And he didn't want to hear just that. What he wanted to hear was: "There goes Billy Conn with his bride. He's the guy who just *knocked out* Joe Louis." Not for himself. That was what Mary Louise deserved.

Billy had a big smile on his face. "This is easy, Moonie," he said. "I can take this sonuvabitch out this round."

Jawnie blanched. "No, no, Billy," he said, "Stick and run. You got the fight won. Stay away, kiddo. Just stick and run, stick and run. . . . " There was the bell for the 13th.

And then it happened. Billy tried to bust the champ, but it was Louis who got through the defenses, and then he pasted a monster right on the challenger's jaw. "Fall! Fall!" Billy said to himself. He knew if he could just go down, clear his head, he would lose the round, but he could still save the day. "But for some reason, I couldn't fall, I kept saying, 'Fall, fall,' but there I was, still standing up. So Joe hit me again and again, and when I finally did fall, it was a slow, funny fall. I remember that." Billy lay flush out on the canvas. There were two seconds left in the round, 2:58 of the 13th, when he was counted out. The *winnah and still champeen.* . . .

"It was nationality that cost Conn the title," the *Herald Tribune* wrote. "He wound up on his wounded left side, trying to make Irish legs answer an Irish brain."

On the radio, Billy said, "I just want to tell my mother I'm all right."

Back in the locker room, Jawnie Ray said not to cry because bawxers don't cry. And Billy delivered the classic: "What's the sense of being Irish if you can't be dumb?"

Maggie lasted a few more days. "She held on to see me leading Joe Louis in the stretch," Billy says.

He and Mary Louise got married the day after the funeral. The last time they had met with Greenfield Jimmy, he said that Billy had to "prove he could be a gentleman," but what did a father-in-law's blessing matter anymore after the 12th and 13th rounds and after Maggie's going?

They found a priest in Philly; a Father Schwindlein, and he didn't care from Greenfield Jimmy or the bishop or whoever. As Mary Louise says, "He just saw two young people very much in love." They had a friend with them who was the best man, and the cleaning lady at the church stood in as the maid of honor. DiMaggio got up to 45 that day in Fenway, going 2 for 4 and then 1 for 3 in a twin bill. Greenfield Jimmy alerted the state police and all the newspapers when he heard what was going on, but Billy and Mary Louise were on their honeymoon in Jersey, man and wife, by the time anybody caught up with them.

"They're more in love today, 44 years later," Michael Conn says. He is their youngest child. The Conns raised three boys and a girl at the house they bought that summer in Squirrel Hill.

THAT WAS it, really. DiMaggio's streak ended the night of July 17 in Cleveland. Churchill and Roosevelt signed the Atlantic Charter four weeks later, and on Nov. 26 the first subs pulled away from Japan on the long haul to Pearl Harbor. Billy was shooting a movie. It was called *The Pittsburgh Kid*, and in it he played (in an inspired bit of casting) an Irish fighter from the Steel City. Mary Louise was so pretty the producers wanted at least to give her a bit part as a cigarette girl, but she was too bashful, and Billy wasn't crazy about the idea himself. Billy did so well that the moguls asked him to stay around and star in the life story of Gentleman Jim Corbett, but the house in Squirrel Hill was calling. And Mary Louise was pregnant. "We were just a couple of naive young kids from Pittsburgh, and we didn't like Hawllywood," she says.

Joey Diven says that if Billy doesn't care for somebody a whole lot, he'll have them over to the house, take them down to the club cellar and make them watch *The Pittsburgh Kid*.

After Pearl Harbor, Conn fought three more times. Nobody knew it then, but he was done. Everything ended when he hit Louis that last big left. The best he beat was Tony Zale, but even the fans in the Garden booed his effort, and he only outpointed the middleweight. It didn't matter, though, because all anybody cared about was a rematch with Louis—even if both fighters were going into the service.

The return was in the works for the summer, a year after the first meeting. It was looked upon as a great morale builder and diversion for a rattled America. The victories at Midway and Guadalcanal were yet to come.

Then, in the middle of May, Pfc. Conn got a three-day pass to come home to the christening of his firstborn, Timmy. Art Rooney was the godfather, and he thought it would be the right time to patch things up between Greenfield Jimmy and his son-in-law, and so he and Milton Jaffe, Conn's business adviser, arranged a christening party at Smith's house and told Billy that his father-in-law was ready to smoke the peace pipe.

On Sunday, at the party, Greenfield Jimmy and Conn were in the kitchen with some of the other guests. That is where people often congregated in those days, the kitchen. Billy was sitting up on the stove, his legs dangling, when it started. "My father liked to argue," Mary Louise says, "but you can't drag Billy into an argument." Greenfield Jimmy gave it his best, though. Art Rooney says, "He was always the boss, telling people what to do, giving orders." On this occasion he chose to start telling Conn that if he were going to be married to his daughter and be the father of his grandson, he damn sight better attend church more regularly. Then, for good measure, he also told Billy he could beat him up. Finally, Greenfield Jimmy said too much.

"I can still see Billy come off that stove," Rooney says.

Just because it was family, Billy didn't hold back. He went after his father-in-law with his best, a left hook, but he was mad, he had his Irish up, and the little guy ducked like he was getting away from a brushback pitch, and Conn caught him square on the top of his skull. As soon as he did it, Billy knew he had broken his hand. He had hurt himself worse against his own father-in-law than he ever had against any bona fide professional in the prize ring.

Not only that, but when the big guys and everybody rushed in to break it up, Milton Jaffe fractured an ankle and Mary Louise got herself all cut and bruised. Greenfield Jimmy took advantage of the diversion to inflict on Conn additional scratches and welts around the neck, wrists and eyes. Billy was so furious about blowing the rematch with Louis that he busted a window with his good hand on the way out and cut himself more. *The New York Times*, ever understated, described Conn's appearance the next day "as if he had tangled with a half-dozen alley cats."

Greenfield Jimmy didn't have a single mark on him.

Years later, whenever Louis saw Conn, he would usually begin, "Is your old father-in-law still beating the s--- out of you?"

In June, Secretary of War Henry Stimson announced there would be no more public commercial appearances for Louis, and the champ began a series of morale-boosting tours. The fight at the christening had cost Louis and Conn hundreds of thousands of dollars and, it turned out, any real chance Conn had for victory. Every day the war dragged on diminished his skills.

The legs go first.

Conn was overseas in Europe for much of the war, pulling punches in exhibition matches against regimental champs. One time, the plane he was on developed engine trouble over France, and Billy told God he would do two things if the plane landed safely.

It did, and he did. He gave $5,000 to Dan Rooney, Art's brother, who was a missionary in the Far East. And he gave $3,000 to Sacred Heart, his old parish in 'Sliberty, to build a statue of the Blessed Virgin. It is still there, standing prominently by the entrance.

Conn was with Bob Hope at Nuremberg when V-E day came. There is a picture of that in the club cellar.

Then he came home and patched up with Greenfield Jimmy and prepared for the long-awaited rematch with Louis. It was on June 19, 1946, and such was the excitement that, for the first time, ringside seats went for $100, and a $2 million gate was realized. This was the fight—not the first one—when Louis observed, "He can run, but he can't hide." And Joe was absolutely right. Mercifully, the champion ended the slaughter in the eighth. In the locker room Conn himself called it a "stinkeroo," and it was Jawnie Ray who cried, because, he said, "Billy's finished."

As Conn would tell his kids, boxing is bad unless you happen to be very, very good at it. It's not like other sports, where you can get by. If you're not very, very good, you can get killed or made over into a vegetable or what have you. Now Billy Conn, he had been very, very good. Almost one-third of his 75 fights had been against champions of the world, and he had beaten all those guys except Louis, and that was as good a fight as there ever was. Some people still say there never has been a better fighter, a stylist, than Sweet William, the Flower of the Monongahela. But, of course, all anybody remembers is the fight that warm June night in the year of '41 and especially that one round, the 13th.

One time, a few years ago, Art Rooney brought the boxer into the Steelers' locker room and introduced him around to a bunch of white players standing there. They obviously didn't have the foggiest idea who Billy Conn was. Conn saw some black players across the way. "Hey, blackies, you know who Joe Louis was?" They all looked up at the stranger and nodded, Conn turned back to the whites and shook his head. "And you sonsovbitches don't know me," he said.

But really he didn't care. "Everything works out for the best," he says in the club cellar. "I believe that." He's very content. They can't ever get him to go to sports dinners so they can give him awards and stuff. "Ah, I just like being another bum here," he says. "I just loaf around, on the corner, different places." Then Mary Louise comes around, and he falls into line. He never moved around much, Billy Conn. Same town, same house, same wife, same manager, same fun. "All the guys who know me are dead now, but, let me tell you, if I drop dead tomorrow, I didn't miss anything."

He's over by the photograph of Louis and him, right after their first fight. He still adores Louis, they became fast friends, and he loves to tell stories about Louis and money. Some guys have problems with money. Some guys have, say, problems with fathers-in-law. Nobody gets off scot-free. Anyway, in the picture Louis has a towel wrapped around a puzzled, mournful countenance. Conn, next to him, is smiling to beat the band. He was the loser? He says, "I told Joe later, 'Hey, Joe, why didn't you just let me have the title for six months?' All I ever wanted was to be able to go around the corner where the guys are loafing and say, 'Hey, I'm the heavyweight champeen of the world.'

"And you know what Joe said back to me? He said, 'I let you have it for 12 rounds, and you couldn't keep it. How could I let you have it for six months?' "

A few years ago Louis came to Pittsburgh, and he and Conn made an appearance together at a union hall. Roy McHugh, the columnist for the Pitts-

Some assignments were born at editorial meetings, others in bars. The most eccentric often came from the writers themselves. Thomas McGuane was moved to confess his brief fling with a motorcycle (*Finally, We Were Left Alone, Just Me and My Bike*) and Jeff MacGregor wanted to see firsthand what went on at a rattlesnake roundup (*Snakes Alive!*)—both far from mainstream sportswriting. Other assignments, such as the third Ali-Frazier fight ('*Lawdy, Lawdy, He's Great*' by Mark Kram), were obvious sports stories. But as an SI writer you didn't just cover the event, or even distill it with analysis, you blew it through as many filters as you could find—both human and cultural. You blew it out.

As the years accelerated and sports (and life) became more complicated, certain SI writers began to adopt the techniques of fiction. Read Deford and later Gary Smith to see how narrative and scene became more and more important; likewise dialogue and even informed speculation about what was going on inside a subject's head. Everything fit, or almost everything, within the "third person, keep-it-hopping" style that Roy Blount Jr. described as "good for my chops." Much has been made of New Journalism, and SI was one of its important cradles. True enough, but the goal was simply great story-telling, pieces that hit something inside people and moved them.

SI has always been mostly staff written, but at the same time has drawn con-tributions from the best writers and journalists outside the magazine. From the first issue, the writers who appeared in SI threw long shadows. Just to list some of their names in a row is powerful beyond the recollection of any spe-cific story: Mitch Albom, Dave Barry, Jimmy Breslin, William F. Buckley Jr., Erskine Caldwell, Richard Ben Cramer, Don DeLillo, Annie Dillard, E.L. Doc-torow, John Dos Passos, William Faulkner, John Feinstein, Ian Fleming, John Fowles, Dick Francis, Robert Frost, Peter Gent, David Halberstam, Jim Har-rison, Ernest Hemingway, John Hersey, Roger Kahn, Garrison Keillor, Tony Kornheiser, A.J. Liebling, Robert Lipsyte, Thomas McGuane, Peter Matthiessen, W. Somerset Maugham, James Michener, Jim Murray, Ogden Nash, Jose Or-tega y Gasset, Anna Quindlen, David Remnick, Mordecai Richler, Philip Roth, Dick Schaap, Budd Schulberg, Wilfrid Sheed, John Steinbeck, John Edgar Wideman, Herbert Warren Wind, Dick Young. John F. Kennedy wrote for the magazine too, and so did Robert Frost and Ted Williams, and many, many others with recognizable names including Edward, Duke of Windsor, who wrote about Arnold Palmer. Almost everybody but Elvis.

They were all fans, even if they were also politicians or athletes or poets. And they all read the magazine, and would no doubt like this book even if they are not all in it. It is a truth about SPORTS ILLUSTRATED that the magazine be-longs to the readers. It's in the DNA of the place. And it's in this book.

—*Terry McDonell*

CONTENTS

CONTENTS

Wild Kingdom

Supporting Players

Playing for Laughs

Personal Fouls

Music to the Ear

Examined Lives

Introduction

THE FACT THAT THE GREAT PIECE HAS SHOWN UP AGAIN AND again in SI is the result of a contentious conspiracy between the magazine's writers and their editors. Writers first, of course. The way magazine journalism is supposed to work is that the best editors match the perfect idea with the ideal writer and wait for a brilliant run of words. This is followed (with plenty of time before deadline) by the simple exercise of hooking paragraphs and helping with the diction here and there. Nothing to it. Right.

To say that there are complications is like suggesting that gambling is occasionally connected to sports. There may also be misunderstandings, like the ones that occur when an editor changes the word *team* to *squad* ("big-and-large editing," as Dan Jenkins used to call it). Writers hate that.

Frank Deford says that when he was coming up as a writer he developed a nonspecific dread of editors: What would they do to his copy next? It was not that he hated them, exactly, but then again maybe he did. He remarked this year, on the occasion of receiving a Lifetime Achievement Award, that during the time he himself was an editor, he couldn't stand Frank Deford.

Arguments over who has or should have the last word—whether the magazine is, in fact, "a writer's magazine" or "an editor's magazine"—have wailed on since the great Andre Laguerre stepped down in 1976, after SI had emerged under his leadership as a literary force. The truth is, there has always been a tricky balance between editors and writers. Good ones make each other better, perhaps not as human beings but certainly as journalists, and the work soars.

George Plimpton says that he was never happier than when he was on assignment for SI, except that he was terrified of Laguerre. Writers worked harder just knowing Laguerre was going to read their copy. "His standards were so high that he *had* to be a great editor," Plimpton says.

The classic SI piece, the so-called "Bonus," was designed (by Laguerre) to push writers beyond the stats and clichés that filled most newspapers, and now loop in numbing rotation on sports television. It wasn't that SI didn't care about scores or that these pieces weren't fundamentally about winning and losing, which they were. But they were also about context, using sport as a prism to view a much wider world of experience and emotion.

burgh *Press*, was there. Billy brought the film of the '41 fight over from Squirrel Hill in a shopping bag. As soon as the fight started, Louis left the room and went into the bar to drink brandy. Every now and then Louis would come to the door and holler out, "Hey, Billy, have we got to the 13th round yet?" Conn just laughed and watched himself punch the bigger man around, until finally, when they did come to the 13th, Joe called out, "Goodbye, Billy."

Louis knocked out Conn at 2:58, just like always, but when the lights went on, Billy wasn't there. He had left when the 13th round started. He had gone into another room to where the buffet was, after he had watched the 12 rounds when he was the heavyweight champeen of the world, back in that last indelible summer when America dared yet dream that it could run and hide from the world, when the handsomest boy loved the prettiest girl, when streetcars still clanged and fistfights were fun, and the smoke hung low when Maggie went off to Paradise.

Yogi

BY ROY BLOUNT JR.

*When the great Yankees catcher and philosopher, Yogi Berra, was hired
as his old team's manager, he contemplated the volatility of his new boss and the
fleeting nature of his job with the serenity of a true yogi.*

Yoga consists in the stopping of spontaneous activities of the mind-stuff.
—YOGI PANTANJALI

How can you think and hit at the same time?
—YOGI BERRA

IS THE NEW MANAGER OF THE NEW YORK YANKEES A TRUE YOGI? That may seem an odd question. Lawrence Peter Berra is the most widely known Yogi in the world, or at least in those parts of the world where baseball is played. (When the Yankees appeared in Tokyo in 1955, "the biggest ovation, including screams from bobby-soxers, went to Yogi Berra," according to the Associated Press.) He loves to sit around reflecting in his undershorts. He almost never loses his cool, except in ritual observances with umpires, during which he has been seen to levitate several inches. And he's being counted on to bring peace and unity—yoga is Sanskrit for union—to baseball's most rancorous team.

Yet, yogis don't tend to appear in the form that is 5' 7½" tall and weighs 190 pounds. Jimmy Cannon, the late sportswriter, said Berra was built like a bull penguin. When Larry MacPhail, the Yankees president from 1945 to 1947, first saw

Berra, he was reminded of "the bottom man on an unemployed acrobatic team."

Whereas yoga springs from Hinduism, Berra is a Roman Catholic who tries to attend Mass every Sunday and who once visited the Pope. Yogi told of his meeting with Pope John XXIII in a now-famous interview:

Reporter: "I understand you had an audience with the Pope."

Yogi: "No, but I saw him."

Reporter: "Did you get to talk to him?"

Yogi: "I sure did. We had a nice little chat."

Reporter: "What did he say?"

Yogi: "You know, he must read the papers a lot, because he said, 'Hello, Yogi.' "

Reporter: "And what did you say?"

Yogi: "I said, 'Hello, Pope.' "

Yoga is an Eastern study, and Berra is Midwestern Italian. Once, at a dinner held so Japanese journalists could get together with American baseball stars, a Tokyo newspaper editor was ceremoniously reeling off a list of Japanese delicacies that he was sure his American guests would enjoy. "Don't you have any bread?" Berra interrupted.

Berra's parents were born in Italy. (On his passport, Yogi is Lorenzo Pietro.) He was born in St. Louis, and his sayings are in the American grain. For instance, after visiting the Louvre and being asked whether he liked the paintings there, Berra said, "Yeah, if you like paintings." Another time, after attending a performance of *Tosca* in Milan, he said, "It was pretty good. Even the music was nice." These remarks are less in the tradition of the *Bhagavad-Gita* than in that of Mark Twain, who observed that the music of Richard Wagner was "better than it sounds." Berra is also supposed to have said, after someone mentioned that a Jewish lord mayor had been elected in Dublin, "Yeah. Only in America can a thing like this happen."

Berra hasn't followed the traditional regimen of a person who gives his life over to yoga. He has never attempted to assume the Lotus, the Plough, the Fish or the touching-the-top-of-your-head-with-the-soles-of-your-feet position. In his playing days, it's true, he so mastered the Bat Swing and the Crouch that he's now in the Baseball Hall of Fame. And this spring, in the Yankees' new flexibility program, he stretched, bent and folded himself pretty well for a man of 58. But when he's asked whether he knows the body toning postures of yoga, he says, "Nahhh. A couple of people wrote me, 'What exercises do you give?' thinking I was a, you know. . . . Ahhh, I don't do no exercises."

In traditional yoga, the practice of meditation is of central importance. But Berra says, "Guys talk about doing this meditating when they go up to the plate. If I'd done that I'd've been worse. I went up there thinking about something *else.*"

And yet there's something inscrutable about a man who said, when he saw the late Steve McQueen in a movie on television, "He must have made that before he died." There's something mystic about a man who said, "You got to be very careful if you don't know where you're going, because you might not get there." And there's something wise about a man who said, "Slump? I ain't in no slump. I just ain't hitting."

Although yoga is "a definite science," the Yogi Paramahansa Yogananda has written, "There are a number of great men, living today in American or European or other non-Hindu bodies, who, though they may never have heard the words *yogi* or *swami* are yet true exemplars of those terms. Through their disinterested service to mankind, or through their mastery over passions and thoughts . . . or through their great powers of concentration, they are, in a sense, yogis; they have set themselves the goal of yoga—self-control."

By dispelling that ignorance of the true self he has realized the Changeless Total Universal Self as his own true form, and through this realization ignorance has been destroyed.

—THE VEDANTASARA
a 15th-century Brahmanical text

I'd be pretty dumb if all of a sudden I started being something I'm not.
—YOGI BERRA

The dynastic Yankees of the 1940s, '50s and '60s knew exactly who they were. They weren't a projection of their owner's ego. "In those days, to be a Yankee, in New York," says Berra, who was the Yankees' best or at least, after Mickey Mantle, next-best immortal of the '50s, "you were treated like a god." Yankees were united by aplomb and *esprit de corps*. Yoga, wrote Jung, is a "method of fusing body and mind together so that they form a unity which is scarcely to be questioned. This unity creates a psychological disposition which makes possible intuitions that transcend consciousness."

Levitate your consciousness to total nothingness.
—YOGI BHAJAN

In baseball, you don't know nothing.
—YOGI BERRA

Anyone who has followed the Yankees over the last 20 years—since 1964, when Berra was fired as manager although New York won a pennant in its first season under him—knows that the franchise has a karma problem: a festering buildup of the consequences of past actions.

"The Yankees made the biggest mistake in their whole career, firing Yogi," says Berra's old teammate Whitey Ford. It took them 12 years to win another pennant, and although they have won four in the last eight seasons, those years have been an Era of Ill Feeling.

"I don't want to play for George Steinbrenner," said star reliever Goose Gossage last December, before he forsook the Yankees for the Padres. Steinbrenner, New York's principal owner since 1973, has fired 11 managers and alienated player after player. It's about as uplifting to go over his wrangles with Billy Martin, whom he fired for the third time after last season, as it is to replay the Watergate tapes. Bad karma accrues when your manager calls your owner a liar or punches out a marshmallow salesman, both of which Martin did. Also when your owner gets into a fight either in an elevator, as Steinbrenner claimed, or with an elevator, as skeptics suggested.

Just this spring training the Yankees' captain, Graig Nettles, decried Steinbrenner's "big mouth" and demanded to be traded. Dave Winfield, New York's best player, who has had various run-ins with Steinbrenner that still rankle on both sides, predicted that 1984 will see more of the same: "Afternoon soaps will have nothing on us. I think people are tired of that. They want to see baseball."

Ah. Yogi is baseball all over. Says his wife, Carmen, "Everything except baseball seems small to him." That "everything" would seem to include himself. There's not much I in Yogi, whom people often call Yog. Perhaps the true meaning of "In baseball, you don't know nothing" is that baseball is a game that humbles those who presume to be authoritative as Martin and Steinbrenner have done. "Yogi is perfect for this club right now," said pitcher Dave LaRoche in camp this spring. "Billy always wanted to be the center of attention. Yogi is satisfied to be a wallflower type."

The iron filings of karma are attracted only where a magnet of the personal ego still exists.

　　　　　　　　　　　　—YOGI PARAMAHANSA YOGANANDA

A good ball club.

　　　　　　　　　　　　　　　　—YOGI BERRA
　　　　　　　　　　　　　　when asked what makes
　　　　　　　　　　　　　　　　a good manager

Since 1960, the Yankees and their fellow New Yorkers, the Mets, have won 11 pennants. Yogi, who served with the Mets as coach from 1965 through '71 and as manager from '72 through part of '75 is the only person who has been a player or a coach or a manager on every one of those pennant-winning teams. When he was fired by the Yankees after losing to St. Louis in the '64 World Series and also when he was fired by the Mets in '75 although his '73 team had won a pennant, Yogi's critics said he had lost control of his players. But a yogi doesn't try to control others. "Every individual," says the Maharishi Mahesh Yogi, "is responsible for his own development in any field." Were the Maharishi a baseball fan, he would add "and at the plate." A yogi attempts to control himself.

Too nice a guy, Yogi's detractors have said of him. But "gentleness of mind is an attribute of a yogi whose heart melts at all suffering," said the Yogi B.K.S. Iyengar. Robert Burnes, a St. Louis baseball writer, once went with Berra to a church father-and-son banquet. Every son received a bat and a ball and came up to have Yogi autograph them. At a corner table were some kids from a local orphanage. They sat there with no balls or bats. "Aren't they getting anything?" Yogi asked. An organizer of the banquet told him that a couple of balls were being sent to the home for the orphans' use. "We think it's enough of a thrill for them just to be here," the man added.

Yogi got up from the head table, went to the orphans' table, sat down and began autographing whatever the orphans had. Someone at the head table finally said, "Yogi, we'd like you to come back up here and say a few words."

"Go on with the program," Yogi snapped. "I'm busy. I'm talking to some friends." And he stayed with the orphans the rest of the evening. As he and Burnes left, Yogi said, "I'll never forget that as long as I live."

When Yogi was promoted to manager this winter—he'd rejoined the Yankees as a coach in '76—Boston sports talk show host Eddie Andelman said that what the Yankees were actually getting was a "designated schmoo." Yogi's shape and good nature may resemble a schmoo's, but he may be more than that. He may be the man of the hour.

The time is now and now is the time.

—YOGI BHAJAN

You mean right now?

—YOGI BERRA
when someone asked him what time it was

TO SPEAK of the history of the Steinbrenner Yankees is difficult, because who wants to wade through all that again? To speak of Berra's history is difficult because so much of what's said about him—no one, including Yogi, seems to know how much—is legend.

Berra has little inclination to dwell upon the past. "I'm sure glad I don't live in them days," he once said, after watching a bloody movie called *The Vikings*. Or he may have said that. He's said to have said it. Trying to establish which of Yogi's famous sayings he actually said is an interesting, but hopeless, endeavor.

Sometimes diligent research pays off. For instance, there's the story about what Yogi told a young Met hitter who had adopted Frank Robinson's batting stance but still wasn't hitting, "If you can't imitate him," Yogi is supposed to have advised, "don't copy him."

But on Jan. 11, 1964, right after Berra had been named Yankee manager and a year before he got to the Mets, a long tape-recorded telephone colloquy between Berra, Casey Stengel and reporter Robert Lipsyte appeared, in transcript, in *The New York Times*. In it Stengel says to Yogi, "If you can't imitate anybody, don't copy him. That's the best advice I can give a new manager." Conceivably, Berra later passed that adage on to a Met, but because Berra spent several minutes one morning this spring chuckling over the kind of things Stengel used to say and wishing he could remember even a few of them specifically, that seems unlikely.

Why not just ask Berra himself whether he said various things he's supposed have said? Well, I did that. It confused matters. For instance, if I hadn't consulted Yogi, I'd be able to report that I pinned down the origin of "Nobody ever goes there anymore; it's too crowded" once and for all. I'd always been told that Yogi said that about a place called Charlie's in Minneapolis. On the other hand, I read somewhere that back in the late '40s Dorothy Parker had said it about Chasen's in Beverly Hills. Then I read that John McNulty had written it in a short story. And sure enough, in the Feb. 20, 1943 issue of *The New Yorker*, in a McNulty story entitled *Some Nights When Nothing Happens Are the Best Nights in This Place*, there occurs this passage.

" . . . a speakeasy, you could control who comes in and it was more homelike and more often not crowded the way this saloon is now. Johnny, one of the backmen outside, put the whole thing in a nutshell one night when they were talking about a certain hangout and Johnny said, 'Nobody goes there any more. It's too crowded.'"

Because in 1943 Yogi was 19 and playing in Norfolk, Va., we can assume that neither McNulty, nor some New York cabdriver stole the line from Yogi.

However. Before I tracked that short story down I discussed Berraisms with Yogi and Carmen. We were relaxing over vodka on the rocks in their nicely appointed parlor in Montclair, N.J. After their three boys grew up, the Berras sold the enormous Tudor house about which Yogi once said proudly, "It's nothing but rooms," and moved into a smaller but still substantial gray-shingled house a few blocks away. It's a home filled with fine antiques, with dropping-by children and grandchildren and with Berraisms which, however, the Berras don't preserve as carefully as they do furniture.

"The kids are always telling me, 'There you go, you said another one,' " Yogi said with a chuckle.

"He said one the other day," said Carmen. "I thought, 'That's a classic. I've got to write that one down.' But I forgot."

"How about the one I said, 'If I didn't wake up, I'd still be sleeping,' " said Yogi.

"I was almost late someplace," he explained. "Another one," he added, and he said something else that I didn't quite catch.

"No, that one wasn't funny," said Carmen.

"Oh," said Yogi affably.

"How about the one about the restaurant being so crowded nobody ever goes there?" I asked. "You didn't really say that, did you?"

Yogi smiled. "Yeah! I said that one," he assured me.

"You did?" I said. "About Charlie's in Minneapolis?"

"Nahhh, it was about Ruggeri's in St. Louis. When I was headwaiter there." That would have been in 1948."

"No," said Carmen, "You said that in New York."

"St. Louis," Yogi said firmly.

So there you are.

"My favorite Yogi story," says Yankee first baseman Roy Smalley, "is about the time be went to a reception at Gracie Mansion [the residence of New York's mayor]. It was a hot day and everybody was sweating, and Yogi strolled in late wearing a lime-green suit. Mayor Lindsay's wife, Mary, saw Yogi and said, 'You certainly look cool,' and he said, 'Thanks. You don't look so hot yourself.' If that isn't true, I don't want to know it isn't."

Nor do I. I feel bound to report, however, that there's at least one other version of the story. Same dialogue, only between Yogi and someone it would be hard for witnesses to confuse with Mary Lindsay: umpire Hank Soar.

Bill Veeck once maintained that "Yogi is a completely manufactured product. He is a case study of this country's unlimited ability to gull itself and be gulled. . . . You say 'Yogi' at a banquet, and everybody automatically laughs, something Joe Garagiola discovered to his profit many years ago."

What Berra says about his sayings, in general, is "I always say I said half of them, and Joe said the other half." This is apt but untrue. Certainly Garagiola, who grew up with Berra in St. Louis on what was known then as Dago Hill and who is working on a book about those days, has done as much for Berra's legend as the Beatles did for the Maharishi's. For one thing, as Berra says, "Joe can remember stories better than I can. I can't remember them." It follows that Yogi isn't the best authority for what he actually said. (And nobody else is, either.) Sometimes he will say, "I could've probably said that." Sometimes he will say he never said things that you wish he wouldn't deny saying. For instance, he claims he never said, "How can you think and hit at the same time?" It's a cold-blooded historian indeed who's willing to take Berra's word for that.

It may even be that Berra did think and hit at the same time. "Any hitter as good as Yogi was had to have an idea up there," says Yankee coach Mickey Vernon, who played against him for years. But when you ask Berra if it's true that he always hit high pitches well, he says, "They told me I did. I didn't know. If I could see it good, I'd hit it. Some of them I'd swing at, and some of them I wouldn't because I didn't see them good." Berra's old teammate Phil Rizzuto claims, "I've seen him hit them on the bounce; I've seen him leave his feet to hit them."

There's no doubt that Berra thought about other people's hitting. Ted Williams says Berra would notice subtle shifts of an opposing batter's feet that no other catcher would notice. "Berra knows how to pitch to everybody in the league except himself," said Stengel. But then, nobody knew how to pitch to Berra. "He could pull anything inside," says Vernon. "They'd try to throw him two pitches inside and hope he'd pull them foul, and then they'd go outside on him. And he'd take that to the opposite field."

Yankee player-coach Lou Piniella, who says, "When I'm feeling good I'm a player, when I'm feeling bad I'm a coach," studies hitting mechanics meticulously with the aid of videotape. He insists that thinking and hitting are thoroughly compatible. However, he concedes that "the paramount thing is to see the damn baseball." And New York outfielder Steve Kemp says, "Baseball is a game that if you think too much, it'll eat you up."

Let us remind ourselves that if Berra did say what he says he didn't say about thinking and hitting, he didn't say you can't think and hit at the same time. He just raised the eternal question "How can you?" And even if he didn't say it, he deserves to be credited with saying it because he's such a great example of the athlete who doesn't distract himself. Berra was so attuned to his batting self that he didn't consciously have to focus his mind on hitting. Asked if he ever studied his swing on videotape, he cringes. "I don't like seeing myself on television," he says. "I don't like it."

Concentration is the narrowing of the field of attention, the fixing of the mental eye upon a chosen object.

—ERNEST WOOD
Seven Schools of Yoga

You only got one guy to concentrate on. He throws the ball.

—YOGI BERRA

MANY PUTATIVE Berraisms are clearly bogus. Jim Piersall, a player of Berra's era, tells banquet audiences that someone once asked Berra, "Why don't you get your kids an encyclopedia?" Yogi answered, "Listen here, buddy, when I went to school, I walked. So can they." In the *New York Mirror* in 1959 Dan Parker wrote that someone once said to Yogi, "Why, you're a fatalist," and Yogi answered, "You mean I save postage stamps? Not me."

There were plenty of firsthand witnesses, however, to Berra's famous remark on the occasion of Yogi Berra Night at Sportsman's Park in 1947: "I want to thank all those who made this night necessary." Isn't that a perfect expression of the ambivalence of one who sincerely feels honored but hates playing the role of honoree? A poetic slip.

Some Berraisms transcend logic because they are simpler than logic. "I'm wearing these gloves for my hands," he said one cold spring-training day.

Others express something too subtle for logic. There was the time when some sportswriters urged Berra to go with them to a dirty movie. "Nahhh," he said, "I don't want to see no dirty movie. I'm going to see *Airport*."

"Come on, Yog, come with us. Let's go see the dirty movie."

"Nahhh. I'm not interested."

"Come on. You can see *Airport* anytime. Let's go see this dirty picture."

"Well," said Yogi, "who's in it?"

Isn't that a trenchant comment on pornography? Dirty movies don't have anyone in them.

There are many stories about Yogi on radio shows. He's supposed to have laid down this ground rule once: "It you ask me anything I don't know, I'm not going to answer." Would that everyone on radio followed that policy.

But my radio favorite is the one about the interviewer who told Berra before the broadcast, "We're going to do free association. I'm going to throw out a few names, and you just say the first thing that pops into your mind."

"O.K." said Berra.

They went on the air. "I'm here tonight with Yogi Berra," said the host, "and we're going to play free association. I'm going to mention a name, and Yogi's just going to say the first thing that comes to mind. O.K., Yogi?"

"O.K."

"All right, here we go then. Mickey Mantle."

"What about him?" said Berra.

Self-control entails avoiding statements that cause unnecessary to-do. Berra is very careful about that. Ask him how he's going to differ from Martin as manager, and he says, "I don't get into that."

But self-control isn't the same as self-editing. Two years ago in Florida, Vernon played with Yogi in a scramble golf tournament (in which all players in a group tee off but thereafter play only the best of the balls). Berra hit a nice drive up the middle. Vernon followed with an almost identical shot. Vernon's drive was a bit better. But Berra lingered next to the ball he'd hit so well. "If I was playing alone," he said wistfully, "I'd play mine."

Most people would have stopped themselves before they said that. They would have had the same feeling, but they would have reflected, "I'm not playing alone, though, so. . . ." Then they would have sorted out all the contradictions in their feelings and said either nothing or something less memorable than what Berra said. Berra reacts more quickly and on two planes of possibility at once.

The posture must be steady and pleasant.

—YOGI PATANJALI

Berra thinks home plate is his room.

—CASEY STENGEL

BERRA, WHO was awkward behind the plate at the beginning of his career, worked hard under the guidance of guru Bill Dickey—"Bill is learning me all his experiences"—and he became an extraordinarily heads-up catcher. Between pitches he was full of chatty hospitality, but while he was distracting the hitter, he wasn't missing a trick himself. Indeed, Berra is computer-fast at adding up gin scores. "He would be a brilliant nuclear physicist," says Garagiola, "if he enjoyed that kind of thing."

And when Berra saw a bunt or a steal of home coming, he would spring forward before the pitch had reached the batter. "If anybody'd swung," he says, "they'd've creamed me." But no one ever did. Berra was especially effective on squeeze bunts. Twice in his career he grabbed the bunt, tagged the batter before he could get away and then dived back to tag the runner coming in from third. That ties him with several other catchers for the lifetime record for unassisted double plays, "I just touched everybody I could," Berra explained after one of them.

On another occasion, Billy Hunter of the Orioles missed a two-strike squeeze bunt attempt on a pitch that was in the dirt. Berra trapped the ball, slapped a sweeping tag on Hunter, who was entitled to run because the third strike had hit the ground, and wheeled to put the ball on Clint Courtney sliding in. Alas, the umpire ruled that Berra had missed Hunter. Otherwise, Berra would hold the catcher's single-handed d.p. record single-handedly. "Hunter was out, too," says Yogi today, "Out as the side of a barn."

The preceding Berraism is one that I just made up. I guess it won't do. It's

Berraesque in that it entails a kind of refreshment of the concept of "out"—a soft-focus version of what E.E. Cummings called "precision which creates movement." (Cummings' own, not very pleasant, example of such precision came from vaudeville: "Would you hit a woman with a child?" "No, I'd hit her with a brick.")

But "out as the side of a barn" doesn't linger in the mind like Yogi's famous re-examination of two ordinary verbs: "You can observe a lot by watching." He actually did say that, except that it may have been "You observe by watching" in the original.

It's hard to make up a good Berraism.

One thing you cannot copy and that is the soul of another person or the spirit of another person.

—YOGI BHAJAN

If you can't imitate him, don't copy him.

—YOGI BERRA

I WAS determined to make up a Berraism for this story. One that would pass for real and go down in lore alongside "How long have you known me, Jack? And you still don't know how to spell my name." (Which is what Berra said—really and truly—when announcer Jack Buck compensated him for appearing on a pregame show with a check made out to Bearer.)

Here is an ersatz Berraism that I worked on for weeks: "Probably what a pitcher misses the most when he doesn't get one is a good target. Unless it never gets there." Nope. It's too busy. A real Berraism is more mysterious, yet simpler. Stengel once asked Berra what he would do if he found a million dollars. Yogi said, "If the guy was real poor, I'd give it back to him."

To come up with a Berraism that rings true, you have to start with some real Berraistic raw material, which, in itself, may *not* ring true. Take the famous utterance, "It ain't over 'til it's over," which is so distinctively descriptive of a baseball game—a football or basketball game is often over with five minutes to go—and which we would like to think is even true of life.

Research through old sports-page clippings indicates that what Berra probably said was, in reference to the 1974 pennant race, "We're not out till we're out." That quickly became "You're not out of it till you're out of it," which somehow evolved into "The game's never over till it's over," which eventually was streamlined into "It ain't over 'til it's over."

But I wouldn't call that a wholly manufactured product. Berra sprouted its seed. And he did so at a time when the expression "The game is never over till the last man is out" had become hackneyed, even if its meaning still held true. One thing Berra doesn't deal in is clichés. He doesn't remember them.

"Yogi gives short answers. And they're all mixed in with grunts," says Rizzuto, who adds, "but that doesn't mean he doesn't know as much as managers who'll talk forever." Usually these short statements aren't eloquent, and often they're more a matter of finger pointing, nudges, scowls, pats, shrugs and ingenious grins than of words or grunts. And yet every time I talked to Berra this spring, he said something or other that I couldn't get out of my mind. For instance, giving me directions to the racquetball club he co-owns in Fairfield, N.J., he said, regarding how long I should stay on one stretch of road, "It's pretty far but it doesn't seem like it."

As I drove to the club, I kept thinking that over. How could he know that a given distance wouldn't seem far to me? I thought it over so much that the distance went by even faster than I'd been prepared for, and missed the turn. I should have remembered what Berra said about taking the subway to Brooklyn, for the World Series; "I knew I was going to take the wrong train, so I left early."

There is a vital difference between an idiot or a lunatic on the one hand, and a yogi striving to achieve a state of mindlessness on the other.
                    —YOGI B.K.S. IYENGAR

People say I'm dumb, but a lot of guys don't make this kind of money talking to cats.
                    —YOGI BERRA
on receiving a residual check from his Puss 'n Boots
catfood commercial, in which the voice
of the puss was played by Whitey Ford.

IN HIS BOYHOOD, Berra was called Lawdie—a shortening of Lawrence. Had that name stuck, would there now be a cartoon character named Lawdie Bear? At any rate, there is one named Yogi Bear, an amiable, rotund figure who assures people he's "smarter than the average bear."

"They came out with that after Yogi won his third Most Valuable Player award," says Carmen. "And yet they claimed it had nothing to do with Yogi."

"Once somebody came up to me and asked, 'Which came first, you or the bear?' " says Yogi.

But how did Lawdie become Yogi? Historians agree it happened in his teens. At least five people, including Garagiola, have been credited for giving Yogi his name. Garagiola has said, "it was because he walked like a yogi." *The New York Times* once said it was because young Lawdie had taken up yoga-like exercises. According to other accounts, it was because nothing ever upset

Berra, or because one day he was wrestling and spun out of his opponent's grasp, and someone said, "He spins like a yo-yo." Then someone else said, "You mean he spins like one of them yogis." The most established version is that Berra used to sit around serenely with his arms and legs crossed, and one of his American Legion teammates, having seen some yogis in a travelogue about India, said he sat like a yogi. Berra told me a few weeks ago that this last version was correct, except, "Nahhh. There wasn't any movie."

And yet this spring I also heard him telling reporters that he had no idea why he'd been dubbed Yogi. "I had a brother they called 'Garlic,' " Berra told one reporter who pressed him for possible explanations of his cognomen, "and his name was Mike." Berra did say that the original dubber was his American Legion teammate Bobby Hofman—one of the few people connected with youth baseball in St. Louis in the '40s who, according to my research, had never been credited before.

So there you are. Taped onto the Berra's refrigerator door in Montclair is a letter from a boy in San Francisco, which Yogi hasn't gotten around to answering.

Dear Yogi Berra,
My name is Yogi, and I am 9. I hate my name because kids at school joke about it a lot. All the time. You are the only other Yogi I ever heard of. Where did you get your name from? My teacher told me about you. I hope that is OK. She said you just about invented baseball. How long did you play? Will you be my friend? I sure need one.

Your friend
Yogi Lisac
P.S. What do your friends call you? Did you ever get so mad you wanted to punch somebody?

WHEN BERRA came into organized ball he, too, was the butt of cruel kidding—people swinging from dugout roofs and calling him Ape was typical of this kind of humor—and he never fought back. He says it never bothered him, but that's hard to believe. Even some of the compliments he got would have upset most people. Cannon wrote that he and Berra were sitting in a restaurant when a woman stopped by the table.

"I don't think you're homely at all," the strange lady said.

"Thank you," replied Berra, sincerely.

In 1949, Cannon reported that some players had theorized that Berra swung at bad pitches because he was afraid of being ridiculed for taking a strike, "Notice how Yogi acts when he misses a ball?" one player was quoted as saying, "He shrinks and closes up. They kid him so much he's afraid of looking bad in the spotlight."

But if that was Berra's motivation for attacking every pitch he could reach, he turned that anxiety into a strength that caused opponents to consider him the Yankee they would least like to face in the clutch. He was always at his best in the late innings. "You give 100 percent in the first half of the game," he's said to have said, "and if that isn't enough, in the second half you give what's left." And you don't look back to add things up.

"He doesn't dwell on mistakes," says Cannon. "When something happens, it's done. His wheels are immediately turning about what to do next. I guess it's a quality that successful men have. I read that about David Rockefeller when he made a bad loan."

Male and female make a union and this complete union is the greatest yoga.
—YOGI BHAJAN

She wasn't the first girl I had ever asked out, she was the third, but I could hardly believe my luck when it turned out that she liked me as much as I liked her.
—YOGI BERRA

IT'S CLEAR, in her 50th or so year, that Carmen Berra will always be a great-looking woman. She and Yogi met in 1947 when he was a budding Yankee and she was a waitress at Stan and Biggie's in St. Louis.

"He was honest. And simple," she says. "Wasn't a show-off. I was dating a lot of college boys at the time and I liked him in contrast."

Her name was Carmen Short. "My family came from England in the 17th century," she says.

"Yeah," says Yogi. "She's got more aunts and uncles!"

At the time, Carmen's family wondered why she wanted to marry a "foreigner" and Yogi's why he wanted to marry an "*Americano*." But it has been a happy marriage, by all accounts, for 35 years.

When asked whether it's true that wise investments over the years have made him very comfortable financially, a near millionaire in fact, Yogi shrugs. "I don't know," he says, "you'll have to ask Carm." But hasn't he been a remarkably successful businessman? "Well," he says, "I guess I've got a smart wife. She's a, whattayacallit, an inquirer. Where I'd say, 'Yeah, go ahead,' she'll say 'Let's wait and took into it.' It's like with the furniture for the house. She's patient. She'll leave the room bare till she gets just the right thing."

Carmen serves on the board of a regional theater group, is on the committee that is working for the restoration of the Statue of Liberty and stays on Yogi's case. "Carmen said if you chew tobacco today, forget it. You don't have anyplace to come home to," says a young blonde employee at Berra's racquetball center. "She knows you chewed this morning, Yogs."

They have raised three solid sons: Larry Jr., 35, who caught in the minor leagues until he hurt his left knee and is now in the flooring business; Tim, 32, who played one season as a wide receiver for the Baltimore Colts in 1974 and now oversees the operation of the racquetball center and Dale, 27, who makes $600,000 a year playing shortstop for the Pittsburgh Pirates. Dale, who has always lived with his parents in the off-season, is about to follow his older brothers' example by getting married and buying a house not far from the New Jersey homestead. What with grandchildren and in-laws, there are as many as 17 people around the Berra table at Thanksgiving. Yogi carves.

When his boys were kids, Yogi says, "They'd try to get me to play ball with them, and I'd say, 'Go ask your brothers. I *got* to play.' " Otherwise, they say, he was a warm, normal father. And now they regard him with evident affection. Because he was already in Florida for spring training, Yogi couldn't make Dale's engagement party this February, but he telephoned his best wishes. After he hung up, Yogi said, "And Dale, you know, he's good. He's good. He said: 'I miss you.' "

"He's masculine," says Carmen of Yogi. "Very strong. Physically and mentally, or I should say psychologically. I think he's very sexy."

Yogi smiles. He doesn't look surprised.

"But he's stubborn. Very stubborn. About everything. I don't even think he's Italian. I think he's German. He's Milanese, from the north of Italy. They're very clipped. Very strong. They have a lot of German in them."

Feldmarschall Steinbrenner, please note.

Man suffers for one reason: Man loses his innocence. When you lose your innocence, you end up with dispute. To regain innocence so that universal consciousness will serve and maintain you is the idea of this yoga.

—YOGI BHAJAN

How can you say this and that when this and that hasn't happened yet?

—YOGI BERRA

BERRA WON'T speculate as to how long he'll last as Yankee manager, except jokingly: "You better get this story out pretty soon." It should be remembered that in 1949 when the Yankees hired Stengel, who lasted as manager for 12 years and 10 pennants, some of the same things were said about him as are said about Berra now: that he was good for public relations, a funny guy, but not really a serious field leader. When Stengel was a player, they said the same thing about him that they said about Berra later: that he wasn't built like a ballplayer.

Stengel used to say of Yogi, "This is Mr. Berra, which is my assistant manager." He also said the Yankees would fall apart without Berra behind the plate, and that Berra was the best player he ever had, except for Joe DiMaggio. Such distinctly ungushy baseball men as Ted Williams, Jackie Robinson and Paul Richards all said Berra was an exceptionally smart player. His managing moves have been questioned in the past, but so have those of every other manager. No one accuses him of not knowing the game.

At the very least, Berra is a link with the old, proud Yankee days. The clubhouse today is full of players whom Steinbrenner acquired for big money after they became established and whom fans tend to think of more as former Reds, Padres and Twins than as Yankees. The team used to be a symbol of permanence. Under Steinbrenner, Yankees have come and gone and been shifted from position to position. Now that the pinstripes are doubleknits, the team lacks real fabric.

Will Berra produce cohesion? "He knows players," says Smalley. "He's made it clear to each guy what's expected. A team takes on the personality of its manager. And Yogi is comfortable."

But not wholly laissez-faire. "Before, we had a Broadway clubhouse in here, all kinds of extraneous people," says Smalley. "Yogi says no visitors except family, and them only at certain times. I asked if I could bring in Bob James, the jazz pianist. Yogi said he'd go out and meet him, he'd give him a hat, but not in the clubhouse. I respected that."

"Everybody likes Yogi," said Steinbrenner when he announced Yogi's appointment, "and . . . respects him." The pause was just long enough to make the "respects" sound grudging. When I try to imagine how Berra and Steinbrenner will relate to one another, I can't shake the unpleasant image of a TV commercial for a New York radio station that Steinbrenner and several uniformed Yankees appeared in a few years ago. When Yogi, who was then a coach, began to say something in this commercial, Steinbrenner glared and snapped, "Just sing, Yogi." Yogi smiled, sang and gave no indication that heavy condescension bothered him. Self-control.

"To say that I don't have any worries or nerves is the opposite of the truth," Berra said in his 1961 autobiography, *Yogi*, written with the aid of Ed Fitzgerald. I worry about getting old, I worry about not getting around on the fastball. . . . ."

Indeed, when Tony Cloninger struck him out three times on fastballs one May day in 1965, Yogi immediately retired as a player. "I didn't go out there to be embarrassed," he says.

"I worry," he went on in the book, "about keeping Carm happy so she won't be sorry she married me, about the kids growing up good, and about keeping out of trouble with God. I worry a lot."

He has always had trouble sleeping on the road. In his playing days his insomnia exhausted many of his mates, including Rizzuto, from whom Berra often demanded bedtime stories. "Three Little Pigs, Three Bears, things like that," Rizzuto says. "He said the sound of my voice put him to sleep. I often thought of that when I started in broadcasting."

"Relaxed?" says Carmen. "I don't know why people think he's so relaxed. He's a basket case."

But it's a well-woven basket. "Some men are kind of hanging in the balance," Carmen says. "It seems like they just might go off the deep end any minute. I don't have to worry that Yogi is going to have a nervous breakdown.

"I look around at our friends. The men are heads of some of the biggest corporations, they're members of the biggest law firms. And Yogi is the envy of all of them. Since Day One, I saw that Yogi was the only man I knew who loved his job."

That in itself, of course, doesn't make him a true yogi. "I am a yogi because it is in your mind," says the Yogi Bhajan. "The problem with man," the Yogi Bhajan also says, "is that he is asked, 'Are you this or are you that?' But you are not this nor that, you are as you are." Yogi Berra has said quite a few things more thought-provoking than that.

The Last
Angry Men

BY RICK TELANDER

Every great NFL linebacker plays with a chip on his shoulder, and the best of them all, the Bears' Dick Butkus, remains a model for those players who, as the author notes, are among the rare human beings who appreciate being called animals.

THE GREATEST LINEBACKER IN FOOTBALL HISTORY SPEARS THE raw flesh with two sticks. He raises the meaty morsel and observes it, then places it in his mouth and eats it with gusto. He spears another slab of uncooked flesh and eats it too. But Dick Butkus, the man who once said his goal was to hit a ballcarrier so hard that the man's head came off, is shattering all myths tonight. Dick Butkus is eating sushi.

Can this be? The hand that used to search through pileups, feeling for eyes to gouge and limbs to twist, now cradles the chopsticks that grasp dainty yuppie food. Beside Butkus is his good buddy Steve Thomas, owner of a BMW dealership in Camarillo, Calif., a man who deals in fancy cars, sharing *ebi* with a man who used to deal in stripped-down pain. The two friends recently finished shooting a commercial for Thomas's dealership, in which Butkus plays a mechanic who is so awestruck by a young woman's ability to fix a noisy Bimmer with a twist of a screwdriver that he backs away from the engine, saying meekly, "I, uh, I'll get the coffee," cracking his head on the open hood in the process.

Good lord. Butkus the wimp? The man even lives in Malibu, a place about as close in texture to Butkus's old Chicago Southside neighborhood as *maguro* is to Polish sausage. Isn't Butkus the savage who once was charged with provoking three separate fights in one game against the Detroit Lions in 1969, who picked up four personal fouls in an exhibition game against the St. Louis Cardinals in 1970, who supposedly in one heated skirmish bit . . . a referee? Dick Butkus, a casualty of Hotel California? Say it ain't so.

And maybe it ain't. Underneath the civility, Butkus seems restless, a caged animal. "I'm sick of all the Beverly Hills crap," he snarls, putting down his chopsticks, wiping his mouth with a napkin clutched in a great right paw scarred by, among other things, crocodile's teeth. Yeah, just a couple weeks ago, he says, he had to put a linebacker's touch on some unfinished business. A big shot who owed Butkus for some entertainment work had sent him two checks in a row that bounced. Dick's wife, Helen, had urged her husband to remain calm, but Butkus shrugged her off, drove to the big shot's office in Beverly Hills, barged in, grabbed the man by the shirt and in front of stunned office workers, shoved the deadbeat out the door and into the man's car. They drove to the bank, whereupon Butkus pushed the miscreant up to the teller and demanded $2,500 in cash. After the fellow withdrew the money from his account, Butkus shoved him back out the door, telling him before they parted that the man was, in Butkus's uncluttered appraisal, an orifice.

"People promising stuff and not coming through. Talking," says the Hall of Fame linebacker. "People tell me, 'That's how people do business in Beverly Hills.' I say, 'Well, I'm not *from* here.'"

Where is Butkus from? Chicago, of course. Chicago Vocational High School, then the University of Illinois in Champaign for a while, then the Chicago Bears for nine years, from 1965 to 1973. But where really? Where are all linebackers really from?

The same place. A world where things are straightforward, yet a little bit skewed, where collisions are embraced, where hitting is a form of chatting. A jittery place of easy provocation and swift retribution. Detroit Lion inside linebacker Chris Spielman once tackled his grandmother when he was just five years old. Why? Spielman doesn't know. "She walked through the door. She went to give me a hug, and I took her out," he says. "I knocked her down, but she bounced back up. You could tell she was a Spielman."

Certainly genetics plays a part in the makeup of a linebacker. "You are born with some type of aggressive streak in you," says Spielman. Linebackers don't end up at their position by accident. No, sir. They are drawn to its possibilities the way foaming dogs are drawn to junkyards. "A linebacker couldn't be an offensive lineman," says Los Angeles Raider coach Art Shell. "Check out the guy's locker. An offensive lineman's locker, you see everything is in order. A linebacker's locker is in total disarray."

Nor can a wannabe linebacker masquerade for long as the genuine article.

"Brian Bosworth thought he was a great linebacker," says Seattle Seahawk defensive coordinator Rusty Tillman with contempt. Tillman, a former NFL linebacker himself, put together a tape of Butkus's big plays to show Bosworth (who had a brief, overhyped career with Seattle from 1987 to '89) "what a great linebacker was really like." A real linebacker would have been bouncing on his chair, cheering the video action, but Bosworth wasn't impressed by the tape. A short time later the Boz and his Mohawk were out of the league seeking work in biker movies.

Real linebackers don't constantly promote themselves. They may talk trash, but during the season they don't have a lot on their minds except nailing people. They are among the rare human beings who appreciate being called animals. How else can one describe a player who gets his greatest high from hitting an opposing quarterback, when, as New York Giant Lawrence Taylor said in his book, *LT: Living on the Edge*, "he doesn't see you coming and you drive your helmet into his back so hard, he blows a little snot bubble." Lovely. Linebackers all have their favorite moments. Former Lion Jimmy Williams used to speak of blindsiding a ballcarrier and hearing "that little moan"; the Houston Oilers' Wilber Marshall says simply, "I like to hear 'em gasp."

To each his own. As Dallas Cowboy hit man Ken Norton puts it, linebacker "is the most badass position on the field." Just repeat the names of the great ones and see if you don't feel like ducking: Ray Nitschke, Mike Curtis, Tommy Nobis, Bill George, Jack Ham, Sam Huff, Joe Schmidt, Lee Roy Jordan, Chuck Howley, Mike Singletary. There's former Kansas City Chief Willie Lanier, his helmet padded *on the outside*, to protect his victims. There's grizzled Philadelphia Eagle Chuck Bednarik nearly cutting golden boy Frank Gifford in two. There's Marshall hitting Lion quarterback Joe Ferguson so hard in 1985 that Ferguson is unconscious before he reaches the Silverdome turf. Is the man dead? Chicago Bear defensive coordinator Buddy Ryan thinks he is. Until Ferguson twitches. The league fined Marshall $2,000 for the blow, even though no penalty was called. "What was I supposed to do?" asks Marshall in disgust. "Hit him softly?"

Bad humor is integral to the position, says Bear linebacker coach Dave McGinnis, because of what a linebacker is asked to do: "He has to diagnose a play, defeat blockers and still be ticked off enough to get the ballcarrier. An offensive lineman is done when his man is blocked. A linebacker is only half done when he's beaten an offensive lineman. He has to have this desire to make the runner pay a price, to make him not want to come up in there anymore. I'd watch Singletary when he'd get stoked up, and he'd be screaming, 'I'm gonna be here! Always! Right here!'"

Linebackers rise out of the football ooze in a curious twist on Darwin: While the primitive stayed below, groveling on all fours, the more primitive ascended to the upright position. Of course in the beginning there were no linebackers at all in football. Because there was no forward pass, there was no need on defense for anything other than seven or eight down linemen who rooted like pigs and three or four defensive backs who could run down any ballcarrier who got past the swine. With the dawn of the pass in professional football in 1906, defensive principles slowly evolved. "Roving centers" started to pop up, and by 1920 something like a modern-day NFL middle linebacker had emerged.

His name was George Trafton and he played for the Decatur Staleys, who became the Bears. There is some dispute as to whether Trafton was the first true linebacker, but he was definitely the first Butkus-like personality in the NFL. Nicknamed the Brute, Trafton was as nasty as they come, despised by rival teams and their fans. In a Rock Island (Ill.) *Argus* account of a Staley game in 1920, Trafton was described as "sliding across the face of the rival center." Against the Independents in Rock Island that same year, Trafton took umbrage at a rumor that an opponent, a halfback named Fred Chicken, was out to get him. The Brute promptly knocked Chicken out with a hit that broke his leg. On the final play, Staleys' coach George Halas sent Trafton running for the exit and a waiting taxi. Angry Rock Island fans mobbed the taxi, and Trafton had to hitch a ride with a passing motorist to get himself safely out of town.

According to Bob Carroll, the executive director of the Professional Football Researchers Association, the first outside linebacker in the NFL was 6' 4" John Alexander, who played for the Milwaukee Badgers. Normally a tackle, one day in 1922 Alexander "stood up, took a step back, two steps out and became an outside linebacker," says Carroll. "He wondered why, as tall as he was, he was always getting down on the ground where he couldn't see."

Alexander would set the evolutionary clock moving, and 60 years later it would bring us to LT himself. Some people think that modern outside linebackers, blitz specialists primarily, aren't really linebackers at all, but gussied-up defensive ends. Some people say that inside linebackers, whether in tandem in a 3–4 alignment or standing alone in the increasingly rare 4–3 (wasn't a big part of Butkus's dark majesty that aloneness?), are the only true linebackers today. But linebacking is really about responsibilities and attitude, not formations.

Pain is the thing that separates linebackers from everyone else on the field—both dishing it out and receiving it. Linebackers dish out pain because it intimidates opponents. Says Butkus, "I was a fullback in high school, and if somebody made a perfect tackle on me, no big deal. But if I got hung up and guys were bear-hugging me and I couldn't use my arms, and somebody came in and nailed me, I didn't like that. So I did that to guys we were tackling in high school, and sometimes their eyes would close or they'd flinch or pull up.

In college I figured punishing the ballcarrier wouldn't intimidate anybody, because the players were better. But it did. Then I *knew* it wouldn't work in the pros. I thought I'd meet guys like me. But there were still guys who were chicken----, guys with big yellow streaks."

Linebackers see the game as superseding all guidelines on basic empathy for one's fellow man. "You want to punish the running backs," says Steeler Pro Bowl linebacker Greg Lloyd. "You like to kick them and, when they get down, kick them again. Until they wave the white flag." Or as Huff of the Giants said to TIME magazine in 1959, "For that matter, we try to hurt everybody."

Even themselves at times. The euphoria that linebackers experience afield comes during the white flash of great collisions—enlightenment literally being a blow to the head. Lloyd split two blockers in a game against the Cleveland Browns last year and then met runner Kevin Mack head-on in the open hole. The ensuing crash overwhelmed Lloyd. "I was dizzy, my head was hurting and my eyes were watering," he says of his condition as he staggered to the huddle. "It felt good."

Where does such lunacy come from? "Off the field I'm quiet, laid-back, calm, relaxed," says Eagle star Seth Joyner. "On the field I talk all kinds of garbage and things like that. I think it's a way to vent your anger."

Anger over what?

Butkus struggles with the question. It's not really anger, he says. It's more a desire to set things right, to prove, as he says, "you don't get something for nothing." Violence can resolve ambivalence and uncertainty. And who doesn't crave certainty in life, a reward for the good, punishment for the bad?

Things are so simple when you're a linebacker. One afternoon while Butkus was practicing at Chicago Vocational with his high school team, he noticed four boys in a car harassing his girlfriend, Helen Essenberg, who was across the street near the school. Without hesitation Butkus ran off the field, chased the car onto 87th Street, dived through the open front window on the passenger side and, in full uniform, thrashed each of the passengers. Then he climbed out of the car and walked back to the field. He never said a word to Helen, who is now his wife. He had done what needed to be done, and it was over. "They could have been her friends, for all I knew," he says.

Singletary broke 16 helmets in four years at Baylor, all of them his own. The school's publicist confirmed that typically two or three football helmets are broken each year at the school, *by the entire team*. Most NFL coaches agree that the perfect size for a linebacker is between 6' 2" and 6' 4" and 240 to 250 pounds, but players such as the 6-foot, 230-pound Singletary and the New Orleans Saints' 5' 9", 225-pound Sam Mills have proved that size is not as important to the position as want-to. Is that the same as craziness?

There are former players like the Steelers' Ham, a Hall of Famer, who says, "I don't think we're any meaner than any other position on the team." But after some thought he admits that the first person he saw eat a glass was former Eagle linebacker Tim Rossovich, and that former Raider star 'backer Ted Hendricks did, indeed, have "this demented look to him." Then there was former Cincinnati Bengals linebacker Reggie Williams, who doubled as a city councilman and seemed the master of comportment, as long as he wasn't on the field. But that is in keeping with the Jekyll and Hyde nature displayed by good linebackers. Off the field they generally keep cool; on the field they explode. Lloyd says linebackers are "deviant" because they change personalities so dramatically. "You wear all different hats," he says. "You're a father, a husband. But on the field, yes, you are that other person."

Marshall marches to his alter ego's battle chant, kill or be killed, but going nuts can lead to disaster, even for an assassin. "You have to be under control, you can't be a complete idiot," says McGinnis. "I've seen tough guys who couldn't make reads just get killed. You have to be tough like a bull but smart like a coyote. You step up too quick and they'll run a power O or a counter, and the tight end will come down and earhole you. Try that some time."

The easiest thing to teach a linebacker is to blitz. It's like cutting the twine on a catapult. The hardest thing to teach is pass defense. Dropping back after reading a play-action fake is not an easy thing for an attacker to do. "It's a discipline thing," says Buffalo Bill assistant linebacker coach Chuck Lester, "because it goes against his nature."

Still linebackers have more freedom than other players. Their job is basically to do whatever is necessary to make all the tackles. And because linebackers are freer to attack and seek the explosions they crave, they seem to miss the game more than other players when they can no longer play. In his book, *Calling the Shots*, Singletary described the splendor of the devastating hit: "The resultant feeling has always been almost indescribable to me, akin to being struck, I suppose, by a bolt of lightning—a blast that, for one brief second, shines through your mind and body like a flash of brilliant white heat." St. Paul would not describe a vision any differently.

Thinking about life after football worries some linebackers. "Right now, with football, I can release all of my frustrations and not too much bad can happen to me," says New England Patriot linebacker Vincent Brown. "Sometimes I wonder what my outlet for those feelings will be after I stop playing."

That worried Butkus. It still does. "What I miss is the violence," he says bluntly. "Life is very boring to me now." He thought he would get into coaching after he retired, keeping the juice flowing that way, but an injury lawsuit he brought against the Bears, which was settled in '76, made him something of a pariah to his old team. His Miller Lite beer commercials led to an acting career, with Butkus mostly playing against type —a funny, sensitive guy in a caveman's body. Acting's O.K., he says, but after football, "hell, you just do what's second best."

Every now and then the demons that can't be exorcised come out, as they did when Butkus went to collect on the bounced checks. As they did last month when he was hosting a quail hunt in Georgia for the *Suzuki's Great Outdoors* series on ESPN. A quail flew at him, and Butkus, holding a shotgun in one hand, angrily forearmed the bird, batting it to the earth as if it were a tipped pass, its feathers drifting down to meet the corpse. The segment did not make the final program. "We didn't think it showed proper safety with a gun," the producer explained.

And so the greatest linebacker ever to play the game is trapped in La La Land. He starts his car, puts a dip of snuff under his lip and heads down the highway toward Malibu, where his neighbors include Cher and Olivia Newton-John.

"There are other things you can accomplish in life," Butkus says, spitting into his cup. "But physically, how do you get that rush again? You're in the middle of it all. You're involved, instead of hanging over the sides, you're *there*. The ball is snapped, somebody is trying to knock your ass off, you're trying to knock his ass off. . . ."

Mountains rise out of the dark air. The ocean is nearby.

"How the hell do you get that feeling again?"

The answer is simple.

The Year, The Moment And Johnny Podres

BY ROBERT CREAMER

There were many worthy candidates when SI chose its second Sportsman of the Year, but none more deserving than the man who delivered the Brooklyn Dodgers to the promised land by beating the Yankees in Game 7 of the World Series.

T HE NINTH WAS JOHNNY PODRES'S INNING. THE ANTICIPATION *of the victory rode on every pitch. The first batter tapped the ball back to the pitcher's mound and Johnny, plucking the ball from the netting of his glove, threw him out. In Yankee Stadium 62,000 people leaned forward to watch Johnny Podres face the next man. He raised an easy fly to leftfield and was out. (Fifty million or so TV watchers were holding their breath now too.) The third man took a called strike (the stadium crowd exploded with noise), took a ball, swung and missed (an explosion from coast to coast), took a second ball high, fouled one, fouled another. The Brooklyn Dodger infield moved restlessly, fidgeting. Podres threw again, a big, fat, arrogant change-up that the batter topped on the ground. After a half century of waiting the Brooklyn Dodgers were champions of the world.*

THE GRANDFATHER of Johnny Podres climbed out of the mines of czarist Russia and came to America in 1904, the year after Cy Young and the Boston Red Sox beat Honus Wagner and the Pittsburgh Pirates in the first World Series. The chances are excellent that Barney Podres had never heard of Cy Young or Honus Wagner, or of the Boston Red Sox or the Pittsburgh Pirates, or of the World Series, or even, for that matter, of baseball. He was 24, and he had been working in the mines for 10 years.

In America he found his way to an iron-mining community in upstate New York in the rough foothills of the Adirondacks near Lake Champlain, married a Lithuanian girl and took his broad back and big hands down into the mines again. Forty-six years, two wives and eight children later he came out of the mines for the last time.

Now he sits in his weather-beaten house in the company village of Witherbee, N.Y., ailing from "the silica," the miner's disease, his great hands folded. His story is neither rare nor extraordinary; it has been repeated in one form or another in millions of American families. But it has a close relationship to the reasons why SPORTS ILLUSTRATED this week salutes the old man's grandson as its second Sportsman of the Year, to succeed Roger Bannister as the one person—of the millions active in sports all over the world in 1955—who was most significant of the year past.

For in the old man's lifetime sports has grown from a minor diversion for a leisurely handful of people to a preoccupying influence in almost every country on earth.

Consider Joe Podres, son of old Barney and father of Johnny, the Sportsman of the Year. Like his father, he went down into the mines in his youth. But working conditions in the mines have improved, like working conditions almost everywhere, and a man has more time that is his own. Joe Podres spent a good deal of his free time playing baseball. He worked all week and played ball on Sundays, or whenever the local team could schedule a game. He was a topflight semiprofessional pitcher for 25 years, until he reluctantly retired three years ago at the age of 43. Sports earned him no money to speak of ("Eight dollars in eight years," is one family joke about it), but the competition and the pride of victory over a quarter century did a great deal to offset the exacting drudgery that goes with simply digging iron ore. And it provided the key that opened the way for his son to make come true a modern version of one of those old legends of beggars and kings and gold pots in the cabbage patch that were told for centuries by miners, farmers, peasants and other wishful Old World dreamers.

Today, even the dream is different. It does not deal with beggar boys becoming kings, or knights on white chargers. The boy kicks a football along Gorky Street and imagines himself booting the winning goal for Spartak in Dynamo Stadium in Moscow. He belts a hurley ball along the rich turf with a stick of Irish ash and thinks how grand it would be in Croke Park in Dublin saving the All-Ireland title for Cork. He stands on the edge of a street in a village in Provence as the Tour de France wheels by and sees himself pedaling into Parc des Princes Stadium in Paris, miles ahead of Louison

Bobet. He throws a ball against the battered side of a house and dreams of pitching Brooklyn to victory in the World Series.

JOHNNY PODRES, with three other high school boys, drove out of Witherbee in August 1949, and 265 miles south to New York City to see the Brooklyn Dodgers play a baseball game with the Boston Braves. It was the first major league game Johnny Podres had ever seen.

"We sat way up in the upper-leftfield stands," Podres recalls. "Newcombe was pitching. The Dodgers had the same guys they have now: Robinson, Reese, Campy, Hodges, Furillo, Snider. I've always been a Brooklyn fan, and that day I made up my mind, I'm going to pitch for Brooklyn."

Johnny planned to see the Dodgers play again the next day but it rained, and the day after that when the Dodgers were playing again, some other youngster was sitting in the upper-leftfield stands daydreaming of playing in the majors. John Podres was back in Witherbee, still a high school kid rooting for Brooklyn. While the Dodgers went on playing, winning and losing pennants, John Podres went on to become captain of his high school basketball team, to pitch his high school team to its league championship, to date, to dance, to hunt deer in the hills outside of town, to fish through the ice of Lake Champlain in the winter.

Then the major league scouts came around and the dream began to come true for John Joseph Podres. Two or three clubs were interested in him for their minor league farm clubs, but for one reason or another John did not sign. His father says, "I think he was just waiting for Brooklyn to come along." Come along they did, and Johnny signed a contract and, in 1951, went off to the Dodgers' farm system. He won 21 and lost five in his first year, later caught the eye of Dodger manager Charley Dressen and in 1953 was indeed pitching for Brooklyn in a World Series. That, however, was far from being the magic moment, because young Podres was driven from the mound by the New York Yankees, who were beating Brooklyn again, for the fifth time in five World Series meetings.

John Podres is on good terms with luck, however, despite a chronic bad back and a midseason appendectomy. Last fall, as most of the world knows, he got a second try at immortality. Fittingly enough, it was on his 23rd birthday. Brooklyn had lost the first two games of the World Series—and Johnny himself had not finished a game since early summer—but he was the right man in the right place that day. The Yankees could not rattle him, nor could they connect solidly against his arrogant blend of fastballs and lazy-looking slow ones. The Dodgers not only won that game but the next two to take the lead in the Series and approach the brink of incredible victory.

Then they lost the sixth game, woefully. People in Brooklyn were saying, "those bums," and not in tones of rough affection. Rather it was an expression of heartbroken anger and frustration, that they should have come so close only to lose again. They had always lost to the Yankees in the World Series. They had always lost to everybody in the World Series. They were losing now. They would always lose.

At this propitious moment the grandson of old Barney Podres stepped forward, bowed to the audience and promptly became the hero of the year. It was the setting of the dream of glory, and Johnny Podres knew exactly what to do. He beat the Yankees for a second time, shut them out without a run in that old graveyard of Brooklyn hopes, Yankee Stadium itself. Johnny Podres pitched with his ears shut. The explosive noise of the crowd, the taunts of the Yankee bench never got through to him. "I guess I didn't really hear the noise," says Johnny, "until I came up to bat in the ninth." By that time the noise was for Johnny Podres, pitcher, and it was time for him to hear it.

In winning—and this was, in retrospect, the most exciting and fascinating thing about the Series—Johnny became the personification, the living realization of the forgotten ambitions of thousands and even millions of onlookers who had pitched curves against the sides of their own houses and evoked similar visions of glory, only to end up at the wheel of a truck or behind a desk in an office. What was happening transcended any game, or any sport . . .

> . . . *The Russian more often than not ends up in a factory turning out heavy machinery for the state; he keeps his emotions under control until he can get to his seat high up on the side of Dynamo Stadium where he can yell his heart out for Spartak. The Irishman puts his hurley stick away and tends dutifully to the farm, except when he can get down to Cork City to shout for Cork against Tip or Limerick. The Frenchman uses his cycle only to ride back and forth from home to shop to cafe; but the day the Tour goes through his village he's back on the curb again, watching, watching, as the wheels fly by. Dreams die hard.*

And so, when the country boy from the small mining village stands alone on the mound in Yankee Stadium in the most demanding moment of one of the world's few truly epic sports events, and courageously, skillfully pitches his way to a success as complete, melodramatic and extravagant as that ever dreamed by any boy, the American chapter of the International Order of Frustrated Dreamers rises as one man and roars its recognition.

There were others in the world of sport eminently fitted for the robes of Sportsman of the Year.

Sandor Iharos set five world records in 1955, astounding records that left track and field aghast. Rocky Marciano broadened his omnipotent rule over heavyweight boxing. Paul Anderson performed Bunyanesque feats of weightlifting that evoked admiration and applause even in Russia. Aging Jackie Robinson retained the fiery spirit of the competitor sufficiently to light an exciting spark of success under his Brooklyn teammates during the pennant race and again in the World Series. Mrs. Mildred (Babe) Didrikson Zaharias brought great credit to sport by the courage, serenity and bright good humor she displayed in the face of a terrifying attack of cancer. Juan Fangio combined magnificent skill and cold, practical courage to drive racing cars faster than anyone else in the world. Otto Graham came out of the ease of retirement to lead the desperate Cleveland Browns to yet another magnificent season. Eddie Arcaro rode a horse as well as ever a horse can be ridden. Ray Robinson wrote a brilliant chapter of climax to the most dramatic comeback in the history of boxing. And dozens of others, with names like Cassady, Tabori, Alston, Russell, Sowell, Stengel . . . the list is endless if you listen to the sincere arguments from every part of the world of sport.

But nowhere else in that vast, heterogeneous and wonderful world did such a moment exist in 1955 as that of the seventh game of the World Series. Nowhere else did a man do what he had to do so well as Johnny Podres did that day. Nowhere else in all the world did sports mean as much to so many people as it did the day John Podres beat the Yankees.

Gifts That God Didn't Give

BY JOHN PAPANEK

As he entered his third pro season, Larry Bird's talent was well-established, but this cover story for SI revealed how the Celtics star—by force of will and tireless labor—was making himself the most complete player since Oscar Robertson.

OUTSIDE THE GYM IT'S A CHILLY AND GRAY BROOKLINE, MASS., evening. Inside it's steamy and hot and marginally violent. It is the first of October, the last day of a rite known as orientation camp, and eight players, including one promising rookie and one has-been, are scrimmaging for their lives against the home team from Hellenic College. The following morning the veterans will check into camp, and soon afterward, most of the members of the orientation class will be checking out. The veterans, after all, are the real owners of the green jerseys—the World Champion Boston Celtics.

It is seven o'clock, and the real Celtics are at once celebrating the official end of summer and dreading the transition from champions to defending champions. No NBA team has successfully defended a title since the 1969 Celtics, so this last night of liberty is to be cherished. But not by Larry Bird, who can't wait until morning.

His premature appearance in the Hellenic College gym, calculated, as always, to be as unobtrusive as possible, is, as always, anything but. The pair of worn sweat pants, the navy-blue sweat shirt and the blue baseball cap bearing the inscription WEST BADEN POLICE that is pulled down over his straw-blond hair (but not his blue eyes) fail to mask Bird's true, 6' 9", ultrawhite identity. There is a palpable skip in the beat of the practice when everyone realizes he is in the gym. All the would-be Celtics nod to him in careful reverence, and what they are thinking shows even more clearly now that *he* is here. Bird knows what they're thinking, but he wants them all to relax. He recognizes his responsibility to them, even though most will never get to play on his team.

"You guys gettin' your asses beat again?" he calls out in his southern-Hoosier twang as he sits down next to some rookies. The tension eases, and the players go even harder as Bird calls out encouragement across the gym from where coach Bill Fitch has been hollering commands all evening. Bird salts his Herb Shriner Hoosierisms with a dash of Redd Foxx vulgarity, and the players love it. Bird is a champion. He has proved it. But more than that, he is what the Creator had in mind when he invented the teammate. For this moment—and for this moment only—all the rookies and free agents and Larry Bird are one. Celtics. Eight minds cry out at once: "Please grant me the chance to play with Larry Bird!"

When the court clears and everyone leaves the gym, Bird ventures onto the floor, alone with a basketball and a goal to shoot at—a creature in his natural habitat if ever there was one.

He begins his routine by setting the ball down by his feet—*lovingly*, if that is possible—and then jumping rope vigorously for five minutes to warm up. When he finishes, he bends down to the ball, but instead of picking it up he gives it a hard slap and it springs to life, leaping up to Bird's hand like an eager pet. He never holds it, just begins striding briskly downcourt while the bouncing ball weaves itself intricately in and out of his legs. He quickens his pace from a walk to a jog; from a jog to a run—stopping, starting, darting, spinning. The basketball is his dancing partner, never causing Bird to reach for it or to break stride in any way. When Bird begins to feel loose, he flings the ball against a wall and back it comes, in rhythm. Off a door, off a chair . . . the ball seems to be at the end of a rubber band attached to his right hand.

Now he finds himself making layups, 10 with his right hand, 10 with his left. No misses. Then hooks from eight feet: 10 and 10, no misses. He backs away along the right baseline for 15-foot jump shots. He misses three in a row; and for the first time the ball goes its own way and Bird has to chase it. When he catches up with it, he flings it, a little bit angrily now, off a wall or a section of bleachers. Once, when he has to go way into a corner of the gym for the ball, he spots a small trampoline lying on its side. *Thwang*—he hurls the ball into the netting and it shoots back to him. A new game. He passes into the trampoline 25 or 30 times, harder each time, until the ball is a blur flying back and forth, powered by nothing but flicks of his wrists.

He catches the last pass from the trampoline, spins and shoots from 35 feet—and the ball hits nothing but net. Three points. Not only is the shot true, but the ball hits the floor with perfect spin and, bouncing twice, comes right into his hands at 15-foot range on the left baseline. With his body perfectly squared to the basket, the fingers of his right hand spread behind the ball, the left hand guiding the launch, he makes another jump shot. He moves three steps to his right and the ball is there—as expected—and he swishes another. He continues to move "around the world," all the way back to the right baseline, making 10 15-footers without a miss and without reaching for the ball. It is always there to meet him at the next spot. Then he goes back the other way and never misses. From 20 feet he makes 16 of 20, and then he begins all over again, running up and down, dribbling the ball between and around his legs, heaving it off a wall every now and then, putting it down for the jump rope, then calling it back into action.

After two hours of this, Bird shrugs off a suggestion that his performance has been slightly short of incredible. "Nah, I was really rusty," he says. "I've missed it. Being out there all alone . . . I've always liked it best that way. At midnight, like that, when it's really quiet, or early in the morning when there's nobody else around."

If Bill Russell symbolized the Boston Celtic ideal of humility, teamwork and excellence through 11 championship seasons, the torch was passed to John Havlicek, then Dave Cowens and now to 24-year-old Larry Joe Bird. Bird, in fact, carries humility to an extreme. He spurns publicity (and untold thousands of dollars) and doesn't enjoy sharing with strangers his innermost—or, for that matter, outermost—feelings. To some, he is every bit what he calls himself: "Just a hick from French Lick." He went through most of his senior season at Indiana State without talking to print reporters because, he explained, he wanted his teammates to get publicity, too. "When Larry makes up his mind to do something, nothing can change it," a Celtic official says. That intense resolve goes a long way toward explaining Larry Bird. "How do you differentiate the great athletes from the good ones?" asks Cowens, sitting in his athletic director's chair at Regis College in Weston, Mass. "It's a savvy, or something. Larry's got it. Something mental that other players with more physical talent don't have. If I were starting a basketball team, I'd look for a great center, but if I couldn't find a great one, I'd take Larry Bird."

The image of the dummy, the hick, is one more thing that Bird uses to his advantage, like his jump shot, or, more to the point, his head-fake. "Like I tell people," he says, "I'm not the smartest guy in life, but on a basketball court I consider myself an A-plus. Not that I'm dumb. I can keep up with 90 percent of the people in this world. I just don't explain myself to people. I want to keep 'em guessing. The way they take me is the way they take me."

This is the way to take Bird: He is the most *complete* basketball player to come along since Oscar Robertson. Bird may not be the best player—at least he doesn't think he is—but no one playing the game today can do as many different things on a court as well as Larry Bird. The year before he joined the Celtics, 1978–79, the team won 29 games, lost 53 and finished last in the NBA's Atlantic Division with the second-worst record in the league. In that season, Bird, averaging 28.6 points and 14.9 rebounds, led Indiana State from obscurity to 33 straight victories and the NCAA finals. In 1979–80, his NBA Rookie of the Year season, Bird averaged 21.3 points, 10.4 rebounds and 4.5 assists; led the Celtics to the NBA's *best* record (61–29); and carried them to the Eastern Conference playoff finals, which they lost to Philadelphia. Last year Bird averaged 21.2 points; upped his rebounding average to 10.9 and his assists to 5.5; led the Celtics to a 62–20 record, tying them with the 76ers for best in the NBA; and then averaged 21.9 points, 14 rebounds and six assists in the playoffs as Boston won its 14th NBA championship. Bird finished second to Philadelphia's Julius Erving in the balloting for the league's most valuable player.

When you thumb through basketball history to find the one player who could score, rebound, pass, play defense, lead a team and—this is Bird's greatest gift—see the court better than all others, your finger stops first at Robertson, the great guard for the Cincinnati Royals and later the Milwaukee Bucks. But then it continues, past Havlicek, past Rick Barry, past Erving, past Jerry West, past Earvin (Magic) Johnson even, and comes to rest at Larry Bird.

At 6' 9", Bird, who plays forward, is four inches taller than Robertson, but height would seem to be Bird's only natural advantage over Robertson or anyone else for that matter. Bird looks like a soft, fleshy adolescent. He is slow as NBA players go, and in the words of an NBA scout—not the only one who thought Bird would be a mediocre pro—he suffers from "white man's disease." That is, he can't jump. How, then, can Bird be so great? "I would say my vision, my court awareness and my height are God-given," Bird says. "Everything else I've worked my ass off for."

Work—at least work on a basketball court—is what Bird loves. It has been that way ever since he was old enough to dribble a basketball up and down the hilly streets to the playgrounds of French Lick, Ind. Because his two older brothers, Mark and Mike, generally dominated the ball and the neighborhood games, Larry had to wait his turn. And when he got the ball—late at night or early in the morning, when no one else wanted to play—he would usually take it to the park by the old high school and work by himself for hours on end, just as he does now. Nothing else mattered to him but mastery of the ball and the game to which it belonged. When Bird gets into a game with four other players, his greatest gift—his court awareness—makes that unit work. He performs as though he not only sees everything as it develops, but also as though he sees everything *before* it develops.

"Larry is the best passing big man I've ever seen," says Celtics president Red Auerbach, who coached nine NBA championship Celtic teams and has been around the NBA since 1946. "Barry was damn good, but he wasn't in a class with Bird. This guy is unique. He's like a Bob Cousy up front, and Cousy, without question, was the greatest passer who ever played the game. Larry will probably go down in history as one of the great forwards of alltime, if not the greatest."

Says Havlicek, "What Larry does doesn't surprise me because our minds think alike. When I watch a game I know what *should* be done, but 99 percent of the time it isn't. When Larry's in there, 99 percent of the time it *is*." Says Bird, "When my teammates get open I hope to God I can get 'em the ball. If you don't get 'em the ball, you'll tell 'em you seen 'em but it was too late. I don't know how many times last year I'd cut right down the middle and [Cedric] Maxwell would pass the ball a second before I was open. And he'd come right to me and say, 'My fault, I missed you.' It just carries over. And I know I might have started that. When you get that going, it means that everybody's always looking for the open man, and that's all they care about. The other teams better watch out."

What most impresses the people who know Bird—from his few new friends in Boston, to those in Terre Haute, where Indiana State is located, to the French Lickers who have known him since he was an itty-bitty thing with a basketball under his arm—is that *nothing* has changed him. Not the celebrity. Not the money ($650,000 per year). Nothing. The quintessential team player in the quintessential team game still wears blue jeans and baseball caps, and he still derives a third of his pleasure from being alone with a basketball and a goal to shoot at. Another third comes from being part of a team. "I've never known another player who is so loyal," says Celtic Kevin McHale. "If you're Larry's teammate, you're one of the most important people in the world to him." The rest of his pleasure comes from winning, mowing his lawn, drinking beer, hunting squirrels, fishing, playing golf and being with friends and family. Those who know Bird have a saying: "That's Larry." And they always say it smiling.

"If I say Larry Bird is the best player," Celtic guard Tiny Archibald comments, "people say, 'He's on your team, that's why you're saying that.' I still say he's the best *all-around* player. He does more things for us than any other player does for his team." Other Celtics echo Archibald's sentiments. Chris Ford: "Larry is a living textbook of basketball." Fitch: "I call him 'Kodak' because his mind is constantly taking pictures of the whole court."

Bird used to crawl into the nearest corner when people said such things about him. He would look down at his feet and, without thinking, mumble whatever words came first—anything to get these stupid questions over with and let's play ball. But during last year's playoffs Bird was the Celtics' most elo-quent spokesman—after Fitch.

Bird doesn't receive star treatment on the Celtics—"That's the way I like it, too"—and always heaps praise upon his teammates: "If it weren't for Tiny, for Max, for Robert Parish . . . you know, I could be out there but we wouldn't have won anything." They, in turn, heap praise upon Bird. Archibald says, "Guys appreciate his talent and what he sacrifices. We know he's the main focus on the team, but everybody on the team likes him because he's just Larry."

There is, however, another side of Larry Bird. When he gets loose, has a few beers and gets himself into comfortable company, he'll sit back, look up rather than down, his blue eyes sparkling and his face shining like a little boy's, and suddenly his Hoosier voice will become musical and full of confi-dence in his own marvelous talent.

"There are a lot of good players in the league," he'll say. "And on any given night any player can get hot and do anything he wants to. Some guys are very consistent and some guys are just great, but there are probably about 20 guys up there all the time. Now, I figure three out of four nights I'm going to play better than anybody else in the game. If you want to know who the best play-er in the league is, I'll put my money night after night on Kareem Abdul-Jabbar. He's the best. After him I'd probably take Julius Erving. And then, when it comes to a player who can do everything consistently, you'd have to say Elvin Hayes. There are just so many good players."

Bird is reminded of a stretch in the middle of last season when the Celtics won 25 of 26 games. "O.K.," he says. "I was playing great basketball for about a month. I reached my potential. For one stretch there, I was averaging about 28 points, 14 or 15 rebounds and seven assists. I felt like I had control of every game I played." But then came a nasty injury—one of Darryl Dawkins' mas-sive knees caught one of Bird's comparatively delicate pink thighs just before the All-Star Game, and Bird's thigh turned ugly purple for two weeks. Bird didn't miss a game, though. Never has, college or pro.

The championship series last year against Houston was supposed to be a for-mality, but the Rockets extended the Celtics to six games. In Game 6 the Rock-ets came from 17 points down in the fourth period, to pull within three with 1:51 left. Bird caught a pass from Archibald and, just as calmly as if he were all alone in a gym at midnight on the first of October, hurled in a three-point-er that put away the championship. "I didn't even know it was a three-point-er," Bird says now. "Heck, when I'm open like that for a shot I usually feel like I *can't* miss it. And when I have a shot like that to get us a game [in this case, a championship], I got to take it because I know I have an excellent chance of making it."

Can Bird feel when a shot is going to go in? And when it's not? "I used to in college, not anymore," he says. "For one thing, I don't like the basketball they use in the NBA [the seams on the pro ball are wider than those on the college ball]. In college I never had to worry about anybody blocking my shot. I could take my time. The defense is so much better in the pros. I always have somebody like Bobby Jones to worry about. You can never fake them out. You just have to make your move and shoot it quick. In college I followed my shot a lot. In the pros you can't afford to. If you follow your shot, you get burned at the other end. And there's one other thing. . . . "

Bird laughs a little bit and holds up his right index finger. "This," he says. The finger is shaped much like a boomerang, permanently bent toward his thumb at a 45-degree angle. Two operations have failed to straighten it; he can bend it only halfway to his palm. "I didn't have this in college," he says. He broke it playing softball the summer before his rookie year, trying to catch a wicked line drive off the bat of his brother Mike. "Mike hit a shot that knuckled like nothing I ever seen and that sucker hit my finger and I dropped it. So I picked it up and threw to second base, only the ball tailed up and away and clear over the second baseman, and Mike went all the way to third base laughing like anything. I had to laugh, too, because I didn't know why the ball did that until I looked down at my hand and saw my finger broken at about a 90-degree angle."

How great a baseball player would Mickey Mantle have been if he hadn't torn up his knee early in his career? One wonders what kind of shooter Bird would be now if he had a straight finger.

"That's what Red was telling me when I was trying to sign," Bird says.

LARRY BIRD was born in French Lick on Pearl Harbor Day, 1956, and he'd just as soon let the personal stuff go at that. The folks in the beautiful old hillside resort town honored their favorite son by renaming Monon Street as Larry Bird Boulevard, and they acknowledge the fact that Georgia Bird had to work all her life to raise her daughter Linda, 26, and five sons, Mike, 29; Mark, 28; Larry; Jeff, 17; and Eddie, 14. (Larry's father and mother were divorced in Larry's junior year in high school; his father committed suicide about a year later.) But they don't say much else. Close friends have been conditioned to say nothing more. Larry is a town treasure, and even though the townspeople would love to use his fame for their own fortune, as their elders once used the famous mineral springs to attract the cream of American society, they refrain. "I could tell some stories about some real nice things Larry has done but I wouldn't unless Larry said it was O.K.," says one close family friend. Another; a restaurateur; has thought of how his business would improve if he renamed his place "The Bird's Nest," but he knows Larry wouldn't go for it.

"I'll say this much," the man says, "you won't find a finer person than Larry. He hasn't changed one little bit. He comes back here in the summer every year and doesn't want anyone to know he's around except his closest friends."

For Bird, the pain of public exposure has been great from the beginning, when all he wanted to do was play ball. He didn't know what to make of the college recruiters who came to town. No sooner had he checked into Indiana University, in 1974 than he checked right out. Same thing at Northwood Institute in West Baden, Ind., a few months later. In his first 18 years Bird never was farther than 40 miles away from French Lick for more than a weekend.

When Bird finally found himself a home at Indiana State in 1975, it was only through the persistence of Bill Hodges, the assistant basketball coach who would become ISU's head coach in Bird's senior season. "If it wasn't for Coach Hodges, who knows what I'd be doing today?" says Bird.

"He'd probably be a bum," says a French Lick friend, "pumping gas or working in the Kimball piano factory like the other boys."

Bird never considered that basketball was something he could excel at and make his living from. "I didn't care either," he says. "I was one of those guys that never looked ahead. When I was younger I played for the fun of it, like any other kid. I just don't know what kept me going and going and going. I remember we used to practice in the gym in high school; then, on the way home, we'd stop and play on the playgrounds until eight o'clock. I played when I was cold and my body was aching and I was so tired . . . and I don't know why, I just kept playing and playing. I didn't know I was going to college until I was there. I never thought about pro basketball until I got there. Now that I am there, I want to make the most out of it that I can. I guess I always wanted, to make the most out of it. I just never knew it."

Bird takes for granted that one doesn't think he's just talking about money. "The way I live, I'd be happy making ten or twelve thousand a year," he says. But his agent, Bob Woolf, thinks in other terms. In his office on the 45th floor of Boston's Prudential Tower, Woolf has one entire rolling file cabinet filled with Larry Bird business. Woolf, a prominent sports attorney and meticulous keeper of scraps of paper and lists, pulls out the hotel bill from Larry's first visit to Boston. "Look at this," he says. "Three nights. Nothing but room and tax. Not a room service charge. Not a phone call."

The chance for Woolf to represent this most prized client came after a bizarre series of meetings set up by a committee of Terre Haute businessmen who "adopted" Bird, and still advise him on his finances. They reduced a list of three final candidates to Woolf after an eight-hour session. When Woolf met Bird over a dinner with the businessmen, he did his best to impress—Woolf wanted everyone to know what he thought Bird was worth, and he shared his insider's knowledge of salaries of basketball, football and baseball players. Woolf mentioned Tommy John of the Yankees, who happens to be a native of Terre Haute. The men on the committee blurted, "Yeah! How much does Tommy make?"

Woolf was about to divulge the numbers when Bird piped up for the first time: "Hey, please, Mr. Woolf. Tommy John's a friend of mine. I don't want to know how much he makes."

Woolf now waits for June 1984, when Bird's five-year, $3.25 million contract expires. "I'm dying to see what kind of money he'll draw on the open market," Woolf says. "He could become the highest-paid athlete in the world! Certainly in the NBA."

Woolf has served as a surrogate father to Bird. When Bird bought a home in the Boston area, he purchased one right next door to Woolfs in Brookline, just two minutes from the Celtics' practice site at Hellenic College. Last summer Bird bought a place on Cape Cod—right across the street from Woolf's. But now that Bird feels a bit more comfortable in the limelight, he no longer hides behind Woolf. Still, his reverence for home, family and charity hasn't changed. He mostly stays out of Boston, preferring the sanctuary of his house, which he shares with a 3-year-old Doberman named Klinger and a longtime girl-friend named Dinah Mattingly. He tends to his lawn and apple trees obsessively. His friends are chosen with caution; sometimes, Bird admits, too much caution.

"I'm not really shy, but it depends on what situation I'm in," he says. "I used to be real bad. I'm not the kind of person to go up and shake hands with somebody, because I'm in a situation where everybody wants to be my friend. I guess I miss out sometimes. I'm just accustomed to a small environment. When I was young, I was never around more than five or ten people at once."

Almost without exception, those people whom Bird has allowed to get close to him treasure his loyalty. He's great with children; for them, he will indulge himself in situations in which he wouldn't give an adult the time of day. His two summer camps—one in French Lick, the other in the Boston area—are strictly labors of love.

He also supplied entire teams of French Lick youngsters with clothing and equipment. And he has—though he would rather not have it known—a compelling affinity for the physically handicapped. "He's got an incredible memory," Woolf says. "If I told him something a year ago and change one word today, he'll catch me. He'll play a golf course once and memorize the location of every tree."

Woolf recalls that when a *Today* show crew came to tape a segment on Bird shortly after last May's playoffs, they wanted to show Larry watching a replay of the championship game against Houston. They threw the videotape on at a random point in the game and Woolf asked Bird if he could tell what part of the game was showing.

"Fourth quarter, 5:40 left," said Bird.

"How can you possibly be that precise?" Woolf asked. There had been no commentary and no score flashed. "The song," Bird said.

"The *song*?" Woolf said.

"That fight song. That's the last time they played it. They played it three times during the game. This is the last time because the crowd is going nuts. Houston came from 17 down and there's about 5:40 left."

"You mean you were aware of the *song*?" Woolf asked incredulously.

"I was *there*, wasn't I?" Bird asked.

"I was there, too, but I don't remember any song," Woolf said. "And I wasn't playing."

Bird chuckled and went on, watching the tape. He proceeded to call each play in perfect detail, about five seconds before it appeared on the tape.

"Larry's not subject to the normal persuasions," Woolf says. "He doesn't react to things the way normal people do."

But he did last spring. Four days after the Celtics won their championship, the financially beleaguered city of Boston turned out en masse to honor its team. Bird told a cheering crowd on City Hall Plaza, "I spent ten minutes in the mayor's office with all these people going around getting autographs, and now I know why Boston is going bankrupt."

There was some nervous laughter, but Bird wasn't finished. Someone in the crowd held up a sign that made a scatological reference to Moses Malone, the Houston center. Bird spotted it and announced to the throng, "I think, after all the hollering and screaming, I look out in the crowd and see one thing that typifies our season. Moses does eat ----!"

Bird later apologized to those he offended, including Malone, but it never occurred to him that the remark would be offensive. "That's me," he says with an impish grin. "I've said a lot of things I wished I never had, but hey, that's me. I'll do a lot more before I get older. There's nothing l can do about it once I've done it. What people think of me could hurt a little if they think bad. I'm sure there are people in this world who hate me, but there are a lot who love me. I'm just me. I try, to be honest.

"Like I told this friend of mine in Terre Haute before I came into the pros: 'One of these days I'll be the best basketball player in the NBA.' I was with the guy last June after it was announced that Julius Erving won the MVP. First thing this guy says to me is, 'Well, hell! You lied to me again! You been in the league two years already and you haven't even come close.' I said, 'Well, maybe this year.' "

That's Larry.

All the Rage

BY RICHARD HOFFER

As Mike Tyson stormed toward a long-awaited showdown with heavyweight champ Lennox Lewis, a writer who had chronicled Tyson's entire career tried to determine whether he was the ultimate psycho-celebrity or the shrewdest self-promoter of his time.

HERE, TAKE A LOOK: MIKE TYSON IS IN HIS BEACHFRONT cabana in Maui, having run his six miles on the sand, in great shape (as far as you can tell) and strangely calm, given the intense nature of his preparations, the desperate state of his professional life, the shambles of his business affairs. He and one of his assistant trainers are hunched at a laptop, poring over a web page, picking out pigeons to buy online. (He has a thousand.) Behind Tyson is a stack of books—*Machiavelli in Hell* by Sebastian de Grazia and the *Ultimate Encyclopedia of Mythology*. Outside, you can hear a gentle surf, maybe 20 yards away. A trade wind moves small clouds across the baby-blue horizon beyond his patio. Tyson looks up as a parade of international writers files in, and paradise be damned, a shape of bitterness suddenly forms in his mind.

"All my antagonists," he says by way of acknowledgment, a Maui menace now. An idea! "I ought to close the gate and beat your f------ asses, you all crying like women. Just close the gate. Kick your f------ asses."

These are his first words as he disengages from the childlike innocence of buying pets. He is not serious, of course; he beats no f------ asses. But he means to demonstrate how easily he can shuck the cloak of civility when it comes to his public life. He is not to be trifled with. A day later, when he meets broadcasters separately (like the writers, handpicked and briefed to a comical fare-thee-well by a nervously grinning New York p.r. man), he tells a young woman reporter from CNN/SI, "I normally don't do interviews with women unless I fornicate with them, so you shouldn't talk anymore, unless you want to, you know. . . . " He is not serious. Of course.

This is what everybody has come to see and hear, and nobody is disappointed. The rage is so ready that it seems practiced, the hatred by now ritual. Is it shtick? Or is it really a horrific unraveling? Questions to think about. Also: Does it matter?

For quite some time now Tyson has coasted on the fumes of his anger, as if it's all he's got left, as if it's all we want. He's long since crossed from boxing into a lurid show business where his chronic inability to exist in normal society has been all the entertainment value we need. Certainly, for years now, he's been satisfied to substitute aberrant behavior for actual athletic performance. And who can blame him? There has been no downside to that, except possibly an artistic or historic one. (He really could have been one of the greatest of all time.) Financially, it's been a bonanza. Outside of the occasional stretch behind bars, which is the acceptable, perhaps necessary, overhead in such a career, his perversity has paid off sensationally. Do you think Mike Tyson is earning a minimum of $17.5 million for his next fight because he's coming off a knockout of Brian (the Danish Pastry) Nielsen? Or because he bit Lennox Lewis on the leg at their last press conference? These days aberrant behavior wins every time.

Hey, it's nothing to get discouraged about. Ours has been a geek-oriented culture for a while, and to blame Tyson and his nervously grinning handlers for a business plan that exploits our low-rent entertainment requirements is hypocritical. He's delivering the goods, best he knows how. Lewis, who likewise is getting $17.5 million for their June 8 fight in Memphis, surely does not complain about having had to get a tetanus shot. (He doesn't even acknowledge it, so fearful is he—is everyone involved—of cancellation.) Showtime and HBO, which are cooperating on the promotion, are also somewhat less horrified than you might imagine as they lick their corporate chops over rising pay-per-view buys. Nor, for that matter, do we complain, even as we set aside our $54.95 for this next catastrophe. That would be hypocritical too.

In fact, aren't we all looking forward to it, a guilty pleasure if ever there was one, the chance to be ringside at some kind of personal disintegration?

This is how it has been with Tyson since he got out of an Indiana state prison in 1995, having served three years for raping Desiree Washington. His boxing career had splendid beginnings and was theatrical in its own right, but it quickly degenerated into a sideshow, and his followers became less fans than voyeurs, craning their necks for a peek at the type of explosive personality that repeatedly makes news for all the wrong reasons. Of course, as anybody who enjoyed the sight of Tyson biting a chunk of Holyfield's ear off might say, if watching a man having a nervous breakdown is wrong, I don't want to be right!

But he's not a complete madman and is, in fact, confoundingly human. Look at him again. Even as he vents, for the sake of performance or just his psychic survival—who knows?—he quickly relaxes into less threatening rants, becoming by turns interesting, funny, sympathetic, highly dramatic, at all times profane. However, it seems to be a given that he must deliver diatribe to remain authentic. This is the sad subtext of his career, even as he careens into Lewis in what may be the most lucrative fight of all time. He has scarcely done anything but talk, not for years and years, and even he knows it. After the Nielsen bout seven months ago (capping a comeback in which he fought just 19 rounds in five years, and against as marginal a lineup of heavyweights as has ever been assembled) he at first said he would need two more tune-up fights before he could ever face Lewis for the championship. That sounded about right.

Economics and age (Tyson will turn 36 this summer, Lewis is already 36), not to mention the unlikely and highly temporary alliance of rivals HBO and Showtime, each controlling one fighter, changed his mind. Tyson owes a fortune (to Showtime mostly, but to others as well) and can hardly defer a huge payday. Plus, inasmuch as he has proved highly unpredictable in the company of women and old men (road-rage assault, four months in jail), and it seems as though women and old men are everywhere these days—even at press gatherings!—any further abeyance is hardly prudent. At Showtime's offices there is actually a countdown clock that ticks off the seconds remaining to this financial absolution. (They wish.)

So, lacking recent bona fides (Lou Savarese? Julius Francis?), Tyson plays his part the only way he knows how. "I wish that you guys had children," he tells the broadcasters during their audience, "so I could kick them in the f------ head or stomp on their testicles, so you could feel my pain."

Oh, you can now add youngsters to that endangered species list. Old men, children and women—mind your asses, testicles and, you know. . . .

Tyson, acting as a sort of aggrieved bully at every opportunity, has encouraged this characterization, but now it's worse. During his three post-prison years under the promotion of Don King, he fine-tuned his portrayal of a fighter who was both dangerously savage and distressingly vulnerable. That was an important part of a comeback that began in August '95 and earned him $112 million for six fights (nearly as much as Tyson's lawyers claim King earned!), up to and including his disqualification in the second Holyfield fight, in June 1997.

His second comeback, begun after he served a "parole" handed down by the Nevada Athletic Commission after the ear-biting debacle, is now the subject of a $100 million lawsuit by Tyson against his former promoter (more on which later) but has otherwise proceeded without the cunning contrivance that King brings to boxing promotion. As a result Tyson's postsanction career has progressed by fits and starts, with one irrelevant bout there (England), an insignificant one here (Michigan). No titles, no legacy, no savings have accrued in the past three years. Only the prospect of a bout with Lewis, in the talking stages since 1996, has kept Tyson at all relevant (and his nervously grinning handlers, in the hole for millions, hopeful). Big, wild talk is required.

Consequently, this latest campaign has been conducted without any subtlety whatsoever. Whether by calculation or by some organic loosening of his id, Tyson has become something of a symbol for prepackaged calamity: Just open and add opportunity. Disaster! Six servings! Against François Botha he tried to break an arm. In the Savarese fight he took on the ref. Two others since the Holyfield disqualification ended as no-contests (one of those not actually Tyson's fault). Of course, this is not to ignore his January press conference with Lewis, at which, in a mix-up during a photo opportunity, a Lewis camp member shoved Tyson, who had menaced the champion, and punches were thrown and legs (well, one) were bitten, forcing a continued exile from Las Vegas and an invitation from Memphis, where the money is presumably not Confederate.

Tyson, who was never one to couch his comments in traditional sports quote, has dialed up the rhetoric accordingly. When he is not threatening old men, women and children, he serves vitriol to Lewis, offering to "smear his pompous brains all over the ring." This is a declamatory upgrade from previous offers, in which he proclaimed himself eager to eat Lewis's (unborn) children. Lewis, by the way, is not as excited by these threats as you might suppose. "He's nothing but a cartoon character," Lewis said when the parade of international reporters visited him for a response.

Still, this is great for the promotion of their fight, which will take place in a sold-out Pyramid in Memphis (although it has been reported that fewer than 2,000 tickets were actually available to the public) and which will certainly generate more than one million pay-per-view buys. (It will not approach the 1.9 million record set by Tyson-Holyfield II because of rampant cable piracy, say broadcasters.) The New York City press conference by itself increased awareness of the fight by a third, according to Showtime boxing chief Jay Larkin, even though as a fighter Tyson remains as suspect as ever.

The question becomes, how much is Tyson promoting the fight (which is in his interest, given that industry insiders believe he still owes Showtime $12 million, a figure that could be recouped only if the bout sells through the roof—and, in any case, he's still living large), and how much is he just going crazy?

Tyson enjoys confounding you here, becoming playful and thoughtful, a guy who might be fun to be around if he weren't periodically promising your destruction. Those books behind you, Mike, you reading those? "You think they're window dressing?" he says, laughing.

And then he goes on to discuss them, purposely poking fun at his own ignorance (in comparison with the better-educated "erudite" sitting beside him) but, at the same time, challenging your perception of him as an unwary brute. It is clear, even if he hasn't read as many books as he might like you to believe, that he has a surprising and wide-ranging curiosity and is capable of more absorption than a testicle-stomping savage ought to be. So he delivers a highly entertaining and informed treatise on John Brown, on Machiavelli. "A fool," he says, "but not a damn fool."

The parade of international media enjoys these departures into feigned normalcy and plays happily along. When Tyson touts de Grazia as "the most sophisticated writer since that impostor, what's his name?"—the clot correctly shouts out, "Shakespeare!"

"I like all those guys, like the Gatsby guy [F. Scott Fitzgerald!] and the guy who shot himself [Hemingway!]," Tyson goes on. "They were cool. Derelicts and drunks. They were hip. They were cool."

You see, he is not canned hatred after all, stir and heat. What he is, he would very much like you to know, is damaged goods, struggling for redemption, for knowledge, just like the rest of us. His excuse, in summary: "I don't know what to do. I'm from the ghetto. I don't know how to act. One day I'm in a dope house robbing somebody; next day I'm heavyweight champion of the world."

This would be more affecting, of course, if it were true. Not to disregard his early upbringing in Brownsville, but he did spend some formative years—age 13 on—in the Catskills refuge of his trainer and surrogate father, Cus D'Amato. Not many of his opponents enjoyed so generous a sponsorship.

His forays into citizenship, anything short of a book group, have sometimes been less than halfhearted, but he has made attempts. He recognizes that, within his life, he had the chance to become a beloved figure. "I would have liked to be Tiger Woods or Michael Jordan or Will Smith," he says. His nature thwarted him, though, because "I like the forbidden fruits, I like to have my d--- sucked." The outrage is not that he's deprived of the reverence bestowed upon that trio but that those three seem to operate above the law, his law, of hypocrisy. It is galling to him that Jordan, who was briefly separated from his wife (to Tyson's mind, because he probably enjoyed forbidden fruits), continues to enjoy respect. "Everybody in this country is a big f------ liar."

Still, he tries. Not too long ago, but well before this fight was announced, Tyson ran into Lewis at Crustacean, a Beverly Hills restaurant. Tyson's wife, Monica (they are in the process of divorce, precipitated by this very event, he says, half joking), suggested he say hello to his compadre. Tyson understood that this is how normal people behave and, forbidden fruits aside this one time, was eager to become part of the social contract—a father, a neighbor, a Muslim, a good citizen, a fighter well-met. Someone beloved. Yet when he tried to perform even this minimal act of civility, he was rebuked. "He looked at me and stared me down like a damn dog," he says. "Made me a punk. You see, I want to be a nice guy, but my wife, she hands him my nuts. Takes my balls away from me." It is exactly that difficult for Tyson, manhood.

He has always been desperate for approval and easily seduced by any interest shown him. From Cus D'Amato, from Don King. It is no great trick, for that matter, for writers, whose asses he would kick, to establish a rapport, however brief and self-serving. Just appear to take him seriously. "Mike," a man asks, "would you say that pigeons are the niggers of the bird world?" The question, while flabbergasting and pointless, is also flattering to Tyson in that it seems to respect his interest, his knowledge of the animal world vis-a-vis race, and, ultimately, his authority. He answers the writer at length, and they are friends for life.

He does want to be a nice guy, does want to be loved. Who doesn't, of course. Yet Tyson, millionaire champion at 20, has come to believe that love must cost. His two marriages—the first, to actress Robin Givens in 1988, the result of Hollywood opportunity; the second, the result of jailhouse visits—will certainly have been pricey. Far more reliable to engage what he calls "strippers and bitches" for purposes of comparatively cut-rate companionship. "No strip clubs here," he says, laughing at himself. "I didn't know that when I came."

Is it a matter of unchecked appetite? "I'm not criminally lascivious, you know what I mean," he says. "I may like to fornicate more than other people, it's just who I am. I sacrifice so much of my life, can I at least get laid? I mean, I been robbed of most of my money, can I at least get my d--- sucked?"

Or is it something sadder than that? "I'll tell a ho, here's some extra money, make me think you love me." He laughs.

Self-pity has always been the big equalizer in Tyson's life, as if it balances his recurring and violent hatred for others. "I hate myself sometimes," he says, slipping into a melodramatic mode that has ensured steady and sympathetic press over the years. What? A surprised scribe asks, "You hate yourself?" Tyson calculates the effect. "Every day of my life," he says.

As you can see, Mike Tyson is a franchise in need of constant tuning, the demands of manhood constantly up for calibration, and the franchise spends a lot of time in the shop. Does he hate Lennox Lewis? "I love Lennox Lewis," he says. "Of course I love him. He has the dignity of any fighter." Or does he hate him? "At that press conference, if I had the right crew, he should have died that night."

But this is a franchise many believe is worth keeping in working order. Showtime may have invested as much as $30 million in this latest comeback—"Let's say," says Showtime's Larkin, teasingly, "we've been supportive at key times"—and is a long way toward breaking even. America Presents, which was Tyson's promoter of record for a while, is on the ropes financially and is still trying to recoup more than $1 million of its loan to Tyson. Others may be on the line.

If past fiscal behavior is any indication, Tyson, too, needs this promotion to work. He is broke. "I've blown a half billion," he says, "money don't be a big issue for me. I like a good time more than money."

Apparently a good time costs money. According to court documents filed in connection with Tyson's suit against King, in which he claims King fraudulently diverted more than $40 million from him, it is not cheap being heavyweight champion of the world or even a defrocked contender. The documents indicate that the fighter was forced into an onerous contract that gave King and "co-managers" John Horne and Rory Holloway a full 50% of his income. King, who was supposed to get 30% (with an additional 10% each to Horne and Holloway), somehow wound up, according to Tyson's lawyers, with $113 million to Tyson's $112 million. "I guess I wasn't giving them my money fast enough," Tyson says.

King's lawyers call Tyson's claim "frivolous and deceptive" and have filed a counterclaim asserting that King had a 10-fight deal with Tyson, which the fighter breached after the second Holyfield bout. Tyson, they say, earned "millions more than he now claims," and King earned "a lot less."

No matter where the truth lies, it's almost impossible to imagine that a more favorable division of income would have left Tyson a nest egg. In the three years before his estrangement from King—from 1995 through '97—Tyson spent heroically. According to court documents, accountant Mohammed Khan set forth Tyson's finances and told the fighter his spending was in the deficit area, accountingwise. "Moe," Tyson told him, "I can't have it and not spend it."

Said Khan, "Mr. Tyson makes his money and he spends his money, and nobody can tell him anything about it."

Here's how to go broke on $112 million: Spend $115 million. Through the 33 months of Tyson's first comeback, Khan's accounting statement shows that Tyson spent $4,477,498 on automobiles and motorcycles. Under the item "cash & personal expenses" (walking-around money), average monthly outlay came to $236,184. Jewelry and clothing: $94,555 per month. He spent $411,777 on pigeons and cats. (He owned a lion, which he famously sparred with; "Oh, my God!" King yelled at the sight of the big cat's swiping at Tyson. "He done give him a right-hand paw!") He gave a birthday party in 1996 that cost $410,822. Taxman? He got $32.4 million. Houses, of course, were expensive. Lawn care for his Las Vegas home (one of three he owned) was $309,133 for that period.

He gave automobiles to 15 women and two men: Alicia, Gabriella, Tiffany, Hillery, Jeannine, Rosalinda, Isadore. . . .

This is magnificent spending, unrepentant spending, championship spending. Did it persist? Well, not likely, considering that his purses after his Nevada suspension totaled an estimated $58 million before anyone, including the government, had gotten a cut. Pagers and cell phones, $7,259 a month? Those were the days.

Still, Tyson has not taken to canning vegetables out of his various backyards. And being Tyson, in certain fundamental ways, will always be expensive. "I need the fancy cars," he explains, "to get the fancy [women]." Apparently, that is not subject to budgeting. "Shouldn't I enjoy my life?"

That has always been the champion's prerogative, but Tyson has not been champion for some time. He and his camp talk as if the title is his due, that the fight amounts to a formality. And, at least until he and Lewis finally step into the ring, he will have his supporters, people who can't imagine Lewis (who has had some uncertain performances himself) fending off a wildly charging Tyson. It's true, Lewis has not faced many fighters as fast as Tyson; David Tua, whom Lewis beat easily, compares in stature but in hardly anything else.

And Tyson's resolve seems impressive. He told one of his current trainers, "I quit fighting 10 years ago; now I'm getting ready to start fighting again."

But Lewis is a strangely confident, if comparatively quiet, athlete, who seems to rouse himself for big fights. (His two losses, in which his chin was proved to be weak, were to lesser opponents and were both conclusively avenged.) His jab might keep Tyson off him, and with his greater size (6' 5" to Tyson's 5' 11") and strength, he may be able to suffocate Tyson as he tries to bore in, which could produce an unexciting but somewhat predictable result.

The thing is, hardly anybody's going into this bout expecting a wonderful athletic event. Is there curiosity as to who the better heavyweight is? Some, but not enough to justify the magnitude of interest in the fight. Six years ago, when Tyson's résumé still had some boxing highlights in it, the bout might have deserved the buildup on its merits. But now, with Tyson long since passed into a weird psycho-celebrity culture, in which his eventual breakup is the entire point, Lewis only serves to legitimize his challenger's notoriety. The pleasure is a little less guilty for Lewis's involvement. You're free to enjoy the vagaries of brain chemistry without hating yourself too much.

Discouraged? Maybe you should be. Tyson is correct to say that we've all exploited him—for the dark thrills he provides, for this little peephole into alternative humanity—and that we should all feel a little disgusted with ourselves. What hypocrisy, that we condemn him as we order ringside tickets. He is boorish, unforgivably irresponsible in the preservation of his talent, a sad case who can't decide if he wants to be loved or hated and who may not even be able to tell the difference anymore. Yet he is utterly irresistible.

But in our defense: The example of a man who chooses to disable his impulse controls is not always a pleasant one, but it's instructive, maybe exhilarating even, to see where such exaggerated independence leads. As if, the pigeons circling to roost, we didn't already know.

The Ring Leader

BY FRANK DEFORD

The greatest team player of all time, Bill Russell was the hub of a Celtics dynasty that ruled its sport as no other team ever has. Thirty years after his first story about Russell, the dean of SI writers revisited the big man.

I T WAS 30 YEARS AGO, AND THE CAR CONTAINING THE OLD RETIRED basketball player and the young sportswriter stopped at a traffic light on the way to the airport in Los Angeles. (Of course, in the nature of things, old players aren't that much older than young writers.) The old player said, "I'm sorry, I'd like to be your friend."

The young writer said, "But I thought we were friends."

"No, I'd like to be your friend, and we can be friendly, but friendship takes a lot of effort if it's going to work, and we're going off in different directions in our lives, so, no, we really can't be friends."

And that was as close as I ever got to being on Bill Russell's team.

In the years after that exchange I often reflected on what Russell had said to me, and I marveled that he would have thought so deeply about what constituted friendship. It was, obviously, the same sort of philosophical contemplation about the concept of Team that had made him the most divine teammate there ever was.

Look, you can stand at a bar and scream all you want about who was the greatest athlete and which was the greatest sports dynasty, and you can shout out your precious statistics, and maybe you're right, and maybe the red-faced guy down the bar—the one with the foam on his beer and the fancy computer rankings—is right, but nobody really knows. The only thing we know for sure about superiority in sports in the United States of America in the 20th century is that Bill Russell and the Boston Celtics teams he led stand alone as the ultimate winners. Fourteen times in Russell's career it came down to one game, win you must, or lose and go home. Fourteen times the team with Bill Russell on it won.

But the fires always smoldered in William Felton Russell, and he simply wouldn't suffer fools—most famously the ones who intruded upon his sovereign privacy to petition him for an autograph. He was that rare star athlete who was also a social presence, a voice to go with the body. Unafraid, he spoke out against all things, great and small, that bothered him. He wouldn't even show up at the Hall of Fame when he was inducted, because he had concluded it was a racist institution. Now, despite the importunings of his friends, he is the only living selection among ESPN's 50 top athletes of the century who hasn't agreed to talk to the network. That is partly because one night he heard an ESPN announcer praise the '64 Celtics as "Bob Cousy's last team." Cousy was retired by then.

Russell says, "They go on television, they're supposed to know."

Cousy says, "What the Celtics did with Russ will never be duplicated in a team sport. Never."

Of course, genuine achievement is everywhere devalued these days. On the 200th anniversary of his death, George Washington has been so forgotten that they're toting his false teeth around the republic, trying to restore interest in the Father of Our Country with a celebrity-style gimmick. So should we be surprised that one spectacular show-off dunk on yesterday's highlight reel counts for more than some ancient decade's worth of championships back-before-Larry&Magic-really-invented-the-sport-of-basketball?

Tommy Heinsohn, who played with Russell for nine years and won 10 NBA titles himself, as player and coach, sums it up best: "Look, all I know is, the guy won two NCAA championships, 50-some college games in a row, the ['56] Olympics, then he came to Boston and won 11 championships in 13 years, and they named a f------ tunnel after Ted Williams." By that standard, only a cathedral on a hill deserves to have Bill Russell's name attached to it.

But then, too often when I try to explain the passion of Russell himself and his devotion to his team and to victory, I'm inarticulate. It's like trying to describe a color to a blind person. All I can say, in tongue-tied exasperation, is, You had to be there. And I'm sorry for you if you weren't.

Russell was right, too. The two of us did go our separate ways after he dropped me at the airport. He left the playing life exactly 30 years ago this week, on May 5, 1969, with his last championship, and my first child was born on May 7. So there were new things we both had to do, and in the years that followed we were together only a couple of times, briefly.

Then a few weeks ago we met at his house in Seattle, and for the first time in 30 years I climbed into his car. The license plate on the Lexus reads KELTIC 6, and on the driver's hands were two NBA championship rings: his first, from '57, and his last, from 12 years later. We took off together for the San Francisco Bay Area, there to visit Bill's father, Charlie, who is 86 and lives in a nursing home. It was 13 hours on the road. We stopped along the way at McDonald's and for gas and for coffee and for a box of Good 'n' Plenty and to pee and to buy lottery tickets once we got over the California line, because there was a big jackpot that week in the Golden State. In Oakland we found a Holiday Inn and ate a fish dinner at Jack London Square, where a bunch of elderly black ladies sat at the next table. "I was thinking they were old," Bill said, nodding his gray head toward them. "Then I remembered, I'm probably their age." I laughed. "Hey, what are you laughing at?" he roared. So, like that, wherever we happened to be going in the car, our destination was really back in time.

Back to the Russell Era. Back to the Celtics and the University of San Francisco Dons, to the Jones Boys and Cooz. Yes, and back to Wilt. To Satch and Heinie and the sixth men. Red, of course. Elgin and Jerry. But more than just the baskets, more than just the '60s. Russell's family experience describes the arc of a century. Why, when Charlie Russell was growing up in Louisiana, he actually knew men and women who had been slaves. He told me about "making marks in the ground" to help his illiterate father calculate. I was baffled by that expression. "It's from the old country," Bill explained. That is, from Africa, centuries before, passed along orally. And as we were talking, and the old man—wearing a jaunty red sweat suit and a green hat—reminisced about more recent times, he suddenly smiled and said something I couldn't quite make out. I leaned closer. "What's that, Mr. Russell? How *what*?"

"No, *Hal*," he said. "All on account of Hal DeJulio." Charlie remembered so well, after all this time. You see, if young William hadn't, by chance, been there on the one day that DeJulio showed up at Oakland High in the winter of '51, none of this would have happened. None of it at all. But life often hangs by such serendipitous threads, and sometimes, like this time, we are able to take them and weave them into a scarf for history's neck.

The long trip to Oakland was not unusual for Russell. He enjoys driving great distances. After all, he is most comfortable with himself and next most comfortable with close friends, cackling that thunderous laugh of his that Cousy fears he'll hear resonating in the afterlife. *Playful* is the surprising word that former Georgetown coach John Thompson thinks of first for Russell, and old number 6 himself always refers to his Celtics as "the guys" in a way that sounds curiously adolescent. Hey, guys, we can put the game on right here!

Cynosure on the court though he was, Russell never enjoyed being the celebrity alone. "I still think he's a shy, mother's son," says Karen Kenyatta Russell, his daughter, "and even now he's uncomfortable being in the spotlight by himself." Maybe that's one reason the team mattered so to him; it hugged him back. "I got along with all the guys," Russell says, "and nobody had to kiss anybody's ass. We were just a bunch of men—and, oh, what marvelous gifts my teammates gave to me."

"He was just so nice to be with on the team," says Frank Ramsey, who played with Russell from 1956 to '64, Russell's first eight years in the NBA. "It was only when others came around that he set up that wall."

Russell loves nothing better than to talk. "Oh, the philosophizing," recalls Satch Sanders, who played with Russell from '60 to '69. "If he started off and said, 'You see,' we just rolled our eyes, because we knew he was going off on something." Yet in more recent times Russell went for years without permitting himself to be interviewed. "If I'm going to answer the questions, I want them to be my questions, the right questions," he says—a most unlikely prerogative, given the way journalism works. O.K., so no interviews. Privacy edged into reclusiveness.

On the other hand, as upside-down as this may sound, Russell believes he can share more by not giving autographs, because instead of an impersonal scribbled signature, a civil two-way conversation may ensue. Gently: "I'm sorry, I don't give autographs."

"You won't?"

"No, *won't* is personal. I don't. But thank you for asking." And then, if he senses a polite reaction, he might say, "Would you like to shake hands with me?" And maybe chat.

Utterly dogmatic, Russell wouldn't bend even to give his Celtics teammates autographs. One time this precipitated an ugly quarrel with Sanders, who wanted a simple keepsake: the signature of every Celtic he'd played with. "You, Satch, of all people, know how I feel," Russell snapped.

"Dammit, I'm your teammate, Russ."

Nevertheless, when the shouting was over, Russell still wouldn't sign. Thompson, who was Russell's backup on the Celtics for two years, is sure that Russell never took pleasure from these sorts of incidents. "No, it bothered him," Thompson says. "But doing it his way, on his own terms, was more important to him. And that's Bill. Even if it hurt him, he was going to remain consistent."

Russell speaks, often, in aphorisms that reflect his attitudes. "It is better to understand than to be understood," he told his daughter. "A groove can become a rut," he advised his teammates. And perhaps the one that goes most to his own heart: "You should live a life with as few negatives as possible—without acquiescing."

So, alone, unbothered, one of the happiest times Russell ever had was driving around the West on a motorcycle in the '70s. When he takes a long auto-mobile trip by himself these days, he listens to National Public Radio, CDs and tapes he has recorded to suit his own eclectic taste. On one tape, for ex-ample, are Stevie Wonder and Burl Ives. On another: Willie Nelson and Aretha Franklin. But also, always, Russell sets aside two hours to drive in complete silence, meditating. He has never forgotten what Huey Newton, the Black Panther, once told him: that the five years he spent in solitary confinement were, in fact, liberating.

Russell returned twice to the NBA after he retired as the Celtics' player-coach following the 1968–69 season. As coach and general manager of the Seattle SuperSonics from 1973 to '77, he built the team that would win the championship two years after he left. A brief tenure with the Sacramento Kings during the '87–88 season was, however, disastrous and unhappy. On the night he was fired, Russell cleaned out his office; returned to his Sacramen-to house, which was contiguous to a golf course; and stayed there, peaceful-ly by himself, for weeks, venturing out only for provisions and golf. He didn't read the newspapers or watch television news. "To this day, I don't know what they said about me," he says. He put his house on the market immediately, and only when it sold, three weeks later, did he return to Seattle, where for 26 years he has lived in the same house on Mercer Island, one tucked away into a sylvan hillside, peeking down at Lake Washington.

Divorced in 1973, Russell lived as a single parent with Karen for several years, until she left for Georgetown in 1980 and then Harvard Law. Alone after that, Russell says, there were times when he would hole up and practice his household "migratory habits." That is, he would stock the kitchen, turn on the burglar alarm, turn off the phone and, for the next week, migrate about the house, going from one couch to another, reading voraciously and watching TV, ideally *Jeopardy!* or *Star Trek*—just bivouacked there, the tallest of all the Trekkies, sleeping on various sofas. He was quite content. The finest team player ever is by nature a loner who, by his own lights, achieved such group suc-cess because of his abject selfishness. You will never begin to understand Bill Russell until you appreciate that he is, at once, consistent and contradictory.

Russell began to emerge from his most pronounced period of solitude about three years ago. Shortly after arriving in Seattle in 1973, he had gone into a jew-elry store, where he hit it off with the saleswoman. Her name is Marilyn Nault. "Let me tell you," she sighs, "working in a jewelry store is the worst place to meet a man, because if one comes in, it's to buy something for another woman." But over the years—skipping through Russell's next, brief marriage, to a for-mer Miss USA—Marilyn and Bill remained friends. Also, she impressed him as a very competitive dominoes player. When Bill's secretary died in 1995,

Marilyn volunteered to give him a hand, and all of a sudden, after more than two decades, they realized they were in love. So it was that one day, when Marilyn came over to help Bill with his accounts, she just stayed on with him in the house on the hill under the tall firs.

There is a big grandfather clock in the house that chimes every hour. Like Bill, Marilyn doesn't hear it anymore. She has also learned how to sleep with the TV on, because Bill, a terrible night owl, usually falls asleep with the clicker clasped tightly in his hand. Usually the Golf Channel is on. Imagine waking up to the Golf Channel. Marilyn has also learned to appreciate long car trips. Twice she and Bill have driven across the continent and back. Their lives are quite blissful; he has never seemed to be so at peace. "They're the ultimate '50s couple," Karen reports. "They have nothing but kind things to say about each other, and it's part of their arrangement that at least once a day, he has to make her laugh."

Yet for all the insular contentment Russell has always sought in his life, his play was marked by the most extraordinary intensity. If he threw up before a big game, the Celtics were sure everything would be all right. If he didn't, then Boston's coach, Red Auerbach, would tell Russell to go back to the toilet—order him to throw up. Rookies who saw Russell for the first time in training camp invariably thought he had lost it over the summer, because he would pace himself, even play possum in some exhibitions, to deceive pretenders to his throne. Then, in the first game of the real season, the rookies would be bug-eyed as the genuine article suddenly appeared, aflame with competition. It was as if the full moon had brought out a werewolf.

Cousy says, "The level of intensity among the big guys is different. You put a bunch of huge guys, seminaked, out there before thousands of people, and you expect them to become killers. But it just isn't in their nature. Kareem [Abdul-Jabbar] probably had the best skills of all big men, and he played till he was 42. If he'd had Russ's instincts, it's hard to imagine how much better he'd have been. But he'd have burned out long before 42."

Sanders: "There's no reason why some centers today couldn't block shots like Russ did. Only no one has the intestinal fortitude. A center blocks one shot now, the other team grabs the ball and scores, and the center stands there pouting, with that I-can't-do-everything look. Russell would block three, four shots in a row—I mean from different players—and then just glower at us."

Russell: "Once I blocked seven shots in a row. When we finally got the ball, I called timeout and said, 'This s--- has got to stop.' " Some years Russell would be so exhausted after the playoffs that, as he describes it, "I'd literally be tired to my bones. I mean, for four, five weeks, my bones would hurt."

Russell believes that Wilt Chamberlain suffered the worst case of big-man syndrome; he was too nice, scared that he might hurt somebody. The year after Russell retired, in the famous seventh game of the NBA Finals at Madison Square Garden, Willis Reed, the New York Knicks center, limped onto the court against the Los Angeles Lakers, inspiring his team and freezing Chamberlain into a benign perplexity. Russell scowls just thinking about it. "If I'm the one playing Willis when he comes out limping," he snarls, "it only would have emphasized my goal to beat them that much worse." Russell would have called Six—his play—again and again, going mercilessly at the cripple, exploiting Reed without remorse. The Celtics would have won. Which was the point. Always.

"To be the best in the world," Russell says, all but licking his lips. "Not last week. Not next year. But right now. You are the best. And it's even more satisfying as a team, because that's more difficult. If I play well, that's one thing. But to make others play better. . . . " He grins, savoring the memory. "You understand what I mean?" Bill often says that, invariably when there is no doubt. It has to do with emphasis more than clarity. In fact, I can sort of visualize him saying that after he blocked a shot. *You understand what I mean?*

Yes.

It is difficult to comprehend whence came Russell's extraordinary will on the court. Karen recalls only once in her life that her father so much as raised his voice to anyone. "I just never saw the warrior in him," she says. "As a matter of fact, as I got to understand men better, I appreciated all the more how much of a feminine side my father has." Ironically it was Russell's mother, Katie, who appears to have given him his fire, while his father, Charlie, instilled the more reflective component.

What do you remember your father telling you, Bill?

"Accept responsibility for your actions. . . . Honor thy father and mother. . . . If they give you $10 for a day's work, you give them $12 worth in return."

Even more clearly, Russell recalls the gritty creed his mother gave him when he was a little boy growing up in segregation and the Depression in West Monroe, La. Katie said, "William, you are going to meet people who just don't like you. On sight. And there's nothing you can do about it, so don't worry. Just be yourself. You're no better than anyone else, but no one's better than you."

One time, when he was nine, William—for that is what he was called till basketball made him just plain Bill—came home to the family's little shotgun shack after being slapped by a boy in a gang. Katie dragged him out to find the gang. She made her son fight every boy, one by one. "The fact is, I had to fight back," Bill says. "It wasn't important whether I won or lost."

When he and I visited his father, Charlie said this about Katie: "She was handsome and sweet, and she loved me, and she showed it by giving me children." Bill was very touched by that, subdued. Then Charlie smiled and added, "She played some basketball too—the bloomer girls."

Bill shot to his feet, screaming, "Daddy, I never knew that!" Then there was such vintage Russellian cackling that the old fellow in the next bed woke up, a little discombobulated by all the fuss.

If Katie Russell had any athletic instincts, though, they paled before her passion for education. It was an article of faith with her, a high school dropout, that her two sons—Charlie Jr., the elder by two years, and William—would go to college. Bill has a vivid memory of his mother taking him to get a library card. That was not mundane; that was a signal event. And this is what he remembers of West Monroe, altogether: "I remember that my mother and father loved me, and we had a good time, but the white people were mean. But I was safe. I was always safe. In all my life, every day, not for one second have I ever thought I could have had better parents."

Then, in 1946, when William was 12, his mother died of kidney failure, with very little warning. Katie Russell was only 32. The last thing she told her husband was, "Make sure to send the boys to college." The last thing she told William was, "Don't be difficult for your father, because he's doing the best he can."

The Russells had moved to Oakland not long before, after Charlie was denied a raise at the mill in West Monroe because he was black. Now the father and his two sons boarded the train with Katie's casket to return to Louisiana to bury her. It was after the funeral that young William heard Katie's sisters arguing about which one of them would take the two motherless boys to raise. That was the custom in these matters. Charlie interrupted. "No," he said, "I won't let you. I'm taking the two boys back with me." Though there was still much protesting from the aunts, that was that.

"I told my two boys they'd lost their best friend," Charlie says, "but we could make it if we tried." The goal remained to get them through college. Charlie Jr. was developing into a pretty good athlete, but his father couldn't spend much time thinking about games. After all, he'd had to quit school to work; unlike Katie, he'd never even been able to play basketball. It certainly never occurred to him that now, for the first time, there were people like Hal DeJulio around, scouting black teenagers, eager to give the best ones a free college education just for playing some ball.

The radar detector on the Lexus beeped. Russell slowed down. A bit. We had driven through Washington and most of Oregon, too. A billboard advertised the Seven Feathers Casino. Ah, fin de siècle America: casinos, cable, cosmetic surgery and scores from around the leagues. Russell, who just turned 65, is fairly pragmatic about the new ways of the world. He never put on any airs—witness that amazing laugh of his, which is the loud leitmotif of his life. "I try not to stifle anything," he says. "It isn't just my laugh. If I have to sneeze, I just let it go. You understand what I mean?"

He is also helped by the fact that even as a young man, he looked venerable. Other players would dart onto the court, all snappy and coltish. Number 6 would stalk out hunched over, stroking that dagger of a goatee, and stand there dark and grim. We always talk about teams "executing." All right, then: Russell appeared very much an executioner.

Jerry West, who was denied about a half-dozen championships strictly because of Russell, remembers. "When the national anthem was played, I always found my eyes going to Bill. He did that just right, stand there for the anthem. He was a statue, but there was a grace to him. Even just standing still: grace."

Whereas Russell is disappointed by much that he sees on the court today, he does not lambaste the players. He is just as prone to blame the coaches for taking so much of the spontaneity out of basketball. "The coaches dumb players down now," he says, clearly irritated. "They're stifling innovation. They're not letting them play outside the system." Pretty soon, it seems, the Celtics' fast break, which was the most gloriously coordinated rapid action in sport, will be nothing more than athletic nostalgia, like the dropkick.

And the players? Well, it's not just them. "All the kids in this generation—they really don't have a clue," Russell says. "They don't know, but they really don't care. A lot of my peers are annoyed that the players accepted a salary cap. I'm not. I know there's not supposed to be a limit on what you can make in America, but then, the NBA may also be the only place where there's a high roof for a minimum. When I speak to the players, I just say they have a responsibility to be caretakers. When you leave, there should be no less for those who follow you than there was when you arrived."

We started up Mount Ashland, whose other side goes down into California. Russell said, "Of course, a lot of my peers are also annoyed with all this money these kids are making. Me? I love it when I see a guy get a hundred million, because that says something good about what I did. You understand what I mean?"

This is, however, not to say that some of the guys making a hundred million—or getting by on only 50 or 60—have a clue about what Bill Russell did. It took years of hectoring by some of his friends to persuade Russell to step out of the safe shadows, to display himself again. His legacy was fading. John Thompson fairly bellows, "Nobody cares when some turkey like me won't give interviews. But Bill Russell! I say, Bill: You owe it to the people you love not to take this to your grave. I want my grandchildren to hear you talk about all you were."

So, while sometimes it mortifies Russell that he is, like everybody else, marketing himself—"I can't believe I'm doing all the things I swore I'd never do," he moans—there is the reasonable argument that truth nowadays must be packaged; otherwise, only the hype will survive as history. So Russell is planning a speaking tour and an HBO documentary about his life, and Karen is working on a book about motivation with her father, and a huge charitable evening to honor Russell is scheduled at the FleetCenter in Boston on May 26, when his number 6 jersey will be ceremonially re-retired. Russell is even selling about 500 autographs a year, and when we went to ship some signed basketballs to a sports collectibles store, I felt rather as if I had gone over to Handgun Control and mailed out some Saturday Night Specials.

So, O.K., it's the millennium, it's a different world. But we're not that far removed from the old one. Look at Bill Russell in 1999. His grandfather Jake was of the family's first generation born free on this continent. When this fading century began, Jake Russell was trying to scratch out a living with a mule. The Klan went after him because even though he couldn't read or write a lick, he led a campaign to raise money among the poor blacks around West Monroe to build a schoolhouse and pay a teacher to educate their children at a time when the state wouldn't have any truck with that.

At the other end of Jake's life, in 1969, he went over to Shreveport, La., to see the Celtics play an exhibition. By then his grandson had become the first African-American coach in a major professional sport. Jake sat with his son, Charlie, watching Bill closely during timeouts. He wasn't quite sure what he was seeing; Celtics huddles could be terribly democratic back then. It was before teams had a lot of assistants with clipboards. Skeptically Jake asked his son, "He's the boss?" Charlie nodded.

Jake took that in. "Of the white men too?"

"The white men too."

Jake just shook his head. After the game he went into the decrepit locker room, which had only one shower for the whole team. The Celtics were washing up in pairs, and when Jake arrived, Sam Jones and John Havlicek were in the shower, passing the one bar of soap back and forth—first the naked black man, then the naked white man stepping under the water spray. Jake watched, agape. Finally he said, "I never thought I'd see anything like that."

Of course, it was hardly a straight line upward to brotherhood. Nor was Bill Russell afraid to point that out to America; he could be unforgiving and sometimes angry, which meant he was called arrogant by those who didn't care for his kind. Russell invested in a rubber plantation in Liberia, and at a time when African-Americans were known as Negroes, and the word black was an insult, Russell started calling himself black. In the civil rights movement he became a bold, significant figure far beyond the parquet.

Thompson says, "It took a long time for me to be able to accept him as a person, as another guy, because I admired and respected him so. Russell made me feel safe. It was not that he was going to save me if anybody threatened me. Somehow I knew it was going to be all right so long as I was with him. I was going to be safe."

Often, edgy whites misunderstood him, though. Once a magazine quoted him as saying, "I hate all white people." Russell walked into the cramped old Celtics locker room, where equality reigned: Every player had one stool and two nails. Frank Ramsey glanced up from the magazine. "Hey, Russell, I'm white," he said. "You hate me?"

The two teammates looked into each other's eyes. "I was misquoted, Frank," was all Russell said. That was the end of it; he and Ramsey remained as close as ever. A few years earlier, too, there had been a big brouhaha in Kentucky, Ramsey's home state. Russell and other black Celtics had pulled out of an exhibition game there because the hotels were segregated. There was a lot of talk that Russell should not have embarrassed Ramsey that way. None of the talk came from Ramsey, though. Then, in 1966, when Russell succeeded Auerbach and became the first black coach (while continuing to play), he accepted the job only after trying to persuade Ramsey to return to basketball, from which he had retired in 1964, and coach the Celtics. Russell thought that would be better for the team than for him to make history.

The Celtics really did get along the way teams are supposed to in sports mythology. Russell threw Christmas parties for his teammates and their families. In 1962 he took the astonished rookie Havlicek around town to get a good price on a stereo. "All of us were strangers in a place far from home," Russell says. "But we made it into a unique situation. Cousy started it. He was absolutely sincere about being a good teammate."

Still, it was different away from the warm cocoon of the Celtics. One night in 1971 the team assembled in the Boston suburb of Reading, where Russell lived, to be with him as the town proudly honored their captain. It was the first time Heinsohn ever saw Russell cry, he was so happy. A few months later some people broke into Russell's house, rampaged, smashed his trophies, defecated in his bed and spread the excrement over his walls. They didn't want any black man in their town. But in the locker room Russell never talked about the terrible things that happened to him so close to the Celtics' city. "He was too proud to let people know," Heinsohn says.

Cousy still feels guilty. "I wish I'd done more to support Russ," he says. "We were so close, as teammates, but we all should have been more aware of his anger." Cousy draws a deep sigh. "But you know jocks—all into the macho thing. Always afraid to let the conversation be anything more than superficial. We mature so much later than anybody else."

So they just had to settle for winning.

Russell drove the Lexus into Oakland. When he was a little boy, after rural Dixie, his big new California hometown seemed such a wondrously exciting place. But Oakland wasn't Valhalla. "I couldn't even go downtown," he says. "The cops would chase the black kids away. And you still have those soldiers in blue in the streets. In terms of economics, things are certainly better in America today. But the criminal justice system hasn't improved."

Still, even if the police ran young William out of stylish Oakland, he grew up in contentment. Even after Katie's death, the Russells enjoyed the sort of family embrace that is denied so many black boys today. Charlie Jr. would graduate from college and become a social worker and a playwright. William, for his part, was a bookworm. For someone who ended up 6' 10", he grew very late and wasn't much noticed on the basketball court. But then, he also wasn't much good. Frank Robinson, the great baseball player, was on the McClymonds High basketball team with Russell, and he says, "He couldn't even put the ball in the basket when he dunked." Russell was scheduled to graduate in January 1951, whereupon it was his intention to get a job in the shipyards and save up to go to college part time.

This is surely what would have happened, too, except that Hal DeJulio, who had played at the University of San Francisco and occasionally steered young players toward the school, went to an Oakland High–McClymonds game one day to help the Oakland coach. USF was a struggling urban Catholic college that didn't even have a gymnasium; the team had to settle for leftovers and overlooks. As a consequence, DeJulio noticed McClymonds' center, the unknown string bean with the incredibly long arms, who had a rare good game that day. A week later DeJulio showed up unannounced at the Russells' house and offered William a scholarship to San Francisco. Only then did he tell Dons coach Phil Woolpert about his find. Woolpert was skeptical but agreed to take William on.

It was that close to there never being a Bill Russell. "It gives me chills," Karen says.

Even as Russell won his first NCAA title, in 1955, his coach—like most everybody else—couldn't yet fathom that Russell was this genius who had, in effect, created a whole new game of basketball. For instance, Woolpert concurred with the conventional wisdom that to play defense you must not leave your feet, "and here I was airborne most of the time," Russell recalls. Although the Dons' victories piled up, Woolpert kept telling Russell he was "fundamentally unsound." He would say, "You can't do that." Russell would respond, "But I just did."

Nevertheless Russell liked Woolpert—"a fine and decent man," he calls the coach—who was being excoriated for starting three black players: Russell,

K.C. Jones and Hal Perry. Woolpert was flooded with hate mail, and rival coaches snidely called him Saperstein, after Abe, the coach of the Harlem Globetrotters. Although the NCAA championship won by the 1965–66 Texas Western team, with five black starters, has over time been painted as a watershed event, the fact is that Russell was as much pioneer as avatar. The African-American domination of basketball traces to two teams, his teams: USF in college, Boston in the pros. Texas Western was but the end product of what Russell inspired—and what he had suffered through—a decade earlier.

K.C. Jones remembers an occasion in Oklahoma City, where USF was practicing, when local citizens threw coins at the players as if they were clowns in the circus. Inside, Jones raged. But Russell, smiling sardonically, picked up the change and handed it to Woolpert. "Here, Coach, hold this for me," was all he said.

"Then," Jones says, "he took it out on the opposition."

"I decided in college to win," Russell says matter-of-factly. "Then it's a historical fact, and nobody can take it away from me. You understand what I mean?"

Indisputably, his race diminished Russell in the eyes of many biased observers, but, withal, it was the rare fair-minded expert who could comprehend the brilliance of this original force. Indeed, even as Russell won every year in the NBA, the fact that Chamberlain averaged skyrocket numbers was more beguiling to the unsophisticated. Meanwhile, in Boston, the stylish—and Caucasian—Cousy continued to hold the greater affection. Auerbach recalls one time when Cousy was injured but the Celtics swept a five-game road trip, with "Russ blocking a million shots." When the team returned home, it was greeted by a headline that made no reference to the victory streak, asking only, WILL COUSY PLAY TONIGHT? "This coulda killed my team," Auerbach says. He felt obliged to order the exhausted players to go directly from the airport to the Garden, there to air the matter as a team.

Russell was a great admirer of Cousy, though, and the two led together. If they called a team meeting, they'd start off by soliciting opinions on how they—Cousy and Russell—were lacking. After that, who could bitch about anybody else? Jones cannot recall a single instance, either in college or in the NBA, when Russell "jumped on anyone's butt. But Bill definitely had his Machiavellian side. Anybody who didn't fit in, he'd just dismiss him."

Russell's simple key to a successful team was to encourage each player to do what he did best. "Remember," he says, "each of us has a finite amount of energy, and things you do well don't require as much. Things you don't do well take more concentration. And if you're fatigued by that, then the things you do best are going to be affected." The selfishness of successful team play—"I was very selfish," he declares—sounds paradoxical, but a team profits if each player revels in his strength. Still, Russell points out, there is a fine line between idealistic shared greed and typical self-gratification. "You must let your energy flow to the team," he says.

And sometimes, of course, you simply must sacrifice. For instance, one of the hardest things Russell had to learn to accept was that if he filled one lane on a fast break and Heinsohn was on the other flank, Cousy would give Heinsohn the ball—and the basket. Every time. "He simply had so much confidence in Heinie," Russell says. "So I had to discipline myself to run that break all-out, even if I knew I wasn't going to get the ball."

Above all, though, the key to Russell's success was that his greatest individual talent was the one that most benefited the team. It was not only that he blocked shots; Auerbach estimates that 80% of the time Russell could also direct the blocked ball into Celtics hands, usually fast-break bound. Moreover—and here is why statistical analyses of Russell's play are meaningless—the mere threat of a Russell block made opponents think twice about shooting, while the other Celtics could gamble aggressively on defense, knowing that number 6 would save them. "Other teams, all you hear is 'Switch!' 'Pick!' 'Help!'" Thompson says. "On the Celtics you'd only hear one word: 'Russ!'"

Although Russell made his *team* nearly invincible, the singular image that survives is of that one extraordinary athlete. That's the trouble with old sportswriters: They remember the beauty they saw far better than people today can visualize it from reading statistics. "It wasn't just that Bill was the whole package—and he was," West says, "but there was such presence he brought to the game."

By himself, in fact, Russell was hugely responsible for changing the way the public thought about big men in basketball. Before Russell, the giants were often dismissed as gawky goons or, like 6, bully-boy Goliaths. But Russell was as comfortable in his shape as he was in his skin, and it showed. "I am tall," he says. "O.K.? And if that's the only reason I can play, that's all right too. Don't deny your biggest asset. I'm a tall black guy. O.K.? No apologies, no bragging." In a game that was much more choreographed than the one today, no one could fail to see the elegance of Russell—this great winged bird swooping about, long angles that magically curved, rising high before your eyes. In fact, Russell saw himself as an artist, his play as a work of art. "If you can take something to levels that very few other people can reach," he says without vanity, "then what you're doing becomes art."

Unashamed, he sought to play the perfect game. "Certain standards I set for that," he says. "First, of course, we had to win. I had to get at least 25 rebounds, eight assists and eight blocks. I had to make 60% of my shots, and I had to run all my plays perfectly, setting picks and filling the lanes. Also, I had to say all the right things to my teammates—and to my opponents." Ironically, the closest he ever came to achieving that ideal was one night when he lived up to all his standards except the most obvious one: He did not make a single basket in 11 attempts.

Never mind. There were many discrete exquisite moments that made up for never quite attaining that comprehensive dream. "Sometimes," Russell told me in the car, breaking into a smile at the recollection, "sometimes if I could do something exactly the way I wanted, it was such an exhilarating feeling that I wanted to scream."

That memory was so joyous, in fact, that he missed the turn to the airport. Yes, 30 years later, he was driving me to an airport again. We had seen his father that morning, so our mission was accomplished. And now Karen was coming up to visit Charlie, so three generations of Russells would be together, Bill in the middle.

Karen returned, not long ago, from her first visit to West Monroe. "We're like so many other Americans, all scattered to the winds," she says, "and it was, for me, like finding my lost tribe. It also put my father's incredible journey into a context I'd never been able to put it before." She visited Katie's grave, and it made Karen think: "She had the vision for my father, as he had the vision for me."

Charlie was touched when Karen hugged him and told him this. Bill looked at them—the father who had a sixth-grade education and the daughter who'd graduated from Harvard Law. There they were, a whole century's worth of one American family. When Bill was young, in his game, players like him were known as pivotmen. Now, in his family, he is something of that again, the axis on which the Russells, ahead and behind him, turn. But then, it was the same way with basketball. Bill Russell was the pivot on which the whole sport turned. You understand what I mean?

II

MAIN
EVENTS

'Lawdy, Lawdy, He's Great'

BY MARK KRAM

The Thrilla in Manila, the climactic bout in Muhammad Ali and Joe Frazier's epic trilogy, inspired one of the most lyrical news stories ever written for SI, a piece truly worthy of the event it memorialized.

I T WAS ONLY A MOMENT, SLIDING PAST THE EYES LIKE THE SUDDEN shifting of light and shadow, but long years from now it will remain a pure and moving glimpse of hard reality, and if Muhammad Ali could have turned his eyes upon himself, what first and final truth would he have seen? He had been led up the winding, red-carpeted staircase by Imelda Marcos, the first lady of the Philippines, as the guest of honor at the Malacañang Palace. Soft music drifted in from the terrace as the beautiful Imelda guided the massive and still heavyweight champion of the world to the long buffet ornamented by huge candelabra. The two whispered, and then she stopped and filled his plate, and as he waited the candles threw an eerie light across the face of a man who only a few hours before had survived the ultimate inquisition of himself and his art.

The maddest of existentialists, one of the great surrealists of our time, the king of all he sees, Ali had never before appeared so vulnerable and fragile, so pitiably unmajestic, so far from the universe he claims as his alone. He could barely hold his fork, and he lifted the food slowly up to his bottom lip, which had been scraped pink. The skin on his face was dull and blotched, his eyes drained of that familiar childlike wonder. His right eye was a deep purple, beginning to close, a dark blind being drawn against a harsh light. He chewed his food painfully, and then he suddenly moved away from the candles as if he had become aware of the mask he was wearing, as if an inner voice were laughing at him. He shrugged, and the moment was gone.

A couple of miles away in the bedroom of a villa, the man who has always demanded answers of Ali, has trailed the champion like a timber wolf, lay in semi-darkness. Only his heavy breathing disturbed the quiet as an old friend walked to within two feet of him. "Who is it?" asked Joe Frazier, lifting himself to look around. "Who is it? I can't see! I can't see! Turn the lights on!" Another light was turned on, but Frazier still could not see. The scene cannot be forgotten; this good and gallant man lying there, embodying the remains of a will never before seen in a ring, a will that had carried him so far—and now surely too far. His eyes were only slits, his face looked as if it had been painted by Goya. "Man, I hit him with punches that'd bring down the walls of a city," said Frazier. "Lawdy, Lawdy, he's a great champion." Then he put his head back down on the pillow, and soon there was only the heavy breathing of a deep sleep slapping like big waves against the silence.

Time may well erode that long morning of drama in Manila, but for anyone who was there those faces will return again and again to evoke what it was like when two of the greatest heavyweights of any era met for a third time, and left millions limp around the world. Muhammad Ali caught the way it was: "It was like death. Closest thing to dyin' that I know of."

Ali's version of death began about 10:45 a.m. on Oct. 1 in Manila. Up to then his attitude had been almost frivolous. He would simply not accept Joe Frazier as a man or as a fighter, despite the bitter lesson Frazier had given him in their first savage meeting. Esthetics govern all of Ali's actions and conclusions; the way a man looks, the way he moves is what interests Ali. By Ali's standards, Frazier was not pretty as a man and without semblance of style as a fighter. Frazier was an affront to beauty, to Ali's own beauty as well as to his precious concept of how a good fighter should move. Ali did not hate Frazier but he viewed him with the contempt of a man who cannot bear anything short of physical and professional perfection.

Right up until the bell rang for Round 1, Ali was dead certain that Frazier was through, was convinced that he was no more than a shell, that too many punches to the head had left Frazier only one more solid shot removed from a tin cup and some pencils. "What kind of man can take all those punches to the head?" he asked himself over and over. He could never come up with an answer. Eventually he dismissed Frazier as the embodiment of animal stupidity. Before the bell Ali was subdued in his corner, often looking down to his manager, Herbert Muhammad and conversing aimlessly. Once, seeing a bottle of mineral water in front of Herbert, he said, "Watcha got there, Herbert? Gin! You don't need any of that. Just another day's work. I'm gonna put a whuppin' on this nigger's head."

Across the ring Joe Frazier was wearing trunks that seemed to have been cut from a farmer's overalls. He was darkly tense, bobbing up and down as if trying to start a cold motor inside himself. Hatred had never been a part of him, but words like "gorilla," "ugly," "ignorant"—all the cruelty of Ali's endless vilifications—had finally bitten deeply into his soul. He was there not seeking victory alone; he wanted to take Ali's heart out and then crush it slowly in his hands. One thought of the moment days before, when Ali and Frazier with their handlers between them were walking out of the Malacañang Palace, and Frazier said to Ali, leaning over and measuring each word, "I'm gonna whup your half-breed ass."

By packed and malodorous Jeepneys, by small and tinny taxis, by limousine and by worn-out bikes, 28,000 had made their way into the Philippine Coliseum. The morning sun beat down, and the South China Sea brought not a whisper of wind. The streets of the city emptied as the bout came on public television. At ringside, even though the arena was air-conditioned, the heat wrapped around the body like a heavy wet rope. By now, President Ferdinand Marcos, a small brown derringer of a man, and Imelda, beautiful and cool as if she were relaxed on a palace balcony taking tea, had been seated.

True to his plan, arrogant and contemptuous of an opponent's worth as never before, Ali opened the fight flatfooted in the center of the ring, his hands whipping out and back like the pistons of an enormous and magnificent engine. Much broader than he has ever been, the look of swift destruction defined by his every move, Ali seemed indestructible. Once, so long ago, he had been a splendidly plumed bird who wrote on the wind a singular kind of poetry of the body, but now he was down to earth, brought down by the changing shape of his body, by a sense of own vulnerability, and by the years of excess. Dancing was for a ballroom; the ugly hunt was on. Head up and unprotected, Frazier stayed in the mouth of the cannon, and the big gun roared again and again.

Frazier's legs buckled two or three times in that first round and in the second he took more lashing as Ali loaded on him all the meanness that he could find in himself. "He won't call you Clay no more," Bundini Brown, the spirit man, cried hoarsely from the corner. To Bundini, the fight would be a question of where fear first registered, but there was no fear in Frazier. In the third round Frazier was shaken twice, and looked as if he might go at any second as his head jerked up toward the hot lights and the sweat flew off his face. Ali hit Frazier at will, and when he chose to do otherwise he stuck his long left arm in Frazier's face. Ali would not be holding in this bout as he had in the second. The referee, a brisk workman, was not going to tolerate clinching. If he needed to buy time, Ali would have to use his long left to disturb Frazier's balance.

A hint of shift came in the fourth. Frazier seemed to be picking up the beat, his threshing-blade punches started to come into range as he snorted and rolled closer. "Stay mean with him, champ!" Ali's corner screamed. Ali still had his man in his sights and whipped at his head furiously. But at the end of the round, sensing a change and annoyed, he glared at Frazier and said, "You dumb chump, you!" Ali fought the whole fifth round in his own corner. Frazier worked his body, the whack of his gloves on Ali's kidneys sounding like heavy thunder. "Get out of the goddamn corner," shouted Angelo Dundee, Ali's trainer. "Stop playin'," squawked Herbert Muhammad, wringing his hands and wiping the mineral water nervously from his mouth. Did they know what was ahead?

Came the sixth, and here it was, that one special moment that you always look for when Joe Frazier is in a fight. Most of his fights have shown this: You can go so far into that desolate and dark place where the heart of Frazier pounds, you can waste his perimeters, you can see his head hanging in the public square, may even believe that you have him, but then suddenly you learn that you have not. Once more the pattern emerged as Frazier loosed all of the fury, all that has made him a brilliant heavyweight. He was in close now, fighting off Ali's chest, the place where he has to be. His old calling card—that sudden evil, his left hook—was working the head of Ali. Two hooks ripped with slaughterhouse finality at Ali's jaw, causing Imelda Marcos to look down at her feet, and the president to wince as if a knife had been stuck in his back. Ali's legs seemed to search for the floor. He was in serious trouble, and he knew that he was in no-man's-land.

Whatever else might one day be said about Muhammad Ali, it should never be said that he is without courage, that he cannot take a punch. He took those shots by Frazier, and then came out for the seventh, saying to him, "Old Joe Frazier, why I thought you were washed up." Joe replied, "Somebody told you all wrong, pretty boy."

Frazier's assault continued. By the end of the 10th round it was an even fight. Ali sat on his stool like a man ready to be staked out in the sun. His head was bowed, and when he raised it his eyes rolled from the agony of exhaustion. "Force yourself, champ!" his corner cried. "Go down to the well once more!" begged Bundini, tears streaming down his face. "The world needs ya, champ!" In the 11th, Ali got trapped in Frazier's corner, and blow after blow bit at his melting face, and flecks of spittle flew from his mouth. "Lawd have mercy!" Bundini shrieked.

The world held its breath. But then Ali dug deep down into whatever it is that he is about, and even his severest critics would have to admit that the man-boy had become finally a man. He began to catch Frazier with long right hands, and blood trickled from Frazier's mouth. Now, Frazier's face began to lose definition; like lost islands reemerging from the sea, massive bumps rose suddenly around each eye, especially the left. His punches seemed to be losing their strength. "My God," wailed Angelo Dundee. "Look at 'im. He ain't got no power, champ!" Ali threw the last ounces of resolve left in his body in the 13th and 14th. He sent Frazier's bloody mouthpiece flying into the press row in the 13th, and nearly floored him with a right in the center of the ring. Frazier was now no longer coiled. He was up high, his hands down, and as the bell for the 14th round sounded, Dundee pushed Ali out saying, "He's all yours!" And he was, as Ali raked him with nine straight right hands. Frazier was not picking up the punches, and as he returned to his corner at the round's end the Filipino referee guided his great hulk part of the way.

"Joe," said his manager, Eddie Futch, "I'm going to stop it."

"No, no, Eddie, ya can't do that to me," Frazier pleaded, his thick tongue barely getting the words out. He started to rise.

"You couldn't see in the last two rounds," said Futch. "What makes ya think ya gonna see in the 15th?"

"I want him, boss," said Frazier.

"Sit down, son," said Futch, pressing his hand on Frazier's shoulder. "It's all over. No one will ever forget what you did here today."

And so it will be, for once more had Frazier taken the child of the gods to hell and back. After the fight Futch said: "Ali fought a smart fight. He conserved his energy, turning it off when he had to. He can afford to do it because of his style. It was mainly a question of anatomy, that is all that separates them two men. Ali is now too big, and when you add those long arms, well . . . Joe has to use constant pressure, and that takes its toll on a man's body and soul." Dundee said: "My guy sucked it up and called on everything he had. We'll never see another one like him." Ali took a long time before coming down to be interviewed by the press, and then he could only say, "I'm tired of bein' the whole game. Let other guys do the fightin'. You might never see Ali in the ring again."

In his suite the next morning he talked quietly. "I heard somethin' once," he said. "When somebody asked a marathon runner what goes through his mind in the last mile or two, he said that you ask yourself why am I doin' this, you get so tired. It takes so much out of you mentally. It changes you. It makes you go a little insane. I was thinkin' that at the end. Why am I doin' this? What am I doin' here in against this beast of a man? It's so painful. I must be crazy. I always bring out the best in the men I fight but Joe Frazier, I'll tell the world right now, brings out the best in me. I'm gonna tell ya, that's one helluva man, and God bless him."

❧

There's Never Been
An Open Like It

BY DAN JENKINS

The past, the future and the present converged on one remarkable day at Cherry Hills in 1960, as Arnold Palmer caught Ben Hogan and Jack Nicklaus in the U.S. Open—and an SI writer was there to catch lightning in a bottle.

THEY WERE THE MOST ASTONISHING FOUR HOURS IN GOLF since Mary, Queen of Scots found out what dormie meant and invented the back nine. And now, given 18 years of reflection, they still seem as significant to the game as, for instance, the day Arnold Palmer began hitching up his trousers, or the moment Jack Nicklaus decided to thin down and let his hair fluff, or that interlude in the pro shop when Ben Hogan selected his first white cap.

Small wonder that no sportswriter was capable of outlining it against a bright blue summer sky and letting the four adjectives ride again: It was too big, too wildly exciting, too crazily suspenseful, too suffocatingly dramatic. What exactly happened? Oh, not much. Just a routine collision of three decades at one historical intersection.

On that afternoon, in the span of just 18 holes, we witnessed the arrival of Nicklaus, the coronation of Palmer and the end of Hogan. Nicklaus was a 20-year-old amateur who would own the 1970s. Palmer was a 30-year-old pro who would dominate the 1960s. Hogan was a 47-year-old immortal who had overwhelmed the 1950s. While they had a fine supporting cast, it was primarily these three men who waged war for the U.S. Open championship on that Saturday of June 18, 1960. The battle was continuous, under a steaming Colorado sun at Cherry Hills Country Club in Denver. Things happened *to* the three of them and *around* them—all over the place—from about 1:45 until the shadows began to lengthen over the same elms and cottonwoods, the same wandering creek, and the same yawning lake that will be revisited this week as Cherry Hills again is host to our grandest championship.

In those days there was something in sport known as Open Saturday. It is no longer a part of golf, thanks to television—no thanks, actually. But it was a day like no other; a day on which the best golfers in the world were required to play 36 holes because it had always seemed to the USGA that a prolonged test of physical and mental stamina should go into the earning of the game's most important title. Thus, Open Saturday lent itself to wondrous comebacks and horrendous collapses, and it provided a full day's ration of every emotion familiar to the athlete competing under pressure for a prize so important as to be beyond the comprehension of most people.

Open Saturday had been an institution with the USGA since its fourth annual championship in 1898. There had been thrillers before 1960, Saturdays that had tested the Bobby Joneses, Walter Hagens, Gene Sarazens, Harry Vardons, Francis Ouimets, Byron Nelsons, Sam Sneads—and, of course, the Ben Hogans—not to forget the occasional unknowns like John L. Black, Roland Hancock and Lee Mackey, all of them performing in wonderfully predictable and unexpectedly horrible ways, and so writing the history of the game in that one event, the National Open.

But any serious scholar of the sport, or anyone fortunate enough to have been there at Cherry Hills, is aware that the Open Saturday of Arnold, Ben and Jack was something very special—a U.S. Open that in meaning for the game continues to dwarf all of the others.

The casual fan will remember 1960 as the year old Arnie won when he shot a 65 in the last round and became the real Arnold Palmer. Threw his visor in the air, smoked a bunch of cigarettes, chipped in, drove a ball through a tree trunk, tucked in his shirttail, and lived happily ever after with Winnie and President Eisenhower.

And that is pretty much what happened. But there is a constant truth about tournament golf: Other men have to lose a championship before one man can win it. And never has the final 18 of an Open produced as many losers as Cherry Hills did in 1960. When it was over, there were as many stretcher cases as there were shouts of "Whoo-ha, go get 'em, Arnie.' " And that stood to reason after you considered that in those insane four hours Palmer came from seven strokes off the lead and from 15th place to grab a championship he had never even been in contention for.

Naturally, Palmer had arrived in Denver as the favorite. Two months earlier he had taken his second Masters with what was beginning to be known to the wire services as a "charge." He had almost been confirmed as The Player of the New

Era, though not quite. But as late as noon on Open Saturday, after three rounds of competition, you would hardly have heard his name mentioned in Denver. A list of the leaders through 54 holes shows how hopeless his position seemed. The scoreboard read:

Mike Souchak 68-67-73—208
Julius Boros 73-69-68—210
Dow Finsterwald 71-69-70—210
Jerry Barber 69-71-70—210
Ben Hogan 75-67-69—211
Jack Nicklaus 71-71-69—211
Jack Fleck 70-70-72—212
Johnny Pott 75-68-69—212
Don Cherry 70-71-71—212
Gary Player 70-72-71—213
Sam Snead 72-69-73—214
Billy Casper 71-70-73—214
Dutch Harrison 74-70-70—214
Bob Shave 72-71-71—214
Arnold Palmer 72-71-72—215

Through Thursday's opening round, Friday's second round, and right up until the last hole of the first 18 on Saturday, this Open had belonged exclusively to Mike Souchak, a long-hitting, highly popular pro who seldom allowed his career to get in the way of a social engagement. His blazing total of 135 after 36 holes was an Open record. And as he stood on the 18th tee of Saturday's morning round, he needed only a par four for a 71 and a four-stroke lead on the field.

Then came an incident that gave everyone a foreboding about the afternoon. On Souchak's backswing, a camera clicked loudly. Souchak's drive soared out of bounds, and he took a double-bogey 6 for a 73. He never really recovered from the jolt. While the lead would remain his well into the afternoon—long after Arnold had begun his sprint—you could see Souchak painfully allowing the tournament to slip away from him. He was headed for the slow death of a finishing 75 and another near miss, like the one he had experienced the previous year in the Open at Winged Foot.

Much has been written about Arnold Palmer in the locker room at Cherry Hills between rounds on Open Saturday. It has become a part of golfing lore. However, there could hardly be a more appropriate occasion for the retelling of it than now. As it happened, I was there, one of four people with Arnold. Two of the others were golfers—Ken Venturi and Bob Rosburg, who were even farther out of the tournament than Palmer—and the fourth was Bob Drum, a writer then with the *Pittsburgh Press*. It was a position that allowed Drum to enjoy the same close relationship with Palmer that *The Atlanta Journal*'s O. B. Keeler once had with Bobby Jones.

Everybody had cheeseburgers and iced tea. We bathed our faces and arms with cold towels. It was too hot to believe that you could actually see snowcaps on the Rockies on the skyline.

As Palmer, Venturi and Rosburg sat on the locker room benches, there was no talk at all of who might win, only of how short and inviting the course was playing, of how Mike Souchak, with the start he had, would probably shoot 269 if the tournament were a Pensacola Classic instead of the Open.

ARNOLD WAS cursing the first hole at Cherry Hills, a 346-yard par four with an elevated tee. Three times he had just missed driving the green. As he left the group to join Paul Harney for their 1:42 starting time on the final 18, the thing on his mind was trying to drive that first green. It would be his one Cherry Hills accomplishment.

"If I drive the green and get a birdie or an eagle, I might shoot 65," Palmer said. "What'll that do?"

Drum said, "Nothing. You're too far back."

"It would give me 280," Palmer said. "Doesn't 280 always win the Open?"

"Yeah, when Hogan shoots it," Drum said, laughing heartily at his own wit. Drum was a large Irishman with a P.A. system for a voice and a gag-writer's knowledge of diplomacy.

Arnold lingered at the doorway, looking at us as if he were waiting for a better exit line.

"Go on, boy," Drum said. "Get out of here. Go make your seven or eight birdies and shoot 73. I'll see you later."

Bob Drum had been writing Palmer stories since Palmer was the West Pennsylvania amateur champion. On a Fort Worth newspaper, I had been writing Ben Hogan stories for 10 years, but I had also become a friend of Palmer's because I was a friend of Drum's.

Palmer left the room but we didn't, for the simple reason that Mike Souchak, the leader, would not be starting his last round for another 15 or 20 minutes. But the fun began before that. It started for us when word drifted back to the locker room that Palmer had indeed driven the first green and two-putted for a birdie. He had not carried the ball 346 yards in the air, but he had nailed it good enough for it to burn a path through the high weeds the USGA had nurtured in front of the green to prevent just such a thing from happening. Palmer had in fact barely missed his eagle putt from 20 feet.

Frankly, we thought nothing of it. Nor did we think much of the news that Arnold had chipped in from 35 feet for a birdie at the second. What did get Bob Drum's attention was the distant thunder which signaled that Arnold had birdied the 3rd hole. He had wedged to within a foot of the cup.

We were standing near the putting green by the clubhouse, and we had just decided to meander out toward Souchak when Drum said:

"Care to join me at the 4th hole?"

I said, "He's still not in the golf tournament."

"He will be," Drum said.

And rather instinctively we broke into a downhill canter.

As we arrived at the green, Palmer was in the process of drilling an 18-foot birdie putt into the cup. He was now four under through 4, two under for the championship, only three strokes behind Souchak, and there were a lot of holes left to play.

We stooped under the ropes at the 5th tee, as our armbands entitled us to, and awaited Arnold's entrance. He came in hitching up the pants and gazed down the fairway. Spotting us, he strolled over.

"Fancy seeing you here," he said with a touch of slyness.

Then he drank the rest of my Coke, smoked one of my cigarettes, and failed to birdie the hole, a par 5. On the other hand, he more than made up for it by sinking a curving 25-footer for a birdie at the par-3 6th. At the 7th, he hit another splendid wedge to within six feet of the flag. He made the putt. And the cheers that followed told everybody on the golf course that Arnold Palmer had birdied six of the first seven holes.

It was history book stuff. And yet for all of those heroics it was absolutely unreal to look up at a scoreboard out on the course and learn that Arnold Palmer still wasn't leading the Open. Some kid named Jack Nicklaus was. That beefy guy from Columbus paired with Hogan, playing two groups ahead of Palmer. The amateur. Out in 32. Five under now for the tournament.

Bob Drum sized up the scoreboard for everyone around him.

"The fat kid's five under and the whole world's four under," he said.

That was true one minute and not true the next. By the whole world, Drum meant Palmer, Hogan, Souchak, Boros, Fleck, Finsterwald, Barber, Cherry, etc. It was roughly 3:30 then, and for the next half hour it was impossible to know who was actually leading, coming on, falling back, or what. Palmer further complicated things by taking a bogey at the 8th. He parred the 9th and was out in a stinging 30, five under on the round. But in harsh truth, as I suggested to Bob Drum at the time, he was still only three under for the tournament and two strokes off the pace of Nicklaus or Boros or Souchak—possibly all three. And God knows, I said, what Hogan, Fleck and Cherry—not to mention Dutch

Harrison, or even Ted Kroll—were doing while we were standing there talking.

Dutch Harrison, for example, had gone out very early and was working on a 69 and 283. And way back behind even Palmer was Ted Kroll, who had begun the round at 216, one stroke worse off than Palmer. Kroll and Jack Fleck had put almost the same kind of torch to Cherry Hills' front nine holes that Palmer had. Kroll had birdied five of the first seven holes, with one bogey included. Fleck had birdied five of the first six, also with a bogey included. Kroll was going to wind up firing the second-best round of the day, a 67, which would pull him into what later would look like a 200-way tie for third place at the popular figure of 283. One last footnote: Don Cherry, the other amateur in contention, was the last man on the course with a chance. There was this moment in the press tent when everyone was talking about Palmer's victory, and somebody calculated that Don Cherry could shoot 33 on the back nine and win. Cherry was due to finish shortly after dark. He quickly made a couple of bogeys, however, and that was that. But, meanwhile, we were out on the course thinking about Palmer's chances in all of this when Drum made his big pronouncement of the day.

"My man's knocked 'em all out," he said. "They just haven't felt the shock waves yet."

History has settled for Bob Drum's analysis, and perhaps that is the truth of the matter after all. The story of the 1960 Open has been compressed into one sentence: Arnold Palmer birdied six of the first seven holes and won.

BUT CONDENSATIONS kill. What is missing is everything that happened after 4 o'clock. The part about Mike Souchak losing the lead for the first time only after he bogied the 9th hole. The part about Nicklaus blowing the lead he held all by himself when he took three ghastly putts from only 10 feet at the 13th. This was the first real indication that they were all coming back to Palmer now, for Nicklaus's bogey dropped him into a fourway tie with Palmer, Boros and Fleck.

But so much more is still missing from the condensation. Nicklaus' woeful inexperience as a young amateur cost him another three-putt bogey at the 14th hole, and so, as suddenly as he had grabbed the lead, he was out of it. Then it was around 4:45 and Palmer was sharing the lead with Hogan and Fleck, each of them four under. But like Nicklaus, Fleck would leave it on the greens. Boros had started leaving it on the greens and in the bunkers somewhat earlier. He was trapped at the 14th and 18th, for instance, and in between he blew a three-footer. In the midst of all this, Palmer was playing a steady back side of one birdie and eight pars on the way to completing his 65. And until the last two holes of the championship, the only man who had performed more steadily than Palmer, or seemed to be enduring the Open stress with as much steel as he, was—no surprise—Ben Hogan.

It was getting close to 5:30 when Hogan and Palmer were alone at four under par in the championship, and the two of them, along with everybody else—literally everyone on the golf course—had somehow wound up on the 17th hole, the 71st of the tournament.

The 17th at Cherry Hills is still a long, straightaway par 5, 548 yards, with a green fronted by an evil pond. In 1960 it was a drive, a layup and a pitch. And there they all were. Hogan and Nicklaus contemplating their pitch shots as the twosome of Boros and Player waited to hit their second shots, while the two-some of Palmer and Paul Harney stood back on the tee.

Hogan was faced with a delicate shot of about 50 yards to a pin sitting al-together too close to the water to try anything risky. Ben had hit 34 straight greens in regulation that Saturday. He needed only a par-par finish for a 69, which would have been his third consecutive subpar round in the tourna-ment. He had to think this might be his last real chance to capture another Open. And nobody understood better than Hogan what it meant to reach the clubhouse first with a good score in a major championship.

Armed with all of this expertise as I knelt in the rough and watched Hogan address the shot, I brilliantly whispered to Drum:

"He probably thinks he needs another birdie with Arnold behind him, but I'll guarantee you one thing. Ben'll be over the water."

At which point Hogan hit the ball in the water.

He made a bogey 6. And in trying to erase that blunder on the 18th with a huge drive, which might conceivably produce a birdie, he hooked his tee shot into the lake and suffered a triple-bogey 7. Sadly, only 30 minutes after he had been a co-leader with just two holes to go, Hogan finished in a tie for ninth place, four strokes away.

Second place then was left to the 20-year-old with the crew cut, and Nicklaus' score of 282 remains the lowest total ever posted by an amateur in the Open.

All in all, these were tremendous performances by an aging Hogan and a young Nicklaus. The two of them had come the closest to surviving Palmer's shock waves.

It was later on, back in the locker room, long after Palmer had slung his visor in the air for the photographers, that Ben Hogan said the truest thing of all about the day. Ben would know best.

He said, "I guess they'll say I lost it. Well, one more foot and the wedge on 17 would have been perfect. But I'll tell you something. I played 36 holes today with a kid who should have won this Open by 10 shots."

Jack Nicklaus would start winning major titles soon enough as a pro, of course. But wasn't it nice to have Arnold around first?

The Day Bobby Hit
The Home Run

BY ROGER KAHN

*In the most thrilling of pennant races, the Giants tied the Dodgers on the
final day of the 1951 season. And then, in a special playoff, a million hearts were
broken—and a million more delighted—on one swing by Bobby Thomson.*

SOME DAYS—THEY COME RARELY—ARE CHARGED WITH PUBLIC
events so unexpected, so shocking, so far beyond the limits
of belief, that the events are not really public at all. Their impact thrusts them into the private lives of millions of people
who forever after remember these events in personal terms.

Pearl Harbor day was like that. ("I was listening to the radio, a football
game, when I heard about the bombing.") There was the day President Roosevelt died. ("I was riding the subway and the conductor told me. He was crying.") Then there was the day, in the most exciting of all baseball seasons,
when Bobby Thomson hit his home run.

The night before nearly everyone slept well. Bobby Thomson was troubled
because he had struck out with the bases full, but after a steak dinner and a
few beers, he relaxed. Ralph Branca fell asleep quickly. He had pitched on
Sunday, the last day of the regular season, and on Monday in the first game of
the playoff. Tomorrow, October 3, 1951, would be Wednesday, and Branca did
not expect that he would be called on to pitch again so soon.

Sal Maglie, who knew he was to start for the New York Giants, spent a comfortable night in his room at the Concourse Plaza Hotel. For all his intensity,
Maglie had learned to control his nerves. So, to a degree, had Don Newcombe,
who was to start for the Brooklyn Dodgers. "I can always sleep," Newcombe

said, a little proudly. "I don't need to take pills like some guys do the night before they pitch."

Charley Dressen, who managed the Dodgers, went out to an Italian restaurant called Rocco's and ate a dinner of clams, mussels, lobsters and spaghetti with hot sauce. A few people asked him how he felt about tomorrow's game and Dressen told them he wasn't worried. "Our ball club is ready," he said.

One man who did feel restlessness was Andy Pafko, the Dodgers' new left-fielder. The Dodgers had traded for Pafko at midseason, in a move the newspapers called pennant insurance, and Pafko, reading the papers, was impressed. Now he felt that the pennant was almost his personal responsibility. Lying in his room at the Hotel St. George in Brooklyn, he thought of his wife, Ellen, in Chicago. He had sent her a ticket to New York so she could watch him play with the Dodgers in the World Series. Next year there would be time to find an apartment together in Brooklyn, but for the moment Andy Pafko was alone. Perhaps it was loneliness as much as pressure that depressed him.

Although New York City was bright with the quickening pace of autumn, none of the ballplayers went out on the town. Everywhere, harboring their energies, they went to bed at about 11 o'clock, and soon, everywhere, they slept.

These were two tough and gifted baseball teams. The Dodgers had been built around such sluggers as Duke Snider and Gil Hodges, and in Jackie Robinson they had the finest competitor in baseball. For months that year the Dodgers won big and won often. On the night of August 11 they had been in first place, a full 13 games ahead of the Giants, who were their closest competitors.

Under Leo Durocher the Giants were combative, strong in pitching and opportunism, concentrated in themselves. Bobby Thomson, like the other Giants, knew none of the Dodgers socially; the teams did not fraternize. He thought that Gil Hodges was a pleasant man but that the rest of the Dodgers were unpleasant. This was a sermon Durocher had preached ceaselessly throughout the last months of the season until finally the ballplayers came unquestioningly to believe their manager.

Durocher's Giants, jelling slowly, spent some of May in last place. It was only when Willie Mays was called up from Minneapolis and Thomson became the regular third baseman that the team began to show fire. Then, from August 11 on, the Giants blazed, winning 37 games and losing only seven under demanding, unrelenting pressure.

The Dodgers, playing .500 ball as some of their sluggers slumped, were nonetheless uncatchable by all the traditions of baseball. But the Giants, establishing a new tradition, caught the uncatchable, forced them into a playoff and won the first game 3–1, defeating Ralph Branca at Ebbets Field. Then Clem Labine, a Dodger rookie, shut out the Giants at the Polo Grounds. The score was 10–0, but the game was close for some time and seemed to turn when Thomson, with bases full, struck out on a 3-and-2 pitch, a jumping curve that hooked wide of the plate.

No one expected the deciding game of the playoff to be easy, but no one, not Thomson, or Branca, or Durocher, or Dressen, felt any dramatic foreshadowing of what was ahead.

The game would be tense, but they'd all been tense lately. That was all. It was against this background of tension, which the players accepted as a part of life, that everyone slept the night before.

Robert B. Thomson, brown-haired, tall and swift, said goodbye to his mother a little before 10 a.m. and drove his blue Mercury to the Staten Island Ferry. The Thomsons lived on Flagg Place in New Dorp, once an independent village, now a community within the borough of Richmond. As he drove, Thomson thought about the game. "If I can just get 3 for 4," he mused, "then the old Jints will be all right." The thought comforted him. He'd been hitting well, and 3 for 4 seemed a reasonable goal.

Ralph T. Branca, black-haired, tall and heavy-limbed, said goodbye to his mother in suburban Mount Vernon, N.Y., the town where he had grown up, and drove off in his new Oldsmobile. He felt a little stiff from all his recent pitching. It would take him a long time to warm up, should Dressen need him in relief.

It was a gray day, darkened with the threat of rain. The temperature was warm enough—in the high 60s—but the crowd, waiting for the gates of the Polo Grounds bleachers to open, was smaller than the one which had waited in bright sunshine the day before.

Most of the players arrived by car, but Andrew Pafko came by subway, an hour's ride from downtown Brooklyn. "I'll beat the crowd," he decided, "so there's no sense wasting money on a cab." The crowd, it was to develop, was scarcely worth beating; 34,320, some 15,000 under standing room capacity.

As a ballpark, the Polo Grounds was unique; oddly shaped and with clubhouses 600 feet from the dugouts. It was, actually, a football horseshoe and as such made strange demands upon pitchers. The foul line in rightfield ran only 250 feet until it reached the lower deck of the grandstands. The leftfield line ran slightly longer, but in left a scoreboard was fixed to the façade of the upper deck, a façade that extended several yards closer to the plate than did the lower stands. A short fly, drifting down toward a fielder, could become a home run merely by grazing that projecting scoreboard.

Both walls fell away sharply, and the fence in centerfield was 485 feet out. The pitching rule was simply to make the batter hit to center, where distance didn't matter. The outfielding rule was to crowd the middle. The right- and left-fielders conceded drives down the line and tried to prevent hits from carrying into the deep alleys in left and right center. At the Polo Grounds, outfielders stood in a tightly bunched row, all seemingly about the same distance from home plate.

Back of centerfield stood an ugly green building which contained the clubhouses, a dining room for the press and an apartment for Horace Stoneham, the Giants' owner. Since both Durocher and Dressen believed in intensive managing, each team was gathered for a meeting in that green building shortly before noon. The announced purpose was to review hitters, although the two teams had played each other 24 times previously that season and there was nothing fresh or new to say about anyone.

"Jam Mueller on the fists," Dressen told Don Newcombe. "Keep the ball low and away to Thomson. Don't let him pull it." Dressen concluded with more warmth than he customarily displayed: "Look, I know it's tough to have to play this game, but remember we did our best all year. So today, let's just go out and do the best we can."

"Don't give Hodges anything inside," Durocher told Maglie. Then, later: "We haven't quit all year. We won't quit now. Let's go get 'em."

During batting practice Branca was standing near the cage with Pee Wee Reese and Jackie Robinson. "You guys get butterflies?" a reporter asked.

"No matter how long you been playing, you still get butterflies before the big ones," Reese said. Robinson laughed and Branca nodded solemnly. Ralph's long face, in repose, was sad or, perhaps, deadpan. One never knew whether he was troubled by what was around him or whether he was about to laugh.

The game began badly for the Giants. Sal Maglie, who had won 23 games and beaten the Dodgers five times that season, walked Reese and Duke Snider in the first inning. Jackie Robinson came up and lined Maglie's first pitch safely into leftfield for a single. Reese scored, and the Dodgers were ahead 1–0.

Newcombe was fast but not untouchable, and in the second inning Lockman reached him for a single. Thomson followed with a sharp drive to left, his first hit, and briefly the Giants seemed to be rallying. But very briefly. Running with his head down, Thomson charged past first base and had almost reached second before he noticed that Lockman had stopped there. Thomson was tagged out in a rundown, an embarrassing end to the threat.

When the day grew darker and the lights were turned on as the third inning began, the ballpark buzzed with countless versions of a joke: "Well, now maybe Thomson will be able to see what he's doing."

During the fifth Thomson doubled, his second hit, and Branca began to throw. Newcombe pitched out of the inning easily, but Branca threw a little longer. He wasn't snapping curves or firing fastballs. He was just working to loosen his arm, shoulder and back.

Branca threw again during the sixth inning, and when Monte Irvin doubled to left in the seventh, Branca began to throw hard. He felt loose by then. His fastball was alive. Carl Erskine, warming up next to him, was bouncing his curve, but Branca had good control and good stuff.

With Irvin at second, Lockman pushed a bunt in front of the plate, and Rube Walker, the Dodger catcher, grabbed the ball and threw to Billy Cox at third. Irvin beat the throw, and now Thomson came to bat with the tying run at third base late in a 1–0 ballgame.

Bearing down, Newcombe threw only strikes. After two, Thomson fouled off a fastball. Then he hit another fastball into centerfield, and Irvin scored easily after the catch. As the eighth inning began, the score was 1–1.

"I got nothing left, nothing," Newcombe announced as he walked into the Dodger dugout. Jackie Robinson and Roy Campanella, who was not playing that day because he had pulled a thigh muscle, took Newcombe aside.

"My arm's tight," Newcombe said.

"Obscenity," Robinson replied. "You go out there and pitch until your obscene arm falls off."

"Roomie," Campanella said, "you ain't gonna quit on us, now. You gonna hum that pea for us, roomie."

While the two built a fire under Newcombe, other Dodgers were making the inning miserable for both Maglie and Thomson. Reese and Snider opened with singles to right, and when Maglie threw a curve in the dirt and past Wes Westrum, Reese scored and Snider sped to third. Then Maglie walked Robinson, and the Dodgers, ahead 2–1, once again had runners at first and third.

Pafko pulled a bounding ball up the third base line and Thomson, breaking nicely, reached backhand for it. The play required a delicate touch; the ball glanced off the heel of Thomson's glove and skidded away from him. Snider scored, making it 3–1 Brooklyn, and Pafko was credited with a single. Then Billy Cox followed with a fierce one-hopper, again to Thomson's sector.

One thought—"Get in front of it"—crossed Thomson's mind. He did, lunging recklessly. There were other times at third when Thomson had thought of hard smashes coming up and hitting him in the face. This time he didn't. He thought only of blocking the ball with his glove, his arm, his chest. But the ball bounced high and carried over his shoulder into leftfield. The Dodgers had their third run of the inning and a 4–1 lead.

Newcombe blazed through the eighth, his arm no longer tight, and Larry Jansen retired the Dodgers in the ninth. "Come on," Durocher shouted as the last of the ninth began. "We can still get 'em. Come on."

Newcombe threw two quick strikes to Alvin Dark. "Got to get my bat on the ball," Dark thought. "Just get my bat on it."

Newcombe threw again, and Dark rapped a bounder into the hole in the right side of the infield. Both Hodges and Robinson broke for the ball and Newcombe ran to cover first base. Hodges, straining, touched the ball with the tip of his mitt and deflected it away from Robinson. Perhaps if he had not touched it Robinson could have made the play. As it was, Dark reached first on a single.

It was then that Dressen made a curious decision. He let Hodges hold the bag on Dark, as though Dark as a base runner were important. Actually, of course, Dark could have stolen second, third and home without affecting the game. The Giants needed three runs to tie, not one, and the Dodgers needed only outs.

Don Mueller, up next, quickly bounced a single through the right side—close to Hodges' normal fielding depth—and the Giants had runners at first and third. All around the Polo Grounds people stood up, but not to leave.

With Monte Irvin coming to bat, Dressen walked to the mound. Branca and Erskine were throwing in the bullpen, and Clyde Sukeforth, the bullpen coach, had told Dressen that Branca was fast and loose. But on the way to the mound the Dodger manager thought about catching, not pitching.

Campanella had a way with Newcombe. He knew how to needle the big pitcher to fury, and this fury added speed to Newcombe's fastball. Walking to the mound, Dressen wondered about replacing Rube Walker with Campanella. There was only one drawback. Foul territory at the Polo Grounds was extensive. A rodeo, billed as colossal, was once staged entirely in the foul area there. Campanella, with his bad leg, could catch, but he could not run after foul pops. Dressen thought of Hodges and Cox, both sure-handed, both agile. They could cover for Campanella to some extent. But there was all that area directly behind home plate where no one would be able to help Campy at all. Dressen thought of a foul pop landing safely, and he thought of the newspapers the next day. The second-guessing would be fierce, and he didn't want that. No, Dressen decided, it wouldn't be worth that. He chatted with Newcombe for a moment and went back to the dugout. When Irvin fouled out to Hodges, Dressen decided that he had done the right thing.

Then Newcombe threw an outside fastball to Whitey Lockman, and Lockman doubled to left. Dark scored, making it 4–2, but Mueller, in easily at third, slid badly and twisted his ankle. He could neither rise nor walk. Clint Hartung went in to run for him, and action was suspended while Mueller, on a stretcher, was carried to the distant Giant clubhouse.

"Branca's ready," Clyde Sukeforth told Charley Dressen on the intercom that ran from dugout to bullpen.

"O.K.," Dressen said. "I want him."

Branca felt strong and loose as he started his long walk in from the bullpen. At that moment he had only one thought. Thomson was the next batter, and he wanted to get ahead of Thomson. Branca never pitched in rigid patterns. He adjusted himself to changing situations, and his thought now was simply to get his first pitch over the plate with something on it.

Coming into the infield, he remembered the pregame conversation with the newspaperman. "Any butterflies?" he said to Robinson and Reese. They grinned, but not very widely.

At the mound, Dressen handed Branca the ball and said, "Get him out." Without another word the manager turned and walked back to the dugout.

Watching Branca take his eight warmup pitches, Thomson thought of his own goal. He had two hits. Another now would give him his 3 for 4. It would also tie the score.

"Boy," Durocher said to Thomson, "if you ever hit one, hit one now." Thomson nodded but said nothing. Then he stepped up to the plate.

Branca's first pitch was a fastball, hip-high over the inside corner. "Should have swung at that," Thomson told himself, backing out of the box.

"I got my strike," thought Branca. Now it was time to come up and in with a fastball. Now it was time for a bad pitch that might tempt Thomson to waste a swing. If he went for the bad ball, chances were he'd miss. If he took it, Branca would still be ready to come back with a curve, low and away. Branca was moving the ball around, a basic point when pitching to good hitters.

The pitch came in high and tight, just where Branca had wanted it. Thomson swung hard and the ball sailed out toward left.

"Get down, get down," screamed Billy Cox as the line drive carried high over his head.

"I got a chance at it," thought Andy Pafko, bolting back toward the wall.

Then the ball was gone, under the overhanging scoreboard, over the high wall, gone deep into the seats in lower left. For seconds, which seemed like minutes, the crowd sat, dumb. Then came the roar. It was a roar matched all across the country, wherever people sat at radio or television sets, a roar of delight, a roar of horror, but mostly a roar of utter shock. It was a moment when all the country roared and when an office worker in a tall building in Wall Street, hearing a cry rise all about her, wondered if war had been declared.

As the ball sailed into the stands, Thomson danced around the bases, skipping and leaping. The Giants crowded from their dugout to home plate. Ed Stanky, the second baseman, ran to Durocher, jumped on the manager's back, wrestled him to the ground and hugged him.

In left, Pafko stood stunned. Then he started to walk slowly toward the clubhouse, telling himself over and over, "It can't be." Most of the Dodgers were walking before Thomson reached second base, but Jackie Robinson held his ground. He wanted to make sure that Thomson touched all bases before conceding that the Giants had won, 5–4, before conceding that the pennant race was over.

Clyde Sukeforth gathered gear in the bullpen, and nearby Carl Erskine turned to Clem Labine. "That's the first time I've ever seen a big fat wallet go flying into the seats," Erskine said.

As Thomson touched home plate, the Giants lifted him to their shoulders. Then, inexplicably, they lowered him, and everyone ran for the clubhouse. Champagne was waiting. "Gee whiz," Thomson said. "Gee whiz."

Wes Westrum and Clint Hartung grabbed Ed Stanky, who liked to boast that he had never been drunk, and pinned him to a rubbing table. Westrum poured champagne into Stanky's mouth. "You're gonna get drunk now," he shouted. Westrum turned to the rubbing table, where Mueller lay, ice packs at his ankle. "Hey, Don," he shouted and emptied a magnum over the injured leg.

"Isn't this the damnedest thing you ever saw?" Durocher said.

"Gee whiz," Thomson said. "Gee whiz."

"How the hell did you go into second with Lockman there?" coach Fred Fitzsimmons said to Thomson. "But the hell with that," he added, and kissed Thomson damply.

"Congratulations," Charley Dressen said to Durocher. "I told you we'd finish one-two. Well, we did, and I'm number two."

"Gee whiz," Thomson said.

In the Dodger dressing room, Branca wept a little, showered slowly and, after submitting to some questioning, asked reporters to leave him alone. Then he went to the Oldsmobile, where his fiancée, blonde Ann Mulvey, was waiting with Father Frank Rowley of Fordham.

"Why me?" Branca said inside the car. "I don't smoke. I don't drink. I don't run around. Baseball is my whole life. Why me?"

"God chose you," the priest said, "because He knew you had faith and strength enough to bear this cross."

Branca nodded and felt a little better.

Thomson went from the ballpark to a CBS studio where he appeared on Perry Como's regular Wednesday night television show. Everywhere he went he was cheered, and always three thoughts ran through his mind. The old Jints had won. He had pushed his runs-batted-in total up over 100. He had got his 3 for 4.

When Thomson reached the house in New Dorp, his older brother, Jim, was waiting for him. "Do you know what you've done?" Jim said, all intensity and earnestness.

Only then, some six hours after the event, did Bobby Thomson realize that his home run was something that other people would remember for all the rest of his days.

A Pay Night
For Old Archie

BY BUDD SCHULBERG

When light-heavyweight champ Archie Moore finally made his debut at Madison Square Garden, he was 37, the veteran of 141 fights. At ringside for SI was the author of The Harder They Fall *and* On the Waterfront, *among other classics.*

ONE EVENING LAST WEEK 8,327 LIVE-FIGHT FANS AND SOME 20 million TViewers around the country watched the Garden debut of old Archie Moore, the goateed tumbleweed from San Diego, St. Louis, Toledo, Baltimore, or wherever the pickings look good. As debuts go, it was eminently successful, for the oldest headliner in the business caught up with his number one challenger, 26-year-old Harold Johnson, in the 14th round with a series of beautifully timed and perfectly thrown right hands that reminded one of well-told stories, short and to the point.

The only trouble with this debut is that Moore was closing in on that age at which Dr. Pitkin argued, questionably, that Life Begins. Archie Moore had to wait until he was 37 years old to see his name go up on a Garden marquee. It had taken him almost 19 years of barnstorm campaigning, from North Adams, Mass., to Panama, from Newark to Tasmania. The boxing story today is often told through likely looking preliminary kids a year or two out of the amateurs who are hustled into Garden main events to keep those razor blades moving. But there was nothing hurried about this maiden appearance of our light-heavyweight champion. Behind him were 141 battles with the toughest middleweights, light-heavies and heavyweights of the '30s, '40s, and '50s.

Putting Archie Moore into his first Madison Square Garden main event at the age of 37 is something like signing Caruso into the Metropolitan in 1920 instead of 1903 when he actually scored the first of his New York triumphs. If Caruso had had to tour the tank towns in moth-eaten opry houses for petty cash while third-raters unfit to carry his music case were pulling down the big notices and the heavy sugar at the Met, he would have become as cynical and money-hungry and unthrilled as Archie Moore seemed to feel in the Garden last week.

When Moore first climbed through the ropes as a pro back in the middle '30s, a 22-year-old Joe Louis was waiting for his shot at Braddock s heavyweight title. FDR was still promising to pull us out of the depression. Carole Lombard was a national idol. Adolph Hitler was training his Arbeitssolldaten with shovels. Mussolini was kicking up a rumpus in Ethiopia. People were singing *Goody, Goody*. The Oakies were pushing their rattletraps along Highway 66. Mickey Mouse and Joe DiMaggio were hitting their strides. And when you said McCarthy it meant little Charlie.

Nearly all the people who were making history when Archie was fighting up and down the West Coast in the late '30s and early '40s have gone back into the ground and the history books. The men who were in there with Moore in the years before Pearl Harbor are old men with stomachs hanging over their belts, and balding heads, living off their scrapbooks and their memories of trial and glory.

Watching old Archie coming on in the later rounds against a clever prime opponent who had taken Ezzard Charles and Nino Valdes and who was nine years old when the champion was belting out tough boys for peanuts in San Diego, you had to admire the old-time moves, the way he got up from an off-balance knockdown and took the fight to the younger man, careful to offer only the smallest pieces of himself and watchful for mistakes on which he could capitalize.

Years ago he had crowded Charles and knocked out Bivins and worked with the tough ones nobody wanted, Charley Burley, Lloyd Marshall, Holman Williams, Curtis Sheppard, Billy Smith. He was good enough in those days to be the light-heavyweight champion of the world, but everybody was looking the other way.

If it had been tennis, his ranking would have top-seeded him into a shot at the champions. But this was boxing, a bitter and slippery business, where the challenger your manager picked for you was the one who guaranteed the high money—and who didn't figure as tough as Archie Moore. An aging Lesnevich would rather have the build-up kid, Billy Fox, or the run-down limey, Freddie Mills. And when Mills got his hands on the title would he rather fight Archie, still the number one at age 33, or Joey Maxim, the Kearns concoction, who never resembles a fighter so much as when he's sitting down between rounds.

It was 1952 and Joey Maxim was in the book as the light-heavyweight champion of the world. At an age (36) when the best fighters in the world can't find their legs or their reflexes, Moore finally got Maxim into the ring with him. The expected happened. It was one of those nights when Moore was in there for the glory alone, and Maxim and Kearns got all the money. There wasn't another light-heavyweight around who could bring in a dollar, so the Moore–Maxim thing became a traveling circus—in Ogden, in Miami. And now they're talking Omaha. And six figures for Archie.

At the end of his long and rocky road Archie is finding the golden vein that eluded him through the best of his fighting days. Last week he and manager Charley Johnston were calling the turn and taking home all the money— around $40,000, including, rumor had it, a fistful out of Johnson's purse.

Moore didn't bother to pick up his check. He's off in his Cadillac and big black cowboy outfit, a dark-skinned, pugnacious Burl Ives, gypsying around the country talking about fighting Rocky Marciano. Or the top heavyweight contenders Valdes and Cockell.

What he's really saying is that after all those years in the financial desert he'd like to linger around the I.B.C.'s oasis. More pay nights like that debut in the Garden. There were times last week when he walked back to his corner like an old man waddling home from a tour of the gin mills. But he's the last of the great journeymen and it's still a pleasure to watch someone who knows his business in a day when under-developed and oversold kids bob up and down the ladder like the popular songs you can never remember once they've slipped off the hit parade.

Duel of the
Four-Minute Men

BY PAUL O'NEIL

When Roger Bannister and John Landy, the first four-minute milers, met in the summer of '54, the fledgling SI sent its star writer to cover the event. His dramatic account of athletic will and human courage set the standard for all SI writers.

THE ART OF RUNNING THE MILE CONSISTS, IN ESSENCE, OF reaching the threshold of unconsciousness at the instant of breasting the tape. It is not an easy process, even in a set-piece race against time, for the body rebels against such agonizing usage and must be disciplined by the spirit and the mind. It is infinitely more difficult in the amphitheater of competition, for then the runner must remain alert and cunning despite the fogs of fatigue and pain; his instinctive calculation of pace must encompass maneuver for position, and he must harbor strength to answer the moves of other men before expanding his last reserves in the war of the home stretch.

Few events in sport offer so ultimate a test of human courage and human will and human ability to dare and endure for the simple sake of struggle—classically run, it is a heart-stirring, throat-tightening spectacle. But the world of track has never seen anything quite to equal the "Mile of the Century" which England's Dr. Roger Gilbert Bannister—the tall, pale-skinned explorer of human exhaustion who first crashed the four-minute barrier—won here in Vancouver last Saturday from Australia's world-record holder, John Michael Landy. It will probably not see the like again for a long, long time.

The duel of history's first four-minute milers, high point of the quadrennial British Empire & Commonwealth Games, was the most widely heralded and universally contemplated match footrace of all time. Thirty-two thousand people jostled and screamed while it was run in Vancouver's new Empire Stadium, millions followed it avidly by television. It was also the most ferociously contested of all mile events. Despite the necessity of jockeying on the early turns and of moving up in a field of six other good men, Bannister ran a blazing 3:58.8 and Lundy 3:59.6. Thus for the first time two men broke four minutes in the same race. (Though far back in the ruck, five other runners finished under 4:08—Canada's Rich Ferguson in 4:04.6, Northern Ireland's Victor Milligan in 4:05, and both New Zealand's Murray Halberg and England's Ian Boyd in 4:07.2.)

Landy's world record of 3:58, set seven weeks ago in cool, still Nordic twilight at Turku, Finland, still stood when the tape was broken. But runners are truly tested only in races with their peers. When the four-minute mile was taken out of the laboratory and tried on the battlefield, Landy was beaten, man to man, and Roger Bannister reigned again as the giant of modern track.

Seldom has one event so completely overshadowed such a big and colorful sports carnival as this year's Empire Games. The Empire's miniature Olympics, for which Vancouver built its $2,000,000 stadium, a bicycle velodrome and a magnificent swimming pool, would have been notable if only for the rugged, seagirt, mountain-hung beauty amidst which they were held. They were further enlivened by the sight of Vancouver's kilted, scarlet-coated Seaforth Highland Regiment on parade, by the presence of Britain's Field Marshal Earl Alexander of Tunis, and—more exciting yet—of Queen Elizabeth's tall, handsome husband, Philip, Duke of Edinburgh.

During seven days of competition 20 of 27 games records were cracked in track and field events alone, and England, by virtue of her peerless distance runners, walked off with the lion's share of glory (scoring by unofficial points: England 514½, Australia 363¾, Canada 339, South Africa 260¾) and served notice on the world of tremendous new strength. Canadians and U.S. tourists alike were startled at the Elizabethan rudeness with which the Englishmen (Oxonians almost to a man, and thus held to be effete) ran their opposition into the ground in races demanding stamina and bottom. They placed one, two, three in the six mile (won by Peter Driver) one, two, three in the three mile (won by amiable, beer-quaffing Chris Chataway, who paced Bannister in the Oxford mile) and one, two, three in the half mile (won by Derek James Neville Johnson).

There were also alarums and sensations. Australia bicycle team protested English tactics, were rebuffed, withdrew from competition in a scandalous huff, cooled off, and duly reentered the lists. Vancouver's world champion weightlifter, Doug Hepburn—who stands 5' 8", weighs 299 pounds, measures 22 inches around the biceps and wears the look of a Terrible Turk—

lifted an aggregate of 1,040 pounds with contemptuous ease while his fellow citizens watched with unsurpassed pride and glee.

Canada's big, beautiful, blond woman shotputter, the Toronto schoolteacher Jackie MacDonald, was barred from competition in mid-meet for publicly endorsing Orange Crush. And the big closing-day crowd in the stadium was treated to one of the most gruesome scenes in sports history after England's marathon champion, Jim Peters, entered the track a mile ahead of his field but almost completely unconscious from strain and weariness. Peters fell as he came in sight of the crowd, rose drunkenly, staggered a few steps and fell again, until he was lifted to a stretcher and thus disqualified short of victory.

But for all this, nothing in the games remotely approached the tension and drama inherent in the mile. The race developed, in fact, amid an atmosphere much more reminiscent of a heavyweight championship fight than a contest of amateurs on the track. This was not unjustified; it was obvious from the beginning that Bannister and Landy would be engaged in a sort of gladiatorial combat, a duel of endurance in which no two other men who ever lived could even have engaged.

At first glance they seemed like an odd pair of gladiators. Like most distance men both look frail and thin in street clothes. Landy has a mop of dark, curly hair, the startled brown eyes of a deer, a soft voice with little trace of the Australian snarl, and a curious habit of bending forward and clasping his hands before his chest when making a conversational point. As a student at Australia's Geelong Grammar School ("A Church of England school," says his father with satisfaction, "where the prefects whack the boys, y'know") John developed a passion for the collection of butterflies and moths and an ambition to become an entomologist (which his father cured by sending him to Melbourne University to study agricultural science).

Roger Bannister is taller (6' ¾" to Landy's 5' 11¼"), slightly heavier (156 to Landy's 150), and slightly older (25 to Landy's 24) but he too would be the last man in the world to be singled out of a crowd as an athlete. He is stooped and negligent in carriage; he has lank blond hair, a high-cheeked, peaked face, and a polite and non-committal upper-class British voice. The face is expressive and can flash with instant animation and warmth. He can use words with precision and humor, and at times, even with a conversational eloquence. But scholarly is the word for Dr. Bannister. It is apt—he is a scholar and a brilliant one. Perhaps 5% of London medical students go through their courses without failing one exam and Bannister was among that small fraction when he received his degree at London's St. Mary's Hospital this year.

But men are seldom what they seem; Bannister, a complex and many-sided person, is both repelled and fascinated by the hurly-burly of big time sport, but for seven years, he has driven himself, stoically as an Indian brave or a man climbing Everest, toward the four-minute mile. So during the last five years has John Michael Landy. Both men have engaged in an endless and grueling effort to explore and push back the furthest boundaries of their own endurance.

Neither has ever been coached—in the casual British club system of competition, unlike the more regimented U.S. college team system, runners are presumed to be able to train themselves. Separately, half a world apart, both Bannister and Landy arrived at curiously identical conclusions; both decided that overtraining and staleness were simply myths and that the more the body endures the more it will endure. Both drove themselves to extremes of exertion (training sessions of 10 to 14 58-second quarter miles with one lap walked between) which would have staggered the average U.S. athlete.

Bannister carried his preoccupation with the mysteries of exhaustion into the world of science when he was a medical student at Oxford in 1951. He ran to the point of total collapse on a treadmill almost daily, with hollow needles thrust into his fingers to measure lactic acid and with an oxygen mask clapped over his face to give him extra fuel. Meanwhile at Oxford, and all through his three years at St. Mary's (where he ducked out to Paddington Recreation Ground and paid three pence to use the cinder paths), he went on with his massive burden of running.

The two four-minute milers developed into unique beings—men whose hearts have enormous capacity and power and whose bodies can utilize oxygen with fantastic economy and resist the inroads of fatigue with fantastic success. Bannister's pulse rate, which was a normal 65 when he was 17, is now 45. Landy's is 50. But there their similarities end. In Vancouver, as the remorseless pressure of the world's excitement pressed down on them, and race day neared, their differences of temperament became obvious. Landy seemed assured, relaxed, cocky. Bannister became quiet, remote, and fled daily to a golf course to train.

But Bannister's teammates were not misled. "Roger hates the idea of having to beat Landy—of having thousands of people expecting him to do it," said one. "But he'll do it. Nobody gets in such an emotional pitch before a race as he does. He's got a cold now, you know. I suspect it is psychosomatic and I suspect he suspects it—he had one just like it before the Oxford mile. Roger may tell you he has slept before a race, but he hasn't. When he goes out to run he looks like a man going to the electric chair. There are times the night before a race when he actually makes involuntary sounds, like a man being tortured. But Roger is a hard man to comfort—if you try he'll give you look that goes right through you."

Whatever their preliminary travail, both runners seemed equally intent and equally oblivious to the rumble and roar of applause as they warmed up on the infield grass in the moments before race time. Bright sunlight bathed the jam-packed stadium. The temperature stood at a pleasant 72, the relative humidity at a pleasant 48. Only the faintest of breezes moved on the track, as the field of milers was called to the mark. Landy, in the green of Australia, stepped quietly into the pole position. Bannister, in the red-barred white of England, had lane 5—he drew one deep, shuddering breath and then leaned forward for a standing start.

The gun puffed and popped and New Zealand's darkhorse Murray Halberg burst into the lead with his teammate William David Baillie at his heals. Landy let them go—he wanted speed, but he wanted top cover if he could get it—and settled into a docile fourth on the turn. He stayed there for less than the lap. The pacesetters slowed, almost imperceptibly, and Landy moved instantly and decisively into the lead. His strategy was simple and savage—to run the first seven furlongs at so blazing a pace that Bannister would be robbed of his famous kick.

As Landy moved, Bannister moved too. They ran Landy first, Bannister second at the end of the stretch and the duel had begun. "Time for the first lap," the loudspeakers grated as they entered the turn, "fifty-eight seconds." Then bedlam began too. It increased as Landy moved away—five yards, ten yards, fifteen yards—in the backstretch of the second lap, and Bannister let him go. "It was a frightening thing to do," said the Englishman later, "but I believed he was running too fast. I had to save for my final burst and hope I could catch him in time."

Landy's time was 1:58 at the half. The groundwork for a four-minute mile had been laid. The field had faded far to the rear. The duelists ran alone in front with Lundy still making the pace. But now, yard by yard, easily, almost imperceptibly Bannister was regaining ground. He was within striking distance as they fled into the last, decisive quarter amid a hysterical uproar of applause. He stayed there on the turn. Two hundred yards from home, Lundy made his bid for decision and victory. But Bannister refused to be shaken, and with 90 yards to go he lengthened his plunging stride. He came up shoulder to shoulder, fought for momentum, pulled away to a four-yard lead and ran steadily and stylishly through a deafening clamor to the tape. He fell, arms flapping, legs buckling, into the arms of the English team manager a split second after the race was done.

"I tried to pull away from him in the backstretch of the last lap," said Lundy after he paused to gasp for breath. "I had hoped that the pace would be so fast that he would crack at that point. He didn't. When you get a man in that sort of a situation and he doesn't crack, you do. From then on I knew it was only a question of time. I looked over my left shoulder to see where he was on the turn, and when I looked back he was ahead of me." He paused, grinned, shook his head and added: "I've had it."

III

SWEET
SPOTS

Finally, We Were Left Alone, Just Me and My Bike

BY THOMAS MCGUANE

For the author, a noted novelist, taking possession of a new motorcycle was a matchless moment, a dream come true—and then a nightmare.

L IKE MANY WHO THINK THEY MIGHT WANT TO BUY A motorcycle, there had been for me the time-consuming problem of getting over the harrowing insurance statistics, the reports on just what is liable to happen to you. But two years of living in California—a familiar prelude to acts of excess—had moved me up to the category of active motorcycle spectator. I watched and identified, and eventually resorted to bikers' magazines, from which I evolved a whole series of foundationless prejudices.

Following the war motorcycling left a peculiar image in the national consciousness: porcine individuals wearing a sort of yachting cap with a white vinyl bill, the decorative braid pulled up over the hat, their motorcycles plated monsters, white rubber mud flaps studded with ruby stars hung from both fenders. Where are those machines now? Surely Andy Warhol can't have bought them all. Not every one of them is a decorative planter in a Michigan truck garden. But wherever they are, it is certain that the ghosts of cretinism collect close around the strenuously baroque plumbing of those inefficient engines and speak to us of an America that has gone.

It was easy for me initially to deplore the big road bikes, the motorcycles of the police and Hell's Angels. But finally even these "hogs" and show bikes had their appeal, and sometimes I had dark fantasies of myself on El Camino

Real, hands hung overhead from the big chopper bars, feet in front on weird-ly automotive pedals, making all the decent people say: "There goes one."

I did it myself. Heading into San Francisco with my wife, our Land-Rover blaring wide open at 52 miles per, holding up a quarter mile of good people behind us, people who didn't see why anybody needed four-wheel drive on the Bayshore Freeway, we ourselves would from time to time see a lonesome Angel or Coffin Cheater or Satan's Slave or Gypsy Joker on his big chopper and say (either my wife or myself, together sometimes): "There goes one."

Anyway, it was somewhere along in here that I saw I was not that type, and began to think of sporting machines, even racing machines, big ones, because I had no interest in starting small and working my way up as I had been urged to do. I remember that I told the writer Wallace Stegner what I intended, and he asked, "Why do you people do this when you come to California?"

"It's like skiing," I said, purely on speculation.

"Oh, yeah? What about the noise?"

But no one could stop me. A simple Neanderthal "gimme" expressed my feeling toward all unowned motorcycles. "I'll have that and those. Me, now."

There was the dire question of money that ruled out many I saw. The English-built Triumph Metisse road racer was out of the question, for exam-ple. Some of the classics I found and admired—Ariel Square Fours, Vincent Black Shadows, BSA Gold Stars, Velocette Phruxtons, Manx Nortons—had to be eliminated on grounds of cost or outlandish maintenance problems.

Some of the stranger Japanese machinery, two-cycle, rotary-valved engines, I dismissed because they sounded funny. The Kawasaki Samurai actually seemed refined, but I refused to consider it. I had a corrupt Western ideal of a bike's exhaust rap, and the tuned megaphone exhausts of the Japanese mo-torcycles sounded like something out of the next century, weird loon cries of Oriental speed tuning. My wife felt they were all unwholesome and only nasty people rode them.

Somewhere in my mind the perfect motorcycle, the Platonic bike, had taken shape. Try to see this period as my time in the desert. Picture me bikelorn, as it were, driving a brutally slow safari vehicle on the crisp, perfect highways of California. Healthful airs are kept from my body by a corrupt capitalist windshield. The front differential is never engaged. Our Land-Rover, I told my wife, gets much worse mileage than almost any motorcycle you could name. "Oh, for God's sake," she said.

THERE IS a blurred moment in my head, a scenario of compulsion. I am in a motorcycle shop that is going out of business. I am writing a check that challenges the entire contents of my bank account. I am given ownership papers substantiated by the State of California, a crash helmet and five gallons of fuel. Some minutes later I am standing beside my new motorcycle, sick all over. The man who sold it to me stares palely through the Thermopane window covered with the decals of the noble marques of "performance." He wonders why I have not moved.

I have not moved because I do not know what to do. I wish to advance upon the machine with authority but cannot. He would not believe I could have bought a motorcycle of this power without knowing so much as how to start its engine. Presently he loses interest and looks for another tormented creature in need of a motorcycle.

Unwatched, I can really examine the bike. Since I have no notion of how to operate it, it is purely an *objet*. I think of a friend with a road racer on a simple mahogany block in front of his fireplace, except that he rides his very well.

The bike was rather beautiful. I suppose it still is. (Are you out there? If you read this, get in touch care of this magazine. All is forgiven.) The designation, which now seems too cryptic for my taste, was "Matchless 500," and it was the motorcycle I believed I had thought up myself. It is a trifle hard to describe the thing to the uninitiated, but, briefly, it had a 500-cc., one-cylinder engine—a "big single" in the patois of bike freaks—and an eloquently simple maroon teardrop-shaped tank that is as much the identifying mark on a Matchless, often otherwise unrecognizable through modification, as the chevron of a redwing blackbird. The front wheel, delicate as a bicycle's, carried a Dunlop K70 tire (said to "cling") and had no fender; a single cable led to the pale machined brake drum. Over the knobby rear curved an extremely brief magnesium fender with, instead of the lush buddy-seat of the fat motorcycles, a minute pillion of leather. The impression was of performance and of complete disregard for comfort. The equivalent in automobiles would be, perhaps, the Morgan, in sailboats the Finn.

I saw all these things at once (remember the magazines I had been reading, the Floyd Clymer books I had checked out of the library), and in that sense my apprehension of the motorcycle was perfectly literary. I still didn't know how to start it. Suddenly it looked big and mean and vicious and no fun at all.

I didn't want to experiment on El Camino Real and, moreover, it had begun to rain heavily. I had made up my mind to wheel it home, and there to peruse the operation manual whose infuriating British locutions the Land-Rover manual had prepared me for.

I was surprised at the sheer inertial weight of the thing; it leaned toward me and pressed against my hip insistently all the way to the house. I was disturbed that a machine whose place in history seemed so concise should look utterly foreign at close range. The fact that the last number on the speedometer was 140 seemed irresponsible.

It was dark by the time I got home. I wheeled it through the back gate and down the sidewalk through a yard turned largely to mud. About halfway to the kitchen door, I somehow got the thing tilted away from myself, and it slowly but quite determinedly toppled over in the mud with me, gnashing, on top of it.

My wife came to the door and peered into the darkness. "Tom?" I refused to vouchsafe an answer. I lay there in the mud, no longer struggling, as the spring rains of the San Francisco Peninsula singled me out for special treatment: take that and now that. I was already composing the ad in the *Chronicle* that motorcycle people dream of finding: "Big savings on Matchless 500. Never started by present owner. A real cream puff." My wife threw on the porch light and perceived my discomfiture.

The contretemps had the effect of quickly getting us over the surprise that I had bought the motorcycle, questions of authorization and so on. I headed for the showers. Scraped and muddy, I had excited a certain amount of pity. "I'll be all right."

NO ONE told me to retard the spark. True enough, it was in the manual, but I had been unable to read that attentively. It had no plot, no characters. So my punishment was this: when I jumped on the kick starter, it backfired and more or less threw me off the bike. I was limping all through the first week from vicious blowbacks. I later learned it was a classic way to get a spiral fracture. I tried jumping lightly on the kick starter and, unfairly, it would blast back as viciously as with a sharp kick. Eventually it started, and, sitting on it, I felt the surge of torque tilt the bike under me. I was afraid to take my hands off the handlebars. My wife lowered the helmet onto my head; I compared it to the barber's basin Don Quixote had worn into battle, the Helmet of Mambrino.

I slipped my toe up under the gearshift lever, lifted it into first, released the clutch and magically glided away and made all my shifts through fourth, at which time I was on Sand Hill Road and going 50, my shirt in a soft air bubble at my back, my Levi's wrapped tight to my shins, my knuckles whitening under the giddy surge of pure undetained motion as I climbed gently into the foothills toward Los Altos. The road got more and more winding as I ascended, briskly but conservatively. Nothing in the air was lost on me as I passed through zones of smell and temperature as palpable transitions, running through sudden warm spots on the road where a single redwood 100 feet away had fallen and let in a shaft of sunlight. The road seemed tremendously spacious. The sound was behind me, so that when I came spiraling down out of the mountains and saw some farm boy had walked out to the end of the road to see me go by, I realized he had heard me coming for a long time. And I wondered a little about the racket.

These rides became habitual and presumably more competent. I often rode up past La Honda for a view of the sea at the far edge of a declining cascade of manzanita-covered hills, empty and foggy. The smell of ocean was so perfectly evocative in a landscape divided among ranches and truck gardens whose pumpkins in the foggy air seemed to have an uncanny brilliance. A Japanese nursery stood along the road in clouds of tended vines on silver redwood lattice. I went past it to the sea and before riding home took a long walk on the ribbed, immense beach.

A fascinating aspect of the pursuit, not in the least bucolic, was the bike shop where one went for mechanical service, and which was a meeting place for the bike people, whose machines were poised out front in carefully conceived rest positions. At first, of course, no one would talk to me, but my motorcycle ideas were theirs; I was not riding one of the silly mechanisms that purred down the highways in a parody of the equipment these people lived for.

One day an admired racing mechanic—"a good wrench"—came out front and gave my admittedly well-cared-for Matchless the once-over. He announced that it was "very sanitary." I was relieved. "Thank you," I said, modestly.

Ultimately, I was taken in, treated kindly and given the opportunity to ride some of the machinery that so excited me: the "truly potent" Triumph Metisse, an almost uncontrollable supercharged Norton Atlas from New Mexico and a couple of road-racing machines with foot pegs way back by the rear sprocket and stubby six-inch handlebars—so that you lay out on the bike and divide a sea of wind with the point of your chin.

One day I "got off on the pavement," that is, crashed. It was not much of a crash. I went into a turn too fast and ran off the shoulder and got a little "road burn" requiring symbolic bandages at knees and elbows. I took the usual needling from the crew at the bike shop, and with secret pleasure accepted the temporary appellation, "Crash Cargo." I began taking dawn trips over the mountains to Santa Cruz, sometimes with others, sometimes alone, wearing a wool hunting shirt against the chill and often carrying binoculars and an Audubon field guide to birds.

Then one day—and here the kettledrums are introduced on the sound track—riding in my own neighborhood, a man made a U turn in front of me and stopped, blocking the road. It was too late to brake and I had to put the bike down, riding it like a sled as it screeched across the pavement. It ran into the side of the car and I slid halfway under, the seat and knees torn out of my pants, scraped and bruised but without serious injury. I had heard the sharp clicking of my helmet against the pavement and later saw the depressions that might have been in my skull.

The man got out, accusing me of going 100 miles an hour, accusing me of laying for a chance to create an accident, accusing me of being a Hell's Angel, and finally admitting he had been daydreaming and had not looked up the street before making his illegal maneuver. The motorcycle was a mess. He pleaded with me not to have physical injuries. He said he had very little insurance. And a family. "Have a heart."

"You ask this of a Hell's Angel?"

At the motorcycle shop I was urged to develop nonspecific spinal trouble. A special doctor was named. But I had the motorcycle minimally repaired and sent the man the bill. When the settlement came, his name was at the top of the stationery. He was the owner of the insurance agency.

Perhaps it was the point-blank view from below of rocker panels and shock absorbers and the specious concern of the insurance man for my health that gave my mortality its little twinge. I suddenly did not want to get off on the pavement anymore or bring my road burn to the shop under secret bandages. I no longer cared if my bike was sanitary. I wanted to sell it, and I wanted to get out of California.

I did both those things, and in that order. But sometimes in the midst of more tasteful activities, I miss the mournful howl of that big single engine as it came up on the cam, dropped revs and started over on a new ratio; the long banking turns with the foot pegs sparking against the pavement and the great crocodile's tears the wind caused to trickle out from under my glasses. I'm behind a sensible windshield now, and the soaring curve of acceleration does not come up through the seat of my pants. I have an FM radio, and the car doesn't get bad mileage.

Call me Gramps.

❧

You'll Not Do That Here, Laddie

BY DAN JENKINS

In order to rewrite the history of Scottish golf in his inimitable style, the author toured his—and the game's—ancestral homeland. Neither golf's sacred shrines nor the reverent keepers of its mythology would ever be quite the same.

> *It is statute an ordinit that in na place of the realme be there usit . . . Golfe or uther sik unprofitabill sportis.*
> —James IV to Parliament in Edinburgh May 16, 1491

I T WAS A GRAY, DRIZZLY DAY LIKE MOST IN SCOTLAND, AND THERE was I, a lonely shepherd, strolling along a swollen dune by the North Sea looking for a wee stane to hit wi' a bit crook. Clumps of heather were up to my knees and the yellow-tipped whin was up to my chest, and I was up to here with my sheep because the little dumplings had wandered away. I had this crooked stick, that I normally used to keep the dumplings in line, in my hand. You know. Firm left side, eye on the tailbone, slow backswing—and whap. But they were gone and I was just ambling along when I saw this chuckie stane, as it was called, this round pebble. I also saw this rabbit scrape, as it was called, through an opening in the heather and whin. So I said to myself, "Self, why don't you take your bit crook and try to knock this here stane into that there scrape? And stay out of the heather because, boy, it'll make your hand ring." Well, I guess I took it back a little outside, because I cut a low one right into the garbage and almost never did find it, but anyhow, this is how I came to invent the game of golf a few hundred years ago.

There are those, of course, who claim that I did not invent golf in another life, nor did any other Scot. Some say the Romans did it long before me and called it *Paganica*, which, between you and me, sounds like a joint over on East 56th with a big tab. Some say the Dutch invented golf, or a game called *kolven*, which was similar. But no way. *Kolven* has to be a roll of veal stuffed with cheese and chives. Some even say that the French originated golf under the name of *jeu de mail*, but, as any European traveler knows, this is a game for the big players in Monaco.

The fact of the matter is, golf is a Scottish game. It is naturally Scottish, as natural to our instincts as the seaside links land is natural to the setting. It was the Scots, after all, who took the game and did something with it when everybody else was busy making crossbows. We made the courses and the clubs, the balls and the rules, the trophies and the tournaments. We invented wind and rough, hooks and slices, bunkers and doglegs, and we were just getting ready to invent the overlapping grip when Harry Vardon, an Englishman, beat us to it.

We looked at the seashores, our links-land, and said this is where the glory's at. Let the wet wind blow in from Denmark or wherever it comes from. Let the incursions of the sea make the giant dunes and the tumbling valleys. Let the birds bring in the seeds that will grow our curious rough—the wiry, purple heather, the bulging whin, the fern we'll call bracken and the broom, that does not have thorns to distinguish itself from whin, or gorse.

No, I don't know what the Romans, the Dutch and the French were doing around the 1450s, but we Scots were playing golfe then and had been. At least we were when the kings would permit it, there being, from time to time, this nagging problem of national service. Had to go fight the English. Cancel my starting time.

There was an afternoon, I recall, when the game came close to being banished forever. As it happened, I was out on a moor at St. Andrews trying out a new Auchterlonie driving spoon at the 11th—the short hole, of course—when a king's guard rose up out of the whin and handed me a scroll signed by our monarch.

The scroll said, "It is decreetid and ordained . . . that the Fute-ball and the Golf be utterly cryit doune, and nocht to be usit."

"Guy never could spell," I said.

The guard pointed his crossbow at me and said that the king, Jimmy the Roman Numeral, meant business.

"The golfe is sik unprofitabill sportis," he said.

"Pal, you got that right," I said. "See that shepherd over there with the cross-handed grip on his bit crook? Well, he's got me out, out, out and one down."

"Don't be abusit," the guard said. "It is statute an ordinit that in na place of the realme be there Golfe in tyme cuming."

"Look," I said. "Smell that air. Gaze over this land. Great, huh? Who would want a guy to be hanging around a drafty castle waiting for an Englishman to scale a wall?"

"Aye," he said. "The aire is guid and the field reasonable feir. But can ya na handle the bow for archerie? Can ya no run or swoom or warstle instead?"

"I don't know, man," I said. "Let me put it your way. Here's the deal. I was drivin' the chuckie stanes wi' a bit stick as sune's I could walk."

He nodded as if he were beginning to understand.

"Here's something else," I said. "I happen to know that a bow-maker in Perth is fixing up a set of clubs for the king right now. Why? Because the king sneaked out the other day to see what this game was all about and the Earl of Bothwell, who plays to a cool 23, brought him to his knees on the back three at Leith. The king's getting a pretty good price, too. Like only 14s's for the set, whatever an s is."

The guard put down his crossbow and said, well, go ahead and play if that was the case. And by the way, he added, did I want to buy "a dussen guid golfe ballis?"

"Hold it," I said. "You got featheries?"

"Aye," he said. "Guid featheries that cum from the Laird of Rosyth. Guid featheries stuffed with flock."

"Four s's," I said. "And not an s more."

"Eight s's," he said.

"They're hot, man. Six s's and we both get out clean," I said.

He went for the six—you can always strike a bargain in Europe—and disappeared back into the whin. And now that I had saved golf, I couldn't wait to try out one of the new high-compression featheries. I heeled up a good lie and gave the shot a full body turn. Wow. There is still a hole in the wind where I hit that shot and I thought to myself, what a happy and golden time, indeed.

In a few more years all of royalty would be playing golfe. There were rumors of Mary Queen of Scots shanking around the fields of Seton when some said she should have been mourning the demise of Lord Darnley. Charles I got a very bad press for being in a match at Leith when the Irish Rebellion broke out. A lot of Jameses and Dukes of York were seen swinging at Musselburgh, which still claims to be the oldest layout in the world and now sits inside a racecourse near Edinburgh. There was a Stuart or two spotted in a putting game at Leith, where The Honourable Company of Edinburgh Golfers got started.

All golfers, I think, are indebted to a small group of us that got together in 1744—The Honourable Company, or The Company of Gentleman Golfers as we called ourselves then. What we did was form the first country club. Not only that, we sat down and wrote the first rules of the game, which we called the *Articles & Laws in Playing at Golf*.

Those first rules have been well-preserved, along with some terribly clever comments I made at the meeting as I spoke keenly above the roar of our first president, Duncan Forbes. Among those rules were:

I You Must Tee your Ball within a Club length of the hole.

(It's going to be uproarious fun, guys, waiting for somebody to drive before you can putt.)

II Your Tee must be upon the Ground.

(Nothing like teeing up the ball in the air for greater distance.)

III You are not to Change the Ball which you Strike off the Tee.

(The caddies will take care of this. When I tried to put down a clean one to putt the other day at St. Andrews, my man, Ginger Johnson, tugged at the sleeve of my cashmere and said, "You'll not do that here, Laddie.")

IV You are not to Remove Stones, Bones or any Breakclub for the Sake of playing your Ball Except upon the fair Green, and that only within a Club's Length of your Ball.

(Well, we'll get some pretty tricky breaks over the stones and bones.)

V If your Ball come among Water, or any Watery filth, You are at Liberty to take out Your Ball, & bringing it behind the hazard, and teeing it, You may play it with any Club, and allow your Adversary a Stroke, for so getting out your Ball.

(Unless your Adversary doesn't see you do it.)

VII At holeing, You are to play your Ball honestly for the Hole, and not to play upon your Adversary's Ball, not lying in your way to the Hole.

(I heard about this across the ocean in a place called Easthampton. They call it croquet.)

VIII If you should lose your Ball, by its being taken up, or any other way, You are to go back to the Spot where you Struck last and drop another Ball, and allow your Adversary a Stroke for the Misfortune.

(And if your Adversary has been seen taking up your Ball, you may strike your Adversary wi' a bit crook, teeing him upon the Ground.)

IX No Man at Holeing his Ball, is to be Allowed to Mark his way to the Hole with his Club or anything else.

(And if you do, man, the greens committee will chew you out.)

XII He Whose Ball lyes furthest from the Hole is Obliged to play first.

(This is a good rule, but I'll tell you, the public course players are going to relax it a little.)

XIII Neither Trench, Ditch or Dyke made for the preservation of the Links, Nor the Scholars' Holes or the Soldiers' Lines, shall be Accounted a Hazard, But the Ball is to be taken out, Teed and played with any Iron Club.

(Oh, swell, Duncan. So how come you let me make eight passes at it yesterday in the Soldiers' Lines with no relief?)

Well, you know what happens. You let one private club get started and down the road another pops up. The nobleman and lairds of Fifeshire couldn't stand it that we had The Company of Gentleman Golfers, and some rules, especially they said, when *everybody* knew St. Andrews was the cradle of golfe. So in hardly any time at all they formed The Society of St. Andrews Golfers, which later would become known as the Royal and Ancient Golf Club. And you know what happened after that. They had the sport by the old gutta-percha and never would turn loose of it.

A lot of arguments have gone on through the years about the history of the game—where it began, who molded the first cleek and so forth. Over at Muirfield, where The Honourable Company still hangs out, they say that the R&A would still be the Greensboro Jaycees if the Edinburgh code of golf hadn't been written. And at the same time, over at Prestwick on the West Coast, they like to say that the R&A wouldn't have anything to do but run the St. Andrews city championship if Prestwick's members hadn't decided to invent the Open Championship and stage it the first 12 years of its existence. The Open Championship, of course, is what a lot of crass Americans would call the British Open today.

All I know is, every time somebody at Muirfield or Prestwick or Troon or Carnoustie goes out and finds an old track iron which had to have been made over 200 years ago, somebody from the R&A will reach down into Hell Bunker or the Swilken Burn and find a club that is older. One envisions genial Laurie Auchterlonie, the honorary professional of St. Andrews, carving and hammering away these days, making an antique putter dated 1742.

What truly matters, of course, is that the whole scene is old—the gray clubhouses and the rolling land, the minute books and the scrolls, the wind and rain, the heather, dunes and swales—everything that makes Scottish golf what it is. It has been said by many that a golfer hasn't played the game until he has gone back where it all was, and where it all still is.

It is a special feeling, I think, that calls the golfer back to Scotland. "Take me to the grave of Old Tom Morris," a voice says. "Drive me around the Road Hole. Show me where the Wee Icemon chipped it in at Carnoustie. Lead me down the long narrow 11th at Troon where Arnie made the 3s. Let me hear the groan of the Spitfire ghosts at Turnberry. Carry me over the Sleepers at Prestwick. Bend me around the archery field at Muirfield. Drown me in these treasures of time."

The Scots themselves relish all this more than anyone. It is in their faces as deeply as it is in their verse. They are constantly writing poems about their bunkers and burns and braes. "The swallows are high in an empty sky, so let's to the tee once more." That kind of thing. It's enough to have a man packing his clubs, tossing his alligators into his suitcase and. . . .

"So let's to the tee once more," I said to the customs official at Prestwick, having deboarded my Pan Am flight from JFK. "The nature of my visit? Well, I have a meeting scheduled with Heather, Whin, Bracken & Broom, one of your very successful brokerage firms."

There was this tour that Keith Mackenzie, the secretary of the R&A, had worked out for me. Fly to Prestwick, an old WWII air base where everybody played *Twelve O'Clock High,* and motor down the West Coast to Turnberry, the Pebble Beach of Scotland. Stay at the Turnberry Hotel, which is the only thing there and covers a hillside overlooking the course and the Spitfire runways. From Turnberry, he said, one could reach two other famous Scottish links—Troon and Prestwick—simply by driving over the Electric Brae, a road that goes up when it appears to be going down. Cover the West Coast first, said Mackenzie, then move to The Old Course Hotel at St. Andrews, where you can play the Old Course, right outside your window, and then journey north toward Dundee and Carnoustie or south toward Edinburgh and Muirfield.

"This is the best possible route for an American," said Mackenzie.

"But I'm Scottish," I said. "I'm just retracing my steps from a few hundred years before."

"Of course, dear chap," he said. "We're all Scottish when it comes to golf."

"Aye," I said.

"Simply marvelous tour," he said. "You'll see a bit of it all. Turnberry, for example, pitched right there on the Firth of Clyde. Tees practically hanging on the water like Pebble. And Prestwick with those slender fairways and blind shots, and seven bloody 5 pars. Too outdated for the Open Championship, of course, but mind you, the Pine Valley of Scotland in a way. And wonderful Old Troon. The Postage Stamp green. One of the first sharp-angled doglegs. I say, Arnie argued a good case there, didn't he?"

"Aye," I said.

"Then to the East Coast. That's your story," Keith said. "You'll quarter in The Old Course Hotel, naturally, right where the railway sheds were on the Road Hole. Walk out on your terrace and spit in the Principal's Nose, by Jove. With the new bridge you can reach Carnoustie in an hour now. Good old somber Carnoustie, the Barry Burn and all that. And then, of course, there's Muirfield. Marvelous place, Muirfield. Not a burn on it, you see. Just 165 bunkers. You'll see a bit of sand there, I'd guess."

"Aye, Aye," I said.

"Best of luck," he said. "See you at St. Andrews. We'll have a bit of port. It goes well in the Big Room."

For some evil reason, some death wish that perhaps is concealed within us all, the first thing a touring golfer is captivated by in Scotland is the plant life adjacent to all fairways. The heather, whin, bracken and broom. Turnberry, my first stop, had all of these other landmarks to dwell upon—holes hanging on the Firth of Clyde, as Mackenzie said, the Spitfire runways now bordered by wild flowers, a bird sanctuary on an island off in the distance, the huge hotel on the hill where *God Save the Queen* reverberates from the orchestra pit in the ballroom at night through all of the tearooms and the RAF monument at the 12th green commemorating those men from Turnberry's aerial fighting and gunnery school who died in combat. But I was preoccupied with the rough.

You find yourself having this running commentary with your caddie as if he's a botanist in his checkered James Cagney cap, his coat and tie and scruffy face that hasn't been shaved since the last air raid. His name is Jimmy or Peter or Ginger or Tip or Cecil and chances are he caddied for Hagen at Hoylake in 1924.

"What am I in here?" I asked my caddie at Turnberry on the very first hole. "Is this gorse?"

"Not likely," he said. "I think that's a bush."

Your caddie is a warm, friendly man who knows his golf. You swing once and he knows your distances. If he says the shot is "a wee seven," you'd better hit it wee-ly or a dozen of you with machetes won't be able to find the ball behind the green.

Such a hole was the 4th at Turnberry, which bears the name Woe-Be-Tide. It is a 175-yard one-shotter. You practically stand on the firth and hit into a crosswind to a green about as big as your golf bag, with more water on the left and the hounds of the Baskervilles on your right.

"What am I in now?" I asked, having hit a firth-lock safely to the right. "Is this heather?"

"That," he said, "is gorse. You ca'na swing softly, Sir, and be way o' the gorse."

"Gorse is whin, right?"

He said, "Aye, the whins we call it. You ca'na plant the whin and neither will the whin die. The whin is just here where it always was."

I took a forceful swing with a sand iron, moving the ball about one foot, and said, "Don't forget to show me the heather when we find some."

"Aye," he said. "That's heather you're in now."

You can't often find the ball in heather. It is a stubby dwarf plant, all tied and wiry, brown at times, purple at others. You can top a shot with a driver and, whereas in America the ball is likely to run for a hundred or so yards, if in Scotland it finds a cluster of heather only a few yards away, it will go flimp—and either disappear forever ever or bound straight back to you.

I could see at least half of the ball there in the heather, and I took a full swipe at it with the wedge, so hard that the caddie counted all of the cleats in my shoes and the veins in my legs, and the noise I made sounded like the Luftwaffe had returned to drop another load on the docks at Glasgow.

And the ball didn't move at all.

"When does my hand stop tingling?" I said.

Turnberry has one hole that is more magnificent than all of the others. It is the 9th, 425 yards with a tee sitting back on an island of jagged rock. Water and rock border it on the left where a lighthouse marks the farthest point of the course from the hotel. Off to the right, beyond the plant life, is part of the Spitfire runway. Behind the green is broom and dabs of bracken, which cows won't eat.

One finds in Scotland, however, that if the botany doesn't confuse you, the scorekeeping will. I drove well at the 9th, which means safely onto the close-cropped fescue grass which dominates all Scottish fairways. I reached the small green with one of my rare unshanked four-irons, and I stole a putt of about 20 feet for a 3. Then the trouble began.

"Is this a par-4 hole?" I asked the caddie.

"No, Sir," he said. "It plays to a bogey-5."

"Then I made an eagle," I said.

"It ca'na be an eagle, Sir," he said.

"Well, what's par for the course?"

He said, "Bogey today is about 76."

"But level 4s is 72," I said. "Shouldn't that be what I would call par?"

He thought a minute and said, "I reckon par to be about 74 today."

"What was it yesterday, for instance?" I asked.

"Oh, in that wind, par must have been 77 or so."

I said, "Well, I think I just made an eagle."

"You did na make an eagle, Sir," he said.

"A birdie?"

"Not exactly a birdie with the helpin' wind, Sir."

"A par?"

"Oh. much better than a par, it was," he said.

"So what the damn hell was it, James Cagney?"

"It was a very good score, Sir. Your first of the round."

There is much to see in the neighborhood of Turnberry and along the route to either Prestwick or Troon, like a castle here and there or a birthplace of Robert Burns, of which there must be a dozen, but never should a visitor miss that hill—that thing—called the Electric Brae. Years ago bicyclists discovered it, one is told. They found themselves forced to pedal sweatily to get uphill when it obviously looked as if the road were going downward into the woods. It is an optical illusion, and you would lose your wallet betting on it. The proof is this: stop the car at a point where you are certain you are headed uphill. Put a golf ball on the road, a shiny new Dunlop 65. It will roll uphill, that's all.

As mysterious as the Electric Brae is, it is no more mysterious than the course at Prestwick, the one where all of those early British Opens were staged beginning in 1860. Your first impression as you gaze out on a wasteland punctuated by a crumbling old stone fence is that this has to be the biggest practical joke in all of golf. "I've got it," you say. You pay your green fee, put down a ball, aim at the world, take four or five steps and are never heard from again.

Consider the 1st hole, only 339 yards. On your right: the stone fence about 10 feet away, separating you from a train that will come chugging by at intervals. On your left: mounds of heather and scrub. Directly in front: wasteland. Absolute wasteland. Small and large clumps of it, sheltered by thin layers of fog. And the caddie hands you a driver. The fairway, presuming one is actually there, can't be more than 20 yards wide but the caddie hands you a driver.

"*Where* is it?" I asked.

"Straightaway, Sir," said Charles, who was distinguished from my caddie at Turnberry by two things. Charles wore a muffler and had his own cigarettes. "It's just there," he said. "Just to the left of the cemetery."

It is asking a lot, I know, to expect anyone to believe that you can bust a drive about 250 yards on a 339-yard hole, have a good lie in the fairway and still not be able to see a green anywhere, but this is Prestwick.

The green was there, all right, as are all of the greens at Prestwick, but you never see them until you are on them, which is usually eight or 10 strokes after leaving the tee. They sit behind little hills, or the terrain simply sinks 10 or 15 feet straight down to a mowed surface or they are snuggled over behind tall wood fences where you have nothing to aim at but a distant church steeple.

You would like to gather up several holes from Prestwick and mail them to your top 10 enemies. I guess my alltime favorite love-hate golf hole must be the 3rd hole of this course. Like most of the holes at Prestwick, it is unchanged from the day in 1860 when Willie Park Sr. shot 174 to become the first Open champion. Quite a good score, I have since decided.

First of all, without a caddie it would take you a week and a half to find the 3rd tee. It is a little patch of ground roughly three yards wide perched atop a stream—a burn, rather—with the cemetery to your back and nothing up ahead except mist. Well, dimly in the distance you can see a rising dune with a fence crawling across it. "The Sleepers," the caddie says. But nothing more. Nothing.

"I'll be frank, Charles," I said. "I have no idea which way to go or what with."

"Have a go with the spoon, Sir," he said.

"The *spoon*?" I shrieked. "Where the hell am I going with a spoon?"

"A spoon'll get you across the burn, Sir, but it'll na get you to the Sleepers," he said.

"Hold it," I said. "Just wait a minute." My body was sort of slumped over and I was holding the bridge of my nose with my thumb and forefinger. "These, uh, Sleepers. They're out there somewhere?"

"Aye, the Sleepers," he said.

"And, uh, they just kind of hang around, right?"

"Aye, the Sleepers have took many a golfer."

Somehow I kept the three-wood in play and when I reached the shot, Charles casually handed me the four-wood. I took the club and addressed the ball, hoping to hit quickly and get on past the Sleepers, wherever they were. But Charles stopped me.

"Not that way, Sir," he said.

"This *is* the way I was headed when we left the tee," I said.

"We go a bit right here, Sir," he said. "The Sleepers is there just below the old fence. You want to go over the Sleepers and over the fence, but na too far right because of the burn. Just a nice stroke, Sir, with the four-wood." Happily, I got the shot up and in the general direction Charles ordered, and walking toward the flight of the ball I finally came to the Sleepers. It was a series of bunkers about as deep as the Grand Canyon. A driver off the tee would have found them and so would any kind of second shot that didn't get up high enough to clear the fence on the dune. A worn path led through the Sleepers, and then some ancient wooden steps led up the hill and around the fence to what was supposed to be more fairway on the other side.

It wasn't a fairway at all. It was a group of grass moguls going off into infinity. It looked like a carefully arranged assortment of tiny green Astrodomes. When Charles handed me the pitching wedge, I almost hit him with it because there was no green in sight. But I got the wedge onto a green that was, sure enough, nestled down in one of those dips, and two-putted for a 5 that I figured wasn't a par just because the hole was 505 yards long. Charles said I had played the hole perfectly, thanks to him, and that I could play it a thousand times and probably never play it as well.

I said, "Charles, do you know what they will say about this hole in America?"

"Sir?" he said.

"This is one of those holes where you hit one bad shot and you're dead," I said.

"Aye, 'tis that," he said.

"You're S-O-L," I said.

"Sir?" said Charles,

"Sure out of luck," I said.

"Aye," said Charles, "You call it S-O-L. At Prestwick we call it the Sleepers."

Prestwick has a number of other charming atrocities. There is a 201-yard 5th hole the caddies call the Himalayas. It plays with anything from a five-iron to a driver, depending on the wind. You flog the shot over a mountainous dune and discover, on the other side, about 100 feet down, a green. You ring a bell when you've putted out. There is a wonderful 15th hole of only 329 yards, straightaway, but the fairway is total heather except for the width of an umbrella, and there is no green at all that I could find. All in all, I would say that Prestwick has 18 holes all right, but I dare any visitor to find more than, say, 12.

Only a couple of graveyards and trash piles away from Prestwick lies Troon. In fact, from the 10th tee at Prestwick you can see Troon better than you can see Prestwick. The course is on the Firth, not so much as Turnberry but more so than Prestwick, and the town is filled with small resort hotels and rooming houses that advertise bed-and-breakfast. Troon is the seaside getaway on weekends for the inhabitants of Glasgow. You can wade there, and hike, and go camping in the drizzle. But the best thing you can do if you are privileged enough is play Old Troon, the championship course of the snootiest club on the West Coast. Mr. A. Sweet, sektry, will arrange the round if he approves the cut of your blazer.

Old Troon is the only Scottish links on the West Coast that the R&A keeps on what Keith Mackenzie terms "the championship rota." These are courses fit to host the British Open. In Scotland they have been narrowed down to St. Andrews, Muirfield, Carnoustie and Troon. And in England they are Birkdale, Lytham and Hoylake. Troon takes immense pride in the fact that it is the jewel of the West and even more pride in the fact that it was the scene of one of Arnold Palmer's most glorious weeks. It was at Troon in 1962 that Palmer won the British Open by six strokes (276) on a course that Gary Player declared "unfair" before departing in rage, and a course that drew such horrid individual holes out of Jack Nicklaus as a 10 and an 8.

For the full haul of 18 holes, Troon is not all that memorable. The rough, for one thing, is more like rugged American rough; you can escape from it in one hearty swing if the waist of your trousers is cinched up. Troon, I found, is what you would call a very pleasant course and perhaps more modern than most Scottish courses, if any layout without the hint of a tree can look modern to all American. This is not to say that Troon is void of character. It has several holes, as a matter of fact, that are as good as any to be found, including the single hardest hole I have ever seen—the 11th—not to forget two others that have been architectural landmarks since they were constructed.

There is the 8th, for example, the famed Postage Stamp. It is so called because the green clings to nothing but the lower half of a heather-covered mound, and a tiny one at that. The hole measures only 125 yards but it can play up to a four-iron if the wind is whipping out of the north. Mr. A. Sweet likes to tell about a member who made a hole in one at the Postage Stamp in a most unusual usual way. His tee shot came to rest atop the mound, he swung at the ball with a wedge from up there and missed it. But the sweep of the club through the grass dislodged the ball and it trickled down the hill into the cup.

"Rightly, of course, the chap made a 2," said Mr. Sweet.

It did not harm the fame of the Postage Stamp that in 1923, when Troon was first used to stage the Open Championship, none other than Walter Hagen made a double bogey 5 there to blow the title by a stroke to Mr. Arthur Havers.

All over Scotland one continually finds par-4 holes where, at one time or another, according to the caddies, Jack Nicklaus was on in one. The hole before the Postage Stamp, Troon's 7th, is such a hole. It is renowned for two other reasons: first, it is supposed to be one of golf's earliest doglegs, since the fairway curves sharply to the right, and it is also considered one of the most beautiful of golf holes.

With the tee up on a bluff furnishing a wide view of the sea, and with the wind usually helping, you can envision how Nicklaus might have driven all 385 yards of it. He caught one just right and strung it out over the sand hills, hit a downslope and burned a path through the whin up to the putting surface.

It might well have been this good fortune back in 1962 that encouraged Jack to take out the driver at Troon's 11th the day he had to sink a good putt for a 10. The 11th hole is 485 yards of railroad track on the right and clusters of whin on the left. The fairway is nothing but moguls all the way with the tiny green hard by another of those old stone fences. This is the hole Palmer won the Open on, for he played it with a 3, two 4s and a 5—four under—by using a one-iron off the tee and a two-iron to the green.

My caddie at Troon, Peter Neil, who happened to have toted Sam Snead's bag in the 1962 Open, gave me the driver at the 11th and when we lost sight of the ball soaring out over the whin, he consoled me the way a good caddie should.

"You're just not with it today, Sir," he said.

Troon makes no claim to being among the oldest clubs in Scotland, seeing as how it wasn't built until just the other day—1878—but like any other self-respecting private domain for gentlemen golfers, it has a set of relics that are said to be the oldest in Britain. Mr. A. Sweet proudly pointed to the trophy case and said those clubs were found in a cupboard wrapped in a newspaper dated 1741.

"I think Laurie Auchterlonie at St. Andrews is getting ready to discover a set from 1740," I said.

Mr. A. Sweet did not laugh.

The crass American would not think much of a clubhouse at a Scottish links, be it Troon or Prestwick or most anywhere. There are no tennis courts, of course, and no swimming pool. There is no Mixed Foursome Grill because there is no mixed. Which means no women or pros allowed inside. The pro stays in his wooden shack nearby, selling rain suits and mending clubs. The main clubhouse itself is for ex-wing commanders to eat lunch in—no smoking until after 2 p.m.—to change socks in before or after their daily 36 holes and to slump over their London *Times* in. If there is a shower stall down some creaking corridor, the water is chilled and hits you with all the force of a leak in the roof. On the walls of the dining room and the reading room, both of which are likely to offer a closeup view of the 18th green, will be portraits of a lot of men who look like George Washington but would rather be dead first. They will be ex-secretaries and ex-captains of the club who not only invented the mashie niblick but were survivors of the Black Hole of Calcutta.

If you are as poor at geography as I, you have to divide Scotland like this. The West Coast, where Troon and Prestwick and Turnberry are, and where I had been, is the Ireland side. From almost any point on those three courses, in other words, if you could see far enough, you would see Northern Ireland. This is also known to me as the Glasgow side which, even to the Scots, is not exactly Sutton Place. Where I was headed now was to the East Coast, the Edinburgh side, to the North Sea, to the more posh area of the country where St. Andrews, Muirfield and Carnoustie are. There is a great deal more to Scotland than just this "golf belt," which embraces the land across the midsection from Troon to Muirfield. There is, for instance, way up north, the links of Dornoch. As good a test as any, according to Keith Mackenzie, but too far away for the R&A to transport its people, chestnut palings, gallery rope, scoreboards and tents for the Open Championship. Thanks, Dornoch, but Carnoustie is as far north as the R&A cares to travel.

Actually, if one could grease himself up and swim like Florence Chadwick, he could get to Carnoustie from St. Andrews in about 30 minutes. It is just across a bay. Driving, however, takes longer because cars have to go through Dundee, which is Yonkers with, as they say, less glamour.

From the viewpoint of providing difficulty for the top professional golfers, Carnoustie is surely the toughest course in Scotland. It is long and windy and wet. It is also smoky, dreary and somber. It is a course with more of a sameness to it throughout than any other. Every hole begins to look like the one you've just played—unreachable. Even the names of the holes are unimaginative, The 2nd: Gulley. The 4th: Hillocks. The 6th: Long. The 11th: Dyke. The 18th: Home.

Carnoustie began to develop a distinction around the 5th hole, I thought. But maybe I felt this because my caddie had me primed. Here was the hole where The Wee Icemon, Ben Hogan, had chipped in for a birdie-3 in 1953 during the last round. It was where he had made the chip from the sand at the edge of the lower left bunker that launched him toward the British Open title the one and only time he ever played in the tournament,

"He stood right here," said Phillip, the caddie. "Aye, it was only a short flick of the wrist."

The 6th, too, had character, most of it provided by an imposing cable fence, down the left side of the fairway. Periodically, there would be a sign in red letters hanging on the fence that said: "Do Not Touch Anything. It May Explode and Kill You." On the other side of the fence was a firing range used by the Ministry of Defense. The hole is 565 yards long and the Scots named it Hogan's Alley in '53, for Ben birdied it the last two rounds.

Phillip stopped at a point far beyond my tee shot down the fairway. "Here," he said, digging his shoe into the turf. "And here." He moved it a couple of inches. "Then here." He moved it another inch. "And over here." He moved his shoe about a foot.

"That's where the Icemon drove it," he said,

From here until near the finish Carnoustie became something of a blur. The wind wouldn't give my four-wood a rest and the steady drizzle turned my under-and-over cashmeres into about 700 pounds of inconvenient weight. The most fascinating landmark near the course, after the firing range, was a factory calling itself Anderson Cranes & Stone-Cutting Machinery.

"Phillip," I said. "Did anyone ever suggest to you that Carnoustie is *not* Antibes?"

Somewhere near the end, I vaguely recall, there is a Barry Burn that you have to cross about 30 times on the last three holes, which happen to be first a 243-yard 3-par into the gale that Jack Nicklaus finally reached with a driver in 1968, then a 438-yard par-4 that you are forced to lay up on off the tee and finally a 453-yard par-4 that I judged to be a driver, spoon and full eight-iron. With dry grips, maybe less.

As it turned out, I finished with a flourish. Good driver, good spoon, good eight-iron, four feet from the cup. Of course in my haste to have Phillip show me the spot where Hogan used to go to wring out his sweaters, I blew the putt. And with a number of people staring at me through the clubhouse window, too.

Muirfield is everything Carnoustie isn't. Muirfield is elegance and class, charm and dignity, convenience and pleasure. There is not a true distance on it, nor a fixed par, nor a name for a hole, but it is a course with a championship quality in the purest sense. There is not a tree or a bush or a burn, but there are those 165 bunkers, and they are trouble enough. It is the only course in Scotland that takes advantage and disadvantage of the full cycle of the wind, for the outgoing nine goes clockwise and back to the clubhouse, and the back nine runs counterclockwise and returns. Par is probably 72, but it is easy to envision days when the winds would make it 76.

Muirfield is on the Firth of Forth between Gullane and North Berwick, not painfully far from Edinburgh. It is on a fine shore surrounded by estates, and one gets the idea that this area is to Edinburgh what the Hamptons are to New York City. Muirfield's clubhouse is noted for its spaciousness in comparison with other Scottish clubhouses, and its kitchen is esteemed for its cuisine. This, after all, is where The Honourable Company of Edinburgh Golfers hangs out.

Directly next door to the huge stone clubhouse with its sprawling veranda and putting green is the Greywalls Hotel, where a member of The Honourable Company would stay. Greywalls fronts on the 9th green, and the Scots have long felt that part of the vast charm of Muirfield is that a fellow can stop after nine holes and grab a tap at Greywalls—the way Americans do at their courses.

The real charm of Muirfield is in its memorable fairness and its splendid pacing, both of which are much on the order of Merion, that gem of a battleground on Philadelphia's Main Line where every club comes out of the bag every round you play. Muirfield has short 5s and long 5s, short, bending 4s and long, narrow 4s, short, tricky 3s and long, reachable 3s. Its fairways are skinny but the lies are perfect, and there are shortcuts to be taken by the brave or long-hitting who wish to flirt with more bunkers than the eye can count.

Because of the eccentricities of the wind and the roll of the fairway, as well as, perhaps, the exaggerations of the caddies, one hears that Jack Nicklaus was able to drive the 407-yard 15th hole when he won the British Open there in 1966. But as they say at Muirfield, "He one-ironed her."

The highest compliment anyone could pay Muirfield I suppose, would be to say that it is a Hogan type of course. Distances are meaningless because of the wind, and Hogan always said they were meaningless, anyhow. Every shot has a look to it, he said, a certain feel. "I might hit a two-iron 150 yards," he often said.

I played Muirfield that way. My two-irons went 150 yards and frequently off the shank of the club to the right.

"This is the course," my caddie said, over and over. "This is the best of the lot."

"I'd like to see it sometime," I said.

There are a number of spectacular holes at Muirfield, but the 6th is perhaps the finest. It is a par-4—sometimes a par-5—of 475 yards, or thereabouts, an uphill-downhill dogleg left that curls around a battered rock wall which separates the course from an archery field. The landing area for the tee shot is no more than 20 yards across and deep bunkers patrol it. With a career drive you can then get close to home with a career three-wood to a rolling green, again framed by bunkers.

"What a hole," I said to the caddie as I stood there considering the three-wood.

"Have a good go with the spoon," he said. "But a word of caution, Sir. A ball played into Archerfield Wood is irrecoverable."

The mystique of Muirfield lingers on. So does the memory of Carnoustie's foreboding. So does the scenic wonder of Turnberry and the haunting incredibility of Prestwick and the pleasant deception of Troon. But put them all together and St. Andrews can play their low ball for atmosphere.

To begin with, St. Andrews is an old university town. Spires rise up over narrow streets littered with shops and cozy pubs. Students wearing red cloaks are bicycling around. Statues confront the stroller. An inn is here and there, and the North Sea just beyond.

There are four golf courses at St. Andrews: Old, New, Eden and Jubilee and they are all available to the Public. The New Course is over 70 years old. Try that on for nostalgia. But no one, of course, is ever concerned about anything but the Old. The Old Course is St. Andrews, the R&A, all of those famed hazards. It is Jones, Vardon, Hagen and Old and Young Tom Morris, and Keith Mackenzie standing on the balcony of his office in the R&A building just above the first tee surveying the layout through a pair of mounted German submarine binoculars.

I was fortunate enough to secure lodging in The Old Course Hotel. Thus I could walk out on my terrace and it was all there directly below me. To my left, the course stretching out to the 11th green, and to my right, a matchless view of the 18th fairway leading up through the Valley of Sin, with Rusacks Hotel standing there as it is supposed to be, and with the great gray edifice of the Royal and Ancient clubhouse forming a backdrop.

The Old Course has been called a lot of things because, at first glance, it looks like nothing more than a flat, green city park. Some Americans have labeled it a "third-rate municipal course," and a "football field," but Bob Jones knew its subtleties better. It was, he said, the one course he would play forever if he could choose just one.

Two things strike the first-timer at St. Andrews immediately. First, the double greens. No less than 14 holes share the enormous putting surfaces, the 2nd also being the 16th and that sort of thing. There are two flags, naturally, and often they will be as far as 80 yards apart, with many a dip and turn between them. The erring shotmaker is apt to find the longest putts in golf at St. Andrews. Secondly, the Old Course has some heavenly aspects for one with a chronic hook. The first nine goes straight out, you see, with all of the heather and the sea on your right. And the back nine returns, parallel, giving the hooker all of those outgoing fairways to land on.

The mystery of why no golfer has ever been able to tear apart the Old Course—278 is the lowest a winner has shot in the British open there—lies in the wind and the putting, and in the fantastically perfect location of such hazards as Hell Bunker, a deep and somewhat inescapable pit at the 14th; the Swilken Burn, a small brook that rushes right up against the green on the 1st hole and catches many a soft nine-iron; and the Valley of Sin, the cavernous lower level of the 18th green from which three-putts, and even four-putts, are commonplace.

I attack the Old Course in the company of Ginger Johnson, who had been caddying there for merely 45 years. For a few holes he thought he had Henry Cotton again. The wind was behind, and my shank, my top, my slice and my putting jerk seemed to have disappeared. Through the 10th I was only one over par, and I said to Ginger:

"I think I'm bringing the Old Course to its knees."

And Ginger said, "Aye, you made a putt or two, Sir. But now we go home into the wind."

In rapid order, I was lost in the Elysian Fields, lost in the Beardies, trapped in Hell Bunker, gouged in the Principal's Nose, over the fence, smothered in heather and even out of bounds on the overhang of The Old Course Hotel at the Road Hole. Finally I limped up the 18th fairway en route to the Valley of Sin. Par for 86.

"You had a wee bit of hard luck," Ginger said. "But it can't spoil the fact that as we cum up the 18th, we sense a wee bit of tradition, don't we?"

Keith Mackenzie peered down from his balcony as I walked onto the green. I putted out: a straight-in four-footer that broke six inches. The secretary motioned me up for lunch in the R&A dining room—no smoking at all. I toured the club and reread the letter that Isaac Grainger, then USGA president, had written to the R&A on the occasion of its 200th birthday.

Grainger said, in part: "What golf has of honor, what it has of justice, of fair play, of good fellowship and sportsmanship—in a word, what is best in golf—is most surely traceable to the inspiration of the Royal and Ancient."

I thought of those words again as I strolled back outside to stand and look at the sea and at the town and all across the gentle green sweep of the Old Course—the oldest course.

I had been there all my life.

The University of Eighth Avenue

BY A.J. LIEBLING

America's most distinguished boxing writer, author of The Sweet Science, *explored the gritty world of Stillman's Gym in New York City, the extraordinary institution that was the center of the boxing universe.*

I N EVERY GREAT CITY CERTAIN QUARTERS TAKE ON THE COLOR OF an industry. Fifty-second Street between Sixth and Fifth Avenues in New York, for example, is given over to strip-tease palaces. In addition to electric signs and posters advertising the Boppa La Zoppas and Ocelot Women inside, it can be identified in the evening by the thin line of males along the curb who stand on tiptoes or bend double and twist their necks into periscopes in what must surely be an unrewarding effort to see through the chinks in the draperies. This is known as the old college try, since it is practiced largely by undergraduates.

Forty-seventh Street between Sixth and Fifth, for another example, is devoted to polishing and trading diamonds. It is lined with jewelers' exchanges, like North African souks with fluorescent lighting, inside which hordes of narrow men rent jumping-up-and-sitting-down space with a linear foot of showcase immediately in front of it. The traders who don't want to sink their funds in overhead stand out on the sidewalk. There is a social distinction even among them: between two-handkerchief men, who use one exclusively for diamond storage, and one-handkerchief men, who knot their diamonds in a corner of their all-purpose *mouchoirs*.

The block on the west side of Eighth Avenue between 54th and 55th street is given over to the polishing of prizefighters. It has a quiet academic charm, like West 116th Street when you leave the supermarkets and neighborhood movie houses of upper Broadway and find yourself on the Columbia campus, with its ivy-hallowed memories of Sid Luckman and Dwight D. Eisenhower. It is a sleepy block whose modest shops are given over to the needs of the student body—a couple of hock shops, a pet store and a drugstore which sells bandages and gauze for taping fighters' hands. A careful etiquette reigns in this student quarter, as it is impossible to know if you can lick even the smallest man looking into the pet shop next door to No. 919 Eighth Avenue, which is the Old Dartmouth, or Nassau Hall, of the University of Eighth Avenue.

Old Stillman, as this building is named in honor of the founder, is three stories high, covered with soot instead of ivy and probably older than most midwestern campuses at that. It is a fine example of a postcolonial structure of indefinable original purpose and looks as if it had been knocked down in the Draft Riots of 1863 and left for dead. It hides its academic light behind a sign which says STILLMAN'S GYM against a background resembling an oilcloth tablecloth from some historic speakeasy specializing in the indelible red wine of the age of F. Scott Fitzgerald and Warren G. Harding. Maybe that is where the artist got the canvas; it is an economical neighborhood. The sign also says TRAINING HERE DAILY, and in smaller letters BOXING INSTRUCTION—SEE JACK CURLEY. This is the university's nearest approach to a printed catalogue. Doctor Lou Stillman, the president, knew when he put out his sign in 1921 that an elaborate plant does not make a great educational institution. In the great schools of the Middle Ages, scholars came to sharpen their wits by mutual disputation. Prizefighters do likewise.

The narrow window of the pet shop is divided by a partition, and the show is always the same. Monkeys on top—which is Stillmanese for "in the feature attraction"—and a tolerant cat playing with puppies underneath, which is Stillmanese for the subordinate portion of the entertainment, as for example a semifinal. Dangling all over the window are parakeets and dog collars. The window draws very good, to stay with the scholastic jargon, before noon when the fighters are waiting for Old Stillman to open and around 3, when the seminars are breaking up. A boy wins a four-rounder, he buys a parakeet and dreams of the day he will fight on top and own a monkey. There was a time when a boxer's status was reflected by the flash on his finger, now it is by his pet. Floyd Patterson, a brilliant star on the light-heavyweight horizon, owns a cinnamon ringtail.

Whitey Bimstein, the famous trainer, had one of the pet-shop monkeys hooking off a jab pretty good for awhile. Whitey, a small bald man with side-hair the color of an Easter chick, would stand in front of the window darting his left straight toward the monk's face and then throwing it in toward the body, and the monk would imitate him—"better than some of them kids they send me from out of town," Whitey says. Then one day he noticed a cop walking up and down the other side of the street and regarding him in a peculiar manner. "I figure he thinks I'm going nuts," Whitey says. "So I drop the monk's education."

"You probably couldn't of got him a license anyway," Izzy Blank, another educator, said consolingly.

The affinity between prizefighters and monkeys is old; the late Jack McAuliffe, who retired as undefeated lightweight champion of the world in 1896, once had one that rode his neck when he did roadwork. Twenty miles was customary in those days—they trained to finish fights—so the monkey and McAuliffe saw a lot of territory together. "The monk would hold on with his legs around my neck, and if I stopped too fast he would grab my ears to keep from falling off," the old hero told me when I had the good fortune to talk to him. McAuliffe was a great nature-lover and political thinker. When he told me about the monkey he was 69 years old and running in a Democratic primary for assemblyman to annoy his son-in-law, who would give him no more money to lose at the races.

"I went into this contest," he said, "because the taxes are too high, the wages of the little fellow are being cut, and nobody has ever went right down to the basis. There are men in our Legislature today who remind me of Paddy the Fig, who would steal your eye for a breastpin." Not drawing a counter in the political department, he told me about the monkey.

McAuliffe in his glory had been a great friend of John L. Sullivan and of a bantamweight named Jack Skelly from Yonkers. The three were engaged to perform in a Salzburg festival of the Sweet Science promoted by the Olympic Club of New Orleans in September 1892. On Sept. 5 McAuliffe was to defend his lightweight title against Billy Myer, the Streator (Ill.) Cyclone. On the 6th, Skelly would try to win the featherweight championship from the incumbent George Dixon, the great Little Chocolate. And on the third, climactic night, the great John L. would annihilate an upstart from San Francisco named Jim Corbett.

"I thought the monk would bring us all luck," the old man said. "He started good. When I knocked Billy out in the fifteenth the monk was up on the top rope as the referee said '10!' and hop, off onto my shoulder before the man got my hand up. I took him and threw him into the air and caught him again, I was so happy.

" 'Oh, you jool of a monkey!' I said, and when I was on the table after the fight he played in the hair on my chest like I was his brother.

"Then Skelly fought Dixon, and when Dixon knocked him out I thought I noticed a very peculiar look on the monkey's face, like he was glad to see Skelly get it. I said to myself, 'I wonder who you are.' I gave him the benefit of the doubt, but when Corbett stopped Sullivan, I grabbed the monkey by the neck and wrung it like he was a chicken. I've often felt bad about it since. God help me, I had a very bad temper."

I cite this only to prove the ring is a continuum with fixed values and built-in cultural patterns like Philadelphia or the world of Henry James.

Monkeys can fight like hell when properly trained, incidentally, and Jacco Maccacco, the Fighting Monkey, weighing 12 pounds, had a standing challenge to kill any 20-pound dog in Jane Austen's England. He had a considerably greater public reputation than Wordsworth.

On the second floor of a taxpayer at the northwest corner of 54th and Eighth, the International Boxing Guild maintains a brand-registry office for the purpose of preventing managers from stealing other managers' fighters and renaming them. They do not nick the kids' ears or cut their dewlaps, but they keep complete files, so if a rustler lures a boxer under contract to a Guild member from, say, Spokane to Toronto, both out-of-town points, word of the theft goes out. Then no Guild manager will fight him. That is to say, of course, no Guild manager will let his chattels fight him. It is a simpler process than going to law, because the rustler may have an edge in his hometown and you cannot carry your own judge with you. It is a handy location, because if anybody smuggled anybody else's fighter into town, Stillman's is where he would be most likely to show up, like a stolen diamond on 47th Street. It is harder to ring a fighter than a horse, because in order to disguise him you have to change his style, which is more trouble than developing a new fighter.

The whole block is handy to the building called Madison Square Garden, at 50th Street and Eighth, where the International Boxing Club maintains offices and promotes boxing matches on Friday nights when the house hasn't been rented out to Ringling Brothers' Circus or Sonja Henie or the rodeo. This is of considerable economic advantage to members of the academic community, since they can drop down to the Garden and talk their way into some complimentary tickets without spending an extra subway fare. It is doubly convenient for managers who are discontented with Billy Brown, the IBC matchmaker, a sentiment they usually communicate by sitting around his office and making faces. By walking down from Stillman's, bumming comps and making a face, they effect a double saving. This advantage is purely fortuitous because when Stillman opened his place in 1921 the Madison Square Garden stood at Madison Square. Not even Stillman contends they tore it down and built the present one just to get near him.

The modest entrance to Old Stillman is the kind of hallway you would duck into if you wanted to buy marijuana in a strange neighborhood. There are posters for the coming week's metropolitan fight shows—rarely more than one or two nowadays since television has knocked out the nontelevised neighborhood clubs. There is a wide wooden staircase leading up to the gym. Although Dr. Stillman locks a steel grille across the doorway promptly at 3, keeps it locked until 5:30, when working scholars come in for the poor man's session, and then locks it again religiously at 7, the joint always smells wrong. Dr. Stillman, like so many college presidents nowadays, is not himself a teacher but rather an administrator, and the smell in the hall makes him feel there are limits to academic freedom. He is a gaunt man with a beak that describes an arc like an overhand right, bushy eyebrows, a ruff of hair like a frowsy cockatoo and a decisive, heavily impish manner. He has the reputation of never having taken any lip off anybody, which is plausible, because he seldom gives the other fellow a chance to say anything. In earlier stages of his academic career he used to speak exclusively in shouts, but now that he is in his latter 60s, his voice has mellowed to a confident rasp. The great educator has never, so far as is known, himself put on the gloves; it might prove a psychological mistake. Stillman excels in insulting matriculants so casually that they don't know whether to get sore or not. By the sixth time Stillman has insulted a prizefighter the fighter feels it would be inconsistent to take offense at such a late stage in their personal interrelationship. When that happens, Stillman has acquired the edge.

Dr. Stillman has not been so styled since birth. His original surname was Ingber, but he got into the gymnasium business by working for a philanthropist named Alpheus Geer who ran a kind of Alcoholics Anonymous for burglars trying to go straight. Geer called his crusade the Marshall Stillman movement, and he thought the best kind of occupational therapy was boxing, so he opened a gym, which young Ingber managed. The burglars got to calling Lou Ingber, Lou Stillman, and after they stole all the boxing gloves and Mr. Geer quit in disgust, Ingber opened a gymnasium of his own, farther uptown than this Old Stillman, and legally adopted his present name.

Occasionally Dr. Stillman has a problem student who does not know when he is being insulted, and then he has to think up some more subtle psychological stratagem. Tommy (Hurricane) Jackson, a heavyweight who has to be driven out of the gymnasium at the end of every session because he wants to punch the bag some more, has been a recent disciplinary challenge. Jackson, who is 6 feet 2 inches tall and of inverse intellectual stature, would occupy a boxing ring all the time if Stillman let him. He would like to box 15 or 30 rounds a day, but this would be of no value to his fellow students, even those who worked with him, because Jackson is a purely imitative boxer. He waits to see what the other follow will do and then does it right back at him until the guy drops from exhaustion. Against a jabber he will jab and against a mauler he will maul; it is the exact opposite of Sam Langford's counsel: "Whatever that other man want to do, don't let him do it. Box a fighter and fight a boxer." Jackson will box a boxer, after a fashion, and fight a fighter, in a way, but he can never decide for himself. Knowing this, most boxers who work with him step in with a right to the jaw, planning to knock him out before he can begin his systematic plagiarism. But he has a hard jaw. Whitey and Freddie Brown, his trainers, who are partners, attribute his lack of originality to an emotional conflict, but it has not yielded to any kind of permissive therapy like buying him a .22 rifle to shoot rats, or letting him drink soda pop on fight nights. "He is not too smart of a fellow," Freddie Brown has concluded.

Jackson, when not exercising, likes to walk around Stillman's with a shiny harmonica at his mouth, pretending to blow in it. A small, white camp follower trails in his wake, completely concealed from anybody in front of Jackson, and plays a real tune on another harmonica. It is Jackson's pose, when detected, that this is an elaborate joke because he could play a tune too, if he wanted to. Dr. Stillman once invited him to play a tune into the microphone with which the president of the University of Eighth Avenue announces the names of students defending theses in the rings. "Give us all a chance to hear you," he snarled invitingly. Tommy backed off, and Stillman grabbed a moral ascendancy. Whenever Jackson is obstreperous now, the good Doctor points to the microphone, and the Hurricane effaces himself.

To gain access to the hall of academe you must pass a turnstile guarded by Professor Jack Curley, the assistant to the president who the sign says is the fellow to see about boxing instructions. The only person who ever did was a follower of Father Divine named Saint Thomas. Curley signed him up as a heavyweight contender before letting him through the gate where the managers could see him. Saint Thomas was a hell of a natural fighter if you believe Curley, but they split on theological grounds such as he wanted Father Divine, *in absentia*, to okay his opponents by emanation. Later he backslid and stabbed a guy, and is now in a place where he has very little opportunity for roadwork. The sign is as sensible as one would be on the door of Yale saying "Instruction in reading and writing, see Professor Doakes." Old Stillman is no elementary school.

There are two ways of getting by Professor Curley. The more popular is to invoke the name of some manager or trainer you know is inside, claiming an urgent business mission. Professor Curley will deny he is there, but if you ask some ingoing fighter to relay the message, the fellow will come out and okay you. Curley will then assume the expression of a baffled witch in a London Christmas pantomime, but he will let you in without payment. The second method is to give him 50 cents, the official price of admission, which he doesn't expect from anybody who looks familiar. Through decades of practice he has trained his facial muscles not to express recognition, but he is violently disconcerted when the other fellow does not demand to be recognized. After you give him the 50 cents he has another problem—whether to say hello. This would be a confession he had known you all along. He compromises by giving you what is known on campus as "a cheap hello," looking over his shoulder as if he might be talking to somebody else.

On the main floor of Old Stillman there are two boxing rings set close together. The space in front of the rings is for spectators, and the relatively narrow strip behind them for boxers and trainers. To get from one zone to the other, the latter must pass directly in front of Dr. Stillman, who stands behind an iron rail leaving a passageway perhaps two feet wide. This is a big help in the collection department because a boxer who is in arrears can't get into the ring to spar unless the president, who doubles as bursar, gives him an extension. When granted, this is usually on the grounds that the delinquent has a fight coming up.

Boxers pay $6 a month for a locker and $11 a month for a dressing room, which means a stall just wide enough for a rubbing table. The de luxe dressing rooms have hooks on the plywood partitions. Stillman has a microphone in back of his stand and in the back of his head a rough list of the order in which fighters will go into the rings. Some fighters he knows by sight; trainers have to prompt him with the names of others. Most of the present crop, the Doctor says, he would like to forget as rapidly as possible. When he says the names into the mike they come out equally unintelligible, so it doesn't matter. Most of the spectators know who the guys are anyway, despite the increasingly elaborate headgears which make them look like Tlingit witch doctors.

In the days when 375 boxers trained at Stillman's and the majority actually had bouts in sight, there was considerable acrimony about the scheduling. Trainers were afraid that some of their boys who needed sparring would be crowded out. Now that fewer fellows use the place and are in less of a hurry, everybody gets a chance. The enrollment at Old Stillman is less than a hundred, which is not bad when you reflect that there are only 241 licensed professional boxers in the whole of New York State and this number includes out-of-state fighters who have had to take out a license for a New York appearance.

The main operating theater at Stillman's is two stories high. There is a gallery which, in the halcyon days before television, used to accommodate spectators, but which now serves as a supplementary gym. The light and heavy bags are up there, and so is most of the space for skipping rope. In pretelevision times Stillman's had an extensive bargain clientele of fans who couldn't afford the price of admission to regular boxing shows, but now these nonholders see their fights free.

Only knowing coves come to Stillman's these days—fellows who have more than a casual interest in boxing or are out to make a buck, like the diamond traders. Few managers today have offices of their own—there are only a half-dozen such grandees—and the rest transact their business walking around Stillman's or leaning against the radiators. There are seats for ordinary spectators, but managers consider it unprofessional to sit down. Even managers who have offices use them chiefly to play klabiash or run up telephone bills; they think better on their feet, in the mingled aura of rubbing alcohol, sweat and hot pastrami-on-the-lunch-counter which distinguishes Old Stillman from a gym run by Helena Rubinstein or Elizabeth Arden.

The prevailing topic of conversation at Stillman's nowadays is the vanishing buck. Boxers are in the same predicament as the hand-loom weavers of Britain when Dr. Edmund Cartwright introduced the power loom. Two boxers on a national hookup with 50 major-city outlets can fill the place of 100 boxers on top 10 years ago, and for every two eliminated from on top, at least 10 lose their work underneath. The boxer who gets the television assignment, though, is in the same spot as the hand-loom weaver who found work driving a power loom—he gets even less money than before. This is because while wads of the sponsors' tease go to networks for time and camera fees, to advertising agencies in commissions based on the purchased time, to producers for creating the drivel between rounds and even to the promoters who provide the boxers, the boxers themselves get no more than they would have drawn in an off night in Scranton in 1929. Naturally, this is a discouraging technological circumstance, but the desire to punch other boys in the nose will survive in our culture. The spirit of self-preservation will induce some boys to excel. Those who find they excel will try to turn a modest buck by it. It is an art of the people, like making love, and is likely to survive any electronic gadget that peddles razor blades.

Meanwhile the contraction of the field has led to a concentration of talent at Old Stillman. These days good feature-bout fighters, who were sure of $10,000 a year not long ago, are glad to sell their tutorial services as sparring partners for $5 or $10 a session. This is particularly true of the colored boys who are not quite champions. Trainers who in the flush times accepted only stars or near-stars as students will now take on any kid with a solvent sponsor. The top trainers, whose charges appear frequently on televised shows, still make out pretty well.

Trainers, like the teachers in medieval universities, are paid by their pupils or their pupils' sponsors. A couple of trainers working as partners may have 15 fighters, all pretty good, if they are good trainers. If they cannot teach, they get no pupils and go emeritus without salary. There are two televised boxing cards originating in New York clubs every week—the St. Nick's on Monday evening and the International Boxing Club show from the Garden on Friday. When the Garden is occupied by other events, the IBC runs its show from out of town, which is a blank margin around New York City, extending for several thousand miles in every direction but east. A team of trainers like Whitey Bimstein and Freddie Brown, or Nick and Dan Florio, or Chickie Ferrera and Johnny Sullo, figures to have at least one man in one of the three features every week, and a couple underneath. The trainer customarily gets 10% of his fighter's end of the purse. Because of their skill as seconds they are also sure to get calls to work in the corners of men they don't train. Noted Old Stillman trainers are called out of town for consultations almost as often as before television, because while there are many less fights, the out-of-town trainer as a species has for that very reason nearly vanished. In most places it is a part-time avocation.

Their reputation is international—last year, for example, Whitey Bimstein was retained to cram a Canadian giant named James J. Parker for a bout for the Canadian heavyweight championship in Toronto. Parker is not considered much of a fighter here—a good banger, but slow of intellection. In Canada, however, he is big stuff—he weighs more than 210 pounds. The Canadian champion (now retired), whom Parker was to oppose, was Earl Walls, also a pretty good banger but a slow study.

Whitey took Parker up to Greenwood Lake, N.Y., where his troubles started when the Canadian insisted on doing his roadwork on the frozen surface of the lake. "He might fall through and roon the advance sale," Whitey said. Not wishing to increase the weight on the ice, Whitey declined to accompany him. He would watch him from a window of the inn where they were staying, prepared to cut loose with a shotgun if Parker slowed to a walk. Trainers blanch when they tell of the terrible things fighters will do to get out of roadwork. Nick Masuras, one of Whitey's friends, once had a fighter up at the Hotel Peter Stuyvesant, across the street from Central Park at 86th, and every morning he would send him out to run a couple of times around the Central Park reservoir, which is right there practically. Masuras would then go back to sleep. By and by the fellow would come in panting and soaking wet, and it wasn't until three days before the fight that Nick learned he had just been sitting on park benches talking to nursemaids, after which he would come in and stand under a warm shower with his clothes on. After that Nick moved to a room on the eighth floor, with a park view. But it was too late. The guy's legs went back on him and he lost the fight. "He done it to himself, no one else," Nick says, mournfully, as he polishes beer glasses in his saloon, the Neutral Corner, which is the Deux Magots or Mermaid Tavern of the fighters' quarter. Instead of training fighters, Nick has taken to feeding them.

Parker, on the other hand, didn't skimp his training. He heeded everything Whitey told him. As a consequence, Whitey says, "He give this Walls a hell of a belting and in the sixth round cut his left eye open so bad that if you were a doctor you had to stop it." The Canadian doctor, however, didn't stop it. "He was pertecting Walls," Whitey says. "The guy could of lost his eyesight." Walls had in his corner another ambassador of culture from Stillman's, Nick Florio. Florio patched the eye up so well that Walls went the distance, 12 rounds. Whitey felt like calling Florio a carpetbagger. The announcer then collected the slips of the two judges and the referee, read them, and proclaimed James J. Parker, Whitey's candidate, "Winner and new champion"—of Canada, naturally. "But," Whitey says, "they take it very serious." Whitey posed for victory pictures, allowing Parker to get into the background, and then led him away to his dressing room. There, five minutes later, another man came in and said the announcer had made a mistake—it was really a draw, so Walls was still champion. "It was a outrage," Whitey says. "They pertected him." He came back from Canada with a bale of Toronto newspapers, which said Walls's cut eye had required 16 stitches. "They were those wide Canadian stitches," Whitey said. "Here they took them kind of stitches to make him look better." The fight, which was not televised, drew $30,000 and the fighters whacked up $18,000. This was much better than they would have done at the Garden, where each would have received $4,000 from television and a purely nominal sum from the almost nonexistent gate.

For most fighters, however, pickings are lean between infrequent television appearances—so lean that they are beginning to recall the stories old-timers tell about the minuscular purses in the 1890s. One of the best lightweights in the world, for example, went up to Holyoke, Mass., from the campus on Eighth Avenue not too long ago and fought on top of the gate against a tough local boy whom he knocked out in five rounds. He had signed for a percentage of the gate which turned out to be $115. After he had deducted railroad fare, the price of a Massachusetts boxer's license and a few dollars for a local helper in his corner, he wound up with $74. Freddie Brown, the trainer, wouldn't accept a fee, and the fighter's manager wouldn't cut the fighter because the guy was broke and he would have had to lend him the money back anyway. He had been out for several months with a broken rib sustained in another fight.

The club in Holyoke, one of the few stubborn survivors, functions Tuesday nights because of television boxing Monday, Wednesday and Friday.

All the great minds of the university have gone a few rounds with this problem, but none has come up with a thesis that his colleagues at the lunch counter couldn't flatten in the course of a couple of cups of tea. One school of savants holds that if the television companies are going to monopolize boxing they should set up a system of farm clubs to develop new talent. Another believes the situation will cure itself, but painfully. "Without the little clubs, nobody new will come up," a leader of this group argues. "The television fans will get tired of the same bums, the Hooper will drop, the sponsors will drop boxing, and then we can start all over again." Meanwhile a lot of fighters have had to go to work, a situation the horror of which was impressed upon me long ago by the great Sam Langford, in describing a period of his young manhood when he had licked everybody who would fight him. "I was *so* broke," he said, "that I didn't have no money. I had to go to work with my hands." Manual labor didn't break his spirit. He got a fight with Joe Gans, the great lightweight champion of the world, and whipped him in 15 rounds in 1903, when Sam says he was 17 years old. The record books make him 23. (They were both over the weight, though, so he didn't get the title.) After the fight he was lying on the rubbing table in his dressing room feeling proud and a busted-down colored middleweight named George Byers walked in. "How did I look?" Langford asked him. "You strong," Byers said, "but you don't know nothing."

Langford wasn't offended. He had the humility of the great artist. He said, "How much you charge to teach me?" Byers said, "$10." Langford gave him $10. It was a sizable share of the purse he had earned for beating Gans.

"And then what happened?" I asked Sam. He said, "He taught me. He was right. I didn't know nothing. I used to just chase and punch, hurt my hands on hard heads. After George taught me I made them come to me. I made them lead."

"How?" I asked.

"If they didn't lead I'd run them out of the ring. When they led I'd hit them in the body. Then on the point of the chin. Not the jaw, the point of the chin. That's why I got such pretty hands today." Sam by that time was nearly blind, he weighed 230 pounds and he couldn't always be sure that when he spat tobacco juice at the empty chitterling can in his hall room he would hit.

But he looked affectionately at his knees, where he knew those big hands rested. There wasn't a lump on a knuckle. "I'd belt them oat," he said. "Oh, I'd belt them oat."

When I told this story to Whitey he sucked in his breath reverently, like a lama informed of one of the transactions of Buddha.

"What a difference from the kids today," the schoolman said. "I have a kid in a bout last night and he can't even count. Every time he hook the guy is open for a right, and I tell him: 'Go twicet, go twicet!' But he would go oncet and lose the guy. I don't know what they teach them in school."

After Sam tutored with Professor Byers he grew as well as improved, but he improved a lot faster than he grew. He beat Gans, at approximately even weights, but when he fought Jack Johnson, one of the best heavyweights who ever lived, he spotted him 27 pounds. Langford weighed 158, Johnson 185. Sam was 26, according to Nat Fleischer, or 25, according to Sam, and Johnson 28. Sam knocked Johnson down for an eight count, Johnson never rocked Sam, and there has been argument ever since over the decision for Johnson at the end of the 15 rounds. Sam's effort was a *succes d'estime* for the scholastic approach to boxing, but Johnson, an anti-intellectual, would never give him another fight.

Johnson, by then older and slower, did fight another middleweight in 1909—Stanley Ketchel, the Michigan Assassin. Ketchel's biographers, for the most part exponents of the raw-nature, or blinded-with-blood-he-swung-again school of fight writing, turn literary handsprings when they tell how Ketchel, too, knocked Johnson down. But Johnson got up and took him with one punch. There was a direct line of comparison between Langford and Ketchel as middleweights. They boxed a six-round no-decision bout in Philadelphia which was followed by a newspaper scandal; the critics accused Langford of carrying Ketchel. Nobody accused Ketchel of carrying Langford. I asked Sam once if he *had* carried Ketchel, and he said, "He was a good man. I couldn't knock him out in six rounds."

Their artistic statures have been transposed in retrospect. The late, blessed Philadelphia Jack O'Brien fought both of them. He considered Ketchel "a bum distinguished only by the tumultuous but ill-directed ferocity of his assault." (That is the way Jack liked to talk.) Ketchel did knock Mr. O'Brien *non compos* his remarkable *mentis* in the last nine seconds of a 10-round bout (there was no decision, and O'Brien always contended he won on points). Jack attributed his belated mishap to negligence induced by contempt. He said Langford, though, had a "mystic quality."

"When he appeared upon the scene of combat you knew you were cooked," Jack said.

Mr. O'Brien was, in five.

Sons of
The Wind

BY KENNY MOORE

*The author, an Olympic marathoner, journeyed to Kenya's Great Rift Valley
to see firsthand how generations of athletes, forged by the customs and rigors of
their homeland, came to dominate distance running.*

T HE MEN'S 10,000-METER RUN IN KENYA'S COMMONWEALTH
Games trials is a race of many departures, many rejoin-
ings. The leaders—exuberantly, incorrigibly Kenyan—surge
and slow and surge again, flying willingly into the distress
such tactics cause. That they race through the thin air of Nairobi's 5,500-foot
altitude seems of no consequence. Most were born and trained at even greater
elevations. With their incessant passing and jostling, they seem to consider the
25 laps not as a single long contest but as dozens of shorter ones. If you don't
know how excruciatingly effective this manner of racing is, you think them impatient children.

By 6,000 meters, under the leadership of 1988 Olympian Moses Tanui, the
front pack has been cut to four. They are three men and a boy.

Kibor, barefoot, shirttail out, the gap in his lower teeth a mark of his Kalenjin tribal upbringing, clings to the pace. Kibor turned 17 only the day before.
This is his first year of competitive running. He had to sell a goat to pay his way
from his home far back in the Cherangani Hills to the preliminary trials in
Kisumu, on Lake Victoria. He is barefoot because he failed in a two-day search
to borrow some spikes.

Each time Tanui surges, Ondoro Osoro and Kibiwott Bitok stick right with
him. But the young Kibor, unpracticed at sprinting and recovering, must let

them go. When they have gained 20 or 30 meters they ease slightly, and Kibor laboriously reclaims what he has lost, his arms swinging high and loose across his chest, his hips cocked back, his heels grazing the back of his shorts.

His form, it happens, is the picture of the young Kipchoge Keino, Kibor's idol and an influence on almost every Kenyan runner. Keino, now 50, is the man who let the world know Kenyans could run. More to the point, he let Kenyans know Kenyans could run.

Keino's world records at 3,000 and 5,000 meters in the mid-1960s and his defeat of Jim Ryun in the '68 Olympic 1,500 gave rise to a river of superb Kenyan distance men. Since Kenya gained independence from Great Britain in '63, its athletes have won 24 Olympic medals in men's running events, despite boycotting the '76 and '80 Games. Ten of those medals were gold, a total second only to the sprinter-blessed U.S.'s.

In recent years the river has deepened and widened. Kenyans won the 800-, 1,500- and 5,000-meter runs and the steeplechase at the 1988 Seoul Olympics and got silvers in the steeple and the marathon and a bronze in the 10,000. The most difficult race in the world is the IAAF World Cross-Country Championships, because it draws together champions from all the distances. Olympic 5,000-meter champion John Ngugi of Kenya has won this race the last four years. Kenya has been the team champion on each occasion. In the '88 race in Auckland, New Zealand, eight Kenyans finished in the top nine.

Traditionally these magisterial runners have come from a very few tribes, notably the Kisii and the Kalenjin, which constitute only 15% of Kenya's 23 million people (52% of whom are under 15 years old). The Kalenjin are actually a group of related tribes. One of them is Kenya's historic cradle of runners, Keino's tribe, the Nandi, most of whom live at an altitude of 7,000 feet or more in a small area near the northeast corner of Lake Victoria.

Nandi athletes have won nearly half of Kenya's Olympic and Commonwealth Games medals. But in recent years, champions have begun to come from other tribes. Ngugi and Julius Kariuki, the steeplechase victor in Seoul, are Kikuyu, as is the 1987 world marathon champion, Douglas Wakiihuri. The 800-meter champion at Seoul, Paul Ereng, who blossomed at the University of Virginia, is of the Turkana, an aloof, nomadic people only now coming to see any value in sport.

Kibor embodies this expanding excellence. He is Marakwet, from the mountainous district to the north of the Nandi. Though Kibor's tribe is of the Kalenjin group, there has never been a superior Marakwet runner. "The Nandi are very tough," Kibor has said. "But I hope to be for the Marakwet what Kipchoge was for the Nandi."

With 600 meters to go, Kibor is still a close fourth. He begins to move up, a development the others find intolerable. Osoro and Bitok cut him off twice, then hurl him three lanes wide. Kibor darts inside and passes, dangerously, on the rail. With a lap to go he is in the lead and sprinting with an expression of terrible anguish. A lap is too far, and he has used too much. He tightens. Tanui passes him on the backstretch, Osoro on the last turn. But Kibor holds third to the end.

His time is 28:51.1, one of the fastest 10,000s ever run by one so young at any altitude. After a vote of the selection committee, Kibor is named to the team that will go to Auckland a month later, in January, for the 1990 Commonwealth Games. He will be the youngest Kenyan male ever to represent the country in a major competition and will finish fifth in the 10,000.

Respectfully amazed, Kibor walks the infield, dripping, holding hands with an official. "Next time I'll wait. I'll sprint only the last 300," he says, the lesson indelible. "My feet are painful now. I do think shoes, spiked shoes, would have helped."

To Westerners, Kibor is a prodigy, but this is a land of prodigies. "We lost another like him two years ago," says Philip Ndoo of Nairobi, who ran at Eastern New Mexico University in the mid-'70s. "A kid named Atoi Boru did 3:42 for 1,500 meters when he was 14. His coach ran him too hard, burned him out. We don't know where he is." A 1,500 in 3:42—need one be reminded?—is equivalent to a 4:00 mile.

The questions are simple and irresistible. How can this be? What land, what history, what life has created such abundance in this specific sporting expression? And why are Kenyans getting even better?

Some factors seem obvious, until you think about them. It's a boon to grow up at high altitude, but lots of societies are located in highlands yet nurture no runners. Where are the Tibetans? The Peruvians?

A statistical case might once have been made for the Nandi's being a genetically superior strain of runner. But no one has found and measured any specific genetic factors that make the Nandi better than anyone else. And now that tribes once thought hopelessly untalented are getting into the act, they seem to be showing that the raw material is wonderful all across the Kenyan tribal spectrum. Perhaps the Nandi were just first to develop it.

Besides, Kenyan tribes have intermarried and absorbed each other so much over the centuries that genetic distinctions are hard to make. Tribal differences are real—are they ever—but they are more cultural than physiological.

This suggests that to understand how Kenya's wellspring of runners has really come about, you must follow one runner home and live a little of his life. To assist in this, fortune offers Joseph Kibor.

Christmas is but two days away, and Kibor is shyly working the small crowd of track fans filing out of Moi International Stadium, casting about for a ride home to Kapchebau village to take the news of his success to his grandmother. Give him a lift, he says, and he will show you the way.

FROM NAIROBI you head northwest over the Ngong Hills and into the Great Rift Valley. Near Lake Naivasha the roadside impalas shine as if groomed and oiled. Zebras standing out among the green acacias don't look natural. They look published. Pink dust drifting over one end of the distant lake turns out to be a cloud of flamingos.

In the car, Kibor takes out his chemistry and geography books—good, demanding texts—from Sambirir Secondary School. He rides along doing problems on his palm with a ballpoint pen. "I am trying very hard in school," he says. "I would like a scholarship to an American college." A couple of hundred Kenyan runners have had such scholarships, but Kibor is not ready. It's an effort for an American ear to process his (and much other) Kalenjin-accented English, and this will need work.

But Kibor is a patient communicator, and gradually it comes out that when, with the encouragement of a coach who has since left his school, he vowed to become a runner, it was an eccentric thing for a Marakwet to do. "Other boys opposed me," he says. "They would say, 'You are chasing air.' But this year I have got my courage. I have been trying hard."

Trying, in Kibor's mind, is very close to succeeding. He began running and immediately won at district, provincial and national levels. Yet his training is astonishingly light. He runs a couple of miles to school in the mornings, and three more after classes. He runs fast, he says, "only in competition, because alone, one person can do nothing. There are no others to push."

Past Nakuru, the land begins to rise and cool. At an elevation of 9,000 feet, amid stands of rushing eucalyptus, you cross the equator. Heading west, you drop through pine woods and maize fields into the Nandi Hills, beautiful for their tea plantations. The pickers seem to wade in verdant foam, their red and violet sweaters fire against the green.

Here, in the hamlet of Kilibwoni, were born the three most distinguished Nandi runners: Keino, Henry Rono (world records at 3,000, 5,000 and 10,000 meters and in the 3,000-meter steeplechase) and Mike Boit (a 3:49.45 mile and a 15-year international career). Boit, up from teaching at Kenyatta University in Nairobi to inspect his family's tea acreage, takes you to a low hill from which you can see the birthplaces of all three. Last summer, Peter Koech broke Rono's 11-year-old record in the steeplechase. Koech, too, is a Nandi from Kilibwoni.

Here is how the Nandi came to be. About 2000 B.C., Cushites from southern Ethiopia began arriving in these highlands. Pastoralists, they displaced or absorbed the region's original hunter-gatherers. Then, during the first 1,000 years A.D., Nilotic people pressed in, again from the north. They intermarried with the Cushites, and the groups combined customs. From the Cushites came circumcision as a rite of passage. The Nilotes contributed the extraction of the lower incisors of adolescents (so they may be fed if they contract lockjaw) and a boundless passion for the milking, bleeding and worship of cattle.

The result of this union, the Kalenjin and related groups such as the Masai and Turkana, spread down the hills and across the plains, reaching their peak about 500 years ago. Then, as the Bantu expanded eastward from Central West Africa, the Kalenjin retreated to their highland strongholds, warred with their neighbors and split into half a dozen subgroups, including the Nandi, who have felt themselves a distinct tribe since the 17th century.

The fixation of all Kalenjin tribes was the cow. The tribes understood themselves to be the chosen of God and therefore the rightful owners of all cattle on earth. They had but to go forth and repossess. This they did, rejoicing. The Kalenjin's—and many other tribes'—incessant raids for cattle and women created a culture in which reputation, wealth and progeny came to the fighting men who could cover long distances quickly.

In the late 19th century, the British colonialists found Nandi raiding parties ranging more than 100 miles from their highlands, striking at night and driving cattle miles toward home before enemy warriors could regroup. Nandi ferocity was such that it took the British five military campaigns over 10 years to subdue the tribe, which they finally did in 1906.

To make men who could run a hundred miles on a handful of millet and a spurt of cow's blood, the Kalenjin tribes employed powerful means. The most potent was ritual circumcision.

To come of age in much of East Africa, a boy between 12 and 20 must command himself to remain stoic while an extremely sensitive part of his body is slowly cut away. Sir A. Claud Hollis, a British diplomat, wrote of Nandi circumcision in 1909: "The boy's face is carefully watched by the surrounding crowd of warriors and old men to see whether he blinks or makes a sign of pain. Should he in any way betray his feelings, he is dubbed a coward and receives the name of *kipite*. This is considered a great disgrace, and no *kipite* may ever attend another circumcision festival." Or claim full rights as an adult.

Boys are prepared with months of seclusion and instruction in the ways of the tribe. "Circumcision parallels what the military does to a draftee," Boit has said. "The elders shave his head, give him a new name and subject him to rigorous discipline, all to remove his individuality and replace it with a new identity of toughness and obedience."

Kibor was circumcised at 14. "Some other boys and I. It was important," he says. "But everybody does it." So how could it be extraordinary? Kibor doesn't think it the most difficult thing he's ever done. It was not as hard, he says, as leaving his childhood home to go to a distant school. The discomfort of running he does not see fit to mention.

"Once you feel the sweetness of winning," Ndoo has said, "running is not what you call pain. The pain is *losing*. Most of them don't even think about what they are feeling . . . until you ask them."

So widespread is circumcision that Kenyans can seem rather offhand about it. CIRCUMCISION RITUALS IN FULL SWING, reads a headline in the *Daily Nation*. "December is always a busy month. . . ."

The story, by Waigwa Kiboi, details how the Kuria tribe near the Tanzanian border practices not only male but also female circumcision, or clitoridectomy, which is outlawed by the government. "As you walk along the roads," writes Kiboi, "you will see young men and women dancing wildly as they surround the initiates, who, despite the pain and bleeding, walk home majestically."

"There is no way," says Nelson Monanka, a farmer, "that girls can command respect here if they are not circumcised and ready for marriage."

Marriage means farm labor and childbearing. Circumcision, one is told, allows women not to be distracted by concern for their own pleasure. It lets them be good wives. In this way, and in many others, the plight of Kenyan women is dismal.

"Parents acquire cows as dowry," says Boit, "as the bride price for a daughter. It makes a wife more of an economic object than a partner in a joint venture."

So Kenyan women are seldom encouraged in sport. Time and again wonderfully talented 14-year-olds have gotten pregnant, married, quit school and given up running. There has never been a female Kenyan Olympic medalist.

Down through the generations, as the raiding life killed off slow runners and made fathers of the swift, the tribes must have distilled their talent. The genes that shape football tackles or sumo wrestlers would have been winnowed away. Always the culture exalted endurance. And so the Kalenjin men became not explosively muscular, but lean and tireless.

Then the British came in and couldn't tolerate all the cattle raiding to which this tirelessness was devoted. So they substituted sport. "They jailed the raiders and put them to work leveling and marking out running tracks," says John Manners, a former Peace Corps teacher in Kenya who has made an extensive study of Kalenjin runners and whose help in preparing this article was invaluable. "Because the Kalenjin, and especially the Nandi, were such frequent offenders, they got a disproportionate number of tracks in their districts and the biggest push to participate."

In the 1920s, British officials began to organize local track meets, putting up blankets and cooking pots as prizes. The Nandi flocked in to race, as much for the competition between younger and older warriors as for the worldly goods. Later, army and police recruiters came to these meets and importuned the victors as they crossed the finish line. Young Kalenjin men entered the ranks in great numbers and found in service careers a way to continue running. Two thirds of Kenya's champions first achieved international renown while in uniform.

The first modern hero was Kiptalem Keter, an 800-meter runner in the 1950s who was a corporal in the tribal police. As a child, Boit was transfixed by the sight of Keter. "He had a long mustache, and he never *lost*," Boit says. "He was always in front. He refused to let anyone else even *lead*." The effect on Boit was transparent. He usually ran exactly the same way.

Boit invites you to make a short side trip from Kilibwoni to the wedding of steeplechaser Joshua Kipkemboi. The party has gathered in corn stubble at sunset, and there is much passing of a celebratory gourd of pungent *mursik*, or curdled milk. The bride's smile and gown are incandescent. Kipkemboi, who will finish second to Kariuki in the '90 Commonwealth Games steeplechase, stands impassive, smooth-faced, and you think of the day in 1981 when Boit married Lillian Maina, a Kalenjin of the Kipsigis tribe.

She had gone to United States International University in San Diego. He was working on his Ph.D. at the University of Oregon in Eugene. When word of their engagement got back to Kenya, Boit's family conveyed a dowry of five cows to Maina's parents.

Maina came down the aisle of Eugene's Central Presbyterian Church in white silk and pearls. Boit stood at her side like a polished spear. When the preacher got to the vows, and Boit began to speak, it was in the dry-reed voice of the Nandi blood oath.

The hair stood up on the back of the guests' necks. The preacher stiffened, the church evaporated and the gathering was transported to hills covered with blazing green tea and thatch-roofed huts. These are not men who falter in ceremony.

DRIVE CAREFULLY says the sign outside Eldoret, BLOODLESS ROAD LOOKS GOOD. Eldoret, not far from where Keino now runs a farm and orphanage, is a fine place to spend the night. Kibor says his secondary school is about 60 miles north, in Chesoi, and his grandmother's house a bit farther on, but it is better to go in daylight.

On Christmas morning you awaken to the cries of hawks and the songs of children, and lie there thinking about how Africa can seem a sieve of afflictions through which only the hardy may pass. The largest, fastest, wildest, strangest beasts are here. Every poisonous bug, screaming bird and thorned shrub has arrived at this moment through the most severe competition. They have a history of overpowering more gentle environments. You think of lungfish, of killer bees, of AIDS. Of men. Of the great Repo Men, the Nandi, turned from their raiding and become runners.

In the rest of the world, sport serves as an initiation, as a true test. In East Africa, initiation is the initiation. Sport is a pale shadow of the competitive life that has gone on forever across this high, fierce, first continent. Is it any wonder that frail European varieties feel threatened?

THERE IS pavement as far as the market town of Iten. Kibor asks twice if, "just for security reasons," you have enough petrol, and grows a little vague about precisely how far it is to Grandmother's house. Moist red paths have been worn on both sides of the road. Upon them walk brightly dressed holiday crowds, iridescent as birds. The people move with a cool economy. They keep a reserve.

But gaze across the land and you catch a different kind of movement. Sheep and goats at first, and then small children in dirty sweaters, running over the hillocks and the fields of dry maize. When you stop to photograph a few children who are tending sheep, they run away. They don't stop or hide. They keep going toward the horizon.

"They are fearing," says Kibor. "They know their faces will be taken to a different country." The remedy is the miracle of Polaroid. Children watch the resolving images with rapt wonder. Their own faces appearing from the clouds. When they get the idea, they pose with an elaborate solemnity.

You are in the Cherangani Hills now, real Marakwet country, so steep that extensive cattle herding is impractical. The Pokot, Kalenjin people who live down in the Rift and despise the cultivation of crops, call the Marakwet *Cheblong*, or the Poor, for their scarcity of cattle.

The road grows steadily worse. Kibor says *matatus*, the crazily crowded, unsafe commercial buses, do make their way up here. One carried him out. Noon comes and goes. At a lunch stop you realize that nowhere in all these hills have you been out of the sound of human voices. They lift, soft and high, from every slope, testimony to the density of humanity here, and its youth. Sometimes kids chase the car, running with a smile and a will, staying there in the dust for long minutes until they make you nervous. After such a childhood, formal athletic training must be just polish, a final pat on the butt.

The subsistence farms give way to a forest preserve of trees hung with vines. Striking black-and-white colobus monkeys hurl themselves through the branches with great, heedless crashes. Across the Aroror River, huts appear again, like mushrooms after a rain. Kibor begins to lean out the window and yell at people. "My classmates," he says. Sambirir School is a brutal climb up a hill from the village of Chesoi. "There is no field at school for practice," says Kibor, pointing out a cluster of huts down in the valley where he lives with cousins while at secondary school. "I run up the hill on a path. It's not far."

Grandmother's house is still quite far away, however, and seems to be receding. The road is now either a sandy track or a faint depression in the animal-cropped grass. Bamboo, laid down for traction in muddy streambeds, cracks and splinters under the tires. At 10 miles an hour, you are slammed around the inside of the four-wheel-drive Isuzu Trooper as if on a small boat in a sickening six-foot chop.

You're above 10,000 feet now, and climbing. Fantastically shaped trees seem like twisted, gesturing spirits. Clouds lie down on the road.

About four o'clock you lurch to a stop at last, before the most beautiful vista of the ordeal: a great, smooth field stretching away to three long buildings, Kibor's primary school. A track is visible on the thick turf. "We cut the lanes," says Kibor proudly, "with pangas."

Beyond, on a dome of green, are the tawny buildings of Kapchebau. The single approach is across a saddle, making the village seem like a medieval fortress. As you reach it, you see that there is nothing beyond but a precipice plunging a mile or more down to the desert floor of the Great Rift Valley.

At once you are surrounded by a dozen weather-burnished people. You have the honor of informing them that their native son made the team. Kibor points out his name in the newspaper account of the trials. The pages are received as if they were illuminated manuscripts.

"We are very happy," says a man. "Now others will come up the way this man has done. He has qualified, you say? We are happy."

From here, you go down on foot, carrying the gifts Kibor has specified: meat, candy and a case of soda. The earth is black mud under the drying maize. You cross a roaring cataract on boulders. "This is where I was running, up this hill to that school," says Kibor. "Jogging, jogging, for eight years."

Even descending you feel dizzy from the altitude. After half a mile you reach a compound of seven huts perched below cypress trees on the lip of the cliff. There, ecstatic in a shiny Christmas dress, is Elizebeth Kokibor, Kibor's grandmother. She hugs you delicately, her eyes tightly shut, and gives you rich, oily tea.

Kibor takes you to a promontory and points out settlements far down at the base of the escarpment. "That is where I was born," he says. "That is where my father and mother are. There are mosquitoes there, malaria, and it's always hot. So when I was small, my parents brought me here, for school and health. I carry stalks of bananas up from my father's. It is a five-hour climb, if you are a good climber."

It was a relative in the valley, he says, who knew that Kibor wanted to run in the Commonwealth Games preliminary trials. "He gave me a goat, and I led it up the mountain to Chesoi (a trek of 15 miles) and sold it there for 150 shillings (about $7), a very low price, because I was in a hurry. Then I took *matatus* to Kisumu. I hitched some and used the money I saved for food." He still had energy enough to run third, advancing to the Nairobi finals.

Kibor introduces his older brother Yano, and his cousins George, maybe nine, and eight-year-old Salome. His nearest neighbor, Benjamin Yator Kisang, 37, was born right here but has worked in Nairobi. "In advertising and design," he says. "But the city. . . . Well, I thought I'd better come back to the good life before I get old."

The Kapchebau life is simple and rigorous. "Our diet is goat's milk and millet," says Kisang. "Sometimes eggs or meat, and always *ugali*. *Ugali* is our staple."

Ugali is the maize porridge that you hear Kenyan runners yearning for wherever they travel. "You plant the maize on May first," says Kisang, "and you harvest January first." By then the kernels are as pale and hard as porcelain. Grandmother shows you her storehouse of millet, the grain a deep variegated red, the door secured by a strong new padlock.

The huts have no electricity or plumbing, but back on the hillside is a small, stone-lined channel of clear, cold water, quite separate from the stream. A spout of split bamboo allows little Salome to fill her jug. This is not a spring but part of a vast network of ancient channels that apportion water to every clan on the escarpment. The Marakwet have lived a thousand years on these slopes, yet they say they inherited the channels from previous users, possibly the lost tribe of the Sirikwa.

The light fades by seven. You are cordially invited to Christmas dinner and to spend the night. You would accept even if there were an alternative.

Chickens roost in the cooking hut. This is where Grandmother sleeps, on a cowhide folded on a cot. Along the dim back wall are round earthenware pots. "She drinks maize alcohol all day, so of course she is happy," says Kibor.

The fire is surrounded by three stones. A fair percentage of the smoke goes out a hole in the roof, after warming and drying green wood in the rafters. Salome sifts ground maize. Yano cuts and washes the meat and puts it in a pot to stew. A chicken lays an egg. Kibor goes to the main hut, which has two rooms, and does a few more chemistry problems by the light of a kerosene lamp before dinner is delivered. He breaks the sad news to the family that he must leave in the morning. He has to get back to the training camp in Nairobi.

Yano pours water so you may soap and rinse your hands. You eat with your fingers. The beef is tough, the sauce delicious. *Ugali* is kind of scratchy on the palate, as if there were some earth in with the corn. It is bland but satisfying. You really dig in, to the contentment of your hosts.

Kibor pours water so you may wash your hands again. Dinner concludes with bottles of orange soda (which Kisang opens with his teeth) and goodwill all around.

You pass the night rolled in a blanket on the hut's immaculately swept earthen floor. It is not as uncomfortable as, say, a night on a 747. The dawn is announced firmly, repeatedly, unnecessarily, by a rooster. You awaken thinking that if you need to know where a man lays his head to understand him, well, now you do.

The Rift Valley is filled with vapor. Clouds shoot up from the gorge as from volcanoes. Breakfast is strong tea and bread. "It was always tea and *ugali* and a run to school," says Kibor with as much nostalgia as a 17-year-old can summon.

"I hope you've seen that it's a good neighborhood," says Kisang. Kibor and his grandmother walk into the fields and grasp each other's forearms in parting. Hiking up the dewy, slippery slope to the village, little George carries your bag. You stumble and sway. He darts and hops. You gasp. He is inaudible. Strength, efficiency and athletic coordination, there they all are, vanishing over the hill.

The ride back seems shorter. At the roadside Chebaimo Hotel and Bakery you get sponge cake, biscuits and corn bread that all taste exactly the same. On the wall is a sign:

"Struggling is the meaning of life. Victory and defeat are in the hands of God, so one must enjoy in struggling."

Kibor, his mouth full of cake, agrees with a nod and laugh. "I do enjoy it," he says, spraying crumbs. "Struggle."

SAFELY BACK in Iten, you call at St. Patrick's High School, a most remarkable institution run by the Patrician brothers, an Irish Catholic teaching order. Brother Colm O'Connell, originally from County Cork, is headmaster and coach. In the 14 years he has been here, the school has sent more than three quarters of its graduates to college and has turned out more than 40 international- level runners.

In the cafeteria, Kibor gazes up at an imposing set of school records. There is a 1,500 of 3:34.9 and a mile of 3:52.39 by Kip Cheruiyot, and a 5,000 of 13:18.6 by his twin brother, Charles. Other boards name the 12 athletes St. Patrick's has sent to the Olympics.

O'Connell's enthusiasm grows as he finds words for it. "My great advantage," he says, "was that when I came, I knew no athletics. I learned about the athletes first, then the sport. Normally, there's not a lot of attention paid talented runners in the schools. We're more successful here because we take a personal interest."

As seems fitting for a man of the cloth, O'Connell encourages runners toward the essential vow. "It helps them if they make up their mind, if they say, 'I am a runner,'" he says. "Joseph here is typical of how quickly they can come to prominence, but many Kenyans are quite late developers. Ibrahim Hussein graduated from here and then New Mexico before he really took it seriously."

When he did, Hussein, one of a small group of Islamic Nandi, won the New York, Honolulu and Boston marathons between November of '87 and April of '88. The key is not age—Hussein was 29 years old when he won those marathons—but resolve.

"It's not just altitude, diet and climate," says O'Connell. "It's a very subtle combination of those with their tradition. They come from great, extended families. You hear them speaking of 'my father and my other father and my other father,' because they're brought up to think uncles are fathers. Cousins are brothers or sisters. The mentality is community. They run for their people, and when they come back they aren't put up on a pedestal. They're absorbed back into the family. That's a great release of pressure for them. They don't have a great fear of losing because the loss is distributed over the group."

As is winning. "When a girl wins a race," O'Connell says, "her first reaction is to run into the middle of the crowd and hide."

Most of O'Connell's runners do not come to him burning with inextinguishable ambition. "If you want to motivate them, they must enjoy it," he says. "If you bring the painful or boring aspects in, they may lose interest. You try to get them over the stage where the novelty's done, to where they say, 'Yes, I'm an athlete.' Then they can be single-minded about it." Then they can tap the deep seriousness their culture has planted within them.

Only rarely does O'Connell burden St. Patrick's boys with running much more than 50 miles a week. They need the energy to study. "And Kenyans have an amazing ability to get fit quickly," he says. "For example, in 1987 John Ngugi finished only 76th in the national cross-country, but he was still selected to the team going to the world championships because he'd won the year before. He had a mere three weeks to prepare. He won easily. It's built into them. In their daily lives a lot of Kenyans are training completely unbeknownst to themselves."

O'Connell swears the talent at St. Patrick's is equaled by that at other schools. He does not recruit. "One season we had fine 400-meter runners. That was the year I told Paul Ereng, 'Go away. You wouldn't even make our relay team.'" Ereng is now the Olympic 800-meter champion.

"I wish I'd taken him," says O'Connell, but his tone is free of regret. "When

I see Kenya's team going off to the world junior championships, I know you can find another group just as good being left behind. It takes a teacher or headmaster, someone to give a boy a lift or a hundred shillings. Joseph, are there others in your school who can run?"

"There are," says Kibor. "But they have no transport. They have no chance of coming to races."

"So what we see," says O'Connell, "is the tip of the iceberg."

O'Connell trains his less talented team members to be assistant coaches. "Peter Rono was coached largely by a classmate," he says. "He was a small boy and always struggling. He ran the 5,000 when he came, which was O.K., but in 1983, Kip Cheruiyot was selected to run with the national team in Helsinki, and suddenly I had no 1,500-meter runner for the Schools Championships. I went to little Peter Rono and said, 'You're going to be a 1,500 runner. I need you.' "

Rono gave his grave consent. "That was his breakthrough. He won the Schools 1,500 and 5,000 double three times. He's really a 5,000 man. He has no hope in a real sprint, but if everybody's tired, he can maintain his speed."

Thus it was that in Seoul little Peter Rono led the last 800 meters of the Olympic 1,500 final and made everybody tired. In the stretch, with Steve Cram and Peter Elliott of Great Britain straining on his heels, Rono smoothly maintained his lead to the finish. He was the first St. Patrick's boy to win an Olympic gold medal.

In his honor, the school planted the Peter Rono tree in the courtyard. It is of the species *Spathodea nilotica*. The Nandi Flame.

KENYAN RUNNERS endure a few things Kibor cannot yet know much about. There have been complaints since Keino's time of Kenyan Amateur Athletic Association (KAAA) officials' pocketing appearance money meant for athletes, but recently, with the growth of de facto professional track, the habit has reportedly grown into serious corruption. KAAA general secretary Robert Ouko, who won a gold medal in the 1972 Olympic 1,600-meter relay, has long been accused by runners of letting them race only in meets where their earnings were paid directly to Ouko or to his minions.

Under IAAF rules, athletes' winnings must be kept in trust funds. At first Ouko refused to set up such funds. Some Kenyans chose to have their trust funds supervised by The Athletics Congress of the U.S. rather than by their own body. They were smart. Ngugi reportedly had $185,000 siphoned from his Kenyan trust fund.

At the 1987 World Championships in Rome, the most impressive Kenyan performance was that of Paul Kipkoech in the 10,000. A Nandi soldier from

Kapsabet, he destroyed a strong field by surging through the last 5,000 meters in 13:25, which was actually 1.44 seconds faster than the winning time of Morocco's Said Aouita in the 5,000.

Immediately afterward, a promoter offered Kipkoech what one source calls "a small fortune" (it was probably about $15,000) to run at a track meet in Rieti, Italy. Kenyan officials, though, insisted that all team members return to Kenya immediately and, according to an official KAAA report, confiscated athletes' passports, including Kipkoech's. Ouko and Kipkoech reportedly came to blows in the Rome airport.

Ouko finally was suspended, along with the KAAA treasurer, Timothy Musyoki, in late 1988, and things are looking up. But Kipkoech, perhaps the most graceful of all Kenyan runners, is said to have abandoned all serious competition.

The KAAA has its share of tribal infighting, too, which explains why a few deserving athletes have been left off some national teams. The country has a chronic shortage of the most basic equipment. Kenyan runners' desperation for shoes is legendary. Asked what size he wore, one runner told Boit, "Eight . . . and up."

Yet all these problems must be kept in perspective. By African standards, Kenya is as stable and prosperous as Sweden. Stray from its borders and you enter regions of famine, war and dislocation: Uganda, Sudan, Somalia, Ethiopia.

Kenya's stability has allowed its athletes to shine despite Kenyan mismanagement. The greatest harm to Kenyan running was done by the 1976 and 1980 Olympic boycotts, which removed the ultimate goal from a generation. But now the runners are better than ever. When Ereng stepped from the plane that brought the triumphant Kenyan team back from Seoul, two things happened. His mother washed his hands, symbolically purifying the son as he returned from the decadence of the outside world. And people began to argue over what tribe Ereng was from.

His parents were of the nomadic Turkana. "But he was raised Nandi," says Boit, "in the town of Kitale. He was circumcised Nandi." The Turkana do not circumcise. So Ereng seemed to affirm that it is culture, not some gene, that makes the difference, and in Kenya the racing culture is making converts of even the nomads.

An hour south of Iten, Kibor bids you stop at Kapsabet Stadium, in Kapsabet. A brick wall surrounds low, roofed stands that have the aspect of cattle barns. This track is the source, the one from which so many great Nandi athletes sprang. It was here that Henry Rono, watching Keino from afar, made his silent promise to become a runner.

Boit is lobbying the IAAF to install a modern all-weather track in Kapsabet, and he has a case if the idea is to place the track in the exact spot in Africa where there is the most interest in running. "The only trouble with that," British distance runner Tim Hutchings has said, "is the rest of the world no longer will have a chance."

Kibor is such a novice that he has never run here, and he wants to put in a few laps of devotion. The track surface is moist sand and clay, and is unaccountably springy. Upon it, Kibor runs like a freshly released antelope.

Soon he goes blazing down the straightaways, and he doesn't slow much in the curves. He obviously has terrific natural speed, which makes it curious that he has never raced anything shorter than a 10,000.

"I watched them running the 1,500, and I saw they ran fast," he says, panting. "I didn't know if I could run that fast, because I had never specialized. And in the 3,000 and the 5,000, too, they looked like they were running fast. But in the 10,000 I saw I could just run along slowly and catch everyone at the end."

He rockets away. "I can run the 1,500," he says when he passes again, "if I specialize."

He has never even done any track training. He has simply grown up Kalenjin in the Cherangani Hills, and come to a decision. Had you known in high school that people like this existed, it would have darkened your dreams of running.

Here, though, it has the opposite effect. The vision of Kibor in full stride has drawn a flock of kids. They watch for a while, poker-faced; then, told it's O.K. to go on the track, they fly into motion like a covey of quail, boys and girls, forming a ragged pack. They're impatient, they surge and elbow and squeal, and when it's time to go, you can't get them stopped. But never again will you quite think of them as children.

Road Swing

BY STEVE RUSHIN

For a year the author cruised the highways of America in search of the soul of sports. He found it in shrines both hallowed and profane—and wrote a book about it all, which SI excerpted.

ORKING PRESS?" A PITTSBURGH PIRATE ONCE SAID to me with a sneer. "That's sorta like jumbo shrimp."

"My favorite oxymoron is *guest host*," I replied chummily. "You know, like they used to have on *The Tonight Show*?" But he didn't know. And he didn't care. In fact he thought I was calling him a moron, so he calmly alit from his clubhouse stool and chloroformed me with his game socks.

But I see his point. My life's work is not work. Indiana basketball coach Bobby Knight likes to say of sportswriters, "We all learn to write by the second grade; most of us move on to bigger things." Most of us stop throwing chairs and calling ourselves Bobby by the second grade, too. But I see his point.

As a writer on the staff of SPORTS ILLUSTRATED, I've had the same day job since I was eight. I was raised in a house with mint-green aluminum siding and spent my days watching ball games in our wood-paneled den. My father loved wood paneling and even had it on the exterior of his station wagon. He'd have preferred mint-green aluminum siding, but it wasn't available on the '74 Ford Country Squire.

Pity, because the Country Squire looked like the crate it was shipped in. Only it didn't run as well. It was not so much a motor vehicle as an oak coffin with a luggage rack, proof that you really can take it with you. Every summer vacation our family of seven was vacuum-packed into that car, and we raced across the country as if through one continuous yellow light, pausing only long enough to attend some big league baseball game—in Houston or Anaheim or Cincinnati. It didn't matter where. The important thing was that for nine innings once every August, Dad forgot the Kafkaesque problems of his suburban existence. Namely, that his house was rusting. And his car had termites.

It all seems so long ago. My brothers and sister grew up and got jobs. I grew up and became a sportswriter, though it is hardly a grown-up pursuit. The naked manager of the California Angels once threw his double-knit uniform pants at me in anger, something that happens all the time to baseball writers and may explain why we're so comfortable wearing polyester. Whereas a similar burst of pantsfire across a conference table at IBM would no doubt be considered inappropriate, especially since the trousers in question were mottled with moist tobacco stains. (Please, God, tell me they were tobacco stains.)

It is hard to believe now, but the heroes of my youth were all as smooth and wholesome as Skippy peanut butter. This surely owes something to the fact that I never saw them naked, that I knew almost nothing about them. I loved a Minnesota Twins catcher named George Mitterwald, but only because I loved the name George Mitterwald. Beyond that, I was faintly aware that his middle name was Eugene and he lived in Orlando. Or that his middle name was Orlando and he lived in Eugene. And I knew that the Fun Fact on the back of his 1974 Topps baseball card said, "George likes to take home movies." If George liked to take anything else—fistfuls of amphetamines, long walks in women's clothing—I was blissfully unaware of it.

For some years now I have wanted to return to that state of blissful oblivion, preferably without a prescription. Which brings us to the story that you hold in your hands. It is an effort to revisit the twin pursuits of my youth: epic car trips and an unhealthy obsession with sports, usually combined. I wanted to get into my Japanese car and drive to American sports shrines for a year, or until I became fully alarmed myself. I wanted to put my finger to the pulse of American sports, and I wanted it to be one of those giant foam-rubber index fingers worn by pinheaded fans across the land.

So I consigned all my worldly possessions to a 6-by-12-foot steel box at one of those U-Lok-It mini storage facilities patronized primarily by serial killers, and I consigned myself to another 6-by-12-foot steel box, a leased Nissan Pathfinder that I loaded with only the barest necessities: 36 compact discs, a set of golf clubs and a dozen foul cigars that might double as road flares in the event of an emergency.

Which is how it was that I arose one stormy July morning in Minneapolis, in the year before my 30th birthday, and embarked on a busman's holiday. I had no fixed itinerary, except to travel the nation in two grand loops, like those in the lowercase *L*'s that punctuate the $295 card-show signature of Bill Russell. My sister-in-law once approached the former Celtic on an airplane and said excitedly, "Mr. Russell, your name is an answer in today's *USA Today* crossword puzzle." To which Russell replied testily that he didn't give a fig. Or words to that effect. I have often since wondered what the crossword clue was: Cantankerous cager? Peevish pivotman?

But I digress, which is half the fun of any journey. Agape on the shotgun seat lay a Rand McNally road atlas, with all its varicose-veined possibilities. I am one of those people who cannot look at a map without feeling a child's sense of wonder at all that awaits me out there: Boos (Ill.) and What Cheer (Iowa), Baskett (Ky.) and Ball (La.), Sliders (Va.) and Heaters (W.Va.). Who knew what I might see?

For now, I could say only this: I wanted all my lunches to be racing-striped in ballpark mustard, noisily dispensed from flatulent squeeze bottles. I wanted to eat all my dinners from Styrofoam fast-food clam boxes that yawned in my lap while I drove 70 mph and steered with my knees. I wanted all my afternoons to dwindle in the backward-marching time of a scoreboard (:10, :09, :08 . . .), that physics-defying device that allows a person lucky enough to mark his or her time by it to grow younger.

I wanted to stave off adulthood. I wanted to see America. I wanted to have fun. Over the next several months, my only calendar would be the multicolored mosaic of one team pocket schedule or another. Shakespeare asserted in *Henry IV, Part I*, "If all the year were playing holidays, to sport would be as tedious as to work." Surely Shakespeare was full of s---, and I intended to prove it. Leisure City (Fla.), here I come.

So I joined Interstate 35 and traveled out of Minneapolis in a cold gray mist. It was like driving into a sneeze. The radio reported 94-mph winds in southern Minnesota as well as golf-ball-, baseball- and softball-sized hail. Wonderful. It was raining sporting goods, and I was following the perforated yellow line of the highway, a trail of dripping nacho "cheez" that would lead me to the lost soul of American sports. Or whatever it was I was looking for.

DYERSVILLE, IOWA

I found Don Lansing reposing on his grand front porch, lemonade and tinkling ice cubes sweating through a tall glass. It was not yet noon and already 94°. Lansing had forgone the wooden porch swing for an aluminum-framed lawn chair, the kind whose nylon latticework leaves your ass looking like a flame-broiled hamburger.

"I think they come for as many reasons as there are stars in the heavens," the farmer said, looking out on his Field of Dreams, a ballpark cut into a cornfield that receives 20,000 tourist pilgrims annually. "Some think that Kevin Costner lives here. A lot of people don't understand that Universal built this field—they think my family built it before there was a movie. And a lot of people don't know that the house is real. They think it's just a movie set."

Wasn't he bothered that some people treat his house as a movie set, taking photos through windows? "Naw," he said. "Usually they respect my little area here. Sometimes at night they'll ask me to turn on the lights"—there are six stanchions around the field—"but I only do that for special occasions." Lansing pointed to a stanchion 280 feet down the rightfield line. "Joe Pepitone hit the top of that one," he said, referring to the ex-Yankee with a toupee like a shag toilet-seat cover. "No one else has done it.

"It's neat to see all the people and where they come from and their reactions to the field," Lansing continued. "We've had 'em from Australia, Japan, all over Europe. Places without baseball."

What could possibly be the appeal to someone who doesn't know baseball? Lansing chewed on that question as if it were cud. The farm has been in his family for 92 years. Lansing played ball on the property with his father, LaVern, and LaVern played ball there with *his* father. "I think," Lansing said at last, "it has a lot to do with fathers and sons."

Now we were getting somewhere.

SPRING GREEN, WISCONSIN

In the early 1940s, a man named Alex Jordan built a weekend retreat on a 60-foot-high chimney of sandstone here. Soon the house sprouted an addition, then another, until it began wandering this way and that, like Don King's syntax, over 40 acres of land. The interior is decorated in the swank '50s lounge style in which I imagine Dean Martin's place was turned out and is kept ridiculously dark, the better to obscure the escape routes when you learn that the entrance fee is $14.50.

It is worth every penny, for the House on the Rock is now a museum housing Jordan's astonishing collection of random junk: the world's largest merry-go-round, a menu from the *Titanic*, a series of old Burma-Shave billboards (HE LIT A MATCH/TO CHECK HIS TANK/THAT'S WHY THEY CALL HIM/SKINLESS FRANK/BURMA-SHAVE). The best display by far, and the reason I had come, is the modest assembly of ancient sepia newspapers flaking on the walls.

Pasted in various corridors are sports pages from the 1930s and '40s with headlines such as BLAME CUB SLUMP ON SLIM SLAB CORPS. (Say it aloud.

It's poetry.) The stories themselves are filled with pitchers who "hurled cypher jobs," batters who "collected clutch bingles," base runners who "expired at the cash register" and visiting pitchers who—I swear to God—"toed the alien humpback." There was a scribe in Pennsylvania who, describing the turning point of any contest, invariably wrote, "That's when Mr. Mo Mentum changed uniforms." This language is ridiculous and incomprehensible, of course, and I must say I love each and every word of it.

It seems to me a shame that it's now as dead as Latin.

HERMITAGE, PENNSYLVANIA

According to a kindly woman who fielded my call at the National Golf Foundation, there were 15,390 golf courses in America. The average parcel of land devoted to each course—excluding clubhouses and parking lots and the like—was 120 acres. In other words, golf holes covered 1,846,800 acres of U.S. real estate. That's an area more than twice the size of Rhode Island, a state that exists expressly to be demeaned in comparisons such as this one.

When you throw in clubhouses, parking lots, golf-supply stores, the National Golf Foundation and touring pro Craig Stadler, golf surely consumes three times as much space as the Ocean State. As the U.S. turns away aspiring immigrants who wash up at its shores half dead on rafts, I wonder: Is this a defensible use of such landmass? The answer, I fear, depends on your handicap.

There is much to be said for a solitary round of golf. For starters, all of the footprints on the dew-soaked greens at Tam O' Shanter Golf Course in Hermitage were mine; they looked like an Arthur Murray dance chart for something called the Four-Putt. Whenever I drove the ball to a heavily foliated corner of the course, which was often, a guy on a riding lawn mower tore off in pursuit of it and returned with a ball that was not even the color of the one I had hit—but that I graciously accepted as my own. Better yet, I rained golf-ball-sized hail on the many homes surrounding the course and felt bereft of self-consciousness in doing so.

In this way golf is legalized vandalism for adults. "Serves 'em right for living on a golf course" said in Latin is a legal defense against breaking windows in 47 states. With a cymbal crash of glass, I once smother-hooked a tee shot through the window of a fairway condominium in Palm Springs. "What should I do?" I asked my partner, who happened to be my father.

"Take a drop," he said with a shrug.

But the best thing by far about my round at Tam O' Shanter was not having to wait for anybody. I failed to break Sam Snead's course record of 65, but I may have set a course speed record, clocking in at less than two hours.

A friend of mine has long insisted that Steve Scott, the great American miler, once played a full round of golf in 27 minutes—putting out on every green, lugging a variety of clubs, stopping (for all I know) for a cigar and a cold beer at the turn—a feat that supposedly put him in the *Guinness Book of World Records*. I have no idea if this is true—I've never read beyond those two fat twins on motorcycles—but Scott seems to me well worth emulating.

If America consolidated all of her courses into a single state called Golf, and those links were all linked in one epic layout, this supercourse would have 226,287 holes—the figure includes both 9- and 18-hole courses—and measure roughly 68 million yards. At a brisk 3½-hour pace per 18 holes, you could finish a round in five years. Steve Scott would require a mere 8½ months. Neither timetable is realistic, of course: You would need time to eat and sleep, and to phone the office every 50,000 holes. But a man's reach should exceed his grasp, right, or what's a heaven for?

COOPERSTOWN, NEW YORK

Baseball was first described as the national pastime in 1857, but by 1881 *The New York Times* was reporting that the sport had been displaced as "the national game" by, of all things, cricket. While I have an excellent true story about cricket involving a West Indian bowler named Michael Holding, an English batsman named Peter Willey and a BBC announcer who actually said, "The bowler's Holding, the batsman's Willey," that is not the point I want to make here.

My point is that baseball may never have been the consensus American obsession that we think it used to be. But I must tell you: The game does exert a strange patriotic hold, especially if you happen to be driving in upstate New York in a Pathfinder, which is the name of the fourth installment of the Leatherstocking Tales, a series of American frontier novels by James Fenimore Cooper, whose father founded Cooperstown, which is 25 miles south of Dolgeville, where lumbermen harvested the Adirondack white ash that became the bat that hit the ball over the fence to win the pennant for the '51 New York Giants.

That bat is enshrined in Cooperstown—at the Baseball Hall of Fame—as the instrument that fired the Shot Heard Round the World. That phrase was penned by Ralph Waldo Emerson to commemorate the Revolutionary War battles of Lexington and Concord, but I daresay it's more often associated (by cretins like you and me, anyway) with Bobby Thomson's dinger at the Polo Grounds. There's nothing wrong with that; the U.S. has a long tradition of recalling its history in this backhanded way. De Soto discovered the Mississippi but is better remembered as a boxy automobile. Ethan Allen is no longer a soldier but rather a furniture store. If I said, "I just devoured an O. Henry," you would think I had been eating, not reading. And you would be right.

The Baseball Hall of Fame had all the elbow room of the Tokyo subway, and the lines moved at the pace of plate tectonics, but so what? Save for a bulletproof display case, I could have touched Lou Gehrig's shabby address book, which was open to a casual notation, in Lou's hand, on the R page: "Babe Ruth, 345 W. 88th St." It was somehow humanizing and awesome at the same time, like a WHILE YOU WERE OUT message slip to Zeus reminding him to call Ares. And similar knee-buckling items were everywhere in the museum.

Sportswriters had their own (out-of-the-way and much ignored) corner of the hall, I am proud to say. It housed an exhibit called Scribes and Mikemen, two coinages of that inane and archaic sportswriterese that I so adore. "By 1900, most sportswriters covered the game from press boxes protected by chicken wire," said a caption beneath a length of chicken wire. Indeed, pecking away at typewriters in a chicken-wire cage, sportswriters could scarcely be distinguished from chickens. An examination of the resulting prose wouldn't clarify matters much, I'm afraid.

A *Sporting News* column called "Clouting 'Em with Joe King" was on display and bore the unutterably euphonious headline SHALLOW HURLING BALKS BUCS 'N' BIRDS. I couldn't get it out of my head, and I strutted around repeating it softly: shallow hurling balks bucs 'n' birds. I looked and sounded a bit like a clucking chicken when at last I left the Hall of Fame and went blinking out into the Cooperstown sunlight.

LOUISVILLE, KENTUCKY

There are 47 stables at Churchill Downs, which is home, in peak season, to 1,400 horses. Among the residents of this equine Levittown is a roan named Rapid Gray. He was 16 years old at the time of my visit—about 55 in human years—and held the track record for seven furlongs. Alas, the Derby is a 10-furlong race, which may be why Gray was never entered in the Run for the Roses. But the fact remains that Rapid Gray was once at the top of his profession.

I met the horse after infiltrating a tour group and was immediately struck by how uncannily he resembled a retired sports star of the human race. His massive upper body was borne by creaky old legs. He scratched out an undignified living greeting fans. They said frank things about him to each other, right in front of his nose, as if he couldn't hear or understand a word of it. Then they came closer and stroked him and whispered sweet nothings in his ear. He was given free shoes for life. He never bought a meal. And women got in line to ride him.

Rapid Gray is expected to spend a few more years growing more gray and less rapid before joining Man o' War and Secretariat in the next life. Indeed, the tour guide was giving an elegy for those two great champions—"Secretariat's heart was three times the size of the average thoroughbred's . . . "—when a hatchet-faced lady in stretch pants piped up: "Is Man o' War stuffed?"

"I beg your pardon?" asked the guide.

"Man o' War. I heard he was stuffed." "No, ma'am," said the guide, harnessing every atom of restraint in his body. "Man o' War was not"—he smiled weakly— "stuffed."

The woman curled her lip in a pout, disappointed that famous thoroughbreds of the Bluegrass had not been taxidermied for her photo-op edification. Her question elicited some head-shaking and eye-rolling among the horsey set on the tour, and when I arched an eyebrow of my own at the woman, she blurted defiantly, "Well. . . . Roy Rogers stuffed Trigger!"

LUMBERTON, NORTH CAROLINA

The South was an alien land. The athletic director at the University of Alabama was Hootie Ingram. The president of the Charlotte Motor Speedway was Humpy Wheeler. The football coach at Lumberton (N.C.) Senior High was Knocky Thorndyke. These were grown men in positions of authority. And yet, if they were to meet, a mutual friend presumably would introduce them to each other by saying: "Humpy, Knocky. Knocky, Humpy. Humpy, Hootie. Hootie, Humpy. . . . "

TUPELO, MISSISSIPPI

The King's Munsingwear pajamas were laid neatly across the back of his brown Barcalounger. Next to his chair was a table, and arrayed on the table were an ashtray, a lighter, two pipes, a reading lamp and a pair of reading glasses. The entire display looked like something from the Eisenhower estate sale. But in fact all of these items were recovered from Graceland and moved here—to the Elvis Presley Museum in his hometown, Tupelo. My eyes fell to Presley's favorite book, which lay unopened for all eternity on the armchair. It was *Great Running Backs of the NFL*, by Jack Hand. Its cover bore the circular seal of the NFL Punt, Pass & Kick Library. I recognized this book. I had read it when I was eight. "Oh, Elvis loved his football," said a sweet old woman who caught me admiring the book and who had offered to answer any questions when I arrived. "He loved all sports. He played some football in high school, when he moved to Memphis. He warn't too good, mind you, but he always joined in. You know, to be one of the fellas."

Several minutes passed in this fashion, the woman leading me around by the elbow as she pointed out the portrait of Mr. F.L. Bobo, who, she said, sold Elvis his first guitar, until at last I applied a sleeper hold to her neck, and she slumped over in a temporary and harmless blackout. I tiptoed out of Tupelo, passing the Tupelo Hardware Co., where the King really did get his first guitar from a Mr. F.L. Bobo, whose name you thought I made up.

From Tupelo I drove to Graceland, 107 miles to the northwest in Memphis, where I learned that Elvis built a one-court racquetball pavilion in his backyard in 1975, at the height of the nation's racquetball boom. There is, predictably, a wet bar and a piano in the viewing gallery, making the King's primary workout facility look like the racquetball-themed piano bar of a Holiday Inn. This is the penultimate point of interest on the Graceland tour—the last stop before visiting the grave.

Alas, it was also E.'s last stop before visiting same. Or very nearly so. To paraphrase the tour audiotape, in August 1977 Elvis had recently returned from weeks of touring, the road having left him tragically out of match shape, when he was seized in the middle of the night by an irrepressible impulse to play racquetball. He rallied with friends for a couple of hours, then repaired to the piano to play what is poignantly called his "last concert"—*Unchained Melody* and *Blue Eyes Cryin' in the Rain*—before retiring upstairs around dawn, at which time he passed away peacefully on the bathroom floor.

The implication was unmistakable, a revisionist revelation that I wanted desperately to believe. It wasn't drugs or alcohol or fried peanut butter and banana sandwiches that killed the King. On the contrary.

Racquetball killed Elvis.

IRVING, TEXAS

The Texas Sports Hall of Fame in Waco houses an assortment of ludicrously named local legends: Honk Irwin, Boody Johnson, Putt Powell, Botchey Koch. In preparation for a Dallas Cowboys game, I venerated Tom Landry's hat and viewed a display on Texas Stadium, the Cowboys' home field, which opened in 1971 with a Billy Graham crusade. The stadium's religious beginning—almost literally a christening—was not accidental. Essentially a dome, Texas Stadium has a long, narrow hole cut in the top, like the coin slot on a piggy bank. According to the display at the Texas Sports Hall of Fame, "Texans believe the hole is there so that God can watch his favorite team."

The Cowboys and their fans have brilliantly co-opted the themes of God and country. I parked in remote lot 17-C at Texas Stadium, next to a guy in a F--- YOU, I'M FROM TEXAS T-shirt. His formidable sound-check-at-Altamont car-stereo speakers boomed the country anthem *God Bless Texas*. The Cowboys are not merely God's Favorite Team but also, famously, America's Team. During the national anthem, the crowd sang, "whose broad stripes and bright *stars*," shouting this last word as homage to the Cowboys' logo.

The anthem was sung by a mononymous Latino superstar named Emilio, and the crowd was informed that "Emilio will be appearing after the game in the American Express Corral Tent." Shortly afterward another announcement was made: "Free bottles of Pepsi will be handed out as you leave the stadium at the conclusion of the game." This was the handiwork of Jerry Jones, the Cowboys' owner, who signed exclusive deals with Pepsi, American Express and Nike in defiance of the NFL's licensing agreement with their competitors. He told the league, though not in so many words, "F--- you, I'm from Texas."

A three-sided sandwich board bearing Nike logos was suspended by wires above the 50-yard-line, and in the first quarter Jones himself materialized in the press box, trailed by a young lady who handed out complimentary Nike coffee mugs to us, the assembled scribes. "If Nike wants to give us something," bitched the grizzled *USA Today* writer next to me, "they should give us shoes." He was eating a free hot dog and drinking a free soda as he said this.

Cowboys fans seated in front of the press box took notice of Jones and turned around to regard him as if he were a tropical fish in an aquarium. "*Jerry! Jer-ry!*" called a guy in a T-shirt that read WENT ON VACATION LEFT ON PROBATION. In response Jones pantomimed a pistol shot with his index finger. He looked like Sinatra playing the Sands. A woman shrieked at Jones while pointing at her chest. She was wearing a T-shirt with a Cowboys logo on one breast and Pepsi and Nike logos sharing the other. "Oh, that's great!" said Jones, giving a thumbs-up. "That's beautiful."

The afternoon passed in a silver-and-blue blur: I remember Emmitt Smith running all over the Arizona Cardinals, and Jones winking and shooting fingers at fans, and a biplane overhead pulling a banner that read RAMSES: ROLL ONE ON, and my Nike mug instructing me to JUST DO IT, and the Dallas Cowboys cheerleaders' high-kicking and the woman with corporate logos on her breasts and my heart going like mad and yes I said yes I will yes. . . .

PAXTON, NEBRASKA

America's original sports bar is a place of legendary and longstanding political incorrectness that goes by a variety of names. OLE'S BIG GAME LOUNGE, 200 MOUNTS, reads a rotting highway billboard in central Nebraska. OLE'S BIG GAME LOUNGE & GRILL, touts a slightly newer sign up the road. When I arrived in Paxton and parked between Swede's Lounge and the American Legion Hall, I saw yet another, grander name on the bar: OLE'S BIG GAME LOUNGE STEAKHOUSE & LOUNGE.

I swallowed hard and entered. A sign above the door said SMOKING IS PERMITTED IN THIS ENTIRE ESTABLISHMENT. Permitted? It is evidently compulsory. Just inside the door I glimpsed, through cumulus clouds of Camel smoke, an 11-foot, 1,500-pound polar bear menacing me from its hind legs. TAKEN BY OLE HERSTEDT MARCH 12, 1969 ON THE CHUKCHI SEA read a tasteful inscription inside the glass case that housed the angry bear so that it looked to be attempting an escape from a carnival dunk tank.

A nearby black-and-white photo showed a barrel-chested man with a rifle standing over the fallen bear in Alaska; another showed the same man, wearing an apron, atop a stepladder in this very bar, pouring champagne into the stuffed bear's open mouth. The jovial man in the photographs was Rosser O. (Ole) Herstedt. On Dec. 5, 1933, Ole opened his Big Game Lounge, waiting until 12:01 a.m. to do so—a full minute after Prohibition had ended. It was his last concession to caution. The first beer kegs were carried by Union Pacific railroad to nearby North Platte and from there conveyed to Ole's in a school bus. Within five years Ole had begun to fill his lounge with trophies from his worldwide killing sprees, a crass menagerie. So here was a bare-chested Ole, framed in another photo, pretending to stab a leopard he had already shot, while the dead animal was made to look as if it were mauling the hunter.

The head of a 15,000-pound elephant, its trunk raised in full trumpet, jutted from the wood paneling above an upright piano. The elephant appeared to be stampeding through the wall, as in a beer commercial. Its tusks were over by the fireplace, five feet of ivory on either side.

"Sometimes people complain," bartender Brent Gries said when I asked what visitors made of the place. "Animal-rights people. Someone will ask, 'What did the fawn think when her mother was shot?' The one we get the most complaints about is the American eagle." Above a row of Bacardi bottles behind the bar soared a golden eagle that Ole bagged in 1940. "That's probably the worst," Gries said, thinking aloud. "We probably shouldn't have that up there." He paused. "We should put that away," he said again, leaving the eagle right where it was.

Gries's friend Tim Holzfaster bought the bar 10 years ago from Ole, who died in 1996. Knute Rockne was a regular at Ole's, and so was Jack Dempsey. USC football coach John McKay and Dodgers great Don Drysdale made it to this no-man's-land. Nebraska senator Bob Kerrey tended bar one night. Gries tended bar today. "When someone asks if we have any local mounts," Gries said, "I always point up there." Above the bar were six 1940s pinups of naked women.

On my way out the door, I signed Ole's guest book. I leafed back through page after page looking for expressions of outrage, but found none. In fact, most every visitor had written the same sentiment in the comments column: *Great food. I'm stuffed!*

ROCK CREEK, MONTANA

It isn't true that you can blink and miss Idaho while driving across the state's panhandle, though I strongly recommend that you try. Regardless, you are very quickly in Montana, where a highway sign advertises the ROCK CREEK TESTICLE FESTIVAL—HAVE A BALL! (Sadly, it was not for another five months.) Up the road a piece is another billboard: WELCOME TO DRUMMOND—WORLD FAMOUS BULLSHIPPERS! You don't see these crude punning signs outside most of the world's municipalities (ENTERING GENEVA—KISS OUR ALPS!), and I say that's too bad. The world would be a better place if it were a little more like Montana, for Montanans have the good sense not to take themselves seriously. After one 49ers Super Bowl victory a town changed its name for a year to Joe: Joe, Montana. I had half a mind to go there, to find an apartment where I might live out my days in exile: a grown man, hopelessly obsessed with sports, avoiding adulthood in Joe, Montana.

But already, for the better part of a year, I had lived a life of epic irresponsibility. I had neglected to pay bills, neglected to call friends, neglected to tell the office where I was going to be, in large measure because I had seldom known my destination more than 10 minutes before arriving there. I had drunk too much, slept too little and eaten exclusively those things that cause swift, painful deaths in laboratory mice. I had watched a fat man in a minor league ballpark in Colorado Springs spoon chopped onions and pickle relish onto his jumbo frank, then turn to me, a complete stranger, and say, "Vegetables." And scarier still, I had shared his pride, for I too had come to view the stadium condiment bar as a veritable vegetable garden.

In short, all my year had been a playing holiday. And I could now say, with absolute certainty, that Shakespeare should have been so lucky.

IV

WILD
KINGDOM

Mirror of My Mood

BY BIL GILBERT

As his dog was growing old, a little deaf, occasionally forgetful, the author of many SI stories about animals turned a naturalist's eye on man's best friend—his own best friend—and wrote a story that is both observant and deeply moving.

THERE ARE SOME FINE, BRIGHT DAYS IN EARLY WINTER WHEN certain things must be done that are pointless or downright impossible much earlier—butchering, starting hard cider, setting muskrat traps, flying passage hawks. Or perhaps cutting wood. You wait till a powder of snow is on the ground and the sun is strong enough to melt the snow by noon. This day is a time that was anticipated months before. In February trees were felled—tulip poplar for kindling and a quick blaze, oak and maple for steady, lasting heat—the timber cleaned, cut into 10-foot lengths and dragged and rolled down the hill. Now the logs are dry and they are wrestled onto a buck to be cut into two-foot lengths for the workshop stove, three-foot lengths for the fireplace in the house. It is not complicated, not even very hard work. It is rather soothing. On the right early winter day, with dry wood, a level buck, sharp saw, a comfortable ax and enough time, there seems to be nothing that you should or would rather be doing than making firewood. You feel you could go on sawing, splitting and stacking until the wood-pile is the size of the Ritz.

An old red dog, Dain, climbs up the hill on stiff legs and eases under the gate. He finds a sunny place on the lee side of the log pile, lowers himself slowly and curls up on a jacket that has been shucked off and thrown there. He remains all day, as long as the work goes on. Sedentary as he is, he is on duty, doing what he has done all his life: being at my heel, on a car seat beside me, on my sleeping bag, under my bed, under my desk. Dain is a companion dog, specifically my companion. Responding to my moods and activities has been his life's work.

Dain watches with mild interest. If he is spoken to or patted during a break, he raises his head and beats his tail on the ground in response. Otherwise he scratches, lifts his nose to catch scents, dozes in the winter sun.

Once he was a burly 100-pound dog who could run by the hour, climb cliffs like a goat, tree a coon and kill it when it came down if that were permitted. Now he is 11 years old and 20 pounds lighter, his flanks gaunt, his hams shaky. His coat, which was once remarkable—a solid red-gold pelt the color of fallen oak leaves, thick as a beaver's—is now thinning, and is flecked with white. He is a little deaf, occasionally forgetful.

His age and infirmities have changed the pattern of both our lives. There will be no hard bushwhacking for a while; it would be cruel to ask him. Now it is a matter of courtesy and respect to tell him a little beforehand that you are going someplace so that he does not have to get up or move quickly to follow. To chat, you sit down with him so that he will not feel obliged to leap up, put his paws on your shoulder or, worse, try and not be able to do so.

As he lies against the woodpile taking the sun, he occasionally groans as he shifts position. Some of the aches are the ordinary ones that come to any big dog with age. But because of how he has used himself and been used, the years have been especially hard on Dain.

When he was two we walked 2,000 miles through the eastern mountains from Georgia to Maine. More accurately, I walked 2,000 miles and Dain perhaps 4,000 miles. He explored side trails, ran ahead, returned, lagged behind to investigate curiosities. Since then he has traveled perhaps another 5,000 miles in woods, mountains and deserts, across rock and ice and through snow. His legs are arthritic now, scarred by limestone and ice shards, by barbed wire, by agave, wait-a-bit and greenbrier thorns.

I remember setting off on a hot June morning to cross 15 miles of high, empty Sonora desert. We carried no water because in my pride I thought I could find water anyplace in that country when I needed it. I was wrong. He padded along, heaving, his tongue lolling. He followed, very nearly to his death, began staggering under the sun and finally collapsed in a coma. He was dragged and packed the last five miles until we came to a stock tank into which I stumbled and sat, holding his head above water until he revived.

One night we slept by a small lake in Maine. Three trout, cleaned and wrapped in leaves, were cached in the fork of a tree for breakfast. The fish drew a midnight bear. Dain rose and went out into the night, and after some back-and-forth ran the bear off through the spruce thickets, but he paid with broken ribs. We cornered a coati mundi in a canyon on the Mexico-Arizona border. On request Dain went in to roust out and hold the animal. He did so even though the fangs of the coati left a jagged scar running from the corner of his mouth almost to his right ear. He has been kicked by a horse, raked by the talons of an imperfectly manned goshawk, bitten by a copperhead. He has fallen in a mine shaft, had his left leg smashed by a truck.

The signs are obvious that he and his time are all but used up. One sign is audible and visible from the place where the wood is being cut. In a barnyard enclosure across the way 11 puppies are gamboling, yapping and annoying their golden retriever dam. The bitch is young and gay, giving promise that she herself will be a reasonably good dog once she has lost her silliness. But she was bought and brought to the place like a slave bride (because of temperament, size and color) as a mate for the old red dog. The largest and reddest of the puppies is being considered as his father's replacement. This pup and the rest of the litter exist because I have been brooding about the dog I will have when Dain is gone, as he soon will be.

Because early winter prompts thoughts about the ending of things, because woodcutting releases the mind, because of the pups, it is an appropriate time to reflect on the fact that the red dog will not see another early winter, to reflect on how things have been between us, to reflect simply on men and dogs.

That partnership began with jackal-like beasts scavenging from Asian nomads. In time these hunters came to realize that scavengers could lead them to prey, flush it, sometimes hold it. They could stir up such a commotion that no intruder could approach a camp surreptitiously. So, little by little, the scavengers were brought in from the cold, their rations regularized, their young protected and petted. From this primitive arrangement and thousands of years of genetic topiary work have come the domestic dog, sight and scent hounds, catch dogs, hole dogs, water dogs, retrievers, pointers, guard dogs, sled dogs, cart dogs, guide dogs, messenger dogs, herd dogs. For room and board we have hired other beasts to perform chores: to carry heavy loads, catch small game, grow fat, lay eggs. However, in complexity and versatility, nothing comes close to equaling the services that we receive from dogs.

The working arrangements between dogs and men are remarkable, but perhaps less astonishing than the capacity for companionship that has evolved. Recently there have been serious attempts to penetrate the inner lives of other species, even to explain ourselves to them. There are dictionaries of wolf, monkey, whale and bird utterances. We have had some success in two-way verbal communication with dolphins and have developed a sign language that can be used between men and chimpanzees. Nevertheless, man-dolphin and man-chimp exchanges are shallow when compared to the capacity of dogs and men to exchange information, respond to each other's moods, know each other's inner feelings.

Dain and I have been good companions, a good example of what is possible. Part of our mutual vocabulary are the traditional man-dog words—sit, stay, come, heel, get it, no. Then there are elementary dog signs—the wagging tail, head in the lap, whine at the door and a variety of yips and barks. As he prowls outside, there is a particular barking response to a stranger passing by on the road, a stranger entering the lane, for people he knows, for those in cars and those on foot. There are certain barks for dogs, for cats and for creatures that are not people, dogs or cats. Dain does not bark in order to pass along specific information, but as an outward manifestation of inner feelings. However, the result is the same as if he were yelling words.

I am usually occupied with natural history projects and enthusiasms. As a rule these involve small mammals. Little by little, through observation, Dain has become a mammalogist's dog. He has learned that I am invariably seeking odd furred creatures and am much more pleased if they are alive and well than mauled, bitten or dead. As we poke about, he lets me know when he comes across an interesting beast, will try to hold it if he can or, if he fails, follow it. While waiting for me to come up he will call out a rough description (usually based on size and formidability) of what he has found—a mouse-type, squirrel-type, raccoon-type, fox-type or deer-type creature. He can be even more specific. During a year that I devoted to a field study of the coati mundi, Dain learned that this was the most prized animal. His coati bark became distinctive.

As time has passed, the vocabulary Dain and I share has become larger and more subtle. One of the first command words any dog should learn is "stay." It is a flat-out order to remain exactly where he is, if necessary until hell freezes over. Dain learned to stay as a pup. However, this blunt command is seldom used between us anymore, being replaced by others that express degrees of "stayness." If I am going to walk down a lane to negotiate with a stranger, I may tell Dain to "stay here," which means he should hang around at this end of the lane, not follow me, but he does not have to remain frozen or immobile. "Stay in the car" means he may not climb out the window, but is free to move from seat to seat. "Stay around" means he can move but not very far. If we approach a woodpile that may have a weasel in it, I may warn him to "stay back," the equivalent of proceed with caution.

Dain will heel through a field of sheep or a chicken yard. He will heel down a strange street, through a yapping gantlet of poodles and boxers. He will heel all day if so asked. At one time he was obsessed with this command. If the magic word was spoken in his hearing, even in a breakfast discussion of dog behavior, he would stop whatever he was doing and rush into position a pace behind. Since then he has grown more sensible about tones and context. And now the term is used infrequently.

From a variety of signs I know when Dain is excited, alarmed, content, fatigued, confused. But he knows all of this about me and more. He recognizes and responds to shades of my anger, joy, uncertainty, fear, triumph, pain, illness, elation, impatience, boredom, satisfaction. During one period we staged large, intemperate New Year's Eve celebrations. I would get up New Year's Day and take a walk in the mountains with anyone so inclined. Nine years ago no one went with me. The house was filled with ugly reminders of the night—dregs of food and drink, bodies sprawled here and there in ugly positions, making ugly sounds. I whistled up Dain, who felt as good as he ever did, and we started off through the fields, into the mountains.

It was one of those days that John O'Hara had in mind when he wrote that before Christmas suicide weather settles over Pennsylvania and hangs on until March. It was overcast and gloomy. I walked along in appropriate agony, mouth tasting terrible, stomach queasy, head throbbing, and mused on weakness of character and general jackassery.

In those, his younger days, unless requested to do otherwise, Dain ranged widely on purposeless walks. He would gallop through the brush, taking canine pleasure in the sounds and scents he encountered. On this New Year's morning, being so preoccupied with myself, I did not pay much attention to him. Then I looked down and saw him walking quietly at my side, head and tail down, a figure of depression. "My God," I remember thinking, "he has a sympathetic hangover."

A companion dog responds to mood by imitating it, functioning as a kind of living mirror. As the years have passed there have been times when Dain, by his behavior, has shown me how I felt. I might not know how high or low, elated or ornery I was feeling until I happened to catch the manner and mood of the dog.

Love, someone said, is the desire for knowledge of another. By this definition, claims that dogs love men are not so maudlin as they sometimes seem. This old red dog knows me in ways and to degrees no other living thing ever has or probably ever will. A dog cannot counsel or argue or criticize. There is no way for him to express such a thing as "You feel bad because you drank too much and are a damn fool. You will not die: you just think you will." There are times when being the object of uncritical love is probably a very bad thing, but also times when it is most pleasurable.

The responsiveness of dogs is not mysterious. The domestic dog is the product of selective breeding, a prime purpose of which has been to produce ever more responsive animals. In part it has been a practical matter. The more sensitive a dog is to man, the easier it will be to teach him to do useful work. However, emotions must have entered in as well. Responsiveness attracts. So it has gone for thousands of generations of dogs.

As with any friends, the more experiences they share the closer man and dog will be. Since Dain was a pup there have been few times and places we could not be together. For the better part of four months when we walked the Appalachian Trail, we were never apart. We drank from the same springs, ate the same food from the same pan, slept in the same place, often close together for warmth. Day after day we saw the same things.

A dog is in some respects the best companion to have in the boondocks—better at finding trails in the dark, keeping varmints out of food sacks, turning up wildlife, than a human companion. Dogs do not complain, rush or delay you or spend hours discussing the merits of health foods. They have their own ways of stimulating, comforting and entertaining. One way has always pleased me. An energetic, confident, curious dog will get up several times during the course of a night and wander off to explore. Lacking the proper sensual equipment, you cannot do what he does, but it is possible to enjoy the night through his senses. By way of example: we bedded down one night 7,000 feet up in the Huachuca Mountains of Arizona in a grove of ponderosa pines. It was cold and the full moon was brilliant. About sundown we had surprised a young mountain lion at a stock tank a quarter of a mile below us. When, after sleeping an hour or so, Dain got up to ramble, I thought about keeping him back. He was a fair hand with bears, coons and woodchucks but inexperienced so far as lions were concerned. He went off up the canyon. By and by he barked in such a way as to indicate he had met up with something moderately formidable, of medium size. It may well have been a ring-tailed cat scurrying in and out of limestone crevices. Whatever it was, he must have soon lost it for I heard nothing more for 15 minutes or so. He must have crossed and descended along the far rim of the canyon for soon he was below our camp, running through the pines with the moonlight glinting off his red coat. He came up and sat down beside me, tongue lolling, tail thumping, grinning as dogs do, telling me as clearly as it can be said that he had had a hell of a fine ramble. I rubbed his ears and told him I was pleased for him.

All canines have well-developed territorial feelings; to a considerable extent what might be called their psychic certainty seems to depend upon their sense of having a homeplace. A dog that has strayed is usually a terrified, confused animal. Possibly because of the nomadic months Dain and I spent in the Appalachians, my person and possessions became his homeplace. Ever since he has held to this notion. So long as we are not far apart he is serenely confident that he is home. This overview has enabled him to retain his cool in many extraordinary places: a jailhouse in New Mexico, a bear hunters' camp in North Carolina where a pen of hounds was howling for his blood, in the midst of a girls' track team, on foreign streets and trails.

A man-dog pair is an intricate craft product that cannot be bought, ordered on demand or mass-produced. Each pair is a unique creation into which has gone time, patience and feeling. But less and less we have the time, patience and feeling for this work. Each year fewer and fewer men and dogs have the opportunity or inclination to walk together for thousands of miles through the mountains, hunt wolves together, go back and forth together between the house, barn, fields and shop.

We go on breeding, buying and keeping dogs for reasons and under conditions that do little justice to either party. We have come to have some 50 million dogs, an inordinate number of which cannot function as evolution intended for them to function and therefore are a kind of aggravation, reproach, even menace, to themselves and to men. Too often we use dogs as keepsakes, to promote nostalgia. We have changed the world, changed ourselves to the point where it and we are not generally fit for a dog. This is not necessarily bad. What is bad is that we cannot face the fact that we and the times have changed so that dogs are becoming obsolete.

This is not a manifesto in support of rural chauvinism. The country is no better, nobler or more truthful place than the city or the suburbs. Rural living does not make or attract more perceptive or kindly people. To decry the passage of the country life-style because it upsets traditional arrangements between dogs and men is as nonsensical as deploring nuclear weapons because they threaten the survival of the whooping crane. Nevertheless the fact remains that the domestic dog is a creature created over a vast span of years principally by and for country men, for country pursuits and pleasures. It is the place where they have scope and range in which to develop.

There is a neighborhood tavern sitting on a northerly hump of the Blue Ridge, where the long chain peters out in southern Pennsylvania. Coming down the ridge one January afternoon we stopped at this place. I took off the pack and laid it against the tavern porch, told Dain to stay with it while I went inside. He curled up, dozed off even though light snowflakes were settling on his coat. Sometime thereafter a man drove up in a truck, parked in front of the tavern and walked up the steps. Being careful not to come uncivilly close, he stopped for a moment to speak to Dain. The dog did not cringe, snarl or quiver with false affection. He raised his head, beat his tail a time or two, answered as politely as he could.

Since there were no other customers, the man, who was the manager of an apple orchard, came over and sat down with me at the bar. He asked me if the dog was mine. I nodded.

"What is he?"

"A collie-shepherd cross."

"That's a good one. You don't get many of those solid red dogs. I like the way he handles himself."

"I've had a lot of them. He's the best I ever had."

"I'd give you a hundred dollars, but I guess you wouldn't want to do that."

"No, you know how it is."

"Sure do, but I tell you what. If you ever get any of his pups let me know. Good dogs aren't easy to find."

A year or so later, Dain braced a Navaho cowpuncher who innocently but unexpectedly tried to walk into the cabin where we were living. So efficiently and calmly did the dog discharge his responsibilities that on the spot the Navaho, pulling off an ornate belt buckle won in a bull riding contest, offered that and again a hundred dollars for the dog.

Neither offer was serious, in the sense that neither man expected to enter into negotiations about the ownership of the red dog. Both were, however, graceful, country-style compliments. They were accepted and are remembered with more pleasure than any ribbon won by the dogs I once showed in a ring.

One night in Arizona events occurred giving me a brief, frightening insight into what Dain might truly be worth to me. We were alone in the cabin where the dog and the Navaho had met. It stands on the side of a large empty canyon that has a very bad rock road winding through. Bad as it is, the road gets a fair amount of nighttime traffic. Dope dealers and therefore narcotics agents are active in these parts. There is an Army post 20 miles away and soldiers, their friends and lovers, occasionally come by simply because it is a lonely place.

This night I was in the cabin working by lantern light on field notes having to do with the behavior of coati mundis. I heard a car below and then voices. Sound travels in this thin air and I heard something about "that light up there." Since it was the only light in the canyon, I assumed my lantern was under discussion. Then there were several gunshots.

There was a rifle in the cabin. We seldom carried guns but this one, ironically, had been brought in the week before to use against a pack of wild dogs running in the canyon that we feared might molest the coatis, whose females were then gravid. I picked up the rifle and went outside with Dain. We walked quietly a little way down the trail, which wound through a dense stand of Emory oak. We could hear voices, then footsteps on the trail below, and saw flashlights. Dain advanced, barking ferociously.

"Get the damn dog," I heard, and then two more shots. Without any reflection, I fired once into the oaks and then began screaming threats of violence.

Thereafter the incident petered out. The voices and sounds retreated, shortly a car door slammed and the car started up. I was left shaky, not so much because of the brush with danger, which probably was minimal, but because of my reaction to it. I was shaking because in the moment of red anger it seemed as if I would have killed another man in defense of a dog. Whether anything is worth that price is an enormous question, but it was the price that for a moment I put on Dain.

As I worked away on the firewood logs, thought about the old red dog, watched him, talked to him as he lay napping in the early winter sun, I reflected on another price that I soon would pay, not ask, for him. One day soon, very likely before the spring comes, in any event before his time and feebleness have become a perpetual humiliation and agony for him, I will kill him. A vet will not do it in a sterile room with a needle. If he can he will follow me and if he cannot I will carry him to a quiet place and I will kill him myself. It will be the last thing we do together and the sobs, the sorrow and loss will be the ultimate price.

Snakes Alive!

BY JEFF MACGREGOR

The annual Rattlesnake Derby in Mangum, Okla., is a lot like a
bass fishing tournament, except you really *don't want to get a bite. What SI*
readers got was a hilarious account of the proceedings—from a safe distance.

YOU CAN TASTE THE MEAN.
 Even when it's battered and seasoned and deep-fried, every rubbery, molar-binding cheekload of barbed rib bones and fast-twitch-muscle meat resists, bites back. This is one oily, ornery little tenderloin. It's an angry flavor, metallic and full of resentment— like having a tiny jailhouse machine shop in your mouth.

Everybody tells you it tastes just like chicken. Maybe, but only if the chicken in question had a neck tattoo, took hostages and died in a police shootout. Rattlesnake. The mutha white meat.

FRIDAY WELCOME, SNAKEHUNTERS! A greeting you might reasonably expect to go your whole life without seeing, is papered all over town. The two-pump gas station/micromart, the motel and the drive-in burger 'n' shake stand all have signs up: COORS LIGHT @$12.99/CASE FOR YOU SNAKE-HUNTERS! and HOWDY! SNAKEHUNTERS! and GOOD LUCK, SNAKE-HUNTER'S! (sic), etc. There's a cockeyed sandwich board hand-lettered red-on-white in front of the barbecue shack too, and big banners draped across the streets, and billboards out along the highway.

The 33rd Annual Mangum Rattlesnake Derby, a celebration of local herpetological superabundance, western diamondback variety, is under way, and

I am circling Mangum, Okla., looking for a place to park. I can't imagine it being much of a problem on any other Friday morning, what with Mangum being plenty small and, like a lot of five-stoplight towns in the rural Southwest, a little down at the boot heels lately. Downtown parking is probably the one thing Mangum has plenty of. Today, though, it's every moderately herpeto-phobic writer for himself. There's no parking anywhere because over the next three days Mangum (pop. 3,200) will entertain 10 times that number of vis-itors. Not counting the snakes. (Although we'll get around to that, too.)

Picture the Rattlesnake Derby as sort of a county fair grafted onto a giant flea market next to a carnival midway, all of it operating contemporaneous to and under the auspices of what amounts to a potentially deadly bass-fishing tour-nament. Like most American regional festivals (honoring cherry/apple/orange blossoms, crawdads or catfish, dairy or spuds, or Ole King Coal) this one at-tracts every mobile vendor in a five-state radius: 80-some-odd booths and motor caravans for corn dogs, funnel cakes, freshly squozen lemonade and various somethings that aren't corn dogs but are still fried up on a stick. More than two-score clattering rockabilly thrill rides and games of hand-eye coor-dination manned by ominously polite carny teens; many hundred wobbly card tables and flapping tarps necessary to house and market the native arts and crafts, solemn velvet portraiture, semismutty novelty T-shirts and dis-count bric-a-brac integral to such a day. Plus a full-sized circus-tented snake pit. At ground zero, across the corner from the ancient and eroding county courthouse, is the main stage, a canopied flatbed trailer, carpeted with As-troTurf, upon which the most important snaky doings will unfold. There is a snake-meat-only restaurant and butcher shop, too. This is an awfully big deal.

Before I left my motel this morning, the TV weatherkid on the station out of nearby Wichita Falls, Texas, said it was going to be a pure-D late April siz-zler today and Saturday. Sunday's a crapshoot. The local forecast calls for po-tent spring thunderstorms by then, a serious threat here in southwestern Ok-lahoma, the business end of Tornado Alley. The prospect of this has my apple-cheeked weatherboy grinning in a happy panic. (None of these guys has been the same since *Twister* premiered.) Now I've got to tote sunscreen, rain gear *and* the tallest, thickest boots I own.

Rooms being impossible to get in Mangum proper during the festivities, I'm billeted two towns over from Snake Central, about 25 miles as the rental car flies. But the drive up is an easy one—feed-calendar pretty farm/ranch country, tall, stark cottonwoods, hawks above the alfalfa, etc.—and gives me plenty of time to nail down my itinerary for the next 72 hours. On the first page of my notebook I write, "Find out how." Next page, "Find out why."

I finally finesse a sweet parking space right behind the American Legion

Hall, just yards from the flatbed stage. Even this early it's hot as a blacksmith's belt buckle. The media credentialing process is quick, though. I leave a note on the dashboard that reads SPORTS ILLUSTRATED PRESS CAR so maybe I won't get towed.

Trying to muscle my car door closed against the breeze, I realize that Rodgers and Hammerstein were mostly mum about the genuine Oklahoma wind. It surely does come right behind the rain, but it also precedes and accompanies it. It's the OK State mantra, a white-noise constant that blows grit up your skirt at 10 or 20 or 30 mph all day, every day.

Through that wind just now I hear the frantic, countertenor shouting that we he-men usually reserve for imminent forklift tip-overs or industrial-solvent accidents. The bottom, I see, has fallen out of a packing crate a couple of guys were unloading at the foot of the stage. I can't make out the words, but a few early gawkers nearby are now moving very purposefully away from the truck. Very purposefully. It takes a few seconds to register that the crate is, or rather was, full of live rattlesnakes. Now they're all over the street. Seventy or 80 of them. Snakes. One poor guy seems suspended in flight, pedaling midair for all he's worth like a cartoon half-wit. That would be me. The ensuing 30 seconds answer my first question re snake hunting, though. Under the word *How* on page 1 of my notebook, I write: "A) Find a snake; B) Pick it up fast with a stick." I'm sure there's more to it than this, but it's hard to write when you're leaning into a hard wind while standing on the hood of your car.

Let me take this moment, while the Derby organizers and city fathers try to talk me down, to explain how the competitive part of the weekend works. It's like a bass-fishing tournament in that there are cash awards for the hunters who bring in, alive, the longest snake and the most snakes and the most (ugh) pounds of snakes. These hunters are mostly semipro types who've been stalking the wily serpent daily since the Oklahoma snake season opened back in early March. That's the best time for 'em, I'm told, because, having just come out of hibernation, they're apt to be out on the rocks in front of the den, lying on their bellies, taking their ease in the warming sun (the snakes, not the hunters).

The best of the best hunters nab rattlesnakes by the hundredweight during these few weeks, box them up with a pan of water in the barn or the basement and then load 'em into their trunk and drive into town for the Derby. There are no time or geographic limits for snake-taking. A few of the most serious hunters, the real Ahabs, will range as far south as Mexico, where the longer "growing season" can produce blue-ribbon rattlers the size of NBA power forwards. There's also a tournament within the tournament: Weekend hunters, mostly tourists and day-trippers, compete for daily awards. (Consensus among the experts is that it'll be slim pickin's this weekend because it's hotter 'n refried hell out here, so the snakes might all be hiding in their dens. This strikes me as a very good thing, but I make a sad face anyhow when I receive the news.)

All of which begs question number 2: Why? A pocket poll of the crowd coaxing me off the hood of my rental car reveals little: Hale fellowship, good exercise, communion with the out-of-doors, thrill of the pursuit, fresh air, etc. Most of which can be had lawn bowling or quail hunting or shopping the sidewalk liquidation sale, but with a greatly reduced chance of being bitten co- matose by a pit viper. A red-bearded bear of a man with a baby-sweet smile and hands the size of smoked hams pipes up with the first answer that makes real sense. Ernie Adams has been snake hunting around here off and on for more than 20 years. Why? "Cuz I don't like 'em in the house."

Funny as that is, it's also a tidy summation of the complex chain of links between local economies and ecosystems. When subsistence farmers started pulling out of here in the '30s (see Depression, the Great), the homes, barns, sheds and untended land they left behind provided a housing boom for the ro- dents upon which rattlesnakes feed. With fewer folks to keep either in check, both populations grew explosively. Furry Stuart Little in the pantry is one thing, but a poisonous snake in the cupboard is another, and by the early '60s Mangum residents saw an opportunity to formalize what they were already spending a lot of time doing freelance: hunting snakes to keep them from showing up in the feed bin or under the porch glider or in the kids' sandbox.

The just-dropped and jaywalking snakes have been corralled by now, round- ed up by the hunters who brought them in and the staff of wranglers who man the stage all weekend for the weigh-ins and flashy/spooky snake-handling demos. Jes' a little hitch in the morning's gitalong, I'm assured as I step gin- gerly to the ground, but the phrase "I *think* we got 'em all" becomes a real knee-slapper for the next few hours.

In any case, it's time for me to go snake hunting with the governors' wives. (I told you this was a big deal.) We meet up at Mexicali's Restaurant on the main drag outside town. Over the devil's own platter of glowing, 500-rad que- sadillas I'm introduced to Cathy Keating, first lady of Oklahoma, and Janet Huckabee, first lady of next-door neighbor Arkansas. Pleasantries and chunky green salsa are exchanged.

Cathy is a small, pretty brunette, sharp and funny, dressed in a Governor's Wife Casual Day outfit that includes just enough Chanel to remind you who you're out there snake hunting with. Janet is wearing jeans and a polo shirt ("It's what we used to wear when we did this back home") and has about her the gracious, good-humored hoot and holler of a gal-buddy you'd like to spend the day yakking with in a duck blind.

The two women are clearly old friends, cracking wise with each other at lunch, laughing it up while responding gaily to the many civilian heys and howdies. The only metaphorical clouds on the figurative horizon come from the bruisers on their security team, whose furrowed and darkling brows might be read as an absence of enthusiasm for the afternoon's snaky high jinks. Still, the bodyguards have guns with them, something I find profoundly reassuring.

On the way out the door to the snaking grounds, I ask Wesley Webb, Mangum's district chief for the Department of Wildlife Conservation and swami-guide for our group, if he has any last-minute tips on hunting snakes with the first spouses. "Just watch where you put your hands," he says. Excellent advice in any number of contexts.

A couple of miles out on the prairie, in a collapsed formation of chalk-soft rock known locally as gypsink (see gypsum, nicknames for), Wes uses a snake catcher (a tonging device similar to what the grocer uses in Manhattan to get cans of pricey coffee down off the highest antitheft shelf) to snare our first diamondback. He is a little shaver, maybe eighteen inches of hiss and vinegar. Still, the first ladies and I all jump when ol' Wes brandishes him comically at us from about 10 feet away. Janet and Cathy have the better vertical leap; having practiced, I have the superior hang time.

Genial adaptability being part of their job description, the F.L.'s are soon hunting happily away under close official supervision and a brutal afternoon sun. From a distance, snake hunting looks just like golf; people repeatedly poking at the grass with sticks, moving slowly across the landscape in a reverential quiet broken only by suggestions shouted from those nearby as to how one might poke at the grass more successfully. Not much appeal for spectators.

The western diamondback rattlesnake (*Crotalus atrox*) ranges throughout the desert and semiarid Southwestern U.S. It's a pit viper; pit referring to the nifty prey-targeting heat-seeker apparatus dimpled into its ugly mug just behind the nostrils. Deaf as a retired roadie (no ears), it can't hear its own rattle. It can grow to seven feet in length, attaining the diameter of a salad plate. That big, it'll have a head the size and shape of an antique flatiron, fangs like 10-gauge drapery hooks and a brain the size of a proton. Rattlesnakes are cold-blooded but not murderous, and they prefer the stealthy escape to the lethal confrontation—unless they're peckish and you're a hamster. Stand real still when you meet one and it'll slither off, thinking you're just a rock or at least a thing too large to eat. Of course, if you surprise one by stepping on it, sitting on it (heard this several times; still not over it) or putting your hands where they don't belong (i.e., under rocks, into holes . . .), you're likely to end up snakebit and off to the hospital, there to experience the complex multisymptomatic wonders of a venom that works at once as a neurotoxin, cytotoxin, hemorrhagic agent and digestive acid. Meaning you'll most likely suffer some pain, swelling, pain, pain, discoloration, pain, bleeding, pain, blistering, nausea, pain, light-headedness, pain and further, persistent acute pain. Statistically speaking, you probably won't die—you'll just want to.

I'm troweling on my sixth coat of sunblock when Cathy K. yelps a well-mannered scream from some nearby rocks. She and Janet have got one cornered. "Grab it right behind the first bend with the catcher," Wes offers. "You don't want to break its neck." The first ladies carefully obey and soon stand triumphant in the howling wind, a bigger-than-average rattler held squirming at twice arm's length. A beat passes. Two. Then Janet gives voice to the question on everyone's mind. "Now what?"

Exactly.

"What" turns out to be a trip back into Mangum with the catch of the day in a locked bucket, there to be weighed and measured for posterity. At 52 inches it is, in fact, Friday's longest snake. Things get extra weird when we all troop over to the butcher shop to learn what becomes of the rattlesnakes rounded up during the Derby. In a stifling garage of a room behind the vacant-storefront Bite-A-Snake restaurant, they've set up bleachers to face a stainless-steel counter behind which is a chopping block and a prefab fiberglass shower stall. Snakes are a cash crop hereabouts—meat (for eatin'), skin (for boots), rattles (for key chains), gallbladders (for amorous Asians), etc., all have their market price, and proceeds are plowed back into the community by the Derby organizers—and the reduction of rattlers to their salable parts is no more or less disturbing to most local viewers than the dismantling necessary to furnish you your osso buco or lemon-roasted chicken.

There's a strange Vegas-lounge-act, Shirley-Jackson-short-story vibe to the whole thing, though, especially when Robert Ray, the Butcher (sporting a tattoo indicating same), smiles and says "Showtime!" right before the ax comes down. The vivid gutting-the-snake-while-it-hangs-in-the-shower process takes on a *Scream3* quality when the first ladies start pitching in. I make my exit when the headless, skinless, innardsless snake carcasses on the counter begin flopping and coiling and generally behaving as though nothing untoward has happened to them in the last 10 minutes. As I'm leaving, I hear the first lady of Arkansas behind me asking the Butcher a question. "Now what?" she says.

Exactly.

There's one more chore I have left to do before I can drag ass back to my motel. I head up the street, tired and sunburned but resigned to my sacred duty as a journalist. I take a table under a fluorescent fixture that buzzes like a tequila hangover, spread a napkin on my lap and, so you won't have to, I eat Southern-fried rattlesnake.

I spend the night dreaming I'm tangled in a closet full of venomous neckties.

SATURDAY. It is way hotter than yesterday. Whole families cower behind fat relatives just for the shade. You could fry a snake on the sidewalk, but it wouldn't taste any better. By noon the crowd is double what it was the day before—there are snake lovers and snake haters here, dudes and thimbleriggers and solid citizens, plowboys and cowboys, big boys and ol' boys (good and bad), biker boys with biker babes, blue-eyed stalwart sweethearts of the rodeo, wranglers and ranch hands and punks and convicts, even some high-mileage motor-coach couples down from Wisconsin. I'm told that somewhere out in the tall grass are first ladies from two of the 50 United States, hunting snakes with the governor of Oklahoma just for the fun of it.

Freud would have gotten a charge out of the knots of 14-year-old girls gathered bug-eyed around the snake pens in front of the main stage. Behind the doubled chicken wire, maybe 500 phallic symbols are rattling and hissing and starting to stink in the sun. "*Eeeeeuw*" is the favored comment. The boys watch the girls watch the snakes.

The big news today is that Cody Easley got bit in the snake pit tent while I was out on safari with the first ladies. The premise of the pit is that you pay a buck to stand around a plexiglass pen about four feet high by 20 feet long by 15 feet wide to see what nearly a thousand rattlesnakes look like when piled two feet deep. There are men (Cody's one of them) who are paid to stand in there with the snakes and explain their habits and so forth while not fainting from the fear or the 120 degree heat. Cody's dad, Rusty, a Richard Boone look-alike and professional snake handler who carries a picture in his wallet of his own "snakebit, swole-up-like-a-kid's-balloon hand" from a while back, tells me his son will be O.K. "He wanted to get out of snake handling about two hours into the pain," Rusty says. "But then this morning he told me he wants to come back. I wish he wouldn't. It's too dangerous." Having so said, Rusty heads back to work in the sweltering tent.

This afternoon, they crowned the 1998 Derby Princess (originally and more euphoniously known as Miss Fang). Her name is Jennifer Ward, a charming, A student high school senior. She receives a sash, a tiara, a plaque and a $400 scholarship to Western Oklahoma State College down in Altus.

Overheard Quotes of the Day: 1) "I can't get the venom off this lens." 2) "Women are attracted to the so-called manly arts. That's probably why I'm divorced right now." 3) "We've never lost anybody dead, far as I know." 4) "Why would I *eat* it? It's a *snake*." 5) "Is there a pet shop around here?"

Best Novelty Dessert Name That Would Also Work for the Middle Act at a Drag Club: Strawberry New Orleans.

No-Surprise File: The kids' petting zoo closed today. No takers.

Cody Easley is propped up in bed watching TV when I visit him. The doctors have had him on morphine since yesterday—this snake's venom wasn't very hot, very toxic; maybe a 5 on a scale of 1 to 10. The doctor told Cody he was lucky because the snake got only one fang into his leg, on the shin. It fanged Cody above the boot. His left leg is the size of a railroad tie. The blister on his shin looks like a plum, and his foot's the size and shape of a catcher's mitt. (When the snake bit him, he was in the middle of a television news interview.) "The pain was pretty incredible. It just throbs mostly now," he says, dreamylike. I ask Cody how he feels about going back to work. "It sure makes you think."

Exactly.

The Derby dance that evening in the livestock show barn on Mangum's tattered outskirts draws more than 900 paying two-steppers and boot scooters. None seem to mind the skull-liquefying acoustics of a band playing under a galvanized tin ceiling. Dancing happens and dripping cans of cold beer are passed from hand to hand. It's too loud to talk. Couples wander in and out of the light by the entrance, headed for the parking lot. Music pours out onto the empty prairie. The sky is black and soft as jeweler's velvet, the stars wheel slow in their course, and a warm wind confuses the grass. Nobody says a word about snakes.

SUNDAY. Rain squalls, a ransacking wind, and it's 40 degrees colder than it was 12 hours ago. By the time I get to Mangum some of the vendors are already striking their tents. The schedule for the day's events is being rejiggered, and not many visitors have shown up yet. The snakes in the pens out front of the main stage are listless in the cold, piled elaborately on top of one another. Imagine Medusa on prom night, and you'll see it.

Notes Made in the Rain: The snake has been a powerful, contrary presence in myth and history from the beginning of time, the good/evil ur-symbol of original sin or of infinite, skin-shedding reinvention and regeneration. We loathe its beauty and perfect efficiency yet can't make ourselves turn away. Still, the storied duality of the serpent in ancient mystery cults isn't something anybody in Mangum thinks about every day. Staying afloat in hard financial times is, however, and it's ironic that the much-reviled western diamondback rattlesnake is now an economic agent in the town's struggle to recover.

The environmental effects of the Derby are a topic of conflict too. Only lately was a study begun to determine its impact on the snake population. Argument runs hot on both sides; the enviros (or bunny huggers, in the local patois) say that too much pressure on the snakes will destroy an important link in the food chain, starving the eagles and hawks and owls that feed on them. Rats and mice will run rampant. Hunters and Derby boosters counter by positing snakes as a renewable long-term resource thanks to liability-conscious ranchers who have closed their land to hunting, thereby offering de facto protection and preservation. Lots of opinions, very few facts.

The day is low and gray, and the awards ceremony is sparsely attended. Everyone is tired and puffy from staying too long at the dance. It's something to see these guys stretch a snake to measure it, though. It takes the well-coordinated effort of seven very serious snake handlers to position each entry in a V-shaped, indexed trough and hold it long enough to shout out the dimensions. They do 10 triple-XL snakes this way looking for a winner, and their concentration exhausts you just watching. Nobody wants the bed next to Cody Easley's.

The Derby's longest snake is 78 inches, hauled in by John Townsend of Muldrow, Okla. Melvin Ishcomer, the Mark McGwire of snake hunting the past few seasons, wins for most snakes and most (ugh) pounds of snakes, 706 and 775, respectively. Melvin is from Eldorado, Okla., just down the road. It's something like his sixth year in Victory Lane. He wins $150 in prize money and will earn $3 a pound when the Derby buys his snakes to process. Interviewed, he uses the lazy-intense language of the sports star and sounds like John Elway post-Super Bowl. "You just have to get out there every day," he says, "and work at it." His advice to young snake hunters: "Whatever you do, don't get bit."

What I'm thinking while he talks: You *drove* here with 700 snakes in your car?

Photo op of the Day: Derby Princess Jennifer Ward has the Longest Snake of the Tournament draped over her shoulders like a stole for some pictures for the local paper. She doesn't get all that loot and attention for doing nothing, apparently. She stands very still. There are several snake handlers gripping Mr. Big as hard as they can so he doesn't move. Teeth are gritted into smiles, and veins bulge. The wind blows. Directly behind Princess Jennifer, crouched just out of the photo, is another snake handler with his hands at her hips. He's poised there to push her off the stage if the snake gets loose. She stands very still. Click. Click. Click. They take the pictures. The snake is taken off her shoulders and put it in a box. People shake hands and laugh and slap each other on the back. In the center of the stage, Jennifer Ward stands very still.

With the twilight gathering late Sunday afternoon, I get the Last, Best Answer to question number 2. It comes from Tony Patterson, 9½-year-old veteran snake hunter, who is standing with his dad on the corner, watching the men dismantle the main stage in the rain. For some reason I'm very sad all of a sudden. Rain patters off my tape recorder. I ask Tony why he enjoys snake hunting. He looks down at the sidewalk. "I don't know," he says. He looks back up at me and narrows his eyes, thinking. "Because it's fun?"

Pure Heart

BY WILLIAM NACK

When Secretariat died in 1989, the man who literally wrote the book on Big Red relived for SI readers the greatest ride of his life: his days covering history's most extraordinary equine athlete.

J UST BEFORE NOON THE HORSE WAS LED HALTINGLY INTO A VAN next to the stallion barn, and there a concentrated barbiturate was injected into his jugular. Forty-five seconds later there was a crash as the stallion collapsed. His body was trucked immediately to Lexington, Ky., where Dr. Thomas Swerczek, a professor of veterinary science at the University of Kentucky, performed the necropsy. All of the horse's vital organs were normal in size except for the heart. "We were all shocked," Swerczek said. "I've seen and done thousands of autopsies on horses, and nothing I'd ever seen compared to it. The heart of the average horse weighs about nine pounds. This was almost twice the average size, and a third larger than any equine heart I'd ever seen. And it wasn't pathologically enlarged. All the chambers and the valves were normal. It was just larger. I think it told us why he was able to do what he did."

IN THE LATE afternoon of Monday, Oct. 2, 1989, as I headed my car from the driveway of Arthur Hancock's Stone Farm onto Winchester Road outside Paris, Ky., I was seized by an impulse as beckoning as the wind that strums through the trees down there, mingling the scents of new grass and old history.

For reasons as obscure to me then as now, I felt compelled to see Lawrence Robinson. For almost 30 years, until he suffered a stroke in March 1983, Robinson was the head caretaker of stallions at Claiborne Farm. I had not seen him since his illness, but I knew he still lived on the farm, in a small white frame house set on a hill overlooking the lush stallion paddocks and the main stallion barn. In the first stall of that barn, in the same place that was once home to the great Bold Ruler, lived Secretariat, Bold Ruler's greatest son.

It was through Secretariat that I had met Robinson. On the bright, cold afternoon of Nov. 12, 1973, Robinson was one of several hundred people gathered at Blue Grass Airport in Lexington to greet Secretariat after his flight from New York into retirement in Kentucky. I flew with the horse that day, and as the plane banked over the field, a voice from the tower crackled over the airplane radio: "There's more people out here to meet Secretariat than there was to greet the governor."

"Well, he's won more races than the governor," pilot Dan Neff replied.

An hour later, after a van ride out the Paris Pike behind a police escort with blue lights flashing, Robinson led Secretariat onto a ramp at Claiborne and toward his sire's old stall—out of racing and into history. For me, that final walk beneath a grove of trees, with the colt slanting like a buck through the autumn gloaming, brought to a melancholy close the richest, grandest, damnedest, most exhilarating time of my life. For eight months, first as the racing writer for *Newsday* of Long Island, N.Y., and then as the designated chronicler of Secretariat's career, I had a daily front-row seat to watch the colt. I was at the barn in the morning and the racetrack in the afternoon for what turned out to be the year's greatest show in sports, at the heart of which lay a Triple Crown performance unmatched in the history of American racing.

Sixteen years had come and gone since then, and I had never attended a Kentucky Derby or a yearling sale at Keeneland without driving out to Claiborne to visit Secretariat, often in the company of friends who had never seen him. On the long ride from Louisville, I would regale my friends with stories about the horse—how on that early morning in March '73 he had materialized out of the quickening blue darkness in the upper stretch at Belmont Park, his ears pinned back, running as fast as horses run; how he had lost the Wood Memorial and won the Derby, and how he had been bothered by a pigeon feather at Pimlico on the eve of the Preakness (at the end of this tale I would pluck the delicate, mashed feather out of my wallet, like a picture of my kids, to pass around the car); how on the morning of the Belmont Stakes he had burst from the barn like a stud horse going to the breeding shed and had walked around the outdoor ring on his hind legs, pawing at the sky; how he had once grabbed my notebook and refused to give it back, and how he had seized a rake in his teeth and begun raking the shed; and, finally, I told about that magical, unforgettable instant, frozen now in time, when he turned for home, appearing out of a dark drizzle at Woodbine, near Toronto, in the last race of his career, 12 lengths in front and steam puffing from his nostrils as from a factory whistle, bounding like some mythical beast of Greek lore.

Oh, I knew all the stories, knew them well, had crushed and rolled them in my hand until their quaint musk lay in the saddle of my palm. Knew them as I knew the stories of my children. Knew them as I knew the stories of my own life. Told them at dinner parties, swapped them with horseplayers as if they were trading cards, argued over them with old men and blind fools who had seen the show but missed the message. Dreamed them and turned them over like pillows in my rubbery sleep. Woke up with them, brushed my aging teeth with them, grinned at them in the mirror. Horses have a way of getting inside you, and so it was that Secretariat became like a fifth child in our house, the older boy who was off at school and never around but who was as loved and true a part of the family as Muffin, our shaggy, epileptic dog.

The story I now tell begins on that Monday afternoon last October on the macadam outside Stone Farm. I had never been to Paris, Ky., in the early fall, and I only happened to be there that day to begin an article about the Hancock family, the owners of Claiborne and Stone farms. There wasn't a soul on the road to point the way to Robinson's place, so I swung in and out of several empty driveways until I saw a man on a tractor cutting the lawn in front of Marchmont, Dell Hancock's mansion. He yelled back to me: "Take a right out the drive. Go down to Claiborne House. Then a right at the driveway across the road. Go up a hill to the big black barn. Turn left and go down to the end. Lawrence had a stroke a few years back, y'know."

The house was right where he said. I knocked on the front door, then walked behind and knocked on the back and called through a side window into a room where music was playing. No one answered. But I had time to kill, so I wandered over to the stallion paddock, just a few yards from the house. The stud Ogygian, a son of Damascus, lifted his head inquiringly. He started walking toward me, and I put my elbows on the top of the fence and looked down the gentle slope toward the stallion barn.

And suddenly there he was, Secretariat, standing outside the barn and grazing at the end of a lead shank held by groom Bobby Anderson, who was sitting on a bucket in the sun. Even from a hundred yards away, the horse appeared lighter than I had seen him in years. It struck me as curious that he was not running free in his paddock—why was Bobby grazing him?—but his bronze coat reflected the October light, and it never occurred to me that something might be wrong. But something was terribly wrong. On Labor Day, Secretariat had come down with laminitis, a life-threatening hoof disease, and here, a month later, he was still suffering from its aftershocks.

Secretariat was dying. In fact, he would be gone within 48 hours.

I briefly considered slipping around Ogygian's paddock and dropping down to visit, but I had never entered Claiborne through the backdoor, so I thought better of it. Instead, for a full half hour, I stood by the paddock waiting for Robinson and gazing at Secretariat. The gift of reverie is a blessing divine, and it is conferred most abundantly on those who lie in hammocks or drive alone in cars. Or lean on hillside fences in Kentucky. The mind swims, binding itself to whatever flotsam comes along, to old driftwood faces and voices of the past, to places and scenes once visited, to things not seen or done but only dreamed.

IT WAS July 4, 1972, and I was sitting in the press box at Aqueduct with Clem Florio, a former prizefighter turned Baltimore handicapper, when I glanced at the *Daily Racing Form*'s past performances for the second race, a 5½-furlong buzz for maiden 2-year-olds. As I scanned the pedigrees, three names leaped out: by Bold Ruler–Somethingroyal, by Princequillo. Bold Ruler was the nation's preeminent sire, and Somethingroyal was the dam of several stakes winners, including the fleet Sir Gaylord. It was a match of royalty. Even the baby's name seemed faintly familiar: Secretariat. Where had I heard it before? But of course! Lucien Laurin was training the colt at Belmont Park for Penny Chenery Tweedy's Meadow Stable, making Secretariat a stablemate of that year's Kentucky Derby and Belmont Stakes winner, Riva Ridge.

I had seen Secretariat just a week before. I had been at the Meadow Stable barn one morning, checking on Riva Ridge, when exercise rider Jimmy Gaffney took me aside and said, "You wanna see the best-lookin' 2-year-old you've ever seen?"

We padded up the shed to the colt's stall. Gaffney stepped inside. "What do you think?" he asked. The horse looked magnificent, to be sure, a bright red chestnut with three white feet and a tapered white marking down his face. "He's gettin' ready," Gaffney said. "Don't forget the name: Secretariat. He can run." And then, conspiratorially, Gaffney whispered, "Don't quote me, but this horse will make them all forget Riva Ridge."

So that is where I had first seen him, and here he was in the second at Aqueduct. I rarely bet in those days, but Secretariat was 3–1, so I put $10 on his nose. Florio and I fixed our binoculars on him and watched it all. Watched him as he was shoved sideways at the break, dropping almost to his knees, when a colt named Quebec turned left out of the gate and crashed into him. Saw him blocked in traffic down the back side and shut off again on the turn for home. Saw him cut off a second time deep in the stretch as he was making a final run. Saw him finish fourth, obviously much the best horse, beaten by only 1¼ lengths after really running but an eighth of a mile.

You should have seen Clem. Smashing his binoculars down on his desk, he leaped to his feet, banged his chair against the wall behind him, threw a few punches in the air and bellowed, "Secretariat! That's my Derby horse for next year!"

Two weeks later, when the colt raced to his first victory by six, Florio announced to all the world, "Secretariat will win the Triple Crown next year." He nearly got into a fistfight in the Aqueduct press box that day when Mannie Kalish, a New York handicapper, chided him for making such an outrageously bold assertion: "Ah, you Maryland guys, you come to New York and see a horse break his maiden and think he's another Citation. We see horses like Secretariat all the time. I bet he don't even run in the Derby." Stung by the put-down "you Maryland guys," Florio came forward and stuck his finger into Kalish's chest, but two writers jumped between them, and they never came to blows.

The Secretariat phenomenon, with all the theater and passion that would attend it, had begun. Florio was right, of course, and by the end of Secretariat's 2-year-old season, everyone else who had seen him perform knew it. All you had to do was watch the Hopeful Stakes at Saratoga. I was at the races that August afternoon with Arthur Kennedy, an old-time racetracker and handicapper who had been around the horses since the 1920s, and even he had never seen anything quite like it. Dropping back to dead last out of the gate, Secretariat trailed eight horses into the far turn, where jockey Ron Turcotte swung him to the outside. Three jumps past the half-mile pole the colt exploded. "Now he's runnin'!" Kennedy said.

You could see the blue-and-white silks as they disappeared behind one horse, reappeared in a gap between horses, dropped out of sight again and finally reemerged as Secretariat powered to the lead off the turn. He dashed from last to first in 290 yards, blazing through a quarter in :22, and galloped home in a laugher to win by six. It was a performance with style, touched by art. "I've never seen a do that," Kennedy said quietly. "He looked like a 4-year-old out there."

So that was when I knew. The rest of Secretariat's 2-year-old campaign—in which he lost only once, in the Champagne Stakes, when he was disqualified from first to second after bumping Stop the Music at the top of the stretch— was simply a mopping-up operation. At year's end, so dominant had he been that he became the first 2-year-old to be unanimously voted Horse of the Year.

Secretariat wintered at Hialeah, preparing for the Triple Crown, while I shoveled snow in Huntington, N.Y., waiting for him to race again. In February, 23-year-old Seth Hancock, the new president of Claiborne Farm, announced that he had syndicated the colt as a future breeding stallion for $6.08 million, then a world record, in 32 shares at $190,000 a share, making the 1,154-pound horse worth more than three times his weight in gold. (Bullion was selling at the time for $90 an ounce.) Like everyone else, I thought Secretariat would surely begin his campaign in Florida, and I did not expect to see him again until the week before the Kentucky Derby. I was browsing through a newspaper over breakfast one day when I saw a news dispatch whose message went through me like a current. Secretariat would be arriving soon to begin his Triple Crown campaign by way of the three New York prep races: the Bay Shore, the Gotham and the Wood Memorial Stakes.

"Hot damn!" I blurted to my family. "Secretariat is coming to New York!"

At the time I had in mind doing a diary about the horse, a chronicle of the adventures of a Triple Crown contender, which I thought might one day make a magazine piece. The colt arrived at Belmont Park on March 10, and the next day I was there at 7 a.m., scribbling notes in a pad. For the next 40 days, in what became a routine, I would fall out of bed at 6 a.m., make a cup of instant coffee, climb into my rattling green Toyota and drive the 20 miles to Belmont Park. I had gotten to know the Meadow Stable family—Tweedy, Laurin, Gaffney, groom Eddie Sweat, assistant trainer Henny Hoeffner—in my tracking of Riva Ridge the year before, and I had come to feel at home around Belmont's Barn 5, particularly around stall 7, Secretariat's place. I took no days off, except one morning to hide Easter eggs, and I spent hours sitting on the dusty floor outside Secretariat's stall, talking to Sweat as he turned a rub rag on the colt, filled his water bucket, bedded his stall with straw, kept him in hay and oats. I took notes compulsively, endlessly, feeling for the texture of the life around the horse.

A typical page of scribblings went like this: "Sweat talks to colt . . . easy, Red, I'm comin' in here now . . . stop it, Red! You behave now. . . . Sweat moves around colt. Brush in hand. Flicks off dust. Secretariat sidesteps and pushes Sweat. Blue Sky. Henny comes up, 'How's he doin', Eddie?' 'He's gettin' edgy'. . . . Easy Sunday morning."

Secretariat was an amiable, gentlemanly colt, with a poised and playful nature that at times made him seem as much a pet as the stable dog was. I was standing in front of his stall one morning, writing, when he reached out, grabbed my notebook in his teeth and sank back inside, looking to see what I would do. "Give the man his notebook back!" yelled Sweat. As the groom dipped under the webbing, Secretariat dropped the notebook on the bed of straw.

Another time, after raking the shed, Sweat leaned the handle of the rake against the stall webbing and turned to walk away. Secretariat seized the handle in his mouth and began pushing and pulling it across the floor. "Look at him rakin' the shed!" cried Sweat. All up and down the barn, laughter fluttered like the pigeons in the stable eaves as the colt did a passable imitation of his own groom.

By his personality and temperament, Secretariat became the most engaging character in the barn. His own stable pony, a roan named Billy Silver, began an unrequited love affair with him. "He loves Secretariat, but Secretariat don't pay any attention to him," Sweat said one day. "If Billy sees you grazin' Secretariat, he'll go to hollerin' until you bring him out. Secretariat just ignores him. Kind of sad, really." One morning, I was walking beside Hoeffner through the shed, with Gaffney and Secretariat ahead of us, when Billy stuck his head out of his jerry-built stall and nuzzled the colt as he went by. Hoeffner did a double take. "Jimmy!" he yelled. "Is that pony botherin' the big horse?"

"Nah," said Jimmy. "He's just smellin' him a little."

Hoeffner's eyes widened. Spinning around on his heels, jabbing a finger in the air, he bellowed, "Get the pony out of here! I don't want him smellin' the big horse."

Leaning on his rake, Sweat laughed softly and said, "Poor Billy Silver. He smelled the wrong horse!"

I remember wishing that those days could breeze on forever—the mornings over coffee and doughnuts at the truck outside the barn, the hours spent watching the red colt walk to the track and gallop once around, the days absorbing the rhythms of the life around the horse. I had been following racehorses since I was 12, back in the days of Native Dancer, and now I was an observer on an odyssey, a quest for the Triple Crown. It had been 25 years since Citation had won racing's Holy Grail. But for me the adventure really began in the early morning of March 14, when Laurin lifted Turcotte aboard Secretariat and said, "Let him roll, Ronnie."

The colt had filled out substantially since I had last seen him under tack, in the fall, and he looked like some medieval charger—his thick neck bowed and his chin drawn up beneath its mass, his huge shoulders shifting as he strode, his coat radiant and his eyes darting left and right. He was walking to the track for his final workout, a three-eighths-of-a-mile drill designed to light the fire in him for the seven-furlong Bay Shore Stakes three days later. Laurin, Tweedy and I went to the clubhouse fence near the finish line, where we watched and waited as Turcotte headed toward the pole and let Secretariat rip. Laurin clicked his stopwatch.

The colt was all by himself through the lane, and the sight and sound of him racing toward us is etched forever in memory: Turcotte was bent over him, his jacket blown up like a parachute, and the horse was reaching out with his forelegs in that distinctive way he had, raising them high and then, at the top of the lift, snapping them out straight and with tremendous force, the snapping hard as bone, the hooves striking the ground and folding it beneath him. Laurin clicked his watch as Secretariat raced under the wire. "Oh, my god!" he cried. *"Thirty-three and three fifths!"* Horses rarely break 34 seconds in three-furlong moves.

Looking ashen, fearing the colt might have gone too fast, Laurin headed for the telephone under the clubhouse to call the upstairs clocker, Jules Watson: "Hello there, Jules. How fast did you get him?"

I watched Laurin's face grow longer as he listened, until he looked thunderstruck: "Thirty-two and three fifths?" A full second faster than Laurin's own clocking, it was the fastest three-furlong workout I had ever heard of. Tweedy smiled cheerily and said, "Well, that ought to open his pipes!"

Oh, it did that. Three days later, blocked by a wall of horses in the Bay Shore, Secretariat plunged through like a fullback, 220 yards from the wire, and bounded off to win the race by 4½ lengths. I could hear a man screaming behind me. I turned and saw Roger Laurin, Lucien's son, raising his arms in the air and shouting, "He's too much horse! They can't stop him. They can't even stop him with a wall of horses!"

I had ridden horses during my youth in Morton Grove, Ill., and I remember one summer I took a little black bullet of a thoroughbred filly out of the barn and walked her to the track that rimmed the polo field across Golf Road. I had been to the races a few times, had seen the jockeys ride, and I wanted to feel what it was like. So I hitched up my stirrups and galloped her around the east turn, standing straight up. Coming off the turn, I dropped into a crouch and clucked to her. She took off like a sprinter leaving the blocks—*swoooosh!*—and the wind started whipping in my eyes. I could feel the tears streaming down my face, and then I looked down and saw her knees pumping like pistons. I didn't think she would make the second turn, the woods were looming ahead, big trees coming up, and so I leaned a little to the left, and she made the turn before she started pulling up. No car ever took me on a ride like that. And no roller coaster, either. Running loose, without rails, she gave me the wildest, most thrilling ride I had ever had.

But that was nothing like the ride Secretariat gave me in the 12 weeks from the Bay Shore through the Belmont Stakes. Three weeks after the Bay Shore, Turcotte sent the colt to the lead down the backstretch in the one-mile Gotham. It looked like they were going to get beat when Champagne Charlie drove to within a half length at the top of the stretch—I held my breath—but Turcotte sent Secretariat on, and the colt pulled away to win by three, tying the track record of 1:33⅖.

By then I had begun visiting Charles Hatton, a columnist for the *Daily Racing Form* who the previous summer had proclaimed Secretariat the finest physical specimen he had ever seen. At 67, Hatton had seen them all. After my morning work was over, I would trudge up to Hatton's private aerie at Belmont Park and tell him what I had learned. I was his backstretch eyes, he my personal guru. One morning Hatton told me that Secretariat had galloped a quarter mile past the finish line at the Gotham, and the clockers had timed him pulling up at 1:59⅖, three fifths of a second faster than Northern Dancer's Kentucky Derby record for 1¼ miles.

"This sucker breaks records pulling up," Hatton said. "He might be the best racehorse I ever saw. Better than Man o' War."

Those were giddy, heady days coming to the nine-furlong Wood Memorial, the colt's last major prep before the Kentucky Derby. On the day of the Wood, I drove directly to Aqueduct and spent the hour before the race in the receiving barn with Sweat, exercise rider Charlie Davis and Secretariat. When the voice over the loudspeaker asked the grooms to ready their horses, Sweat approached the colt with the bridle. Secretariat always took the bit easily, opening his mouth when Sweat moved to fit it in, but that afternoon it took Sweat a full five minutes to bridle him. Secretariat threw his nose in the air, backed up, shook his head. After a few minutes passed, I asked, "What's wrong with him, Eddie?"

Sweat brushed it off: "He's just edgy."

In fact, just that morning, Dr. Manuel Gilman, the track veterinarian, had lifted the colt's upper lip to check his identity tattoo and had discovered a painful abscess about the size of a quarter. Laurin decided to run Secretariat anyway—the colt needed the race—but he never told anyone else about the boil. Worse than the abscess, though, was the fact that Secretariat had had the feeblest workout of his career four days earlier when Turcotte, seeing a riderless horse on the track, had slowed the colt to protect him from a collision. Secretariat finished the mile that day in 1:42⅘, five seconds slower than Laurin wanted him to go. Thus he came to the Wood doubly compromised.

The race was a disaster. Turcotte held the colt back early, but when he tried to get Secretariat to pick up the bit and run, he got no response. I could see at the far turn that the horse was dead. He never made a race of it, struggling to finish third, beaten by four lengths by his own stablemate, Angle Light, and by Sham. Standing near the owner's box, I saw Laurin turn to Tweedy and yell, "Who won it?"

"You won it!" Tweedy told him.

"Angle Light won it," I said to him. "Angle Light?" he howled back. But of course! Laurin trained him, too, and so Laurin had just won the Wood, but with the wrong horse.

I was sick. All those hours at the barn, all those early mornings at the shed, all that time and energy for naught. And in the most important race of his career, Secretariat had come up as hollow as a gourd. The next two weeks were among the most agonizing of my life. As great a stallion as he was, Bold Ruler had been essentially a speed sire and had never produced a single winner of a Triple Crown race. I couldn't help but suspect that Secretariat was another Bold Ruler, who ran into walls beyond a mile. In the next two weeks Churchill

Downs became a nest of rumors that Secretariat was unsound. Jimmy (the Greek) Snyder caused an uproar when he said the colt had a bum knee that was being treated with ice packs. I *knew* that wasn't true. I had been around Secretariat all spring, and the most ice I had seen near him was in a glass of tea.

All I could hope for, in those final days before the Derby, was that the colt had been suffering from a bellyache on the day of the Wood and had not been up to it. I remained ignorant of the abscess for weeks, and I had not yet divined the truth about Secretariat's training: He needed hard, blistering workouts before he ran, and that slow mile before the Wood had been inadequate. The night before the Derby, I made my selections for the newspaper, and the next day, two hours before post time, I climbed the stairs to the Churchill Downs jockeys' room to see Turcotte. He greeted me in an anteroom, looking surprisingly relaxed. Gilman had taken him aside a few days earlier and told him of the abscess. Turcotte saw that the boil had been treated and had disappeared. The news had made him euphoric, telling him all he needed to know about the Wood.

"You nervous?" he asked.

I shrugged. "I don't think you'll win," I said. "I picked My Gallant and Sham one-two, and you third."

"I'll tell you something," Turcotte said. "He'll beat these horses if he runs his race."

"What about the Wood?" I asked.

He shook me off. "I don't believe the Wood," he said. "I'm telling you. Something was wrong. But he's O.K. now. That's all I can tell you."

I shook his hand, wished him luck and left. Despite what Turcotte had said, I was resigned to the worst, and Secretariat looked hopelessly beaten as the field of 13 dashed past the finish line the first time. He was dead last. Transfixed, I could not take my eyes off him. In the first turn Turcotte swung him to the outside, and Secretariat began passing horses, and down the back side I watched the jockey move him boldly from eighth to seventh to sixth. Secretariat was fifth around the far turn and gaining fast on the outside. I began chanting, "Ride him, Ronnie! Ride him!" Sham was in front, turning for home, but then there was Secretariat, joining him at the top of the stretch. Laffit Pincay, on Sham, glanced over and saw Secretariat and went to the whip. Turcotte lashed Secretariat. The two raced head and head for 100 yards, until gradually Secretariat pulled away. He won by 2½ lengths. The crowd roared, and I glanced at the tote board: 1:59⅖! A new track and Derby record.

Throwing decorum to the wind, I vaulted from my seat and dashed madly through the press box, jubilantly throwing a fist in the air. Handicapper Steve Davidowitz came racing toward me from the other end. We clasped arms and spun a jig in front of the copy machine. "Unbelievable!" Davidowitz cried.

I bounded down a staircase, three steps at a time. Turcotte had dismounted and was crossing the racetrack when I reached him. "What a ride!" I yelled.

"What did I tell you, Mr. Bill?" he said.

I had just witnessed the greatest Kentucky Derby performance of all time. Secretariat's quarter-mile splits were unprecedented—:25$\frac{1}{5}$, :24, :23$\frac{4}{5}$, :23$\frac{2}{5}$ and :23. He ran each quarter faster than the preceding one. Not even the most veteran racetracker could recall a horse who had done this in a mile-and-a-quarter race. As quickly as his legions (I among them) had abandoned him following the Wood, so did they now proclaim Secretariat a superhorse.

We all followed him to Pimlico for the Preakness two weeks later, and he trained as if he couldn't get enough of it. He thrived on work and the racetrack routine. Most every afternoon, long after the crowds had dispersed, Sweat would graze the colt on a patch of grass outside the shed, then lead him back into his stall and while away the hours doing chores. One afternoon I was folded in a chair outside the colt's stall when Secretariat came to the door shaking his head and stretching his neck, curling his upper lip like a camel does. "What's botherin' you, Red?" Sweat asked. The groom stepped forward, plucked something off the colt's whiskers and blew it into the air. "Just a pigeon feather itchin' him," said Sweat. The feather floated into the palm of my hand. So it ended up in my wallet, along with the $2 pari-mutuel ticket that I had on Secretariat to win the Preakness.

In its own way Secretariat's performance in the 1$\frac{3}{16}$-mile Preakness was even more brilliant than his race in the Derby. He dropped back to last out of the gate, but as the field dashed into the first turn, Turcotte nudged his right rein as subtly as a man adjusting his cuff, and the colt took off like a flushed deer. The turns at Pimlico are tight, and it had always been considered suicidal to take the first bend too fast, but Secretariat sprinted full-bore around it, and by the time he turned into the back side, he was racing to the lead. Here Turcotte hit the cruise control. Sham gave chase in vain, and Secretariat coasted home to win by 2$\frac{1}{2}$. The electric timer malfunctioned, and Pimlico eventually settled on 1:54$\frac{2}{5}$ as the official time, but two *Daily Racing Form* clockers caught Secretariat in 1:53$\frac{2}{5}$, a track record by three fifths of a second.

I can still see Clem Florio shaking his head in disbelief. He had seen thousands of Pimlico races and dozens of Preaknesses but never anything like this. "Horses don't *do* what he did here today," he kept saying. "They just don't *do* that and win."

Secretariat wasn't just winning. He was performing like an original, making it all up as he went along. And everything was moving so fast, so unexpectedly, that I was having trouble keeping a perspective on it. Not three months before, after less than a year of working as a turf writer, I had started driving to the racetrack to see this one horse. For weeks I was often the only visitor there, and on many afternoons it was just Sweat, the horse and me in the fine dust with the pregnant stable cat. And then came the Derby and the Preakness, and two weeks later the colt was on the cover of TIME, SPORTS ILLUSTRATED and *Newsweek*, and he was a staple of the morning and evening news. Secretariat suddenly transcended horse racing and became a cultural phenomenon, a sort of undeclared national holiday from the tortures of Watergate and the Vietnam War.

I threw myself with a passion into that final week before the Belmont. Out to the barn every morning, home late at night, I became almost manic. The night before the race I called Laurin at home, and we talked for a long while about the horse and the Belmont. I kept wondering, What is Secretariat going to do for an encore? Laurin said, "I think he's going to win by more than he has ever won in his life. I think he'll win by 10."

I slept at the *Newsday* offices that night, and at 2 a.m. I drove to Belmont Park to begin my vigil at the barn. I circled around to the back of the shed, lay down against a tree and fell asleep. I awoke to the crowing of a cock and watched as the stable workers showed up. At 6:07 Hoeffner strode into the shed, looked at Secretariat and called out to Sweat, "Get the big horse ready! Let's walk him about 15 minutes."

Sweat slipped into the stall, put the lead shank on Secretariat and handed it to Charlie Davis, who led the colt to the outdoor walking ring. In a small stable not 30 feet away, pony girl Robin Edelstein knocked a water bucket against the wall. Secretariat, normally a docile colt on a shank, rose up on his hind legs, pawing at the sky, and started walking in circles. Davis cowered below, as if beneath a thunderclap, snatching at the chain and begging the horse to come down. Secretariat floated back to earth. He danced around the ring as if on springs, his nostrils flared and snorting, his eyes rimmed in white.

Unaware of the scene she was causing, Edelstein rattled the bucket again, and Secretariat spun in a circle, bucked and leaped in the air, kicking and spraying cinders along the walls of the pony barn. In a panic Davis tugged at the shank, and the horse went up again, higher and higher, and Davis bent back, yelling, "Come on down! Come on down!"

I stood in awe. I had never seen a horse so fit. The Derby and Preakness had wound him as tight as a watch, and he seemed about to burst out of his coat. I had no idea what to expect that day in the Belmont, with him going a mile and a half, but I sensed we would see more of him than we had ever seen before.

Secretariat ran flat into legend, started running right out of the gate and never stopped, ran poor Sham into defeat around the first turn and down the backstretch and sprinted clear, opening two lengths, four, then five. He dashed to the three-quarter pole in 1:09⅘, the fastest six-furlong clocking in Belmont history. I dropped my head and cursed Turcotte: *What is he thinking about? Has he lost his mind?* The colt raced into the far turn, opening seven lengths past the half-mile pole. The timer flashed his astonishing mile mark: 1:34⅕!

I was seeing it but not believing it. Secretariat was still sprinting. The four horses behind him disappeared. He opened 10. Then 12. Halfway around the turn he was 14 in front ... 15 ... 16 ... 17. Belmont Park began to shake. The whole place was on its feet. Turning for home, Secretariat was 20 in front, having run the mile and a quarter in 1:59 flat, faster than his Derby time.

He came home alone. He opened his lead to 25 ... 26 ... 27 ... 28. As rhythmic as a rocking horse, he never missed a beat. I remember seeing Turcotte look over to the timer, and I looked over, too. It was blinking 2:19, 2:20. The record was 2:26⅗. Turcotte scrubbed on the colt, opening 30 lengths, finally 31. The clock flashed crazily: 2:22 ... 2:23. The place was one long, deafening roar. The colt seemed to dive for the finish, snipping it clean at 2:24.

I bolted up the press box stairs with exultant shouts and there yielded a part of myself to that horse forever.

I DIDN'T see Lawrence Robinson that day last October. The next morning I returned to Claiborne to interview Seth Hancock. On my way through the farm's offices, I saw one of the employees crying at her desk. Treading lightly, I passed farm manager John Sosby's office. I stopped, and he called me in. He looked like a chaplain whose duty was to tell the news to the victim's family.

"Have you heard about Secretariat?" he asked quietly.

I felt the skin tighten on the back of my neck. "Heard what?" I asked. "Is he all right?"

"We might lose the horse," Sosby said. "He came down with laminitis last month. We thought we had it under control, but he took a bad turn this morning. He's a very sick horse. He may not make it.

"By the way, why are you here?"

I had thought I knew, but now I wasn't sure.

Down the hall, sitting at his desk, Hancock appeared tired, despairing and anxious, a man facing a decision he didn't want to make. What Sosby had told me was just beginning to sink in. "What's the prognosis?" I asked.

"Ten days to two weeks," Hancock said.

"Two weeks? Are you serious?" I blurted.

"You asked me the question," he said.

I sank back in my chair. "I'm not ready for this," I told him.

"How do you think I feel?" he said. "Ten thousand people come to this farm every year, and all they want to see is Secretariat. They don't give a hoot about the other studs. You want to know who Secretariat is in human terms? Just imagine the greatest athlete in the world. The greatest. Now make him six foot three, the perfect height. Make him real intelligent and kind. And on top of that, make him the best-lookin' guy ever to come down the pike. He was all those things as a horse. He isn't even a horse anymore. He's a legend. So how do you think I feel?"

Before I left I asked Hancock to call me in Lexington if he decided to put the horse down. We agreed to meet at his mother's house the next morning. "By the way, can I see him?" I asked.

"I'd rather you not," he said. I told Hancock I had been to Robinson's house the day before, and I had seen Secretariat from a distance, grazing. "That's fine," Hancock said. "Remember him how you saw him, that way. He doesn't look good."

Secretariat was suffering the intense pain in the hooves that is common to laminitis. That morning Anderson had risen at dawn to check on the horse, and Secretariat had lifted his head and nickered very loudly. "It was like he was beggin' me for help," Anderson would later recall.

I left Claiborne stunned. That night I made a dozen phone calls to friends, telling them the news, and I sat up late, dreading the next day. I woke up early and went to breakfast and came back to the room. The message light was dark. It was Wednesday, Oct. 4. I drove out to Dell Hancock's place in Paris. "It doesn't look good," she said. We had talked for more than an hour when Seth, looking shaken and pale, walked through the front door. "I'm afraid to ask," I said.

"It's very bad," he said. "We're going to have to put him down today."

"When?"

He did not answer. I left the house, and an hour later I was back in my room in Lexington. I had just taken off my coat when I saw it, the red blinking light on my phone. I knew. I walked around the room. Out the door and down the hall. Back into the room. Out the door and around the block. Back into the room. Out the door and down to the lobby. Back into the room. I called sometime after noon. "Claiborne Farm called," said the message operator.

I phoned Annette Covault, an old friend who is the mare booker at Claiborne, and she was crying when she read the message: "Secretariat was euthanized at 11:45 a.m. today to prevent further suffering from an incurable condition. . . ."

The last time I remember really crying was on St. Valentine's Day 1982, when my wife called to tell me that my father had died. At the moment she called, I was sitting in a purple room in Caesars Palace, in Las Vegas, waiting for an interview with the heavyweight champion, Larry Holmes. Now here I was, in a different hotel room in a different town, suddenly feeling like a very old and tired man of 48, leaning with my back against a wall and sobbing for a long time with my face in my hands.

Grim Reapers of The Land's Bounty

BY JIM HARRISON

A poet and novelist issued this indictment of anglers and hunters who violate fish and game codes—who snag trout with gang hooks and jacklight deer—destroying the spirit as well as the substance of outdoor sport.

PICTURE THIS MAN ON A COOL LATE SUMMER MORNING, BARELY dawn: gaunt, bearded, walking through his barnyard carrying a Winchester 30-30, wearing a frayed denim coat and mauve velvet bellbottoms. He is broke and though able-bodied he thinks of himself as an artist and immune to the ordinary requirements of a livelihood. Perhaps he is. He is one of the now numberless dropouts from urban society, part of a new agrarian movement, the "back to the land" bit that seems to be sweeping young writers. But he hankers for meat rather than the usual brown rice. I myself in a fatuous moment have told him of my own 200-gram-a-day protein diet—meat, meat, meat, lots of it with cheese and eggs, plus all the fruit you can lift from neighboring orchards and all the bourbon you can afford during evening pool games. Who needs macrobiotics.

Anyway, back to the barnyard. The killer lets the horses out of the paddock and they run off through the ground mist. The morning is windless and the grass soaked with dew, ideal conditions for poaching a deer. He walks up the hill behind his house, very steep. He is temporarily winded and sits down for a cigarette. Thirty miles out in Lake Michigan the morning sun has turned the steep cliffs of South Fox Island golden. There is a three-foot moderate roll, the lake trout and coho trollers will be out today in all of their overequipped glory. Later in the season he will snag lake trout from the Leland River, or perhaps even catch some fairly. He thinks of the coho as totally contemptible—anyone with a deft hand can pluck them from the feeder streams.

About 500 yards to the east, clearly visible from the hill, is a deserted orchard and a grove of brilliantly white birch trees. Beautiful. He will walk quietly through a long neck of woods until he is within 100 yards of the orchard. Except in the deepest forest, deer are largely nocturnal feeders in Michigan, but they can still be seen in some quantity at dawn or dusk if you know where to look. During the day they filter into the sweet coolness of cedar swamps or into the rows of the vast Christmas tree plantations. He sits and rests his rifle on a stump. He immediately spots a large doe between the second and third rows of the orchard, and farther back in the scrubby neglected trees a second-year buck, maybe 130 pounds, perfect eating size. He aims quickly just behind and a trifle below the shoulder and fires. The buck stumbles, then bursts into full speed. But this energy is deceptive and the animal soon drops. My friend hides his rifle, covering it with dead leaves. If you do happen to get caught—the odds are against it—your rifle is confiscated. He jogs down to the deer, stoops, hoists its dead weight to his shoulder and heads back to the house.

A few hours later his pickup pulls into my yard. I am in the barn wondering how I can fix one of the box stalls when my brother has bent the neck of my hammer pulling spikes. I hear the truck and when I come out into the yard he hands me a large bloody package. Everything is understood. We go into the kitchen and have a drink though it is only 10 in the morning. We slice the buck's liver very thin, then drive to the grocery store where I have some inexpensive white Bordeaux on order. When we get back my wife has sautéed the liver lightly in clarified butter. We eat this indescribably delicious liver, which far exceeds calf's liver in flavor and tenderness. A hint of apple, clover and fern. We drink a few bottles of wine and he goes home and I take a nap. That evening my wife slices a venison loin into medallions, which she again cooks simply. During the afternoon I had driven into Traverse City to splurge on a bottle of Châteauneuf-du-Pape. The meal—the loin and a simple salad of fresh garden lettuce, tomatoes and some green onions—was exquisite.

End of tale. I wouldn't have shot the deer myself. But I ate a lot of it, probably 10 pounds in all. I think it was wrong to shoot the deer. Part of the reason I would not have killed it is that I am no longer able to shoot at mammals. Grouse and woodcock, yes. But gutting and skinning a deer reminds me too much of the human carcass and a deer heart too closely resembles my own. My feelings are a trifle ambivalent on this particular incident but I have decided my friend is a violator only barely more tolerable than the cruder sort. If it had been one of the local Indians—it often is—I would have found it easy to bow to the ancestral privilege. But my friend is not a local Indian.

Game hoggery is not the point. The issue is much larger than human greed. We have marked these creatures to be hunted and slaughtered, and destroyed all but a remnant of their natural enemies. But fish and mammals must be considered part of a larger social contract, and just laws for their protection enforced with great vigor. The first closed deer season in our country due to depletion of the herds occurred in 1694 in Massachusetts. Someone once said, "The predator husbands his prey." The act of violation is ingrained, habitual; it represents a clearly pathological form of outdoor atavism. Not one violator out of a hundred acts out of real need or hunger. The belief that he does is another of many witless infatuations with local color.

I HAVE AN inordinate amount of time to think and wander around. Poets muse a lot. Or as Whitman, no mean fisherman, said, "I loaf and invite my soul." Mostly loaf. I have always found that I can think better and more lucidly with my Fox Sterlingworth, or any of a number of fly rods, in hand. I'm a poor shot, but I really do miss some grouse because I'm thinking. Recently I was walking along a stream that empties into Lake Michigan within half a dozen miles of my farm. It was late October, with a thin skein of snow that would melt off by afternoon. There were splotches of blood everywhere and many footprints and small piles of coho guts. The fish were nearly choking the stream, motionless except for an errant flip of tail to maintain position. And there were some dead ones piled up near a small logjam. They stank in the sharp fall air with the pervasive stench of a dead shorthorn I had once found near the Manistee River. Oh, well. Sport will be sport. No doubt someone had illegally clubbed a few for his smokehouse. Clubbed or pitched them out with a fork or shovel as one pitches manure. They are surprisingly good if properly smoked, though you must slice and scrape out the belly fat because of the concentrated DDT found there. But in the stream, in their fairly advanced stage of deliquescence, with backs and snouts scarred and sore and whitish, they looked considerably less interesting than floundering carp. How could a steelhead swim through this aquatic garbage to spawn? Tune in later, maybe another year or two folks.

I walked back to my car and drove west two miles to the stream mouth. This confluence of waters has never produced any really big trout, but it is fine for close-to-home fishing. I rigged my steelhead rod, put on my waders and began casting into a mild headwind, which required a low-profile turnover. Around here one learns to appreciate anything less than 15 knots, though if the water is too still the fishing is bad. I am not a pretty caster and my ability to double-haul, thus increasing lind speed, is imperfect; when you flunk a double haul the line whips and cracks, then collapses around your head and you are frustrated and sad as only a flycaster can be, glad only that no one was watching. I hooked two small fish on an attractor pattern and lost them after a few jumps. Then I hooked a larger fish on a lightly weighted Muddler and within an asthmatic half hour of coaxing I beached it. I was breathless, insanely excited. A steelhead, maybe six pounds with a vague pink stripe and short for his weight, chunky, muscular, a very healthy fish.

Three more fishermen came along and began casting in my spot with huge treble-hooked spoons. One of them quickly changed to a heavy bell sinker to which he had attached large hooks. They were using what is known in Michigan as the "Newaygo Twitch"; three easy turns of the reel and then a violent reef. It is a fine method for foul-hooking and snagging coho and chinook, even spawning steelhead and lake trout. The Michigan Department of Natural Resources has submitted to political pressure and ruled that foul-hooked salmon can be kept rather than released and this ruling has encouraged bozos by the thousand to use the twitch method to the exclusion of all the other styles of fishing. I have seen sportsmen snag upwards of 200 pounds of lake trout—incredibly far over the legal limit—in the Leland River where the fish are in layers devouring their own aborted spawn below the dam. And these people have been led to think they are fishing. Anyway, I left the beach immediately. I stopped into Dick's Tavern to calm my abraded nerves. I often fantasize about bullwhipping these creeps as Mother Nature's Dark Enforcer. When my imagination for vengeance is depleted I think about moving to Montana where such yuks, I suppose, are as plentiful, but seem at least less visible. It is strange to see a government agency sponsoring acts that are a degradation of the soul of sport. It is as if the National Football League were to encourage and promote face-mask tackling. Take a firm grasp and rip his damn head off.

It is a silly mistake, I've found, to assume that rules of fair play are shared. I have met and talked at length with men who harry and club to death both fox and coyote from snowmobiles. It should not seem necessary to pass laws against so base and resolutely mindless a practice, but it is necessary. I suppose that in simplistic terms our acquisitive and competitive urges have been transferred directly to sport—one can "win" over fish or beast but, unlike what happens in other forms of sport, the violator disregards all the rules. A certain desolate insensitivity persists: I know some seemingly pleasant enough young men who in the past have gathered up stray dogs to use as target practice to hone their skills. This is not the sort of thing one can argue about. Neither can one question the logic of the hunting club members who bait deer with apples, corn and a salt lick, and then on the crisp dawn of the first day of the season fire away at the feeding animals. Or marksmen who hang around rural dumps to get their garbage bear. Or those who wander around swamps adjacent to lakes in the spring collecting gunny sacks of spawning pike; usually they are the same people who tell you that fishing "isn't what it used to be." To be sure, the majority of sportsmen follow the laws with some care, but the majority is scarcely overwhelming. More like a plurality with a grand clot of the indifferent buffering the middle. And silent, at best. Not to mention the chucklewink aspect, the we're-all-cowpokes-ain't-we attitude, of so many judges who mete out wrist-slap fines to game-law violators.

I think I was about 14 when the problem first became apparent to me. It was late in November near the end of the deer season, very cold up in Michigan with a foot of fine powder snow, not bad to walk in as it burst around one's feet like weightless down or fluff. I was hunting along a ridge that completely encircled a large gully forming a bowl. At the bottom of the bowl there was a small marsh of tag alder, snake-grass, dried-up cattails and brake, and perhaps four or five slender tamarack. I sat down on a boulder to eat my lunch and watch the swale, thinking it might hold a large buck or even a young spikehorn. Across my lap I held an antique 38-40, the accuracy of which was less than profound but better anyhow than the shotgun and slug my friends used, which was an embarrassment to them. After an hour of sitting and staring, staring so hard that my eyes tried to trace the shapes I wanted to see, four deer calmly walked out of the far side of the swale. I looked at them quickly through my peepsight. All female. They picked their way cautiously single file toward a sumac thicket on the side of the hill, trying to minimize the time spent in the open. But then an explosion, a barrage, a fusillade. The first doe made the thicket and bounded up and over the ridge. The second dropped in her tracks but the third, shot probably in the hindquarters, tried to drag herself back to the swale by her forefeet. Then she was hit again and was still. The fourth doe ran in narrowing, convulsive circles until she dropped.

I don't remember thinking anything. I only watched. Three men walked down the hill and looked at the deer. They were talking but were too far away for me to hear distinctly. I sat very still until their red forms disappeared. I didn't go down the hill and look at the dead deer. I thought the game warden might come along and think I had shot them and the fine for shooting a doe would be enormous for someone who earned at best $2 a day for hoeing potatoes. I hunted without thought for a few more hours, getting a hopeless shot at a distant buck, and then walked to the car where I was to meet my father when it began to get dark. All the staccato noise of the rifle shots had served to remind me of the Korean war and what it must sound like. Pork Chop Hill was much in the news in those days.

I THINK IT was Edward Abbey who coined the phrase "cowboy consciousness" to describe that peculiar set of attitudes many Americans still hold: the land is endless, unspoiled, mysterious, still remaining to be overcome and finally won. So shoot, kill, bang-bang-bang. WOW! And city dwellers, it seems, who come to the country during the hunting and fishing seasons, are now more guilty of these attitudes than their rural counterparts, who sense the diminishing wilderness around them, the truncated freedom of movement. Every dentist and machinist and welder and insurance adjuster in Michigan either owns or wants to own 20 posted acres "up north."

But we are hopeless romanticists about this imaginary Big Woods—it simply no longer exists in any faintly viable form. Even one of the far corners of creation, the North Slope of the Brooks Range, is littered with oil drums. It seems funny, too, to discover that every American in the deepest little synapse in his brain considers himself a natural at hunting and fishing, a genetic Pete Maravich of the outback, wherever that is. We always tell each other that the deer are on the ridges today or in the swamps or clustered in the grape arbors or frittering away the morning behind the woodpile despite the fact that few of us could identify five trees at gunpoint. And every little rural enclave has its number of wise old owls who have spent a lifetime sipping draft beer and schnapps and are rife with such witticisms as "you greenhorns couldn't hit a bull in the butt with a banjo. Now back in 1928, why. . . ." The point is that in the old days the rivers were stiff with giant bull trout and deer wandered the countryside in grand herds like Idaho sheep. You didn't even have to aim. This cowboy consciousness is so ingrained and overwhelming in some violators that they will suffer any risks. A poacher near here was arrested for the 20th time, fined $1,000 and given 165 days in jail. An equal punishment was given to two men who dynamited a rainbow holding pond at a weir. I somehow doubt that this will discourage them.

I FEEL A very precise melancholy when I hear rifle shots in the middle of a September night; the jacklighters are at work after a tepid evening at the bowling alley. Picture this recent local case. A yellow cone of light is shining into a field. It is a powerful beam and nothing animate within a hundred yards escapes its illumination. Three teen-agers are sitting in an old Mercury playing the light against the backdrop of woods and field as they drive slowly along a gravel road. One of them has a loaded rifle. If a deer is spotted the light paralyzes it hypnotically. The deer will stare without motion into the light and even the shabbiest marksman can pick his shot. But this will prove an unfortunate night for shining deer. A car approaches from the rear at high speed and swerves in front of the hunters to block any escape. It is Reino

Narva, the game warden, to the rescue. In this particular instance all of the culprits are juveniles and first offenders and the sentences are light.

There is nothing inscrutable about the matter of violation. I fancy myself an amateur naturalist and have hot flashes when I think of the sins of my past, harmless and usual though they may be. I think of the large brown trout I caught at age 12 by illegal set line in the Muskegon River. Turtles had eaten all but its head by the time I pulled the line in. I nailed the head to the barn alongside my pike and bass skulls as if I had caught the fish by fair means. Or the roosting grouse stalked and shot with a .22. Or diving into a lake for weeks on end with a knife, handle in mouth, to carve the heads off turtles we flushed from logs. We thought they were killing our fish. Or shooting crows. Or shooting at deer in midsummer with bow and arrow, though I don't remember ever coming close. All the mindless sins of youth committed in the haze of reading Edgar Rice Burroughs, Zane Grey, James Oliver Curwood, Jack London and Ernest Seton; wanting to be a steely half-breed Robert Mitchum type with hatchet, revolver, cartridge belt and a long mane of hair trained with bear grease.

GENTLE READER, rules will never stop the jacklighter and snagger, the violator. It is not so much that enforcement of the law is inept, but that respect for the spirit of the law is insufficient. And in Michigan there are fabulous ironies; a portion of any fine for a game violation is earmarked as "restitution to the state." But you might well be shining your deer in an opening in a forest that has been ravaged by the oil interests—public land doled away for peanuts by conservationists in a state with boggling population and recreation problems. Or you might get caught snagging a trout in Manistee Lake where a paper company belches out thousands of gallons of fluid waste daily into public waters so rank that a motorboat scarcely can manage a wake. Who is violating what? Or as René Char said, "Who stands on the gangplank directing operations? The captain or the rats?" Not a very subtle distinction, hereabouts. The problems seem, and perhaps are, insuperable. The political-business-conservation relationship in Michigan often reminds one of old-style Boston politics; everyone gets a piece of the action but the pie itself suffers from terminal rot. Of course, this is ho-hum stuff now. Pollution is "in committee" everywhere and government is firming up its stand, a la kumquat jelly, with a lid of yellow paraffin. I have a dreamy plot afoot for a court test to be decided on Saturn wherein the Constitution and Bill of Rights would be made to apply to fish and mammals.

Finally, it is a very strange arrogance in man that enables him to chase the last of the whales around the ocean for profit, shoot polar bear cubs for trophies, allow Count Blah-Blah to blast 885 pheasants in one day. It is much too designed to be called crazy or impetuous.

Those lines of Robert Duncan's about Robin Hood come back to me now: "How we loved him/in childhood and hoped to abide by his code/that took life as its law!" The key word here is "code." Sport must be sporting. We have a strong tendency to act the weasel in the hen house. At dawn not a single cluck was heard. It might be preposterous to think we will change, but there are signs. Judges are becoming sterner and people are aware of environmental problems to a degree not known in this country before. Game wardens get more cooperation from the ordinary citizen than they used to. Violating is losing its aura of rube cuteness.

The true violator, though, will persist in all of his pathological glory. Even if there were no game left on earth, something would be devised. Maybe a new sport on this order: ganghooking Farmer Brown's pigs. A high-speed power winch mounted on a vehicle hood is required, and a harpoon with large hooks. You shoot the harpoon over the pig's back and press the winch button. Zap! You've got yourself a squealer. Precautions: make sure Farmer Brown is away for the day, and take your finger off the winch button in time or the pork will really fly.

We Are Destroying
Our National Parks

BY WALLACE STEGNER

*Almost 50 years ago, a noted novelist and authority on conservation
reported in SI that our nation was steadily laying waste to its magnificent
wilderness. To this day, his words remain disturbingly relevant.*

YOSEMITE VALLEY, A SEVEN-MILE SETTING FOR THE GREAT
granite jewels of El Capitan, Half Dome and Clouds Rest, is
veined with bright water and has grown to the loveliest of
forests. The climate is perfect, access easy. Result: On any
summer day the Valley entertains between 20,000 and 32,000 people. Its
population, at three or four thousand per square mile, is three or four times
as dense as that of Java, one of the most densely populated countries on earth.

Here is dramatically illustrated the dilemma of the National Park Service,
whose legal duty is "to conserve the scenery and the natural and historical
objects and the wildlife. . . . and to provide for the enjoyment of the same in
such manner and by such means as will leave them unimpaired for the enjoyment of future generations."

GUARD AGAINST fire, clean up after the litterbugs. Protect and restore the
wildlife, even wolves and mountain lions, in order to keep the balance of nature, but do it in a show window where millions can thrill to see it. Offer high-
grade adult education to all who ask for it and many who don't. Rescue
climbers trapped or injured on the cliffs, tourists wounded by the bears they
have been (against the rules) feeding.

Do what you can about America's slop-happy habit of defacing signs, tearing up shrubs and wild flowers and throwing candy wrappers, bottles and beer cans in creeks and springs and geysers. Be patient when tourists bawl you out for something "because I pay taxes for this." Do it all on a pitifully inadequate budget, with collapsing equipment and an overworked and under-manned staff and *smile.*

The picture is gruesome, but it is neither sensational nor exaggerated. If the men of the park service had only the vacationing hordes to contend with, maybe they would be able to cope with their problems. But there are other groups—the entrepreneurs who want to open the parks for exploitation, federal agencies which would build dams in them, and Congress, which likes the parks but will not pay for them. Together, all four groups represent almost every living soul in America. They are at once the friends and the enemies of the system of national parks that gained its first great strength under the vigorous championship of President Theodore Roosevelt and has since stood as a model of democratic conservation for the rest of the world to copy. While most of the people of the United States love their parks, the parks might be destroyed.

The entrepreneurs would cut timber, dig metals, graze the ranges, drill for oil and install ski lifts. Once a great threat, they are now reduced to a minor one. To Joe Smith, average citizen, reading of proposed raids on the timber of Olympic National Park or the watershed ranges of Yellowstone, the choice seems a simple one between good and bad. But the threat from private interests has been replaced by the threat posed by government bureaus whose philosophy of land-use runs counter to the strict conservation policy of the national parks. The Corps of Engineers and the Bureau of Reclamation both want to build dams in some of the parks and monuments. When they are well planned, such dams mean fewer water-starved areas, greater flood control, more electric power. These are obviously very good things. But are they good enough to warrant the destruction of incomparable wildernesses? Joe Smith is confused; it seems to him the choice is not between good and bad but between varying degrees, varying kinds of good.

Our Mr. Smith, who has been battered by arguments from all sides, is only ordinarily informed; he may even have been misinformed. But he may suspect that the value of preserving a wilderness may outweigh the value of hydro-electric power, especially when it seems likely that the same amount of power could be produced at alternate sites, or more cheaply by steam-coal plants, and when the potential of atomic power casts a big shadowy question mark on all expensive hydroelectric installations. Joe may even end up thinking that these dam-building bureaus are the worst enemies of the national parks.

He would be close to right. But let us not forget the Congress and the people of the United States.

It means little that both Congress and the people think themselves the parks' best friends. Congress has been friendly in principle and stingy with money ever since it established Yellowstone in 1872. The American people love their parks and threaten to trample them to death. The more successful the Park Service is in keeping a park wild and beautiful, the more people it will draw and the more it has to contend with a thundering herd.

Everything in a primeval park ought to be preserved just as God made it: everything except man, who is an intruder and has to be educated. That is the Park Service's job. It is more than a clean-up job, though refuse disposal is a desperate problem in all the popular parks, and a park ranger in summer often finds himself little more than a garbage man working a 15-hour shift. Worse than dirty public habits is the public's failure to understand what a national park is.

Its failure is understandable, for too many kinds of things are included in the 24 million acres which the Park Service must administer in 38 states, the District of Columbia, Alaska, Hawaii, Puerto Rico and the Virgin Islands. There are 180 parks, monuments, battlefields, historic sites, memorials, cemeteries, parkways, National Capital Parks and recreational areas.

The Park Service takes care of everything from F.D.R.'s Hyde Park home to the parkways through the Great Smokies and the campgrounds on some reclamation reservoirs. No wonder Joe Smith is confused; no wonder he sometimes falls for the notion that the parks ought to be "developed." There are swimming pools in Yosemite, and a bandstand from which dance music bounces off the cliffs. There are several tows for skiers at Hidden Valley in Rocky Mountain National Park, and Seattle businessmen are asking for more of the same on Mount Rainier.

None of these things ought to be there; they are contrary to the spirit and the letter of the law establishing the National Park Service. A national park is not a playground and not a resort, though it may be ideal for such activities as hiking, riding, climbing, hunting with a camera, fishing and cross-country skiing—sports which demand no installations, attract no spectators and leave no scars. The real purpose of the national parks—to preserve scenery, beauty, geology, archaeology, wildlife, for permanent use in living natural museums—is not affected by these, but it cannot be made compatible with weekend dances, ski tournaments, speedboat races and a million people a year. And if the parks are not protected against people who insist on using them as resorts, they are shortly going to look like Settembrini's Picnic Ground after the annual Lions Outing.

In 1954 Yosemite had 1,008,031 visitors; Rocky Mountain 1,425,635; Great Smoky more than two and a half million, Yellowstone almost a million and a third, Grand Teton more than a million. Nearly 26 million in the national parks and monuments alone, over 54 million in all the Park Service areas. The total has steadily increased by more than a million each year. By 1975, when according to demographers the population of the United States will be 200 million and that of California 20 million, visitors to the national parks may well run to more than 100 million every year.

If Yosemite looks now like the rush hour at Hollywood and Vine, how will it be in 1975? And where shall we go then for our inexpensive and restorative family vacations? Not to Sequoia or Rocky Mountain or Lassen Volcanic. Their beauty will be lost to us, as Yosemite's is already to many because of the crowds. We will have to seek quieter and wilder places where there is rest for soul and eye. Such places are scarce now. They are getting rarer, and there are no more where they came from.

Every one of them is unique and beyond price. We need not fewer such protected areas but more of them. House and Senate have not agreed on the Service's 1956 appropriation as this is written. The approximately $33 million budget for 1955, though supplemented by a little more than $10 million in contract authorization for roads and parkways and by a half million to match the same amount of donated Rockefeller money for land purchases, was only a fraction of what was needed. In presenting his budget for 1954, Director Conrad Wirth noted a long-term trend of slow starvation. What the Bureau of the Budget had allotted him would provide 15% fewer man-years of work than the budget of 1941, yet "in 1953 we have 8% more areas, 10% more acres, 32% more miles of roads, 35% more miles of trails and 100% more visitors than we had in 1941."

The 1955 budget, though better than 1954, provided for less than 5% of the backlog of construction that every year is more frantically needed as the visitor load increases. For our National Park System we dedicate only seven-tenths of one percent of our land area, and then we refuse to provide even 5% of what is needed to develop it. Many nations, all of whom learned the national park idea from us, do better by it than we do. Even Japan, overpopulated and land-starved, has set aside 4% of its territory.

Our parks are like a child whose teeth have been neglected. Look at that smile, we say. See how white and pretty? Hardly any decay showing. But keep her away from the dentist another few years. Let maintenance and construction be postponed as they have been ever since the stand-by years of World War II. Put off renovating the museums, do without the extra rangers and naturalists. Don't bother moving the campgrounds, though they ought to be moved about as often as a turkey run, and for similar reasons. Let it all go, and pretty soon we will not ask the child to smile.

The service which Congress established in 1916 to care for its national parks has been, in spite of starvation budgets, a destructive public and persistent outside enemies, one of the best agencies of public service that any people ever had. Today there are more trees, flowers and wildlife in Yosemite, in spite of the thundering herd, than there were a generation ago. They are there because the Park Service takes its job seriously. Park Service employees have a resilient morale, a morale that is always threatened but never caves, despite meager pay, high rent for park housing and unpaid overtime. They are men of high ability who have sacrificed better pay and ambition to do a job they like.

JOE SMITH is going to have to get used to some restrictions, even if Congress should decide in the future to deal kindly with the parks. Already most campgrounds have a 15- or 30-day limit; already concessionaires may restrict the stay of their lodge and motel guests. Admission cards to pitch a tent in campgrounds, good for the whole season, will probably have to go. And the recreation activities, spectator sports, concerts and swimming pools and organizational picnics, maybe even ski lifts, will have to be left to the resort areas where there is little of the real wilderness left to spoil.

We can't, as has been bitterly proposed, close our national parks and thus force Congress to put up money for their proper operation. We can't close up something that 54 million people want. But we can destroy their beauty, and hence their reason for being, and perhaps we will. It would take a 10-year construction and rehabilitation program of $60 million a year to bring the parks back to what they should be, and an annual operating budget at least twice that of 1955 to keep them there.

That sounds like a lot of money, and is. But the money will produce returns of another kind: health and sanity and the profound and personal sense of belonging to something good and beautiful that cannot be measured in dollars. A primeval park offers values that are close to the values of religion.

V

SUPPORTING
PLAYERS

'There Ain't No Others Like Me'

BY MARK KRAM

By the time Joe Frazier and Muhammad Ali were preparing for their Thrilla in Manila, Don King was nearly as prominent as the heavyweights he promoted—a latter-day P.T. Barnum, up from the gutter and reaching for the stars.

S PACE IS NOT SPACE BETWEEN THE EARTH AND THE SUN TO one who looks down from the windows of the Milky Way." He pulls on a Montecruz Supreme, releasing a smoke ring that flutters above his head like a broken halo. "It was but yesterday I thought myself a fragment quivering without rhythm in the sphere of life. Now I know that I am the sphere, and all life in rhythmic fragments moves within me." Having rid himself of these thoughts, the big man, the main man, the "impresario of the Third World" (name him, and you can have him, say his critics) turns and booms, his voice ripping across the skyline of Manhattan, "Yes, I do have an ego! I am an ego! I am!" Then, humbly, he adds, "But no man is an island, ya deeg?"

One could swear he hears the world sigh with relief, so glad it is that the orator admits to being human. "I am quintessential!" he begins again. He does not say of what he is quintessential, and it does not matter, his eyes seem to say; the word fits his mood. Words are always hovering above anyone who happens to be within ocean's distance of Don King, words fluttering in the air like crazed bats. But nobody waits for the next word, his next sentence of impeccable incoherence. They wait for his next move, that next gale of a gamble that knocks reason senseless and has powered him in a few short years from a busted-out life to the summit of his business—which you can also have, if you can name it.

Call him a boxing promoter, but that does not explain what he does; it only gives him a label. Nobody knows exactly what he does or how he does it, and his adversaries, who underestimated him so badly, now flinch at the sound of his impact. The clattering telex in his office tells much more: Baby Doc Duvalier, the president for life, hopes that King can visit Haiti to discuss a situation of mutual interest; a spokesman for President Mobutu Sese Seko of Zaire has shown much interest in King's idea for a future project. King does not deal much with private capital, he works with governments, Third World countries whose rulers find King to be a useful catalyst. He says, "Henry Kissinger can't get in the places I can."

The power of the world, says King, "is slowly shifting, and you don't have to be no prophet like . . . who was that old dude? Yeah, Nostradeemusss. It's right in front of your nose, if you wanna look. But I don't care about politics. Just call me a promoter. Not the first black one. Not the first green one. But *theeee* promoter, Jack. There ain't no others, 'cause they've only had three in the history of the world; P. T. Barnum, Mike Todd, and you are lookin' at the third. Nobody kin deny it. They mock me at their peril."

Some do, though—with passion. They look upon him as a blowhard, a mountebank—and look at the way he dresses, like an M.C. in a cheap nightclub. "Just an uppity nigger, right?" says King. But the facts bite back in his defense; he has raised $35 million in less than a year for his boxing spectaculars; he has made more money for Muhammad Ali "than Ali done in all his previous fights in his whole career." With the Ali-Foreman fight—and for only $14 million ("most of which they got back")—he brought "dignity and recognition and solidarity" to Zaire, a place "where people thought it was ridden with savages." And in a few weeks King will bring to the universe Ali vs. Joe Frazier for the heavyweight title in Manila. How's that for quintessential, his long pause seems to ask.

What he did not do and what he might do in the future are equally dramatic, according to King. With oil money from Saudi Arabia, he was on the brink of buying Madison Square Garden before deciding it was a bad investment. "It's become a turkey of a building," he says. He is now thinking of purchasing a major movie company. But more immediate is his sudden thrust into big team sports and music as a packager and manager of careers. He says that he has already signed 85 black pro football players, with more to follow in basketball and baseball. Overnight, it appears, he could become one of the most powerful men in all of sports.

"I won't be creatin' any wars," he says. "We just wants in on the middle of all that high cotton."

But for now, right this minute in Tokyo, or Zaire, or Cairo, or London, or in the back streets of Cleveland, whether among the rich and polished sportsmen, or those who leg the numbers up dark alleys, Don King is boxing, the man with the show, the man with the fistful of dollars and the imagination to match. Quickly, with a lot of street genius, enough brass for a firehouse and the messianic support of Herbert Muhammad (Ali's manager, who has an inscrutable genius of his own), King has managed to reduce the ring's power structure to rubble, and he is left all alone in his cavernous office atop Rockefeller Center to commune with the gods and play with his own ideas as if they were toys.

Boxing promoters have seldom been so singular; most of the big ones have been nearly invisible as personalities. The color, it seems, was left to the scufflers who kept their offices under their hats, would step on a nickel if a kid dropped it and would smoke a cigar down to its last gritty and defiant end. In one sense, the big ones weren't promoters, not in the way of a Tex Rickard, his mind as sharp as his familiar diamond stickpin, or a Mike Jacobs, with his clacking false teeth and pawnbroker's shrewdness—they were names who worked up front. In the last decade or so, all those who have come along have been moneymen who happened to be in control of the heavyweight champion. The list is long: Roy Cohn, the Bolan brothers, the Nilon brothers, Bill Fugazy and that most resilient of night creatures, Bob Arum.

Limousines, hot dogs, the law, these were their businesses, and they drifted like clouds across a big moon. The ring was an amusing subsidiary, a playground in which to exercise their already fully developed roguishness; they left nothing behind, and if they were not completely anonymous, they were as dull as their gray suits. Now there is Don King, who used to stick out like a single hatchling turtle trying to make the sea in full view of sly crabs and deadly frigate birds. That image has been smashed, replaced by something close to King Kong skipping across the jagged teeth of Manhattan's skyline. He will be heard. He will be seen. He thinks a low profile is something you get in a barber shop.

"Nobody wanted to be up front before me," says King. "They all wanted to sit back, collect their money and play their dirty tricks on each other and even the ones who worked for them. But I'm out there, Jack. You can see me, and if you don't, then you're color-blind. My name's on everything. This ain't no NoName Productions. It's Don King Productions. I *perform*. And when I don't perform, then I gotta go, too."

All right, let's look at the record over the 1½ years King has been a front-rank promoter. First, there was Foreman vs. Ken Norton in Venezuela; give it a rating of two garbage cans. Norton was timid, King's partners behaved like sharks, and Foreman was his usual self, that is to say, his presence did not radiate. It was pure chaos. Next, Ali vs. Foreman in Zaire. Give it three stars. It was a brilliant victory for Ali, cerebrum over inept strength; it was genuinely exciting, and if the figures did not excite accountants, they did not disappoint them, either. On the negative side was government censorship, and again the attitude of some of King's associates, who tried (and in some cases managed) to cheat the press out of a charter-plane refund. King went on his own with Chuck Wepner vs. Ali, Foreman vs. the Infirm Five up in Toronto, Ron Lyle and Ali in Las Vegas, and Ali against the catatonic Joe Bugner in Malaysia.

The artistic merit of these four productions is dubious. "How did I know Foreman would go berserk in Toronto?" says King. "But I'll take the blame. It was a good idea, but I didn't think George would make a farce of it." The business aspect is brighter. Wepner took a loss, but television picked up the tab for the Toronto show and Lyle; Toronto held its own against Connors vs. Newcombe in the TV ratings, and the Lyle fight had an enormous pull in numbers. Bugner in Malaysia lost a few dollars, too. "What can you do?" says King. "Here's a big strong dude with the chance of a lifetime and he stands in the ring like a 1,000-year-old mummy."

Essentially, King works for Muhammad Ali, the hottest property in the world, and for Herbert Muhammad, a hard realist who could not care if King's skin was Technicolor; when Herbert looks at a promoter, he sees only green. Herbert gave King his chance, but he would not stay with him if King didn't produce. Herbert never really believed King would deliver, yet he could not deny a black brother a chance to fail. But King did not fold, and as Herbert watched, King produced the figures, the action, the credibility, the continuity that Herbert demanded. "He's a hard taskmaster," says King, "but he's taught me much." King has survived.

The trio gets along well. Ali introduced King as "a businessman—and former gangster." Often bemused, Herbert looks on quietly from the background. He is sensitive to any nuance suggesting that King is the brains behind Ali. Recently, when Ali conned the press into thinking he was retiring, King said he was going to Malaysia to intercede, to use his influence on him. "What's this?" asked Herbert. "You got everybody thinking you're the manager of Ali. I'm paranoid 'bout that, Donald." Herbert tries to tone down the excessive side of King, and that is like trying to rein a runaway team of Clydesdales. The excesses, the props, have become King's style.

Harold Lloyd had his lensless glasses, W.C. Fields his voice and Clark Gable those ears. Several distinctions—familiar things that have become a part of his character—mark Don King. His hair looks like a bale of cotton candy just retrieved from a coal bin. He must hold the record for time spent in a tuxedo; he easily beats out Tony Martin, the recognized champion. Then, there is his jewelry. To look at King is to look into the sun or to gaze at a mobile Cartier's. On one finger is a meat block of a diamond ring that cost $30,000, on his pinky is a $3,000 number and on his wrist is a $9,000 watch. Add to all of this his voice and language, a thunderous roll that blends black slang with newspeak words like infrastructure, interface and input, a grandiloquent soliloquy that he will suddenly interrupt to summon up the ghosts of the Apostle Paul, François Villon, the moonstruck Khalil Gibran and King's favorite, Shakespeare.

Now King, at age 44, has found a headquarters, an address to match the man. The suite of offices, including two boardrooms, is located on the 67th floor of the prestigious RCA Building, just two floors up from the famous Rainbow Room and close enough to the sky to grab a star. The rent is $60,000 a year, and the furniture cost him $40,000. The move by King shook those who follow such things, not to mention the fight mob, which was used to dealing in the back rooms of bars, or in five-story walkups. "I'm not walkin' up to the top of that place," said one manager. Clearly, the offices have done what King hoped they would do.

"They're all out there wonderin'," he says. "They're wonderin' what's that crazy nigger doin' up there. He must be doin' somethin'. The place has become a magnet."

King has made people pay attention, so much so that his reception room looks like the last lifeboat leaving the *Titanic*, and his messages run to 200 a day. He tries to see everyone—from inventors who have machines with strange powers or a solution to the aging process of the body, to the lowliest fight managers who look up and around the place as if they were in a spaceship—all of the schemers and dreamers looking for that peg to hang the world on. King spends an average of 15 hours a day in his office, some of it in the effort of staying atop office intrigue. And well he should, for he has made himself vulnerable.

King's high command is a good example of how things work in boxing promotion. For instance, one never lets a grudge get in the way of making money. Working with him are Henry Schwartz, and, of all people, Bob Arum, once King's avowed enemy. Schwartz was King's former boss at Video Techniques. He first brought King on the scene, made him a vice president and thought of him as "my black interface." Which, as King says now, was another way of saying "chump." But King could not be held on a leash, and soon he went on his own, leaving behind such disgraceful practices as extra charges for equipment; closed-circuit exhibitors were badly mauled by Video on the Zaire fight. "Schwartz has got nothin' to do with the business end now," says King, "but he's valuable when it comes to technical stuff like satellites."

Malitz is a familiar face; he was long the right arm of Bob Arum. Malitz is a pro. He has no equal as an orchestrator of closed-circuit television. He knows where the money is, and he knows how to collect. King needs Malitz, but why Arum? "He has a brilliant legal mind," King says unconvincingly. The fact is that King has no choice but to cut Arum in on the promotion. The Manila connection, a personage named Thomas Oh, had dealt with Arum first, having been led to believe that Arum could deliver Ali. King had been trying to put the fight on in New York. Failing, he went to his sources in Manila, who did not have the clout of Thomas Oh. Finally, learning that Arum did not have Ali, Oh had to deal with King. Now Arum's only chance was to bring Thomas Oh and King together. They sat down, but King held out as long as possible, looking for money elsewhere, mainly because of Arum's presence in the deal. Herbert Muhammad was impatient. He wanted a contract from King, or else be was going with still another rival promoter, Jerry Perenchio.

King saved promotional face by hooking up with Thomas Oh at the last minute, so Arum, the man who used to "control" Ali in a promotional sense is once more in the thick of things. King fought long and hard to break Arum's grip, and here Arum is, back in the middle of the money, right in the middle of King's own operation, sitting on his shoulder like a wise and patient owl observing a field mouse who has gotten too big.

But a hired hand in King's office says, "There's no way King's going to get hurt. So far he's done the impossible for Herbert and Ali. If Herbert ever does sink him for a white man, he's going to look pretty bad after the way King's performed. And as far as this promotion is concerned, King won't be caught napping. The secret of closed circuit is who gets to the money first, and that's King now. King and Arum have absolutely nothing in common. King has his faults. He's too loud. His tired black line can wear you out. But he's a decent human being generous and sensitive. One day he must have had his driver 20 hours. So he's going into his hotel, and then turns back and presses a $100 bill in the driver's hand. Another promoter would have borrowed $20 from the driver."

The main person King must keep an eye on is himself. It is an old truth that the bigger the man, the easier the con. King's feathers must be preened, his ego stroked; grafters with larger plans usually jump at the chance, and then they become much more. Loyalty is almost nonexistent in boxing, but King has what little there is. He did not have to ask for it, or pay for it. It was given to him because he was strong and fair, and his followers saw him as a deliverer from the tyranny of Madison Square Garden. "He's made a mole out of Teddy Brenner, and he's put Mike Burke in his pocket," says Paddy Flood, a manager. "The Garden doesn't count anymore." But there are some who believe King's ego and his ambition have leaped out of hand. "He don't listen too good anymore," says another manager.

"It's all subjective," says King. "They don't understand that up here is like being in a war every day. I'm so tired most of the time I goes home and falls into bed."

It is a Sunday afternoon. He sits beneath a large portrait of Ali. He has been talking about his early life, about the roaches in the tenement that he would spray furiously with bottles of white poison, and still they kept coming; about all the days he spent running to deliver squalling chickens from Hymie's Chicken Shack to the slaughterhouse knife; about his reign as the regent of the numbers in Cleveland; about Benny, one of his predecessors, who used to equip his numbers runners like an army preparing for winter invasion. "He used to buy a whole supply of galoshes and hats and overcoats and hand them out to his men," says King.

King is not wearing a shirt, and his massive chest is moist with sweat. It is hot day in New York and he does not like air conditioning. An angry scar crawls up his chest, a gift from his prison days when an incompetent doctor turned a simple cyst surgery into an awful mess. It is obvious, as he stretches and prowls throughout the room, that he likes the space of his office. King knows all about space, for it was only six years ago that he was put into the hole at the Ohio Penitentiary with only bread and water and a Bible and darkness; he read the Bible by light that slithered through cracks, and then he would use it as a pillow. "I had no trouble in prison, except for that one time a guy hit me in the mouth," says King. "They don't need much excuse to do anything they want to you."

King was in prison because he killed one of his runners in a fistfight, just an ordinary scrap. The memory of it haunts him and so do the four years he got, a severe sentence for the kind of charge that a lot of people have beaten over the years.

"I went up on manslaughter," says King, "and I expected to be paroled early. But they made me do four years in the joint. These parole flops cut the heart right out of me. My numbers reputation was held against me."

The details, the moments of prison life, are engraved in his mind: being led by foot chains off the bus; the 60-man floor at Marion Reformatory where nightmares came to life in sound, and King would stay awake as long as he could so he would not have to enter subconscious hell; the 6-by-12 cell, where they made you wash out of the toilet bowl, and the smell of sulphur in the water made you sick; the look on the face of his wife, who drove 400 miles every weekend to see him—and the riot.

"It was over," says King, "and we're standin' there naked, and a guy named

Bradshaw was standin' there, too . . . just standin' there, I'll never forget how the kid from the National Guard got nervous. Bradshaw, he was doin' what he was told, but the kid got scared and he pulled the trigger, and there was Bradshaw's stomach running down to his crotch. Solitary? Perversions? You don't know the kind of depravity that stalks a prison!"

King looks over at a picture of his wife and kids taken on his big farm in Ohio. "That's the only place where the war stops," he says. His wife Henrietta runs the farm. "She don't go for no nonsense," he says, recalling how once his son's marks in school tailed off, and she personally shaved off all his hair.

King gets up and walks out onto the balcony. Down below, 67 floors, evening falls on the town like a dirty handkerchief. High up there, he is a long way from a 6-by-12 cell, he is a man with the power to raise $35 million in a year, the man who can deliver Muhammad Ali—for now. And then he shouts up to the sky, "If I do not perform, Mr. Rockefeller, I will not jump off your building!" Raising his hand as if he were Emperor Jones, his voice booms again, "But if the Milky Way were not within me, how should I have seen it or known it?"

A star winks back at him.

He says. Winking.

Master of the Joyful Illusion

BY WILLIAM BARRY FURLONG

*Bill Veeck was baseball visionary, a major league owner who believed he owed
fans not just a good team but all the pleasures and delights a ballpark had to offer.
This entertaining profile did justice to the game's master showman.*

IN THE SECRET REACHES OF HIS PRIVATE UNIVERSE, THERE IS
little that the dreamer in Bill Veeck says can't be done. His success, his failures, his joys, his sorrows have created an extravagant legend that even for him tends to obscure reality. To the public, Bill Veeck, president of the Chicago White Sox baseball club, is a brashly
clamorous individual who has fashioned a brilliant career out of defying the
customs, conventions and crustaceans of baseball. It is an authentic yet one-
dimensional view. For Veeck is also an intelligent, impetuous, whimsical,
stubborn, tough-fibered, tireless individual with a vast capacity for living and
a deep appreciation for humanity. He is full of the humor that springs from the
unsuppressed human being. To Veeck, baseball is not an ultra-constitutional
mission, a crusade, a holy jousting for men's minds, souls and pocketbooks,
but simply an exhilarating way to make a living. His approach to the game
is seasoned with an almost visceral irreverence, a wit that is sometimes droll,
sometimes raffish, sometimes wry or macabre, and sometimes abusive. A few
months after emerging from the hospital where his right leg had been amputated, he threw a "coming-out" party. The high point of the party was
achieved when Veeck ripped off his artificial leg and flourished it before the
startled eyes of his guests. "It itches," he said.

He has the wit and the grace to make fun of what Veeck hath wrought.

When he took over the St. Louis Browns in 1951, he warned the fans to "stay away unless you have a strong stomach." Naturally, many fans rushed out to the ballpark to see what he was talking about. "They came out to see if the ball club was as bad as I said," he says, "and it was." Later on, while making a public appearance in New York, he apologized for his nervousness. "As operator of the St. Louis Browns," he explained, "I am not used to people." He outlined his strategy for making the Browns a pennant contender, "We've sold half of our ballplayers and hope to sell the rest," he said. "Our secret weapon is to get a couple of Brownies on every other team and louse up the league."

Behind this façade is a man with a highly perceptive vision of baseball's appeal. "This is an illusionary business," Veeck said not long ago. "The fan comes away from the ballpark with nothing more to show for it than what's in his mind, an ephemeral feeling of having been entertained. You've got to heighten and preserve that illusion. You have to give him more vivid pictures to carry away in his head." The most exalted illusion of all is satisfaction about the game ("The only guarantee of prosperity in baseball is a winner"), but that illusion, says Veeck, must be augmented by a feeling that it was fun to be at the ballgame. In support of this conviction, Veeck has given fans live lobsters, sway-back horses, 30,000 orchids, a pair of uncrated pigeons and 200 pounds of ice. He has staged circuses and brought in tightrope walkers and flagpole sitters and jugglers and the Harlem Globetrotters to perform between games of a double-header. He has shot off several kilotons of fireworks after night games. ("If you win, it's a bonus for the fans on top of the flush of victory; if you lose, they go away talking about the fireworks, not the lousy ballgame.")

At the age of 46, Veeck retains many of the elfin enthusiasms of his youth, though the years have thinned his once-bushy, pinkish-blond hair to a pair of tracks and a tuft of straw, and his face has assumed the rutted dignity of a mask done in clay by a slightly arthritic sculptor. But there has been a quickening of the currents and contradictions that make up the man. He is an omnivorous reader who likes to talk out his thoughts. He is a gregarious companion with an introspective streak. He is an undisciplined spirit of spontaneous inspirations, yet he is hard-working—he rises at 4 or 5 o'clock virtually every morning and works 16 to 20 hours a day. He is intensely competitive. Even though he has only one leg, he continues to play tennis and paddleball. "Does a man stop smiling because he wears false teeth?" he asks. He is painstakingly unpretentious. He works in a onetime reception room in Comiskey Park, answers all his mail himself (writing in longhand on the margins of the letters) and takes phone calls at all hours of the day and night.

Unlike most larger-than-life personalities, Veeck exhibits in public a self-deprecatory air and in private a remarkable sense of charity of heart and purse.

At times he is as insistent and impetuous in his charities as in his business dealings. When one friend refused to allow Veeck to buy him a much-needed automobile, Veeck phoned a children's home in which the friend was interested and announced he would buy anything it needed. "Take a little time to think it over," he said. "Take six hours."

Veeck has studied—*studied*, not browsed in—accounting, architecture and "at law." (He discovered a few years ago that some states still offer admission to the bar to persons who study, as Abraham Lincoln did, under a lawyer's guidance and tutoring.) He reads four books a week, has written a novel ("50,000 words and now they want me to put in dialogue!") and played a role in an allegedly professional production of *The Man Who Came to Dinner*. "Putting me on the stage was like putting Sarah Bernhardt on second base," he said at the time. "The theater people would think she was out of place and the baseball people would know it." His conversation ranges restlessly over a seemingly limitless mental horizon, from baseball to philosophy and back again.

It was this restlessness that touched off, some 11 years ago, the intellectual revolution that led to his becoming a convert to Roman Catholicism. "I'd studied everything from Buddhism to Magna Mater," he says. "In fact, I gave quite a bit of thought to Judaism." He approached Catholicism with a healthy skepticism, challenging and even dropping instruction when it did not respond to his intellectual need. "He had the toughest mind I've ever encountered," says the Rev. George Halpin of Chicago, the priest who ultimately brought Veeck into the Church. "He was a great student of comparative religions. He never asked an ordinary question." When Veeck voiced doubts about a single footnote in a 600-page volume on Catholicism, Father Halpin spent three days and probed through 13 books with him in an effort to establish its intellectual validity. "It was a most interesting three months," says Father Halpin of the period of Veeck's instruction.

All this mental activity takes place on a sort of subterranean level, the generative but not always visible level of Veeck's nature. On the surface, he remains invincibly The Clown and The Irritant. His volcanic relations with the other owners in baseball stem not so much from his picaresque approach to the game as to his unsheathed candor. His feud with the New York Yankees started years ago as a professional matter and quickly became a personal one. "George Weiss is a sensitive man and I am an outspoken one," he says. "I'm sure that when I say George is a fugitive from the human race he does not think it is funny." Many owners profess to find his Midas touch distasteful. "He is nothing but a capital-gains gypsy," says one whose own disaffection for money is not pronounced.

That Veeck has a gypsy nature is indisputable. "I've had seven children and no two of them have been born in the same state," he says. That his ball clubs make money is also indisputable. In Cleveland, by Veeck's own testimony, his backers got back $20 for every $1 they put into the club. At St. Louis, Veeck bought stock at $7 a share and sold it 2½ years later for $12 a share; even when the huge operating losses are included, the transaction netted Veeck and his backers a 38% profit. In Chicago the appraised value of the White Sox rose from $195 a share to $450 a share in the first year of Veeck's management. But that he shuffles franchises for profit motive alone *is* disputable. Veeck sold the Milwaukee Brewers in 1945 because he thought he might restore health to his ailing legs and ailing marriage by dropping out of baseball. He sold the Cleveland Indians in 1949 to raise enough cash to provide trust funds for his three older children and for a final settlement on his divorce. He sold the St. Louis Browns in 1953 at the insistence of an American League cabal led, he claims, by the Yankees.

None of this negates the alienation of Veeck from the community of owners or the real reasons for that alienation: that Veeck is a person of greater dimensions and grander vision than his contemporaries. All this would be tolerable if Veeck fitted the baseball men's image of such an individual—*i.e.*, a failure. But his success offers a suggestion of their own inadequacy and threatens some of the longtime institutions of baseball, such as the domination of the American League by the Yankees. For if other clubs in the league continue to find Veeck's club a better draw than the Yankees, they may undergo a polar shift from domination by the Yankees—who, through the years, have offered them so much money that they couldn't defy Yankee wishes in league councils—to domination by Veeck.

The hostility of the owners is not shared by their players. Veeck is probably the most popular "players' owner" in history. He speaks the players' language without condescension and tends their needs without personal or financial reserve. Once in Milwaukee, Harry (Peanuts) Lowrey, an outfielder demoted to the Brewers by the Chicago Cubs, explained that his poor performance in Milwaukee was due to the fact that he and his family couldn't find a home there. "Move into my place," said Veeck—and promptly moved his own family out so Lowrey's could move in. Another time, Veeck spent $10,000 arranging for the birth and adoption of illegitimate children sired by three of his ballplayers. "I'd handled about 15 cases like this before but never three in one season!" he says—and then spent $100,000 of his own money fighting various legal actions just to keep the players' names secret. "We were trying to keep their families from breaking up," he says, "and we did."

Historically, Veeck is perhaps the most notable mutation in baseball. He developed his bizarre techniques out of a sturdy tradition of conservative training and heritage. The only employer he ever knew was Philip K. Wrigley, the correct, conservative owner of the Chicago Cubs. Of him Veeck says: "A very bright man, more about things than about people, but very bright nevertheless." Veeck's father, for 15 years president of the Cubs, was a dignified person who, says Veeck, "was basically in favor of many of the same things I stand for—a clean ballpark, a happy atmosphere. The kidding part I do—well, you must remember we operate in different eras. When my daddy started with the Cubs [as a vice president in 1917] baseball was just about the only mass sport there was. This meant that your competition was a lot less and of an entirely different nature from today. You didn't have much golfing. You didn't have the huge race tracks and legalized betting of today. You didn't have hunting and fishing in reach of everybody, or sailing and boating. You didn't have radios that you can carry around on a golf course so you can listen to the games but never have to go to one. You didn't have television. It's true, certain things I do would be completely foreign to my father's nature. But he was indoctrinated in a different era and he reacted to it in a different way."

The elder Veeck was a sportswriter working under the name Bill Bailey on the Chicago *American* when Bill was born on Feb. 9, 1914. Bill had an older brother, Maurice, who was killed in a childhood shooting accident playing cops and robbers. He still has an older sister, Peggy Krehbiel, who lives in Downers Grove, a suburb near Chicago. In his sportswriting days, the senior Veeck was a trenchant critic of the Cubs. "My infant son can throw his bottle farther than this team can hit," he said of one Cub team. Thus needled, the Cubs took Veeck into the organization as a vice president and, after the 1918 season, raised him to president.

It was in these years that young Bill became attuned to the hidden tempos and secret life that make a ballpark pulse with personality. When he was 11, he was helping mail out tickets for ladies' day, a novelty brought to Chicago by his father. In his teens he worked in the stockroom, in the concession stands, in the grandstand hawking popcorn and programs, with the ground crew, any place where his exceptional energies could be harnessed. (In 1929 he lost $10,000 worth of tickets to the World Series and didn't find them until two months after the season was over.) After hours he went rollicking with many of the players, a raucous, hard-drinking crew. From them he learned all the facts of life and the childlike enthusiasm with which ballplayers explore them. "One thing I tell our sons," says Veeck's wife, Mary Frances, "is that there is nothing they need to keep from their father. There isn't any kind of trouble they can get into that he hasn't seen."

His own father did not approve of all this. When Mr. Veeck took his wife and daughter partying, Peggy would have to rush into the speakeasy and flush the teen-age Bill and his friends out the back way before the elder Veeck walked in. "Bill could never understand why, if it was illegal for his father to be there, it was *more* illegal for *him* to be there," says Peggy.

In September 1933 the elder Veeck became ill with leukemia and on October 5, he died. Bill dropped out of Kenyon College and went to work as an office boy for the Cubs at $17 a week. Eight years later, still in his 20s, he was treasurer of the Cubs and earning $17,000 a year. He was also a husband and father; in 1935 he had married Eleanor Raymond, a childhood friend from Hinsdale whose horsemanship won her a role as a bareback rider in the Ringling Brothers Circus. "I thought when I married Bill I was leaving the circus," she was quoted as saying some years later. She was wrong. Ideas were burgeoning in Veeck's mind, ideas that won no welcome from the Cubs. "It got," Veeck has said, "so that when Mr. Wrigley saw me coming, he automatically said, 'No.' "

IN 1939, when he was only 25 years old, Veeck had tried unsuccessfully to buy the White Sox. Two years later, on June 21, 1941, with nothing but $11 and a ticket to Milwaukee in his pocket, Veeck quit the Cubs. In Milwaukee he blew $10 partying with newspapermen to celebrate his liberation and imminent purchase of the Milwaukee Brewers of the American Association. At the time the Brewers were, if possible, in worse financial shape than Veeck. They were close to bankruptcy, the league had taken over the franchise, and the bank was about to foreclose. Veeck hurried to the bank to buy the club and get an extension on the loan. He persuaded the bankers that all he really wanted to borrow was time, and he got it. On the strength of this he talked some more and asked for $50,000. He got that too.

On the night that Veeck took over the Brewers, they drew a total of 22 fans. "They were all people who liked to attend hangings," says Veeck. Within 24 hours he had brought in Charlie Grimm as manager and started building the Legend of Bill Veeck. He shuttled players in and out on almost daily schedules. He cleaned up the ballpark. He rocked staid Milwaukee with his zany stunts. He began throwing money around as if he were the last of the great spenders. "Fortunately, in Milwaukee it didn't take an awful lot of money," he says. The ball club remained an indomitable last in 1941, but the next year it shot to within a game of first place. Veeck wiped out all but $17 of the club's $135,000 debt, then started earning large profits as the Brewers won three straight American Association pennants and began setting minor-league attendance records. In October 1945, after spending 22 months in the Marines ("I was a four-time buck private"), Veeck sold the Brewers at a personal profit of

$275,000. With this, he temporarily retired from baseball, bought a ranch in southern Arizona and moved there with Eleanor and their three children.

While Veeck had been fighting with the Marines on Bougainville during World War II, both his legs were attacked by a jungle rot that threatened to dissolve the bones. In addition, his right leg was injured in the recoil of an anti-aircraft gun. Veeck underwent 10 operations, had bone grafts taken for both legs ("I now have very little bone in my right hip"), and suffered as many as 24 penicillin shots a day for five months while lying in traction. Ultimately his left leg was saved but his right leg was amputated about six inches below the knee in November 1946. Since then, Veeck has had seven more operations to pare off more and more of the bone—the last only a week ago. This time the knee itself was sacrificed, and Veeck may virtually have to learn to walk again.

If Arizona partially saved his legs, it could not save his marriage. Eleanor was an intelligent young woman who, as it developed, was considerably more introverted than her husband. "Eleanor just didn't understand Bill's moods," says one of Veeck's close friends. After a period of separation, the couple was divorced in 1949. At about that time Bill met Mary Frances Ackerman, a one-time drama student who was a press agent for the Ice Capades. They dated almost daily for two weeks, then Bill asked her to marry him. The proposal was enormously complicated by the fact that Mary Frances was a Catholic and Bill a divorced man. Ultimately, the Church made a thorough investigation of Veeck's first marriage and found that a civil but not a sacramental union had taken place: Neither Bill nor his first wife had been baptized nor had they been married in a church, so he was granted the Pauline Privilege to rewed. In the meantime, as a test of his faith and his love, Veeck refrained from seeing Mary Frances for six months. They finally were married by Father Halpin in the Cathedral at Albuquerque in the spring of 1950.

LONG BEFORE that he had returned to baseball. In June 1946, less than a year after selling the Brewers, he acquired the Cleveland Indians for $1,750,000. "The team looked hopeless," he says, "so I bought it." Within 2½ years the Indians had won their first pennant in 28 years, won the World Series and set an alltime attendance record of 2,620,627. Because of his need for cash, Veeck sold the Indians for $2.2 million in 1949 and then, almost as if he had a drive for self-immolation, bought the cellar-bound St. Louis Browns for $1.5 million in mid-1951. "They were the worst-looking collection of ballplayers I've ever seen," he said. "It hurt to look at them." Very few people did.

By the end of 1952, however, attendance was up 60%, and the Browns were outdrawing the Detroit Tigers, Chicago White Sox and Philadelphia Athletics on the road. Veeck, meanwhile, was learning some harsh facts of economic life. He was, in fact, engaged in a fight for survival. In February 1953, Fred Saigh, who was about to go to prison on an income tax evasion charge, sold his St. Louis Cardinals to the Anheuser-Busch Brewery. That altered the balance of power in St. Louis. Veeck felt he could compete against the limited resources of Saigh, but he knew that he could not compete against the virtually unlimited resources of the brewery. His only alternative was to move the Browns out of town. In March 1953 he asked permission of the American League to move to Baltimore and saw a unanimous agreement turned into a 5–3 vote against him. He traced the switch to the Yankees. "Let's put it nicely," he has said. "They figured they could beat my brains out—and they did."

The technique was simple: By forcing Veeck to remain in St. Louis, where he was now unpopular because of his plans to move, they could force him to near bankruptcy. They were right. Within a few weeks Veeck found he was getting three cancellations for season tickets for every new one be sold. He had to sell some of his players, then he had to sell his ballpark to the St. Louis Cardinals for $900,000 and rent it back for $175,000 a year. He sold his stocks and bonds, his ranch in Arizona, his annuities and much of his personal property. Rudie Schaffer, long his closest aide, mortgaged his own home to help meet payrolls. Unable to raise more than 10% of the $30,000 asking price for a likely-looking shortstop in the Negro league, Veeck told the Cubs about Ernie Banks "to keep him out of the American League." By June, attendance had dropped 87%, Veeck had lost $400,000 of his own money in the club and he was being hanged in effigy regularly at the Browns' ball games. "It was the most difficult year of my life," he says.

At length, their sense of duty only half-fulfilled, the Yankees relented. They allowed the American League to allow the Browns to move to Baltimore if Veeck did not move with them. He and his backers agreed to sell out for $2.5 million.

It was a cankerous personal defeat for Veeck, but within two weeks he was back in baseball as a $1,000-a-month special assistant to Phil Wrigley, seeking ways of getting major-league baseball to the West Coast. Veeck spent 14 months and $75,000 of his own money on the project. At one point, in the hope that American League owners loved money more than they hated him, Veeck teamed up with hotel man Conrad Hilton and construction man Henry Crown to try to buy the foundering Philadelphia Athletics and move them to Los Angeles. But the league blocked him and arranged for the club to be sold instead to the late Yankee landlord, Arnold Johnson, who moved the Athletics to Kansas City.

Subsequently Veeck failed in a bid to buy the Cleveland Indians again ("We were really setting a price so that Hank Greenberg could sell his stock"), saw his high bid for the Detroit Tigers ($5.5 million cash or $6 million "on time") turned down for a lower bid ("Sometimes you run into riverboat gamblers," he said bitterly) and failed to buy the Ringling Brothers Circus for $21.1 million.

Not until Dorothy Comiskey Rigney tired of her bitter legal battle with her brother Charles over control of the White Sox did Veeck get his chance to acquire a club again. In the winter of 1958–59 he moved in swiftly and with half a dozen backers bought the 54% of the club controlled by Dorothy for $2.7 million.

The fiery illusions of fun he built around the game in Chicago—notably the exploding scoreboard, which fires off $60 worth of skyrockets and aerial bombs every time a White Sox player hits a home run—are now part of the durable Veeck legend. But some others of Veeck's changes were quite subtle. "Anything that happens in a ballpark, from the moment a fan arrives to the moment he leaves, can ruin the impression of fun that you're trying to build," he says. "This requires an attention to detail." He offers, as an example, the metamorphosis of the dun-colored roach pit that was Comiskey Park. "If you remember, it was dark and dank when you came in; it was like going into a dungeon," he said. "So we painted everything under the grandstand white, tore down a few useless pillars and ripped out everything that hung overhead, that loomed over you. We wanted to get away from that dungeonlike atmosphere to one of cleanliness and airiness." Other details he labored over ranged from putting cloth towels in the washrooms instead of paper towels (cost: $500 a month just "to get a little extra class") to establishing contact with the radar screen around Chicago in order to get early warning of approaching rainstorms so ushers could hand out plastic rain capes to fans in rain-exposed areas. "The important thing is to give them the capes before it starts raining, not after they've got wet," he says. "The intrinsic value of the capes [they cost 4½ cents apiece] is nothing. But the fact that you went out of your way to protect people is important to the fans."

The impact of his methods was demonstrated in an important area; banishing the historic dislike women had for Comiskey Park. To overcome this attitude, Veeck worked on a variety of details. He stationed ushers just inside the gates to look for women who appeared confused and to escort them personally to their seats. He cleaned up and redecorated the once-nauseating powder rooms. He installed lighting in them that was subtly flattering ("A woman likes to think she's looking her best when she goes back into the world") full-length mirrors ("so she can check her seams") and different levels of vanity tables. He gave away orchids and roses, let mothers in free on Mother's Day, gave away green stamps (instead of cigars or beer) on certain Sundays. The result was that the number of women attending games at Comiskey Park tripled (to about 420,000) and the proportionate number went up from less than 20% to more than 30%.

By far the most vivid part of the illusion which Veeck built up, however, was the bravura defiance of destiny by the 1959 White Sox. Employing an anachronistic philosophy of speed, pitching and defense, the White Sox won their first pennant in 10 years and drew 1,423,144 fans to Comiskey Park, double the attendance of 1958.

Ever since moving to Chicago in March 1959, the Veecks have lived in a three-bedroom apartment on the ninth floor of a lake-front hotel on Chicago's South Side. They have four children, ranging from 21 months to 9 years old. At home, as in baseball, the impact of Veeck's personality is electric ("All of our children learned to say 'Daddy' first," says Mary Frances) but, in her own way, Mary Frances exercises the tyranny of the weak over the strong with great subtlety. She does all the personal buying for her husband, from toothbrushes to the 50 white sport shirts and the half dozen identical blue sports coats and slacks that Bill needs every year ("I haven't bought anything in 10 years," says Bill. "Not even a razor blade"). But she has never insisted that Bill wear a tie, not even at their nuptial Mass. She has achieved only one change: She succeeded in switching Bill from tan sports clothes to navy blue because navy blue was simply more practical for handling by the wife in this family.

The only routine that Veeck follows is early in the morning. Usually he spends 60 to 90 minutes bathing the shrunken stump of his right leg. This is the time when he gets chance to read and reflect, when the reality of Bill Veeck—the substance behind and beyond the legend—becomes apparent and the far reaches of his private universe are explored. "I'm for the dreamer," he said not long ago. "The only really important things in history have been started by the dreamers. They never know what can't be done."

The Coach and
His Champion

BY ALEXANDER WOLFF

John Wooden's UCLA teams won 10 NCAA titles in 12 seasons but what mattered most to him was his wife of 53 years. Once she was gone, SI's longtime basketball writer found that all the memories turned bittersweet for the game's most revered coach.

JOHN WOODEN WILL NOT BE IN SEATTLE THIS WEEKEND. INSTEAD, the greatest basketball coach ever—the man who so completely made the Final Four his private reserve that the fans and the press and the rest of the college game couldn't get in on the fun until he retired—will be at home, in Encino, Calif., in what is called the Valley.

He will not stay home because he is unwelcome in Seattle. Men like Bob Knight and Dean Smith have implored him to come, to grace with his presence the annual meeting of the National Association of Basketball Coaches, which is held at the Final Four. But their entreaties have been unavailing. "We need him at our convention," says current UCLA coach Jim Harrick, who is the sixth man in 14 years to try to wear Wooden's whistle. "He is a shining light. My wife and I have offered to take him. I hounded him so much that he finally told me to lay off. The more you badger him, the more stubborn he gets. But I can see his point. The memories would be really difficult."

To most coaches, memories of 10 NCAA championships in 12 years, including seven in a row, would be sweet and easy. Indeed, this spring marks the 25th anniversary of Wooden's first title, the championship won by UCLA's tiny Hazzard-Goodrich-Erickson team, the one he likens to his first child. But beginning in 1947, when he was coaching at Indiana State, and continuing for 37 consecutive years, Wooden attended the coaches' convention and the Final Four in the company of his late wife, Nell. At 78 he's not about to start going alone, not now.

Nell was perennial, consensus All-Lobby. She knew the names that went with the faces, and she would whisper cues to her husband as well-wishers approached. He needed her with him, for she was as outgoing as he was reserved. A few coaches didn't cotton to Nell's presence, for they had left their own wives at home and knew that the usual boys-will-be-boys shenanigans would never pass unnoticed before Nell's Irish eyes. But her husband wasn't for an instant to be talked out of bringing her, just as today he isn't to be talked into going without her.

So Wooden will spend college basketball's premier weekend in much the same way he passes all his days now. The games on TV will be mere divertissements. He will take his early-morning walk, past the park, the eucalyptus trees and the preschool his great-granddaughter attends. Each evening he will speak to Nell in apostrophe before retiring. He may whisper the lines from Wordsworth that he finds so felicitous: "She lived unknown, and few could know/When Lucy ceased to be;/But she is in her grave, and, oh,/The difference to me!"

Sunday will be for church, for the long drive to Nell's grave in Glendale and for their children, their children's children, and their children's children's children. At night he will repair to the bedroom of the condominium he and Nell shared, in which virtually nothing has been altered since her death four years ago. Wooden sleeps fitfully these days, as if expecting a call. He talks often of death but does not fear it. "No fear at all, absolutely none," he says. "I'll confess that prior to losing Nellie I had some."

Upon finishing his morning constitutional—a doctor prescribed it in 1972 because of heart trouble—he often will sit down in his study, underneath the pictures of the 10 national championship teams that were hung, at Nell's suggestion, to form a pyramid, and a poem or aphorism will take shape. He remarks on how effortlessly this one flowed from him one morning:

The years have left their imprint on my hands and on my face;
Erect no longer is my walk, and slower is my pace.
But there is no fear within my heart because I'm growing old;
I only wish I had more time to better serve my Lord.
When I've gone to Him in prayer He's brought me inner peace,
And soon my cares and worries and other problems cease;
He's helped me in so many ways, He's never let me down;
Why should I fear the future, when soon I could be near His crown?
Though I know down here my time is short, there is endless time up there,
And He will forgive and keep me ever in His loving care.

And how did you imagine John Wooden spending his later years? The mind, the values, the spring in his step—they're all still in place. He could probably take over a misbegotten college varsity, demonstrate the reverse pivot, intone a few homilies and have the team whipped into Top 20 shape in, oh, six weeks. He continues to stage summer basketball camps in which you won't necessarily meet famous players but you may actually learn the game. He answers his own mail, in a hand that you'll remember from grammar school as "cursive writing."

He books most of his own speaking engagements, although several outfits have solicited his services. Audiences rarely ask about Nell, but he tends to bring her up anyway. He usually refers to her as "my sweetheart of 60 years, my wife of 53, till I lost her." The cards he sends to family and the checks he makes out for the children's trusts, he signs in both their names. "That pleases Nellie," he says.

His life is lived to that end. "I won't ever leave here, because I see her everywhere," he says in his—their—living room. "I miss her as much now as I ever have. It never gets easier. There are friends who would like to see me find another woman for the companionship. I wouldn't do it. It would never work."

He takes the morning walk in part because she insisted he take it. He has continued to participate in the camps because his share of the profits goes into the trusts, and family was so important to her. He gives the speeches, usually on his Pyramid of Success—a homespun collection of life principles—because, if you riffle back through the Norman Rockwell scenes of their life together, back to high school in Martinsville, Ind., you'll see it was Nell who persuaded taciturn Johnny Wooden to take a speech class to help him out of his shell. He struggled until the teacher, Mabel Hinds, who knew of his fondness for poetry, gave him a copy of Thomas Gray's *Elegy Written in a Country Churchyard*, which made the speaking easier.

He still knows Gray's *Elegy* cold, and in Martinsville in January, at a banquet on the eve of ceremonies to dedicate the 12-year-old high school gym in his name, he recited it. With all manner of acclaim being slung at him, he intoned this stanza as if raising a shield to protect himself:

The boast of heraldry, the pomp of pow'r,
And all that beauty, all that wealth e're gave;
Awaits alike th' inevitable hour:
The paths of glory lead but to the grave.

"And they do," he added from the dais. "We're all going to go someday."

AS A COACH, did you ever lose your temper?"

The postprandial question comes from the audience in Martinsville. Wooden's answer provides a lesson about self-control: "I always told my players to control their tempers, and I couldn't very well expect them to if I wasn't setting a good example myself. I lost my temper once in a while. But I never lost control. I never threw anything. I never threw a chair."

Not 20 miles from Bloomington, within the pale of Bob Knight, the banquet hall erupts with approval.

The sphinx of the Pyramid of Success rests his left forearm against his stomach, parallel to the ground. His left hand is a socket for his right elbow. His right forearm forms a hypotenuse leading to his chin, where the index finger sticks upright, hovering just over his mouth. When speaking, Wooden strikes this pose frequently and unconsciously. A photograph of him in the same pose—Nell's favorite—hangs in their bedroom.

It is an enigma, that finger to the mouth. Is it the stern Midwestern schoolteacher, meting out discipline, admonishing the class? Or is it the kindly grandfather, guiding the wayward and confused young, giving them assurances that everything will be all right?

Or is it both? Wooden's greatest achievement isn't the 10 in 12, or seven in a row, although such a feat will surely never be accomplished again. It is rather that he did all this during the roily years from 1964 to '75—an era in which 18- to 22-year-old males were at their most contrary—at UCLA, a big-city campus awash in the prevailing freedoms.

Your star player lies down in rush-hour traffic to protest the Vietnam War. (Stand up for what you believe, Bill Walton's coach always said, but be willing to accept the consequences.)

Four of your players ask to use your office after practice to conduct meditation sessions. (You let them.) One asks your permission to smoke marijuana, saying he'd heard it would relieve the pain in his knees. (I am not a doctor, you tell Walton. All I know is it's against the law.)

College players still take drugs, but none today go in to discuss it with the coach beforehand. What was it about Wooden that caused Walton to broach this subject? "Decisions are more apt to be accepted when you've listened to suggestions first," says Wooden. "I wanted them to see the reason behind what I asked of them, not to do things just because I said so."

Yet Wooden threw down the clipboard when he had to. Former UCLA center Steve Patterson remembers the day, in the fall of 1970, that he and forward Sidney Wicks asked to be excused from practice to show solidarity with a nationwide rally protesting the Vietnam War. "He asked us if this reflected our convictions, and we told him it did," says Patterson. "He told us he had his convictions, too, and if we missed practice it would be the end of our careers at UCLA.

"We blinked. I don't think he was necessarily unsympathetic to the statement we wanted to make. He may even have agreed with us. But I see the connection. I didn't at the time, but I do now. He continually challenged you about your attitude toward the team as a whole. He set the standards. He didn't let us set the standards, even though we wanted to."

Wooden's practice gym was a sort of one-room schoolhouse, transported from the Indiana plains. For two hours in the afternoon his pupils listened to material that seemed to have emerged from a time warp. They listened because they knew they would win if they learned their lessons. The fundamentals came complete with hoary precepts: Failure to prepare is preparing to fail. Be quick, but don't be in a hurry. Don't mistake activity for achievement. The purpose of discipline isn't to punish but to correct. Things turn out best for those who make the best of the way things turn out.

One sentiment is so dear to Wooden that he has mined the anthologies for two renderings of it. "The journey is better than the end" comes from Cervantes. And Robert Louis Stevenson said, "To travel hopefully is a better thing than to arrive." Says Wooden, "I appreciated that notion more later, after we started to win championships. The saying that it's tougher to stay on top than to get there—I don't believe it. It's very tough to get there. And along the way you learn, as Lincoln would say, not just what to do, but what not to do.

"People say we could never win those championships again, what with parity. But I'm not so sure it couldn't happen today. Winning breeds winning. If we had had freshman eligibility during the 1960s, we would have won another one (with Lew Alcindor, now Kareem Abdul-Jabbar, in 1965–66). When everyone has good players, teaching will be a telling difference."

Wooden taught basketball according to the simplest pedagogical principles. He used what he calls the whole-part method. Show the whole and then break it down, "just like parsing a sentence," he says, "or solving a math problem." He followed his four laws of learning: explanation, demonstration, correction and repetition. For 16 years there was talk of a new gym, and when UCLA finally opened Pauley Pavilion in 1965, Wooden made sure he didn't get just an arena, but a classroom with bleachers that roll back.

Wooden taught English at South Bend Central High before heading to Indiana State for two seasons and then to Westwood for the rest of his coaching life. He always preferred the practices to the games. The games were just exams, when the teacher's work was done. "There again," he says, "the journey's better than the end."

Piggie Lambert, Wooden's coach at Purdue, preached that the team making the most mistakes would win, for good things come to those who risk error by taking the initiative. Thus, initiative is part of Wooden's Pyramid. You would think, given his success, that someone might still coach his way today. But rare is the coach who doesn't have a tight rein, a hard derriere or both. How can a real teacher not indulge mistakes? "George Patton is not my idol," Wooden says. "I prefer Omar Bradley."

As he sees all the games the networks satellite-dish out, Wooden concludes that, besides turning the young men into dogs and ponies, television has transformed the coaches into showmen. Coaches today overcontrol. Instead, they should teach players the game and let them play it. Goodness gracious sakes alive—you may hear that truncated to Gracious sakes, but from Wooden you'll hear no stronger oath—coaches nowadays haven't even hit their 40's before they're writing books with titles like *A Coach's World* and *Born to Coach*.

Wooden's first book is still in print. Published in 1966, it's called *Practical Modern Basketball*. Read it and you'll learn that basketball is a game of threes: forward, center, guard; shoot, drive, pass; ball, you, man; conditioning, skill, teamwork. These last three elements made up Lambert's hoops trinity, and they are the three blocks at the heart of the Pyramid. The Wooden text also holds that the way to play the game—soundly, and with balance—isn't a bad way to live your life.

"You might have thought of that as a golden time, when you've climbed to the top of the mountain. But we were at the top of the mountain when we showed up." Greg Lee is talking about the Walton era, the three seasons Lee played at guard, between 1971 and '74. "Half the time we didn't even know who our opponent would be," he says. "Winning 88 straight games—that's not normal. It would have been better if we'd have struggled."

When Lee and his classmates were precocious sophomores, Wooden warned them that, as seniors, they would be intolerable. Headstrong young men like Walton, guard Tommy Curtis and Lee—"I'd like to be able to say I didn't contribute to the problems," Wooden says, "but I did"—didn't prove him wrong. But Wooden bent too much, and his normally steady hand seemed to waver. He relaxed some of the inviolable principles on which he had always insisted. He excused Walton from practice on Mondays and Tuesdays because of the center's aching knees. Detecting inconsistency, the team took advantage.

That March, as if to vindicate 25 years' worth of strictures suddenly allowed to go flaccid, UCLA squandered a seven-point lead in the second overtime of the NCAA semifinals and lost to North Carolina State. "Bill was such a megastar he probably didn't need to practice," says Lee. "But maybe the team needed him to practice."

Lee, now coach at a high school near San Diego, has learned that lesson in discipline in retrospect. But Wooden, even if he denies it today, relearned it then and there. The next season, with the Bruins again playing on his exacting terms, they became champions once more.

SINCE HIS retirement, the catty strains of Wooden revisionism have made their way through the coaching fraternity. Unlikely as it may seem, between 1948 and 1963 Wooden did not win an NCAA crown at UCLA, and during this period the critics accused him of being a jockey of referees and opposing players. They said that he overheated the old "B.O. Barn," the Bruins' second-floor gym, because he knew his teams could stand it. They said that he had two sets of standards, one for stars and another for everybody else. But the most persistent whisper has always been that the cornerstone of the Pyramid was no middle-American verity, not conditioning or skill or teamwork, but a Los Angeles contractor and UCLA booster named Sam Gilbert.

Gilbert was everything Wooden wasn't. Worldly and wealthy, he offered players advice and, in violation of NCAA rules, gave them gifts and paid for their girlfriends' abortions. Black players, in particular, received healthy doses of his street wisdom and regular invitations to the lavish spreads at his house on Sunday mornings. "I remember we were on a road trip in Chicago, and five guys all got on the bus together wearing matching coats with fur-lined collars," says Lee. "It was pretty conspicuous. It's not like Coach was an ostrich about Sam, but he wouldn't confront the problem."

Wooden insists that no one enrolled at UCLA because of Gilbert. But once a player became a Bruin, few were denied his largess. With the inertia born of a successful program, and with Wooden's lack of interest in matters outside the gym or the classroom, Gilbert went unchallenged. After becoming the UCLA coach in the late '70s, Larry Brown, who resented Gilbert's sway with his players, tried to run him off. Gilbert responded by threatening not only to cut off Brown's testicles but also to do it "without him even knowing it." In 1987 a Florida grand jury, unaware of Gilbert's death four days earlier, indicted him in a drug-money-laundering scheme.

In the simplistic analogy, Gilbert is the hoodlum on the fringe of the school yard, and Wooden is the teacher who can only tell his pupils to Just Say No. "I warned them, but I couldn't pick their friends," says Wooden. Today Wooden owns up to breaking NCAA rules himself. He invited players to have meals with him and Nell during in-season school vacations so they would not be alone in dormitories on campus. He helped pay the rent of a player with a child and a sick wife. He bailed out of jail another player who had been picked up for delinquent parking violations. These transgressions all conformed to Wooden's higher rules.

"I honestly feel Sam meant well," says Wooden. "He felt whatever he did was right, even if it was against the rules." As different as he and Gilbert were, Wooden felt much the same way.

"I never had a smarter player than Mike Warren," Wooden frequently says. He also says, "I never had a better athlete than Keith Erickson." This is a salutary lesson about race, from a man who grew up in Indiana, then a hotbed of the Ku Klux Klan. Warren, who later starred in *Hill Street Blues*, is black; Erickson, white. In a sport infected with racial code phrases like "heady ballplayer" and "great athlete," Wooden's comments are March on Washington stuff. But he says he isn't the slightest bit aware of their stereotype-busting implications. Wisdom subdues bigotry. With the experience to judge, one need not prejudge.

By her husband's count, Nell was twice at death's door before she finally succumbed. A heart attack, which she suffered while undergoing a hip-replacement operation in 1982, put her in a coma. Friends and family took turns visiting St. Vincent's Hospital in downtown Los Angeles, not to see Nell in her quiet as much as to succor her husband. He spent 10- and 12-hour days at her bedside, and he might not have found time to eat were it not for their solicitude.

"The doctors told me to talk to her," says Wooden. "They said that I might not see any signs, but in her subconscious she might be hearing me." Three months after Nell entered the coma, as her body lay suctioned and plugged with intravenous tubing, he took her hand and squeezed it, and he felt a squeeze back. There are no nets to cut down when something like that happens.

But shortly thereafter Nell had to go back into the hospital to have her gallbladder removed, and that, the doctors said, was a no-hoper. No way she could weather the trauma. Yet she survived the surgery, recovering enough to live life rather than just muddle through it. She even made one last Final Four—Seattle, in fact, in 1984. She was in a wheelchair but was still alert and vivacious, still matching the names with the faces. "It was," the coach says, "the last enjoyable thing she did."

That is why this weekend in Seattle would have been so difficult. Early on Christmas morning in 1984, Nell had to be rushed to the hospital. By then a number of ailments, including cancer and emphysema, had gotten ornery. At 73 she just wasn't going to pull off any more miracles. Nell fought on through the rest of the winter, playing out the season. She died on the first day of spring.

Before every tip-off back at Martinsville High, Wooden had looked up from his guard position and caught her eye in the stands, where she played the cornet in the band. She would give him the O.K. sign and he would wave back. They kept up that ritual even as Johnny Wooden (Hall of Fame, inducted as a player in 1960) became John R. Wooden (Hall of Fame, inducted as a coach in 1972). He's the only person with the old one-two combo. Few knew that he clutched a cross in his hand. Fewer knew that she clutched an identical one in hers. She took it with her to the grave.

The reclusiveness that ruled Wooden's first year as a widower alarmed doctors, family and friends alike. Former players and assistant coaches conspired to telephone regularly until Wooden's granddaughter, Caryn, gave birth to a girl, Cori, and he brightened somewhat. "I try to be thankful for the time Nellie and I had together," says Wooden. "But sometimes you wonder what you could have done. There's a certain amount of second-guessing that goes on."

He never went off to scout opponents, never brought the practices home and didn't make more than a dozen recruiting trips in his entire career. What could so faithful and doting a husband possibly regret? "We did things because I wanted to, not because she did," he says. "We never went to Ireland. Nellie always wanted to go to Ireland. We had planned to, too. But something would always come up. And Nellie loved to dance. I was not a dancer, you know."

He averts his eyes, betraying his small-town bashfulness. That's what Nell, at 13, had to crack; that's what she and her friend Mary Schnaiter would talk about when they repaired to the quarries outside town. Of course, Johnny was already smitten. "She was as cute as can be," says Mary. "Little, with a turned-up nose. She could do just about anything she wanted."

And my, the life John and Nell spent together. You can almost hear Alistair Cooke in the voice-over: Johnny, born in Hall, Ind., in 1910, one of four sons of a simple and devout couple, spent much of his youth in a farmhouse with a three-holer outhouse out back. His father forged the iron goal he learned to shoot at. John and Nell waited out his four years at Purdue, only to have their savings—$909 and a nickel—wiped out in a bank failure on the eve of their wedding.

So rock-solid a couple was grossly misplaced amid the shifting-sand values of Los Angeles. When John and Nell left Indiana State for UCLA, they found the support of two familiar Midwestern pillars. Wales Smith, the minister at the church they joined in Santa Monica, had been in Wooden's class at Martinsville High. Ralph Irwin, the doctor they chose, had performed an emergency appendectomy on Wooden in Iowa City. With a pastor and a doctor they could trust, John and Nell needed little more. "Oh, you're from back East!" people would say. Crossly, Nell would correct them.

She would speak up at times when John wouldn't. She upbraided the fans who she thought were too greedy. She threw withering looks at the caviling men along press row. She badgered J.D. Morgan, UCLA's shrewd and parsimonious athletic director, about her husband's insulting salary and the anemic retirement package awaiting them. "I know John Wooden never lies," one coach said during the early '70s, "but he can't be making twenty-nine-five." At the time he was. And he never made more than $32,500.

He had no shoe contracts or courtesy cars, either. In the early days, before all the titles, before Pauley was built, Wooden's Bruins practiced amid the gymnasts and wrestlers and shared a locker room with the other men's sports. The dust from all the gym classes would build up by practice time, and Wooden and his managers had to mop the floor themselves. The undisciplined circumstances under which he was asked to teach ate away at him, but he and Nell never really considered going elsewhere, even as offers from NBA teams and several schools in the Big Ten came his way. Their son, Jim, had fallen for surfing; their daughter, Nan, for Hollywood, where she and her girlfriends staked out the stars, autograph books clutched to their breasts. Soon enough Wooden made peace with the broken promises and his chaotic classroom. "I whipped it," he says, "by recognizing it."

Some people think Wooden was too deferential to Morgan. Certainly, the same couldn't be said of Nell. "She really thought they were taking advantage of him," says Nan. "And Daddy never wanted to complain, because he never wanted for anything. But Daddy didn't have to get mad. He could stay very serene, because his other half was getting it out. Nobody was his champion the way Mother was."

Championing a champion took its toll. During his early days as a coach, Wooden would stop smoking the day practice began and forswear cigarettes for the balance of the season. In 1955, he quit entirely. But it wasn't so easy for Nell. From the time she first acquired a taste for cigarettes, Nell had relied on smoking to help her cope with the stress. Her husband desperately wanted her to give up the habit that would hasten her departure from him, but she played games with him: stashing butts in her purse, retiring to her daughter's house to get a fix.

As the dynasty pushed into the '70s, success was spoiling what should have been glorious times and edging Wooden toward retirement. "Sometimes I'm very slow making up my mind," he says. "But once I make it up, I'm very slow to change it."

On the floor of the San Diego Sports Arena in 1975, after Wooden had won his last NCAA title, a booster sought him out and said, "Great victory, John. It makes up for your letting us down last year." The attitude implicit in that statement disgusted him. There would be no second thoughts, no regrets, about retiring. He didn't want to step down. He had to. "Daddy's job wasn't fun for us," says Nan. "It really wasn't."

HERE IS A lesson about learning. Back in the late '60s, when he was in the midst of winning those seven straight titles and had little reason to question himself about anything, Wooden attended a press conference at which the Los Angeles Lakers announced that they had traded for Wilt Chamberlain.

A reporter asked Wilt about his reputation for being hard to handle. Would the Laker coach have problems handling him? "I am not a thing," Chamberlain said. "You handle things. You work with people."

Upon returning home that day, Wooden opened a copy of *Practical Modern Basketball*. He turned to the section titled "Handling Your Players," crossed out "Handling" and wrote in "Working With." He phoned his publisher and asked that the change be made in all subsequent printings.

"John was a better coach at 55 than he was at 50," says Pete Newell, the former coach at Cal and San Francisco, who has known Wooden for more than 40 years. "He was a better coach at 60 than at 55. He's a true example of a man who learned from day one to day last."

In the outer lobby of the old Martinsville High gym hangs a picture of the Artesians' 1927 state championship team. "Gone," says Wooden, pointing to the player in the top left-hand corner. "Gone, gone, gone, gone," he continues, moving his finger from teammate to teammate. "Almost gone," he says, his finger finally coming to rest on his likeness.

When speaking engagements take him east, he'll route himself through Indianapolis, rent a car, drive the highway south and slip into the various graveyards around Martinsville, where his and Nell's forebears are buried. At each one he'll say a prayer. The neighboring gravestones are graced with names like Way and Byroad and Schoolcraft, names that sound as if they came from a novel about Puritans.

His preoccupation with death lifts only when Cori, 3, and her cousin, John, who's pushing three, come by to visit. Cori is the philosophical one, and little John is the instigator. It was John who got Papa, as they call their great-grandfather, to turn off all the lights and play a flashlight game that the kids call Ghostbusters. Nell must have been cackling from behind the credenza.

Meanwhile, over the hill in Westwood, a variation of the same game goes on. "The problem we're having is John Wooden," a Bruin named Kenny Fields said a few years ago. "He won too much. Now our fans can't accept anything less."

Wooden has scrupulously avoided commenting on the performance of any of his many successors. Indeed, Harrick says he has to crowbar advice out of him. Watch Wooden watching the Bruins, from his second-row seat across from the UCLA bench, occasionally with Cori and John scrambling around him: He claps rhythmically to the pep band during timeouts, but otherwise he betrays little reaction to the basketball before him.

Wooden won't say this explicitly, but the man UCLA should have hired back in 1975, the man the old coach praises whenever he has a chance, is Louisville's Denny Crum. That single move might have forestalled all the Bruins' recent travails. But Morgan refused to consider him as Wooden's replacement simply because Crum, a former UCLA player and assistant coach, had been divorced. Such were the impossible standards of John's and Nell's legacy.

SO WE COME to the lesson of the peaks and the valleys. If you should catch one of those Final Four historical shows on late-night cable, be sure to study Wooden's Bruins in victory. They're happy campers, storming the floor and cutting down the nets, but always they hold something back. "Of course, I will have reminded them in a timeout," says Wooden, "for every artificial peak you create there is a valley. I don't like valleys. Games can be lost in them."

He had seen Phil Woolpert win back-to-back national championships at San Francisco in 1955 and '56 and then struggle in the crucible of trying to keep winning. Then he saw Ed Jucker also win two in a row, at Cincinnati in '61 and '62, only to leave coaching because of similar pressure. That's when he resolved never to exult unduly in victory or to languish in defeat. "One's life," he says, "should be the same."

But with Nell's death his very faith wavered. Never mind that a favorite plaque of theirs hangs in his study and reads GOD NEVER CLOSES ONE DOOR WITHOUT OPENING ANOTHER. "He did not want to live," says Gary Cunningham, his old assistant. "A lot of us were worried, and disappointed, too. What he had instilled in our lives he wasn't practicing in his own." All that winning, and look what one loss did.

A few weeks ago Cori and Papa looked up as an airplane passed overhead. "See that airplane, Papa?" said Cori. "I'm going to take that airplane and fly all the way to heaven and get Mama and bring her back, so Papa won't be lonely anymore."

Gracious sakes, Cori, no. Stay right here with Papa. For later, there, he'll have Mama. For now, here, he has you and John, two previous generations of Woodens, and—should he ever change that mind that's so hard to change once it's made up—a convention full of rudderless coaches of basketball, who desperately need to learn how to teach the game.

Before this extraordinary life gets played out, before the buzzer sounds, won't someone please call timeout to remind him? He has taught so many of us such wonderful lessons. He has one more lesson, his own, to study up on.

'I Managed Good, but Boy Did They Play Bad'

BY GILBERT ROGIN

For 11 years Rocky Bridges played (more or less) for seven major league teams and always got more laughs than hits. In the summer of '64, SI's future managing editor was on hand to chronicle Bridges's managerial debut in the minor leagues.

T O BEGIN WITH," SAYS ROCKY BRIDGES, THE MANAGER OF THE San Jose Bees, "I'm a handsome, debonair, easygoing six-footer. Anyway, that's what I told them at the Braille Institute. As *you* can see, I'm really a five-foot-eight-and-a-halfer and I weigh 190, but what you know is that my weight is very mobile—it's moved around in front of me."

This is Rocky's first year as a manager, but he has come prepared, for he is one of the best stand-up comics in the history of baseball. "I'm back in the California League, where I started my slump," he says, "I'm the only man in the history of the game who started his career in a slump and stayed in it. I could play here as well as manage, but I have no guts. In 1947 I hit .183 for Santa Barbara and I'll be damned if I'll try again. I always wanted to be a baseball player. Now that I've quit playing, I still entertain that idea."

No man ever had a greater love for the game of baseball than Rocky Bridges. He considered it a privilege just to sit on the bench in the big leagues, which is a good thing because that was his usual position. "It was like being a little boy forever," he says. "I got a big charge just out of *seeing* Ted Williams hit. Once in a while they let me try to field some of them, which sort of dimmed my enthusiasm." Rocky's glove was mightier than his bat, but he could always handle a one-liner better than a line drive.

Rocky played (more or less) in the majors for 11 years and coached for two more. All told, he was on seven different teams: Brooklyn (1951–52), Cincinnati (1953–57), Washington (1957–58), Detroit (1959–60), Cleveland (1960), St. Louis (1960) and the Los Angeles Angels (1961–63). "I've had more numbers on my back than a bingo board," says Rocky. "My wife had to write to me care of Ford Frick. He was the only one who knew where I was. It's a good thing I stayed in Cincinnati for four years—it took me that long to learn how to spell it."

Rocky was a shortstop and second baseman by trade, a third baseman out of desperation and a left fielder for a third of an inning. "If I did anything funny on the ball field it was strictly accidental," he says. "Like the way I played third. Some people thought it was hilarious but I was on the level all the time. When Charlie Dressen asked me if I could play third, I said, 'Hell, yes. I'll mow your lawn for you if you like. I want to stay up here.' "

Rocky endured in the majors because of his enthusiasm, his versatility and his hustle. "If I told him to go up and get hit on the head," Birdie Tebbetts once said, "he'd do it." For the most part, Rocky was a utilityman, cheerfully accepting bit parts as a pinch runner or late-inning defensive replacement. For instance, in 1956 he appeared in 71 games but had only 19 at bats. And hustle, he says, "is not running out of the dugout, as some of my troops at San Jose think."

Rocky's best year was 1958, when he was chosen for the All-Star team. "I was hitting .307 at the break," Rocky recalls, "but then I checked out Frank Lary's fastball on my jaw. The trouble with having a wired jaw is that you can never tell when you're sleepy—you can't yawn." Rocky didn't play in the All-Star Game, nor did he play in the 1952 World Series, when he was with the Dodgers. "I've been a paid spectator at some pretty interesting events," he says, "and I've always had a good seat. I guess they figured there was no point in carrying a good thing too far."

Rocky has a .247 lifetime average and hit 16 home runs during his career. In fact, about his only statistical distinction is that he started triple plays in both leagues. "There used to be a rule against hitting me or walking me," Rocky says. "They had a lot going for them if I swung. I never figured myself an out man—I always swung, let it go wherever it wanted. Like I tell my troops, swing the bat. You never know what might happen. Two might get together." In 1961, after hitting his first homer in two seasons, Rocky said: "I'm still behind Babe Ruth's record, but I've been sick. It really wasn't very dramatic. No little boy in the hospital asked me to hit one. I didn't promise it to my kid for his birthday, and my wife will be too shocked to appreciate it. I hit it for me."

All of which adds up to the kind of record that leads a man whose life is baseball back to the California Leagues of the world, and Rocky is not crying in his Lucky Lager. He was asked the other day whether he thought he had reached his full potential as a baseball player. "I might have gone beyond it," he said.

Rocky finds that the league has changed a shade since he compiled an .884 fielding average in 19 games for Santa Barbara before being put out of his misery with a broken leg. "Reno wasn't in it," Rocky says. "That helped. The last time the Bees were in Reno, I lost the bus and two outfielders, but I won a shortstop and a bat."

The bus is leased from the Santa Cruz Transit Company. "It's not a brand-new bus," says Jack Quinn, general manager and president of the Bees, "but it's not an antique. I don't want to put any laurels in my pocket, but it's as good as any bus in the league."

"The bus isn't air conditioned," says Rocky. "It is if you open the window. Every so often we have to tell the driver to throw another log on the air conditioner. We take a lot of interesting trips in our bus. Reno to Bakersfield—that's 10 hours. We stay at a lot of interesting hotels, too. In one hotel lobby they have an artificial plant. Now, it wasn't always artificial. It's just that it's been there since the Stone Age. In another hotel they have television sets which only receive vertical lines. We play in some interesting ball parks, too. In one— well, I don't want to say the mound's high, but when I pitch batting practice I got to chew gum.

"There are three things the average man thinks he can do better than anybody else," says Rocky Bridges, "build a fire, run a hotel and manage a baseball team." Managing in the California League is something else, however.

"In one game," Rocky recalls, "there is a man on first, one out and my pitcher is up. 'If you don't bunt him over on the first pitch,' I tell him, 'hit-and-run on the second.' He misses the bunt, takes the next pitch and the guy's thrown out. 'How can you blow a sign when I told it to you?' I ask him, 'Well,' he says, 'I forgot.' Four days later there's a man on first, one out and my pitcher is up. Different pitcher. 'If you don't bunt him over on the first pitch,' I tell him, 'hit-and-run on the second.' He misses the bunt, takes the next pitch and the guy's thrown out. 'How can you blow a sign when I told it to you?' I ask him. 'Well,' he says, 'I forgot.' Now, some guys might get teed off at that, but it halfway struck me as kind of funny, For the life of me, I couldn't see how they could do it twice within a week."

Rocky manages the Bees from the third-base coach's box. "I pick one of the older guys on the club, 22 or 23—one thing that bothers me about this job is that I might come down with the croup—and put him on first base. I don't think anyone listens to him. I try to dream up strategy and things on third—like please hit the ball. The first game I managed good, but boy did they play bad.

"You got to treat the troops as pros but in the back of your mind remember they're novices. They do things you probably did and forgot. Of course, some of them it's easier to tell to go out and get an honest job. The other day my leftfielder saw some guys rob a liquor store near the ball park and chased them until he got their license number. Afterwards, he told me that he'd always wanted to be a cop. 'Don't give up hope,' I said."

Rocky is an admirably patient and gentle manager. "I always said I'd never forget I was a player if I became a manager, but I wanted to see if I would. How many times you hear of a manager keeping the guys sitting in front of their lockers for an hour after the ball game? That's an insult to their intelligence. I can't see bringing out the tambourine and jumping up and down, either. You can be a good guy and still have their respect. Of course if they start to goof off, they can be handled in a different way."

"I know when Rock's mad at me," says Lon Morton, a San Jose pitcher now *hors de combat* with a sore arm. "He puts his arm around Lon Morton and says, 'I'm mad at you.' " Morton alternately fascinates and exasperates Rocky. "There's a questionnaire all the players have to fill out," Rocky says. "One of the questions is what is your ambition. Every player but Morton put down 'big-league ballplayer.' Morton wrote, 'Hall of Fame.' Then there's Peraza, my lefthanded pitcher who can also throw right, and Cotton Nash, the big Kentucky basketball star I got on first. Nash could be an interesting individual. I'm small, but I still like the big ones. Nash offers an interesting target for some of my infielders. Some of my infielders make interesting throws. It makes it very interesting, but then I was sent down here to learn the pitfalls of managing—not winning."

Rocky Bridges was born in Refugio, Texas, on Aug. 7, 1927 under the name of Everett LaMar Bridges Jr. When he was one, his maternal grandparents took him to Long Beach, Calif., where he has lived ever since. Rocky never learned to swim, however. "My uncle dumped me in the ocean when I was six," he says, "I think I walked back underneath the water. I know I didn't walk on top." But then Bridges has always been a prodigious walker. He did not own a car until he got married. The day he signed with the Dodgers he had previously signed with the Yankees, but walking home he thought it over and tore up the Yankee contract. He then took a bus to the Dodger scout's house and walked all the way home with that contract intact—a total of four miles.

Rocky has always had to scuffle. "When I was a kid," he says, "I sold newspapers, delivered them, stole them." Even when he was a big-leaguer, he was still making it the hard way. He worked winters for a foundry pouring centrifugal die castings, for Boraxo cleaning out furnaces and sacking soap, and for a pipeline outfit. "I drove a Mexican diesel," he says, "that's a wheelbarrow. I was on a jackhammer, I dug holes. It not only kept me in shape but, more important, it kept me in money." Since he has been with Los Angeles (the Bees have a working agreement with the Angels) life has been sweeter. Last winter, for instance, Rocky worked for Oscar Gregory, a Paramount, Calif., Chevrolet dealer. "I do lip flappers [luncheon and banquet speeches]," he says. "I'm very big with the Elks."

Rocky is married to the former Mary Alway. "We're just like everybody else," he says, "cat, dog, four kids and debts. I used to lead the league in windows [the envelopes that bills come in]." His children are: Melinda, 11, Lance, 9, Cory, 6 and a baby, John Roland. Rocky can not recall where the name Lance came from. "I don't remember a bar by that name," he says. "I married my wife on her birthday to cut down on expenses. One kid was born on December 30 so I could claim the deduction. We're a family of conveniences."

Rocky is not handy around the house. "I couldn't fix a track meet," he says. He does like to cook, however. He carries a recipe for veal parmigiana in his wallet that he clipped from a home magazine. Rocky's major diversion is golf. "I play at it," he says. "I know that people who have seen me out on the course find it mighty hard to believe that golf's my hobby. Actually, it's not a hobby. It's an ordeal. I'd do much better if they'd build golf courses in a circle. You see, I have this slice. . . . "

This season Rocky Bridges is living alone at a Holiday Inn in Sunnyvale, 11 miles from the Bees' ball park. "It's a more lonely life than I'm used to," he says. "You can't run around with the troops, and I miss my wife and kids. I write her, but she says I put more on the envelope than in the letter." Rocky sits by the motel pool with the papers until Larry Klaus, the team trainer, comes by to pick him up. In the majors, Rocky was always the first one in the clubhouse. He's still an early bird, getting to the park at 3 for an 8 p.m. game. "Rocky's lost away from a ball park," says Klaus.

At Municipal Stadium, Rocky puts on a pair of shorts and shower clogs, sticks a chaw of Beechnut in his check, sets up a chair in the sun behind third and reads *Better Homes and Gardens* or *House Beautiful*. His view is the outfield fence, which is decorated with ads for Berti's Bail Bonds, Robbie's Wheel Service and the Moderne Drug Co., and beyond it the Santa Cruz Mountains.

"I started chewing in this league," Rocky says. "Guy got me chewing tobacco and smoking cigars the same night. I like a fat cigar. It's easier to chew, I used to have my trips measured by cigars. From Cincinnati to Long Beach was 40 cigars. It was 50 from Washington. I can't chew much around the house. I'm a closet chewer. I always liked to chew when I played ball. When you slide headfirst, you're liable to swallow a little juice, though. A lot of my troops be chewing lately, but not many be buying. I expect to get irate letters from their moms any day now. It's like a PTA meeting when the moms come around. I always manage to think of something good to tell them their sons are doing." The moms try to please Rocky, too. One day he got a note from a mother thanking him for letting her son off to go to his sister's high school graduation. Accompanying the note was a gift-wrapped five-pack of cigars.

One afternoon, as Rocky was climbing into his uniform, Al Coutts, an All-America second baseman from Los Angeles State, joined the team.

"Here's our new stooge, Larry," said Rocky.

"What size uniform you take?" asked Larry.

"Thirty-two," said Coutts.

"We got 38s and 40s," said Larry.

"You'll never make it on this club," said Rocky. "We go by sizes."

"Anyone we can option out wear a 32?" asked Larry.

"Don't be surprised by the umpires, Coutts," said Rocky. "I'm tired of complaining. What I'm really tired of is running. I pick my spots now. When they're close by. Another thing, you won't hear too much yelling out there. It's kind of a mutes' convention. As long as they play good, though, I don't care if they yell good."

"What time do I report here tomorrow?" asked Coutts.

"Around 6," said Rocky. "This is a kind of a do-it-yourself ball club."

"I don't have a sweat shirt," said Coutts.

"Here, take one of mine," said Rocky, reaching in his locker. "I hope you don't mind if it's a little damp."

Jack Quinn, the general manager, came in. Jack is the son of John Quinn, the general manager of the Phillies, and Rocky says Jack's so thin he could tread water in a test tube. Jack came to San Jose in 1962, the first year the franchise had been active since 1958. Jack won the pennant, drew 62,000 and was named minor league executive of the year (lower division) for performing those feats "in the shadow of Candlestick Park." The Giants' park is only a 45-minute drive up 101 from San Jose. ("We ought to advertise that there's good reception for all Giant games at Municipal Stadium," says Rocky.) Carried away, Jack bought the franchise and sold 300 season tickets. ("He ought to have a saliva test," says Rocky.) The Bees finished seventh in 1963, and last winter Jack could only sell 204 season tickets to such San Jose concerns as The Nite Kap, Ann Darling Bowl, Unicorn Pizza, Mid City Magnesite and O'Brien's Almaden Liquors. By midseason Jack Quinn always seems to be looking forlornly over his shoulder. He gets that way watching foul balls vanish into the parking lot. "There goes another $1.50," he has been known to sigh many times a night. Jack's baseball bill is $1,700 per annum.

There was no batting practice that night for the Bees or their opponents, the Modesto Colts, as the field was being used first for a Pony League game and then for a Little League game. "You know what the Little League is?" Rocky said, watching the kids play. "Something to keep the parents off the street. I bet you don't know what's the first question Little Leaguers always ask me. 'How much money do you make?' "

After infield practice Rocky joined his troops for a supper of hot dogs and Cokes at a concession stand. Then the Bees went out and beat the Colts 18–0. The first man dressed was Vic LaRose—a utility infielder. Two nights before, when the Bees lost 1–0, LaRose had finally gotten into the game as a pinch runner in the bottom of the ninth but had been stranded on first. He was the first man dressed then, too.

"He do get dressed remarkable quick," Larry had said when LaRose came in for his watch and wallet.

"It's amazing," said Rocky. "He ran all the way in from first."

"You better take a salt pill," Larry told LaRose. "You're bound to get dehydrated dressing so quick."

When he was dressed Rocky joined some of the fans, the two umpires and the Modesto manager in the Bee Hive. The Bee Hive is a club for box-seat holders which has been set up in an old trainer's room under the stands. Free whisky and beer are served for an hour before and an hour after each game.

"Eighteen to 0!" a fan said. "What happened, Rock?"

"I don't know," said Rocky, "but I'm for it."

Someone spilled a beer on the floor and asked the bartender for a sponge.

"Give me that sponge," said Rocky. "I'm the manager here." He bent down and mopped up the floor.

An hour later, Larry was driving him back to the Holiday Inn.

"I haven't got it made yet," said Rocky. "You know when you know you got it made? When you get your name in the crossword puzzles. But I've gotten a big charge out of it. The troops don't come to you asking advice about getting married when you're coaching for the Big Club. I'm a white-knuckles artist when I fly, so I don't mind the bus. There's a good pinball machine in Modesto, too. I'm real lucky to be here. But, as Branch Rickey said, 'Luck is the residue of design.' "

Baseball's Babbling Brook

BY HUSTON HORN

As the voice of the New York Yankees, Mel Allen drowned many a fan in his endless flood of chatter. And while he inspired the same feelings of devotion and revulsion as the team he covered, he was clearly the top dog in the sportscasting game.

WHILE THERE WAS VERY LITTLE OF LASTING INTEREST about an editorial in the *Birmingham Age-Herald* endorsing the presidential candidacy of James M. Cox one fall day in 1920, the newspaper's words had a galvanic effect upon an Alabama shopkeeper named Julius Allen Israel. "I remember that as I heard the words my hair stood up on end," Israel takes pleasure in relating today, "and goose bumps popped up all over my body." To appreciate the man's agitation, it is necessary to know that Israel was being read to at the time by his son Melvin, a little fellow not yet a month enrolled in the first grade. The revelation that the child could read the Birmingham papers, let alone the ponderous editorial pages, was an eye-opening experience from which the father has not yet completely recovered. "I had known all along that Melvin was brighter than most," says Israel with paternal candor, "but he'd never let on just how smart he really was. He was always such a modest and quiet little boy."

Modest he still is—he has not forgotten how to blush and, when asked for his autograph, never fails to say, "Thank you"—but quiet he is not, for the boy Melvin Israel has since grown up to become the man Mel Allen. As such he is the most successful, best known, highest paid, most voluble figure in sportscasting, and one of the bigger names in broadcasting generally. In New

York City, his base of operations, Mel Allen has a following that only a politician, which Allen in some ways is, could love. There are people to whom his voice is a comfort, his handshake a benediction, his autograph an heirloom. "Write 'Good luck, George' and sign your name," a man named George demanded of Allen not long ago, and a bartender insisted that Mel sign a $5 bill, "This is illegal," said Allen, scribbling away.

"For this," said the bartender, "I don't mind dying."

To such a weird and wonderful estate, which over the past dozen years has annually paid him more than $100,000, most of it already spent, Mel Allen has risen on the strength of an indefatigable, hinged-in-the-middle tongue, an unsurpassed knowledge of and almost mystical involvement in sports. Riding the pinstriped coattails of his employers for the last two decades, the New York Yankees, has helped. Moreover, he has merrily made his way to the top of a field of limited opportunities without deceit, without guile, without cynicism and without, it would seem, half trying, fame having stalked him more than the other way around. His formula has been simply an open-faced and honest ambition to fulfill himself and to believe in himself.

Since self-satisfaction has always eluded Mel Allen, he sits today uncomfortable in his eminence, wondering what it amounts to and knowing at the same time that, whatever its worth, he has, in the words of a friend, "only one direction left—down." Goaded by this unnerving intelligence—and spurred along by loneliness that befalls him as a 49-year-old bachelor hopelessly embroiled in his job—Allen is a tireless worker, driving himself to accept as many obligations, commitments and duties as daylight and dark will allow and, like a tightrope walker, resisting the impulse to look beneath him. "He has so many things going for him," says fellow sportscaster Joe Garagiola, "that if he ever got the flu he'd be a one-man Depression." And one of Allen's favorite stories, one of the thousands he knows and cherishes, takes on the flavor of a morality play when he tells it. The story concerns a onetime major league pitcher named Bobo Holloman who had the bad luck to pitch a no-hitter for the St. Louis Browns on his very first start in the majors. By the end of the season they were saying, "Bobo? Bobo who?"

Bobo's flaw, says Allen, was a sore arm and serenity, and while a sore throat may now and then indispose Mel Allen it won't be complacency that goes before his fall. Attaching a peculiarly negative significance to the mark he has made, he lost his once abiding respect for *Who's Who in America*, he says without coyness, when it requested his biography 10 years ago. Allen frankly protests that "if the New York Yankees had been an eighth-place team all the time I'd been with them I'd be an eighth-place announcer." Since the Yankees have done very well altogether during the 21 years, so has their official spokesman. Yet Allen, like a spinster with a rich daddy and a poor boyfriend, wonders bleakly how much he is liked for himself and how much for his association with affluence. Says Julius Israel: "What Mel needs is the swelled head he deserves."

WHETHER OR not Allen's popularity is as mercurial and subject to whim as he supposes, it is sufficient nowadays to keep him occupied on radio, television and motion picture film 600 hours each year, pitching athletic sweat, beer, smokes, razor blades, oatmeal, autos, soap, gasoline and lip balm. More than half of that time, of course, is devoted to Allen's folksy, garrulous descriptions of 162 Yankee ballgames, while most of the remainder is parceled out to the World Series broadcasts, college football and Rose Bowl games, a three-hour, $3-a-minute segment of NBC Radio's *Monitor* on Saturday mornings and baseball All-Star games (his 23rd comes up next Tuesday).

Twice each week he lends his voice to the soundtrack of Fox Movietone sports newsreels. To earn his $12,000-a-year salary for that job, Allen is obliged to write as well as talk the scripts. He does both after a quick look at the film, with speed and efficiency, having a practiced ear for the catchy, punny phrasing that is the pattern of most newsreel features. ("The hull thing makes a fellow keel over from sheer delight," he wrote shamelessly for a girlie documentation of New York's winter boat show.) Somehow Allen has enough energy left over to write an occasional magazine article, to pick an All-America team for a magazine and to work away, somewhat desultorily, at his second book, which, like his first, will be a collection of uplifting sports stories. With so many demands on his reportorial sense, it is no wonder that his capacities are sometimes taxed to the limit, as they were several years ago when he tried his hand at song lyrics. "Let's play ball, play ball, you all," his song began—and went downhill from there.

Happy in his work, Mel Allen is likewise happy in his relative leisure, liking nothing better than to fill it by making speeches—which he makes often for free and always at the drop of the invitations that come in daily. His format, by and large, is the presentation of sports stories—straight-from-the shoulder, sometimes gamy stories for adults, inspirational stories for youngsters. He even makes speeches when no one has asked him to, in bars, on street corners, wherever there is an attentive—or captive—ear.

Mel Allen is the only sportscaster known to the modern world who has had his day in a major league ballpark, in this case Mel Allen Day in Yankee Stadium in 1950, when he received clothes, a Cadillac and $10,000—which he in turn gave to Columbia and the University of Alabama for scholarships. He is certainly one of the few broadcasters who can draw better crowds leaving a stadium than many ballplayers, and is one of the few whom young boys and old women alike have smothered to the sidewalk in excessive shows of partiality.

To offset such effusions, Allen has a solid corps of detractors, too, one of whose doughtiest said gleefully not long ago: "Mel Allen talks more than a magpie—which isn't saying much." More specific critics point out that Allen dearly loves to labor a point or overwork a pet phrase ("How about that?"), that his voice, deep, rich and mellow as it is, has an irritating edge on it, and that his stifled but not fully hidden enthusiasm when the Yankees are winning violates his rights to the air waves. Sober, industrious and otherwise well-adjusted men have been known to fall into gargling, sputtering rages as, sitting helplessly before their TV sets, they feel themselves assaulted by Allen's tedious, drawn-out explanations ("For the benefit of those not so familiar with the game, the infield fly rule states that, with first and second base or first, second and third occupied and less than two out, a ball which in the judgment of the umpire," etc., etc.), by his excessively elated descriptions of everyday Yankee catches, by his strangling compulsion to qualify, modify and amplify nearly every general truth he utters, "International Falls is the coldest spot in the U.S.," he said on TV once. "Temperaturewise, that is." And because New York teems with people who love baseball but refuse to pledge allegiance to the Yankee pennant, Allen's "objective but pro-Yankee" broadcasts can turn a ruly roomful of people into a hating, shouting, blaspheming mob. "In New York, Mel's like the drinking friend who takes home the town drunk," says Lindsey Nelson, a fellow sportscaster and a friend of Allen. "Since the anti-Yankees aren't able to change the team, they hit the nearest thing—Mel Allen—with a rolling pin." Says raconteur Tex O'Rourke: "Mel is Alabama's answer to Tennyson's babbling brook."

AFTER WINNING a radio-TV "best sportscaster" award in 1952, Allen's first reaction was to say, "It's nice, but what if I don't win it next year?" The fact is, he's won it, wonderingly, every year since. He can no more understand this unqualified praise than he can understand the ire and vitriol of his critics. He seeks to show the same courtesy and restraint in replying to both. If accused of favoring the Yankees, for instance, he answers that his technique is one he has carefully considered for many years, and he would do as much for anyone he worked for. If he is accused of being unfavorable to the opposite team, he bridles and denies it. "You listen," he will say, proudly professional. "I call a Colavito home run the same as I call a Mantle home run. The guy who doesn't think so didn't want Mantle to hit that home run in the first place." Only when accused of talking too much does Allen admit that perhaps he has a problem. "Somewhere," he says, "there must be a middle ground: enough explanation for those who don't understand the game and not too much for those who do. If I don't qualify everything I say, here come the letters. I have lain awake nights wondering where that happy medium is. I do the best I can."

Allen's best, as it turns out, is still this side of prolixity. Phrases like, "That brought the crowd to its collective feet," and, "There's no room for margin of error," will suggest why. Like most people who talk a lot, Allen exposes himself to easy ridicule. *The New York Times* once characterized him as a connoisseur of the obvious on the cliché matinee. A quotation the late John Lardner once attributed to Allen—and it sounds more like Allen than Lardner—found him in one of his typical on-the-one-hand-this-on-the-other-hand-that situations (a result, says Allen, who happens to be a law graduate, of his legal training). Lardner's quote, picked from a game several years back, went like this: "By sending Mize to the bat rack, Stengel may have kept Boudreau from replacing Brown, because—You see, Collins is a lefthanded hitter—Well, we've got a righthanded pitcher in there now, but if Boudreau had called in a southpaw—Of course, Collins is a lefthanded hitter, too. But what this might mean—Well, of course, it may mean nothing at all."

Sometimes Allen joins the Allen critics, "When somebody tells me I've done a good job making a bad ballgame sound good," he says, "I know I've failed some way. They mean it as a compliment, but it's really a criticism. I never try to inflate a game. Instead I try to ride it like a boat on waves, and to make it sound like no more than it is. My job is reporting, not making up a press agent's release." Like any reporter, he sometimes falls on his face. Afterward he will brood about these gaffes for years. His worst mistake to date occurred in the seventh game of the 1960 World Series, when he prematurely blurted, "It's going foul," on a three-run homer by Yogi Berra. Stung by the recollection still, he takes some comfort from the fact that SPORTS ILLUSTRATED at the time called it the biggest boner "since Clem McCarthy's historic miscall of the 1947 Kentucky Derby."

"That," says Allen with relish, "was their biggest boner since Clem McCarthy's historic miscall of the 1947 Preakness."

Because he is usually sitting behind a microphone, Allen is pictured by most people as a short and dumpy man. He is not. Unbent, he stands taller than six feet, weighs about 200 and wraps his large, bearish frame in loose-fitting casual jackets and slacks. Like his father and his brother, he is balding, but unlike them he disguises the truth with a hairpiece. He has heavy features, translucent blue-gray eyes and is handsome in an aging way. He looked like a cupid when he was born on St. Valentine's Day in 1913.

Mel Allen's grandfather, William Israel, was a Russian Jew who came to the U.S. when he was 35, settled in West Blockton, Ala., where he ran a dry goods store and raised a family of seven. One of his sons, Julius Allen, Mel's father, re-members West Blockton as a tough mining town, and the meanest man around was an outlaw lyrically named Bart Thrasher. Julius Israel also remembers his father as a stern patriarch unfavorably disposed toward boyhood idleness and particularly inimical to baseball, since it interfered with Julius' chores. "How do you reckon he would like it if he knew his grandsons were making their living just looking at baseball games?" says Julius delightedly. Julius's other son, Larry, is a statistician and spotter on Mel's staff.

Mel Allen's mother, Anna Leibovitz, the daughter of a cantor, was born in Russia and came to this country when she was 9. She married Israel in 1912 and, by the time Melvin was born, Julius was well-established in the dry goods business in Johns, Ala., a small mining town 30 miles southwest of Birming-ham. Continuing to prosper, Julius moved his business and his family first to Sylacauga, Ala., later to Bessemer, a large steel-producing center, where he opened a ladies' ready-to-wear shop. It was in Bessemer that young Melvin began flabbergasting his elders by reading the papers, particularly the sports pages, and by reciting, at the slightest provocation, current batting averages, RBIs and ERAs of popular major league players.

Hit hard by the postwar depression, Bessemer's economy collapsed, and so did Julius Israel's business. In 1922 he moved it to Cordova, Ala., where things went sour again. The Ku Klux Klan, a phoenix in a dirty bed sheet, was reemerging at about that time, and high on the Klan's list of un-American activities was being Jewish. Cordova's citizens began to boycott the Israel store, and before long, the $20,000 Israel had salvaged from his Bessemer operation was gone and, in declining health, he turned to selling shirts on the road. Bitter as Allen's mother is about Cordova's Klan, she cannot forget a second disappointment that took place there. Her ambitions that Melvin should become a concert violinist were shattered when he just about cut off his left forefinger while paring a peach.

By the time Julius Israel moved the family to Greensboro, N.C., the siren call of a career in major league baseball had become a real and vital thing to Melvin, age 11, and he got a job as bat boy with the Greensboro Patriots. Al-ready beginning to spread his time thin, he also delivered dry cleaning on roller skates and spent Saturday afternoons at the corner cigar store posting baseball scores on a blackboard. "Always it was baseball this or that," Anna Is-rael recalls.

Two years later Julius Israel moved his family again—this time to Birmingham—and there Melvin finished high school, dated the prettiest girl on the block and enrolled in the University of Alabama in Tuscaloosa. He was only 15 years old and, because of his precocity, they called him Skyrocket. To save the expense of putting him up in a dormitory, the Israel family moved to Tuscaloosa, too. "About all I was able to afford was a roof over his head," says Julius Israel.

Characteristically, Mel Israel spent little time under that roof. Tall, skinny and physically immature, he was cut quickly from the varsity baseball team. He turned instead to intramural baseball, to writing sports for the school paper, to the drama club and, when necessary, to his books. To help his father meet expenses, he worked Saturday in Brown's Dollar Store selling shoes. After a good day he would take five of Brown's dollars home.

By the time he was a senior, Mel had entered law school, was teaching a class in speech and was sports editor of both the student paper and the annual. He was also earning his varsity A as student manager of the baseball team, working as sports stringer for out-of-town Alabama papers, writing scripts for the football coaches' radio show, playing sandlot baseball and announcing downs and yards to go on the P.A. system at Alabama football games. One fall afternoon in 1935 the late Frank Thomas, the football coach, got a call from a Birmingham radio station. It had suddenly lost its sportscaster for Alabama and Auburn football games. Did Thomas have any suggestions? Sure he did, Mel Israel.

"I wasn't really interested," says Allen now, "but it was a sure $5 a game if I got the job." To see that he did, Allen prepared for his audition by boning up on an earlier Rose Bowl game that he hadn't seen, and came to the station to deliver a stirring account of how Alabama tied the score against Stanford in the last minutes. Charmed as much by Allen's account as by the recollection of that happy day in Pasadena, the station manager hired him.

Allen was already in his third year of law school, and he got the job again the next season, but was unavailable the one after that. He was busy instead on the CBS network. The following fall he called the first baseball games he'd ever seen from a broadcasting booth: the 1938 World Series.

As he had done in Birmingham, Allen got his job with CBS almost accidentally. In New York on a skylarking Christmas vacation, he strolled into the CBS studio one evening to see a program being broadcast. He mentioned his association with the CBS affiliate in Birmingham to a night supervisor, and for no better reason than curiosity let himself be induced to audition. The next question he heard was, "When can you start?"

"Gosh damn," says Allen, using one of his wild expressions (others are "dad gummit" and "jiminy cricket"). "I like to fell over when they said that. I didn't want to start anytime, I told them. I was a graduate lawyer, ready to start my practice most any day. And besides, I had a job teaching speech at the university and getting $1,800. So they said, $45 a week, think it over."

Mel thought it over when he got home. "I told him it was plain foolishness for a boy to go all the way through law school just to talk on the radio," says Julius Israel. "And I told him if he went he'd never come back." Neither was the elder Israel friendly to the network's suggestion that Mel change his name for, as they put it, a more euphonious sound and one not so—uh—inclusive of all the tribes. Mel answered his father that, well, he meant only to go on for a year. The experience would broaden him, he said, give him a bigger outlook on things. Oh, let the boy go, Mel's mother put in. What did it matter what he did for one year, and what did it matter what he called himself for that time? Call yourself Morgan Hall, a solicitous friend suggested, thinking of a euphoniously named building an the university campus. Or call yourself Mel Thomas, suggested Frank Thomas. So Melvin Israel, who has always liked travel and mellifluousness, packed his bags, borrowed his father's middle name and went north. He honestly meant to be home 12 months later, but he never made it.

Mel Allen began broadening his outlook by getting up in time to open the network at 6 a.m., introducing to the stirring nation organ stylings on the Mighty Wurlitzer. Three weeks later he was assigned to a sponsored nighttime show (his salary spurted up to $95 a week), and a couple of months after that he broke into sports.

A prerequisite for sports announcers is an ability to carry things along without benefit of script, and Allen demonstrated an unapproachable talent for that on his first assignment. In a day when networks pirated events from one another, CBS sent Allen aloft in a DC-3 to describe a Vanderbilt Cup race on Long Island. Circling over the course, Allen was obliged to talk for 52 minutes, describing nothing at all because the race was being delayed by a rain shower. The race never did get away, but from then on Mel Allen's career in sports announcing was off and running.

His first full season of baseball began in the spring of 1939, when he was the No. 2 announcer after Arch McDonald, broadcasting both for the Yankees and the New York Giants. The next season McDonald went to the Washington Senators, and Allen moved up. Allen was in the infantry from 1943 until early in 1946; in a rare burst of intelligence the Army made use of his broadcasting experience by assigning him to a public relations program. When he came back to New York he signed a contract with the Yankees (for $17,500 then, for he's not saying how much now) and has been with the club ever since. Along the way, he has also broadcast basketball games, tennis matches, dog shows and horse races. Once he recorded the offstage voice for the game sequence in the Broadway production of *Damn Yankees*, and in a movie called *The Babe Ruth Story* Allen's voice described Ruth's then remarkable

60th home run. "The fact that I was only 14 years old when Ruth hit that homer didn't seem to faze the director," says Allen of the movie. "That gives you a rough idea of what kind of movie it was."

Inasmuch as Mel Allen has been doing basically the same job for more than two decades, it would be reasonable to suppose that much of his enthusiasm has faded. But for Allen, with no wife or children, no hobbies and, with the exception of popular fiction and magazines, no interests beyond sport, it isn't so. Each game he sees is a new and challenging experience. He doesn't just look at it, he lives it. "My work as a sportscaster, dad gummit, is a creative thing," he says. "The players on the field are the actors, and I, in a sense, am the narrator putting the things they do into a story." Allen sometimes gets so carried away by his narration that he paws the air and gesticulates, pounds his neighbors and shifts to the edge of his seat. It is a technique that leaves him completely bushed after a game.

"In a business never known for hard work, Mel has built a reputation for hard work that makes us all uneasy," says Lindsey Nelson. "In the early days of radio it was enough for the announcer to say, 'The sky is blue, folks, and the band sounds mighty pretty, so let's listen.' Now the listeners are too sophisticated for that, and Mel spends far more time getting ready for a broadcast than he does giving it. He gives the listener everything he could ask for."

Once Mel Allen got over the idea of returning to a law practice in Alabama and accustomed his family to the same thing, he moved them all to New York in 1940. His sister has married and gone her own way, his brother works for him and his mother and father live with Mel in a $75,000 house in Westchester County. It is a close-knit family, and everybody is fairly happy, except perhaps Mrs. Israel. She openly resents the fact that her son "never married anybody but those New York Yankees." She has seen Mel woo and abandon possible brides, and she doesn't laugh at the crack made by a friend: "Here comes Mel Allen with the future Miss Jones." And she begrudges the demands made on him by his public.

But, she is asked, would she wish her son Mel to be anything less than the success he is? Anna Israel answers with rue: "I wish he was a shoemaker. A married shoemaker."

VI

PLAYING FOR LAUGHS

Absolutely, Positively the Best Article Ever Written

BY BRUCE NEWMAN

Hype, in many forms and under many names, has long been a fixture in sports. But in an era in which every fight was billed as the Fight of the Century, the author took a hard look at all that overinflation, and wryly put a pin to it.

WHEN MIKE TYSON LEFT DAPPER DAN'S BOUTIQUE sometime after 4 a.m. on Aug. 23, he was carrying the new custom-made leather jacket that he had come to Harlem that morning to pick up. Tyson is one of those impulse shoppers who never know when they're going to wake up in the middle of the night and realize they're running dangerously low on leather coats. "He ordered a jacket, and we told him to pick it up anytime he wanted," explained Dapper Dan, New York's all-night *couturier des pugs*.

After months of headlines about his bizarre public behavior and his equally unusual private life—some of the stories were almost certainly plants to help promote his June 27 title fight with Michael Spinks—Tyson was ready to make a fashion statement, and he knew that the salon of the ever-tasteful Mr. D carried plenty of clothes with writing on them. Tyson had just picked up his $850 white jacket, with the words DON'T BELIEVE THE HYPE in gold and black applique across the back, when he had the bad luck to stumble on that other noted shops-till-he-drops heavyweight, Mitch (Blood) Green.

The funny thing about people who have nicknames like Blood is that they are likely to do anything at four in the morning; you can't reason with them. First thing you know, Green was calling the heavyweight champion of the world a "homo." Then he fractured Tyson's fist with his eye, which resulted in several postponements of Tyson's next fight, which were followed in turn by bouts of depression, which may have accelerated his breakup with his wife, actress Robin Givens, and her mother, Ruth Roper. Perhaps Tyson's fashion statement was worth all that to him, but even if he wishes people wouldn't believe the hype, he probably wouldn't want to do away with it entirely, either. For while his iron fists have led him to an undefeated record in the ring, hype is what made it possible for him to earn more than $50 million in purses by the age of 22.

As recently as 1981, *Webster's Third New International Dictionary*, a 2,662-page colossus, didn't even acknowledge the existence of the word hype as slang for hyperbole. In fact, hype—in its many forms and under many names—has been with us for a very long time. Among other things, hype is what makes it possible for sports teams to fill their arenas game after game despite relatively small advertising budgets. "Hype is almost intrinsic to the coverage of sports," says Vince Doria, sports editor of *The Boston Globe*. "We provide the teams with free advertising on a daily basis. That's what we're there to do."

Hype dresses itself up in Armani jackets these days, and it has grown far more sophisticated since Gregory Peck appeared in *The Man in the Gray Flannel Suit* in 1956. "I don't know much about public relations," Peck told another p.r. man. "Who does?" the man replied. "You got a clean shirt, you bathe every day, that's all there is to it."

The sporting press takes an indulgent view of hype, to say the least. When events come along that have no intrinsic value of any sort (a partial list of these: the week before the Super Bowl; virtually anything that happens before a major prizefight; all intergender grudge matches, such as the Bobby Riggs-Billie Jean King fiasco of 1973), rather than simply ignoring them, the press behaves as if it were guided by an invisible hand to hype them. This often requires the seeker of truth to suspend disbelief. "Let's face it, the media like talk of all kinds, even if they know in their hearts they're being put on," says Mike Brown, assistant general manager of the Cincinnati Bengals. "The media actually seek out some of these stories."

In the mid to late '60s, when television began in earnest to deliver games into people's living rooms—remember when the expression "Live and in color!" really meant something?—and later, when news was delivered for the first time in sound bites, the trick for the hypemasters was to make sure their message wasn't lost in the babble. The most outlandish of them was arguably a young publicist named Andy Furman, who specialized in theme-night stunts. While working at Oral Roberts University, Furman conducted such promotions for the Titans basketball team as Bulgarian Night (anyone of Bulgarian ancestry would be admitted free) and Satan-Worship Night (when Oral Roberts was taking on the DePaul Blue Demons and all self-avowed devil worshippers were let in at no charge). Furman finally went one tasteless step too far while working at Monticello (N.Y.) Raceway, in 1980, when he fired off an invitation to a local klavern of the Ku Klux Klan proposing that the Klan take advantage of the track's group party plan package. One must assume that the idea was to have more than the usual number of horses' asses standing in the winner's circle, wearing bedding. "All I did was write a letter to the head of the Klan and suggest he and his boys take a night off and come out to the track," Furman explained shortly before being fired.

Now hype is everywhere. It's the Iowa caucuses and the New York Marathon (but not the New Hampshire primary or the Boston Marathon). Hype is a pitching statistic called the quality start (but not earned run average). So much of sports has become hype that it's a challenge to recognize something good and true when we see it. The message on Mike Tyson's jacket actually comes from the rap tune *Don't Believe the Hype* by Public Enemy, which could replace *The Star-Spangled Banner* as the pregame anthem for the 1990s.

Suckers, liars, get me a shovel
Some writers I know are damn devils
For them I say
Don't believe the hype . . .
Don't . . .
Don't believe . . .
Don't believe the hype.

GREAT MOMENTS IN HYPE 1: It was supposed to be just another payday for a boxer named Dummy Mahon, nothing special, until a promoter came up with the harebrained notion that if Mahon, who was stone deaf, were to parachute out of an airplane, the sudden change in air pressure as he fell from the sky might make his ears pop open and restore his hearing. It was felt that such a miracle was just what was needed to get Mahon's name in the papers and get ticket sales moving for his upcoming bout. The press did its part by turning out in force on the day of the jump. In fact, the whole stunt would undoubtedly have been a rousing success if Mahon's chute had opened. Looking at it from the promoter's point of view, of course, the results were mixed. On the one hand, Mahon no longer had a hearing problem. On the other, the promoter had undeniably violated the first canon of hype: Never kill your attraction.

At the start of P.T. Barnum's career as a showman, he encountered rival 19th-century hypemaster Johann Nepomuk Maelzel, who took note, admiringly, of the way Barnum was able to help promote his attractions by obtaining free publicity. "I see that you understand the press," Maelzel told Barnum, "and that is the great thing. Nothing helps the showman like the types and the ink."

No one has ever worked the ink-stained wretches of the sporting press better than Irving Rudd, who, at 71, is one of the few characters left in the publicity dodge who can accurately be described as Runyonesque. Rudd—also known by his *nom de plug*, Unswerving Irving—believes there's no substitute for a good hype job. "Nothing sells itself," Rudd says. "Even the Bible had to have a p.r. man."

He learned his craft in small fight clubs like the Coney Island Velodrome and then became a publicist for the Brooklyn Dodgers, who were owned by Walter O'Malley, a man Rudd recalls as having "deep pockets and short arms." After O'Malley moved the Dodgers to Los Angeles in 1958, Rudd went to work at Yonkers Raceway, a thriving harness track just outside New York City. While driving up to the track one day, he noticed that workmen were hanging giant lettering on the side of the new clubhouse. It's not known if the force of inspiration caused Irving to swerve, but he certainly rushed to the foreman of the work crew and issued new instructions. The two men argued briefly, and then the sign was hung, per Rudd's orders, so that in letters 3½ feet high, stretching 84 feet, it read YONKERS RACEWYA. Rudd was ecstatic, and when the track's switchboard nearly exploded with calls pointing out the error, he grew happier still. Within days, virtually every newspaper in New York City had run a picture of this supposed blunder, and wire service shots of the sign eventually appeared in newspapers across the country. It was as pure a piece of malarkey as Rudd had ever put over on an unsuspecting public.

Rudd learned early on that if he could somehow create news—or at least something that passed for it—he could reach far more people than he could by paying for an ad. "Advertising can be very effective, but it's still only an ad," Rudd says. "If a guy picks up a newspaper and reads a story about a boxer with a bionic fist, it becomes a real situation in his mind." The Bionic Fist was in fact—or, more accurately, in fantasy—another of Rudd's inventions, something he dreamed up to help sell tickets to the 1979 WBA heavyweight championship bout in Pretoria between John Tate of the U.S. and Gerrie Coetzee of South Africa. After reading that Coetzee had undergone an operation on his right hand, during which eight steel pins had been implanted and smashed bones had been fused, Rudd persuaded Tate's manager to register a protest and demand a prefight examination of Coetzee's "bionic fist." The story of the protest was reported without question or qualification in newspapers all over the world. "The protest went nowhere," says Rudd, "but it made the papers, it said Tate-Coetzee, and it gave the date of the fight. As long as these things are somewhat tongue in cheek, and there's some relevancy to reason and reality, where's the harm?"

No other sport gives Rudd the freedom to simply make up the rules as he goes along the way boxing does. "Boxing is the last of your freebooting, buccaneering sports," he says. "Unlike baseball or football, boxing has no continuity. Any guy off the street with a Q-tip in his shirt pocket can call himself a manager." To become a boxing *promoter* you don't even have to pass the Q-tip test. After carefully studying the record of one of his fighters, Don Elbaum, a promoter in Akron, Ohio, once sold advertising for an Italian restaurant on the soles of the pug's shoes. The theory was that the tomato can's number—and the sponsor's name—would come up at some point during the fight. This technique never caught on, raising, as it did, troubling practical and esthetic questions about which way the punched-out billboard might fall.

Much as he loves a good plug, Rudd has never taken much joy in hyping the heavyweight division's seemingly endless succession of not-so-great white hopes, the most recent example of whom was Gerry Cooney. "He can't fight to keep warm," Rudd says of Cooney (who, incidentally, was never his client), "but he's a nice kid." The essence of boxing hype, though, is trying to sell the members of the public the notion that they're seeing mythic masters of the ring, when in reality they are seeing pugs like Cooney—who earned an estimated $18 million in the ring despite the fact that he didn't really like to box and never beat anybody of consequence except Ken Norton. "Sometimes it's a sore and trying thing," says Rudd. "You try to put the best face on it you possibly can."

Surprisingly, these face jobs often work. "Boxing panders to the worst instincts in us," says *Los Angeles Times* sports editor Bill Dwyre. "We deal in serious issues, and we want people to take us seriously. If we cross that line and allow ourselves to willingly be had, if we buy into the myths knowing they're myths, then we're really in trouble."

GREAT MOMENTS IN HYPE 2: In addition to inventing the Bionic Fist, Rudd brought in two witch doctors to help promote the Tate-Coetzee fight. So when he brought in only one witch doctor to hype a fight in which Ayub Kalule, a native of Uganda, would defend his WBA junior middleweight title against Sugar Ray Leonard in 1981, it actually appeared that Rudd was cutting back. "I called the Ugandan mission and asked if they had any witch doctors," he says. The mission sent Ben Mugimba, whom Rudd identified for the press as a medicine man from Uganda. "This guy from Uganda was the goods," insists Rudd, who does concede that to help make ends meet during the slack season for medicine men, Mugimba "ran a Gulf station in Kinshasa." Which is in Zaire, by the way.

Rudd dressed Mugimba up in a ceremonial headdress and robe for what would be his first news conference, if you didn't count interviews after the occasional filling station holdup. Mugimba rattled bones. Mugimba chanted. Mugimba swung a chicken over his head. Mugimba was hexing away with impressive verve when a radio reporter named Rock Newman jumped to his feet and stormed angrily out of the room, dismissing the demonstration as a farce that promoted racism. On the way back to his hotel room, Newman was attacked by a huge crow that pecked violently at his head. To escape the crazed bird, he was finally forced to leap, fully clothed, into the hotel swimming pool.

"Everybody likes hype, but it's tough to live up to every night," says Magic Johnson, whose very name is a hype. "Some of it's real, a lot of it's not, but you try to use it all to your advantage."

Coaches do this all the time, of course. Before he retired this month, Georgia football coach Vince Dooley used his weekly press conferences to practice a form of hypespeak known as "poor-mouthin'." Dooley rhapsodized so poetically about the obscure strengths of upcoming opponents that after a while you began to feel sorry for any of the Bulldogs brave enough to take on such juggernauts. Dooley once warned the press, "We've never seen a team kick off quite like Vanderbilt. It has the greatest variety of kickoffs I've ever seen." In Dooley's final years at Georgia, he was often referred to in the press as Poor Mouth of the South. Herewith, some of his choicest licks.

September 1980, opponent Texas A & M: "This is a real good football team. Mike Mosley is the best quarterback we've faced since Archie Manning was at Ole Miss." Game result: Mosley passed for 62 yards as Georgia won 42–0.

October 1982, opponent Memphis State: "Their offense can break a big play at any time. They have tremendous speed. If we don't play well, we'll get beat." Game result: Georgia handed the Tigers their 15th straight defeat, 34–3.

October 1983, opponent Temple: "Temple has quality personnel. We've noticed on film that they have one of the finest snappers in the country." Game result: Georgia beat Temple and its fine snapper, 31–14.

GREAT MOMENTS IN HYPE 3: It was June 24, 1980, and the idea was to celebrate the 50th anniversary of the opening of a Cleveland skyscraper called Terminal Tower. The stunt was a reenactment of one performed by the Cleveland Indians years earlier, in which they dropped baseballs off the top of the building. Ted Stepien, the owner of the Cleveland Cavaliers at the time, participated (presumably as part of his ongoing effort to promote his NBA franchise, not to mention his newly established slo-pitch softball league). Now, Stepien's stewardship of the Cavaliers, the team that care forgot, was marked by repeated public relations gaffes, but none matched his willingness to drop softballs off Terminal Tower and have six members of his softball team, the

Competitors, on the ground trying to catch them. With an expectant crowd gathered below, gazing at the rooftop, Stepien stood proudly at the precipice of disaster and threw the first pitch out a 52nd-floor window. That ball smashed into a car 708 feet below. The second pitch hit a bystander, badly bruising his shoulder. Stepien fired another ball earthward, this time breaking the wrist of a pedestrian. The next pitch hit the street below the tower and bounced 40 feet in the air (calculations showed that the ball was traveling at 144 mph). At that point, bystanders began to flee for their lives, leaving a scene of twisted metal and mangled limbs.

No other event generates the intensity of hype that the Super Bowl does every year, despite the fact that with a few notable exceptions, the games themselves have been either badly played or dull. Last year more than 2,200 media credentials were issued for Super Bowl XXII, which meant that for each of the men on the field for the kickoff, there were 100 media people there to record his every thought and hiccup. The two weeks of interrogation that precede the Super Bowl can create a fairly apocalyptic atmosphere, which is how it came to pass in 1971 that Dallas Cowboy running back Duane Thomas made his classic pronouncement about the Super Bowl. Thomas did not speak often, but it was sometimes worth the wait. When asked if this was the ultimate game, he replied "Well, they're playing it next year, aren't they?"

Thomas was on the right track there, but he may have missed the larger point. "Here is the truth of it," wrote *Chicago Tribune* columnist Bernie Lincicome a few years later. "The Super Bowl is the ultimate game because the press says it is. And the Super Bowl belongs to the press like no other sporting event."

None of this happened by accident. When the Super Bowl came into existence in 1967, former public relations man and NFL commissioner Pete Rozelle was the unchallenged czar of pro football. Rozelle's two top assistants, Jim Kensil and Don Weiss, were also p.r. men. Though the first Super Bowl was not a sellout and got relatively minimal press coverage, by 1973, when the unbeaten Dolphins met the Redskins in Los Angeles, *The Washington Post* sent 13 staffers to cover the game. This was a watershed event in the history of hype, the point at which editorial overkill became the rule, not the exception. Because of the resulting press bloat, the following year—and every year since—the players have been required to sit behind little tables with their names on them for interview sessions several times in the week before the game. "The press conference used to be kind of an informal thing," says Dolphin coach Don Shula, recalling a kinder, gentler America. "You'd sit around in the hotel lobby and that would be the press conference."

Three years ago, the *Chicago Tribune* and *The Boston Globe* set a new standard for wretched excess when they were granted a combined total of 52 working press credentials for the Patriots-Bears Super Bowl in New Orleans. The *Tribune*, a paper that at no time had more than three reporters in Vietnam, sent a crew of 28 to that game. The Super Bowl obviously isn't as important to the commonweal as war and peace, but it is the only event in American life besides the world wars upon which Roman numerals have been bestowed. Fred Dryer, then a defensive end with the Los Angeles Rams, got it about right when someone asked him in 1980 if the Super Bowl was as big as death. "Bigger," Dryer said. "At least it comes in a bigger box."

"I find it hard to believe anything is more overblown than the Super Bowl," says San Francisco 49er center Randy Cross, who expects to play in his third one this year. "It's a lot like a feeding frenzy with sharks."

The extra week between the conference championship games and the Big One is always hardest on linemen, largely because the press rarely has even the vaguest notion who any of them are or what they do. But at the Super Bowl it doesn't really matter who you are or what you say, as long as you keep saying something. "It's like going to the dentist three times a week and having the same tooth filled," Dolphin defensive tackle Manny Fernandez once said.

When the 49ers played the Dolphins in the 1985 Super Bowl at Stanford Stadium, just 30 miles south of San Francisco, there occurred one of the great hype orgies of all time. "An amazing number of trees had to die to feed it," says Glenn Schwarz, sports editor of *The San Francisco Examiner*. "It bordered on the obscene." That border may have been crossed the following year when the *Globe* devoted massive coverage to the meaningless buildup to the game and then got caught in what sports editor Doria describes as "an extremely tough situation" involving a drug story the *Globe* had but didn't run. The Pats had discovered that several of their players were using cocaine, and although the *Globe*'s Ron Borges caught wind of the story from sources on the team, he eventually agreed to hold it until after the season, which came when the Patriots lost the Super Bowl 46–10. "The one story that was there to be had that entire week didn't come out until two days after the Super Bowl," says L.A. sports editor Dwyre. Which is not to say that Dwyre—or anyone else, for that matter—invariably sees straight during the blizzard of Super Bowl hype. When the game was in Pasadena the following year, one of Dwyre's reporters spent her day covering the ladies' restroom.

GREAT MOMENTS IN HYPE 4: Before the first 1987 meeting between the Seattle Seahawks and the Denver Broncos, Seattle linebacker Brian Bosworth announced that he wanted to injure Denver quarterback John Elway. During that same week, thousands of Boz buster T-shirts were sold in Denver—T-shirts manufactured by 44 Boz Inc., a company owned by Brian Bosworth (who, out of the goodness of his heart, donated the profits to charity).

Major media events generate their own kind of hyper-reality, in which no question is so tasteless that it can't be asked. At the World Series one year, a winning pitcher was explaining to the press that his wife had been unable to come to the game because she was at home feeding their newborn baby. Without hesitating for even a moment, someone shouted out, "Breast or bottle?"

And players end up telling their life stories so often that a certain numbness finally sets in. When Oakland Raider quarterback Jim Plunkett made his first Super Bowl appearance, in 1981, one particularly earnest wire service reporter asked him, "For the record, Jim, is it blind mother, deaf father, or the other way around?"

The hunt for a "fresh" angle (defined at the Super Bowl as anything that hasn't already been the theme of a *Geraldo!* show) often leads to roommates of star players, as Cincinnati offensive lineman Dave Lapham found out before the 1982 Super Bowl. Lapham roomed with Ken Anderson, then the Bengals' quarterback, and he was eager to oblige when reporters inquired about Anderson's personal habits. Lapham told them what a meticulous person Anderson was, mentioning (apocryphally) how "he would even hang his socks on individual hangers in the closet." This news, of course, spread like wildfire, and before dawn the story was on doorsteps all over America. "All of a sudden we were the Odd Couple, Oscar and Felix," Lapham says. "He was the neat one, and I was the slob."

Quarterbacks are such obvious targets during Super Bowl week that John Elway spent almost his entire stay last year in San Diego hiding in his hotel room, running up a room-service bill of nearly $600, just to avoid the fans and press he knew would be in the lobby. When he did emerge for one of the mandatory interview sessions, Elway was immediately engulfed in a sticky sea of Minicams, microphones and mousse. From the moment he stepped onto the field at Jack Murphy Stadium, where the interviews were held, reporters followed him step for step as he strolled from one end zone to the other, pressing around him in a pitched battle for position, so that if he should suddenly repeat some witticism uttered by his room-service waiter, they could tell their editors they got it.

When Elway finally settled into a seat in the bleachers, the crowd around him expanded until its radius reached fully 40 feet. Then commenced a merciless grilling. "What do you think of this crowd?" asked one flinty-eyed interrogator. "How come we're all over here talking to you? Why are the defensive guys not worth talking to?" While this was going on, a radio reporter was flitting from player to player asking, "If you were a tree, what kind of tree would you want to be?"

Rozelle evidently believes if that tree falls in the forest and there aren't at least 2,000 journalists there to hear, it can't possibly make a sound. "The Super Bowl, a few people say, 'Well, it's hype. . . .' " Rozelle said at his annual pre-Super Bowl State of the Game press conference a few years ago. "But I think it's tremendous. I've often said if the American public didn't have an entertaining emotional outlet, we'd have trouble. We'd be a sick society."

GREAT MOMENTS IN HYPE 5: "I'd like to address myself to the five percent of you who are sick," said Evel Knievel, addressing himself, in fact, to the press. "I know who these people are, and after I make my jump, when I'm traveling around the country, I'm going to see those sick people, and they're going to look into my eyes and see my disgust for them, and they will get a lump in their throats and a knot in their stomachs, and their chutes will not open."

"Uh-oh," someone muttered, "Evel Knievel has an enemies list."

Less than a month after the resignation of Richard Nixon, Knievel had gone to Idaho to jump the Snake River Canyon on his so-called Sky-Cycle—a motorcycle dramatically modified so that it was more like a rocket, with fins and a parachute—and 130-odd reporters had gone along for the ride. At some point in this endeavor, however, the hype had not only taken on a life of its own, but it had also begun to create its own strange reality. On the day of the jump, for instance, the promoters estimated the size of the multitudes around the canyon rim and made provisions to "evacuate" the press from the launch site by helicopter because of the massive crowds supposedly choking the exit roads. Almost everyone wrote about these throngs, but they were never there. The state police later put the size of the crowd at about 13,000—a realistic estimate—but reporters, faced with a choice between believing the hype or believing their own eyes, went with the hype almost every time.

An hour before the jump, Knievel made his peace with the press, saying he had counted up all the good things about them and all the bad things about them, and the good had outnumbered the bad a million to three. "A million to three?" one reporter grumbled. "I guess the late returns haven't been counted yet."

All of this has produced a lot of thumb-sucking in newsrooms and at press seminars. At the AP Sports Editors' conference in Kings Island, Ohio, in 1985, a panel was convened to try to answer the question "How much is too much?" The sports editors of some of the foremost newspapers in America were called upon to explain their suffocating coverage of major events. "We were all there because we had allegedly overdone something," says Dwyre. The debate eventually degenerated into self-justification and ended in chaos when the panelists finally refused even to acknowledge there was a problem.

GREAT MOMENTS IN HYPE 6: "I think Bill Veeck was the founding father of hype," says Tim Leiweke, a vice president of the Minnesota Timberwolves, an NBA expansion team that will begin play next season. "He knew how to create an atmosphere for an event and still not overwhelm the event itself. For the most part." Leiweke hesitates for a moment, then adds mournfully, "Disco Demolition Night crossed the line."

Veeck was owner of the Chicago White Sox in 1979 when a disc jockey at an album rock station who abhorred disco music proposed the idea of admitting to Comiskey Park for 98 cents each fan who brought a disco record to be blown up on the field between games of a July 12 doubleheader with the Detroit Tigers. The promotion drew a sellout crowd of more than 50,000, many of whom began tossing firecrackers and records onto the field during the first game. After the game, the detonation of thousands of records in a giant container in the outfield touched off a melee during which an estimated 7,000 fans poured onto the playing field. A stunned White Sox spokesman later reported clashes between disco and antidisco groups.

"This is our generation's cause," one antidisco firebrand said. After a 76-minute delay and 37 arrests, the umpires declared the field unplayable, and the Sox had to forfeit the second game.

"Hi, it's Suzy Chaffee!" says Suzy Chaffee, sounding for a moment as if she can't quite believe it herself. She's speaking to the maitre d' of an excruciatingly fashionable restaurant in Santa Monica, the sort of place that's on the cutting edge of Eurotrash cuisine and hostile valet parking. They know her there, she had announced, her voice pealing like a bell, as she dialed the phone. "I'm having lunch with SPORTS ILLUSTRATED, and I need a table for two!" she now explains to the maitre d'. There's a long silence. Then, in a slightly more subdued voice, she says again, "Chaffee."

Again there is a lengthy pause. An unpleasant kind of recognition has begun to settle in. "E-E," she says at last.

Chaffee was one of the favorites to win the gold medal in the women's downhill at the 1968 Winter Olympics in Grenoble, France. On the day of her race, however, she used the wrong wax on her skis and finished 28th. "But I still got the second-most publicity of anybody there," Chaffee says, "next to Peggy Fleming."

Chaffee had spent her entire life preparing for this odd achievement, studying advertising, photography, cinematography, acting and journalism in school—"all the things I would need later," she says. "I had to take total responsibility for my career. I studied photography so that now I can take a nonphotographer and line up a totally hot shot."

It hasn't always been easy. Several years ago, when filmmaker Warren Miller was shooting one of his annual ski movies in Vail, Colo., Chaffee kept barging into his shots, wearing a skintight bodysuit with 10-foot colored streamers flapping from her arms and legs. At one point she kicked a ski back behind her head in a maneuver called a Reuel and got it tangled in her ribbons while she was moving at high speed. "I thought, Oh, great, I'm going to die doing this for this jerk who doesn't even give a ----," Chaffee says.

She promoted herself so hard that if—within 10 years of the Grenoble Games—you had asked most Americans which of their countrywomen had the most Olympic skiing medals, they might very well have answered Suzy Chapstick (confusing Chaffee's real name with the one she used in her most conspicuous product endorsement). When she participated in the drafting of a highly critical 10-point reform plan for the Olympics in 1972, she was confronted by an outraged Avery Brundage, then president of the International Olympic Committee. "You perjured yourself," Brundage admonished her, referring to the Olympic oath she took in order to be eligible, which stated, among other things, that she had not been in a training camp for more than 60 days in the past year and had received no government or private funding. "If you did that, you must give back your medals."

"But, Avery, I have no medals," she replied. "I have only principles."

Chaffee has worked tirelessly for worthy causes. She claims rumors that she was having an affair with Teddy Kennedy helped get the Amateur Sports Act of 1978 passed by the Congress. "The gossip got the bill through," Chaffee says. She's smiling now, absentmindedly pushing a sun-dried tomato around her plate. "One thing I've inadvertently done is be controversial," she says. "Unfortunately, people's ears weren't always open to the intellectual side, so I had to lean a little more toward the sex appeal side. If there's one thing I've learned about the hype that's involved, you have to give a little to get a little."

And with that she's off to valet parking. Waiting for her car, Chaffee notices a group of raffish homeless men who have taken up residence in seaside Palisades Park, just across the street from the restaurant. "They look like they're having fun out there," she says cheerfully, "camping out on the beach!" She waves, she smiles, then she's gone.

Don't . . .
Don't believe . . .
Don't believe the hype.

Ring Tossed

BY STEVE RUSHIN

An SI columnist traveled to Germany for a crash course in high-speed driving on the Nürburgring—once the world's most treacherous racetrack, now a pedal-to-the-metal playground—risking life and limb for the sake of our amusement.

THE MOST UNSETTLING THING ABOUT DRIVING 142 MPH ON the German autobahn in James Bond's convertible with the top dropped is not the sudden realization that your head juts above the windshield, so that any airborne object—a pebble, a lug nut, the shedding payload of a flatbed truck—will forever be embedded in your coconut, like the coins and keys you sometimes see in the hot asphalt of city streets. Nor is it the banana-yellow Porsche GT3 that draws even with you in the passing lane, lingering off your left flank for 30 seconds, as if attempting the in-flight refueling of a Stealth bomber, while its leering driver hand-gestures you to drag-race him. (That terror passes quickly enough when the pilot of the Porsche loses patience and leaves you in his vapor trail at one fifth of Mach 1.) No. What makes a man vow to change his life, to say nothing of his underpants, should he survive such a journey is this: The journey hasn't even begun.

For you have come to test your driving skills not on the speed-limit-less autobahn but on the Nürburgring, the ribbon of road that Germans drive when they find the autobahn too tame; the ribbon of road that racing legend Jackie Stewart called, without hyperbole, "the Green Hell"; the ribbon of road that a 24-year-old German named Mika Hahn told me, with furrowed brow, "is very, very dangerous"—far too dangerous for *him* to drive on, and he's a likely future world champion of speedway motorcycle racing.

The Nürburgring has long been too harrowing for Formula One racing. Since 1927 the picturesque Grand Prix track has lain, like a gold necklace on a rumpled bedspread, in the Eifel Mountains of western Germany. But over the decades, as cars became faster, the 14-mile, 170-turn course became deadlier: It closed forever to F/1 racing in 1976, after Austrian star Niki Lauda was famously set alight there when he crashed on the approach to a turn known as Bergwerk. By 1983 the 'Ring prudently had been closed to nearly every form of professional racing. Yet—and here's the rub—the Nürburgring remains open, as it ever has been, for the general public to drive on as fast as it pleases for as long as it pleases in whatever it pleases: race cars, jalopies or crotch-rocket motorcycles, many of which have become sarcophagi for their drivers.

Why on earth would anybody want to race there? "If you studied piano all your life and had a chance to play Carnegie Hall on a Steinway, you would want to do that," says Dan Tackett, 42, a financial services manager from San Diego who has made 11 trips to the Nürburgring in the past 16 years. "This is the most difficult, challenging and rewarding racetrack in the world. For serious drivers, it remains the Holy Grail."

It is Everest in asphalt—"the single greatest piece of motor racing architecture in the world," says *Motor Sport* magazine of England—and it demands equipment that is up to the task. Which is how it is that I'm heading for the Nürburgring in a cherry-red BMW Z8, the model driven by 007 in *The World Is Not Enough* but piloted at this moment by English photographer Bob Martin, who is not licensed to kill and is, truth be told, barely licensed to drive.

We retrieved this astonishing feat of automotive engineering at the world headquarters of the Bayerische Motoren Werke in Munich. The company's skyscraper is a kind of architectural pun, constructed of four cylinders. Directly across the street is the 1972 Olympic athletes' village. The site where 11 Israelis were taken hostage at the Summer Games is now the world's most poignant apartment complex. Mesmerized by the view, I absentmindedly signed a three-page document in German that rendered me legally responsible for returning, scratch-free, the $125,000, 400-horsepower, eight-cylinder, zero-to-60-in-4.5-seconds dream car that Bob was soon driving off the lot in the giddily overmatched manner of someone who has been given the keys to the space shuttle.

Or rather Bob, a giant of a man, was not so much driving the two-seater as he was wearing it. He looked like a man in a kayak. A very happy man: As we negotiated the streets of Munich, Bob began speaking in tongues about the "Zed 8" and its "bloody brute" of an engine, its "stop-on-a-sixpence" brakes and, "oooh!—all the beautiful bulgy bits" on its chassis. By the time we entered the autobahn and were swept away like a raft on rapids, all of Bob's bulgy bits were aflame with excitement. He was fearless in his phallic chariot. "BMW!" Bob cackled, merging into traffic, throwing down the hammer, the wind whining in our ears. "Bob Martin's Wheels!"

"BMW," I muttered darkly, not liking the looks of this at all. "Bob Martin's *Willy.*" But he didn't respond. So, with an ever-deepening sense of disquiet, I shut up and rode shotgun toward a 'Ring of Hell unlike any imagined by Dante.

We overnight in the Alps and discover, in the morning, that our five-hour route to the 'Ring will take us roughly from Ulm to Bonn—from the birthplace of Einstein to the birthplace of Beethoven—in a vehicle that weds science and art. Construction of Ulm's Munster cathedral began in 1377. Its 536-foot steeple remains the tallest in the world. Mankind, alas, no longer builds such wonders. Or do we? "I think that cars today are almost the exact equivalent of the great Gothic cathedrals," French social critic Roland Barthes wrote of postwar Western civilization. "I mean the supreme creation of an era, conceived with passion by unknown artists, and consumed in image if not in usage by a whole population which appropriates them as a purely magical object."

Nowhere is the automobile more talismanic than in Germany, the country that gave us the concept of wanderlust, the word *fahrvergnügen* ("joy of driving"), the world's top driver (F/1 king Michael Schumacher) and high-performance automakers Mercedes-Benz, BMW, Porsche and Audi (as well as mid-performance automakers Opel and Volkswagen, and nonperformance automaker Trabant). Americans think of themselves as car crazy, but they don't know the half of it. "Germany is a car culture," says Tackett, the American 'Ring veteran. "America is a drive-through culture of convenience."

"In America cars are appliances," adds U.S. Air Force captain Todd Fry, 26, a motorcycle-riding F-16 pilot based at Spangdahlem Air Force base, an hour's ride from the Nürburgring. "Here, cars are the objects of passion."

So Bob and I continue hammering toward the village of Nurburg. Two hours south of the Green Hell, when we cross the Rhine at Karlsruhe, a black Mercedes SL 500 convertible with full body kit and mag tires appears suddenly in our rearview. Bob takes little notice, for he is dozing, an alarming prospect given that he is—at the same time—driving 100 mph with the top down.

In our cramped cockpit (we will later discover) Bob's right leg is mashed against a button that activates his electronic seat warmer. It is 95° on this afternoon, and Bob is being bum-toasted by red-hot coils hidden beneath his seat. He is being lulled into a coma by heatstroke and highway hypnosis when the Benz—headlights strobing madly—gets on our back bumper like one of those KEEP HONKING, I'M RELOADING stickers so popular in the U.S.

We are both nodding like junkies when the horn sounds behind us. Bob snaps to attention. In a panic, he reflexively jerks the wheel. We career into the right lane, and the Benz passes. But as soon as it does, the middle-aged maniac in the driver's seat (Bob is now calling him a "plonker") maneuvers the Merc into the right lane, decelerates and begins to ride our *front* bumper. After 200 yards of this mouse-and-cat game, he exits the autobahn slowly, so that we can see him pointing at the exit sign as we pass. The man is laughing through his elaborate mustache. (The men—and not a few women—of this German region all have mustaches like the CBS golf announcer Gary McCord.) The plonker keeps pointing at the exit sign—a sign, we now see, for the Daimler-Benz complex in Worth. The man in the Merc, evidently in the employ of that automaker, grins as if he's just won something. Perhaps he has. Still we're 150 miles from the Green Hell. If drivers on the autobahn are hypercompetitive and brand-loyal, what kind of psychotics await us at the Nürburgring? "They are people who enjoy the sheer pleasure of driving," says BMW event manager Werner Briel when we pitch up at the 'Ring's parking lot. "They are concerned not only with velocity but with . . . *style*." Then, holding on to his homburg, he leans over and strokes his sweatered pet dachshund, Katya.

The Nürburgring drivers, in turn, attract an audience of rubberneckers almost as interesting as the motorists themselves. "They come to see the cars, they come to see the crashes," says Reinhard H. Queckenberg, whose name sounds like that of a Groucho Marx character but in fact belongs to the owner of a small racetrack not far from the Nürburgring. "It is living theater."

The elevation changes 1,000 feet along the track's 14 miles. The road rolls out, like a rucked red carpet, over hill and dale and through primeval forest. Three towns and a 12th-century castle are contained within the Nürburgring's infield. But then you have already, no doubt, seen the circuit: Countless car commercials are filmed on it, the kind that carry the disclaimer, PROFESSIONAL DRIVER ON A CLOSED TRACK. DO NOT TRY THIS YOURSELF.

Yet, every year, thousands of drivers *do* try it. Each of them pays 21 deutsche marks—about $9.50—per lap and joins the 100-plus vehicles that are allowed on the loop at any one time. For most of its length, the road is little more than two lanes wide. Unlike modern F/1 circuits, the Nürburgring doesn't have a thousand yards of run-off area beyond its shoulders. Rather, it has no run-off area. If you leave the road, you collide with a tree or a cyclone fence or steel guardrails. Crash through the guardrails, and you, or your estate, must pay to have it replaced.

One ambulance and one flatbed wrecker truck are forever on standby at the 'Ring's starting line. Drivers sign no waiver and are given no warnings. "This could never happen in the States," says Roger Scilley of Laguna Beach, Calif., whom we meet 10 minutes after arriving. "Lawyers wouldn't allow it. But over here, you're responsible for your own actions."

Which isn't to say that there are no warnings whatsoever at the Nürbur-gring. No, all along the perimeter of the track are signs that shriek, LEBENS-GEFAHR! (Mortal Danger!), but those are for the *spectators*—and the ones behind the fencing, at that. There are no words for those race fans, like the four teenagers we'll encounter on our second day at the track, who watch the festivities, with a cooler full of beverages, from *inside* the guardrails. Imag-ine enjoying the Indy 500 while standing against the wall of Turn 2. Now imagine doing so when all the drivers are *amateurs*.

But then Germans are, generally speaking, better drivers than Americans. "In Germany," says Louis Goldsman, a 57-year-old retiree from Mission Viejo, Calif., on pilgrimage at the 'Ring, "you're required to attend a driving academy for four months before you can get a license. It costs the equivalent of $2,500 to obtain a license, and you can't get one until you're 18. Insurance is more ex-pensive. All this makes for more serious drivers. The average 18-year-old Ger-man girl can outdrive the typical testosterone-polluted American male any day."

Goldsman has come to the Nürburgring with a group from the BMW Club of America. At 10 a.m. Eastern time on Monday, March 6, many of the club's 55,000 members called a toll-free number in hopes of getting one of the 72 available spots on the trip. Richard George speed-dialed the number 240 times from Dal-las before securing one of the berths, which sold out in three hours. The trip cost each driver $2,500, plus airfare, and required him (or her) to have attend-ed at least three high-performance driving schools. "We're freaks," says a woman who underscores the point by giving her name as Robyn McNutt. "*Freaks*."

The club has rented the track for three days. The first two days were de-voted to learning the line of the course, mile by mile. Bob and I stumble upon these people on the final day, as they are grimly preparing to put the pedal to the metal and make their "graded lap" of the Nürburgring, at full speed, as expert judges stationed about the circuit make notations on their clipboards.

"We will be graded on a scale of one to 10, one being good and 10 being what the Germans call *totalkaos*," says Tackett, the club's best driver and de facto leader, in a pre-lap speech to his fellow motorists. "Now, you've all had some hot laps in practice, maybe even incurred the need for some laundry attention. You might want to slow it down a little this time: I have pictures of a car that rolled here to show you that this is serious business."

"Two years ago," whispers Dan Chrisman, a 53-year-old from Austin, "one driver on this trip took out 30 feet of fencing and wound up on his top in a BMW 328." The driver of that car suffered nothing more than a cut, and his passenger walked away uninjured, but not all cars are that safe. Thirteen kilo-meters into the clockwise course is an infamous hairpin turn called the Karus-sell. It is a concrete former drainage ditch that drivers plunge into, leaving the track looming above them, like a paved wave threatening to break through the right-hand windows. "I have seen families in camper vans out on the course," says Chrisman, a three-time veteran of the circuit. "I've gone into the Karussell and looked above me to see a double-decker tour bus with little old ladies on the upper level looking down at me through their cameras."

There will be two hours of public racing after the BMW club completes its graded laps on this Friday evening, and already some heavy artillery is massing in the parking lot: Lancias, Porsches, Mercs, Ferraris, Vipers, a Lamborghini Diablo, a rare Dutch Donkervoort, a Fiat Uno with valve springs popping through the bonnet. Many cars have but a single seat, with a racing harness. There are racing motorcycles of every description, their leathered riders doing push-ups in the parking lot. "Those bikes," points out Mike Valente, a veteran English motor-sports photographer, "will be going 180 miles an hour on the final straight-away. On two wheels. Each wheel has a footprint the size of your shoe."

I am told to expect madness when the track opens to the public. "The Germans who live locally," says Tom Doherty, 41, an Indianapolis native who has attended every Indy 500 since 1966, "are all driving souped-up BMW M3s"—modified racing cars—"and they drive *blindingly* fast out here."

But before the public can have a go, Tackett has agreed to take me as a passenger on his graded lap. Everyone tells me that I'm lucky, that Tackett is the best American driver on site. But bad juju is confronting us everywhere as I hop into Tackett's BMW 523i sedan and we make our way to the starting chute.

Before Tackett and I set out, BMW of America Club member McNutt points to a spot on her map of the Nürburgring. "That's where Niki Lauda," she volunteers brightly, "had his barbecue."

Fritz-Jurgen Hahn, a 59-year-old member of an auto club in Dusseldorf, fondly recalls for me the first time he raced on the Nürburgring. "It was in 1963, in a Porsche Spyder," he says. That is the car James Dean died in.

"The track was built in 1927 as the German equivalent of a WPA project," Tackett says, attempting to soothe my nerves with conversation as we wait for a starting flag. "There are 170 turns, and I'm going to alert you to every one of them in advance, not to bore you, but to protect the interior of my car." With that, a flag drops and Tackett accelerates and the world goes by in a blur. I find myself riding a rail-free roller coaster at 125 mph, and I won't have a single coherent recollection—apart from removing my bucket hat and holding it over my mouth—of that first circuit.

"It's just a red fookin' mist out there, innit?" says Tom Thompson, an English motorcyclist we shall meet in a moment. "It is brain out, brick in."

Tackett takes me for two more laps when the course opens to the public. Though he follows the line expertly, the ride is sickening. For most of it I stick my head out the window like a black Lab. Ahead of us Bob Martin rides in the backseat of a convertible, facing backward through 170 turns at up to 140 mph, gamely taking pictures of the cars behind him. His shirt is pulled up over his mouth: At these speeds—and I am as serious as a heart attack here—a shower of vomit on a car windshield may prove fatal to the showeree. Bob had the Wiener schnitzel for lunch.

Bikes and cars flash past on either flank. The Nürburgring is exactly like a Grand Prix video game sprung to life, only instead of getting a GAME OVER message after crashing, you die. Drivers must exit the circuit after each lap. Following my second shotgun lap with Tackett, one hour into public racing, cars are suddenly forbidden to go out again. The P.A. announcement in German states that the track is being cleared. The ambulance and the flatbed wrecker are dispatched, sirens wailing. Vague reports come back from the last drivers to cross the finish line that a yellow car spun out somewhere in the red fookin' mist. The wrecker truck will take 15 minutes to reach the far side of the track, seven miles away. After 10 minutes, a second ambulance sets out from the starter's chute, followed by a police car. The silence is hideous.

Twenty minutes later, a black Opel GTE crosses the finish line, its driver ashen, evidently having lingered at the site of the accident. He drives through the parking lot and off into the dusk without telling any of us what he saw.

Many drivers at the Nürburgring mount video cameras in their cars. A young German who has just recorded his ride cues up the video for a crowd in the parking lot. About halfway through the circuit, as a diabolical turn comes into view, a spot of yellow begins to take shape on the shoulder. We view the tape in super-slow motion until three Zapruder-like frames reveal everything: a yellow Lancia marooned askew on the outside shoulder, its rear left wheel jammed all the way up into its well, the car's driver and passenger standing next to it, miraculously unharmed. The flatbed does not take the wreckage through the main gate, where all the drivers are parked waiting for the track to reopen. The driver of the Lancia is also spirited out some side gate. An announcement is made that the Nürburgring is closed for the night, but it will reopen on Sunday for 10 hours of public racing.

Tonight's public racing lasted 62 minutes before a near-catastrophe occurred. But we will be back on Sunday. We want to see the cars. We want to see the crashes. Reinhard H. Queckenberg was right. It *is* living theater.

A modern F/1 track has been constructed next door to the Nürburgring, and on Saturday it hosts an extraordinarily dangerous event: vintage motorcycle-and-sidecar racing. The sidecars are really just square metal platforms bolted to the bikes. Sidecar passengers, called monkeys, ride a foot off the pavement at 135 mph, sometimes prone, sometimes supine, their helmeted heads an inch off the track when leaning into turns. "Last year at this race, there was a bad accident," says Mika Hahn, a sometime monkey. "Four side-cars went into a turn together, two touched and over-rolled. One person was totally killed and had to be—how you say?—reanimated. He survived."

"The perfect sidecar passenger should weigh six stone [84 pounds] and have a pointed nose for aerodynamics," says a 6' 7" 40-year-old biker whom I meet in the pits, "but I got this one: six-foot-seven and built like a brick s---house." He hooks a thumb at his towering 17-year-old son, who wears a black leather jumpsuit with his nickname stitched to the back: TINY.

"At least," says Tiny, "I got the nose."

Tom and Tiny Thompson are from Bulkington, England. Cheryl Thompson—Tom's wife, Tiny's mother—is a petite woman with painted nails who also wears full leathers. She too is a monkey. When her husband was 28, she explains, he rode his 1938 Triumph 250 everywhere. "He's so tall, he looked ridiculous on it," says Cheryl, a former sales executive with Prudential in London. "Like an elephant on a matchstick." She told him he needed an "out-fit"—a sidecar—for aesthetic balance. "Get an outfit and I'll ride it," she promised, though she had no intention of doing any such thing. "Blimey if two weeks later he doesn't come home with a sidecar," says Cheryl. "I thought, *Crikey.*" The couple painted THOMPSON TWINS on the Triumph. "The Thompson Twins," she says sheepishly of the new-romantic '80s band, "were popular at the time."

Cheryl sighs and says of Tiny, her only child, "He could ride a bike before he could walk." In 1983, Tom rigged a remote-control accelerator to his bike, tied a rope to its frame and let Tiny ride in a circle around him. Says Tom, "He was nine months old at the time."

"The other mothers in the park went mad," says Cheryl. "They said, 'Look at him, with no helmet!' I said, 'You *try* finding a helmet for a nine-month-old!' "

Tiny was allowed to drop out of school at 14—"They didn't want me back," he explains—and now spends the summer traveling from race to race with his parents, living in the back of a rented van. He loves his parents, and they clearly love him. How many 17-year-olds would be willing to spend the summer with their parents, sharing a single mattress? Tiny may have quit school, but the Germans have a phrase that fits him well: *Reisen bildet.* "Travel educates."

The Thompsons are protective not only of each other but of their fellow amateur racers as well. "We take calculated risks," says Cheryl. "The last thing you need is some barmy git out there who's trying to kill people. But you do get them. At [England's] Mallory [Park speedway], on a hairpin, someone tried to push us out—to take a hole that wasn't there—and he smashed into my right hand. I could have killed him. Afterward, he looked at my hand and said to me, 'At least you can still peel the potatoes, luv.' I wanted to punch him out.

"We took a nasty bump at the gooseneck bend on [England's] Cadwell Circuit," Cheryl says with classic British understatement. "This chap was going full out, and his stupid idiot passenger rolled onto the track, and it was either hit the passenger and kill him or go into the wall. So we hit the tire wall at 90 miles an hour." Cheryl says she was "black from top to toe" for two months. Tom was catapulted over the tire wall and lay motionless for 30 seconds with a ruptured kidney and three broken ribs. He slowly returned to consciousness and shouted, "I'm alive!" He wiggled his toes: "My legs work!" He wiggled his fingers: "My arms work!" Then, after a pause, he wailed to his wife, "Oh, my God, I'm blind!"

"There was mud in his helmet," says Cheryl, rolling her eyes.

The point is, they risked their lives to save a monkey, and that says something hopeful about human nature. "We are all ever so close," Cheryl says of the amateur vintage sidecar community, "no matter what nationality. At the start of every race, we all look at each other and cross our fingers—we get sorta jinxy-like. Solo riders aren't like that. But sidecar racers have camaraderie."

The Thompsons' enthusiasm for amateur racing renews my desire to get behind the wheel on the 'Ring of Hell the next day. I am—how you say?—reanimated. Before leaving the vintage bike rally, I buy a Red Baron helmet and goggles from a Swiss trafficker in old-time driving gear. (His business card says, somewhat salaciously, that he also purveys "accessories in leather.") Cheryl kindly cuts a piece of fabric from the Triumph's tarpaulin, creating a white scarf that will billow behind me as I whip the Zed 8 'round the Nürburgring on a public-racing Sunday.

"I would never ride over there," Tiny says as Bob and I prepare to take our leave. "They say one a week goes over there." By *goes* he means *dies*. Then Tiny bids us a cheery farewell.

On Sunday I see it all: a man doing 110 with his dry-cleaning hanging in a back window; an Opel Kadett hammering into an S-turn while its gas cap flaps against the rear quarter panel; a guy getting airborne at Kilometer 4, his children's dolls looking impassively out the rear windshield; three teenage girls smoking in an Opel Swing hatchback, the driver applying lipstick in the rearview while idling in the starting chute; and a man in a drop-top whose hat flies off at the Flugplatz. Happily, the hat doesn't suction itself to the face of a biker behind him. Heaven knows it could.

Todd Fry, the young Air Force captain, likes to race his Honda CBR 900 RR Fireblade around the Nürburgring. "I'm not one of these guys who's an adrenaline junkie," says Fry, of Pompton Plains, N.J., roasting in his red-white-and-blue leather jumpsuit. "I've scared myself more often on the motorcycle than in an F-16. But fear is a good thing to have. Fear is life insurance out here."

If so, I am well insured. As Fry and I speak, an Opel Esona race-prepared road car blazes by on the track. A dozen Lotus Elises go into the starting chute together. A pink-and-white tour bus full of seniors from Kaiserslautern enters the raceway, hazard lights blinking absurdly. A ding-a-ling in a camper van survives two passes around the 'Ring, both times plunging into the Karussell turn. "Just pass him," advises Fry. "Everyone has a right to be out there. For the most part, you're just racing the road anyway."

Tell that to the driver of the Porsche GT2, an earlier, *more aggressive* version of the car whose driver wanted to drag-race Bob and me on our first day in the Alps. Tell that to the pilot of the Nissan Skyline GT-R, a Japanese-only supercar that was probably towed over here from England, street-illegal as it is. Tell that to the nutter in the purple Lamborghini Diablo. Tell that to all the mustachioed Germans doing 160 on their Italian-made Aprilia racing bikes.

"The biggest rush is when you're fully leaned over into a turn and you're scraping your knees on the track," says Mike Leong, 24, an Air Force lieutenant from Cincinnati who rides a Yamaha YZF-R1 racing bike. "When you take a turn right, you have 440 pounds and 150 horsepower and all those G's acting on you." He shows me the deep scuffing in the plastic guards sewn over the knees of his leathers. "That," he says, "is how you know you've made a good turn."

The Zed 8 beckons from the parking lot. I have been reluctant to drive it even on the rural highways around the Nürburgring, which attract almost as many racing bikers as the raceway. Everywhere on those roads are signs that say RACEN IST OUT! (Racing Is Out!) above a silhouette of a biker sliding off his cycle into oblivion. "You know it's a good road," says Leong, without a trace of false machismo, "when you see those signs."

Leong and Fry have the Right Stuff for the Nürburgring. Michael Schumacher, who was winning the Canadian Grand Prix in Montreal on this Sunday afternoon, has the Right Stuff. Eighteen-year-old girls in Opel Swing hatchbacks have the Right Stuff. James Bond has the Right Stuff, and I have his car. But the question remains: Do I have the Right Stuff?

I came to the Nürburgring to test my driving skills—which is to say nerve—on the most difficult roadway in the world, the San Diego Freeway on acid. Of course, I really came to learn deeper truths about my courage under extreme duress. From afar, it seemed as if it would be good for a laugh. But this is what I've learned: I will not drive 125 mph on an automotive minefield in a borrowed car costing more than I'm worth, solely for the momentary diversion of a magazine editor back in New York City. Now I know. *Reisen bildet.* Travel educates.

I call that courage. You call me a wuss. Fine. But you'll have to say the same to Tiny, and trust me, you don't want to do that.

We All
Had a Ball

BY ROY BLOUNT JR.

This is the story of a bunch of over-35 guys—including the author,
a frequent SI contributor—who lived out their fondest athletic fantasy: playing
baseball with the '69 Cubs.

I HAVE A T-SHIRT AND TWO SWEAT SHIRTS THAT SAY "I PLAYED baseball against the 1969 Cubs." This intro lets me get on with the rest of the story. "Hello, my name is Blat, Blong, Blough—whatever, it doesn't matter—and the very fact that Ferguson Jenkins was playing me deep enough to catch a ball hit 350 feet tells you something," is how I usually begin.

"Excuse me?" people reply.

"I hit a ball 350 feet," I say.

"Where?"

"Pulled it dead to left. It was caught over the shoulder, but still, he must have been playing me pretty deep—by Ferguson Jenkins. He was in left at the time. You know how guys over 35 are; they like to live out their fantasies, and Jenkins probably always wanted to rob a sportswriter of extra bases. Earlier in camp, he called me—just a minute, I think I have the exact wording somewhere . . . here it is: 'A good hitter.' O.K., you *could* say that's the kind of thing he might say to his nephew, but still. . . ."

"No, I mean where, like in, what park?"

"Scottsdale Stadium. Arizona. Which was strangely appropriate, because. . . ."

"Oh. Thin air."

Thin air. I may have to get another T-shirt that says I HIT A BASEBALL 350

FEET AND WHY IS IT THAT EVERYONE'S REACTION IS 'THIN AIR'? The whole trouble with my baseball career, and my life, is that my T-shirts have to have too many words on them.

My game shirt, the authentic Chicago away uniform shirt I was wearing when I hit the ball 350 feet, has only one word on it: CUBS. The All-Star Baseball School's weeklong camp last month for men over 35, which culminated with a game against some of the '69 Cubs, was the closest I will come to fitting myself into that word, that one round patch.

How close was that?

What? Who are you with?

This was an oft fantasized experience you had, right? So this is your oft fantasized interview.

About time.

You weren't satisfied with your press coverage at the camp?

No. TIME magazine unaccountably attributed my 350-foot shot to Art Lessel, a 63-year-old pilot.

Yeah, but what about the thin air?

I'll tell you about thin air. Thin air is when Randy Hundley, who was one of the former Cubs I played against, pops a ball incalculably high into what we call the Big Arizona Sky. Being camped under a fly in Arizona is like looking over the side of a boat after a camera you just dropped into Lake Michigan. And I'll tell you something else about thin air. Thin air is when I, the third baseman, fresh from the triumph of hitting a ball 350 feet, find myself in the position of having to come to grips with a pop-up that resembles the average person's concept of a pop-up about as much as Ralph Sampson resembles your gym teacher.

In other words, a tough chance.

But that's not all. To try to catch it, I have to drift toward the same spot where, in 1970, I had my darkest day as a sportswriter, when Leo Durocher—who managed the Cubs then and was managing them again in this game—branded me as the anti-Cub right there in front of the whole team. Anyway, I miss it.

Really? The pop-up? Why do you miss it?

I don't miss it now. I missed it then. And three days later it's on national TV. At least my friends and I think that's me we see, though I find out much later it's some other guy missing a different pop-up. But by then, the damage to my psyche and reputation had been done.

What were you called? You and the other 62 men over 35 who for $2,195 each lived out a boyhood dream by working out with major leaguers?

"Campers." I would have liked "prospects" better. By the way, two or three guys under 35 slipped in. Can you imagine how far I would have hit the ball if I'd been their age? I'm 41! True, I never hit a ball that far when I was under 35. That was the longest ball I ever hit in my life. And maybe the last. What a way to go out! But what if I'm getting better? What if I have yet to come into my oft fantasized own? Baseball! You just won't let go! I might say, however, that it was never my boyhood dream to miss a pop-up in front of thousands of people.

The All-Star School, which is operated by Hundley and Chicago entrepreneur Allan Goldin usually instructs kids, right?

Yes, we were the historic first middle-aged campers. And we seem to have struck a chord. Every television network was all over us. Another Cub camp, also in Scottsdale, is planned for April, and a company called Baseball Fantasies Fulfilled has announced an April camp in Tempe featuring old Dodgers.

How did the Cub camp work?

Very well. We had the Scottsdale facilities that the Cubs formerly used for spring training, and we were drilled in fundamentals by '69 Cubs Hundley, Jenkins, Billy Williams, Ron Santo, Ernie Banks, Glenn Beckert, Jim Hickman, Rich Nye, Ken Rudolph and Gene Oliver, and by slightly later-vintage Cubs Jose Cardenal and Steve Stone. The old Cubs also played with us in intrasquad games. Nobody wanted to look like a jerk in front of them. Take away the Cubs and the camp would have degenerated into middle-aged doctors, lawyers, brokers and businessmen rolling around on the ground fighting over whose bat it was. There should be Cubs at the U.N.

And on the last day of camp, in Scottsdale Stadium—where the fences are all deeper than 350 feet—before around 4,200 fans and a host of media folks who don't really care about the longest ball a person ever hit in his entire life, the old Cubs beat us 23–6.

Does that mean you were 17 runs short of being as good as a team of major-leaguers, one of whom, Jenkins, is still active, and, incidentally, six-foot-five and is the guy who caught your soaring drive over his shoulder?

It's hard to say. I do know that I came within 15 inches of catching what you would call a major-league pop-up. I remember saying to myself, while drifting over to the spot in foul territory where I first met Durocher in 1970, "Oh, well, God, I guess . . . mine." Privately I hoped that Jimmy Stuart, a commodities trader in Chicago who won the plaque for Most Aggressive Camper, would hustle pushily over from shortstop and call me off of it, and I would've given him a look of annoyance and let him have it. But he didn't.

I looked up at that thing. And what struck me was, "This pop-up doesn't care who I am." Also, the sun was in my eyes. "The sun is in my eyes," I thought. "And I *still* don't know what made Durocher say what he said in 1970. And anyway, what in the hell am I supposed to do with this thing? I'm a writer. I'm 41 years old. And I was never all that good when I was 21. And it's not even really spring yet. The pop-ups are ahead of the third basemen. And. . . ."

And you missed it. . . . Could you give us an idea of what a typical day in camp was like?

Thank you for changing the subject. First of all, we take a bus from our hotel to the '69 Cubs' spring workout fields (now used by the Giants) on Hayden Road, where we enter a dressing room and don big league uniforms. Right? Most of us would have been willing to die at that point. All right, my pants were too big. But if angels offered me a golden robe, would I say, "Only if you've got it in a 44 long"? And the old Cubs are sitting around telling stories about Durocher, their manager in '69 (as well as '70, when I met him), and how hard he was on non-regulars, whom he referred to as "the rest of you bleep." There was the time Lee Thomas went up to pinch hit and Durocher sat on the bench saying, "Look at that bleep bleep bleep. He can't run, he can't hit, I don't know why the bleep bleep bleep I got him. Look at him! He's going to pop up." And sure enough, Thomas popped up. Durocher swore for several minutes, then turned to Ted Savage and told him to pinch-hit next. "Why should I go up there," said Savage, "and subject myself to abuse?"

Would you say you were subjected to big league baseball without the abuse?

Well, to some extent. In all candor, I would have to say that this was where the $2,195 came in. Half of that may have been for overhead and the other half for not having Durocher come in until the end of the week. But there was some abuse, after all. There were all those reporters. And aerobics.

Aerobics were led by Susie Warren who is what you might call lithe. And she made us campers do terrible things with our bodies, to music. Cardenal would accompany us, using a bat as a baton and crying *"No más! No más!"* Otherwise, the Cubs grunted and groaned with the rest of us. I have found it possible to live a normal life without reflecting upon the fact that I have hamstrings. I did not find this possible while performing aerobics.

Hamstrings a-twang, we would leave Susie and take on the easier part of the day: playing hardball. We would divide into five squads and rotate from field to field and Cub to Cub. Williams showed me that I'd been holding a bat wrong all my life. You're supposed to hold it up in the forward, or fingers, part of the hand, not back up against the pad. Because when—or if—you hit a ball thrown at big league batting-practice speed with the bat held back up against your pad, your right pad, if you bat righthanded, turns various shades of blue. This subject arose when I asked Williams why I had developed indigo hand.

It was Santo who explained why I'd developed it on my left hand, too. That was because I've been holding the glove wrong all my life. You're supposed to hold it so that the ball always hits in the webbing, he said. This was a piece of advice I was unable to use. I feel I'm doing well when I catch a ball with any part of the leather. Playing third base, I also developed indigo shoulder, chest and thigh.

Hickman and Jenkins also explained to me that I'd been holding the ball wrong all my life. If you hold it along the seams, it veers. This is what Jenkins usually does, because as a pitcher he usually wants it to veer. This is what Hickman never did, because as a fielder he didn't want it to. This is what I, as a fielder, have often done down through the veers.

There are a great many intangibles in baseball, aren't there?

Yes, and I wonder whether I will ever get a feel for them.

What else would you do on a typical day of training, after finding out that you've always been holding everything wrong?

Go back to the dressing room. Sit around sweaty. Take a shower with a member of the Hall of Fame, Banks, who's saying, "There is a vast reservoir of potential in all of us waiting to be tapped!" Stiffen up. Walk out toward the bus like somebody who just got off a horse. Yet feel *primed*. Feel *bodily*.

And go back to the hotel and sit in the whirlpool with the Cubs. Santo tells about the time Rogers Hornsby went through the Cubs' minor league camps checking out all the hitters. Hornsby called a bunch of them together in some bleachers and went down the rows. The first guy was black. "You better go back to shining shoes," Hornsby said, "because you can't hit." And he said more or less the same thing to one prospect after another. Santo and Williams were sitting together. "If he says that to me," Santo said to Williams, "I'm going to cry."

And Hornsby came to Williams. "You," Hornsby said, "can hit in the big leagues right now." And he said the same thing to Santo.

Later Santo was up in the bigs, in the All-Star Game. "And there are McCovey and Aaron and Mays, and Ron Santo, and some photographer is taking a picture of us together!" Santo says, beaming. We beam with him. Not only campers but also Cubs are returned to their youth.

Would you say that rejuvenation was a theme of the camp?

Yes. But also fading. The '69 Cubs, you know, were the team that blew the National League East title to the Miracle Mets. The Cubs looked as if they were going to run away with it. Until September. On the first day of camp, Hundley gave Stone, who was to be our coach in the big Friday game against the Cubs, a chance to address us. "Just stay close to them till Thursday," Stone advised. "These are the '69 Cubs. They fade."

I asked Banks how he knew when it was time to retire. "You lose your quickness," he said. "And you hear whispers. Rumors. 'He used to make that play.' 'He used to hit that pitch.' Or maybe they don't say anything, but you can see it when they look at you. You can see it in their eyes."

That sounded like what I had been going through since I was 12. In my last Little League season I was pretty good, but since then it has been only flashes. Moments. Inklings of what it feels like to be a player.

Did you have any of those inklings with the Cubs?

I had so many inklings, I may never sort them out. "You look like you've played some ball," Hundley told me, and to give you some idea how that made me feel, here's a story. A reporter at the camp overheard some of the Cubs saying that Ken Schwab, a 55-year-old Illinois grain-farm owner, looked pretty good. After asking another camper to point out Schwab, the reporter went up to another person he thought had been indicated and said, "Hey, the Cubs are saying you took pretty good." The guy nearly fainted. "My lifelong dream!" he cried. "You can't imagine what this means to me. For a big league player to say, 'Irvin Singletary looks pretty good!' " (I have changed his name.) Here's how I felt: 1) "I have played some ball! I *have* played some ball. I must have! All those years, some of the time, anyway, that was actually *ball* I was playing!" And 2) "*Me?*"

Then, too, there were simpler moments. Grounder hit at me, bing-bing-tapocketta, it's in my glove, I'm up with it smoothly, throwing, zip, it's over to the first baseman chest high, a couple of murmurs among the campers: "Got an arm."

"Don't throw too hard too soon," Santo tells me. And the next day he asks me, "How's your hose?"

It wouldn't have sounded much sweeter if it had been Jessica Lange asking. *How was your hose?*

My hose was there, all right. My hose wasn't dead.

You sound surprised.

The irony of all this is that before the opportunity to play with the Cubs arose, I had planned to retire from organized ball. I had given Willie Stargell, who is my age, the chance to hang it up first. I didn't want to steal any of his thunder. This spring I was going to make a simple announcement.

There had been certain telltale signs. For instance, when the slo-pitch soft-ball team that you think you belong to fails to inform you that the season is under way, you begin to wonder. That happened two seasons ago. Then, too, I had doubts about my hose.

The one thing I've had in baseball was an arm from third base. Aside from a tendency to hit, at best, singles to right and on defense to stare off into space, I've been, since Little League, a classic third baseman: too slow to run or to hide. And when the ball bounced off some part of my body, I could pick it up and make that throw. If my hose wasn't out of sorts.

Also, I could never hit slo-pitch softball pitching, which was the only kind I seemed likely to face again. I don't like a pitch that goes way up in the air. When I go to bed at night and either pitch or bat myself to sleep, I see curves, sliders, screwballs and hummers. I can't hit pitching that I never see in my dreams.

You were going to confine yourself to fandom, then?

No, I thought I might go on as a sort of pitcher in the rye. Throwing batting practice to the young. You groove the ball to somebody, and he or she hits it on the nose and you both feel good. And so do people watching. It's like a comedy act. And it's interesting, because you can fail at it. In Scottsdale I threw b.p. to Santo, and I pressed too hard and didn't get the ball where he or I wanted it, and he kept popping it up. I got the feeling he was pressing, too, trying to hit pitches he should've laid off so I wouldn't feel bad. I pressed harder. It was like strained conversation. I wonder whether something like that wasn't going on between the '69 Cubs in the stretch, when they let each other down.

Do you have much experience throwing batting practice?

Ah. At the highest level of serious competition I reached, high school, that was my forte. Somebody once told me he'd run into my old high school coach, Ray Thurmond, who remembered me as a pitcher. I was, of course, a third baseman, but it was at throwing batting practice that I shone. I wore a hole in my right high school baseball shoe throwing b.p. without a pitcher's toe. Those are the spikes I wore against the Cubs.

The shoes of a congenial player, a giving player.

Many people might prefer that their old coach remember them the way Durocher remembers Eddie Stanky, as one of those "scratching, hungry, diving ballplayers who come to kill you."

That's the kind of player I wanted to be. Scrappy. I remember the only time I ever broke up a double play. I was playing intramural softball, in college. Hit the second baseman just right, flipped him up into the air. Didn't hurt him, though. I actually think he enjoyed it, too. This is a terrible thing for someone who pretends to understand serious ball to say, but my deepest desire in sports isn't to win but to share a good time. Maybe that's why Durocher seemed outraged at the very sight of me, that day in 1970.

This was the incident that occurred over in foul territory near the third-base dugout, where you missed the pop-up?

I wish you wouldn't keep harping on that pop-up. To me, if I *catch* a pop-up that goes as high as the Washington Monument, that's news. Or if I hit a ball

350 feet. But to my critics and friends, the idea of me camped not quite under a pop-up, and tilting slightly to the left, and tilting slightly farther to the left, and then the ball coming down well beyond my grasp—that's their idea of something worthy of comment. What people usually say to me now, if I'm unable to start the conversation off on the right note, is "I hear that you missed a pop-up."

I'm sorry. There are so many other things I wanted to ask you. Like, how did you prepare for the Cubs?

For the first time in my life, I worked out. I hate to work out. You have an angel on one shoulder saying "Go, go, go" and a devil on the other saying "Stop, stop, stop," and there you are in between, bored to death with the whole argument and wallowing in sheer, but not pleasant, kinesthesia.

I like to play ball. A ball takes you out of yourself. Of course, if you miss a ball, you snap back into yourself pretty quick, but then you have a lot to talk over with yourself. Even while you are out of yourself, you can be narrating semiconsciously. "He can still hit," you can be saying, referring to yourself in the third person. "Ball was in on him but he got that bat head out in front. . . . " The main reason I cover sports is so I can keep the vocabulary of my semiconscious narration up-to-date.

Now looming ahead of me was a shot at living that narration. I was there to write about it, sure, but it meant a lot more to me than that. So, do you know what I did? I lifted weights. Not only do I not like lifting weights, I deplore it. However, a person doesn't get many chances later on in life to whang a well-pitched baseball or to snag a well-hit one. A person doesn't want to come back from such a chance to report to his family, "I was overpowered."

My son has 10-pound dumbbells lying around the house. I started pumping them and swinging them and going through throwing and batting motions with them, and I didn't stop even when my daughter would collapse—her prerogative—in helpless laughter. I also split two cords of firewood down to the biggest pile of kindling in Massachusetts.

When you first encountered the wily hardball in Arizona, how did you feel?

Overpowered.

A hardball is a thing that, when you have not seen one with steam on it in many years, is upon you before you know it. And in the field I was lost in the complexity of hops. Grounders were like logarithms. Also, I didn't seem to hinge in the same places I used to. And my throwing was so zipless the first day that it moved me to compose a blues song:

I used to have a rifle,

I used to have a gun.

Lord, Lord.

I used to have a rifle,
I used to have a gun.
Now that ball floats over
Like a cinnamon bun.

But you said your hose wasn't dead.

Several things happened. One is that our trainer, Harry Jordan, manipulated my arm and discovered that the tendon over the funny bone had popped out. At least that's what he claimed. He popped it back in. I've never heard of anyone being plagued by funny-bone-tendon problems before, but I know that as he worked, Harry made terrific deep crunching noises in his throat that served to keep some of the fainthearted campers out of the training room altogether, so I'm willing to believe that Jordan was a funnybonologist.

Another thing that kept me going early in camp was my chewing. I was chewing good. I talked chewing on a knowledgeable basis with Jenkins, who bites right into an open can of snuff with his lower front teeth. I could chew with the big boys. I even chewed during aerobics. This helped.

Also, nobody was yelling at anybody. The spirit of Durocher wasn't in the camp. I don't respond to being yelled at. It distracts me from yelling at myself.

Then too, I had all of my clichés working.

I thought sportswriters are supposed to eschew clichés.

Sportswriters, yes. Ballplayers use them to hone their concentration.

I was being interviewed by a TV crew. Most campers were interviewed so many times that they eventually stopped calling their wives to tell them to turn on the VCR.

"Are you feeling the pressure?" I was asked.

"Nah," I lied. "When the bell rings, the juices will flow."

And I spat. Television likes visual touches. If you want to get a statement heard and seen all across the land, remember to spit right after making it.

Then, all of a sudden, I picked up a ball the way the first caveman picked up the first good fist-sized rock. And I felt my hose start to fill with water again. I felt leaner, stronger, springier, *glad* to have hamstrings. The downside of this was that my pants became even baggier. But I wore a psychic T shirt that said, PLAYING MYSELF INTO SHAPE.

And then you went on a tear, right?

No. Then I reached my nadir. I thought I had reached my nadir years ago, several times, but in the very first intrasquad game I hit another new low.

Because I let the guys down. "We are here," Banks had announced one day behind the batting cage, "to ameliorate the classic polarization of the self-motivated individual and the ideology of the group."

Excuse me. Did Banks say things like that often?

Banks said things that came from the Big Arizona Sky. When someone asked him whether he felt he had come along too soon, before the days of astronomical baseball salaries, he said, "No. Wish I'd been born sooner. With the philosophers. Days of Plato, and Socrates, and Alexander Graham Bell." When I asked him what would be a thrill for him, comparable to the thrill we campers were getting, he said, "To sing in the Metropolitan Opera."

What Banks most often said was "*Veez*-ualize yourself hitting a home run!"

"Ernie," said a camper, "I thought we were just supposed to meet the ball, and it would take care of itself."

"No," he said. "It won't. It will not take care of itself. You have to see yourself inside the ball when it is in the pitcher's hand, and you're thinking, 'Time to take a long ride.' "

But don't change the subject. I'm ready to discuss my nadir.

You have a lot of heart as an interviewee, you know that?

Yes, but in the first intrasquad game, I made several plays of the kind that kill infield chatter. Here I was feeling, "Give me Jimmy Stuart and Bob Margolin and Bill Mitchell and Dennis Albano and Wally Pecs (best ballplayer's name in camp) and Dennis Ferrazzano and Tim Tyers and Scott Mermel and George Altemose and Dave Schultz and Steve Heiferman and the Arnold, Crawford and Patti brothers, and I could take on anybody in the world." And what do I do in the first intrasquad game? I drop a line drive hit right at me. A third baseman who can't catch a line drive at his sternum is as dependable as a frog that can't balance on a lily pad. And I let an easy grounder go under my glove. That's like letting a baby's head bob around. And Margolin, who in real life runs a vanity press but is no one's vanity catcher, whips a throw down to nip a guy stealing third, but I don't dig it out of the dirt. In Arizona a lot of thin air can get between a person and the ball and between a person and his mates, even if they don't yell at you.

And the first time at bat, I dribble into a double play. The next time, Stone is pitching. "Can you hit a curveball?" he asks me.

"No," I say.

He throws me a curveball.

And you miss it?

No. Worse. I take it on the inside corner. And this is what I hear, from Oliver on the other bench: "That's a hanger, Roy." I've just taken a hanging curveball for a strike! What Stone has done is throw me a curve that I could hit. And I took it! That's like Jack Benny giving you a straight line and you saying, "Oh. Excuse me. I wasn't listening." Like I say, nobody yelled at us campers, but every now and then one of the big-leaguers would give us a quiet, chastening line, like "Got to have that one" or "That's where we need you, big man." The social fabric. The ideology of the group.

The next pitch from Stone isn't a hanger. Not a curve. It's down the pipe. And I go after it. "All right!" I think.

The ball intersects with my bat about three inches from my hands. It pops weakly to the catcher. I feel as if I've reached out for a proffered ice-cream cone and found it in my armpit. "Well," I think, "I am losing my mind."

That was your nadir?

Yes. It didn't help that I had margarita tongue from the night before.

Ah, I've always wondered about the big league night life. What did you do that night?

For one thing, talked to Cardenal about creekus.

What are creekus?

"You know, creekus," Cardenal said. "Little things." He made sawing motions with his arms like a cricket producing sounds. "One time in Chicago I come to the park with my eyes swollen shut. 'Cause I couldn't sleep. 'Cause creekus was in my room all night. So I can't play. And Mike Royko in the paper, ohhh, he got on me.

"And last night in my room? Creekus again. I find seven of them behind the toilet. I kill them all. I go back to bed. I hear more creekus. I turn the light back on. I find five creekus behind the television. I call the desk. 'You got to send the exterminator!' If Royko had been there! I could have shown him creekus!"

But, you came back from that nadir, right?

Let me put it this way. The next evening I'm in the coffee shop. I eat a well-earned sandwich. I sign the check. And there's a place on the check for "comments." So I write, "I went three for five today." There not being much room, I didn't bother to add, "and fielded flawlessly."

What turned you around?

After my nadir, I talked to Stone. He told me about his Cy Young season with Baltimore in 1980, after which he had nothing left. "I threw over 60 percent breaking balls," he said. "I knew it would ruin my arm, but I was winning 15 games in a row. One year of 25 and 7 is worth five of 15 and 15." Before a game, he said, he would take a Percodan if he felt he would need it in addition to the four aspirin he would routinely take every three innings. And he kept breaking off those hooks.

"Well," I sighed, "your straight one was too tough for me."

"No, that was my forkball," he said.

"Oh!" I said. My heart leapt. "What does it do?"

"Drops off like a spitball and moves in on you. Nobody can hit it."

No wonder you didn't hit it.

Precisely. Not only that, but I'd had a real major league experience. I'd popped up a forkball. The next day, when we played our next intrasquad game, I was ready.

Would you like to tell us about it?

Single to right off Dr. Harry Soloway, the Chicago shrink who became nationally famous by telling the *Today* show that he wasn't giving any more interviews because the last reporter he talked to called him "the most inept ballplayer I have ever seen, man or boy." Except for his fame, a single to right off Dr. Harry Soloway is not an enduring achievement, but a solid single is a solid single. Then, off Cardenal, I ground out and single up the middle. Then, off Beckert, I fly to left. I'm pulling the ball!

A portent. For the 350. . . .

Although I don't realize it at the time. But now we get down to the last inning. Bases loaded. Beckert, who has been moving painfully and saying "Now I remember why I retired," wants to get the game over. He's working in and out on me. This feels like actual baseball! Three and two. Comes in with a high, tight fastball. Too close to take. I foul it back. This is probably a thrill for Beckert, too: a second baseman getting a chance to work on a hitter. He delivers a funny-looking pitch on the outside corner.

And what do you do with it?

Rip it. On a line. But not a straight line. More satisfying than that. A line like a scimitar blade. Over the first baseman's head, and it bites the ground three feet fair. It goes blisteringly on its way, and I say to it, "Burn!"

A double. And such a double! I am most of the way to third when I see the runner ahead of me running toward me. Fortunately, he's heading back toward third, not second. He has become conservative and decided he can't score. But this is such a double that I am able to turn around and go 70 feet back into second standing up. I have hit the equivalent of a triple and a half.

That must have been a thrill.

I'll tell you the thrill. The thrill is what Beckert exclaims.

What does Beckert exclaim?

Beckert exclaims, "How did you hit that pitch?" He turns to Jenkins, who's umpiring. "Slider right on the outside corner!" he says. "And I had him set up!" "I was looking for it," I reply.

"That's right!" says Jenkins. "That's a good hitter."

Wow! You were looking for it?

No. I lied. The truth was I had found my strength as a hitter. Which turned out to be very similar to my strength as a defensive back in football—which is that I am too slow to take a fake. My strength as a hitter, I now realize, is that I haven't got sense enough to be set up. Why do you think a person becomes a writer? It's because he can never figure anything out until afterwards. In baseball down through the years I've often been trying, during the seventh inning, to figure out what happened in the fifth. And what happened was that I wasn't paying attention because I was wondering what I did wrong in the third. And what I did wrong in the third was boot one because I was thinking, "I've got to concentrate with every fiber of my being. Hmm, interesting phrase. I wonder what all the fibers of my being in concert would look like? A nice wool shirt?" Oh, those rare great moments in sports when my mind isn't working and my body is!

Another thing I do in this game is throw four guys out with my hose. My mind is a blank then, too.

Did you talk your triple and a half over with Beckert and Jenkins later?

No, not exactly. But I will say this. In my time I'd exchanged various glances with ballplayers. And a major league manager once mistook me for a member of the Hall of Fame. That was when I called Billy Martin on the phone, and hearing my voice, he cried, "Mick? Mick? Is it the Mick?" He thought I was Mickey Mantle. When he realized I wasn't, we were both very disappointed.

But I had never exchanged a glance with a ballplayer that contained any hint that I, too, was a part of the actual ballplaying experience. One time a Venezuelan sportscaster, Juan Vené, and I told Manny Sanguillen, when he was catching for the Pirates, that we had played baseball on opposing press teams.

"Softball?" asked Sanguillen.

"No, hardball."

Sanguillen was one of the most gracious ballplayers I've ever met. But Sanguillen shook his head and said, "You guys!"

That evening in Scottsdale after the second intrasquad game, I exchanged glances with Beckert and Jenkins that, to me—and I am talking in terms of diamond experience now—contained a hint of "us guys."

Tell me. This is another thing I have always wondered about. Do you ballplayers put your pants on one leg at a time, like everybody else?

I can only speak for myself. The answer in my case is: not always. After that intrasquad game, I got tired putting one leg on, stopped for a while and worked on the other one.

But you were ready for the big game the next day in Scottsdale Stadium?

Did I tell you I hit a ball 350 feet?

In passing, but tell me more about it.

I have always gotten on well with veterinarians. Rich Nye, who won 26 games in the big leagues, is now a veterinarian. If I didn't live so far from Des Plaines, Illinois, I'd send my dogs to him. Nye threw me a good pitch to hit.

Every camper got one at bat in the big game. By the time I got up, in the ninth or 10th of many innings, it had become clear that a few winded old Cubs are better than wave after fresh wave of old brokers, law professors and salesmen. The crowd was diminished and restive.

"Representing SPORTS ILLUSTRATED," blared the loudspeaker, "Ray" and a mispronunciation of my last name. I strode to the plate and realized I didn't have on a helmet. I ran back and got one. I strode to the plate and realized that the flap covered the wrong ear. I ran back and got a left-eared one. Fan reaction indicated a doubting of my expertise. I dug in.

"Coming right down the middle," said Rudolph, who was catching.

All you selfless, unrecognized batting practice pitchers out there, Keep it up! Your service will be repaid. Someday a veterinarian will lay one in there for you. In practice, Nye had shown me his real 80-mile-per-hour fastball, which I nearly hit. This one was a notch slower. Later he said he wished he'd thrown it harder; I would have cleared the fence. But I'll take my 350 feet, and the sound of a crowd that came to scoff and stayed to eat its heart out.

Anything else you'd like to say?

Yeah. I got my longest hit ever against a team managed by Leo Durocher.

Did I tell you about the first time I met Leo? It was in Scottsdale Stadium in the spring of 1970 that I, a cub reporter, innocently introduced myself to him. And he, standing outside the third-base dugout, pointed his finger at me and began to address, at the top of his lungs, the players who, a few months before, had been the '69 Cubs: "I want everybody to hear this! I'm not talking to this guy! I'm not saying a word!"

Just before he disappeared under the stands, he turned and added, "And he knows why!"

I didn't then and don't now. But it got to me. I loved baseball, and Durocher went all the way back through Willie Mays and Coogan's Bluff and the Gashouse Gang to Ruth. I couldn't shake the feeling that there must be something about me that didn't fit into the national pastime.

Did you ever run into Durocher again?

Not until camp week 13 years later. At the banquet after the big game, he took the occasion to make an emotional talk. He confessed why the '69 Cubs folded: "They didn't give me 100 percent."

What a thing to say at this point! Would the man never let up?

"They gave me 140 percent." Ah. The Cubs had pressed. Durocher was conceding that he'd chewed on them too hard.

He also apologized publicly for embarrassing Santo nastily in a celebrated 1971 clubhouse meeting. After the banquet, Durocher and Santo embraced.

Durocher didn't apologize to me. He glared at me once but with no hint of recognition. He had relieved me, however, of one burden. I still don't know what made me anathema, but I do know it wasn't my fault that the Cubs didn't win in '69.

"Winning the pennant that year might have been anticlimactic for the kind of love we had on that team," said emcee Gene Oliver from the podium. However that may be, in 1969 Durocher seems, oddly enough, to have forged a team that couldn't win but did learn how to share a good time.

So you have no complaints?

No complaints? No complaints? What madman built a stadium whose fences are nowhere shorter than 355 feet?

Let me quote to you the testimony of Steve Stone, and also of longtime Chicago baseball writer Richard Dozer, now of *The Phoenix Gazette*, who was as much of an official scorer as we had: "The ball is out in Fenway."

But . . . the air in Fenway isn't thin.

Yeah, and Hundley's pop-up doesn't go nearly so high, and I catch it and toss it over to Leo.

The Curious Case
Of Sidd Finch

BY GEORGE PLIMPTON

The straight-faced publication of this fabulous tale—the greatest stunt in
SI history—created enormous buzz among credulous baseball fans across the country.
The tip-off to observant readers: The issue's cover date was April Fools' Day.

THE SECRET CANNOT BE KEPT MUCH LONGER. QUESTIONS are being asked, and sooner rather than later the New York Mets management will have to produce a statement. It may have started unraveling in St. Petersburg, Fla., two weeks ago, on March 14, to be exact, when Mel Stottlemyre, the Mets' pitching coach, walked over to the 40-odd Mets players doing their morning calisthenics at the Payson Field Complex not far from the Gulf of Mexico, a solitary figure among the pulsation of jumping jacks, and motioned three Mets to step out of the exercise. The three, all good prospects, were John Christensen, a 24-year-old outfielder; Dave Cochrane, a spare but muscular switch-hitting third baseman; and Lenny Dykstra, a swift centerfielder who may be the Mets' leadoff man of the future.

Ordering the three to collect their bats and batting helmets, Stottlemyre led the players to the north end of the complex where a large canvas enclosure had been constructed two weeks before. The rumor was that some irrigation machinery was being installed in an underground pit.

Standing outside the enclosure, Stottlemyre explained what he wanted. "First of all," the coach said, "the club's got kind of a delicate situation here, and it would help if you kept reasonably quiet about it, O.K.?" The three nodded. Stottlemyre said, "We've got a young pitcher we're looking at. We want to see what he'll do with a batter standing in the box. We'll do this alphabetically. John, go on in there, stand at the plate and give the pitcher a target. That's all you have to do."

"Do you want me to take a cut?" Christensen asked.

Stottlemyre produced a dry chuckle. "You can do anything you want."

Christensen pulled aside a canvas flap and found himself inside a rectangular area about 90 feet long and 30 feet wide, open to the sky, with a home plate set in the ground just in front of him, and down at the far end a pitcher's mound, with a small group of Mets front-office personnel standing behind it, facing home plate. Christensen recognized Nelson Doubleday, the owner of the Mets, and Frank Cashen, wearing a long-billed fishing cap. He had never seen Doubleday at the training facility before.

Christensen bats righthanded. As he stepped around the plate he nodded to Ronn Reynolds, the stocky reserve catcher who has been with the Mets organization since 1980. Reynolds whispered up to him from his crouch, "Kid, you won't believe what you're about to see."

A second flap down by the pitcher's end was drawn open, and a tall, gawky player walked in and stepped up onto the pitcher's mound. He was wearing a small, black fielder's glove on his left hand and was holding a baseball in his right. Christensen had never seen him before. He had blue eyes, Christensen remembers, and a pale, youthful face, with facial muscles that were motionless, like a mask. "You notice it," Christensen explained later, "when a pitcher's jaw isn't working on a chaw or a piece of gum." Then to Christensen's astonishment he saw that the pitcher, pawing at the dirt of the mound to get it smoothed out properly and to his liking, was wearing a heavy hiking boot on his right foot.

Christensen has since been persuaded to describe that first confrontation:

"I'm standing in there to give this guy a target, just waving the bat once or twice out over the plate, He starts his windup. He sways way back, like Juan Marichal, this hiking boot comes clomping over—I thought maybe he was wearing it for balance or something—and he suddenly rears upright like a catapult. The ball is launched from an arm completely straight up and *stiff*. Before you can blink, the ball is in the catcher's mitt. You hear it *crack*, and then there's this little bleat from Reynolds."

Christensen said the motion reminded him of the extraordinary contortions that he remembered of Goofy's pitching in one of Walt Disney's cartoon classics.

"I never dreamed a baseball could be thrown that fast. The wrist must have a lot to do with it, and all that leverage. You can hardly see the blur of it as it goes by. As for hitting the thing, frankly, I just don't think it's humanly possible. You could send a blind man up there, and maybe he'd do better hitting at the *sound* of the thing."

Christensen's opinion was echoed by both Cochrane and Dykstra, who followed him into the enclosure. When each had done his stint, he emerged startled and awestruck.

Especially Dykstra. Offering a comparison for SI, he reported that out of curiosity he had once turned up the dials that control the motors of the pitching machine to maximum velocity, thus producing a pitch that went approximately 106 miles per hour. "What I looked at in there," he said, motioning toward the enclosure, "was whistling by another third as fast, I swear."

The phenomenon the three young batters faced, and about whom only Reynolds, Stottlemyre and a few members of the Mets' front office know, is a 28-year-old, somewhat eccentric mystic named Hayden (Sidd) Finch. He may well change the course of baseball history. On St. Patrick's Day, to make sure they were not all victims of a crazy hallucination, the Mets brought in a radar gun to measure the speed of Finch's fastball. The model used was a JUGS Supergun II. It looks like a black space gun with a big snout, weighs about five pounds and is usually pointed at the pitcher from behind the catcher. A glass plate in the back of the gun shows the pitch's velocity—accurate, so the manufacturer claims, to within plus or minus 1 mph. The figure at the top of the gauge is 200 mph. The fastest projectile ever measured by the JUGS (which is named after the old-timer's descriptive—the "jug-handled" curveball) was a Roscoe Tanner serve that registered 153 mph. The highest number that the JUGS had ever turned for a baseball was 103 mph, which it did, curiously, twice on one day, July 11, at the 1978 All-Star Game when both Goose Gossage and Nolan Ryan threw the ball at that speed. On March 17, the gun was handled by Stottlemyre. He heard the pop of the ball in Reynolds's mitt and the little squeak of pain from the catcher. Then the astonishing figure 168 appeared on the glass plate. Stottlemyre remembers whistling in amazement, and then he heard Reynolds say, "Don't tell me, Mel, I don't want to know. . . . "

The Mets' front office is reluctant to talk about Finch. The fact is, they know very little about him. He has had no baseball career. Most of his life has been spent abroad, except for a short period at Harvard University.

The registrar's office at Harvard will release no information about Finch except that in the spring of 1976 he withdrew from the college in midterm. The alumni records in Harvard's Holyoke Center indicate slightly more. Finch spent his early childhood in an orphanage in Leicester, England, and was adopted by a foster parent, the eminent archaeologist Francis Whyte-Finch, who was killed in an airplane crash while on an expedition in the Dhaulagiri mountain area of Nepal. At the time of the tragedy, Finch was in his last year at the Stowe School in Buckingham, England, from which he had been accepted into Harvard. Apparently, though, the boy decided to spend a year in the general area of the plane crash in the Himalayas (the plane was never actually found) before he returned to the West and entered Harvard in 1975, dropping for unknown reasons the "Whyte" from his name. Hayden Finch's picture is not in the freshman yearbook. Nor, of course, did he play baseball at Harvard, having departed before the start of the spring season.

His assigned roommate was Henry W. Peterson, class of 1979, now a stockbroker in New York City with Dean Witter, who saw very little of Finch. "He was almost never there," Peterson told SI. "I'd wake up morning after morning and look across at his bed, which had a woven native carpet of some sort on it—I have an idea he told me it was made of yak fur—and never had the sense it had been slept in. Maybe he slept on the floor. Actually, my assumption was that be had a girl in Somerville or something, and stayed out there. He had almost no belongings. A knapsack. A bowl he kept in the corner on the floor. A couple of wool shirts, always very clean, and maybe a pair or so of blue jeans. One pair of hiking boots. I always had the feeling that he was very bright. He had a French horn in an old case. I don't know much about French-horn music, but he played beautifully. Sometimes he'd play it in the bath. He knew any number of languages. He was so adept at them that he'd be talking in English, which be spoke in this distinctive singsong way, quite Oriental, and he'd use a phrase like "pied-à-terre" and without knowing it he'd sail along in French for a while until he'd drop in a German word like "angst" and he'd shift to that language. For any kind of sustained conversation you had to hope he wasn't going to use a foreign buzz word—especially out of the Eastern languages he knew, like Sanskrit—cause that was the end of it as far as I was concerned."

When Peterson was asked why he felt Finch had left Harvard, he shrugged his shoulders. "I came back one afternoon and everything was gone—the little rug, the horn, the staff. . . . Did I tell you that he had this long kind of shepherd's crook standing in the corner? Actually, there was so little stuff to begin with that it was hard to tell he wasn't there anymore. He left a curious note on the floor. It turned out to be a Zen koan, which is one of those puzzles which cannot be solved by the intellect. It's the famous one about the live goose in the bottle. How do you get the goose out of the bottle without hurting it or breaking the glass? The answer is, 'There, it's out!' I heard from him once, from Egypt. He sent pictures. He was on his way to Tibet to study."

FINCH'S ENTRY into the world of baseball occurred last July in Old Orchard Beach, Maine, where the Mets' AAA farm club, the Tidewater Tides, was in town playing the Guides. After the first game of the series Bob Schaefer, the Tides' manager, was strolling back to the hotel. He has very distinct memories of his first meeting with Finch: "I was walking by a park when suddenly this guy—nice-looking kid, clean-shaven, blue jeans, big boots—appears alongside. At first, I think maybe he wants an autograph or to chat about the game, but no, he scrabbles around in a kind of knapsack, gets out a scuffed-up baseball and a small, black leather fielder's mitt that looks like it came out of the back of some Little League kid's closet. This guy says to me, 'I have learned the art of the pitch. . . .' Some odd phrase like that, delivered in a singsong voice, like a chant, kind of what you hear in a Chinese restaurant if there are some Chinese in there.

"I am about to hurry on to the hotel when this kid points out a soda bottle on top of a fence post about the same distance home plate is from the pitcher's rubber. He rears way back, comes around and pops the ball at it. Out there on that fence post the soda bottle *explodes*. It disintegrates like a rifle bullet hit it—just little specks of vaporized glass in a *puff*. Beyond the post I could see the ball bouncing across the grass of the park until it stopped about as far away as I can hit a three-wood on a good day.

"I said, very calm, 'Son, would you mind showing me that again?'

"And he did. He disappeared across the park to find the ball—it had gone so far, he was after it for what seemed 15 minutes. In the meantime I found a tin can from a trash container and set it up for him. He did it again—just kicked the can off the fence like it was hit with a baseball bat. It wasn't the accuracy of the pitch so much that got to me but the speed. It was like the tin can got belted as soon as the ball left the guy's fingertips. Instantaneous. I thought to myself, 'My God, that kid's thrown the ball about 150 mph.' Nolan Ryan's fastball is a changeup compared to what this kid just threw.

"Well, what happens next is that we sit and talk, this kid and I, out there on the grass of the park. He sits with the big boots tucked under his legs, like one of those yoga guys, and he tells me he's not sure he wants to play big league baseball, but he'd like to give it a try. He's never played before, but he knows the rules, even the infield-fly rule, he tells me with a smile, and he knows he can throw a ball with complete accuracy and enormous velocity. He won't tell me how he's done this except that he 'learned it in the mountains, in a place called Po, in Tibet.' That is where he said he had learned to pitch . . . up in the mountains, flinging rocks and meditating. He told me his name was Hayden Finch, but he wanted to be called Sidd Finch. I said that most of the Sids we had in baseball came from Brooklyn. Or the Bronx. He said his Sidd came from 'Siddhartha,' which means 'Aim Attained' or 'The Perfect Pitch.' That's what he had learned, how to throw the perfect pitch. O.K. by me, I told him, and that's what I put on the scouting report, 'Sidd Finch.' And I mailed it in to the front office."

The reaction in New York once the report arrived was one of complete disbelief. The assumption was that Schaefer was either playing a joke on his superiors or was sending in the figment of a very powerful wish-fulfillment dream. But Schaefer is one of the most respected men in the Mets organization. Over the past seven years, the clubs he has managed have won six championships. Dave Johnson, the Mets manager, phoned him. Schaefer verified what he had seen in Old Orchard Beach. He told Johnson that sometimes he, too, thought he'd had a dream, but he hoped the Mets would send Finch an invitation so that, at the very least, his own mind would be put at rest.

When a rookie is invited to training camp, he gets a packet of instructions in late January. The Mets sent off the usual literature to Finch at the address Schaefer had supplied them. To their surprise, Finch wrote back with a number of stipulations. He insisted he would report to the Mets camp in St. Petersburg only with the understanding that: 1) there were no contractual commitments; 2) during off-hours he be allowed to keep completely to himself; 3) he did not wish to be involved in any of the team drills or activities; 4) he would show the Mets his pitching prowess in privacy; 5) the whole operation in St. Petersburg was to be kept as secret as possible, with no press or photographs.

The reason for these requirements—he stated in a letter written (according to a source in the Mets front office) in slightly stilted, formal and very polite terminology—was that he had not decided whether he actually wanted to play baseball. He wrote apologetically that there were mental adjustments to be made. He did not want to raise the Mets' expectations, much less those of the fans, and then dash them. Therefore it was best if everything were carried on in secret or, as he put it in his letter, "in camera."

At first, the inclination of the Mets front office was to disregard this nonsense out of hand and tell Finch either to apply, himself, through normal procedures or forget it. But the extraordinary statistics in the scouting report and Schaefer's verification of them were too intriguing to ignore. On Feb. 2, Finch's terms were agreed to by letter. Mick McFadyen, the Mets' groundskeeper in St. Petersburg, was ordered to build the canvas enclosure in a far corner of the Payson complex, complete with a pitcher's mound and plate. Reynolds's ordeal was about to start.

Reynolds is a sturdy, hardworking catcher (he has been described as looking like a high school football tackle). He has tried to be close-lipped about Finch, but his experiences inside the canvas enclosure have made it difficult for him to resist answering a few questions. He first heard about Finch from the Mets' general manager. "Mr. Cashen called me into his office one day in early March," Reynolds disclosed. "I was nervous because I thought I'd been traded. He was wearing a blue bow tie. He leaned across the desk and whispered to me that it was very likely I was going to be a part of baseball history. Big doings! The Mets had this rookie coming to camp, and I was going to be his special catcher. All very hush-hush.

"Well, I hope nothing like that guy ever comes down the pike again. The first time I see him is inside the canvas coop, out there on the pitcher's mound, a thin kid getting ready to throw, and I'm thinking he'll want to toss a couple of warmup pitches. So I'm standing behind the plate without a mask, chest protector, pads or anything, holding my glove up, sort of half-assed, to give him a target to throw at . . . and suddenly I see this windup like a pretzel gone loony, and the next thing, I've been blown two or three feet back, and I'm sitting on the ground with the ball in my glove. My catching hand feels like it's been hit with a sledgehammer."

He was asked: "Does he throw a curveball? A slider? Or a sinker?"

Reynolds grinned and shook his head. "Good questions! Don't ask me."

"Does it make a sound?"

"Yeah, a little *pft, pft-boom!*"

Stottlemyre has been in direct charge of Finch's pitching regimen. His own playing career ended in the spring of 1975 with a rotator-cuff injury, which makes him especially sensitive to the strain that a pitching motion can put on the arm. Although as close-lipped as the rest of the staff, Stottlemyre does admit that Finch has developed a completely revolutionary pitching style. He told SI: "I don't understand the mechanics of it. Anyone who tries to throw the ball that way should fall flat on his back. But I've seen it. I've seen it a hundred times. It's the most awesome thing that has ever happened in baseball."

Asked what influences might have contributed to Finch's style and speed, Stottlemyre said, "Well, *cricket* may have something to do with it. Finch has taken the power and speed of the running throw of the cricket bowler and has somehow harnessed all that energy to the pitching rubber. The wrist snap off that stiff arm is incredible. I haven't talked to him but once or twice. I asked him if he ever thought of snapping the *arm*, like baseball pitchers, rather than the wrist: It would increase the velocity.

"He replied, very polite, you know, with a little bob of the head: 'I undertake as a rule of training to refrain from injury to living things.'

"He's right, of course. It's Ronn Reynolds I feel sorry for. Every time that ball comes in, first you hear this smack sound of the ball driving into the pocket of the mitt, and then you hear this little gasp, this *ai yee!*—the catcher, poor guy, his whole body shakin' like an angina's hit it. It's the most piteous thing I've ever heard, short of a trapped rabbit."

Hayden (Sidd) Finch arrived in St. Petersburg on Feb. 7. Most of the rookies and minor leaguers stay at the Edgewater Beach Inn. Assuming that Finch would check in with the rest of the early arrivals, the Mets were surprised when he telephoned and announced that he had leased a room in a small boardinghouse just off Florida Avenue near a body of water on the bay side called Big Bayou. Because his private pitching compound had been constructed across the city and Finch does not drive, the Mets assigned him a driver, a young Tampa Bay resident, Eliot Posner, who picks him up in the morning and returns him to Florida Avenue or, more often, to a beach on the Gulf where, Posner reports, Finch, still in his baseball outfit and carrying his decrepit glove, walks down to the water's edge and, motionless, stares out at the windsurfers. Inevitably, he dismisses Posner and gets back to his boardinghouse on his own.

The Mets management has found out very little about his life in St. Petersburg. Mrs. Roy Butterfield, his landlady, reports (as one might expect) that "he lives very simply. Sometimes he comes in the front door, sometimes the back. Sometimes I'm not even sure he spends the night. I think he sleeps on the floor—his bed is always neat as a pin. He has his own rug, a small little thing. I never have had a boarder who brought his own rug. He has a soup bowl. Not much, is what I say. Of course, he plays the French horn. He plays it very beautifully and, thank goodness, softly. The notes fill the house. Sometimes I think the notes are coming out of my television set."

Probably the member of the Mets staff who has gotten the closest to Finch is Posner. When Posner returns to the Payson complex, inevitably someone rushes out from the Mets' offices asking, "Did he say anything? What did he say?"

Posner takes out a notebook.

"Today he said, 'When your mind is empty like a canyon you will know the power of the Way.' "

"Anything else?"

"No."

While somewhat taxed by Finch's obvious eccentricities, and with the exception of the obvious burden on the catchers, the Mets, it seems, have an extraordinary property in their camp. But the problem is that no one is sure if Finch really wants to play. He has yet to make up his mind; his only appearances are in the canvas enclosure. Reynolds moans in despair when he is told Finch has arrived. Sometimes his ordeal is short-lived. After Finch nods politely at Reynolds and calls down "*Namas-te!*" (which means "greetings" in Sanskrit), he throws only four or five of the terrifying pitches before, with a gentle smile, he announces "*Namas-te!*" (it also means "farewell") and gets into the car to be driven away.

One curious manifestation of Finch's reluctance to commit himself entirely to baseball has been his refusal to wear a complete baseball uniform. Because he changes in his rooming house, no one is quite sure what he will be wearing when he steps through the canvas flap into the enclosure. One afternoon he turned up sporting a tie hanging down over the logo on his jersey, and occasionally—as Christensen noticed—he wears a hiking boot on his right foot. Always, he wears his baseball cap back to front—the conjecture among the Mets officials is that this sartorial behavior is an indication of his ambivalence about baseball.

In hopes of understanding more about him, in early March the Mets called in a specialist in Eastern religions, Dr. Timothy Burns, the author of, among other treatises, *Satori, or Four Years in a Tibetan Lamasery.* Not allowed to speak personally with Finch for fear of "spooking him," Burns was able only to speculate about the Mets' newest player.

According to sources from within the Mets organization, Burns told a meeting of the club's top brass that the strange ballplayer in their midst was very likely a *trapas*, or aspirant monk.

A groan is said to have gone up from Nelson Doubleday. Burns said that Finch was almost surely a disciple of Tibet's great poet-saint Lama Milaraspa, who was born in the 11th century and died in the shadow of Mount Everest. Burns told them that Milaraspa was a great yogi who could manifest an astonishing phenomenon: He could produce "internal heat," which allowed him to survive snowstorms and intense cold, wearing only a thin robe of white cotton. Finch does something similar—an apparent deflection of the huge forces of the universe into throwing a baseball with bewildering accuracy and speed through the process of *siddhi*, namely the yogic mastery of mind-body. He mentioned that *The Book of Changes*, the *I Ching*, suggests that all acts (even throwing a baseball) are connected with the highest spiritual yearnings. Utilizing the Tantric principle of body and mind, Finch has decided to pitch baseballs—at least for a while.

The Mets pressed Burns. Was there any chance that Finch would come to his senses and *commit* himself to baseball?

"There's a chance," Burns told them. "You will remember that the Buddha himself, after what is called the Great Renunciation, finally realized that even in the most severe austerities—though he conquered lust and fear and acquired a great deal of self-knowledge—truth itself could not necessarily be found. So after fasting for six years he decided to eat again."

Reached by SI at the University of Maryland, where he was lecturing last week, Burns was less sanguine. "The biggest problem Finch has with baseball," he said over the phone, "is that *nirvana*, which is the state all Buddhists wish to reach, means literally 'the blowing out'—specifically the purifying of oneself of greed, hatred and delusion. Baseball," Burns went on, "is symbolized to a remarkable degree by those very three aspects: *greed* (huge money contracts, stealing second base, robbing a guy of a base hit, charging for a seat behind an iron pillar, etc.), *hatred* (players despising management, pitchers hating hitters, the Cubs detesting the Mets, etc.) and *delusion* (the slider, the pitchout, the hidden-ball trick and so forth). So you can see why it is not easy for Finch to give himself up to a way of life so opposite to what he has been led to cherish."

Burns is more puzzled by Finch's absorption with the French horn. He suspects that in Tibet Finch may have learned to play the *rkang-gling*, a Tibetan horn made of human thighbones, or perhaps even the Tibetan long trumpet, the *dung-chen*, whose sonorous bellowing in those vast Himalayan defiles is somewhat echoed in the lower registers of the French horn.

The Mets inner circle believes that Finch's problem may be that he cannot decide between baseball and a career as a horn player. In early March the club contacted Bob Johnson, who plays the horn and is the artistic director of the distinguished New York Philomusica ensemble, and asked him to come to St. Petersburg. Johnson was asked to make a clandestine assessment of Finch's ability as a horn player and, even more important, to make contact with him. The idea was that, while praising him for the quality of his horn playing, Johnson should try to persuade him that the lot of a French-horn player (even a very fine one) was not an especially gainful one. Perhaps *that* would tip the scales in favor of baseball.

Johnson came down to St. Petersburg and hung around Florida Avenue for a week. He reported later to SI: "I was being paid for it, so it wasn't bad. I spent a lot of time looking up, so I'd get a nice suntan. Every once in a while I saw Finch coming in and out of the rooming house, dressed to play baseball and carrying a funny-looking black glove. Then one night I heard the French horn. He was playing it in his room. I have heard many great horn players in my career— Bruno Jaenicke, who played for Toscanini; Dennis Brain, the great British virtuoso; Anton Horner of the Philadelphia Orchestra—and I would say Finch was on a par with them. He was playing Benjamin Britten's *Serenade*, for tenor horn and strings—a haunting, tender piece that provides great space for the player— when suddenly he produced a big, evocative *bwong* sound that seemed to shiver the leaves of the trees. Then he shifted to the rondo theme from the trio for violin, piano and horn by Brahms—just sensational. It may have had something to do with the Florida evening and a mild wind coming in over Big Bayou and tree frogs, but it was *remarkable*. I told this to the Mets, and they immediately sent me home—presuming, I guess, that I was going to hire the guy. That's not so far-fetched. He can play for the Philomusica anytime."

Meanwhile, the Mets are trying other ways to get Finch into a more positive frame of mind about baseball. Inquiries among American lamaseries (there are more than 100 Buddhist societies in the U.S.) have been quietly initiated in the hope of finding monks or priests who are serious baseball fans and who might persuade Finch that the two religions (Buddhism and baseball) are compatible. One plan is to get him into a movie theater to see *The Natural*, the mystical film about baseball, starring Robert Redford. Another film suggested is the baseball classic *It Happens Every Spring*, starring Ray Milland as a chemist who, by chance, discovers a compound that avoids wood; when applied to a baseball in the film, it makes Milland as effective a pitcher as Finch is in real life.

Conversations with Finch himself have apparently been exercises in futility. All conventional inducements—huge contracts, advertising tie-ins, the banquet circuit, ticker-tape parades, having his picture on a Topps bubble-gum card, chatting on *Kiner's Korner* (the Mets' postgame TV show) and so forth—mean little to him. As do the perks ("You are very kind to offer me a Suzuki motorcycle, but I cannot drive"). He has very politely declined whatever overtures the Mets have offered. The struggle is an absolutely internal one. He will resolve it. Last week he announced that he would let the management know what he was going to do on or around April 1.

Mets manager Davey Johnson has seen Finch throw about half a dozen pitches. He was impressed ("If he didn't have this great control, he'd be like the Terminator out there. Hell, that fastball, if off-target on the inside, would carry a batter's kneecap back into the catcher's mitt"), but he is leaving the situation to the front office. "I can handle the pitching rotation; let them handle the monk." He has had one meeting with Finch. "I was going to ask him if we could at least give him a decent fielder's mitt. I asked him why he was so attached to the piece of rag he was using. 'It is,' the guy told me, 'the only one I have.' Actually, I don't see why he needs a better one. All he will ever need it for is to catch the ball for the next pitch. So then I said to him, 'There's only one thing I can offer you, Finch, and that's a fair shake.' "

According to Jay Horwitz, the Mets' public-relations man, Finch smiled at the offer of the fair shake and nodded his head politely—perhaps because it was the only nonmaterial offer made. It did not encroach on Finch's ideas about the renunciation of worldly goods. It was an ingenious, if perhaps unintentional, move on the manager's part.

Nelson Doubleday is especially hopeful about Finch's ultimate decision. "I think we'll bring him around," he said a few days ago. "After all, the guy's not a nut, he's a Harvard man."

In the meantime, the Mets can only wait. Finch periodically turns up at the enclosure. Reynolds is summoned. There are no drills. Sometimes Finch throws for five minutes, instantly at top speed, often for half an hour. Then he leaves. Security around the enclosure has been tight. Since Finch has not signed with the Mets, he is technically a free agent and a potential find for another club. The curious, even Mets players, are politely shooed away from the Payson Field enclosure. So far Finch's only association with Mets players (other than Reynolds) has been the brief confrontation with Christensen, Cochrane and Dykstra when the front office nervously decided to test his control with a batter standing in the box. If he decides to play baseball, he will leave his private world of the canvas enclosure and join manager Johnson and the rest of the squad. For the first time Gary Carter, the Mets' regular catcher, will face the smoke of the Finch pitch, and the other pitchers will stand around and gawk.

The press will have a field day ("How do you spell Siddhartha? How do you grip the ball? How do you keep your balance on the mound?"). The Mets will try to protect him from the glare and help him through the most traumatic of culture shocks, praying that in the process he will not revert and one day disappear.

Actually, the presence of Hayden (Sidd) Finch in the Mets' training camp raises a number of interesting questions. Suppose the Mets (and Finch himself) can assuage and resolve his mental reservations about playing baseball; suppose he is signed to a contract (one wonders what an ascetic whose major possessions are a bowl, a small rug, a long stick and a French horn might demand); and suppose he comes to New York's Shea Stadium to open the season against the St. Louis Cardinals on April 9. It does not matter that he has never taken a fielding drill with his teammates. Presumably he will mow down the opposition in a perfect game. Perhaps Willie McGee will get a foul tip. Suppose Johnson discovers that the extraordinary symbiotic relationship of mind and matter is indefatigable—that Finch can pitch day after day at this blinding, unhittable speed. What will happen to Dwight Gooden? Will Carter and the backup catchers last the season? What will it do to major league baseball as it is known today?

Peter Ueberroth, baseball's new commissioner, was contacted by SI in his New York office. He was asked if he had heard anything about the Mets' new phenomenon.

No, he had not. He had heard some *rumors* about the Mets' camp this spring, but nothing specific.

Did the name Hayden (Sidd) Finch mean anything to him?

Nope.

The commissioner was told that the Mets had a kid who could throw the ball over 150 mph. Unhittable.

Ueberroth took a minute before he asked, "Roll that by me again?"

He was told in as much detail as could be provided about what was going on within the canvas enclosure of the Payson compound. It was possible that an absolute superpitcher was coming into baseball—so remarkable that the delicate balance between pitcher and batter could be turned into disarray. What was baseball going to do about it?

"Well, before any decisions, I'll tell you something," the commissioner finally said, echoing what may very well be a nationwide sentiment this coming season. "I'll have to see it to believe it!"

Lake Wobegon Games

BY GARRISON KEILLOR

*Even in this aptly named fictional community—created for a radio
show that became wildly popular during the '80s—the townspeople watched in awe
and wonder as a dying Babe Ruth stepped shakily to the plate.*

OUR LAKE WOBEGON TEAMS DID NOT DO WELL IN 1986,
the Whippets with no pitching finishing dead last, the
Leonards pitiful and helpless in the fall even with a 230-
pounder to center the offensive line, and now it's basket-
ball season again and already the boys are getting accustomed to defeat. When
they ran out on the floor for the opener versus Bowlus (who won 58–21), they
looked pale and cold in their blue and gold silks, and Buddy had the custodian
turn up the heat, but it was too late. These boys looked like they were on death
row, they trembled as their names were announced.

It's not defeat per se that hurts so much, we're used to that; it's the sense of
doom and submission to fate that is awful. When the 230-pounder centered
the ball and it stuck between his tremendous thighs and he toppled forward
to be plundered by the Bisons, it was, I'm sure, with a terrible knowledge in
his heart that this debacle was coming to him and it was useless to resist.
Two of the basketball players are sons of players on the fabled 1958 squad
that was supposed to win the state championship and put our town on the
map, but while we looked forward to that glorious weekend our team was
eliminated in the first round by St. Klaus. None of us ever recovered from
that disappointment. But do our children have to suffer from it, too?

As Harry (Can O' Corn) Knudsen wrote: "In the game of life we're playing, people now are saying that the aim of it is friendship and trust. I wish that it were true but it seems, for me and you, that someone always loses and it's us."

Can O's inspiration came from playing 11 years for the Whippets, a humbling experience for anyone. The team is getting trounced, pummeled, whipped, and Dutch says, "Come on, guys, you're too tense out there, it's a game, go out there and have fun," and you think, *This is fun? If this is fun, then sic your dogs on me, let them chew me for a while, that'd be pure pleasure.* But out you trot to rightfield feeling heavyhearted and not even sure you're trotting correctly so you adjust the trot and your left foot grabs your right, *you trip on your own feet,* and down you go like a sack of potatoes and the fans are doubled up in the stands, gasping and choking, and you have dirt in your mouth that you'll taste for years—is this experience good for a person?

Some fans have been led to wonder if maybe our Lake Wobegon athletes are suffering from a Christian upbringing that stresses the unworthiness angle and is light on the aspect of grace. How else would boys of 16 and 17 get the feeling that they were born to lose, if not in Bible class? And the uneasiness our boys have felt about winning—a fan can recall dozens of nights when the locals had a good first half, opened a nice lead, began to feel the opponents' pain and sympathized and lightened up and wound up giving away their lunch. Does this come from misreading the Gospels?

Little Jimmy Wahlberg used to sit in the dugout and preach to the Whippets between innings, using the score of the ball game to quote Scripture, e.g., John 1:1: "In the beginning was the Word, and the Word was with God, and the Word was God" or Matthew 4:4: "Man shall not live by bread alone, but by every word that proceeds from the mouth of God." That was fine except when he was pitching. God had never granted Little Jimmy's prayer request for a good curveball so this fine Christian boy got shelled like a peanut whenever he took the mound, and one day Ronnie Decker came back to the bench after an eternal inning in centerfield and said, "First Revelations 13:0: Keep the ball down and throw at their goddam heads."

Ronnie is Catholic, and they have more taste for blood, it seems. (Was there ever a *Methodist* bullfighter?) In St. Klaus, the ladies chant, "Make 'em sing and make 'em dance/Kick 'em in the nuts and step on their hands." The boys are ugly brutes with raw sores on their arms and legs and with little ball-bearing eyes who will try to hurt you. A gang of men stands by the backstop, drinking beer and talking to the umpire, a clean-cut Lutheran boy named Fred. Fred knows that the week before, Carlson called a third strike on a Klausie, dashed to his car, the men rocked it and let the air out of the tires but couldn't pry the hood open and disconnect the spark plugs before he started up and rode away on the rims.

For a Golden Age of Lake Wobegon Sports, you'd have to go back to the

'40s. The town ball club was the Lake Wobegon Schroeders, so named because the starting nine were brothers, sons of E.J. Schroeder. Nine big strapping boys with identical mops of black hair, big beaks, little chins and so shy they couldn't look you in the eye, and E.J. was the manager, though the boys were such fine ballplayers, he only sat in the shade on a white kitchen chair and grumbled at them, no matter what.

E.J. was ticked off if a boy hit a bad pitch. He'd spit and curse and rail at him, and then R.J.'d go up and pound one out of the park (making the score 11–zip) and circle the bases and the old man'd say, "Boy, he put the old apple right down the middle, didn't he? Blind man coulda hit that one. Your gramma coulda put the wood on that one. If a guy couldn't hit that one out, there'd be something wrong with him, I'd say. Wind practically took that one out of here, didn't even need to hit it much"—and lean over and spit. When the Schroeders were winning every game, E.J. bitched about how they won.

"Why'dja throw to first for, ya dummy?"

"But it's the third out, Dad. We won the game."

"I know that. You don't have to point that out to me. Why'ntcha get the guy at third?"

"It was easier to go to first."

"Easier! *Easier*??!!"

The 10th son, Paul, had a gimpy right leg but still tried to please his dad and sat in the dugout and kept statistics (1.29, for example, and .452 and .992), but E.J. never looked at them. "That's history," he said, spitting, "I am interested in the here and now."

So his sons could never please him, and if they did, he forgot about it. Once, against Freeport, his oldest boy, Edwin Jim Jr., turned and ran to the centerfield fence for a long long long fly ball and threw his glove 40 feet in the air to snag the ball and caught the ball and glove and turned toward the dugout to see if his dad had seen it, and E.J. was on his feet clapping, but when he saw the boy look to him, he immediately pretended he was swatting mosquitoes. The batter was called out, the third out. Jim ran back to the bench and stood by his dad. E.J. sat chewing in silence and finally he said, "I saw a man in Superior, Wisconsin, do that a long time ago but he did it at night and the ball was hit a lot harder."

What made this old man so mean? Some said it happened in 1924 when he played for the town team that went to Fort Snelling for the state championship and in the ninth inning, in the deepening dusk on Campbell's Bluff, Lake Wobegon down by one run, bases loaded and himself the tying run on third, when the Minneapolis pitcher suddenly collapsed and writhed around on the mound with his eyes bulging and face purple and vomiting and foaming and clawing and screeching, everyone ran to help him, including E.J., and he jumped up and tagged them all out. A triple play, unassisted. *What a sick trick*, but there they stood, a bunch of rubes and all the slickers howling and whooping their heads off, so he became mean, is one theory.

And he was mean. He could hit foul balls with deadly accuracy at an opponent or a fan who'd been riding him or a member of the fan's immediate family, and once he fouled 28 consecutive pitches off the home-plate umpire, for which he was thrown out of the Old Sod Shanty League.

"Go! Hence!" cried the ump.

"For foul balls?"

The umpire and the sinner were face to face. "Forever!" cried the ump. "Never again, so long as ball is thrown, shall thy face be seen in this park."

"Foul balls ain't against any rule that I know of!"

The umpire said, "Thou hast displeased me." And he pointed outerward and E.J. slouched away.

So he coached his boys. He never said a kind word to them, and they worked like dogs in hopes of hearing one, and thus they became great, mowing down the opposition for a hundred miles around. In 1946 they reached their peak. That was the year they disposed easily of 15 crack teams in the Father Powers Charity Tournament, some by massacre, and at the closing ceremony, surrounded by sad little crippled children sitting dazed in the hot sun and holding pitiful flags they had made themselves, when E.J. was supposed to hand back the winner's check for $100 to Father Powers to help with the work among the poor, E.J. said, "Fat chance!" and shoved away the kindly priest's outstretched hand. That was also the year Babe Ruth came to town with the Sorbasol All-Star barnstorming team.

The Babe had retired in 1935 and was dying of cancer, but even a dying man has bills to pay, and so he took to the road for Sorbasol and Lake Wobegon was the 24th stop on the trip, a day game on Nov. 12. The All-Star train of two sleepers and a private car for the Babe backed up the 16-mile spur into Lake Wobegon, arriving at 10 a.m. with a blast of whistle and a burst of steam, but hundreds already were on hand to watch it arrive.

The Babe was a legend then, much like God is today. He didn't give interviews, in other words. He rode around on his train and appeared only when necessary. It was said that he drank Canadian rye whiskey, ate hot dogs, won thousands at poker and kept beautiful women in his private car, *Excelsior*, but that was only talk.

The sleepers were ordinary deluxe Pullmans, the *Excelsior* was royal green with gold and silver trim and crimson velvet curtains, tied shut—not that anyone tried to look in; these were proud country people, not a bunch of gawkers. Men stood by the train, their backs to it, talking purposefully about various things, looking out across the lake, and when other men straggled across the field in twos and threes, stared at the train and asked, "Is he really in there?" The firstcomers said, "Who? Oh! You mean the Babe? Oh, yes, I reckon he's here all right—this is his train, you know. I doubt that his train would go running around without the Babe in it, now would it?" and resumed their job of standing by the train, gazing out across the lake. A proud moment for them.

At noon the Babe came out in white linen knickers. He looked lost. A tiny black man held his left arm. Babe tried to smile at the people and the look on his face made them glance away. He stumbled on a loose plank on the platform and men reached to steady him and noticed he was hot to the touch. He signed an autograph. It was illegible. A young woman was carried to him who'd been mysteriously ill for months, and he laid his big hand on her forehead and she said she felt something. (Next day she was a little better. Not recovered but improved.)

However, the Babe looked shaky, like a man who ate a bushel of peaches whole and now was worried about the pits. He's drunk, some said, and a man did dump a basket of empty beer bottles off the train, and boys dove in to get one for a souvenir—but others who came close to his breath said no, he wasn't drunk, only dying. So it was that an immense crowd turned out at the Wally (Old Hard Hands) Bunsen Memorial Ballpark: 20 cents per seat, two bits to stand along the foul line and a dollar to be behind a rope by the dugout where the Babe would shake hands with each person in that section.

He and the All-Stars changed into their red Sorbasol uniforms in the dugout, there being no place else, and people looked away as they did it (nowadays people would look, but then they didn't), and the Babe and his teammates tossed the ball around, then sat down and out came the Schroeders. They ran around and warmed up and you could see by their nonchalance how nervous they were. E.J. batted grounders to them and hit one grounder zinging into the visitors' dugout, missing the Babe by six inches. He was too sick to move. The All-Stars ran out and griped to the ump but the Babe sat like he didn't know where he was. The ump was scared. The Babe hobbled out to home plate for the ceremonial handshakes and photographs, and E.J. put his arm around him as the crowd stood cheering and grinned and whispered, "We're going to kill ya, ya big mutt. First pitch goes in your ear. This is your last game. Bye, Babe." And the game got under way.

It was a good game, it's been said, though nobody remembers much about it specifically, such as the score, for example. The All-Stars were nobodies, only the Babe mattered to the crowd, and the big question was Would he play? He looked too shaky to play, so some said, "Suspend the rules! Why not let him just go up and bat! He can bat for the pitcher! Why not? It wouldn't hurt anything!" And nowadays they might do it, but then you didn't pick up the bat unless you picked up your glove and played a position, and others said that maybe it wouldn't hurt anything but once you start changing the rules of the game for convenience, then what happens to our principles? Or do we change those, too?

So the game went along, a good game except that the Babe sat sprawled in the dugout, the little black man dipping cloths in a bucket of ice and laying them on the great man's head—a cool fall day but he was hot—and between innings he climbed out and waved to the fans and they stood and cheered and wondered would he come to bat. E.J. said to Bernie, "He'll bat all right, and when he comes, remember the first pitch: hard and high and inside."

"He looks too weak to get the bat off his shoulder, Dad. He looks like a breeze would blow him over. I can't throw at Babe Ruth."

"He's not sick, he's pretending so he don't have to play like the rest of us. Look at him: big fat rich New York son of a bitch, I bet he's getting $500 just to sit there and have a pickaninny put ice on him. Boy, I'd put some ice on him you-know-where, boy, he'd get up quick then, he'd be ready to play then. He comes up, I want you to give him something to think about so he knows we're not all a bunch of dumb hicks out here happy just to have him show up. I want him to know that some of us *mean it*. You do what I say. I'm serious."

It was a good game and people enjoyed it, the day cool and bright, delicious, smelling of apples and leather and wood smoke and horses, and a blaze of majestic colors as if in a country where kings and queens ride through the cornfields into the triumphant reds and oranges of the woods, and men in November playing the last game of summer, waiting for the Babe, everyone waiting for the Babe as runs scored, hours passed, the sky turned red and hazy. It was about time to quit and go home, and then he marched out, bat in hand, and 3,000 people threw back their heads and yelled as loud as they could. They yelled for one solid minute and then it was still.

The Babe stood looking toward the woods until everything was silent, then stepped to the plate and waved the bat and Bernie looked at him. It was so quiet you could hear coughing in the crowd. Way to the rear a man said, "Merle, you get your hands off her and shut up now," and hundreds turned and shushed *him*. Then Bernie wound up. He bent way down and reached way back and kicked up high and the world turned and the ball flew and the umpire said, "BALL ONE!" and the catcher turned and said, "Be quiet, this doesn't concern you," and the umpire blushed. He knew immediately that he was in the wrong. Babe Ruth was not going to walk to first base, he would sooner strike out and would do it himself, with no help from an umpire. So the umpire turned and walked away.

The Babe turned and spat and picked up a little dirt and rubbed his hands with it (people thought, Look, that's our dirt and he's putting it on his hands, as if the Babe might bring his own) and then stood in and waved the bat and Bernie bent way down and reached way back and kicked high and the world turned and the ball flew and the Babe swung and missed, he said *huhhhnnnn* and staggered. And the next pitch. He swung and cried in pain and the big slow curve slapped into the catcher's mitt.

It was so still, they heard the Babe clear his throat, like a board sliding across dirt. They heard Bernie breathing hard through his nose.

The people were quiet, wanting to see, hear and smell everything and remember it forever: the wet fall dirt, the pale white bat, the pink cotton candy and the gentlemen's hats, the smell of wool and the glimmer of a star in the twilight, the touch of your dad's big hand and your little hand in it. Even E.J. was quiet, chewing, watching his son. The sun had set beyond right-field, darkness was settling, you had to look close to see—Bernie took three steps toward home and pointed at the high outside corner of the plate, calling his pitch, and the Babe threw back his head and laughed four laughs. (People were glad to hear he was feeling better, but it was scary to hear a man laugh at home plate, everyone knew it was bad luck.) He touched the corner with his bat, Bernie climbed back on the mound, he paused, he bent down low and reached way back and kicked real high and the world turned and the ball flew and the Babe swung and it cracked and the ball became a tiny white star in the sky. It hung there as the Babe went around the bases in his famous Babe Ruth stride, the big graceful man trotting on slim little feet, his head down until the roar of the crowd rose like an ocean wave on the prairie and he looked up as he turned at third, he smiled, lifted his cap, strode soundlessly across home plate looking like the greatest ballplayer in the history of the world. The star was still in the sky straight out due northwest of the centerfield fence where he hit it. The ball was never found, though they searched for it for years.

"Did you see that?" your dad says, taking your hand.

You say, "Yes, I did."

Even E.J. saw it and stood with the rest and he was changed after that, as were the others. A true hero has some power to make us a gift of a larger life. The Schroeders broke up, the boys went their own ways and once they were out of earshot, E.J. sat in the Sidetrack Tap and bragged them up, the winners he produced and how they had showed Babe Ruth a pretty good game.

He was tolerated. Babe Ruth was revered. He did something on that one day in our town that made us feel we were on the map of the universe, connected somehow to the stars, part of the mind of God. The full effect of his mighty blow diminished over time, of course, and now our teams languish, our coaches despair. Defeat comes to seem the natural course of things. Lake Wobegon dresses for a game, they put on their jockstraps, pull on the socks, get into the colors, they start to lose heart and turn pale—fear shrivels them.

Boys, this game may be your only chance to be good, he might tell them. You might screw up everything else in your life and poison the ones who love you, create misery, create such pain and devastation it will be repeated by generations of descendants. Boys, there's plenty of room for tragedy in life, so if you go bad, don't have it be said that you never did anything right. Win this game.

The Worst Baseball Team Ever

BY JIMMY BRESLIN

The newborn Mets and their matchless manager, Casey Stengel, were testing the limits of futility when New York's favorite columnist chronicled for SI the team's ineptitude and the city's affection for its lovable losers.

IT WAS LONG AFTER MIDNIGHT. THE BARTENDER WAS FALLING ASLEEP, and the only sound in the hotel was the whine of a vacuum cleaner in the lobby. Casey Stengel banged his last empty glass of the evening on the red-tiled bartop and then walked out of this place the Chase Hotel in St. Louis calls the Lido Room.

In the lobby the guy working the vacuum cleaner was on his big job, the rug leading into a ballroom, when Mr. Stengel stopped to light a cigarette and reflect on life. For Stengel this summer, life consists of managing a team called the New York Mets, which is not very good at playing baseball.

"I'm shell-shocked," Casey addressed the cleaner. "I'm not used to gettin' any of these shocks at all, and now they come every three innings. How do you like that?" The cleaner had no answer. "This is a disaster," Stengel continued. "Do you know who my player of the year is? My player of the year is Choo Choo Coleman and I have him for only two days. He runs very good."

This accomplished, Stengel headed for bed. The cleaner went back to his rug. He was a bit puzzled, although not as much as Stengel was later in the day when the Mets played the St. Louis Cardinals in a doubleheader.

Casey was standing on the top step of the dugout at Busch Stadium and he could see the whole thing clearly. That was the trouble.

In front of him the Mets had Ken Boyer of the Cardinals in a rundown between first and second. Marvin Throneberry, the marvelous first baseman, had the ball. Boyer started to run away from him. Nobody runs away from Marvin Throneberry. He took after Boyer with purpose. Marv lowered his head a little and produced wonderful running action with his legs. This amazed Stengel. It also amazed Stan Musial of the Cardinals, who was on third. Stanley's mouth opened. Then he broke for the plate and ran across it and into the dugout with the run that cost the Mets the game. (Throneberry, incidentally, never did get Boyer. Charlie Neal finally made the putout.) It was an incredible play. It also was loss No. 75 of the season for the Mets. In the second game Roger Craig, the Mets' starter, gave up so many runs so quickly in the seventh inning that Casey didn't have time to get one of his great relief pitchers ready. The Mets went on to lose No. 76.

Following this, the team flew to New York, where some highly disloyal people were starting to talk about them. There seems to be some sort of suspicion around that the New York Mets not only are playing baseball poorly this season but are playing it worse than any team in the modern history of the sport. As this week began, the Mets had a record of 28 won and 79 lost and seemed certain to break the modern record for losses in one season. This was set by the 1916 Philadelphia Athletics, who lost 117 games—an achievement that was challenged by the Boston Braves of 1935, who lost 115 games and were known as The World's Worst Team. But, by using one of the more expensive Keuffel & Esser slide rules, you discover that the Mets, if they cling to their present pace, will lose 120 games. You cannot ask for more than that.

Figures, of course, are notorious liars, which is why accountants have more fun than people think. Therefore, you just do not use a record book to say the Mets are the worst team of all time. You have to investigate the matter thoroughly. Then you can say the Mets are the worst team of all time.

"I never thought I would have an argument," Bill Veeck says. "I was always secure in the knowledge that when I owned the St. Louis Browns, I had the worst. Now it's different. You can say anything you want, but don't you dare say my Brownies were this bad. I'll prove it to you. There are still a few Browns in the major leagues and this is nine years later. How many Mets do you think are going to be around even two years from now? I'm being soft here. I haven't even mentioned my midget, Eddie Gaedel."

Reporting from Philadelphia is Pat Hastings, proprietor of the Brown Jug bar and a man who has sat through more bad baseball than anybody in America. For consistency, Philadelphia baseball always has been the worst. On nine occasions during Pat's tenure at old Baker Bowl and Shibe Park, both the Phillies and A's finished in last place.

But Pat, who has viewed the Mets on several occasions this season, refuses to put any team in a class with them. "The 1916 Athletics had Stuffy McInnins, you got to remember that," he says. "And some of them Phillies teams could hurt you with the bat pretty good. There was players like Chuck Klein, Virgil Davis, Don Hurst—I seen 'em all. Why, we used to make jokes about Buzz Arlett. He played rightfield for the Phillies in 1931. People used to go out and get drunk if they seen him catch a fly ball. I feel like writing the fellow a letter of apology now. Why he done more fielding standing still than some of these Mets I seen do at full speed."

In Brooklyn there is Joseph (Babe) Hamberger, who once associated with the old Dodgers and vehemently denies he ever saw a Brooklyn club as bad as the Mets.

"When Uncle Robbie [Wilbert Robinson] was managing, he didn't even know the names of the players," Babe says. "But he won two pennants and was in the first division a couple of times. Casey was over here, too. Ask him. He'll tell you. It got rough, but never like now."

Now all this is not being pointed out as an act of gratuitous cruelty. Quite the opposite. The Mets are so bad, you've got to love them. Name one true American who could do anything but root for a team that has had over 135 home runs hit against it. In New York a lot of people root for the Mets. They are mainly old Brooklyn Dodger fans and their offspring, who are called the "New Breed" in the newspapers. They are the kind of people who, as San Francisco Giant publicist Garry Schumacher once observed, never would have tolerated Joe DiMaggio on their team at Ebbets Field. "Too perfect," Garry said.

The Mets are bad for many reasons, one of which is that they do not have good players. The team was formed last year when the National League expanded to 10 teams. ("We are damn lucky they didn't expand to 12 teams," manager Stengel says.) The other new team, the Houston Colt .45s, has done a bit better than the Mets. It's in eighth place, 11½ games ahead of New York. For players, the Mets were given a list of men made available to them by the other eight National League teams. The list was carefully prepared and checked and rechecked by the club owners. This was to make certain that no bonafide ballplayers were on it.

"It was so thoughtful of them," Stengel says. "I want to thank all of them owners who loved us to have those men and picked them for us. It was very generous of them."

Actually, the Mets did wind up with a ballplayer or two. First baseman Gil Hodges was fielding as well as ever before a kidney ailment put him in the hospital. Centerfielder Richie Ashburn, at 35, is a fine lead-off hitter, although he seems to be on his way to getting some sort of a record for being thrown out while trying to take an extra base. If Jim Hickman, an outfielder, ever learns to swing at good pitches he might make it big. Here and there Al Jackson and Roger Craig produce a well-pitched game. And Frank Thomas can hit. But all this does is force the Mets to go out of their way to lose.

And once past these people, the Mets present an array of talent that is startling. Most of those shocks Casey talks about come when his pitchers throw to batters. There was a recent day in St. Louis when Ray Daviault threw a low fastball to Charley James of the Cards. James likes low fastballs. He hit this one eight rows deep into leftfield for the ballgame.

"It was bad luck," Daviault told the manager after the game. "I threw him a perfect pitch."

"It couldn't have been a perfect pitch," Casey said. "Perfect pitches don't travel that far."

One of Casey's coaches is the fabled Rogers Hornsby. Rajah was a batting coach during spring training and for the early part of the season. But all of his work now is done with prospects out on the farms. Which is good, because Hornsby hates to lose. Oh how he hates to lose. One day he was sitting in the dugout at the Polo Grounds before a game and you could see him seething. The Mets had been losing. So was Hornsby. He couldn't get a thing home and he was in action at three or four different major tracks around the country.

"You can't trust them old Kentucky bastard trainers," he confided.

The general manager of the Mets is George Weiss, who was let go by the Yankees after the 1960 season because of his age. He is 68 now. George spent all of last year at his home in Greenwich, Conn. As Red Smith reported, this caused his wife, Hazel, to announce, "I married George for better or for worse, but not for lunch." She was pleased when George took over the Mets this year and resumed his 12-hour working day away from home.

The Mets also have many big-name sports reporters who write about them. This may be the hardest job of all. As Barney Kremenko of the *New York Journal-American* observes, "I've covered losing teams before. But for me to be with a *non-winner!*"

There are some people, of course, who will not stand still for any raps at the team. They say the Mets have a poor record because they lose so many one-run games. They point out that the Mets have lost 28 games by one run so far. However, this figure also means the Mets lost 51 other games by more than one run.

One who advances the one-run theory is Donald Grant, the Wall Street stockbroker who handles ownership details for Mrs. Joan Payson, the class lady who put up the money for the Mets. It is Mr. Grant's job to write letters to Mrs. Payson, explaining to her just what is happening with the Mets.

"It is annoying to lose by one run, but Mrs. Payson and I are pleased with the team's progress," Grant says. "She is perfectly understanding about it.

After all, you do not breed a Thoroughbred horse overnight." Grant obviously doesn't know much about horse racing.

Whether the Mets lose by a run or by 14 runs (and they have done this, too), it doesn't matter. They still lose. They lose at night and in the daytime and they lose so much that the only charge you can't make against them is that their pitchers throw spitters.

"Spitters?" Stengel says. "I can't get them to throw regular pitches good."

Basically, the trouble with the Mets is the way they play baseball. It is an unchanging style of walks, passed balls, balks, missed signs, errors, overrun bases and bad throws. You see it every time. It doesn't matter what day you watch the Mets play or if they win or lose. With this team, nothing changes. Only the days.

On July 22, for example, the Mets were in Cincinnati for a doubleheader. They not only lost both games, but they also had four runners thrown out at home plate in the course of the day. Nobody could remember when this had happened before—probably because it hadn't. What made it frightening was the ease with which the Mets brought the feat off. You got the idea that they could get four runners thrown out at the plate any day they wanted to.

In the first game Choo Choo Coleman was out trying to score from second on a single to left. In the second game Stengel jauntily ordered a double steal in the second inning. He had Cannizzaro on first and Hot Rod Kanehl at third. Cannizzaro took off and drew a throw. Kanehl broke for the plate. The Cincinnati shortstop, Cardenas, cut it off, throw home, and that took care of Kanehl. In the fourth inning Elio Chacon tried to score from first when the Reds messed up a fly in the outfield. But Vada Pinson finally got to the ball, and his throw home beat Chacon by a couple of steps. In the fifth inning Jim Hickman was on third. He broke for the plate as Rod Kanehl hit the ball. Kanehl hit the ball square at third. The throw had Hickman by a yard.

The day before that, Roger Craig, the team's version of a big pitcher, had gone over to Stengel and volunteered for relief pitching in the doubleheader, if he were needed. Stengel nodded. It was nice of Craig to say he would work between starts. And the next day the Mets certainly did need Craig. Going into the ninth inning with a 3–3 tie against the Reds, Stengel called on Roger to save the day. Roger took his eight warmup pitches. Then he threw two regular pitches to Marty Keough of the Reds. Keough hit the second one eight miles, and the Reds won 4–3.

Two days later in the first inning of a game in Milwaukee, the Braves had runners on first and second. Henry Aaron hit the ball hard, but Chacon at shortstop made a fine backhanded stop. As Chacon regained balance, he saw Roy McMillan of the Braves running for third. Chacon yelled to Felix Mantilla, the Mets' third baseman. He was going to get McMillan at third on a sensational play. Mantilla backed up for the throw. Then he backed up some more. By the time Chacon threw, Mantilla had backed up three yards past the base and when he caught the throw all he could do was listen to the crowd laugh. McMillan had his foot on third.

The Mets fought back, however, and had the game tied 4–4 in the 12th. Casey called on a new pitcher to face the Braves in this inning. He was R.G. Miller, making his first appearance as a Met. At the start of the season, R.G. was managing a car agency and had no intention of playing baseball. Then Wid Matthews, the Mets' talent scout, came around to talk to him. Miller, Matthews had found, needed only 18 days in the major leagues to qualify as a five-year man under the baseball players' pension. R.G. had spent a couple of years with Detroit before deciding to quit.

"Go to Syracuse for us," Matthews said, "and if you show anything at all we'll bring you up. Then you can put in your 18 days. When you reach 50, you'll get about $125 every month until they put you in a box."

Miller went out front and spoke to the boss. The job would be waiting for him after the season, Miller was told. So Miller went to Syracuse. He pitched well enough to be brought up. Now he came out of the Mets' bullpen to take on the Milwaukee Braves.

Miller loosened up easily, scuffed the dirt, looked down and got the sign and glared at Del Crandall, the Milwaukee batter. Then Miller threw a slider, and Crandall hit a home run. Miller, with his first pitch of the year, had lost a game.

"He makes the club," everybody on the Mets was saying.

Marvin Throneberry, the fast-running first baseman, has had his share of travail this year, too. In fact, anytime you meet some old-timer who tries to bore you with colorful stories, you can shut him up quickly with two Marv Throneberry stories for every one he has about players like Babe Herman or Dizzy Dean. Throneberry is a balding 28-year-old who comes out of Memphis. He was up with the Yankees and once even opened the season as a first baseman for them. After that, he was with the Kansas City A's and the Orioles. Throneberry is a serious baseball player. He tries, and he has some ability. It's just that things happen when he plays.

Take the doubleheader against the Cubs at the Polo Grounds early in the season. In the first inning of the first game Don Landrum of Chicago was caught in a rundown between first and second. Rundowns are not Throneberry's strong point. In the middle of the posse of Mets chasing the Cub, Throneberry found himself face to face with Landrum. The only trouble was Marvin did not have the ball. During a rundown the cardinal rule is to get out of the way if you do not have the ball. If you stand around, the runner will deliberately bang into you, claim interference and the umpire will give it to him.

Which is exactly what happened to Marv. Landrum jumped into his arms and the umpire waved him safely to first. Instead of an out, the Mets now had to contend with a runner on base—and that opened the gates for a four-run Chicago rally.

Marv had a big chance to make good when the Mets came to bat. With two runners on, Marv drove a long shot to the bullpen in right-centerfield. It looked to be a sure triple. Marv flew past first. Well past it. He didn't come within two steps of touching the bag. Then he raced toward second and careened toward third. While all this violent motion was taking place, Ernie Banks, the Cubs' first baseman, casually strolled over to umpire Dusty Boggess.

"Didn't touch the bag, you know, Dusty," Banks said. Boggess nodded. Banks then called for the ball. The relay came and he stepped on first base. Across the infield Throneberry was standing on third. He was taking a deep breath and was proudly hitching up his belt when he saw the umpire calling him out at first.

It was suggested to Throneberry on a recent evening that his troubles, and those of the entire Mets team, come from unfamiliarity. A year of playing together might help the team considerably, Throneberry was told. Marv took this under consideration.

"I don't know about that," he allowed. "They's teams been established for 30, 40 years and they's still in last place."

Marv has been rankled only once all year. It involved Ed Bouchee, whom Stengel put on first for a couple of games. In San Francisco, Roger Craig, who has a fine pickoff motion for a righthander, fired to first and had Orlando Cepeda of the Giants clearly nailed. But Bouchee dropped the throw. Two windups later, Craig again fired to first. He had Cepeda off the bag, with all his weight leaning toward second. It was an easy pickoff. The ball again bounced out of Bouchee's glove.

Back in New York, when Bouchee stepped out on the field at the Polo Grounds, the fans gave him a good going-over.

"What are you trying to do, steal my fans?" Throneberry complained.

It is a long summer, but the man who is probably finding it longest is Weiss. He is a pale-eyed, bulky, conservative old baseball business man who, as he was saying a couple of weeks ago, is not used to losing.

"I've been in baseball since 1919," George said, "and this is only the second time I have had a second-division team. My first year in baseball I had the New Haven club and we finished seventh. That was in the Eastern League. This year is, I must say, a bit of an experience with me. No, it is certainly not a funny thing to me. But you could say I am not doing things halfway. When I finally get in the second division, I really get there.

"The job this year was simply to get a club started. Why, we couldn't even hire office personnel at first because we didn't have an office. Now we have what I think is the finest office in the majors. Of course we don't want to confine ourselves to leading the league in office space. The future depends on how hard we work now. The main thing is to build up our scouting staff. We had great scouts with the Yankees. Kritchell, Devine, Greenwade. We have Wid Matthews now, but we have to wait until contract time and some of the other good scouts become dissatisfied with their organizations. Then we can make moves. But right now all we can do is hope the players come along and it gets a little better. Anyway the manager is doing a fine job, isn't he?"

The manager certainly is. This is, everybody agrees, Casey Stengel's finest year. When he was running the Yankees and winning 10 pennants and becoming a legend, Casey never really struck you as the one they wrote of in the newspapers. His doubletalk was pleasant, but it had a bit of show business lacquer to it. And he could be rough on young players. Norman Siebern, at one time a tremendous outfield prospect, never really got over a couple of tongue-lashings from Casey. And Bobby Richardson and Clete Boyer were not the most relaxed players in the world under Stengel.

But here with the Mets, at age 73, Stengel is everything you ever read or heard about him. The man has compassion, humor and, above all, class. There is no grousing, and no screaming that players are letting him down. Mr. Stengel came to baseball this year ready to stand up no matter how rough it became. Well, it has become awful rough and he is standing up as nobody ever has. And trying. He talks to the players and he makes all the moves he knows. When they do not work out, he simply takes off his cap, wipes his forehead, then jams it back over his eyes and takes it from there.

In the rare instances when he does have the material to work with in a situation, that old, amazing Stengel magic is still there. Two weeks ago in St. Louis, the Mets won two of a five-game series against the Cards and one of the games was a result of Stengel's moves.

Curt Simmons, a lefthander, was pitching for the Cards, and Stengel sent up Gene Woodling, a lefthanded hitter, to pinch hit. Normally, this is not protocol. But Simmons had been coming in with a screwball as his best pitch. In a left-against-left situation, a screwball breaks toward the hitter and is easy to follow. Simmons had to go with a fastball. Woodling hit it on top of the roof in right and the Mets had two runs and a ballgame.

"I remembered another thing," Casey said after the game. "Once when I had Ford goin' for 20 games over with the Yankees, Woodling beats him with a home run down in Baltimore. What the hell, don't tell me he can't hit a lefthander. I remember him doin' it, and that's why I put him in there."

A few lockers down, Woodling was talking about the manager.

"I was with him for five championships with the Yankees," he was saying, "and he and I had our differences. It's nothing new. Everybody knew that. But I've never seen anybody like him this year. This is a real professional.' "

You could see it a day later, when Casey and his Mets came into the dressing room after losing a doubleheader to the Cards. The manager had a wax container of beer in his hand and he was growling about a call that he said cost him the first game.

"The man don't even know the rules," Casey was saying. "My man was in a rundown between third and home and when he tries to go to home the catcher trips him right on the baseline. You could see the chalk was all erased. The umpire don't call it. Costs me a game. It was an awful thing."

He kept talking about this one play, as if nothing else had happened during the long afternoon. He was going to give "my writers," as he calls newspapermen, something to put in the paper the next day. And maybe it would give these 25 beaten players getting dressed in the room with him something to get mad about. Maybe it would help a little.

When he stopped rasping about the play for a moment, he was asked about a couple of particularly costly plays by Throneberry and Charlie Neal.

"Aaahhh!" Casey said. "Bonehead. They was bonehead plays. Damn bonehead plays." His eyes flashed.

Then he leaned back and spoke in a soft voice. "Look," he said, "I can't change a man's life. I got four or five guys who are going to make it up here. The rest of them, we just got to get along with. I'm not goin' to start breakin' furniture because of them. It's the man and I got him and I can't change his life."

Then he got dressed and a guy named Freddie picked up his suitcase and led him out of the dressing room. They had a taxicab waiting across the street, in front of an old, one-story brick-front place named Gus & Marge's Tavern. Casey pushed through the crowd and got into the taxi. He was carrying on a running conversation with the crowd as he shut the door and the taxi started to pull away.

It was, you figured, the way it should be. For over 50 years now, Casey Stengel has been getting into taxis in front of old saloons across the street from a ballpark. He has done this with great teams and with bad teams. Now he has the worst outfit anybody ever saw. But even if the players don't belong, Stengel does. He'll be back next year.

God help him.

On the Winter Tour With Harry Sprague

BY HERBERT WARREN WIND

In this series of letters from a fictional golf pro to his backer, reporting on his first swing around the circuit, the author, renowned for his elegant formality, gave readers a glimpse of his comic side—and of a seldom seen side of the pro tour.

D EAR MR. PARMENTER   Jan 7nt

I am writing to you from the writing room in the Del Monte Lodge which you can see from the printing on top is in Pebble Beach where we pros are playing the Crosby turnament this week. It is very noisy in here because an awful racket is going on in the bar and if I make any errors in spelling it will be because of the racket and how it effects a persons cordination. Before I left Mass I promised you I would write you a regalar report which is the least I can do since you are my backer and are backing me on the winter tour. So Im going to get this letter off and will treat the racket just like a galery which I did fine in the LA Open or else would I have tied for 14nt place. Thanks for sending your tellergram (spelling?). It was sure good hearing from you Mr Parmenter.

That was a good daybue finishing tied for 14nt. I could have won the whole shoot and match if I had my touch on the greens. I was paired with Dutch Harrison one round and with Walter Burkemo another round and I am not being conceeded when I tell you I outplayed them every hole from tee to green but they got the putts and I couldent buy one for love of money which is what I hear happens on the tour. Meaning that the real golfers cant putt these aradic greens. I blew a couple of easy birdie putts on 14nt and 15nt that was the differents between tieing for 14nt and a tie for 7nt but as you say a person has got to be a pholossifer (spelling?) if hes going to be a golfer and I did hole 2 40 footers so I feel like a pholossifer about those 2 putts.

For a sample I got one of those alpacker sweaters which you push up the sleeves on and makes you look extra rugged and proey.

Some pros had to cancell out of the Crosby so I was invited to play here on the strenght of my showing at LA which I am grateful (spelling?) for and told them so seeing it is my first year on the tour. The pros are very regular guys both the old fellows like Harrison and Littler and the young fellows you never heard of because I never did. However I am strictly unimpressd by their golf. Harrisons swing is no better than Mrs Proutys but he is almost as old as she is so maybe he was better when he was young. That figures. As I wrote you above the pros are very freindly. Al Besselink for exsample let me use one of his sports jackets on a big date I had in LA and it was sure nice of him even though the jacket was kind of small thru the shoulders. I bougth some new clothes here in a habadashry in Pebble so I exspect to do better with the females from now on.

Wait till your boy starts putting

Yours truly
Harry

Jan. 21, 1958

Mr. Walt Parmenter
Parmenter Enterprises Co.
148 So. Main Street
Micawba, Mass.

Dear Mr. Parmenter,

Like you asked me to in your telegram last week, I have got in touch with a public stenographer, so all the words in this letter will be clear which apparently they was not in my handwriting due to the racket coming from the bar at the Del Monte Lodge. Also they will be spelled right. I am sitting in a chair in an office here on the main drag in Palm Springs on the second floor of a building above a store where they sell nothing but moccs and loafers but are still in business apparently. They are playing the Thunderbird Invitational here this week, and I am giving this dictation like I was Adolph Menjou to a lady name of Lorna Thomas who is going to stick in the periods and the other dots and dashes when she types the letter up. She is a nice-looking lady with white hair like Mrs. Prouty which is the best description I can give you under the present playing conditions, if you catch.

Well, Mr. Parmenter, you have probably been wondering how come your boy wasn't in the money since your last letter. So have I because I have been hitting it a ton. That is one of those slang expressions all the pros use. When you ask a pro how he played, he answers one or two things.

"I was hitting it a ton," he says or he says, "I was playing like a Gangbusters" which also means good. They got a lingo of their own out here, like bankers, and that's all they talk. I'll give you a sample of what I mean. No pro calls a golf course a golf course. That's strictly bush. You call a course a track. Another sample. When you get into a sand trap and someone asks you where your ball is, you don't say, "I'm in the trap." You say, "I'm on the beach." Another good sample for you is if you see a pro or anyone else whose name you don't remember just then, you call him "Old Buddy." You can pick up this lingo pretty quick like I did in a couple of weeks if you have got any brains at all. I don't want to lose my own personality which has always been my trademark at the driving range, like you keep telling me, and I think this is the reason for my popularity with my colleague pros. They think I'm a pretty good lingoist, too, is what I mean.

Like at Thunderbird, where I am not entered this week since only something like the top 40 money-winners get invited and I wasn't on the circuit last year, I played a practice round with Burke, Souchak, and Demaret who are all from Texas except Souchak. I had a nice little 66 and took the boys for a few bucks, so when we finished I said, "Okay, you guys, let's adjourn to the 10th Hole and I'll buy you all a Moxie." They got a great kick out of this because though we call the bar the 10th Hole at the Micawba Country Club—who knows better than you, Mr. Parmenter?—apparently if you have an 18-hole course you change around and call the bar the 19th Hole of which I get the point.

Jimmy Demaret can be a serious fellow sometimes, though. He was out practicing the other afternoon and because I like to help the fellows out like I did Dick Mayer with his putting stroke last week, I told Jimmy, "Jimmy, you are cutting across the ball. That is why you are getting that fade at the end on those irons. Would you like a couple of tips, old buddy?"

"Harry," he says, "I've always played the ball from left to right. I better stick with it and just do the best I can."

I told Jimmy not to think about it and I could fix him up in a jiffy like I did Mr. Callahan last summer who had the same kind of slice. "Harry," Jimmy says to me, "It's a shame Snead and Hogan are not on the tour 'cause they been looking for years for someone to straighten them out on the golf swing." When the tour goes through Texas maybe I will get the time to go up to Fort Worth and check Ben's swing for him which I would be glad to do for an old buddy.

What your boy can't understand is why I'm not scoring out here, Mr. Parmenter. It's got to be the tracks. El Centro where we enlisted men had a little tournament this week is just a desert. Tijuana down in Mexico where we played the week before has fairways with no clover in them at all. Pebble and Cypress where we played before that are trick tracks. If you hit the ball a ton like I was there, you get penalized where a short hitter like Middlecoff can't reach the ocean. I was paired with Cary one round and I outdrove him on every hole including the short ones, but he was putting and I wasn't so he gets a 69 and I get an 80, which is backwards. Cary told me after the round I was trying to hit the ball too hard. Now I don't like to accuse a colleague pro of throwing sour grapes but you probably saw in the papers that right after he played with me in the Crosby, Middlecoff left the tour and went back to his club in Florida which is more than a coincidence, hey?

I expect to break into the money in a big way at Phoenix next week. All your boy needs is a couple of putts. A little more female companionship wouldn't do me any harm neither but we keep moving like gypsies and when we hit the new towns the name pros get all the name women and before a guy can get his bearings we move on again.

Yours truly
Harry Sprague

Feb. 1, 1958

Mr. Walt Parmenter
Parmenter Enterprises Co.
148 So. Main Street
Micawba, Mass.

Dear Mr. Parmenter,

I am dictating this letter from Tucson which is also in Arizona which as far as I can see is just one big sandtrap or beach. There are plenty of public stenographers in this town because lots of people come out here to retire among which is a nice-looking lady name of Rhoda Richards who is taking my dictation. She came out here 20 years ago and she is a real veteran, if you follow my drift.

How come I am here in Tucson when the tournament is still going in Phoenix? Well, I ran into some tough breaks in Phoenix, Mr. Parmenter, and missed the cut by two strokes, meaning that my total for the first two rounds was two shots too high to get me into the low sixty scores and ties who qualify for the last two rounds. I think I am maybe spending too much time helping the other pros instead of working on my own game. A good sample of this is Palm Springs and Phoenix where I gave Ken Venturi some tips on competition psychology and, as you read in the papers, Venturi steps right out after that and wins both tournaments, though his game still needs an awful lot of polishing. Where I had my tough break at Phoenix is that a terrific looking blonde with one of those brown suntans came out to watch me and Ford and Finsterwald finish our second round. I introduced myself very politely and I bet her, just to make some conversation, I would get three birds on the last three holes. I guess I gambled too much going after those birds 'cause I finish boge, boge, double boge and that killed me. I learned a lesson from this like you learn on the tour which is this: You have got to putt, old buddy, or you're dead.

I drove down here from Phoenix last night to get used to the track where we fellows who have to qualify in a qualifying round even to get into the Tucson Open qualify on Tuesday. I am now traveling with two other young colleague pros, a great little putter from Indiana name of Pete Grissom and a fellow from Seattle name of Albie Vickary who is a hell of a scrambler. They both made the cut at Phoenix so I took off in the car and they will pick up rides and meet me here Sunday night at the Gila Monster Motel. Vickary, Grissom, and myself have formed a syndicate and we will be splitting our prize money up three ways. I don't know if this is such a smart move for me and I would appreciate your idea about it since you are a real pro with finances.

This reminds me, Mr. Parmenter, to bring up something that's been on my mind for some time now, if you don't mind. Pete, Albie, and a lot of the other pros including the old guys tell me that my finances arrangements with you aren't a fair shake. They say that they never heard of any backer making a deal where he pays a pro's expenses on the winter tour and in return the pro works for him and runs his driving range from April to November for no salary. I told them under our arrangement I get to keep two-thirds of what I make on the lessons I give at the range and that I gave many numerous lessons, but they still say you are giving me less money than what I should be paid for it. I explained that you are a big man in Micawba and got a connection with many enterprises, but all they say about this is it figures. So I will be looking forward to hear what you say about this.

Well, Mr. Parmenter, I'm going out to the practice range now seeing that I never did stir up an acquaintanceship with that blonde with the suntan, so from now on I'll be playing a more conservative type golf.

Yours truly
Harry Sprague

Feb. 15, 1958

Mr. Walt Parmenter
Parmenter Enterprises Co.
148 So. Main St.
Micawba, Mass.

Dear Mr. Parmenter,

I'm going to make this a short letter because I need to get out on the course
and get some practicing in. I am giving the dictation in Houston, Texas, to a
nice-looking lady name of Sue Atherton who, she tells me, is a native of Houston, Texas, and was living here when it was no more an acropolis than Micawba, Mass., or whatever is the foreign name for a city with lots of tall buildings and women's clothes stores. As is getting to be my usual, I arrived in this
next town on the tour a couple of days before the rest of my colleague pros
who made the cut at San Anton' and are still there playing the third round of
the Texas Open today. That was where the roof really hit me, Mr. Parmenter.
If it wasn't bad enough not making the cut in any tournament for a month
now, at San Anton' I didn't even qualify in the qualifying round to get into
the tournament. Those Scotchmen are right when they say this is a humble
game because I never felt punker in my life.

I don't know if I told you I am taking my whole swing apart which is why
I am doing so much practicing on the practice tee. My two old buddies, Albie
Vickary and Pete Grissom, been telling me a long time now I don't get my left
hand on the club correctly and which is why I am hitting from the top all
right side and spraying my shots all over the place. Demaret and some of the
other veteran pros like Barber and Boros also have been trying to show me
changes I ought to make, like the lining up the shot, but for a while I just
thought they were only trying to throw me off my game because this is for
real bucks out here. I am convinced now they were aiming to do me a good turn
all along, and I'm working on a new grip and a whole different swing and
action which nobody perfects overnight even if I am a natural athlete. So I
have decided not to go up to Fort Worth. Hogan will just have to work on his
own game best he can himself till I get going again.

I never knew there was so much bare country with no trees and just plain
dirt in the world as there is in this part of the United States where we cut
across on the winter tour. It's like being an enlisted man in the French Foreign
Legion. I ran into a knockout babe with a convertible Jaguar car in Tucson
when we were both picking up our cleaning and pressing, but my timing

must have been off for she said she was catching a plane that night. Also would appreciate it if you would let me know if we can make some new finances arrangements like I wrote you about which you did not say anything about in your last letter.

Yours truly
Harry Sprague

Mar 1nt

Dear Mr Parmenter

I am writing you in New Orleans and you see I am back to using my own hand writing which is because my funds are getting low. My two buddys Grissom and Vickary are making me follow a budjet with no more spending on habadashry and stenos till I start winning again. Funny thing about those stenos. Where ever you go they all have names like movie starlits and you walk up the stairs to the office exspecting you are going to meet a real live doll with a car and every time what do you see in front of you. One of those old aljebur teachers with pins stuck all over her head who is old enufh (spelling?) to a been an air raid warden in the civel war.

Your boy is finaly hitting it again Mr. Parmenter. I dident qualify for the last 36 at Baton Rouge but I was hitting it so good that George Bayer who I was paired with one round was twenty thirty yards behind me off some tees and pressing to get that close. The Hebert brothers Jay and Lionel who call it something like Aibair in french are very regalar guys and came over and told me my actiun (spelling?) looks way improved and to stick with it and before long I will be taking the boys just like Grant took rich men. Which is what a lot of the other pros came over and slapped me on the back and said. They are a real good bunch. I dont want to knock myself but they also were right when they were telling me I wasnt getting my putts to drop because I am a charjer and keep charjing the hole and have got to work for a smoother stroke or tap. Thats exsperiense and you dont get it unless you go out and play aradic golf and learn some thing from your mistakes hey. This is a funny game turnament golf. Being a big hitter like myself gives you an edge but you also have got to be solid which is why those old pros who are vetran enufg (spelling?) they could open up steno offices keep right on going year after year. The other thing is tempermint which I always had as you know from watching me starring in three sports for Micawba High and winning those driving contests at the range and the Micawba Open.

About those finances arangements Mr Parmenter. I would like to get them fixed up so that I can save some money this year at the range from a salary in-sted of always being in hock to you for the previus season. In your last letter you say my head is getting too big for my hat and I dont know how well off I am with you backing me with loans. My coleague pros say they can swing me an assistance job for me that will give me a much better deal all the way. I just as soon come back to the range where all the gang knows me but let us talk over a new arangement in your next letter. Okay.

You probly noticed that some of us enlisted men are getting in the money like Albie Vickary did at Baton Rouge with that 68 on the last round so our sindy-cut had a big party at a nite club and I got up and sang a couple of songs at the mike to show the folks I am a real pro material.

Your Truly

Harry

March 24, 1958

Mr. Walt Parmenter
Parmenter Enterprises Co.
148 So. Main St.
Micawba, Mass.

Dear Mr. Parmenter,
I got your telegram congratulating me on my performance in tieing for eighth (8th) place in the Pensacola Open which I certainly appreciated since it is the first dough I have won since LA. My prize money share came to six hun-dred dollars ($600) from which I am mailing you a mail order for two hun-dred ($200) as part payment down on the funds you loaned me as my backer on the winter tour which I am leaving now.

I am dictating this letter in St. Pete not to steno but to an old girl friend of mine from Micawba, Marian Haydock, who you probably remember when she used to live on Depot Street. This is why it is all typed up with every thing dotted and spelled correctly again. To make a long story short, Marian has been down here, which I didn't know, for two years working in the office of a real estate outfit in St. Pete; and I ran into her at the tournament here last week.

As you probably read in the papers, I missed the money here by four (4) shots but all my old "Buddies" now tell me: "Harry, you are looking like a player now" or "You are really moving it, 'man' "; which is my pro colleagues' way of saying I am really moving it.

Marian is looking like a million dollars ($1,000,000). She always had it in that dep't but not so much, like I tell her. We are hitting it off like "Gang Busters," and what a relief it is after all these months to bump into a "babe" who talks my language; which Marian does seeing she was a soph and saw every basketball game the year I broke the high school scoring record by "tossing" in those thirty-three (33) points—thirteen (13) field goals and seven (7) fouls—against Braintree High.

Now if we can discuss the other mutual business of ours, Mr. Parmenter. First off, I have decided not to come back to work for you at the range. Mr. Amos A. Tabor who runs the Otter Lake Resort and Country Club up in the state of northern Michigan signed me up as an ass't pro, for which I thank my old "Buddies" on the tour who introduced me to him after my showing at Pensacola. Otter Lake is a real big resort with twenty-seven (27) holes. It doesn't open until middle of May so I latched onto a job instructing at a driving range here in St. Pete where I will make my headquarters until then. Mr. Tabor is going to have me represent Otter Lake on the tour next winter when the course is closed up with snow and unseizable weather. It is all in the contract on paper, and Vickary, Grissom, and my other colleague pros tell me it is a wonderful deal for me. I am enclosing the mail order for two hundred dollars ($200) and you will receive the rest on a monthly installment plan Marian says she will work out.

So that's the good news. I'd appreciate it a lot if you would mail me the photo in the shop of me and you standing in front of the old driving range and pointing at the sign on top, so I can hang it in the pro shop at Otter Lake to show people where I got my start before I became a veteran. Marian has a car and if we go up to the Masters for a day or two I will get some photographer to shoot a picture of me with Bobby Jones and Gene Sarazen with our arms around each other at the first tea, which would be a nice thing to look up and see for the members at Otter Lake when they are having a birch beer or something at the old 28th Hole.

Yours truly
Harry Sprague
Ass't Pro, Otter Lake C.C.

VII

PERSONAL
FOULS

⟡

The Case Against Brian Spencer

BY PETE DEXTER

When a former NHL player was charged in a tawdry Florida murder case, SI sent an acclaimed novelist to cover the story. What he found was an ambitious prosecutor, a man facing execution and a single shaky witness.

ARLY ON THE AFTERNOON OF FEB. 4, 1982, A TRUCK DRIVER named Albert Brihn, on the way to a sewage-treatment plant off PGA Boulevard just outside Palm Beach Gardens, Fla., noticed something lying in a clearing of pine trees 60 feet off the road connecting the treatment plant to the street. It looked like a dummy.

Mr. Brihn delivered his load and headed back out. On the way, the thing in the clearing caught his eye again. Then something else—a buzzard, floating over it, banking again and again in those grim buzzard circles. Suddenly the thought broke, and Mr. Brihn knew what the thing was.

He stopped the truck and walked to the body. It was a man dressed in a black bikini bathing suit. There was a gold chain around the neck threaded through an Italian horn of plenty. He studied the body—there was a hole to the right of the nose, another at the right temple, both with muzzle burns, and there was a tear between the nose and the mouth where a bullet fragment had passed going out. As he stood there, the chest rose and fell twice. It was 1:30 in the afternoon.

A little more than 10 minutes later, the paramedics from Old Dixie Fire Station No. 2 arrived in an ambulance. If you believe the signs you see coming into town, Palm Beach Gardens is the golf capital of the world. It is home to a large retirement community—in this case a financially secure retirement community—so when one of its citizens expires, serious efforts are made toward not leaving the body lying around. Certainly not long enough to attract buzzards.

This particular body, of course, did not belong to someone of retirement age. The paramedics were there in 10 minutes anyway, and took it, the chest still rising and falling, to Palm Beach Gardens Community Hospital, where, at 3:36 p.m., the chest went suddenly still. Michael J. Dalfo was 29 years old, and the coroner's report would say he died of two .25-caliber bullets, shot at close range into his head.

There is not much to say here about Michael J. Dalfo. He lived with his brother, Christopher, in a condominium in the Glenwood section of PGA National, a golf resort and residential development. His father had some money, and he and Christopher and his mother once owned a restaurant, Christopher-Michael's Ristorante. A year after they sold it, investigators say, someone torched the place.

Michael Dalfo had a mustache and a girlfriend, and he apparently spent a lot of time with other girls, ones he had to pay. He also apparently used cocaine.

On the night he was shot, according to police, Dalfo called the Fantasy Island Escort Service three different times. A woman named Diane De Lena had come over first, sometime before midnight, and stayed an hour. Dalfo, in the words of an assistant state attorney, "hadn't been able to get things going" and tried to talk his visitor into staying another hour. He wrote her a personal check for $75, but she refused to take it and left.

Dalfo called Fantasy Island again, this time ordering two more girls. When they arrived he told them that they were "dogs," and they left.

"He was very untactful," one of the escorts would later tell police.

Forty-five minutes later he called Fantasy Island again and ordered a fourth girl. When the service didn't send one, he ordered yet another—this one from a different outfit, Rainbow Escorts—who showed up at about 3:30 in the morning and found the door to Dalfo's condominium open. She told police she walked in and found no one home. She used Dalfo's phone to call Rainbow & Escorts and report she had been stood up. Then she left.

And the next person known to have seen Michael Dalfo was a truck driver named Albert Brihn, who wasn't even looking for him.

ALMOST FROM the beginning, the investigation into Dalfo's death centered on the woman named Diane De Lena. Sheriff's investigators say they found matchbooks on Dalfo's coffee table with the names and numbers of several escort services printed on the backs, Fantasy Island among them. They found Fantasy Island's phone number written on a check, made out to cash, for $75. They also found a small quantity of cocaine.

Within a week, a detective from the sheriff's department got in touch with De Lena, who, in tape-recorded interviews, admitted that she had been with

Dalfo on the night he was killed but said she had left him, healthy, sometime around midnight and gone to a West Palm hotel for her next appointment. She said she hadn't seen him again and, according to prosecutors, stuck to that story for almost five years.

It was not just De Lena, though, who caught the investigators' attention. At the time of the murder, Diane De Lena was living with a man who had once been a major league hockey player. His name was Brian Spencer, and he had spent more than eight years in the National Hockey League—with Toronto, the Islanders, Buffalo and Pittsburgh. He was an aggressive player without exceptional talent, scrambling to stay even, scrambling to stay in the league. A scrappy 5 foot, 11 inch, 185-pound left wing, Spencer did not produce dazzling numbers but was still a favorite of the fans; he was even voted the most popular Islander by the team's booster club in 1973. By 1979, however, the popularity and the scrambling weren't enough, and he was sent by Pittsburgh to the minors, where he stayed a season and a half and then left the game. His marriage dissolved, and he got in his car and drove to Florida.

The assistant state attorney says the sheriff's department "knew" Spencer had done the actual shooting all along. Spencer and De Lena had lived in a trailer on Skees Road, at the far western edge of West Palm Beach. The place may not be officially designated as a swamp, but the mosquitoes come in clouds, the ground is wet all the time, and anything you step on that doesn't bite you or go "squish," crumbles.

Spencer must have liked the swamps. Two, maybe three years later, he began to build a house and a shop in Loxahatchee, which *is* officially a swamp, but he ran out of money and ended up building neither. He was good with his hands, he seemed to understand the way things worked and could fix them when they didn't. He met De Lena, in fact, when he did some repair work on her car.

During the time he and De Lena lived together, he worked as a mechanic for an electrical contracting company, Fischbach And Moore. His Florida friends say the mechanical work was enough, that it had replaced whatever he had in hockey. Spencer had loved the game and the life of a big league professional. "I loved the travel, the people; I loved it all," Spencer said. But when it was over, he wanted to leave it behind—the game, the people. And in the end, leaving was failure. "Even Gordie Howe, at 52, was seen as a failure," Spencer said.

"He used to talk about playing," said a friend named Dan Martinetti, "but he loved working with his hands—fixing equipment—more than hockey. He went from nothing to having everything, and then he went back to chopped bologna. But he didn't care about money, he still doesn't. You could give him $100,000—he'd look at it and then go spend it on tools and equipment."

Diane De Lena, now Diane De Lena Fialco, has a different story. Offered immunity and threatened with jail for contempt if she did not testify, she has told the state attorney that Spencer bragged constantly about his days in the NHL. She has said that he roughed her up. She draws a picture now of a frustrated and violent man and says she was afraid of him.

Diane De Lena Fialco says a lot of things, and the assistant state attorney who until three weeks ago was handling the case—a woman named Lynne Baldwin—thought that a jury would believe her. Baldwin laid the groundwork in the newspapers, referring to Fialco by her working name, Crystal, in order to protect her for as long as possible from the scrutiny of the press. "She's a very beautiful young girl and, even though she worked for an escort service, there's something about her that makes her seem vulnerable, sort of like Marilyn Monroe. . . ." the prosecutor told the *Palm Beach Post* in February. "Because of this incident, she got out of that kind of life and is working a good job and has a family."

The state attorney's office needs Diane Fialco, and needs her to be credible. Without her, there is no case. There seems to be no other evidence linking Spencer to Michael Dalfo—no gun, no blood, no witness save Diane De Lena Fialco herself.

And on the testimony of this one witness, who reminds the prosecutor of an actress, Spencer was indicted by a Florida grand jury on charges of first-degree murder and kidnapping. And on her testimony, the state of Florida is willing to end Brian Spencer's life.

THERE IS a temptation here to set Brian Spencer's life on the table, the way museums set out antique silverware and plates and glasses in an Early American dining room and pretend that the setting is somehow what pioneer life was like.

The trouble, of course, is that a life isn't one way or another. A lot of things happen, and the reflections of those things are shaded by time and mood, and are lost and invented even if you were there. Even if you happen to be a professional athlete and thousands of people see what you do, and remember. But the moment becomes private as soon as it is over, because it is dependent on your other moments. And it is not so much the glory itself that follows you later—reminding you of a way things will not be again—but its reflections.

And so when a friend, for instance, who grew up with Brian Spencer in Fort St. James, B.C., tells you, "He was always smiling, he was always happy," it is hard to see that you are entitled to write, "Brian Spencer had a happy childhood." Or when you learn that 12 years ago in Buffalo, Spencer was charged with assaulting a motorist after a traffic accident and wound up paying the other driver an undisclosed sum in an out-of-court settlement of a civil suit—the criminal charges were dropped—you are not then entitled to write, "Brian Spencer has a violent temper."

And the idea of catching up with such a life, halfway through its 38th year, at the Palm Beach County jail, and then picking through the newspaper clippings and the reflections of friends and wives (there have been two) and teammates for some thread of cause and effect is ambitious beyond what can honestly be accomplished.

It *can* be said that somewhere along the line, Brian Spencer was not careful enough about his roommates, but beyond that you're on your own.

Spencer, of course, is not saying much. He has denied killing Dalfo in a letter sent to this magazine and at least one other publication, but the purpose of the letter was less to explain anything that has happened than it was simply to ask for mail.

"I sit here [in jail] with two passions, really two wishes that you in your charity might help fulfill. First, I hope you find it in your heart to think a kindly thought and to say a prayer for me. . . . Second, if you could, please write. . . . Maybe the 'glory days' are over, but not my memory of how incredibly uplifting the fans are."

The man who represents Spencer, public defender Barry Weinstein, will not discuss the case with reporters. "This is a person's life," he said. "I take this seriously. I'm not going to open it up to the kind of mistakes and misrepresentations that occur when you start trying your case in the press."

Spencer was born in Fort St. James, which is a long way north of anywhere you are, in September 1949. He was a twin, although he and his brother, Byron, do not look much alike. The father's name was Roy, the mother's is Irene. She had been a schoolteacher, and then did office work for the Hudson's Bay Co. Roy had a gravel pit, and drove the boys to hockey practice. Twenty miles, round-trip, even when he was sick.

The family lived outside town and owned a generator that was their only source of electricity. When Roy's emphysema gave him trouble breathing, they would start it to run the oxygen machine.

The boys fished in the summer and played hockey all winter. They went to the only school in town—it was three or four rooms in the beginning—through grade 10. There was no high school in Fort St. James, so they began grade 11 in Vanderhoof—a 40-mile bus ride.

Like a lot of NHL players from small towns, Spencer did not finish high school. He quit, devoting himself to the sport, and in December 1970, he was called up to the Toronto Maple Leafs from Tulsa.

On Saturday, Dec. 12, the Leafs were at home against Chicago. The Canadian Broadcasting Corporation televised that game to eastern Canada. In the west, however, the CBC was carrying the Vancouver Canucks versus the Oakland Seals.

Angry that his son's game was not being broadcast by CKPG Television in Prince George, Roy Spencer got into his car and drove the 110 miles to the station, where he pulled a 9-mm pistol and, holding the news director and the program director and six other employees against a wall, ordered them to take the station off the air.

The station shut down, and Roy Spencer told the program manager, "If the station comes back on the air again, I will hold you responsible. I am very upset about the CBC coverage."

Then he backed out of the studio and ran for the door. He was crossing the sidewalk outside the station when the police told him to drop his gun. He turned, 15 feet away, and shot one of the policemen in the foot, another in the holster. The police returned fire, hitting Roy Spencer in the shoulder, the armpit and the mouth, and he was dead on arrival at Prince George Regional Hospital.

Two of the police officers involved would comment later, at the coroner's inquest, on the exceptional length of time it took Roy Spencer to fall.

ON NOV. 27, 1984, a 25-year-old man named Leslie Raymond Fialco was married in a civil ceremony to Diane De Lena. According to prosecutor Baldwin, Fialco had no hint that his new wife had ever worked for an escort service or that she had been involved in a murder case then 2½ years old. The couple settled into Palm Beach Shores and started a family. According to Baldwin, the marriage has produced two children.

Two years passed, and then one day at work Mrs. Fialco looked up from her desk and found herself being handed a subpoena. It had been a long time since the sheriff's deputies had questioned her about the Dalfo murder, and she did not realize at first what the subpoena was for.

When she walked into the state attorney's office on 3rd Street in West Palm Beach, however, and saw all the old, familiar faces, she broke into tears. According to the assistant state attorney, she cried, "I thought this was over."

Now, one of the many things that is still hazy about this case is exactly what leverage the sheriff's investigators and the state attorney's office used on Diane Fialco to get her to hand them Spencer. She was given "use" immunity, meaning she could not be prosecuted for the murder based on her own statement and would go to jail if she failed to testify, and perhaps that was leverage enough.

Lynne Baldwin has said, "The police knew they [De Lena and Spencer] did it all along, but they just couldn't prove it," and she has acknowledged that part of the deal to get Diane De Lena Fialco to testify was her promise to do what she could to shield Diane from publicity.

There is no question that the Palm Beach County Sheriff's Department wanted Spencer for the Dalfo murder. Here is Lieut. Pat McCutcheon of the sheriff's detective division: "From the outset of the investigation, we looked at him as a suspect. But because of the lack of cooperation [from De Lena] we couldn't implicate him. A couple of times we thought she would testify, but she changed her mind. Maybe out of affection, maybe out of fear."

Fear, of course, can come from a lot of different directions, and in the end Diane Fialco, apparently afraid of something, gave the prosecutors what they wanted. The story she has told, in a sworn statement, goes like this:

On the night Dalfo is killed, she drives to his condominium sometime before midnight, leaving the keys in the car, and stays about an hour. She always leaves the keys in the ignition except when Spencer drives her to a job and waits—a precaution against having to leave without her purse.

While she is there, Dalfo is snorting a lot of cocaine and, according to Baldwin, finds himself impotent. He asks her to stay an extra hour and offers to write her a check.

Staying beyond the agreed time and accepting checks, however, are both against Fantasy Island rules, and she starts to leave. Dalfo stops her, writes the check anyway, payable to cash, and puts it in her hand. She gives it back. He drops the check on the coffee table, angry now, and she walks out the door. She is afraid.

She drives from Palm Beach Gardens back to the trailer on Skees Road, but Spencer isn't home. She goes over to the Banana Boat—a bar where Spencer likes to drink—and tells him what has happened at Dalfo's. She also tells him that she is afraid that Dalfo may have followed her home. She then drives to the hotel in West Palm and sees another customer.

An hour or so later she meets Spencer at home, and he gets upset and wants to go to Dalfo's place. Diane De Lena wants to forget the whole thing, but Spencer won't. She is afraid of Spencer—"Spencer had hit his women," Lynne Baldwin says. "Another woman he knew showed up for work with her face bruised. She said she had been in a car accident. Her boss was suspicious." De Lena thinks he only wants to talk, or at the outside, to rough Dalfo up. She does not think Spencer wants to kill him.

So they head over to Dalfo's. De Lena's plan now is to tell Spencer she can't remember which condominium Dalfo lives in. As all the condominiums at PGA National look the same, this is not a bad plan. There is, however, a built-in flaw: Because the condominiums do look alike, it is Dalfo's habit to wait outside his place for visitors from the escort service, and so when Spencer and De Lena arrive, Michael Dalfo is standing out front in his black bikini swimsuit and his gold chain, waiting for his fourth "escort" of the evening.

Spencer asks Dalfo to get into the car. (When Diane De Lena told this version of the story to the police, she did not remember Spencer's using a gun. In a more recent version, Baldwin says, that detail came back to her.) At any rate, Dalfo, Spencer and De Lena drive out of PGA National to PGA Boulevard, turn west and travel six-tenths of a mile and then come to a white sand road. There is a sign at the junction:PGA WASTEWATER TREATMENT PLANT, SEACOAST UTILITIES.

Four hundred feet up the road, Spencer stops at a spot where the trees recede from the road, creating a weedy clearing. A sign says NO DUMPING.

Spencer tells De Lena to get out of the car. Spencer and Dalfo begin to argue and Dalfo says, "If you touch me, I'll call my lawyer." This infuriates Spencer, and the arguing gets louder. Diane De Lena, who is afraid, begins to run up the road, in the direction of PGA Boulevard. Dalfo is alive when she leaves. She runs, but she never hears any shots. And so when Spencer picks her up in the car a few minutes later, she assumes he has beaten Dalfo up and left him.

They drive back to the trailer. According to Baldwin, Spencer then tells De Lena to take off all her clothes. She does that, gives them to Spencer, and never sees them again. She believes they were burned or buried.

A week later, the sheriff's department is asking her questions about Michael Dalfo's murder. This, of course, scares Diane De Lena. More than Michael Dalfo scared her, more than Spencer used to scare her before Dalfo was killed. She tells the sheriff's investigators nothing except that she was with Dalfo the night he was killed.

And while she will not turn Brian Spencer in, says Baldwin, De Lena now makes plans to leave him. She does not want him to think it is because of the Dalfo murder, however, so she distances herself from him gradually over the next several months, and then she moves out.

Four and a half years later, about 8:30 on a Sunday night—Jan. 18 of this year—Spencer is sitting in the El Cid bar, drinking a gin and tonic with one of his friends. The El Cid, since closed, was one of the few bars left in South Florida attached to a beauty parlor. Anyway, halfway through Spencer's first drink, his friend stands up, goes to the pay phone and calls a cab for Spencer. A few minutes later, the driver, a thick-chested man named William Springer, walks in and calls, "Taxi."

Springer is an undercover sheriff's detective. His picture, in fact, hangs in the lobby of police headquarters as 1986's Officer of the Year. Spencer takes the cab around the corner to the Mt. Vernon Motor Lodge and tells the driver to wait. He speaks to someone inside, then heads back to the cab.

Waiting for him are a helicopter with search lights, the undercover detective, a K-9 cop, a K-9 dog, and as much backup as the Palm Beach County Sheriff and the West Palm Beach police have available. In the lights and the noise Spencer struggles with police, but there are too many of them in too many places, and in a few moments he is in handcuffs.

And, for the next three months, Spencer sits in the Palm Beach County jail. And that is it, the case against Brian Spencer.

THE CASE was kept in a folder a couple of inches thick, which was balanced across the lap of assistant state attorney Lynne Baldwin. She was going through the papers inside, one by one, reading bits and pieces out loud.

Interviews with other girls from escort services, interviews with Spencer's friends.

A report of a possum that Spencer was supposed to have killed with a .25-caliber automatic—the same caliber that killed Dalfo—which initiated a number of searches of his backyard. No possum, no bullets, no gun.

A woman's shoe prints leading away from the scene of the killing.

Lie detector tests of numerous subjects, none of them Diane De Lena or Brian Spencer.

Dalfo's bank statements, which indicate he spent what Baldwin called "a lot of money."

More searches for the dead possum.

The office itself is beautiful, in a comfortable way. Plants, good furniture, a huge antique globe in the corner. And there are signs, one over the light switch in particular: ATTITUDES ARE MORE IMPORTANT THAN FACTS.

"Is what you have," she was asked when she has finished with the file, "anything more than an ex-prostitute who has lied through this whole thing?"

"I don't think it's fair to say she's lied all along," Baldwin said. "She's tried to tell the truth, she's turned her life around. A couple of weeks ago, *The Miami Herald* ran a story about this and called her a 'former call girl' and she called me up, just bananas. . . ."

"I'll tell you something," she said. "They [the Fialcos] came into this office together and sat right in those chairs, and we went through it all. And for a while, it was pretty tough going. He is a very Germanic sort of guy, very stiff and proper, and you could see he didn't like it at all.

"But once it was all out in the open, he accepted it. He supports her now, and I think that someone like that, sitting there supporting you, lends credibility. Do you remember John Dean's wife sitting behind him at those hearings? It gave him a kind of credibility. . . ."

So lined up against Spencer we now have exactly one witness and her very proper husband, who has forgiven her. And we have a question. Couldn't the "untactful" Dalfo have had acquaintances even more untactful than himself? And couldn't a taste for paid escorts and cocaine, and a habit of spending surprising amounts of money have gotten him into enough trouble with one of these untactful acquaintances that he ended up dead? If, let us say, De Lena knew about an execution committed by such an untactful acquaintance—who we can assume would not look kindly on her cooperating with the police—who is she going to give to the state attorney's office when Lynne Baldwin comes around 4½ years later, threatening to put her in jail? That is what we have.

What we do not have are two tapes of the statements made by Diane De Lena when she was originally questioned by the sheriff's investigators five years ago. "Deputies," Baldwin said, "they're always running out of tapes. So when they need one, they sometimes borrow it from another file, something they aren't working, and tape over whatever was on it."

"A murder case? They taped over evidence in a murder case?"

She nodded her head.

What we also do not have is any proof that Dalfo was ever in the car that was supposed to have taken him to the clearing where he died. "The detectives, for the most part, did a very thorough job," Baldwin said. "They interviewed all these prostitutes, administered all these lie tests, conducted searches for the possum. One thing they forgot to do was search the car."

Lynne Baldwin sat dead still for a moment in her beautiful office. Beautiful office, beautiful clothes, beautiful globe. It is always surprising, the places where things are decided. Baldwin listened to a hard assessment of her case against Brian Spencer. Her expression never changed. "We may lose," she said, "but my job is different from a private attorney's. I don't always have to win." She thought for a moment, and then she said, "I get a lot of cases that aren't as clear-cut as you would like them to be, and I win my share."

That much was evident. Lynne Baldwin is the last person you want to see talking about you to a jury. Or the newspapers.

And then she said, "I'll tell you this, he'll know he's been in a fight."

Perhaps. Two weeks later Baldwin would pull out of the case when she was promoted—"I got rid of that mess," she says—and turned it over to Fred Susaneck, another assistant state attorney. After a bond hearing on April 24, Spencer was released from the jail out on Gun Club Road on $50,000 bail, posted by some old Islander teammates and friends. Still, as he waits for a murder-and-kidnapping trial scheduled to begin in the fall, you can't help thinking of Brian Spencer and of the time he has already spent in jail—a place full of reflections—and of the little that is known of the things that happened to him on the way there. And you think that Brian Spencer has been struggling all his life.

It is hard to imagine, though, that he needs this murder trial to know he has been in a fight.

Postscript: Five months after this story appeared in SI, Brian Spencer went on trial for murder and was acquitted. A year later, he was shot to death in a roadside holdup in South Florida.

Total Loss
Weekend

BY DON DeLILLO

*The subject is a man whose passion is action. It's Saturday, and his bets
are down, his curtains drawn, TV and radio tuned to the games. The author, a
prominent novelist, is on hand to observe the remarkable vigil that follows.*

CJ LIVES IN YONKERS NOW. THE SIGN ON THE TRAIN STATION
reads Mount Vernon but I know this is Yonkers, a place
strong and settled in its facelessness. There is a second level
of weather here, subterranean and dangerously mild. I think
of Los Angeles, Brasilia and the moon, places known not for their landscapes
as much as for their fundamental beings, what they seem to represent.

The large apartment building where CJ lives is only five minutes from
the train station (13 minutes from Yonkers Raceway), and after I ring the
outer bell, get buzzed into the lobby, take the elevator to four and walk
through the long, dim hall, he opens the door and leads me into the living
room. I notice the TV sets, two of them, both turned on. CJ himself, T-
shirted and unshaven, nearing 40, seems the least animate thing in the
room right now, not yet having reached his Saturday afternoon glow point.
He appears eager enough for the siege of events but, as always in times
like this (the beginning of ordeals), his very flesh reflects a pale stain of
trepidation and doubt.

CJ is a gambler. He likes to bet on sporting events, almost any kind, and
the dark crawling horror of Total Loss Weekend is never very distant. Mis-
givings and dread. Panic, remorse and deep trauma. A fumbled punt in
Knoxville, a missed sign in Oakland, foul trouble in Baltimore, a slow track at

Monticello. That is Total Loss Weekend, when it all comes apart at once, and the fragments of many such weekends are standard parts of CJ's life.

The living room is long and narrow. At the far end are the televisions. The larger one is a color set assembled by CJ himself over a period of some five weeks, with parts and materials ordered from a manufacturer in the Midwest. The smaller one is a black-and-white portable that sits on the floor. CJ and I are cousins and as we take our respective places in front of the TV sets we exchange views on disease, poverty and madness in our family. We stick to recent developments and keep it brief. CJ sits in a swivel chair that has been covered in plastic ever since he purchased it. I sit a few feet away on a sofa also equipped with a plastic slipcover and for this reason suggestive of a giant slug deep in slumber. This is appropriate because the humans in the room are also about to enter a kind of sleep. The color set is tuned to the Pirates-Reds in Game 1 of the playoff series, and the smaller model to pregame films of Notre Dame and Michigan State in action against other teams.

The blinds are down. CJ puts on a pair of dark glasses. Then he reaches behind the swivel chair for a portable radio, which he places on his lap. He tunes to Columbia-Princeton and the weekend begins.

GAME TIME 1

"Hi, sports fans, it's Saturday, Oct. 7th and this is Chuck White with Bud Brown alongside me bringing you a daylong sports cavalcade of misery, paranoia, bitterness and defeat."

Sound from these three sources, I learn, deepens the feeling of submersion. TV, radio, TV. It is as though we are listening to tapes of the electrical discharges of some rare species of fish. But CJ needs plenty of action today. He spent the previous evening at Yonkers Raceway and was shut out, dropping nearly $200. One way or another, today's action will obliterate all those miscarried Exactas.

An outfielder pauses under a fly ball as a voice says: "Here are the Spartans of Michigan State." And it's true, they're coming out of the runway, the Spartans of Michigan State, black and white for the moment, none of them aware that the game they are about to play is only part of the true contest, the interior contest, the struggle that takes place within and beyond the limits of the point spread.

CJ is getting 15½ points with Michigan State and he has them 20 times. He also has the Reds 20 times, (one "time" equals $5). As we discuss his other bets for the day, he suddenly switches stations (radio) from Columbia-Princeton (he has Columbia, minus eight points, 20 times) to a simulated broadcast (delayed) of the first race at Belmont (he has $20 on numbers 8–3 in the double), and we listen to the announcer calling the race as if it were taking place now instead of half an hour ago, a practice not meant to fool anyone but designed merely to give bettors a measure of action, and I see the idea justify itself when CJ bounces slightly in the chair as his selection, Izadore, the 8-horse (OTB letter H), finishes first. He will remain in his chair for most of the weekend. But he is engaged in *action*. He has action. The action is his.

CJ switches to football on the color set, baseball on the smaller one. The auxiliary set isn't working well and a note of cubism is introduced into the baseball game. It is hard to tell whether a particular figure represents one or two players. An infielder's upper torso is situated at a 45-degree angle to the rest of his body. On the radio we have been away from Belmont Park and back to football for fully 10 minutes, but we are only now becoming aware that we are listening to Army-Lehigh instead of Columbia-Princeton. CJ has no action on Army-Lehigh. He does have action on five college games in addition to Columbia-Princeton and Notre Dame-Michigan State, and throughout the afternoon, the evening and much of the night he will spin the radio dial repeatedly between WINS (scores every half hour) and WCBS (scores 12 minutes after the hour and 12 minutes after the half hour). He will curse the announcers for their stupidity, their cheerfulness, the commercials they must read and the public service messages they are inclined to give—messages about puppet shows at Gimbels or talks sponsored by the Young Lawyers' Committee of the New York County Association—always when CJ is waiting for a crucial score. It is in these ways that bureaucracy crushes the dreamer.

The Reds trail 5–1. Michigan State trails 6–0 but seems to be doing things right as the second quarter progresses. With perfect timing CJ switches (radio) from Columbia-Princeton (no score) to the re-creation of the second race at Belmont. With 70 yards to go a horse named Siberian Native threatens to take the lead from CJ's selection, Early Judgement, but the 3-horse holds on to win by a head, and CJ has his double—a sign, an omen, an early-warning signal. He clenches his fist, nods his head firmly and then gets up and switches to baseball on the color set, football on the black and white. "I gamble because when I don't gamble I feel sick," he says.

What does CJ have in his pockets?
1) Tiny pieces of paper.
His selections for the day are written on these mangled straps. The teams, horses, odds, point spreads and sums wagered are all recorded, very lightly, tentatively, in pencil. It is as though he wants it all to disappear before the weekend is over.
2) A form letter from his finance company.

"As a valued 'Paid-in-Full' customer with a splendid payment record, you are listed on our records as a Gold Star account. This means of course, that your credit is 'Triple-A'—and you can get up to $— more money right now."

Handwritten neatly in the blank space is the figure 800.

3.) An OTB telephone account card.

With this card CJ is able to call the Off-Track Betting Corp., give his code name, find out how much he has in his account and then place a bet—all in the same telephone call. However, he has nothing in his account. The $250 he deposited originally was gone after two phone calls, and now there are zero dollars left. CJ knows this and OTB knows it, too.

4) A box score torn out of a newspaper.

We dissolve to summertime. Picture it. CJ has the Cubs 40 times. They are playing at night in San Diego. He sits in the swivel chair with his radio and waits for scores from the Coast. In the top of the fourth the Cubs take a 2–0 lead. Nothing for a long time but news, commercials, scores of other games. CJ cannot even relax with a cigarette because he stopped smoking in 1970 on the night the Celtics led the Royals by 11 points with a minute to go. But now San Diego scores twice in the seventh inning to tie it. CJ decides to stick it out because he knows the score will not make the morning papers and he will have to wait until early afternoon, and he's got the Cubs 40 times, and it's nearly one in the morning and he can't have a cigarette. He dials from WCBS to WINS and back, hoping the announcers on duty will realize the Cubs-Padres game is not just another negligible event played before a few thousand people and of interest to absolutely no one in the whole world, hoping they'll realize that someone out there is really listening, someone is interested, someone really cares what they say, these affable babbling fools whose voices circulate through the mortal sadness of Yonkers. Then he hears it. The Cubs score three in the ninth and he is ahead 5–2 with only three outs left, and the Padres are one of the worst teams in baseball. But why does it take so long for the final score to come in? Why does he have to keep switching the dial to get word of those three final outs? If the Padres are one of the worst if not the worst, why is he seized by Transylvanian dread? Because it is a busy bottom of the ninth, that's why. Because the Padres get men on base. Because the Cubs have to change pitchers. Because God makes it happen, a four-run ninth, a 6–5 final score, officially reported at 2:09 a.m., and the next day CJ rips the box score out of the newspaper and vows to save it as a reminder of death, hatred, plague and all those bloodsucking ills which keep people up after their bedtime. He saves this piece of paper that reads "two out when winning run scored." He carries it everywhere because this event, in its way, is even more notable than the time he had the Vikings as part of a $90 round robin, and the two other games were over and won, and the Vikings were sailing along against the 49ers when somebody fumbled and Jim Marshall of the Vikings picked up the ball and ran the wrong way, and even though the Vikings won the game they didn't beat the spread because Jim Marshall ran the wrong way with a recovered fumble, the wrong way, he ran the wrong way. But that wasn't as bad as this. CJ had waited for this victory. He had sat up and turned the radio dial through half the night. He had *participated* in that ball game being played 2,500 miles away and he had it won, he had it in his hands, he felt it in his fingers as he changed stations, the Cubs 40 times, the tough gritty Cubs, veteran ball club, and that's why it was worse than Jim Marshall, worse than all the near misses on Exactas and Superfectas, worse than the night he stopped smoking, with the Celtics ahead by seven points and only four seconds left in the game. He saves the box score so he can look at it and hate it.

5) A football betting ticket.

Almost everybody has seen one of these. Pick four teams and get 10-to-1 odds. CJ lets nothing go by.

6) A tout sheet.

This is a piece of paper that CJ has been carrying around for months. Under the heading "Turf Analyst," there is a name and phone number. Beneath these the full text reads: "Please telephone me this Friday, June 30th after 10 a.m. regarding a sensational piece of information."

WE ARE sitting in the midst of static. The room is dim. CJ takes off his sunglasses, rubs his eyes and then replaces the glasses. The Reds have lost. This is bad. With 5:23 left in the game, Michigan State still trails 6–0. This is good, almost excellent. On the black-and-white set we see a drum-and-bugle corps in Oakland, prelude to the Tigers-A's playoff game.

I notice that scores given on radio and scores given on TV do not always match. Sometimes the talk is gibberish. An announcer says a football player is 6' 4" and 250 years old. I hear rain falling. Columbia-Princeton ended 0–0, and the radio is now used exclusively to harvest scores. We hear from the Appalachians, the Ozarks, the Mississippi Delta. In the Rockies they are nearing the end of the first half. Here it is all over, the land in shadows, but in California there is sunlight everywhere, captive happiness and soft beginnings, a flurry of first-period scores. The radio is an instrument of geography. Beyond the numbers it gives, there is a sense of prairie mystery.

Notre Dame tries a field goal. It looks wide but the official raises his arms. CJ responds with a trenchantly obscene remark. We both know what that field goal means. First, it means the score is now 9–0. Second, it means the Spartans of Michigan State had better hold onto the football because there are still a few minutes left in the game and CJ is getting 15½ points, and if the Fighting Irish score another touchdown and kick the all-important extra point, they will have exactly 16 points. We both know it will happen. It is destined to happen. God will make it happen

On the smaller set the Tigers and A's are lined up for the national anthem. The A's are wearing their chorus boy uniforms, and practically all of them have mustaches that seem to have been penciled on by not very well-coordinated children. (Michigan State fails to hold onto the football.) Although everyone in the ball park in Oakland has been invited to join in the singing of the national anthem, nobody on the A's is singing, nobody on the Tigers is singing, the umpires are not singing, and a stray groundkeeper looks sluggish as glue. Baseball and basketball players never sing. Hockey players don't sing either. Prizefighters don't sing. Football players sing.

"I'm dead," CJ says.

He is dead because with 41 seconds left the Fighting Irish have reached the six-yard line. They lose two on a sweep and it is fourth and goal at the eight, and if there are any lingering doubts about whether or not betting on college football is a form of Armenian water torture, they are quickly dispelled when Notre Dame calls time out. Ahead by nine points. Seconds left in the game. They call time out. Who is aiming this sorrowful arrow at CJ's heart? Who is behind this wanton event? Whims are supposed to be things flitting suddenly to mind but this one has been engineered by a deterministic intelligence. The fourth-down play now unfolding represents the concentrated essence of betting on sports. Of course they go for the touchdown. Of course they score. Of course they kick the all-important extra point. Unless you believe in truth, beauty and sportsmanship, the interior game is the only one that matters.

Baseball takes over on the color set. On the auxiliary set we watch cars smashing into each other other. What does this mean? An announcer uses the phrase "demolition derby." Then we see a fat cowboy running toward a herd of cows. It seems to make no sense. The announcer calls this "wild cow milking."

CJ is dead in East Lansing. He is dead and buried in Pittsburgh. He is long dead in New York. He is dying a slow death in Oakland. Before the night is over he will have died in Kentucky, in Mississippi and in Oklahoma. Through the radio he breathes the air of our mysterious and lonely continent.

What did CJ discover 10 years ago?

Ten years ago: CJ discovers a way to prolong the glorious agony of checking results in the newspaper.

With a matchbook, paper napkin or the human hand, he covers the results in question and then slowly moves the shielding device across the page, oh so gradually disclosing the outcome. For football or basketball he moves the matchbook across the line score from quarter to quarter until there is nothing left but victory or defeat. Baseball takes longer, inning to inning, nine panning movements to the final score. Race results are best because as you move vertically up the list of finishers without exposing the name of your own selection, the odds that you've got a winner begin to grow increasingly favorable. Once you get to the show horse, the sense of action is almost dizzying.

Some of CJ's greatest moments in gambling have occurred as he sipped his morning coffee and oh so slowly moved a matchbook across an inch of small print. At times he has stopped just short of the final result in order to savor this moment of action, to draw it out of real time into some secret hourglass of gambler's sand. He walks around the room; he stands at the window for a while; he returns to the table and drinks all but one swallow of his coffee; he sits for a few more minutes and then, slowly and lovingly and with a feeling of total happiness and despair, he moves the matchbook one more notch and brings this splendid scrap of action to its end. After this there is nothing to do but finish off the coffee and go to work.

ON SATURDAY evening CJ calls in his bets for the next day. To the bookmaker's multiple answering service he says: "I want Pickwick Realty." Since he is calling from home, be merely leaves his first name. If he had been phoning from another number, he would give the last three digits of that number in reverse. While we wait for the bookie to return the call, CJ tells me that one day a few years ago he phoned, confirmed the point spreads, placed his bets and then said: "So long, Bernie."

"Don't call me Bernie anymore," the bookie said. "From now on call me Sherm."

CJ ends the day by watching NHL highlights, a half hour of the Rangers–Red Wings, and then a movie called *Marooned* with Gregory Peck. He has no action on either of these.

GAME TIME 2

In which it becomes ever so obvious that this, indeed, is Total Loss Weekend, despite the powerful swamp magic of an unexpected guest wearing imaginary shoulder pads.

On Sunday the auxiliary set fails to work—no picture or sound. We watch yesterday's college highlights on the color set. This is a warmup for the Browns-Chiefs game. The radio is tuned to the Giants-Saints.

CJ does not talk about Saturday's losses. Past action is voided matter, to be discussed only when it includes elements of the fabulous or legendary, and even then only after a suitable amount of time has passed.

The gambler's life is a rhythmic tale of numbers, premonitions, symbols and dreams. He worships magic, and is magic's willing victim. He wins and loses in seasons. But within all these cycles and prismatic mysteries, he must fight to maintain a fingerhold on ordinary reality. In the past, when CJ gambled much more heavily than he does now, when it was getting away from him and threatening to lead to a form of nondrinker's delirium tremens, when he was afraid of seeing pterodactyls come flying out of his TV set—yes, in those days of superstition and bad acid magic, it finally came to him that he was traveling beyond action and into the realm of the unreal. He came out of it like a diver surviving a rapture of the deep, and since then he has lived in a state of carefully controlled enchantment.

Behind his dark glasses he scans Municipal Stadium in Cleveland. He has the Browns plus 7. In New York he has the Saints plus 10½. He has action on six other pro games (all 20 times) and the Bears and 49ers in a $60 parlay. In baseball he has the Reds and Tigers.

The Saints fumble on radio and the Browns fumble on TV. As time passes CJ becomes so repelled by the Saints that he switches to the Jets-Dolphins, even though he has no action on this game—an almost unprecedented move. A bit of stray sunlight forms a bright swatch on the TV screen and CJ puts a piece of cardboard under the blinds to reinforce the dimness. But the Browns are not worth looking at this day. They are playing bouncy-ball all over the field and it is becoming clear that CJ's weekend will have few redeeming features.

No hope remains in the games being broadcast, so he is reduced to waiting for scores of other games. Radio scores seem to predate TV scores and we concentrate on the latter, tracing the course of distant games by trying to digest the numbers that pulse on the screen for a second or two before vanishing. This is never very pleasurable, and compared with CJ's classical discovery of moving a matchbook across a line score, the electronic method is too fleeting. The scores are gone before the mind can interpret them. Did we really see what we thought we saw? How can the Cards be leading the Vikings late in the second quarter? *Pulse.* Look at the Redskins, scoreless at the half. *Pulse pulse pulse.* Scores from Atlanta, scores from Baltimore, scores from Green Bay. We find ourselves pointing at the screen every time a score materializes. This enables us to pin the score, remember it, interpret it, hate it and fear it. CJ needs two touchdowns in Minnesota. He needs a touchdown and a field goal in Green Bay. He needs divine intervention in Washington. *Pulse pulse.* He has fallen behind in Cincinnati. He is virtually dead in Minnesota. He is coming back to life in Atlanta and Baltimore, but it is all too sudden, happening too fast, final scores beginning to flood the screen, and now we are confronted by the man at Network Control who manipulates a revolving scoreboard, and CJ is trying to read around corners, *pulse pulse*, mugged in Washington, slashed in New York, drawn and quartered in Cleveland, his stomach fluids gradually carbonating, his heartbeat interrupted by each new score, *pulse pulse pulse pulse pulse.*

In baseball the Reds (untelevised) have held on to win, and we now prepare to go back and forth between Tigers-A's and Rams-49ers. CJ is stretched out on the rug in front of the color set. He is still unshaven, his glasses off, right arm over his eyes, stale air clinging to his rumpled body. As the Rams begin their destruction of the 49ers, an almost unimaginable thing happens. The doorbell rings. We have been so insulated in our flotation capsule that very little sense of an alternate environment has managed to penetrate. CJ goes to the door and opens it. In walks Kool, his younger brother, fresh from the Jersey swamps. It is the first time I've seen him since the right side of his face totally collapsed following a Saints-Redskins game in 1971.

How does CJ respond to news from the real world?
When CJ reads or hears about an unusual event, such as two ships colliding in mid-ocean with great loss of life, or a Latvian brother and sister separated during World War I who learn they have been living on the same street in Bridgeport for the past 47 years, he usually says: "What's the odds on something like that?"

What does CJ fear most in this life and in the life to come?
CJ fears the weather most. He remembers waking up on the morning of Dec. 31, 1967, and turning on the radio and hearing a voice that sounded like the judgment of God (Him again). The voice said: "It is 13° below zero in Green Bay, Wis., site of today's NFL title game." Bad weather usually favors the underdog because it tends to neutralize superior strength, to atomize and equalize. CJ has the Packers 100 times and he is giving seven points and God has made the temperature drop to 13° below. The Packers win in the last few seconds but they fail to beat the spread.

CJ tries to use the weather like a a tribal conjurer. One day the radio reports tornadoes in Kansas. It is Saturday evening and CJ tries desperately to find a college football game being played in Kansas that night. Finally he comes up with two small, small colleges—names he no longer remembers. He wants the points. He's dying to take the points. He will sit by the radio, all night if necessary to wait for the final score of what is bound to be a windswept and topsy-turvy game. He feels sure the underdog will come through for him because he knows, he has always known, it has been basic knowledge for many years that bad weather favors the underdog because it is a neutralizer of ability, experience and talent, an atomizer and equalizer, and he is ready to wire his mind into the desolate roar of Kansas, for a full night if need be. But his bookmaker,

Bernie Sherm, has no line on the game in question because the two schools are exceedingly tiny, obscure and pathetic, assuming they exist at all.

How did CJ stop smoking?
The year is 1970. CJ has the Boston Celtics 40 times against the Cincinnati Royals. He is giving 5½ points. With a minute left in the game, he leads by 11. With four seconds left, he leads by seven. He has possession of the basketball. The ball is his. Suddenly he loses the ball. The ball is lost. The other team has the ball. A man on the other team heaves a wild shot from a crazy angle. The ball falls in the basket as the buzzer sounds. Bzzzzz. CJ gets up, opens a cabinet, takes out a carton of cigarettes and in a morosely romantic and live-enhancing gesture he quietly strangles the carton before throwing it away.
"Something good had to come of that game," he says.

KOOL GREETS CJ by butting pads with him. He throws a shoulder, backs off, lunges again. Three times he does this, deadpan. It means they are together in this thing, and it is a manly thing, and they are not unlike the players themselves, fond of mock pummeling, doing work heroic enough to require ritual, and it is good luck besides.
Kool has made three bets. All look bad at the moment. Through the years he has been so consistently wrong that CJ often uses him as a guide, betting against the teams his brother selects as winners. Kool lives in a remote part of New Jersey, where he walks the moors in a half-trance before making his betting selections for the week. This trek is meant to empty his mind, enabling him to pick up vibrations from NFL cities.
The brothers begin to ridicule each other's bets. CJ keeps dialing between baseball and football on the color set. Speaking of the weekend to come, or perhaps the one after that, he says something about law of averages, change of luck, help of God.
Kool tells me about the time he and CJ took the Redskins minus 14 against New Orleans. "We had them big," he says. "We were so sure they would romp we called in a second bet just before kickoff. Everything goes pretty much like we figured up to the last few minutes. Then the Saints begin to move. They can't win the game. They're out of the game. But if they get a touchdown, we lose. And now they're moving down the field. We can't look. We're afraid to watch. First we turn off the sound. Then we go into the kitchen and take turns peeking out at the game. The Saints are definitely moving. They're running, they're throwing, they're full of life. The Redskins don't care. They got the game won. CJ and me, we start arguing about who picked the Redskins. Then we start laughing. We're afraid to look and we start laughing and coughing. The Saints call time out to conserve the clock. I can't stop coughing. I take a peek and the Saints

are still moving, and I'm laughing and coughing and my eyes are full of tears.

Grown men, they began tickling one another, then throwing punches to the arm and chest. Neither would volunteer to go out, look at the game and report back. The tickling intensified and they tried to push each other out of the kitchen. Forced into the living room, unable to stop coughing and laughing, Kool finally looked at the set long enough to see one of the Saints standing in the end zone with the football. The next day he woke up to find that his face had slid down on one side and gone completely numb. The right corner of his mouth hung open. His right eye was at a slant. His voice took on a faintly metallic tone and every time he spoke his mustache dipped far to the right but nothing else moved, making it seem as though some kind of mechanism had rusted in his head. The doctor said it was nothing more than a nervous condition brought on by anxiety, and in 10 days Kool was back to normal.

Everything is normal in Yonkers as well, fatigue and defeat in the air, and all that remains is to ask CJ how he feels at the end of a weekend like this.

"Tomorrow's Columbus Day," he says. "I'm going with the Reds 20 times and the Raiders 20 times."

The general feeling about gamblers is that they are characters—colorful, funny, gregarious. The ones I've known have been solitary men who had little to say about their gambling. Here is CJ sitting in a dark room wearing sunglasses, watching two TV sets and monitoring the progress of an obscure event by radio, an earplug strung into his head. At a certain point he becomes material originating in the most pessimistic minds of modern literature. But a hero of this mode. He transcends Yonkers. He is independent of the power of money. He is not afraid to venture in the spaces between the lines that set the logical boundaries of his life.

On the train that takes me back, I think of him five years ago when he was putting together his color-TV set, night after night for well over a month, working his way through a 187-page assembly manual, struggling with oscillator coils and dual selenium diodes.

"Insert the free end of the yoke through the large chassis cutout and insert the octal plug in the socket marked YOKE."

It was a monumental achievement, and all through these past two days, as I watched little figures of men running and leaping, I found it easy to imagine that they too were constructed by CJ with his own hands and in his own time.

On Monday evening he walks to Yonkers, where he stays long enough to lose the daily double and two Exactas. This done, he jogs home in time to catch all but the first six minutes of the Oilers-Raiders on TV.

The Game
Of the Name

BY FRANZ LIDZ

Sports history is full of lovable rogues, but this is the tale of a rogue who brashly assumed the names of athletic celebrities and tried to convert their fame into his fortune.

L EROY BROWN OCCUPIES CELL 3 OF THE NATCHITOCHES, LA., parish jail, but he's not the baddest man in the whole damn town. The guy three cells down has a better claim. He's a bloated, Detroit-born bunko artist with teeth as crooked as his reputation. He answers to Bill Russell and Marv Fleming, and occasionally to John Mackey, but only reluctantly to Arthur Lee Trotter, the name on his FBI rap sheet.

Trotter, 49, changes identities faster than Woody Allen in *Zelig*. But he's more discriminating. He impersonates athletes almost exclusively. Trotter has been arrested 23 times since 1954, mostly for fraud, forgery and impersonation. This summer he claimed to be Bill Russell, the former great center of the Boston Celtics. But Trotter forgot he was eight inches too short for the role. On July 16 police arrested him for attempting to pull a confidence scam after he allegedly told a woman he was Russell and sold her a $2,500 share in a restaurant chain that had never heard of him. The police were listening in an adjoining room of the woman's house when the following conversation took place.

Woman: "You don't took like Bill Russell."

Trotter: "I got into a car accident and had to have plastic surgery."

Woman: "I was expecting someone much taller."

Trotter: "I had 10 inches of bone surgically removed from my shins. I wanted to fit easier into my new Mercedes. And I was tired of having my legs hang off motel beds."

Trotter offered to show her the scars. The cops offered to show him the parish jail.

At the station house, police say, Trotter quit being Russell and identified himself as Marv Fleming, the former tight end with the Green Bay Packers (1963–69) and Miami Dolphins (1970–74). He had a driver's license, insurance policies and personal checks as apparent proof. Snapshots found in the trunk of his car showed him holding up jerseys from the Packers and Dolphins with Fleming's number on them. He explained why he thought Vince Lombardi was a better coach than Don Shula. And he told of how Jim Mandich had beat him out in Miami, and of how he still resented it.

"How were we supposed to know he wasn't the real Marv Fleming?" says Natchitoches detective Larry Vaughn. "He didn't have his Super Bowl ring on, but then again, he was posing as a basketball player."

The local police checked him out by calling the number of the real Marv Fleming in Marina del Rey, Calif. Fleming, 41, is now an actor who does commercials—"I have perfect teeth," he says—and had a one-line speaking part in *Heaven Can Wait*: "Hey, Mr. Farnsworth, did you ever play college football?" He had just come back from shooting rapids on the Colorado River.

"Hey, babe," he'd said to his girlfriend, Karma Anderson, earlier that day when she'd met him at the airport. "What's happening?"

"Don't you know what's happening?" Anderson had snarled.

"Huh?"

"Bill Russell?"

"Bill Russell?" Fleming had repeated. "Did he . . . did he die?"

When she showed him a newspaper account of what had happened, Fleming's reaction had been, "Uh oh, he's at it again. That guy's been living off my name since 1974." But Fleming's lawyer advised him to keep his mouth shut, so when the Natchitoches police called, Fleming told them, "Marv Fleming isn't available."

"I can tell you why Mr. Fleming's not available," said the cop excitedly. "We have him locked up three blocks down the street in jail. Ain't that right, boys? We got him. We got him." Apparently, this case was fast becoming the biggest thing to hit Natchitoches since Jim Croce's plane crashed there 10 years ago.

Finally, Fleming relented and told the police that he was Marv Fleming. The police tested him. "Who beat you out?" asked the cop. "Our Fleming says Jim Mandich."

"Mandich didn't beat me out," Fleming exploded. "I got traded, and he took my place." Actually, Fleming lost his job when he injured a thigh a year before he was dealt to the Redskins.

Fleming can't understand how anyone could mistake an overweight con man for him. "I mean, I'm handsome," he says. "I've heard this Trotter is pig-ugly. And I'm too intelligent to tell somebody I cut 10 inches off my leg. For $2,500? No way."

Fleming became aware that someone was using his name during the 1974 season. Sitting in the Dolphins' locker room reading fan mail, he came upon a bill for a week's stay in an Oakland hotel. "I thought, wait a minute. That couldn't be. I was in Europe then." The hotel told him that somebody claiming to be Marv Fleming, the football player, had stayed there. Later that year he got a letter from a woman in Oakland that said, "The baby has arrived." He called her and said, "You've got the wrong guy."

Trotter impersonated Fleming three years ago in Tyler, Texas, and on that occasion was arrested for selling phony stock in NFL teams. That time he said he was really John Mackey, the former Baltimore Colts tight end (1963–71). He pleaded guilty to felony theft and was sentenced to three years in prison.

Tyler is about 40 miles from Longview, where the real Fleming was born, and only 10 miles from Lindale, where in May of 1978 the Lindale High newspaper, the *Eagle Eye*, ran an exclusive interview with Trotter entitled: EX-PRO MARV FLEMING TALKS WITH THE EAGLE EYE.

Fleming/Trotter talked expansively to the paper about his best season, 1966, argued that Denver wasn't really a Super Bowl team, said that playing against the Minnesota Vikings was so easy it was "like cutting grass" and told how he gave his first pro paycheck to his mother to buy a house. He also promoted his new venture, Fleming Foods. There was even a photo of the counterfeit Fleming with his "fiancée," Vickie Lynn Banks, a senior at John Tyler High in Tyler. Fleming/Trotter told the interviewer that he'd gotten Vickie Lynn's name and address from the personals column of *Soul Teen* magazine.

"At first," the *Eagle Eye* reported, "Marv says her letters were very short, and he thought she either was 'stupid or couldn't write.' . . . Well, one thing led to another, and they have been seeing each other for 23 months now."

"One day he just got up and left," says Banks, who still lives in Tyler. "It was strange. Until I read about him getting arrested in Louisiana, I always thought he was Marv Fleming."

Trotter is willing to talk now, which is something he didn't do much at a press conference in July. "Listen, Marv or Arthur or whoever you are," Vaughn had said to him then, "would you like to talk to some reporters?"

"Sure," said Trotter. But when he saw the TV cameras, he clammed up.

"Are you the Marv Fleming who played for the Packers and the Dolphins?" was the first question.

"I'll take the Fifth Amendment," he said,

"Are you Arthur Lee Trotter?"

"I'll take the Fifth Amendment."

"What's the Fifth Amendment?" he was asked after invoking it more times than a Watergate burglar.

"I don't want to talk about it."

"That's pretty close, Marv," said Vaughn.

Trotter now sits in Cell 6-B in his bright-orange prison issues and explains how everybody got it wrong. He says Arthur Lee Trotter is just an "a.k.e. [sic] alias. I haven't used that since I was a peewee." He says he sometimes goes by Bill Russell because "My foster father's name was William T. Russell; Bill Russell and I grew up in Oakland together, and young kids in the neighborhood used to call me Billy The Kid." Besides, he insists, his real name is Marv Xavier Fleming. The former Packer's middle name is Lawrence.

As for posing as Mackey, he just giggles. "I don't know," he says. "That's a new one on me."

Actually, he says, he played tight end for five years in the Canadian Football League.

Which team?

"Heh, heh," he says, flashing a broad and fishy grin. "Ain't no way you can get me to tell you *that!*"

And how about that shin surgery?

"They were supposed to take eight inches out of just the one leg," he says earnestly, "but it looked stupid having one side of me 6' 11" and the other 6' 3". So they sawed off part of my left shin to make my legs even.

"It's a sham, a whitewash, a frame-up," he shouts with curious glee. "I'm being persecuted because Natchitoches is a Jim Crow, KKK town." It's sure not an Arthur Lee Trotter, a.k.e. town.

He says it'll all be clear when his lawyer arrives.

Who's that?

"Melvin Belli," he says.

Crime and Punishment

BY GARY SMITH

After high school hoops star Richie Parker was convicted of sexual abuse,
a succession of people tried to salvage—or savage—his basketball career, and, one
by one, they were scarred by the experience.

O NE
HERE IS a man. Barely a man; he just ran out of ado-
lescence. He stands alone, 2,000 miles from home, beside
a swimming pool, in a stucco-walled apartment complex,
in a city built on an American desert.

Seton Hall chancellor Thomas R. Peterson buckled under to intense pressure
from media and alumni yesterday when he denied admission to star basketball re-
cruit and admitted sex felon Richie Parker.
                                                        —NEW YORK POST Jan. 24, 1995

It's too hot to run. But he must run. He strips to his trunks. He steps into the
pool. His body leans forward.

The University of Utah ceased its recruiting of former Manhattan Center bas-
ketball star Richie Parker in light of a barrage of media criticism and pressure from
the university president regarding Parker's sexual abuse conviction.
                                                        —NEW YORK NEWSDAY
                                                        May 6, 1995

His hands ball up. His left elbow draws back, pushing against the water. Slowly his foot begins to rise from the floor of the pool.

George Washington University officials informed high school basketball star Richie Parker yesterday they "regrettably" would stop recruiting him and blamed "unbalanced publicity" for a wave of criticism that hit the school for pursuing the youth, who had pleaded guilty to a sexual assault.

—THE WASHINGTON POST
June 30, 1995

His foot gradually descends to the bottom of the pool. His other foot begins to push off. His shoulders tighten. The water pushes back.

Richie Parker will never wear a UTEP basketball uniform. UTEP has bowed out of its recruitment of the controversial basketball player, athletic director John Thompson announced Friday.

—EL PASO HERALD-POST
Feb. 24, 1996

His knee slowly lifts again. His arms silently pump.

USC on Wednesday terminated its recruitment of former New York City All-America point guard Richie Parker, a convicted sex offender. The decision came after . . . two days of sometimes heated exchanges among athletic department personnel.

—ORANGE COUNTY REGISTER
March 28, 1996

He climbs out finally and pants for air, in the desert that once was the bottom of an ocean.

TWO

HERE IS a periodic table. It's the one you would see near the blackboard in any high school chemistry class, a listing of the 109 elements according to atomic number. Why is it being inflicted on you here, in a sports magazine? *Patience.* Remember, this is a story about higher education.

Near the lower lefthand corner of the chart is an element named cesium. Among its own—the metals surrounding it in the chart, such as sodium and potassium—cesium is a quiet, unassuming element. But because it has just one electron on its outer shell, one electron aching to leap to any atom that is lacking a full outer shell of electrons, cesium is a bomb in a suitcase when it leaves its neighborhood. On contact with oxygen, cesium will cause an explosion. Introduce it to chlorine, fluorine, iodine or bromine and look out! Almost everywhere it goes, trying to rid itself of the baggage of that one electron, another eruption occurs, and only those who understand what cannot be seen can make any sense of it at all.

THREE

H E R E I S an assistant principal. She works at Manhattan Center, the East Harlem high school Richie Parker once attended. Teenagers deposit their leather jackets in Ellen Scheinbach's closet in the morning for safekeeping, come to her at lunchtime for oatmeal cookies and advice. The phone's constantly ringing, teachers are always poking in their heads. "A lunatic asylum!" she calls her office, ambling about with her spectacles dangling from a neck chain. But now there's silence, and it's Richie's mother, Rosita, shuffling on her bad knees, clutching her envelope of articles clipped from the *New York Post* and the *Daily News*, extending them toward the assistant principal and asking her to explain.

Ellen Scheinbach is an authority figure, one of the few Rosita knows. Surely she can explain how *all this* could result from that one day in this building, in January 1994, when Rosita's 6' 5" son, a junior then—a well-liked boy known for his silence, his gentle nature and his skill on a basketball court—was walking through these halls, having gone to the nurse's office with a sprained ankle and having found the nurse not there, was returning to class when he paused . . . and turned. And headed toward the bottom of a stairwell in the back of the school, where he and a schoolmate, Leslie Francis, soon compelled a 16-year-old freshman girl to perform oral sex on them. And how 15 minutes later, the girl came running up the stairwell, sobbing, and soon thereafter Richie and the other boy were being led away in handcuffs. And how from that moment on, virtually everywhere Richie would turn to rid himself of the baggage of those 15 minutes, another explosion would occur. How careers would be smashed, men fired, dreams destroyed. How some relationships would splinter and others almost spontaneously be fused. How secrets would burst from hidden places, and rage and fear would tremble in the air behind her lean, quiet son. The assistant principal can explain all this to Rosita, can't she?

Ellen throws up her arms. The incongruity of it all still confounds her. Richie Parker? Richie didn't drink. Richie didn't curse. Richie didn't get into arguments or fights; he had never even gotten detention. She knew lots of kids who would play peek-a-boo with a toddler in the bleachers for a few minutes, but Richie was the only one she knew who would do it for an hour. The only time she had ever seen him exert his will—to *force* any issue—was on a basketball court, and even there he did it so softly, so smoothly, that she would be startled to learn at the end of a game that he had scored 35 points. He would be rated one of America's top 50 high school seniors in 1995, a notch or two below Georgia Tech signee Stephon Marbury in New York's schoolboy hierarchy.

Two investigations—one conducted by a George Washington University lawyer and another by the lawyer of the stairwell victim, not to mention the searchlight sweep of Richie's life by the media—failed to turn up a single thread that would indicate that those 15 minutes in the stairwell were part of a larger pattern. Richie himself had insisted on his innocence at first, but eventually he pleaded guilty when the charges were lowered from first-degree sodomy to first-degree sexual abuse in January 1995. His sentence was five years of probation. So now Rosita's standing on the other side of Ellen's desk, holding a half-dozen full-back-page pictures of her son under screaming SEX FELON headlines, asking her what the world has come to that one rotten act by a 17-year-old could take on such monstrous proportions and why Seton Hall has just reneged on its promise of a scholarship for Richie as long as he didn't get a prison sentence . . . and it's only the beginning, because now the great American morality play is ready to hit the road, with actors and actresses all across the land raring to perform their roles, eager to savage or salvage the teenager from 110th Street in Manhattan—often knowing nothing more of him than his name. Ellen keeps shaking her head and blinking. Sports, having somehow become the medium through which Americans derive their strongest sense of community, has become the stage where all the great moral issues have to be played out, often rough and ugly, right alongside the games.

Ellen had tried to protect Richie from that. She had tried to smuggle him out when the media surrounded her school. She sat beside him at games when he could no longer play, to shield him from the media's popping cameras and questions. She went to Seton Hall and told administrators that she would trust Richie with her daughter, if she had one. But it was hopeless. In the same way that cesium needs to rid itself of that one dangling electron on its outer shell, Richie needed to take his sin to a university, to one of America's last "pure" places, and have it absolved so he could find his way to the promised land, the NBA. In the same way that fluorine longs for that extra electron to complete itself, the universities and their coaches were drawn to the basketball player who could enhance their profile, increase their alumni contributions and TV revenues. And the mutual attraction would keep causing explosions, hurling Richie and yet another university far apart, and Rosita would keep returning to Ellen, her eyes filling with tears. Hasn't her son, she would ask, done everything demanded of him?

Yes, Rosita, yes, he fulfilled the requirements of the criminal justice system and of the out-of-court settlement of the victim's civil lawsuit. He had met monthly with his probation officer, met regularly with a counselor, made both a private and a public apology to the victim, an acknowledgment that regardless of the details of the incident, he had done something profoundly wrong in that stairwell. He had promised to speak out against sexual abuse and to make financial restitution to the victim with a percentage of any money he might generate one day in the NBA. He had earned A's and B's at Manhattan Outreach Center, the school he was sent to in the wake of the court ruling, met NCAA qualifications on his fourth try with an SAT score of 830 and enrolled at Mesa (Ariz.) Community College, which refused to let him play ball but allowed him to be a student. And, yes, both the victim and her lawyer had requested that the country's media and universities let him move on. "He's rare among people who've committed a sexual offense," says Michael Feldman of Jacoby & Meyers, the victim's attorney. "He admitted that he did something wrong and committed to help the victim. How does it assist women to refuse him an opportunity now?"

"We believe Richie is truly sorry," the girl's father had told the *Daily News.* "We're religious people who believe in redemption. We don't believe in third chances. We do believe in second chances."

So how can Ellen explain to the 49-year-old woman with the envelope full of news clippings that the second chance, the fresh start, the comeback, the stuff of magazine covers and made-for-television movies, the mother's milk that immigrant America was nursed on and cannot—to its everlasting credit and eternal confusion—seem to wean itself from, has been denied to her son?

"What can I do?" Ellen cries. "I can't get the reporter from the *New York Post* fired. I can't speak to women's groups who are saying he shouldn't have the right to go to college and play basketball. What is a women's group, anyway? I know plenty of women, but what's a women's group? I can't call [Georgetown coach] John Thompson and tell him to give Richie a chance— you think he's going to listen to some little old Jewish lady? So I'm just left with this horrible frustration. It's like trying to comfort the survivor of a plane wreck when Rosita comes here. There's nothing I can do.

"He was 17 when this happened. For 15 minutes of rotten judgment, he's been crucified! These women's groups are talking about O.J. Simpson and Mike Tyson, and they're using Richie's name. When teachers here heard what he was accused of, they said, 'Are you kidding?' This is a kid who always tried to fade into the background, who wouldn't push back if you pushed him. Even when he wanted something, he'd just stand there and wait till you *asked* what he wanted. Look, I don't know what happened in that stairwell, but if he did it, he must've had a brain lesion. This kid is not a threat.

"If he were white, would this story have been written this way? But no, he fit the perfect stereotype. He has no money, and he's a black male teenager, so they could have a field day. What do people want—for him to fail, so he's out on a street corner? Are they saying you can never redeem yourself? If he wanted to be a doctor instead of a basketball player, would they say, 'You can't take biochemistry class'? Basketball is his talent, and while he's on probation he's entitled to play that the same way he'd be entitled to be a musician or an artist. Everyone thinks the NCAA is so macho. I've never seen so many wimpy men in my life."

Once, just once in the 2½ years of watching everything around Richie go to pieces, has Ellen feared that he might go to pieces too. She had never seen him cry, never heard him blame anyone else, never sensed a chip on his shoulder. But when it was clear that the board of education was about to suspend him from Manhattan Center in the middle of his senior season and that the media swirl was sucking down his teammates too, he came to her office with his mother and read his letter of resignation from the team. When he finished, he finally broke down and clutched his mother. "If not for you," he sobbed to her, "I don't think I could make it."

In the end, Ellen decides, perhaps there isn't much she can do to help Rosita, but there's something Rosita has done to help her. "I've learned a lot from her," says Ellen. "I've learned that no matter how frustrated and upset you get, you just keep turning to your kid and saying, 'I love you, and no matter what happens, there's one place for you that's safe.' When my son has a problem now I just try to hug him and say, 'Whatever decision you make I'll stand by you.' Because it *works*. I've seen it work. It saved Richie Parker."

FOUR

HERE IS a copy editor on the sports desk of a major city newspaper. She's smart, and she's funny, and if an office push-up contest or footrace suddenly breaks out, hopefully after deadline, she's the one you want to put your money on. Of course, because she's a woman, the sensitive stories go to Jill Agostino for editing. Anguish? That's a Jill piece. Morality issue? Absolutely Agostino. Not that it's ever actually stated in a sports department that men are bereft in those areas. It's just sort of understood.

So she gets the Richie Parker stories to polish for *Newsday*. And as she's scanning the words on her computer screen in early 1995, she begins to feel something tightening inside her. It's the old uneasiness, the one she dreads, the one she has no time for here, now, as the clock hands dig toward deadline; the one she might try to run into the ground tomorrow when she's doing her five miles, or scrub away in the quiet of her Long Island apartment, or stow away and convert to fuel someday, something to help flog herself through an extra hour of work when she has to prove her worth to some sexist idiot who dismisses her as a token woman in a man's world, a newspaper sports desk. But not now. Not here. No way.

She begins to sense it here and there between the lines—the implication that Parker is being treated unfairly—and her uneasiness starts to turn to quiet anger. She doesn't sleep much that night, doesn't feel like eating the next day. Another Parker story comes her way a few evenings later, then there's an afternoon drive to work listening to radio talk-show callers chew the issue to death, some of them actually sticking up for the kid, and her quiet anger curdles into a rage that no one knows, no one sees.

The writers like Jill. She's not one of those editors who must tinker with a story to justify their existence. One *Newsday* reporter writes an article that comes right out and says Parker is a good kid who made a mistake and deserves a second chance, and he calls Jill as she's editing it, cheerfully asking her how she likes his piece. There's silence on the phone. And then it erupts from her, something she has never even been able to tell her family.

"I've been raped," says Jill. "I don't agree with you."

"Oh, I didn't . . . Jill, I'm sorry," he says.

She feels like a jerk for making the reporter feel like a jerk, but it's too late now, the anger's out on the table, and it's not finished. Mistake? How can anyone call it that? Leaving your headlights on or forgetting your keys, that's a mistake—not humiliating a woman the way Jill had been nearly nine years earlier, at age 22, by a man on a boat on Queechy Lake in upstate New York. She goes into her boss's office, seething at a society where a man like Mike Tyson can walk out of jail a few years after raping a woman and be greeted by a thunderous roar and a paycheck worth millions of dollars, and TV commentators can blather on about all that *Tyson* has been through, as if the perpetrator was the victim and the real victim was yesterday's oatmeal. "I want to write a column," she tells her boss. "People need to know what it's like for the victim. I was raped."

His jaw drops. Well . . . uh . . . sure, Jill, but. . . .

She barely sleeps that night. Her husband, Michael, says that if she's sure she wants to do this, he's behind her. She's sure. She sits on the couch the next day with a red pen, a blue pen and a notepad. The red ink is for her pain—the italicized sections interspersed in the column that recount that night on the lake where she swam as a little girl: *"I wanted to throw up every time I smelled the mixture of Grand Marnier and tobacco smoke on his breath as he held me down. . . . "* The blue ink is for Richie Parker: "How often do you think Parker will think about this incident once he's on a college basketball court? For the victim, not a day will go by without that memory. . . . Parker's punishment should last until his victim is able to walk alone up the street, or through a parking lot, or down a dimly lit hallway and feel safe. Until the nightmares cease. Until a day goes by and she doesn't think about the horrible things these boys made her do. But it won't."

What are you doing? a voice inside her asks when she has finished writing. To her, this is not an act of courage, as some would take it. To her, this is Jill Agostino publicly admitting her most private pain just on the chance that it will make some men begin to comprehend how it feels to be violated, how it eats into a woman's life forever, how it can make her hold her breath when a stranger steps into an empty elevator with her, make her want to run when a man rolls down his car window and asks her for directions, make her stare into a mirror some days and hate her body because somehow it betrayed her.

She can't surrender to the urge to crumple up the notepad paper, because if she does, the man in the boat wins again, and she can't let him keep winning. He has won too many times, at night when she sits up rigid in bed from nightmares she can never quite recollect—only raw terror and the faint echo of all the world's laughter. He won every time she bought another size 8 blouse for a size 4 body, every time she froze when a colleague she didn't know well threw an arm around her shoulder, every time she couldn't sleep and had to caffeinate and will herself through the next day so that no one, except perhaps her husband, would ever dream that she was anything but the sharp, competitive woman that the world always sees.

Now comes the next agony. She can't let her family find out in a newspaper story. She must call her mother and father and brother and sister and tell them about the rape and why she buried it. She must listen to her mother cry and feel guilty for not protecting her daughter from something she couldn't possibly have protected her from. A few days later the story appears. Seven hundred and fifty thousand readers learn Jill's secret, and countless thousands more—including old boyfriends, old co-workers, old roommates—come across it in the newspapers across the country that run the story. Some of her colleagues are moved to tears by her column. Some confess to her their own buried stories of rape.

The eddies never seem to end. Radio talk shows call her to be a guest and ask her about her rape, and she has to keep reliving the worst moment of her life.

The victim's lawyer calls to compliment her story and asks her if she would testify in his client's civil lawsuit against Parker. When that's settled out of court, he asks if she'd consider doing that in another lawsuit in which the jury needs to feel the long ripple of a rape, and she says yes, because how can she refuse to help someone who has endured what she has or allow so many people to keep insinuating that it's the violated woman who is to blame? SPORTS ILLUSTRATED calls a year later and asks to interview her, and she has to worry how that will affect the way her colleagues at her new workplace, *The New York Times*, will look at her, worry that *this* is who she is now to people, this is *all* she is. Each new episode will mean another week of barely eating, barely sleeping, a few more nightmares and 10 or 15 extra miles of running, but she can't back down. She has never met Richie Parker and no doubt never will, but Jill Agostino is paying for his crime, oh, yes, she's paying.

FIVE
HERE IS an assistant coach from the University of Utah. Once Donny Daniels, too, was a black teenager from a crowded city who lived to play basketball. And so even though he is the 40-year-old father of three, including two daughters, on this spring day in 1995, he is walking into his past when he walks into the Parkers' apartment. He finds Richie just as quiet and respectful as all his sources vowed. He sits in the living room with the 108 basketball trophies that take Rosita hours to dust. He looks into the kitchen where she cooks pots and pans full of baked chicken, ziti, collard greens, banana pudding and sweet-potato pies on Sundays and has half the neighborhood into her house, just like it used to be when she was growing up in North Carolina. He gazes around the home where Rosita and Richie's ever-so-quiet father, Richard, and Richie's two older sisters, Monica and Tanya, who have both attended college, eat and tease each other and laugh.

Donny talks to Rosita, who for years telephoned after Richie to make sure he had gone where he said he was going, who tried to seal her son from all the bad choices blowing around outside the window. No, Donny can't see her running a half-dozen times to the emergency room with high blood pressure at each twist her son's story takes; can't see her bent in half with chest pains six months after Richie's arrest, paramedics rushing through that front door and clamping an oxygen mask over her mouth, driving an IV needle into her arm, pushing a nitroglycerine pill under her tongue, trying to stave off the heart attack or stroke that's on the verge of occurring as her son watches, even more scared than he was on that long night when he lay awake smelling urine in a New York City jail. He can't see her lying in the hospital, realizing that if she doesn't stop letting the newspaper stories affect her so deeply, they're going to kill her. But listening to the mother and the son, he can feel it.

And it's all that feeling that Donny lets out when the *New York Post* reporter gets a tip and calls him a few days later to ask, "How can Utah consider rewarding a sex felon with a scholarship?" All that feeling from a man who senses that his and his university's integrity is being assaulted. Of course, he has never walked into the *victim*'s house and felt what a heart might feel there. "There are two victims here," he tells the reporter. "He doesn't evaporate into the atmosphere. He's not a piece of dirt. He has feelings and emotions. . . . They both made a mistake; they shouldn't have been there. But everyone's worried about the girl. What about him? . . . You don't see her name or picture, but Richie Parker is plastered all over. . . . She probably will get a doctorate and marry a successful guy and live in the Hamptons. . . . Will he ever be able to forget it? . . . Who's hurt more for life?"

Imagine the explosion this quote causes back in Salt Lake City, the ripping apart of molecules. Imagine how rapidly the college president and athletic director must run from that quote, how swiftly Richie's chance to attend Utah vaporizes, how many columns are written citing Richie as the prime example of America's coddling of athletes and Neanderthal treatment of women. Imagine how tightly doors shut to discuss what must be done with Donny.

He is luckier than others will be. He is placed on probation for a year and ordered to attend sensitivity training sessions with a director from the Women's Resource Center on campus. He gets a second chance.

A year later, when a writer from SI calls, Donny says he was wrong for saying what he did but wishes to say nothing more, and his boss, coach Rick Majerus, the most affable of men, seals his lips as well. Better to fence off the area and let the pieces lie where they fell, to be covered by the sediment of time.

SIX

HERE IS a university president. Here is the picture of Teddy Roosevelt on his office wall. Which is which? Who's who? Mustache. Spectacles. Hair combed back. Eyes atwinkle. Robust body. Bent for bold action. Oh, so *that's* how you tell the two of them apart: Stephen Trachtenberg's the better politician.

He's the man who transformed the University of Hartford and George Washington, the one who gives big-idea speeches and writes ethics essays for books, magazines and newspapers. He knows something about everything. Even chemistry.

Yes, he's going to do it. He's going to give this Parker kid another chance, and he's going to satisfy the alumni and faculty and the women's groups and the media and the talk-show callers, and even the victim. He's going to introduce cesium to fluorine, and—*eureka!*—nothing's going to go *ka-boom!*

And why not? He's a master at problem-solving, a genius at persuasion. "He has a tremendous capacity to anticipate a whole variety of outcomes and the implications of those outcomes," says George Washington vice president Bob Chernak, "and then calculate how to move an issue toward the most favorable one. He's always three steps ahead of you. He's thinking of ideas in his sleep."

Stephen inherited a university with a profound identity crisis, not to mention a 1–27 basketball team, in 1988. In the wake of his brainstorms, applications have nearly doubled, contributions have soared, average SAT scores have rocketed, and the hoops team has become an NCAA tournament fixture. A new challenge? Bully! A fray? Fine! He would wade right into it and convince people he was right, the way he did during the student sit-ins at Boston University back in the 1960s as a bearded associate dean, persuading protesters not to risk a violent confrontation with police. He has built up a tall pile of chips at George Washington, and he's willing to ante up for Richie Parker.

Sure, he's eager to help his basketball team, but it's also something else. Sure, he's the son of one hell of a Brooklyn life insurance salesman, but he's also the son of a social activist, a mother who sent him to summer camps with black kids and wanted him to become a doctor who would treat the poor, not to mention the grandson of a Ukrainian Jew who fled to America for a second chance. His record of helping kids out of deep holes is long. At Hartford he gave a scholarship to a young man with an eighth-grade education who had been convicted on drug-dealing and burglary charges. That man, John Richters—who played no sport—went on to graduate summa cum laude and get a Ph.D. in psychology and now works as a program chief at the National Institutes of Health in the study of chronically antisocial children.

A young deer—that's the image that forms in the university president's head when Richie enters his office in May 1995. Barely audible, Richie expresses contrition and an earnest desire to attend George Washington, and he's so hopeful that he buys a school hat and T-shirt. All the questions march through Stephen's head as Richie walks out of his office. Is it a college's job to mete out more punishment than the legal system does? Perhaps not, but isn't it a university president's job to make sure that a parent doesn't send an 18-year-old daughter to live in a dorm room next door to a sex offender? What if it were *his* daughter? If a sex felon shouldn't get a basketball scholarship, what about an academic scholarship? What about a thief, a mugger, an embezzler? A custodian or a waiter can return to his normal life after the legal system passes judgment, but a gifted basketball player cannot? Pro sports are fine for felons to play, but not college athletics? What kind of message does it send out when a sex offender gets a scholarship? When you remove the emotion from the question . . . but maybe you shouldn't remove the emotion from the question. All this confusion, does it signal a society lost in the wilderness . . . or one finally mature enough to look at questions it has always shut its eyes to? His mind gnaws at the bone, at every last bit of gristle. Beneath it all, he can sense what's going on, the vague feeling people are beginning to have that their love of sports—the sense of escape and belonging that they provide—is doubling back on them like some hidden undertow, pulling them all out to sea. It's not the ripest time for redemption.

But he takes a deep breath and begins constructing a master plan. He sends a university lawyer, a woman, to New York City to compile a massive dossier on Richie. If she finds any smudge, besides the stairwell incident, George Washington can retreat—but he keeps checking with her, and she doesn't. Shrewder still, he decides that he won't decide Richie's fate; he'll leave that to a blue-ribbon committee, one that he structures as if he were a supplicant at a Hindu shrine, bowing to a dozen different gods, to every possible political correctness: seven blacks and eight whites, seven females and eight males, including a professor of law, an assistant chief of police, a minister, a campus chaplain, an academic coordinator, a faculty clinical psychologist, a director of multicultural student services, a superintendent of schools, two judges, two trustees and three students. "A Noah's Ark committee," he calls it. If the menagerie chooses to accept Richie, Stephen will have him redshirted for a year, ease him into campus life, save him from the jackals waiting at enemy arenas. And then, as the frosting on the cake, even before the committee makes its recommendation on Richie, he offers the victim, a valedictorian of her junior high class, a scholarship when she graduates from high school. A university lawyer warns him that one won't look pretty in a tabloid headline, but Stephen is determined. Win-win for everyone, right?

Do you recall Chernobyl? It all begins to rain down on Stephen Trachtenberg: the *New York Post* reporter, radioactive telephone calls, faxes and letters, scalding editorials, icy questions from the board of trustees, student petitions and condemnation from the faculty senate. Stephen, the father of George Washington University, is being called immoral, a fool, a calculating liar. Even his wife, Francine, in his corner all the way, warns him that he has underestimated what he's up against, that, politically speaking, he has made the wrong call. He's losing sleep. It's usurping his entire day and all of his night. The story moves to *The Washington Post*'s front page—*that's* trouble. If only he could buy enough time for his plan to incubate, for the score of Richie's last SAT test to arrive and the Noah's Ark committee to see the results of the nearly complete investigation, but no, Stephen looks to one flank, then the other and sees a remarkable alliance closing in on him. The feminists *and* conservatives, "the forces of the left and the forces of the right," he says, "coming together like the teeth of a vise." Eight years of working 12-hour days to build George Washington's image is being frittered away, and image is money. And he can't even try to persuade the public that he's right—the NCAA gag rule preventing school officials from discussing a recruit has stripped him of his greatest gift. Could he even lose his job over this, if the teeth keep closing? Could he?

One by one, those in his inner circle who admire the risk he has taken, or have simply indulged it, urge him to halt, even as his investigator's reports on Richie keep coming in, convincing him more than ever that it's right to go on. Finally it's just Stephen out there, hanging onto Richie by his fingernails as everything around them shakes. At last, he has to let go. Stephen looks at himself in the mirror. It's not Teddy he sees. It's not the man who could persuade almost anyone of anything. "I gave Richie Parker a moment of hope," he says, the light going out of his eyes, "and then I took it away."

SEVEN

HERE IS the victim. No, here the victim is not. She has never emerged from the shadows of that stairwell. She will not emerge now. Of her you shall only know this: For months after the incident she endured nightmares and telephoned threats from people who blamed her. She is an excellent student, but her grades dipped, and the taunts from schoolmates forced her to transfer from one high school, then another. She undergoes therapy. As she gets ready for her senior year, her family will not even reveal the borough where her current school is located.

She hopes to become a doctor. Her father is a social worker who deals with abused children, her mother a hospital nurse. Six years ago they and their daughter left Ghana and came to America, looking for another chance.

EIGHT

HERE IS a number. Such a nice, plump number. Say it: *500.* Let them scoff at Dave Possinger, let them cringe at his intensity, let them ask him, like wise guys, to total up the traffic lights in the towns where he has coached, but this would be proof he could clutch all the way to the coffin: *500.* One more win is all he needs. One more.

And no, this won't be 500 by dint of sheer endurance, a box turtle's milestone. Eighteen years is all it took Dave, an astonishing average of 28 victories a year. He is the best coach you never heard of, a 52-year-old man marooned in the bush country of NAIA and junior college basketball by bad luck and an old whiff of scandal. But it's summer, and the 1995–96 season is just a few months away, and on opening night his Sullivan County (N.Y.) Community College team will no doubt pulverize Dutchess C.C. as it does every year, and he will join that invisible club: 500.

He has envisioned the moment all summer, even as the man he has just chosen as his assistant coach, Charles Harris, has begun to grow intrigued by the never-ending newspaper accounts of a kid in New York City named Richie Parker. Richie is the last thing on Dave's mind. Dave has just coached his team to the national junior college Division III championship and is loaded to repeat in 1995–96, and he has no reason to think that Richie will end up with him in the bush country, at a low-level community college. Start making contacts and see what's out there, especially for the year after this, is all he has asked of Harris, a likable 40-year-old black man who Dave is sure will make a superb recruiter.

Everywhere Dave goes that summer, even on his vacation in the Philippines, he imagines the magical night that is coming: The limousine his girlfriend is renting to take him to the game. The official hoisting of the national-championship banner, his second in four years at the junior college in Loch Sheldrake, N.Y. Former players converging to congratulate him, a capacity crowd rising to recognize him. The plaque, the ringing speeches, the commemorative T-shirts, the late-night dinner for 100 in the Italian restaurant. "It dominated my thoughts every day," Dave recalls. "Even in places in the Philippines where there was no running water, no electricity, I'd see kids playing basketball and I'd think about 500. It would stand for all the years, all the kids, all the hard work." It would stand for his nine seasons at a New York NAIA school named St. Thomas Aquinas, where his 295–49 record helped make the program the country's winningest of the 1980s, on *any* level—yes, Dean Smith at North Carolina was second to Dave Possinger. It would stand for his four-year run of 133–5 at Sullivan County and ease the pain from the '89 scandal that forced him out after one year at Western Carolina, his one shot as an NCAA Division I coach, even though it was his assistant, not him, who was cited for minor recruiting violations. Perhaps 500 wouldn't mean quite so much if he had a wife and children, but no, it's just him and his basset hound Free Throw, and 500 stands for his life.

A few hours drive south, at a showcase game for unrecruited players, his soon-to-be-named assistant Harris is watching the one obvious jewel on the floor, Richie Parker. It's crazy, thinks Harris, who remembers inmates from the local prison taking classes from Sullivan County when he was enrolled there in the 1970s. "Everyone has something in their closet they're not proud of," Harris says, "and everyone deserves a second chance." A long shot, but what a coup if he could offer the kid the second chance that the four-year colleges wouldn't.

Harris gets clearance, he says later, from Sullivan County's athletic director, Mike McGuire, to have Richie apply to the school—not as a scholarship student but as any normal student would. Searching for a way to contact Richie, Harris calls the *New York Post* reporter. It's like the mouse asking the cat for directions to the cheese.

McGuire says now that if he heard the name Richie Parker, it didn't register. And that he definitely never gave Harris permission—even though Harris had been unofficially approved to go on contract in two months and had already invested countless hours and a few hundred dollars from his own pocket on phone calls and recruiting trips—to present himself to a *New York Post* reporter as a Sullivan County assistant coach and declare that Sullivan County was "committed to working" with Richie Parker.

You know what happens next. You know about the reporter's call to the president, asking if he knows that Sullivan County is recruiting a sex felon. You know about the next day's headlines, the ducking for cover. Richie, of course, will never play at Sullivan County. Harris's fate will hang in the balance for a few months while the school wrings its hands. In October, after he has spent weeks monitoring the players in study hall and working at practices without pay, hoping for the best, Harris is told he won't be hired.

Harris, with head-coaching dreams of his own, is crushed. Dave, who feels responsible for Harris, is devastated. There have been other slights from his superiors at Sullivan County, he feels, but to do this to a well-meaning man trying to give a kid a second chance—how can he go on working there and live with himself? But then, how can he walk out on his team two weeks before the season opener and deprive himself of the Holy Grail: 500?

Simple, Dave's friends tell him. Win the opener, then quit. What a scene it would be, the man of the hour strolling to the microphone, saying, "Ladies and gentlemen, thank you. *I quit!*" But Dave's conscience won't let him do it. "If I start something," he tells his friends, "I have to finish it."

Five days before the opener, he quits. He can't sleep. A few days later he smirks and tells a reporter, "Your job is to tell me why I shouldn't jump off a building." His team goes on to win the national championship again, without him.

His record hangs there, rolling around the rim—499 wins and 116 losses—but athletic directors look right past him, searching for a younger man. Eight months later he still hasn't even received an interview. He takes a job as a regional director for National Scouting Report, a service designed to help high school kids get—what else?—college scholarships. "But there's still a claw in the back of my throat," he says, "a claw telling me, 'You are a basketball coach.' "

A week after he quits, Dave goes to his dresser drawer. He opens it and stares at what he purchased in the Philippines a few months earlier, and he makes a decision. Damn the math, they can't take it from him. It's there now, glittering in 18-carat gold from a chain around his neck: *500*.

NINE

HERE IS the girlfriend of the boy who has pleaded guilty to sexual abuse. She's tall and lean, a beautiful girl whose demeanor is so composed that everyone always assumes she's older than she really is, until that day when people are running to her in the hall, telling her to come quickly, something terrible has happened, and Richie's in the principal's office talking so helter-skelter that none of it makes sense, and the police are on their way, and she's nearly in hysterics.

He's the schoolmate Jaywana Bradley fell in love with in 10th grade, the one who taught her to play basketball so well that by her senior year she will be named by the *Daily News* as one of the best schoolgirl players in Manhattan. Who knew, perhaps they would go off together to trumpets, the king and queen of Manhattan hoops moving on, hand in hand, to set up court on a college campus . . . until this.

But what, exactly, *is* this? Jaywana keeps finding herself in bed, crying, wondering. People keep asking her, "You gonna leave Richie?" Some call her a fool if she sticks with him, and a few boys walk right up to her and say, "Why you going out with a rapist?"

She can't quite answer that. Maybe it's because her mother and father believe in Richie, her dad accompanying the Parkers to court hearings. Maybe it's just sitting there in the Parker apartment all those evenings, playing spades with the family and watching TV, feeling that relentless presence of Rosita— like a rock, a magnetic rock. Listening to Rosita talk about the past, telling how her father died when she was one, how her mother died of diabetic complications when she was 13, how her twin sister stepped in front of a car and was killed when they were five, leaving Rosita clutching the sleeve of the coat with which she had tried to yank back her twin. Maybe Jaywana, just like Richie, just keeps absorbing Rosita's relentless message: "Make your life what it's meant to be, and don't let anyone or anything stop you."

Maybe it's two young people pulling closer and closer together the more that forces try to drive them apart. Maybe she's a sucker for that playful, silly Richie, the side he only shows close family and friends. And maybe it comes from holding him, wiping away his tears the way she does when George Washington closes the door on him and she ends up getting the big-time basketball scholarship to Massachusetts that was supposed to be his.

He goes off to Mesa, to the junior college that decides not to let him play basketball, and she goes off to UMass, and they don't see each other for a long while. He has time to sort out what's essential, what he needs, *now*, sooner than he ever dreamed. When they come home for Christmas, he asks her to come over, calls her to his room and asks her to close her eyes. When she opens them, he's on his knee, asking her to marry him, and she says yes. And later, when she asks him when, he says, "As soon as we're done college."

More and more now, Jaywana finds herself daydreaming of a future. There is no city or people there, just her and Richie in a house surrounded by land and trees as far as the eye can see, a place where no one can touch them. Why the two of them against all odds? She can't explain. "I don't know what made me stick through it with him," she says. "All I know is that nothing anybody can ever say or do can pull me apart from him."

TEN

HERE IS death. Now, wait a minute—no one is going to be foolish enough to blame Richie Parker's 15 minutes in the stairwell or the administration of Mesa Community College or even the media for the death of a coach's father, but every event in life is chained to the next, and how do you ever separate the links?

This was supposed to be the year that Rob Standifer gave his father, Bob, a gift—perhaps the last one—in exchange for the gift his father had given him. All Rob's life his dad had awakened at 3 a.m. and reported to work three hours early at a construction company, logging 12- to 14-hour shifts. It didn't matter how badly his dad felt, with his bad back, his diabetes or his weak heart. Work made his father feel good, and his father had a knack of passing that feeling all around. The lesson Rob took into his bones was the old American one: Outwork everyone and you'll succeed in life.

And it seemed true. As a kid Rob was always the first one on the basketball court as a point of pride, shooting 1,000 shots a day, and sure enough, he found himself playing for the Mesa Community College team that nearly won the junior college title in 1987, finishing third in the national tournament in Hutchinson, Kans. He worked for nothing as a high school assistant and then for next to nothing for five years as an assistant at Mesa, and he was rewarded with the head-coaching job two years ago. He was only 27, but his dream, to coach a major-college team, was no longer quite so far away.

The pantry was bare his rookie year, but Mesa went 15–15. Then, doing it his dad's way—his typical off-season day ran from 7 a.m. to 10 at night—he ran the summer league, organized a computerized scouting system, cultivated his high school coaching contacts, recruited at hours when other coaches relaxed, pushed his players through an exhaustive weightlifting program and then nurtured them at night with so many phone calls that his friends called him Ma Bell. He was single and on fire. "I could be a maniac," says Rob, "and I was."

The pantry filled fast. Twice in the summer league in 1995 his players whipped a team with four former Arizona State starters on it, and Rob's target was clear. He was going to take his father and his team back to Hutchinson and this time win the whole damn thing.

Richie? He would sure make things easier. Rob had seen him play in the annual summer tournament at Arizona State, which Richie's New York City club team, Riverside Church, traveled to each year. Just like all the other coaches, Rob was struck by the distance between Richie and the world's image of Richie. Just like all the other coaches, he got that same feeling in the pit of his stomach when he saw a talented high school player—if you didn't get him dunking *for* you, he might soon be dunking *on* you. Besides, Rob knew Ernie Lorch, the Riverside director, and already had taken a few of Lorch's kids at Mesa. And so Rob, too, was drawn in. Mesa would be Richie's safety net, the faraway junior college where he could go to heal himself and play ball if all the Division I scholarship offers went up in smoke.

And because there was so much smoke, and Richie kept hoping and waiting for the next Division I chance, his decision to go to Mesa occurred at the last minute, just a few days before the start of school last August. And because Richie waited, Rob had to wait, and by the time he found out Richie was coming, there was no chance for cool heads to sit and debate this and perhaps construct a plan. Rob told the story of Richie Parker to three women—his mother, his girlfriend and his girlfriend's mother, and they all agreed with him. "What Richie did was flat wrong," Rob says, "but are you going to be part of the problem or part of the solution?" And he insists—*are you crazy?*—that of course he notified his superiors, two of them, about Richie and his baggage.

But the Mesa athletic director, Allen Benedict, says he was told nothing of Richie's past, that all he got was a 9 p.m. call from Rob telling him that a great player was coming from New York. The next morning, while Richie was at 30,000 feet heading west across the heart of America, the junior college president was on the phone with Benedict, saying, "Why did a reporter from the *New York Post* just call me . . . and who is Richie Parker?" And then the National Organization for Women was checking in, and cameras were peering inside the gym for a peek at Richie, and a TV truck was pulling up to Benedict's house. "Whether you do something wrong or not isn't the point sometimes," says Benedict. "It's the perception."

Rob was called in to a meeting less than two weeks before the first practice and forced to quit. Richie called Rob, nearly in tears at what he had wrought.

As for Richie, he could stay, but he couldn't play basketball. College athletics, Mesa president Larry Christiansen reasoned, are like a driver's license—a privilege, not a right. What the westward trip and the open spaces had done for so many others, they couldn't do for Richie Parker.

Richie had to decide, then and there, what was most important in his life. He chose to stay at Mesa, take courses and learn who he was without a basketball. He would work the shot clock at games, like one of those earnest guys in glasses that no one ever notices, and by the end of the year the administrators at Mesa would all say good things about him.

Rob had to tell his father the terrible news. He knew his dad was on the edge of the cliff—doctors had said that if not for the zest that Bob derived from his work, his heart would've likely given way three or four years before—so the son tried to shrug and keep his face a blank, so he wouldn't give his father that nudge. Bob was devastated, but as with all his other pain, he tried to keep it inside. He was bewildered, too. The ethic he had passed on to his only child—outwork everyone and you'll succeed—had failed, been displaced, it seemed, by a new one: Image is everything.

Rob didn't eat for three days after that, unless you count the antacid medication. He wouldn't even show his girlfriend, Danelle Scuzzaro, how badly this hurt. On the fourth day after he was let go, he picked up a diamond ring at the jeweler's and took Danelle to dinner. Afterward, he dropped to his knee—cesium is the damnedest thing—and asked her to marry him. She said yes, and thank god.

Two weeks later, at 5:15 a.m., he got the call from his mother. His father's heart had stopped, at the age of 61. It might well have happened then anyway. "What happened to me didn't kill him," says Rob, "but it didn't help."

There was only one thing to be said for the timing. All the tears Rob had held back after losing his job could finally come out, and they did . . . again . . . and again . . . and again. . . .

ELEVEN

WAIT A moment. What about the reporter from the *New York Post*—isn't he here too? Sure, just a moment, he's still on the telephone. Gosh, look at him, just a kid, wouldn't even pass for 25. Just started at the *Post*, covering high school sports, when suddenly—*whoa!*—he has his teeth into the story of his life, and his incisors are wonderful.

Look at Barry Baum rolling out of bed in his Manhattan apartment and running, literally, to the newsstand at the corner of 79th and Broadway to check if the *Daily News* has scooped him on the Parker story. That has actually happened before, so Barry knows that sinking feeling. See him getting that 10 a.m. call from his editor, groggily picking up the phone—a medic on call in a tabloid war. "So what's goin' on with Parker today?" his editor demands. And Barry says, "I'll let you know," then shakes off the cobwebs and begins working the phones, looking for a tip. He loves this part, the detective work. And the most amazing thing keeps occurring. Because there's such an innocent charm about Barry, people *want* to help him.

Some high school scout or basketball junkie with his ear to the streets keeps slipping him the name of the next university showing interest in Richie, and then Barry plays his role, just as the university administrators and the coaches and the women's groups and the loved ones do. He becomes the Bunsen burner, the heat that agitates the cesium and fluorine molecules into rapid movement, more-violent collision. He leaps to call the university president and the campus women's center to ask that 64-megaton question—"How do you feel about your school recruiting a sex felon?"—and if they say they don't know who Richie Parker is, so they can't comment, he faxes them a pile of his Parker stories, and suddenly they have a comment. And all at once the coach and the athletic director are being called onto the president's carpet, or what's left of it, and then there's a follow-up exclusive story to write when they all abandon Richie, and there's no time to consider all the layers, all the moral nuances, because the editor's on the phone barking, "O.K., hurry, rewrite that for the second edition!"—just like in the movies. And then street vendors are snaking between the cars bottlenecked at the bridges and tunnels leading into the city the next morning, catching drivers' eyes with thick SEX FELON headlines, and every person who contributes his 50 cents confirms the Post editor's instincts and becomes another link in the chain.

"There were nights when I couldn't sleep, an adrenaline I had for a long time," says Barry. "I'd lie in bed, realizing I'd come to New York and made an impact on one of the biggest stories of the year."

Hadn't his editor at the *Post* told him, "We're going to put your name in lights," when he hired Barry in August 1994? Wasn't that music to his ears? Even as a little kid in Brooklyn Heights, he had dreamed of busting back-page stories for the New York tabloids. At 15 he talked his way into becoming the Knicks ball boy by rat-tat-tatting 10 letters to the team trainer, and then he parlayed that job into his own cable-TV show in Manhattan, *Courtside with Barry Baum*, by convincing the station of the wonderful access to big-name Knicks that a precocious 16-year-old ball boy had. He appeared on the televised dating show *Love Connection* three times, and when one of his dates sniffed about Barry's making the wrong turn on their evening out, he brought down the house by sniffing back, "Get a load of Miss Rand McNally, never made a wrong turn in her life!"

And then suddenly the kid who grew up calling *New York Post* and *Daily News* columnists with kudos and beg-to-differs is being lauded for his own back-page *Post* scoops on New York radio talk shows, being asked to appear on the all-sports station, WFAN, and invited to speak at a journalism symposium at Madison Square Garden with a poster board full of his Parker stories. Adrenaline, yes, but anguish, too, stuff you don't talk about when you're a guest on WFAN. Because the nasty phone calls to Barry's desk have begun, people hissing, "Leave Richie Parker alone!"

Then, when he's a guest on a radio talk show one day, a caller says, "Don't you see what you're doing? This is a black kid who comes from nowhere, and you're a white guy who probably comes from a lot of money." Barry blinks. "It hits me," he says. "That's true. I've always had everything, and I'd never even thought of the race factor." New York City high school coaches, his contacts, start saying, "C'mon, Barry, back off. What are you trying to prove?" Even his own father, Bruce, finally says, "Leave him alone already, Barry," and that stings.

"That even someone who knew me that well wouldn't realize that I'm just trying to do my job. . . . " he says. "I mean, don't give me credit for keeping Richie Parker out of college, but don't blame me for it either. And the more people tell me to *stop* reporting a story, the more it means it *is* a story, right? But I keep wondering about Richie. All that time, I couldn't talk to him because his lawyer wouldn't let me, so I couldn't feel him. Finally they let me. You know, it changes things once you talk to him. Before that he was an object, and it was easy to write, 'Richie Parker, sex felon,' because I didn't know him. He was the predator and the girl was the victim, right? I talked to him at a Rucker League game last August, and he actually smiled at me. A smile is a big thing.

"Look, I've never had a problem with Richie playing college basketball. It's not the colleges' job to punish him further. He should be allowed to play—but not without students and their parents being notified, maybe by a letter from the university administration. You know, like Megan's Law, notifying people that a sex felon is in their neighborhood. It's funny. It's like *I've* become Megan's Law for these universities. I'm the one who tells them he's coming. It was amazing how quickly it played out with Oral Roberts. I reported that the school was interested, the story breaks across the country, the TV reporters arrive on campus—and the school announces it has already pulled out! It was like the fire trucks coming, and there's no fire, the local residents have already put it out. These universities have no backbone! Every university president I talk to, except for maybe Stephen Trachtenberg, it's like talking to the same guy. Every one of them says, 'I can't believe my coach did this and that isn't what we stand for and blah-blah-blah. I'm convinced there's only one college president in the United States: He just keeps changing his name!"

One major-college coach, off the record, asks Barry what will happen if he takes the risk on Richie. What's Barry supposed to do, lie? He tells the truth, the coach says thank you and backs off, and—*poof!*—the chance is gone, the chemical reaction begun and finished before anyone ever even smelled it occurring. And it begins to dawn on Barry: "Somehow, I'm *in* this story. I'm not just the observer. People are making decisions based on my reporting. There I am, 25 years old and playing the part of deciding if this kid's going to get into college or not, and maybe, if he's good enough, even into the NBA. I have no agenda or angle at all, but he'd probably be playing now if I hadn't called Utah or GW or. . . .

"So where is the line? I've never been taught that line. I keep wondering, Am I doing the right thing? But I shouldn't have to make that choice. I started compiling a list in my mind of all the people whose lives I've affected, the people who have gotten fired, all the universities. And it tears me apart, because the last thing I want to do is hurt anyone. But I know if I stop reporting it and the *Daily News* gets the story, which you know they will, then my editor will call me and say, 'What's goin' on with Parker? What happened? Where are the words?' and what am I going to say? I can't win. So people blame me. It's like I was the one in the stairwell."

He stares off at the wall, catches his breath. "And it's not over yet," Barry says. "It's not over until I find out where Richie Parker's going."

TWELVE

ONE DAY about a month ago Richie Parker stepped into an airplane in Arizona. The plane rose, and he looked through the window one last time at the desert and flew back across America, with no idea what would happen next. "I've learned I can survive without basketball," he said last month. "I've learned how the real world is and that I'm stronger than I knew I was. There's less fear now. I know myself more. I trust people less, but that doesn't make me sad. Just more aware of things. I can still live a good life." And he said a lot more, but it would be improper to let him do it here, for it might mislead the reader into thinking this was a story about Richie Parker.

This land is vast, and it contains so many kinds of people, and that is its grace. Two weeks ago Gale Stevens Haynes, the 45-year-old provost of the Brooklyn campus of Long Island University—and the black mother of three teenage daughters—offered Richie Parker a basketball scholarship to her Division I school. She didn't pull the offer back when the *New York Post* reporter found out, and Richie accepted it. When asked why she did it, she said, "Unless there's an island that I don't know about, where we send people forever who have done something wrong, then we have to provide pathways for these people so they can rejoin society. If we don't, it can only explode. It can only explode in *all* of our faces."

Broken Promise

BY S.L. PRICE

He was the philosopher king of tennis, a gutsy champion with a social conscience, but when a sex scandal reduced Boris Becker to tabloid fodder, an SI writer who'd witnessed his rise and fall told the tale of a man trying to put the pieces back together.

HE FERRY SWINGS INTO MIAMI'S GOVERNMENT CUT, AIMING for the island. In a van parked on board, Boris Becker sits up in the passenger seat, the front row for an almost unnerving blast of postcard beauty: the buttery dying sunlight, the churning surf. He sees none of it. He has lived through enough South Beach springs to take such a vista for granted, and besides, he's distracted. First, there's that young woman in the back of the van, and yes, Becker is sure he knows why she is there.

Haven't months of headlines pronounced him Germany's most famous satyr? Isn't everyone trying to soften him up? Becker takes great pride in his ability to read all the angles, and he figures it's no mistake that every time he goes on a photo session lately, the photographer shows up with an attractive assistant/makeup artist/gofer. A week ago, at a shoot in Europe, the photographer brought a female assistant and two women with no apparent task. Next time, they joked, we'll bring 10 girls to help you relax. "As if that's all I'm interested in," Becker says.

Still, the makeup artist in the back of the van—who was brought along only to apply makeup—is gorgeous, and the 15-minute ride from Miami Beach to Fisher Island goes slowly. Becker twists around to give the young woman his full attention. For a time, he treats her every word as if it were dipped in gold.

His heart isn't quite in it, though. Becker trusts no one these days, and the ferry is his most immediate reminder why.

He has been making this trip often lately. His sons, seven-year-old Noah and one-year-old Elias, live in a luxury apartment on Fisher Island with his ex-wife, Barbara, and sometimes Becker spends the night there and wakes up like a ghost in what was, only a few months ago, his home. Passing through those rooms, he sees the mundane things—chairs, forks, bedsheets—that he once could lay a hand on and say, Mine. He sees Noah, growing fast. "This is the one loss I have," Becker says. "The fact that I cannot go in the bedroom at night and sneak up on him kills me sometimes. Just to be with him, hold him, smell him. . . . "

Instead, on this blustery March afternoon, Becker drifts. At 33, the greatest male champion in German history spends most of his time in the air or on the road, jetting from Munich to Majorca to Miami, adding to his $100 million fortune, looking to seal the deal that ignites the second act of his life. He looks drawn, thinner than he used to be, and his famous self-confidence comes and goes.

Talk in the van drifts to dating. Becker turns back in his seat. Someone jokes that a man is better off getting a prostitute. As the ferry chugs alongside Fisher Island, Becker stares at the thick green lawns, the impeccable quiet hovering ever closer. He nods. "It's more honest," he says. "Because at the end of the day, you always pay."

He waves a weary hand, describing in that feeble arc all he knows and doesn't know about love and women and his own stupidity. "You see?" Becker says, pointing to the shore. "That's my old apartment."

ONCE, BORIS BECKER was the most important man in tennis. Not just because of his popularity, which reached astounding levels, in and out of Germany, before he retired in 1999. And not just because of his success, though he made huge amounts of money and won plenty of tournaments. In fact, it's easy to discount Becker's stature as one of the game's historic figures: His six Grand Slam singles titles aren't half of Pete Sampras's total. Still, at a time when pro tennis seems to be swimming in an especially shallow pool, it's clear that the sport misses Becker for reasons beyond gate appeal. Sex has become tennis's driving force: The women sell cheesecake; the men rally under the banner of NEW BALLS PLEASE. Looks trump talent. The tour has become the world's richest high school.

Becker flew above all that. He never acted his age. In 1984 he arrived at his first Wimbledon at age 16 and, after tearing ankle ligaments in his third-round match against Bill Scanlon, insisted on hobbling over to shake his opponent's hand before being carried off on a stretcher. The next year he became the youngest man to win at the All England Club, hurling his massive body at the ball, shouldering past veteran Kevin Curren in the final as if Curren had no right to step on the same grass. A few weeks later, as his fame mushroomed and 200,000 German Kinder flocked to play tennis, the new teen idol told TIME magazine that the blind worship he saw in his fans' eyes had him worried. For the first time, Becker said, he understood how Hitler had happened.

This, of course, was a dangerous thing for an athlete to say. Becker risked alienating his public just as it was starting to love him, but he didn't care; gossip and play-by-play bored him. He wanted to engage the world beyond tennis, beyond the era's preoccupation with McEnrovian bile, and his earnestness elevated the conversation. "Those years—'85, '86, '87—Becker was the most natural, crystal-clear youngster I ever saw," says Ion Tiriac, Becker's former manager. "He didn't know how to lie, didn't need to lie, didn't need to find excuses or hype, or cry when he was losing. That's what made human beings around the world identify with him."

On the court Becker would curse himself and bleed from the knees, dive on the grass and scream. Off it, he provided a counterpoint to the bombastic Germans seen in one World War II movie after another. He was a philosopher king in shorts, complaining when British newspapers headlined any of his wins as a BLITZKRIEG and musing, after losing his Wimbledon crown at 19, "I didn't lose a war. Nobody died." He proclaimed solidarity with Amnesty International and with squatters in Hamburg, wore a Greenpeace patch where other players sported sneaker logos. He had charm, an outsized ego and, at times, real guts. In 1992, ignoring his nation's euphoria over reunification, Becker refused to serve as ambassador for Berlin's bid to host the 2000 Olympics, saying he feared a triumphant Germany might stir its citizens' old fantasies about a master race.

"He thinks about the big picture, which is very unusual these days," says Billie Jean King. "He's thoughtful, and he cares. Of his generation he was the only one. Tennis misses him."

However, as the white, straight, middle-class son of an architect from Leimen, Becker lacked the authority of a King or an Arthur Ashe. Yes, his parents had met in a displaced persons' camp after the war, but he was a child of privilege who could never embody his causes. Ivan Lendl dubbed Becker "the limousine radical," and it was true. Becker had strong opinions but no struggle. He had never really put himself on the line.

Then he fell in love. In the fall of 1991 Becker met Barbara Feltus, a model and aspiring actress, the daughter of an African-American serviceman and a white German woman. By that time Becker, at 23, had achieved all a tennis player could ask for: three Wimbledon titles, one U.S. and one Australian Open championship (a second Australian crown would come in 1996), two Davis Cup titles, a stint at No. 1. "She was spontaneous, very lively," Boris says of Barbara. "I was moody, didn't know whether I should continue tennis, and she brought sunshine into my life. She was the complete opposite of how I was."

At a New Year's Eve party in Australia, Becker decided to go public with the romance. Just before he and Barbara ventured downstairs and danced together for all to see, he stood in a hotel room and told her, "Tomorrow your life will be completely different—for the rest of your life."

Barbara had no idea how bad it could be. Death threats poured in. People shouted at tournaments that Barbara was a gold digger, a "black witch." Becker, Germany's most famous man, adored for his so-called Germanic blond looks and furious game, had betrayed something deep. One headline wailed WHY BORIS? WHY NOT ONE OF US? Neither Boris nor Barbara flinched. Fifteen months later he secreted a diamond ring in her whiskey sour and proposed. They shocked Germans by posing nude for a photo on the cover of the weekly magazine *Stern*. Becker threatened to leave Germany if the racist rants didn't stop.

After they married in 1993 and Noah was born and their devotion showed no sign of abating, a sea change occurred. By the mid-'90s Boris and Barbara had risen to a high station in German society, serving as liberal poster parents, "a symbol of the new Germany," Becker says. Now when he spoke out, he had all the authority he could handle. "I wasn't just talking about it; I lived it," he says. "I've felt racism because of her, because of Noah. Because they look a little different, they get treated differently, so it's credible if I talk about it now." "He was a kind of social hero," says Paul Sahner, a longtime friend of Becker's and a writer for *Bunte* magazine. "They were a glamour couple. Many people lived their dreams through Boris and Barbara."

So much so that, by 1997, when Becker curtailed his tournament play and their marriage started crumbling, Boris and Barbara still put on a perfect face. "We almost had no choice but to play along," says Becker, "and it put more pressure on the relationship than already existed. That's probably why we're divorced today. We started to play roles to please everyone."

The marriage ended with a spectacular crash. On Nov. 9, 2000, the 62nd anniversary of the Nazi attack on Jews known as Kristallnacht, Becker marched with 200,000 others through the streets of Berlin to protest Germany's rising tide of racist violence. He was the very picture of a serious man. Only one month later, he was an object of ridicule around the world.

Becker had no one to blame but himself. Since the previous March, he had been quietly pressed by a London-based Russian waitress-model for up to $5 million to support a daughter she claimed was his. Boris and Barbara agree that this didn't cause their split, but it didn't help that Barbara first learned of the baby when she took a call at home last August from the Russian woman herself.

On Nov. 23 Becker told his wife he wanted a separation, touching off a hurricane of marital nastiness. He says divorce was the furthest thing from his mind, but less than a week later Barbara flew to Miami with their sons, and on Dec. 8 she applied in Dade County Circuit Court for financial protection, child support and use of the $3 million Fisher Island condominium—in effect sidestepping a prenuptial agreement that entitled her to a single $2.5 million payoff. Charges and countercharges flew, sending the German media into what the weekly *Der Spiegel* called a "state of emergency."

Out spilled one revelation after another. In early December the press linked Becker with a German rap star named Sabrina Setlur after they were seen checking into the same Black Forest hotel at which Boris and Barbara had honeymooned in 1993. On Jan. 12 the Russian waitress-model, Angela Ermakova, went public, claiming that she and Becker had had sex in a broom closet at London's Nobu restaurant on the last night of June 1999. Becker called Ermakova's story "false," and—though he never elaborated—a flurry of reports appeared saying Becker planned to claim that the two had engaged only in oral sex and that Ermakova had transferred his semen to her womb as part of a blackmail scheme. The tabloids pounced. BECKER: RUSSIAN MAFIA TRIED TO STEAL MY SPERM.

On Feb. 4 Becker publicly blamed his divorce on Barbara's friendship with a racy group of Munich women who dubbed themselves the Tits and Ass Club. By contrast, he told *Der Spiegel*, "I took the job of father earnestly." He also told a German newspaper that the love between him and Setlur was a "little plant that must be fed." (Becker and Setlur have since broken up.) On Feb. 7 DNA tests confirmed his paternity of Ermakova's child, and Becker agreed to make payments to Ermakova that will eventually total about $1.5 million. "I take responsibility," he said in a statement to the press. "Children are the most innocent people in our world."

"If Boris had more than just charm and balls," says Samuel I. Burstyn, Barbara's divorce lawyer, "he'd really be dangerous."

It ended, as these things will, in a tawdry mess—and one in which Becker views himself as the greater victim. Divorce has a way of narrowing the broadest mind, and for the moment Becker's admits only his perspective. He has been deceitful but feels deceived. He admits affairs but insists that marriage should be bigger than infidelity, that it was his and Barbara's diverging priorities that led to the split.

"People kissed her ass, and she started to enjoy it," Becker says. "We didn't have enough time for us. There was too much party. She wanted to become a singer, and I'd say, 'We shouldn't forget family.' I'm not saying I was the best husband. I spent too much time away. But I was trying to make her aware that it's only the four of us. We're the boat, and we shouldn't rock the boat."

Barbara declined to be interviewed, but Burstyn says Boris's peccadillos alone set the boat rocking, and his rendezvous with Setlur at the honeymoon hotel convinced Barbara that the marriage was done. Boris, meanwhile, is sure Barbara had plotted to leave him for months. "On the other hand," he says, "I'm proud she is a smart lady and knows exactly what she's doing. I have more respect for her now than I had before."

This sounds odd, but then Becker also dined daily with his wife and kids during the legal maneuverings. On Jan. 4 he took the stand in a pretrial hearing and answered two hours of questions while Burstyn made him look like a cad for a live TV audience in Germany. That night, Becker went back to Fisher Island and, he says, told Barbara, "[If we go to trial], it's your turn. And not for two hours: My lawyer's going to grill you for six." Becker says she agreed to settle the case then, but Burstyn insists that two days before Becker was to give a deposition about his financial affairs, he called Burstyn at home and surrendered.

Either way, Becker lost. The boys would live with Barbara, she and Boris would share custody, and Barbara would get a package widely reported to be worth $14.4 million. Becker's consolation prize: On Jan. 18, Noah's seventh birthday, he spent the night at the Fisher Island condo for the first time since November, using a guest bedroom—an informal arrangement that will continue indefinitely. "We live during the day like a family," Becker says. "Then I sleep in my room, and she sleeps in hers. It's very, very weird."

There are times, he says, when he and Barbara ask each other, "What did we do?" Sometimes, he adds, they talk about getting back together, maybe even getting married again. "I love her," Becker says, "but that was a big hurt in December. I have made a lot of mistakes, some I will regret the rest of my life, but I would never do anything to purposely hurt my family. This woman had my heart. For her to do something like she did showed a side of her I didn't know. I'm scared. I'm basically scared of the woman."

SEVEN MIRRORS stand waiting on the stage. Becker takes his position before them, and the photographer starts snapping, belting out commands to the assistants who stand behind each mirror, adjusting. "Number 4, you're making him look like a giant," the photographer says.

"I am a giant," Becker says, and whether he is being serious is unclear. As a player, he assumed regal prerogatives, took massages during bathroom breaks, set up to receive serve only when he was good and ready. Of Wimbledon, he'd say, "This is where I live," and before each match that's how he would act.

"The attendants used to come in and say, 'Mr. Becker, five minutes,' " says Nick Bollettieri, who coached him in 1994 and '95. "He was in his jogging clothes, didn't pay attention. 'Mr. Becker, four minutes.' He would take the clothes off, fold them piece by piece. Go into the bathroom. 'Mr. Becker, it's time.' He would come out, slowly put on his tennis clothes. 'Mr. Becker, it's *time*.' But he wouldn't pay attention, and no referee said a word. They were scared s---less."

There are signs—a telltale use of the third person, a low-grade paranoia—that Becker's sense of his own importance has not diminished with the end of his career. If anything, two months on the front page of German newspapers have convinced him that he still takes up much space in the public imagination, his travails a delight for the masses.

"Finally: a little payback," he says. "Becker was the winner for so long. 'The best in tennis with the best-looking wife, beautiful kids, money, he's smart—whatever he touches is gold!' In Germany they thought they had me in a box, and they can't cope with the fact that I'm 33, single, so they stir it up. Because I am so much in that country."

Even now, Becker is the biggest name in Germany, eclipsing singers and chancellors. In the 20 months that he has been spokesman for America Online-Germany, the public's awareness of the brand has more than doubled, and his signature line, *Ich Bin Drin!* (I'm in!), has become the country's catchall phrase for going online. "I don't know if a Michael Jordan comparison is strong enough," says AOL-Germany marketing director Phillipp Schindler. "Boris's sympathy levels are outstanding. He is *the* German superstar."

This can carry Becker far, obviously, and he will need it. By the end of his playing days, the youthful clarity that so pleased Ion Tiriac had been muddied. Becker didn't train as hard as before, he bullied opponents with his stature. "I can describe Boris very quickly," says Bollettieri. "He knew a lot; what he didn't know, he thought he knew; and he would intimidate people into thinking that he knew it."

Becker has done well with his three Mercedes dealerships outside Berlin and by lending his name to AOL, DaimlerChrysler, Volkl rackets and the RTL television network. But his stint as Germany's Davis Cup manager ended in failure in 1999, largely because he couldn't get along with one of the country's leading players, Nicolas Kiefer. That same year Becker was the front man for a $300 million bid by the London-based agency Prisma to market the ATP Tour, but Prisma lost out because Becker demanded too much control. His short stint advising Australian star Mark Philippoussis at last year's Wimbledon fizzled too.

"He said he wanted to coach me and to help me with all sorts of things outside tennis," says another pro, Germany's Tommy Haas. "He promised two years ago that he would come to all the Masters Series tournaments because he had to go to them anyway [to do TV commentary]. That promise never came through." Becker's explanation: He wanted not just to advise Haas part time but to take charge of all decisions—coaching, marketing, scheduling—since, he reasoned, any failure would be blamed on him anyway. But Haas didn't want to split with IMG, and it's probably just as well: By then Becker's life had frayed at every seam.

Just as his marriage started to crumble, Becker's longtime business manager and close friend, Axel Meyer-Wolden, died of cancer in 1997. Two years later Becker's father, Karl-Heinz, died. Boris, a star since he was 16, had never indulged in the usual experimentation nor made the usual mistakes of a boy's late teens. Few were surprised when, at 32, he began indulging himself as never before.

His final day as a player, at Wimbledon in 1999, stands like a doorway between his glorious past and his soiled present. Becker, who'd made his name serving and volleying, lost in straight sets in the fourth round to Pat Rafter, the game's last serve-and-volley specialist. Becker knew he was done. He had liked sitting in the locker room during the rain delays that day, talking to older players back for seniors matches, but he felt removed from the whole scene, as if watching someone else complete his career. After losing he met with the press and began drinking. Barbara was seven months pregnant with Elias. She wanted to spend the night alone with Boris, but he had other ideas.

"This is the night!" Becker recalls. "I'm officially out, no way back, and I'm celebrating with my buddies, and we drink and drink. I have a big argument with her, and she goes crazy and I go crazy, and I say, 'This is a very important day of my life. On this night, I don't want to fight; it's not allowed.' But she went on and I went on, and I drink more. I was crazy."

He ended up at Nobu with friends, and there was Ermakova, the colossal blunder he didn't make until his career's last day. He was still buzzing with the thrill of his final match, still wanting a piece of the action. Then he was in a closet; standing outside himself for the second time that day, he watched someone named Boris Becker drunkenly sire a daughter. "I had no idea what I was doing," he says. "It wasn't an affair. It was just *poom-bah-boom!*"

Ever since, Becker has tried to keep busy. He has cooked in a high hat with chef Paul Bocuse in one TV special, hung out with designer Karl Lagerfeld in another. He owns half of Volkl and is trying to expand its market share.

He is doing plenty of interviews. Still, for a man so apt to see all kinds of signals of his own greatness, his world is sometimes dominated by a frivolousness that is almost painful to see.

One night in March, Becker went to a South Beach club called Bed, where dinner and drinks are served to customers as they loll about on giant beds. In walked Sean (Puffy) Combs, fresh from New York City and his recent acquittal on gun charges. Becker and Combs compared notes on their rides through the celebrity courtroom circus. "I was in bed with Puffy, actually—and a beautiful Indian girl and a Hungarian girl," Becker says. "They bring us a meal, the food, appetizers, fruit, champagne. Continental cuisine."

As his friend Sahner sees it, "Until 1999, Boris didn't have too much of a fun life. In Germany there's a lot of talk that he's running to find his lost childhood. Now he must find his way. If he continues to do what he did the last two years, it will be very dangerous for him and his image."

"He looks lost," says Haas. "He would like to have a family, but on the other hand he feels good about being free so he can do what he wants. It's tough: When you're on the tour for as long as he was, as successful as he was, as committed, you miss out on some things. Now he's really got nothing."

Yet, there are flashes. Becker is a member of the Europe-based Laureus World Sports Academy, a foundation devoted to achieving social change through sports, and when he heard about its support of the Richmond-based Midnight Basketball program, he insisted on seeing it in action. A barely publicized event in mid-April promised Becker little in the way of image-polishing, but he went to Richmond anyway, attended a workshop, gave a pep talk, borrowed some socks and sneakers and played ball—all before an audience of only 100 people. A month earlier, he had spent two days working in a Berlin program for juvenile delinquents. He still wants to make a difference.

"Boris is a serious man," says former U.S. track star Edwin Moses, chairman of the World Sports Academy. "We talk about social issues all the time. He's taken a beating, but with his strength and character, he'll come back and do some fantastic things."

The same objectivity that allowed Boris to admire Barbara even as she took him apart also enables him to see that his career created an entity beyond himself—a creature of fame named Boris Becker—that threatens to trap him in a life of fraudulence. He can't decide if his life is a Wagnerian opera or a Beckett farce, so he takes himself too seriously and pokes fun at himself, often at the same time. He recently finished shooting a movie in Germany, playing himself. "Yeah, myself," Becker says. "Whatever Boris I'm supposed to be that day."

A few nights later, Becker is at a dinner with Volkl retailers. He poses for pictures, jokes about his woman trouble, patiently answers the same old questions. "You still have that glow," says one man. "For my wife and her friends, you still have it. It's a blessing."

"And sometimes a curse," Becker says.

BECKER IS speeding down I-95, rushing to catch a flight to Los Angeles for the Academy Awards, during which he'll wander about with a TV crew and draw huge ratings in Germany. Earlier today, however, at a gathering with Volkl retailers on a tennis court at a Miami resort, he picked up a racket and swung it behind and over his head, tossing an imaginary ball. "It's still there," a retailer said. Becker nodded.

He still wants to play. He has scheduled a series of seniors events in the next few months, and there's persistent talk about a showcase match against John McEnroe after the women's final at this year's U.S. Open. Most of all, Becker wants one more taste of Wimbledon, wants to play doubles in the main draw—not this summer but next, when his game is in better shape. Becker knows he will never do anything as well as he played tennis. He has found only one thing that even brings him close.

"That Sunday afternoon: You're in the Wimbledon final, it's the third set, and you're about to win," Becker says. "Those 20 minutes and then that night and the next couple weeks are just heaven. This is something I miss. Because even with a great business deal, it's not the same sensation. Tennis is an art form. I feel as if I'm performing on a stage in front of millions of people, and I was sometimes able to fascinate them for two weeks. This culminates with a Sunday final, match point, and then all the celebrations. It's like a long foreplay that ends with a huge orgasm. That's what it is."

He does not laugh. Tennis is sex and sex is tennis; never mind that the last time he mixed the two, he ended up in a broom closet. Without one, life is dull for him. Without both, life is death. Becker would like to fall in love again. For now, though, he's thinking about the green grass of England, and giving the world one more big bang.

O Unlucky Man

BY WILLIAM NACK

*Fortune never smiled on Sonny Liston—not when he ruled the
heavyweight division with an aura of menace, and certainly not when he stepped
into the ring with Cassius Clay.*

S OMEDAY THEY'RE GONNA WRITE A BLUES SONG JUST FOR
fighters. It'll be for slow guitar, soft trumpet and a bell.
—*Charles (Sonny) Liston*

IT WAS already dark when she stepped from the car in front of her house
on Ottawa Drive, but she could see her pink Cadillac convertible and Sonny's
new black Fleetwood under the carport in the Las Vegas night.

Where could Charles be? Geraldine Liston was thinking.

All through the house the lamps were lit, even around the swimming pool
out back. The windows were open too, and the doors were unlocked. It was
quiet except for the television playing in the room at the top of the stairs.

By 9:30 p.m. on Jan. 5, 1971, Geraldine had not spoken to her husband for
12 days. On Christmas Eve she had called him from St. Louis after flying there
with the couple's seven-year-old son, Danielle, to spend the holidays with her
mother. Geraldine had tried to phone him a number of times, but no one had
answered at the house. At first she figured he must be off roistering in Los
Angeles, and so she didn't pay his absence any mind until the evening of
Dec. 28. That night, in a fitful sleep, she had a vision so unsettling that it
awakened her and sent her to her mother's room.

"I had the worst dream," Geraldine says. "He was falling in the shower and calling my name, 'Gerry, Gerry!' I can still see it. So I got real nervous. I told my mother, 'I think something's wrong.' But my mother said, 'Oh, don't think that. He's all right.'"

In fact, Sonny Liston had not been right for a long time, and not only for the strangely dual life he had been leading—spells of choirboy abstinence squeezed between binges of drinking and drugs—but also for the rudderless, unfocused existence he had been reduced to. Jobless and nearly broke, Liston had been moving through the murkier waters of Las Vegas's drug culture. "I knew he was hanging around with the wrong people," one of his closest friends, gambler Lem Banker, says. "And I knew he was in desperate need of cash."

So, as the end of 1970 neared, Liston had reached that final twist in the cord. Eight years earlier he was the undisputed heavyweight champion of the world— a 6 foot, 1½ inch, 215-pound hulk with upper arms like picnic roasts, two magnificent, 14-inch fists and a scowl that he mounted for display on a round, otherwise impassive face. He had won the title by flattening Floyd Patterson with two punches, left hooks down and up, in the first round of their fight on Sept. 25, 1962; 10 months later he had beaten Patterson again in one round.

LISTON DID not sidestep his way to the title; the pirouette was not among his moves. He reached Patterson by walking through the entire heavyweight division, leaving large bodies sprawled behind him: Wayne Bethea, Mike De-John, Cleveland Williams, Nino Valdes, Roy Harris, Zora Folley et al. Finally, a terrified Patterson waited for him, already fumbling with his getaway disguise, dark glasses and a beard.

Before the referee could count to 10 in that first fight, Liston had become a mural-sized American myth, a larger-than-life John Henry with two hammers, an 84-inch reach, 23 knockouts (in 34 bouts) and 19 arrests. Tales of his exploits spun well with the fight crowd over beers in dark-wood bars. There was the one about how he used to lift up the front end of automobiles. And one about how he caught birds with his bare hands. And another about how he hit speed bags so hard that he tore them from their hinges, and ripped into heavy bags until they burst, spilling their stuffing.

"Nobody hit those bags like Sonny," says 80-year-old Johnny Tocco, one of Liston's first and last trainers. "He tore bags up. He could turn that hook, put everything behind it. Turn and snap. Bam! Why, he could knock you across the room with a jab. I saw him knock guys out with a straight jab. Bam! In the ring, Sonny was a killing machine."

Perhaps no fighter had ever brought to the ring so palpable an aura of menace. Liston hammered out danger, he hammered out a warning. There was his fearsome physical presence; then there was his heavy psychic baggage, his prison record and assorted shadows from the underworld. Police in three cities virtually drove him out of town; in one of them, St. Louis, a captain warned Liston that he would wind up dead in an alley if he stayed.

In public Liston was often surly, hostile and uncommunicative, and so he fed one of the most disconcerting of white stereotypes, that of the ignorant, angry, morally reckless black roaming loose, with bad intentions, in white society. He became a target for racial typing in days when white commentators could still utter undisguised slurs without Ted Koppel asking them to, please, explain themselves. In the papers Liston was referred to as "a gorilla," "a latter day caveman" and "a jungle beast." His fights against Patterson were seen as morality plays. Patterson was Good, Liston was Evil.

On July 24, 1963, two days after the second Patterson fight, *Los Angeles Times* columnist Jim Murray wrote: "The central fact . . . is that the world of sport now realizes it has gotten Charles (Sonny) Liston to keep. It is like finding a live bat on a string under your Christmas tree."

The NAACP had pleaded with Patterson not to fight Liston. Indeed, many blacks watched Liston's spectacular rise with something approaching horror, as if he were climbing the Empire State Building with Fay Wray in his hands. Here suddenly was a baleful black felon holding the most prestigious title in sports. This was at the precise moment in history when a young civil rights movement was emerging, a movement searching for role models. Television was showing freedom marchers being swept by fire hoses and attacked by police dogs. Yet, untouched by image makers, Liston steadfastly refused to speak any mind but his own. Asked by a young white reporter why *he* wasn't fighting for freedom in the South, Liston deadpanned, "I ain't got no dog-proof ass."

Four months after Liston won the title, *Esquire* thumbed its nose at its white readers with an unforgettable cover. On the front of its December 1963 issue, there was Liston glowering out from under a tasseled red-and-white Santa Claus hat, looking like the last man on earth America wanted to see coming down its chimney.

Now, at the end of the Christmas holiday of 1970, that old black Santa was still missing in Las Vegas. Geraldine crossed through the carport of the Listons' split-level and headed for the patio out back. Danielle was at her side. Copies of the *Las Vegas Sun* had been gathering in the carport since Dec. 29. Geraldine opened the back door and stepped into the den. A foul odor hung in the air, permeating the house, and so she headed up the three steps toward the kitchen. "I thought he had left some food out and it had spoiled," she says. "But I didn't see anything."

Leaving the kitchen, she walked toward the staircase. She could hear the television from the master bedroom. Geraldine and Danielle climbed the stairs and looked through the bedroom door, to the smashed bench at the foot of the bed and the stone-cold figure lying with his back up against it, blood caked on the front of his swollen shirt and his head canted to one side. She gasped and said, "Sonny's dead."

"What's wrong?" Danielle asked.

She led the boy quickly down the stairs. "Come on, baby," she said.

ON THE AFTERNOON of Sept. 27, 1962, Liston boarded a flight from Chicago to Philadelphia. He settled into a seat next to his friend Jack McKinney, an amateur fighter who was then a sportswriter for the *Philadelphia Daily News*. This was the day Liston had been waiting for ever since he first laced on boxing gloves, at the Missouri State Penitentiary a decade earlier. Forty-eight hours before, he had bludgeoned Patterson to become heavyweight champion. Denied a title fight for years, barred from New York City rings as an undesirable, largely ignored in his adopted Philadelphia, Liston suddenly felt vindicated, redeemed. In fact, before leaving the Sheraton Hotel in Chicago, he had received word from friends that the people of Philadelphia were awaiting his triumphant return with a ticker-tape parade.

The only disquieting tremor had been some other news out of Philadelphia, relayed to him by telephone from friends back home, that *Daily News* sports editor Larry Merchant had written a column confirming Liston's worst fears about how his triumph might be received. Those fears were based upon the ruckus that had preceded the fight. *The New York Times*'s Arthur Daley had led the way: "Whether Patterson likes it or not, he's stuck with it. He's the knight in shining armor battling the forces of evil."

Now wrote Merchant: "So it is true—in a fair fight between good and evil, evil must win. . . . A celebration for Philadelphia's first heavyweight champ is now in order. Emily Post probably would recommend a ticker-tape parade. For confetti we can use shredded warrants of arrest."

The darkest corner of Liston's personality was his lack of a sense of self. All the signs from his past pointed the same way and said the same thing: dead end. He was the 24th of the 25 children fathered by Tobey Liston, a tenant cotton farmer who lived outside Forrest City, Ark. Tobey had two families, one with 15 children and the other with 10; Charles was born ninth to his mother, Helen. Outside the ring, he battled his whole life against writers who suggested that he was older than he claimed he was. "Maybe they think I'm so old because I never was really young," he said. Usually he would insist he was born on May 8, 1932, in the belly of the Great Depression, and he growled at reporters who dared to doubt him on this: "Anybody who says I'm not 30 is callin' my momma a liar."

"Sonny was so sensitive on the issue of his age because he did not really know how old he was," says McKinney. "When guys would write that he was 32 going on 50, it had more of an impact on him than anybody realized. Sonny didn't know who he was. He was looking for an identity, and he thought that being the champion would give him one."

Now that moment had arrived. During the flight home, McKinney says, Liston practiced the speech he was going to give when the crowds greeted him at the airport. Says McKinney, who took notes during the flight, "He used me as sort of a test auditor, dry-running his ideas by me."

Liston was excited, emotional, eager to begin his reign. "There's a lot of things I'm gonna do," he told McKinney. "But one thing's very important: *I want to reach my people.* I want to reach them and tell them, 'You don't have to worry about me disgracin' you. You won't have to worry about me stoppin' your progress.' I want to go to colored churches and colored neighborhoods. I know it was in the papers that the better class of colored people were hopin' I'd lose, even prayin' I'd lose, because they was afraid I wouldn't know how to act. . . . I remember one thing so clear about listening to Joe Louis fight on the radio when I was a kid. I never remember a fight the announcer didn't say about Louis, 'A great fighter and a credit to his race.' Remember? That used to make me feel real proud inside.

"I don't mean to be sayin' I'm just gonna be the champion of my own people," Liston continued. "It says now I'm the world's champion, and that's just the way it's gonna be. I want to go to a lot of places—like orphan homes and reform schools. I'll be able to say, 'Kid, I know it's tough for you and it might even get tougher. But don't give up on the world. Good things can happen if you let them.' "

Liston was ready. As the plane rolled to a stop, he rose and walked to the door. McKinney was next to him. The staircase was wheeled to the door. Liston straightened his tie and his fedora. The door opened, and he stepped outside. There was no one there except for airline workers, a few reporters and photographers and a handful of p.r. men. "Other than those, no one," recalls McKinney. "I watched Sonny. His eyes swept the whole scene. He was extremely intelligent, and he understood immediately what it meant. His Adam's apple moved slightly. You could feel the deflation, see the look of hurt in his eyes. It was almost like a silent shudder went through him. He'd been deliberately snubbed.

"Philadelphia wanted nothing to do with him. Sonny felt, after he won the title, that the past was forgiven. It was going to be a whole new world. What happened in Philadelphia that day was a turning point in his life. He was still the bad guy. He was the personification of evil. And that's the way it was going to remain. He was devastated. I knew from that point on that the world would never get to know the Sonny that I knew."

On the way out of the airport after a brief press conference, Sonny turned to McKinney and said, "I think I'll get out tomorrow and do all the things I've always done. Walk down the block and buy the papers, stop in the drugstore, talk to the neighbors. Then I'll see how the *real peoples* feel. Maybe then I'll start to feelin' like a champion. You know, it's really a lot like an election, only in reverse. Here I'm already in office, but now I have to go out and start campaignin'."

That was a campaign that Liston could never win. He was to be forever cast in the role of devil's agent, and never more so than in his two stunning, ignominious losses to Cassius Clay, then beginning to be known as Muhammad Ali. In the history of boxing's heavyweight division, never has a fighter fallen faster, and farther, than did Liston in the 15 months it took Ali to reduce him from being the man known as the fiercest alive to being the butt of jokes on TV talk shows.

"I THINK HE died the day he was born," wrote Harold Conrad, who did publicity for four of Liston's fights. By the nearest reckoning, that birth would have been in a tenant's shack, 17 miles northwest of Forrest City and about 60 west of Memphis. Helen had met Tobey in Mississippi and had gone with him to Arkansas around the time of World War I. Young Charles grew up lost among all the callused hands and bare feet of innumerable siblings. "I had nothing when I was a kid but a lot of brothers and sisters, a helpless mother and a father who didn't care about any of us," Liston said. "We grew up with few clothes, no shoes, little to eat. My father worked me hard and whupped me hard."

Helen moved to St. Louis during World War II, and Charles, who was living with his father, set out north to find her when he was 13. Three years later he weighed 200 pounds, and he ruled his St. Louis neighborhood by force. At 18, he had already served time in a house of detention and was graduating to armed robbery. On Jan. 15, 1950, Liston was found guilty of two counts of larceny from a person and two counts of first-degree robbery. He served more than two years in the Missouri state pen in Jefferson City.

The prison's athletic director, Father Alois Stevens, a Catholic priest, first saw Liston when he came by the gym to join the boxing program. To Stevens, Liston looked like something out of *Jane's Fighting Ships.* "He was the most perfect specimen of manhood I had ever seen," Stevens recalls. "Powerful arms, big shoulders. Pretty soon he was knocking out everybody in the gym. His hands were so large! I couldn't believe it. They always had trouble with his gloves, trouble getting them on when his hands were wrapped."

In 1952 Liston was released on parole, and he turned pro on Sept. 2, 1953, leveling Don Smith in the first round in St. Louis. Tocco met Liston when the fighter strolled into Tocco's gym in St. Louis. The trainer's first memory of Liston is fixed, mostly for the way he came in—slow and deliberate and alone, feeling his way along the edges of the gym, keeping to himself, saying nothing. That was classic Liston, casing every joint he walked into, checking for exits. As Liston began to work, Tocco saw the bird tracks up and down Liston's back, the enduring message from Tobey Liston.

"What are all those welts from?" Tocco asked him.

Said Liston, "I had bad dealin's with my father."

"He was a loner," Tocco says. "He wouldn't talk to nobody. He wouldn't go with nobody. He always came to the gym by himself. He always left by himself. The police knew he'd been in prison, and he'd be walking along and they'd always stop him and search him. So he went through alleys all the time. *He always went around things.* I can still see him, either coming out of an alley or walking into one."

Nothing was simpler for Liston to fathom than the world between the ropes—step, jab, hook—and nothing more unyielding than the secrets of living outside them. He was a mob fighter right out of prison. One of his managers, Frank Mitchell, the publisher of the *St. Louis Argus*, who had been arrested numerous times on suspicion of gambling, was a known front for John Vitale, St. Louis's reigning hoodlum. Vitale had ties to organized crime's two most notorious boxing manipulators: Frankie Carbo and Carbo's lieutenant, Frank (Blinky) Palermo, who controlled mob fighters out of Philadelphia. Vitale was in the construction business (among others), and when Liston wasn't fighting, one of his jobs was cracking heads and keeping black laborers in line. Liston always publicly denied this, but years later he confided his role to one of his closest Las Vegas friends, Davey Pearl, a boxing referee. "He told me that when he was in St. Louis, he worked as a labor goon," says Pearl, "breaking up strikes."

Not pleased with the company Liston was keeping—one of his pals was 385-pound Barney Baker, a reputed head-cracker for the Teamsters—the St. Louis police kept stopping Liston, on sight and without cause, until, on May 5, 1956, 3½ years after his release from prison, Liston assaulted a St. Louis policeman, took his gun, left the cop lying in an alley and hid the weapon at a sister's house. The officer suffered a broken knee and gashed face. The following December, Liston began serving nine months in the city workhouse.

Soon after his release Liston had his second run-in with a St. Louis cop. The officer had creased Liston's skull with a nightstick, and two weeks later the fighter returned the favor by depositing the fellow headfirst in a trash can. Liston then fled St. Louis for Philadelphia, where Palermo installed one of his pals, Joseph (Pep) Barone, as Liston's manager, and Liston at once began fighting the biggest toughs in the division. He stopped Bethea, who spit out seven teeth, in the first round. Valdes fell in three, and so did Williams. Harris swooned in one, and Folley fell like a tree in three. Eddie Machen ran for 12 rounds but lost the decision. Albert Westphal keeled in one. Now Liston had one final fight to win. Only Patterson stood between him and the title.

Whether or not Patterson should deign to fight the ex-con led, at the time, to a weighty moral debate among the nation's reigning sages of sport. What sharpened the lines were Liston's recurring problems with the law in Philadelphia, including a variety of charges stemming from a June 1961 incident in Fairmount Park. Liston and a companion had been arrested for stopping a female motorist after dark and shining a light in her car. All charges, including impersonating a police officer, were eventually dropped. A month before, Liston had been brought in for loitering on a street corner. That charge, too, was dropped. More damaging were revelations that he was, indeed, a mob fighter, with a labor goon's history. In 1960, when Liston was the No. 1 heavyweight contender, testimony before a U.S. Senate subcommittee probing underworld control of boxing had revealed that Carbo and Palermo together owned a majority interest in him. Of this, Liston said, he knew nothing. "Pep Barone handles me," he said.

"Do you think that people like (Carbo and Palermo) ought to remain in the sport of boxing?" asked the committee chairman, Tennessee Senator Estes Kefauver.

"I wouldn't pass judgment on no one," Liston replied. "I haven't been perfect myself."

In an act of public cleansing after the Fairmount Park incident, Liston spent three months living in a house belonging to the Loyola Catholic Church in Denver, where he had met Father Edward Murphy, a Jesuit priest, while training to fight Folley in 1960. Murphy, who died in 1975, became Liston's spiritual counselor and teacher. "Murph gave him a house to live in and tried to get him to stop drinking," Father Thomas Kelly, one of Murphy's closest friends, recalls. "That was his biggest problem. You could smell him in the mornings. Oh, poor Sonny. He was just an accident waiting to happen. Murph used to say, 'Pray for the poor bastard.' "

But even Liston's sojourn in Denver didn't still the debate over his worthiness to fight for the title. In this bout between good and evil, the clearest voice belonged to *New York Herald-Tribune* columnist Red Smith: "Should a man with a record of violent crime be given a chance to become champion of the world? Is America less sinful today than in 1853 when John Morrissey, a saloon brawler and political headbreaker out of Troy, N.Y., fought Yankee Sullivan, lammister from the Australian penal colony in Botany Bay? In our time, hoodlums have held championships with distinction. Boxing may be purer since their departure; it is not healthier."

Since he could not read, Liston missed many pearls, but friends read scores of columns to him. When Barone was under fire for his mob ties, Liston quipped, "I got to get me a manager that's not hot—like Estes Kefauver." Instead, he got George Katz, who quickly came to appreciate Liston's droll sense of humor. Katz managed Liston for 10% of his purses, and as the two sat in court at Liston's hearing for the Fairmount Park incident, Liston leaned over to Katz and said, "If I get time, you're entitled to 10 percent of it."

Liston was far from the sullen, insensitive brute of the popular imagination. Liston and McKinney would take long walks between workouts, and during them Liston would recite the complete dialogue and sound effects of the comedy routines of black comedians like Pigmeat Markham and Redd Foxx. "He could imitate what he heard down to creaking doors and women's voices," says McKinney. "It was hilarious hearing him do falsetto."

Liston also fabricated quaint metaphors to describe phenomena ranging from brain damage to the effects of his jab: "The middle of a fighter's forehead is like a dog's tail. Cut off the tail and the dog goes all whichway 'cause he ain't got no more balance. It's the same with a fighter's forehead."

He lectured occasionally on the unconscious, though not in the Freudian sense. Setting the knuckles of one fist into the grooves between the knuckles of the other fist, he would explain: "See, the different parts of the brain set in little cups like this. When you get hit a terrible shot—*pop!*—the brain flops out of them cups and you're knocked out. Then the brain settles back in the cups and you come to. But after this happens enough times, or sometimes even once if the shot's hard enough, the brain don't settle back right in them cups, and that's when you start needing other people to help you get around."

So it was that Liston vowed to hit Patterson on the dog's tail until his brain flopped out of its cups. Actually, he missed the tail and hit the chin. Patterson was gone. Liston had trained to the minute, and he would never again be as good a fighter as he was that night. For what? Obviously, nothing in his life had changed. He left Philadelphia after he won the title, because he believed he was being harassed by the police of Fairmount Park, through which he had to drive to get from the gym to his home. At one point he was stopped for "driving too slow" through the park. That did it. In 1963 he moved to Denver, where he announced, "I'd rather be a lamppost in Denver than the mayor of Philadelphia."

At times, in fact, things were not much better in the Rockies. "For a while the Denver police pulled him over every day," says Ray Schoeninger, a former Liston sparring partner. "They must have stopped him 100 times outside City Park."

He'd run on the golf course, and as he left in his car, they'd stop him. Twenty-five days in a row. Same two cops. They thought it was a big joke. It made me ashamed of being a Denver native. Sad they never let him live in peace."

Liston's disputes were not always with the police. After he had won the title, he walked into the dining room of the Beverly Rodeo Hotel in Hollywood and approached the table at which former rum-runner Moe Dalitz, head of the Desert Inn in Las Vegas and a boss of the old Cleveland mob, was eating. The two men spoke. Liston made a fist and cocked it. Speaking very distinctly, Dalitz said, "If you hit me, nigger, you'd better kill me. Because if you don't, I'll make one telephone call, and you'll be dead in 24 hours." Liston wheeled and left.

The police and Dalitz were hardly Liston's only tormentors. There was a new and even more inescapable disturber of his peace: the boisterous Clay. Not that Liston at first took notice. After clubbing Patterson, he took no one seriously. He hardly trained for the rematch in Las Vegas. Clay, who hung around Liston's gym while the champion went through the motions of preparing for Patterson, heckled him relentlessly. Already a minor poet, Clay would yell at Liston: "Sonny is a fatty. I'm gonna whip him like his daddy!" One afternoon he rushed up to Liston, pointed to him and shouted: "He ain't whipped nobody! Who's he whipped?" Liston, sitting down, patted a leg and said, "Little boy, come sit in my lap." But Clay wouldn't sit; he was too busy running around and bellowing, "The beast is on the run!"

Liston spotted Clay one day in the Thunderbird Casino, walked up behind him and tapped him on the shoulder. Clay turned, and Liston cuffed him hard with the back of his hand. The place went silent. Young Clay looked frightened. "What you do that for?" he said.

" 'Cause you're too ------- fresh," Liston said. As he headed out of the casino, he said, "I got the punk's heart now."

That incident would be decisive in determining the outcome of the first Liston-Clay fight, seven months later. "Sonny had no respect for Clay after that," McKinney says. "Sonny thought all he had to do was take off his robe and Clay would faint. He made this colossal misjudgment. He didn't train at all."

If he had no respect for Clay, Liston was like a child around the radio hero of his boyhood, Joe Louis. When George Lois, then an art director at *Esquire*, decided to try the black-Santa cover, he asked his friend Louis to approach Liston. Liston grudgingly agreed to do the shoot in Las Vegas. Photographer Carl Fischer snapped one photograph, whereupon Liston rose, took off the cap and said, "That's it." He started out the door. Lois grabbed Liston's arm. The fighter stopped and stared at the art director. "I let his arm go," Lois recalls.

While Liston returned to the craps tables, Lois was in a panic. "One picture!" Lois says. "You need to take 50, 100 pictures to make sure you get it right." He ran to Louis, who understood Lois's dilemma. Louis found Liston shooting craps, walked up behind him, reached up, grabbed him by an ear and marched him out of the casino. Bent over like a puppy on a leash, Liston followed Louis to the elevator, with Louis muttering, "Come on, git!" The cover shoot resumed.

A few months later, of course, Clay handled Liston almost as easily. Liston stalked and chased, but Clay was too quick and too fit for him. By the end of the third round Liston knew that his title was in peril, and he grew desperate. One of Liston's trainers, Joe Pollino, confessed to McKinney years later that Liston ordered him to rub an astringent compound on his gloves before the fourth round. Pollino complied. Liston shoved his gloves into Clay's face in the fourth, and the challenger's eyes began burning and tearing so severely that he could not see. In his corner, before the fifth round, Clay told his handlers that he could not go on. His trainer, Angelo Dundee, had to literally push him into the ring. Moving backward faster than Liston moved forward, Clay ducked and dodged as Liston lunged after him. He survived the round.

By the sixth, Clay could see clearly again, and as he danced and jabbed, hitting Liston at will, the champion appeared to age three years in three minutes. At the end of that round, bleeding and exhausted, he could foresee his humiliating end. His left shoulder had been injured—he could no longer throw an effective punch with it—and so he stayed on his stool, just sat there at the bell to start Round 7.

There were cries that Liston had thrown the fight. That night Conrad, Liston's publicist, went to see him in his room, where Liston was sitting in bed, drinking.

"What are they sayin' about the fight?" Liston asked.

"That you took a dive," said Conrad.

Liston raged. "Me? Sell my title? Those dirty bastards!" He threw his glass and shattered it against the wall.

The charges of a fix in that fight were nothing compared with what would be said about the rematch, in Lewiston, Maine, during which Liston solidified his place in boxing history. Ali, as the young champion was now widely called, threw one blow, an overhand right so dubious that it became known as the Phantom Punch, and suddenly Liston was on his back. The crowd came to its feet in anger, yelling, "Fake! Fake!"

Ali looked down at the fallen Liston, cocked a fist and screamed, "Get up and fight, sucker! Get up and fight!"

There was chaos. Referee Joe Walcott, having vainly tried to push Ali to a neutral corner, did not start a count, and Liston lay there unwilling to rise. "Clay caught me cold," Liston would recall. "Anybody can get caught in the first round, before you work up a sweat. Clay stood over me. I never blacked out.

But I wasn't gonna get up, either, not with him standin' over me. See, you can't get up without puttin' one hand on the floor, and so I couldn't protect myself."

The finish was as ugly as a Maine lobster. Walcott finally moved Ali back, and as Liston rose, Walcott wiped off his gloves and stepped away. Ali and Liston resumed fighting. Immediately, Nat Fleischer, editor of *The Ring* magazine, who was sitting next to the official timer, began shouting for Walcott to stop the fight. Liston had been down for 17 seconds, and Fleischer, who had no actual authority at ringside, thought the fight should have been declared over. Walcott left the two men fighting and walked over to confer with Fleischer. Though he had never even started a count, Walcott then turned back to the fighters and, incredibly, stepped between them to end the fight. "I was never counted out," Liston said later. "I coulda got up *right* after I was hit."

No one believed him, of course, and even Geraldine had her doubts. Ted King, one of Liston's seconds, recalls her angrily accusing Sonny later that night of going in the water.

"You could have gotten up and you stayed down!" she cried.

LISTON LOOKED pleadingly at King. "Tell her, Teddy," he said. "Tell her I got hit."

Some who were at ringside that night, and others who have studied the films, insist that Ali indeed connected with a shattering right. But Liston's performance in Lewiston has long been perceived as a tank job, and not a convincing one at that. One of Liston's assistant trainers claims that Liston threw the fight for fear of being murdered. King now says that two well-dressed Black Muslims showed up in Maine before the fight—Ali had just become a Muslim—and warned Liston, "You get killed if you win." So, according to King, Liston chose a safer ending. It seems fitting somehow that Liston should spend the last moments of the best years of his life on his back while the crowd showered him with howls of execration. Liston's two losses to Ali ended the short, unhappy reign of the most feared—and the most relentlessly hounded—prizefighter of his time.

Liston never really retired from the ring. After two years of fighting pushovers in Europe, he returned to the U.S. and began a comeback of sorts in 1968. He knocked out all seven of his opponents that year and won three more matches in 1969 before an old sparring partner, Leotis Martin, stopped him in the ninth round of a bout on Dec. 6. That killed any chance at a title shot. On June 29, 1970, he fought Chuck Wepner in Jersey City. Tocco, Liston's old trainer from the early St. Louis days, prepared him for the fight against the man known as the Bayonne Bleeder. Liston hammered Wepner with jabs, and in the sixth round Tocco began pleading with the referee to stop the fight. "It was like blood was coming out of a hydrant," says Tocco. The referee stopped the bout in the 10th; Wepner needed 57 stitches to close his face.

That was Liston's last fight. He earned $13,000 for it, but he wound up broke nonetheless. Several weeks earlier, Liston had asked Banker to place a $10,000 bet for him on undefeated heavyweight contender Mac Foster to whip veteran Jerry Quarry. Quarry stopped Foster in the sixth round, and Liston promised Banker he would pay him back after the Wepner fight. When Liston and Banker boarded the flight back to Las Vegas, Liston opened a brown paper bag, carefully counted out $10,000 in small bills and handed the wad to Banker. "He gave the other $3,000 to guys in his corner," Banker said. "That left him with nothing."

In the last weeks of his life Liston was moving with a fast crowd. At one point a Las Vegas sheriff warned Banker, through a mutual friend, to stay away from Liston. "We're looking into a drug deal," said the sheriff. "Liston is getting involved with the wrong people." At about the same time two Las Vegas policemen stopped by the gym and told Tocco that Liston had recently turned up at a house that would be the target of a drug raid. Says Tocco, "For a week the police were parked in a lot across the street, watching when Sonny came and who he left with."

On the night Geraldine found his body, Liston had been dead at least six days, and an autopsy revealed traces of morphine and codeine of a type produced by the breakdown of heroin in the body. His body was so decomposed that tests were inconclusive—officially, he died of lung congestion and heart failure—but circumstantial evidence suggests that he died of a heroin overdose. There were fresh needle marks on one of his arms. An investigating officer, Sergeant Gary Beckwith, found a small amount of marijuana along with heroin and a syringe in the house.

Geraldine, Banker and Pearl all say that they had no knowledge of Liston's involvement with drugs, but law enforcement officials say they have reason to believe that Liston was a regular heroin user. It is possible that those closest to him may not have known of his drug use. Liston had apparently lived two lives for years.

Pearl was always hearing reports of Liston's drinking binges, but Liston was a teetotaler around Pearl. "I never saw Sonny take a drink," says Pearl. "Ever. And I was with him hundreds of times over the last five years of his life. He'd leave me at night, and the next morning someone would say to me, 'You should have seen your boy, Liston, last night. Was he ever drunk!' I once asked him, 'What is this? You leave me at night and go out and get drunk?' He just looked at me. I never, ever suspected him of doing dope. I'm telling you, I don't think he did."

Some police officials and not a few old friends think that Liston may have been murdered, though they have no way of proving it now. Conrad believes that Liston became deeply involved in a loan-sharking ring in Las Vegas, as a bill collector, and that he tried to muscle in for a bigger share of the action. His employers got him drunk, Conrad surmises, took him home and stuck him with a needle. There are police in Las Vegas who say they believe—but are unable to prove—that Liston was the target of a hit ordered by Ash Resnick, an old associate of Liston's with whom the former champion was having a dispute over money. Resnick died two years ago.

Geraldine has trouble comprehending all that talk about heroin or murder. "If he was killed, I don't know who would do it," she says. "If he was doing drugs, he didn't act like he was drugged. Sonny wasn't on dope. He had high blood pressure, and he had been out drinking in late December. As far as I'm concerned, he had a heart attack. Case closed."

There is no persuasive explanation of how Liston died, so the speculation continues, perhaps to last forever.

Liston is buried in Paradise Memorial Gardens, in Las Vegas, directly under the flight path for planes approaching McCarran International Airport. The brass plate on the grave is tarnished now, but the epitaph is clear under his name and the years of his life. It reads simply: A MAN. Twenty years ago Father Murphy flew in from Denver to give the eulogy, then went home and wept for an hour before he could compose himself enough to tell Father Kelly about the funeral. "They had the funeral procession down the Strip," Murphy said. "Can you imagine that? People came out of the hotels to watch him pass. They stopped everything. They used him all his life. They were still using him on the way to the cemetery. There he was, another Las Vegas show. God help us."

In the end, it seemed fitting that Liston, after all those years, should finally play to a friendly crowd on the way to his own burial—with a police escort, the most ironic touch of all.

Geraldine remained in Las Vegas for nine years after Sonny died—she was a casino hostess—then returned to St. Louis, where she had met Sonny after his parole, when he was working in a munitions factory. She has never remarried, and today works as a medical technician. "He was a great guy, great with me, great with kids, a gentle man," says Geraldine.

With Geraldine gone from Las Vegas, few visit Sonny's grave anymore. Every couple of minutes a plane roars over, shaking the earth and rattling the broken plastic flowers that someone placed in the metal urn atop his headstone. "Every once in a while someone comes by and asks to see where he's buried," says a cemetery worker. "But not many anymore. Not often."

VIII

MUSIC TO THE EAR

King of the Sports Page

BY RICK REILLY

When this moving tribute by a former colleague and longtime admirer was published, Jim Murray was America's premier sports columnist, a man who left 'em laughing even as he endured unthinkable losses.

THE THING ABOUT JIM MURRAY IS THAT HE LIVED "HAPPILY" but somebody ran off with his "ever after." It's like the guy who's ahead all night at poker and then ends up bumming cab money home. Or the champ who's untouched for 14 rounds and then gets KO'd by a pool-hall left you could see coming from Toledo.

Murray is a 750-word column, and 600 of those are laughs and toasts. How many sportswriters do you know who once tossed them back with Bogie? Wined and dined Marilyn Monroe? Got mail from Brando? How many ever got mentioned in a governor's state of the state address? Flew in Air Force One?

How big is Murray? One time he couldn't make an awards dinner so he had a sub—Bob Hope.

Murray may be the most famous sportswriter in history. If not, he's at least in the photo. What's your favorite Murray line? At the Indy 500: "Gentlemen, start your coffins"? Or "[Rickey Henderson] has a strike zone the size of Hitler's heart"? Or that UCLA coach John Wooden was "so square, he was divisible by four"? How many lines can you remember by any other sportswriter?

His life was all brass rails and roses—until this last bit, that is. The end is all wrong. The scripts got switched. They killed the laugh track, fired the gag writers and spliced in one of those teary endings you see at Cannes. In this one, the guy ends up with his old typewriter and some Kodaks and not much else except a job being funny four times a week.

They say that tragedy is easy and comedy is hard.

Know what's harder?

Both at once.

Murray on Large People

MERLIN OLSEN: " . . . went swimming in Loch Ness—and the monster got out."

FRANK HOWARD: " . . . so big, he wasn't born, he was founded . . . not actually a man, just an unreasonable facsimile."

BOOG POWELL: " . . . when the real Boog Powell makes . . . the Hall of Fame, they're going to make an umbrella stand out of his foot."

BILL BAIN: "Once, when an official dropped a flag and penalized the Rams for having 12 men on the field . . . two of them were Bain."

ARNOLD PALMER had two of them bronzed. Jack Nicklaus calls them "a breath of fresh air." Groucho Marx liked them enough to write to him. Bobby Knight once framed one, which is something like getting Billy Graham to spring for drinks. Since 1961, a Jim Murray column in the *Los Angeles Times* has been quite often a wonderful thing. (He's carried by more than 80 newspapers today and at one time was in more than 150.) Now 66, Murray has been cranking out the best-written sports column this side (some say that side) of Red Smith. But if a Smith column was like sitting around Toots Shor's and swapping stories over a few beers, a Murray column is the floor show, a setup line and a rim shot, a corner of the sports section where a fighter doesn't just get beaten up, he becomes "sort of a complicated blood clot." Where golfers are not athletes, they're "outdoor pool sharks." And where Indy is not just a dangerous car race, it's "the run for the lilies."

In press boxes Murray would mumble and fuss that he had no angle, sigh heavily and then, when he had finished his column, no matter how good it was, he would always slide back in his chair and say, "Well, fooled 'em again."

Murray must have fooled all the people all the time, because in one stretch of 16 years he won the National Sportswriter of the Year award 14 times, including 12 years in a row. Have you ever heard of anybody winning 12 *anythings* in a row?

After a Lakers playoff game against the SuperSonics in 1979, Muhammad Ali ran into Murray outside the locker room and said, "Jim Murray! Jim Murray! The greatest sportswriter of all time!"

Which leaves only one question.

Was it worth it?

On Grouches

NORM VAN BROCKLIN: " . . . a guy with the nice, even disposition of a top sergeant whose shoes are too tight."

PAUL BROWN: " . . . treated his players as if he had bought them at auction with a ring in their noses. . . . "

CONRAD DOBLER: former guard for the St, Louis Cardinals: "To say Dobler 'plays' football is like saying the Gestapo 'played' 20 Questions."

WOODY HAYES: "Woody was consistent. Graceless in victory and graceless in defeat."

Marilyn Monroe and Murray were having dinner at a Sunset Boulevard restaurant. This was not exactly an AP news flash. Murray was TIME magazine's Hollywood reporter from 1950 to 1953, and you could throw a bucket of birdseed in any direction at Chasen's and not hit anybody who didn't know him. He has played poker with John Wayne ("he was lousy"), kibitzed with Jack Benny (who gave him an inscribed, solid-gold money clip) and golfed with Bing Crosby (later, Crosby sent him clippings and column ideas).

On this particular night, somewhere around dessert, Monroe started looking as if she'd swallowed her napkin. "What's wrong?" Murray asked. "Jim," she said, "would you mind if I left with someone else?"

"Not as long as you introduce me."

"O.K." She waved to a man across the room, who, sheepishly, made his way to the table.

"Jim, I would like you to meet Joe DiMaggio."

Not bad company for a kid who came up through the Depression in his grandfather's standing-room-only house in Hartford, Conn., where, at various times, the roster consisted of himself, his two sisters, his divorced father, his grandparents, two cousins and two uncles, including, of course, Uncle Ed, the one who cheated at dice, a man so bored by work that "he couldn't even stand to watch" people work.

For his part, Murray liked to write, and his first critical success was a 50-word essay on his handpicked American League all-star team. For winning the contest, he received a razor. He was 10.

Murray devoured any book featuring European history, and so, after graduating from Trinity College in Hartford and working a city-side stint at the *New Haven Register*, it is no wonder that when a real war came along and history was being made, he wanted to see it up close. But as a youth, he had had rheumatic fever, and that made him 4-F. He was so disappointed that he wouldn't be seeing Europe that he took the first and farthest-going train out to see distant parts of his own country. Besides, "I wanted to be as far away as I could when the casualties started coming in," he says. "I didn't want any mothers leaning out the window and saying, 'Here's my son with a sleeve where his arm used to be. What's the Murray boy doing walking around like that?' "

The train was bound for Los Angeles, where Murray talked his way into a job as a reporter and eventually became a rewrite man for the Hearst-owned *L.A. Examiner*. Those were gory, glory days for Murray. "There was seldom a dull moment," he wrote in *The Best of Jim Murray*. "And if there were, the front page of the *Examiner* never admitted it."

He specialized in murders. He wrote ". . . we slept with our socks on, like firemen waiting for that next alarm." But Murray never could get used to the blood. Once he covered a story about a little girl who was run over by a truck and lost a leg. Murray took the $8 he had left from his $38 paycheck and bought her an armful of toys.

That figured. Murray always was a sucker for a pretty face. And in those days, in a town with pink stucco houses and restaurants shaped like brown derbies, every nightclub window was filled with pretty faces. One night, Murray and a cohort were entertaining two of them when Jim went to call his best friend. The friend had good news.

"You know that girl over at the Five Seventy Five Club that you're always saying melts your heart? The one who plays the piano?"

"Yeah, so?" Murray said.

"If you can get over here in the next five minutes, she said she'd like to meet you."

Murray threw $2 on the table, grabbed his coat and headed for the door. Outside, his nightclub buddy caught up with him.

"I'm coming, too," he said.

"Why?" Murray asked.

"Because those two girls were mad enough to kill one of us, and it wasn't going to be you."

Murray married the girl at the piano, Gerry Brown, and theirs was a 38-year date. Folks say you've never seen two people carry on so. The Murrays appeared to be happiest at the piano, with Gerry playing (she was an accomplished pianist) and Jim belting out maudlin Irish songs. "If the phone rang at two in the morning, you knew who it was," says Tom McEwen of *The Tampa Tribune*.

"It was the Murrays saying, 'All right, what do you want to hear?' And you'd say, 'Well, whatever you feel like.' And Murray would break into *Galway Bay*."

Murray longed to be a foreign correspondent—"and wear a trench coat and carry a Luger"—but when TIME called with $7,000 a year, he took it. Over the years he worked on a dozen cover stories on such subjects as Mario Lanza, the Duke, Betty Hutton and Marlon Brando.

"You'd go knock on Brando's door," Murray says, "and you'd knock and you'd knock for an hour and he'd never answer it. But as soon as you walked away, he'd fling it open and cackle like a rooster."

Humphrey Bogart became a friend, too. "He was the kind of guy who'd get nasty after a couple of drinks. What's the old line? 'A couple of drinks and Bogart thinks he's Bogart.' That's how he was. . . . But I remember when he was dying, his wife, Lauren Bacall, would allow him only one drink a day, and if I was coming over he'd wait, because he knew I'd have it with him."

When a sports assignment in Los Angeles came up at TIME, Murray got it—by default. His proclivity for sports was so strong that, in 1953, when Henry Luce decided to launch a sports magazine, Murray was asked to help start it up. He did, and a year later SPORTS ILLUSTRATED was in print. Although Murray did return to TIME for a while, he eventually became SI's West Coast correspondent. In 1961 he jumped to the L.A. *Times*, where he was ready to take on the daily world of sports. Unfortunately, that world was not ready to take him on.

Letter from a Rookie's Wife

Dearest Darling:

How are you? . . . I am working now at the Bon Ton Grill. . . . All the fellows from the box works ask for you and say, 'Boy, I bet if that old husband of yours could only see you in them net stockings he'd bat a thousand. . . . '

The other night was election night and the bar had to be closed; so I had the whole gang over to our house. . . . The party wasn't as noisy as the papers said. . . . I didn't see why the police came. . . .

I sure want you to meet Cesar [a new roomer]. . . . [He] feels terrible he had to take this long business trip just the time you come home. . . . He'll come back. He has to; he has the car.

Faithfully yours, Cuddles.

BACK IN 1961, before the Computer Age, writers on the road would type hard copy and Western Union would wire it to the home papers. Except for Murray's stuff. The guys from Western Union would come back to Jim looking befuddled.

"Hey, Murray," they would ask, "you *sure* you want to say this?"

Says Murray, "I think they kept waiting for 'and then, his bat flashing in the sun, the Bambino belted a four-ply swat,' and it never came."

What came instead were one-line snapshots that a hundred fulminations couldn't top. Elgin Baylor was "as unstoppable as a woman's tears." Dodger manager Walt Alston would "order corn on the cob in a Paris restaurant."

It was the kind of stuff that the guy with a stopwatch hanging from his neck hated, but almost everybody else liked—especially women. "I love your column," one female fan wrote him, "even when I don't know what you're talking about."

Murray became nearly as famous as his subjects. Once, during a tournament, Arnold Palmer's golf ball rolled into a gully, leaving him an impossible shot out of a thicket. Just then he saw Murray in the gallery. "Well," Palmer said, "you're always writing about Hogan. What would Hogan do in a situation like this?"

Said Murray, "Hogan wouldn't *be* in a situation like that."

In 1969 Texas and Arkansas met in Fayetteville in a classic battle for number one, a football game attended by President Nixon. After the game Murray was slammed into a chain link fence by a Secret Service man who apparently thought Murray looked suspicious. Murray found himself a foot off the ground, suspended only by his collar. Just then, Nixon walked by.

"How ya' doin', Jim?" Nixon said.

"I'd be better," Murray said, "if you could get this monkey to put me down."

On Cities

LONG BEACH: "The seaport of Iowa . . . a city which, rumor has it, was settled by a slow leak in Des Moines."

SAN FRANCISCO: " . . . it's not a town, it's a no-host cocktail party. If it were human, it'd be W .C. Fields. It has a nice, even climate. It's always winter."

CINCINNATI: "They still haven't finished the freeway outside the ballpark . . . it's Kentucky's turn to use the cement mixer."

ST LOUIS: " . . . had a bond issue recently and the local papers campaigned for it on a slogan 'Progress or Decay,' and decay won in a landslide."

OAKLAND: " . . . is this kind of town: You have to pay 50 cents to go from Oakland to San Francisco. *Coming* to Oakland from San Francisco is free."

THE TWIN CITIES: " . . . didn't like each other and from what I could see I didn't blame either of them."

BALTIMORE: " . . . a guy just standing on a corner with no place to go and rain dripping off his hat. Baltimore's a great place if you're a crab."

LOS ANGELES: " . . . underpoliced and oversexed."

Murray and nuclear waste dumps have a lot in common. Everybody likes them until one shows up in the backyard.

Take the state of Iowa. When the University of Iowa got stuck on its ear in the Rose Bowl this year, Murray felt for the visiting vanquished:

" . . . I mean, you're going to have to start covering your eyes when these guys come to town in the family Winnebago with their pacemakers and the chicken salad. . . . They're going home, so to speak, with a deed to the Brooklyn Bridge and a watch that loses an hour a day and turns green on their arm."

That ruffled Iowans so much that two weeks later Governor Terry Branstad began his state of the state message (as if he didn't have more pressing issues) with a comment for Murray: "Jim, we're proud to be Iowans. . . ." the governor said. "We're tough and we're coming back."

No, no, no, Governor! You're taking it all wrong. To have your nose tweaked by Murray is to be hockey-pucked by Don Rickles. Look on it as a privilege. You're one of the lucky ones. Some people roast celebs. Murray roasts America. He has zinged and zapped every place from Detroit (". . . should be left on the doorstep for the Salvation Army"), to Munich, West Germany ("Akron with a crewcut!").

In fact, Murray maintains Spokane once got to feeling neglected and wrote in asking for the treatment. Always helpful, Murray wrote: "The trouble with Spokane . . . is that there's nothing to do after 10 o'clock. In the morning. But it's a nice place to go for breakfast."

Besides, if Murray had dropped dead as thousands have asked him to, sports wouldn't be the same. He has championed dozens of causes, many as stark as black and white, and they've made a difference in the nation's landscape. It was Murray's badgering of the Masters, for instance, that helped that tournament change its Caucasians-only stance. "It would be nice to have a black American at Augusta in something other than a coverall. . . . "

He was incredulous that Satchel Paige was having difficulty being inducted into the Hall of Fame: "Either let him in the front of the Hall—or move the damn thing to Mississippi."

He championed the cause of the beleaguered, retired Joe Louis: "As an economic entity, Joe Louis disappeared into a hole years ago and pulled it in after him. He cannot tunnel out in his lifetime. He owes the United States more than some European allies."

Crazy, isn't it? For a man who is half blind, Murray sure could see.

I lost an old friend the other day. He was blue eyed, impish, he cried a lot with me, laughed a lot with me, saw a great many things with me. . . .

He had a pretty exciting life. He saw Babe Ruth hit a home run when we were both 12 years old. He saw Willie Mays steal second base. . . . He saw Rocky Marciano get up. . . . You see, the friend I lost was my eye. . . .

July 1, 1979

The beginning of the end announced itself one morning in Miami, three days before the 1979 Super Bowl, in the form of Dallas Cowboys linebacker Thomas (Hollywood) Henderson.

"Funny how dusty the air is in Miami," Murray told Henderson. "Been like this all week."

"What do you mean, Jim?" Henderson said. "It's as clear as a bell out."

The retina in Murray's left eye had become detached—and that was his good eye. The right one had carried a cataract since 1978, leaving him only peripheral vision. Now both eyes were out and Murray was legally blind. Over the next year five operations on the left retina could not restore it.

"At that point, I did not care," Murray says. "I would like to have died, actually. When you're blind, there's no quality to life."

I guess I would like to see a Reggie Jackson with the count 3 and 2 and the Series on the line, guessing fastball. . . . Rod Carew with men on first and second and no place to put him, and the pitcher wishing he were standing in the rain someplace. . . . Muhammad Ali giving a recital, a ballet, not a fight. Also, to be sure, I'd like to see a sky full of stars, moonlight on the water, and yes, the tips of a royal flush peeking out as I fan out a poker hand. . . . Come to think of it, I'm lucky. I saw all of those things. I see them yet.

Funny, he didn't feel lucky, even as sympathies stacked up in his hospital room. Once, when Murray had just come out of surgery and was not allowed visitors or phone calls, the phone did a funny thing. It rang anyway.

"Hello?"

"Hello, Jim? You O.K.?"

"How'd you get through?"

"Persistence."

Reggie Jackson does, after all, have a heart.

As for Murray, he had lost his and it wasn't until six months later that he got it back. Unable to see the keys on a typewriter, he began to use a tape recorder. Writing a column with only the sound of your voice is something like assembling a 1932 Ford roadster wearing boxing gloves. "It wasn't very good," Murray says. "But to me, it was a hell of an achievement."

With no chance to repair the left eye, doctors in December 1979 decided to remove the cataract from his right. That worked until the retina detached from it, too. Retinas 2, Murray 0. The right retina was finally repaired on Jan. 18, 1982, and Murray's vision, albeit tunneled, one-dimensional and precarious, came back.

Who knew that there would be times when he wished it hadn't?

To my three sons, Ted, Tony, and Ricky, who have never read my columns and doubtless won't read this book, and my daughter, Pammy, who won't, either. To their mother, Gerry, who not only read, but, bless her, laughed at all the jokes.

The Best of Jim Murray
Dedication, 1965

Rearing teenagers in the late '60s and early '70s was a bitch, though the Murrays seemed to have done O.K. Tony pitched for Cal and, at one time, had scouts bird-dogging his games. Ted and Pam were good kids, and Ricky, the baby, was a delight. "He could play the piano like an angel," Murray says.

His father got him a job in the nuts-and-bolts end of the *Times*, and everything seemed fine. Many were the days Ricky would call his dad and laugh it up about that day's column.

"I don't know what happened," Murray says. "Dedication is hard on the marriage, hard on the family life. Maybe it was the column. Maybe it was the Malibu beach scene. Maybe it was all of it."

In the early evening of June 6, 1982, Jim and Gerry came home to find a business card sticking out of the door. It was from the county coroner. CALL RE: CASE NO. 82-7193.

Case No. 82-7193 was better known as Ricky, age 29, dead from an overdose.

"I think about it all the time," Murray says, fingering that card, wrinkled from the years it has been in his wallet. "I don't know if I should say this, but it was always easy for me, the column. It's not like I spent long, long hours on it. I had plenty of time to be with my family. . . . But I don't know. You lose a son and you think, 'Was I a lousy father?' But then, when you're a semi-famous father, that's another load to bear."

There was one load yet to go.

It wasn't supposed to be this way. I was supposed to die first. . . . I had my speech all ready. I was going to look into her brown eyes and tell her something I should have long ago. I was going to tell her: "It was a privilege just to have known you.

I never got to say it. But it was too true.

April 3, 1984

TOWARD THE end, because of the treatments, Gerry wore a wig. One day, on the way to Palm Springs, they stopped at a coffee shop and, for some reason, she wanted a milkshake, the first she'd had since high school. They sat there and had a few laughs. And when they'd stopped laughing, Gerry tipped her wig cockeyed for a few more laughs.

Two nights later, she got up in the middle of the night and fell; she faded into a coma and stayed there from January through March.

Four times a week, Murray would write his column, get an interview at lunch and then spend the rest of the time at the hospital at Gerry's bedside. Sitting down at the typewriter with sorrow staring back at him was de rigueur for Murray. Through Ricky, through blindness, through Gerry, the show went on.

"I have sat down and attempted humor with a broken heart," he says. "I've sat down and attempted humor with every possible facet of my life in utter chaos. . . . *Carmen* was announced. *Carmen* will be sung."

What was hard was trying to write over those infernal voices, trying to forget the doctor's voice on the phone. The first X rays showed the cancer hadn't spread. But there had been a mix-up at the radiology clinic, just like in the movies. What in fact had happened was just the opposite. "Sorry," the doctor said. "The cancer has metastasized."

The cancer has metastasized.

"The most terrible collection of syllables in the language," Murray says.

Gerry died on April 1.

That figures. You write punch lines your whole life and then the last joke is on you.

Writing a column is like riding a tiger. You don't want to stay on, but you don't want to get off either.
March 12, 1961

Not 10 minutes down the hill from Murray's house is the Hotel Bel-Air, where a famous low-calorie beer company is holding a dinner for the stars of its next 60-second sports celluloid extravaganza. Murray is invited, so he arranges for a ride (he can't drive at night) and makes an appearance. What the hell, as Murray says, might be a column in it.

Walking in, Murray turns heads. For some in the sports world, seeing Murray come into a room without a guide is sufficient reason for a celebratory dinner. "How ya' feelin', Jim?" asks Red Auerbach. "How you makin' out, Jim?" asks Bob Lanier. "Everything O.K. with you, Jim?" asks Bob Uecker.

Over in the corner, Boog Powell cannot quite get up the courage to say hello. "I haven't ever met him," says Powell, "but I've been reading his stuff for many years. And he's written about me, I don't know, half a dozen times, but I've seen him in a locker room only twice. He's a great man. I'm one of his biggest fans."

This is how it is now for Murray. He is in that the-legend-walks-and-talks-and-eats-breakfast stage. The Last King of Sportswriting, boys, sitting right over there.

But Murray the writer has seldom seemed younger. He was named the nation's best columnist for 1984 by the Associated Press Sports Editors. Odds are that Murray will go on winning awards three years after he is buried.

Why he has never been awarded the Pulitzer Prize is an unsolved mystery. Then again, only three sportswriters have won it—Red Smith, Dave Anderson and Arthur Daley—and all three worked for *The New York Times*. "If Murray worked for the *Times*," says Dan Jenkins, author of *Semi-Tough*, "he'd already have three."

Murray doesn't care. "Gerry's gone. So what?"

He misses her. "I'll be watching TV once in a while and I'll see somebody we knew and I'll say, 'Gerry, come take a look at . . .' And then I'll catch myself."

Two years after Gerry died, friends are still telling him, "Why don't you move out of that house? It'll help you to forget." And he answers, " 'Cause I don't want to forget."

So he fills his days at home, in a house that is far too big for him, the lights always turned on low. He's a steel ball in a giant pinball machine, banging around off the walls, nothing much in the refrigerator, stacks of books and untended mail cluttering up the counter space. No room in the house really means much to him anymore except the corner of a small downstairs bedroom where he writes his column by the light of a lamp and a window. It strained his eyes to make out the tiny print on his portable computer, so someone hooked up a magnifying monitor. It is chilling to watch him with his back to the door, his shoulders hunched over an eerie green light, writing jokes for the greater Los Angeles area.

And Murray never misses a column. "What else would I do?" he says.

A tour of the house is really more of a tour of Gerry—here we are at the Masters, at Pebble Beach, at the Dunes, at Madison Square Garden—until you arrive at a 3-by-5 on the piano.

"This is my favorite," he says. "I don't know if she'd like it or not. But I like it. Look at those eyes. Look at them. There's just no jealousy in those eyes."

He fingers the frame, clears his throat.

"The final curtain is pretty bad, isn't it? The last scene, the last act, is pretty bad." Pause.

"Put it this way," he says. "It'll never sell in Dubuque."

You laugh. But Murray doesn't. He just smiles.

Fooled 'em again.

Then My Arm
Glassed Up

BY JOHN STEINBECK

*When senior editor Ray Cave asked one of America's foremost writers to
contribute an essay to SI, the author—while acknowledging that "sports get into
everything"—wrote the following letter to explain why he couldn't possibly do so.*

DEAR RAY CAVE:
 I have your letter of August 29, and it pleased me to
know that you think of me as a sportsman, albeit perhaps an unorthodox one. As you must know, I get many
requests for articles, such as, "You got to rite my term paper for my second yer
english or they wun't leave me play on the teem." Here is a crisis. If I don't
rite his term paper I may set sports back irreparably. On the other hand, I
don't think I am a good enough writer to rite his term paper in his stile well
enough to get by his teacher. I remember one time when a professor in one of
our sports-oriented colleges had in his English composition class a football
player whose excellence on the playing field exhausted his capabilities, and yet
a tyrannical scholasticism demanded that he write an essay. Well, he did, and
the professor, who was a friend of mine, was utterly charmed by it. It was one
of Emerson's best, and such was the purity of approach on the part of the
football player that he had even spelled the words correctly. And he was as-
tounded that the professor could tell that it was not all his own work.
 Early on I had a shattering experience in ghostwriting that has left its mark
on me. In the fourth grade in Salinas, Calif., my best friend was a boy named
Pickles Moffet. He was an almost perfect little boy, for he could throw rocks
harder and more accurately than anyone, he was brave beyond belief in steal-

ing apples or raiding the cake section in the basement of the Episcopal church, a gifted boy at marbles and tops and sublimely endowed at infighting. Pickles had only one worm in him. The writing of a simple English sentence could put him in a state of shock very like that condition which we now call battle fatigue. Imagine to yourself, as the French say, a burgeoning spring in Salinas, the streets glorious with puddles, grass and wild flowers and toadstools in full chorus, and the dense adobe mud of just the proper consistency to be molded into balls and flung against white walls—an activity at which Pickles Moffet excelled. It was a time of ecstasy, like the birth of a sweet and sinless world.

And just at this time our fourth-grade teacher hurled the lightning. She assigned us our homework. We were to write a quatrain in iambic pentameter with an a b a b rhyme scheme.

Well, I thought Pickles was done for. His eyes rolled up. His palms grew sweaty, and a series of jerky spasms went through his rigid body. I soothed him and gentled him, but to show you the state Pickles was in—he threw a mud ball at Mrs. Warnock's newly painted white residence. *And he missed the whole house.*

I think I saved Pickles' life. I promised to write two quatrains and give one to him. I'm sure there is a moral in this story somewhere, but where? The verse I gave to Pickles got him an A while the one I turned in for myself brought a C.

You will understand that the injustice of this bugged me pretty badly. Neither poem was any great shucks, but at least they were equally bad. And I guess my sense of injustice outweighed my caution, for I went to the teacher and complained: "How come Pickles got an A and I only got a C?"

Her answer has stayed with me all my life. She said, "What Pickles wrote was remarkable for Pickles. What you wrote was inferior for you." You see? Sports get into everything, even into versewriting, and I tell this story to myself every time I think I am getting away with something.

As I started to say, I get many requests for articles, and sometimes the letter of refusal is longer than the article would have been. I have always been interested in sports, but more as an observer than as a participant. It seems to me that any sport is a kind of practice, perhaps unconscious, for the life-and-death struggle for survival. Our team sports simulate war, with its strategy, tactics, logistics, heroism and/or cowardice. Individual competition of all kinds has surely ingredients of single combat, which was for x millions of years the means of going on living. The Greeks, who invented realism and pretty much cornered the market, began the training of a soldier by teaching him dancing. The rhythm, precision and coordination of the dance made the hoplite one hell of a lot better trooper. In this connection, it is interesting that the hill men of Crete in their all-male dancing go through the motions of using shield and spear, of defense and dodge and parry, of attack, thrust and retreat. I don't imagine they know this, but it is what they do.

The very word "sport" is interesting. It is a shortening of "disport" (OED: "disportare, to carry away, hence to amuse or to entertain"). From earliest times people played lightly at the deadly and serious things so that they could stand them at all—all, that is, except the Greeks, who in their competitions were offering the gift of their endurance, their strength and their spirits to the gods. Perhaps our values and our gods have changed.

My own participation in sports has been completely undistinguished. I once threw the javelin rather promisingly until my arm glassed up. Once I was fairly good at boxing, mainly because I hated it and wanted to get it over with and to get out. This is not boxing but fighting.

My feeling about hunting has made me pretty unpopular. I have nothing against the killing of animals if there is any need. I did, can and always will kill anything I need or want to eat, including relatives. But the killing of large animals just to prove we can does not indicate to me that we are superior to animals but a kind of deep-down feeling that we are not. A room full of stuffed and glass-eyed heads always gives me a feeling of sadness for the man so unsure of himself that he has constantly to prove himself and to keep the evidence for others to see. What I do admire and respect is our memory of a time when hunting was a very large part of our economy. We preserve this memory intact even though we now have a larger mortality in hunters than in game.

I must admit that I have enjoyed two stuffed specimens on public display. They were in Moscow in Red Square, and thousands of people went by to see them. Since then the more dangerous of the two has been removed from public view, but for the wrong reasons.

I find the so-called blood sports like fox hunting charming and sometimes ravishingly beautiful. Besides, fox hunting serves the useful purpose of preventing population explosion in the gentry and increasing the number of fine horses. The fox population doesn't seem to be affected one way or another.

I love a certain kind of fishing above all other so-called sports. It is almost the last remaining way for a man to be alone without being suspected of some secret sin. By fishing without bait it is even possible to avoid being disturbed by fish. I am surprised that the dour brotherhood of psychoanalysts has not attacked fishing, since it seems to me it is in competition. Two hours with a fishing rod is worth 10 hours on the couch and very much less expensive.

My passion for fishing does not extend to big game fishing. While I admire the strength, skill and endurance of the men who do it well, I have found that after a time the cranking in of sea monsters becomes damned hard work. And many a man who would resist to the death carrying a bucket of coal up to a second-floor fireplace will break his heart struggling with a fish he is going to kill, photograph and throw away. I have studied fish both zoologically and ecologically, and once long ago I worked for the California Fish and Game Commission, where I helped at the birth and raising of a good many millions of trout. At that time I learned to admire them but not greatly to respect their intelligence. And it has seemed to me that a man who can outthink fish may have a great future, but it will be limited to fish. His acquired knowledge will do him little good at a Sunday-school picnic or a board meeting.

Nearly all sports as we know them seem to be memories and in a way ceremonial reenactments of situations that were once of paramount importance to our survival. For example, jousting in the 16th century was an expensive and mannered playback of the tactics of the heavy armed cavalry of the late Roman Empire. Our own once noble cavalry, which was eliminated by the machine gun and the armoured car, became the tank corps. It is interesting how symbols persist. Tank officers, at least until a few years ago, still wore spurs with their dress uniforms.

Not only are our former triumphs remembered in sports, but some of our ancient fears. The hatred and terror of sharks familiar to all sailors in history have made shark hunting very popular. There is almost a feeling of glory and sacrificial punishment in the shark hunter. He kills these great and interesting animals not only with glee but with a sense of administering justice to a cruel and hated enemy. The carcasses are usually thrown away after photographing. There is utterly no understanding that sharks may well be factors in an intricate ecological balance. Edible sharks, such as the leopards, the whites and the makos, are rarely eaten, and it is never considered that the increase in the shark population has not to do with a shark dynamism but rather that we are dumping more and more shark-edible garbage at sea.

You see, my interest in sports is catholic but cool. I don't expect you will believe that I once sent for a mail-order course in alligator wrestling complete with a practice alligator, so I will not tell you this.

Yes, my interest in sports is quiet but deep. I am particularly drawn to the game of rounders, which we call baseball. I would be wrong to call it a sport. I don't think the players have a real sporting attitude toward it. Mostly they want to win because if they win they get more money. In baseball I like the audience almost better than the game. I guess that is why I am a Met fan. But for many years our household was torn to pieces emotionally every year. My wife was a Dodger fan born and bred in Fort Worth, which is, or was, a Dodger farm. Every year, she went through the fervency, the hope, the prayer, the shining eyes and the loud and raucous voice and, finally, after the season the dark and deadly gloom and despair that lasted clear into spring-training time. I guess our family devoted more pure spiritual energy to the Dodgers than to any other religious organization. This, of course, was before they defected to the West. Any kind of skulduggery and ineptness my wife could forgive and even defend, but treason she could not take. She is a Met fan now, and our house is whole again.

Early on, to save arguments, I became an Oriole fan and even bought a little stock in that club. If you were for anyone else you got an argument, but if you said you were an Oriole fan people just laughed and let you alone. I thought I had a guarantee that they would stay on the bottom, but now they have double-crossed me by climbing up. I nearly went to the Senators, because there is a federal law which forbids them to win. Then the Mets happened, and I was stuck.

Baseball brings out a kind of pugnacious frustration in foreigners. Once as guests of a very old and dear friend in London, we were at Lord's watching a sedate and important cricket match. When a player let a fast ball go by, my wife yelled, "Git it! What ya got, lead in ya pants?" A deathly silence fell on the section around us, and it was apparent that our host would have to resign from all his clubs. Afterward he lectured her gently. "My dear," he said, "we don't do it."

"Peewee Reese would of got it," said my elegant *moglie*.

"Don't tell me about baseball," said our host. "It's only rounders, and I know all about it. Don't forget, I, too, have been to *Egbert's Field*." There is no way to explain that baseball is not a sport or a game or a contest. It is a state of mind, and you can't learn it.

You will be aware by now of my reasons for not being able to write a piece about sports for SPORTS ILLUSTRATED. My interests are too scattered and too unorthodox. But I do find the American cult of youth, violence and coronaries a little unreasonable. It does seem to me that "as life's shadows lengthen" our so-called senior citizens should have competitive sports, but that the pace should be reduced. Turtle racing won't do, because it is dull. But, being lazy, I invented some years ago a sport which satisfied my ego and my sense of competition and matched my inclination. It is called vine racing. Each contestant plants a seed beside a pole of specified height, and the first vine to reach the top wins. There are, however, some furious vines which have been known to grow 10 inches a day—which might in some owner-managers raise the blood pressure. For these passionate ones, among whom am I, I have laid out the ground rules for an even more sedate and healthful contest. This is oak-tree racing. Each of the eager players plants an acorn. The obvious advantage of this contest is that, depending on the agreed finishing height, it may go on for generations. At the cry, "They're off!" the fancy could enjoy all semblance of growth and renewal until the checkered flag came down 300 years later. By that time the original contestants should be represented by large numbers of descendants, for tree racing allows one the leisure to indulge in other sports, the darlings.

I should like to mention one more activity which only the Anglo-Saxons consider a sport and hate and attend in droves. That is bullfighting. In this I have gone full course, read, studied, watched and shared. From the first horror I went to the mortal beauty, the form and exquisiteness from *véronica* to *faena*. I have seen a great many bullfights (it is only called a fight in English). I even saw Manolete fight a number of times, which is more than Ernest Hemingway did. And I have seen a few great and beautiful things in the bullring. There are only a few, and you must see very many fights to see the great one. But I suppose there are very few great anythings in the world. How many great sonnets are there? How many great plays? For that matter, how many great wines?

I think I have been through most of the possible feelings about tauromachy, rising eventually to the sublime conception that the incomparable bravery of the matador somehow doled out courage to the audience. Oh! this was not blind and ignorant celebration. I hung around the rings. I knew about the underweight bulls, the sandbags on the kidneys, the shaved horns and sometimes the needle of barbiturate in the shoulder as the gate swung open. But there was also that moment of what they call truth, a sublimity, a halo of the invincible human spirit and unspeakable, beautiful courage.

And then doubt began to creep in. The matadors I knew had souls of Toledo steel for the bull, but they were terrified of their impresarios, pulp in the hands of their critics and avaricious beyond belief. Perhaps they gave the audience a little courage of a certain kind, but not the kind the audience and the world needed and needs. I have yet to hear of a bullfighter who has taken a dangerous political stand, who has fought a moral battle unless its horns were shaved. It began to seem to me that this superb courage could be put to better uses than the ritual slaughter of bulls in the afternoon. One Ed Murrow standing up to take the charge of an enraged McCarthy, one little chicken-necked Negro going into a voting booth in Alabama, one Dag Hammarskjold flying to his death and knowing it—this is the kind of courage we need, because in the end it is not the bulls that will defeat us, I am afraid, but our own miserable, craven and covetous selves.

So you see, Ray Cave, it was a mistake to ask me to write an essay about sports. Hell, I don't even know the batting average of Eddie Kranepool.

—*John Steinbeck*

◆⧫

The Heavyweight Champion of the Word

BY JEFF MACGREGOR

In an era when America's great sportswriters were as big as the athletes they covered, W.C. Heinz may have been the best of the bunch. This is the story of that storyteller, a superb piece of writing that stands as a fitting tribute to Heinz.

Maybe this is how it begins.

The boy, eight years old, is asleep in his room, curled fast into the pillow, breathing softly. He looks fragile and small beneath the bedclothes, fine-boned, with a long, elegant face that seems determined and earnest even at rest. In the kitchen his mother has washed and dried and put away the dinner dishes. Standing at the sink in her patterned apron, a damp dish towel over one shoulder, she scours the last few imperfections from the white enamel roasting pan. Through the swinging door she can hear the men in the dining room fussing with the radio.

It is a crystal set, a homemade job, bright copper coil and wires and vacuum tubes, as complicated and fickle as a human heart. The boy's father, a salesman, built it himself. With the headphones placed in the cut-glass fruit bowl at the center of the dining-room table to amplify the sound, the family can draw close, lean in over that dark polished wood and listen. Some nights they can hear KDKA all the way from Pittsburgh, the radio signal booming out of the sky across Pennsylvania, crashing over the Alleghenies and down into this trim little house in Mount Vernon, N.Y. Tonight the signal is weak, and the ghostly voices coming from the Polo Grounds, from just a few miles south in New York City, seem distant, interplanetary. The salesman and the bank clerk from around the corner and Schlosser, the German butcher from next door, will have to take turns with the awkward Bakelite headphones, describing to each other what they can hear from beneath that sea of static. It is Sept. 14, 1923, and tonight Dempsey, the lethal Dempsey, is fighting Luis Firpo for the heavyweight championship of the world.

The butcher sits wearing the headset for the opening bell, knitting his thick fingers as he carefully intones the announcer's call to his friends, but within seconds he is on his feet, red-faced and sputtering, repeating again and again that "Vurpo ist down! Vurpo ist down!" until, without sense or segue, eyes wide, he shouts, "Tempsey ist down now too! Out of de ring and down!" The boy's father grabs the headset from the butcher, trying to make sense of what's happening. It's the wildest round in heavyweight history! Impossible but true! Firpo's been down seven times in the first, Dempsey twice, once even tumbling through the ropes. In the second round, with that stadium crowd of 85,000 roaring murder into the night and echoing in those tiny headphones, Dempsey knocks Firpo cold with a couple of short lefts and a hard, anesthetic right, and it's over.

Upstairs, the boy sleeps on, peaceful. Maybe the fight comes to him through the walls, as if in a dream, a riot of giants. *Vurpo ist down!* Maybe, thanks to radio and newsreels and the sports pages, the heavyweight championship of the world is in the very air, and he breathes it in by the lungful.

The next morning, at the breakfast table, his father tells him about the apocalyptic Dempsey-Firpo fight, about the broadcast and the static, and about the bright-red face of the tongue-tied German butcher from next door. The boy will remember all this, and more than three quarters of a century later, it is one of the stories he tells me.

W.C. Heinz is a writer, and he tells his stories the way Heifitz fiddled or Hopper painted, or the way Willie Pep boxed—with a kind of lyrical understatement, with an insistent and inspired economy. His work has been rediscovered only recently, a happy by-product of all those end-of-the-millennium anthologies and sports shows. Pulitzer Prize–winning journalist David Halberstam calls him a pioneer, one of the innovators of what came to be called New Journalism and the literary godfather to men like Gay Talese and Tom Wolfe and Frank Deford.

Heinz will tell you, chuckling at the pun, that he is "last in his class," a writer from a long-gone generation of American greats, the sportswriters of mid-century who come down to us now every bit as ancient and sepia-washed as the athletes and events they covered: Grantland Rice, Damon Runyon, Red Smith, Jimmy Cannon, A.J. Liebling and Frank Graham and Paul Gallico and all those Lardners. Before television, when newspapers and magazines had a heft and resonance unimaginable today, these were the master craftsmen of sporting prose. And Bill Heinz, byline W.C., was perhaps the purest writer among them, the writer other writers read. "At his best," Frank Graham said, "he's better than any of us."

There were 39,827 people there and they had paid $342,497 to be there and when Graziano's head came up out of the dugout they rose and made their sound. The place was filled with it and it came from far off and then he was moving quickly down beneath this ceiling of sound, between the two long walls of faces, turned toward him and yellow in the artificial light and shouting things, mouths open, eyes wide, into the ring where, in one of the most brutal fights ever seen in New York, Zale dropped him once and he dropped Zale once before, in the sixth round, Zale suddenly, with a right to the body and left to the head, knocked him out.
—THE DAY OF THE FIGHT, 1947

He still has that long, elegant face, determined and earnest when he comes to the door, smiling now, his glasses set across the prominent emperor's nose, wide on his face between the pale blue-green eyes, the feathery white hair combed back off the broad forehead; the lines drawn there and down from the high cheeks and at the eyes and up from the corners of his mouth are as deeply etched as a carving, a medieval woodcut of a man at his last age. It takes a long time to earn a face like this. The head is large on his body—he is still fine-boned and slender, somewhere between a super bantam and a light-weight, maybe 130 pounds in his shoes. He stands 5' 8" or 5' 9", a bit short-er after all these years, but unbent by the weight of his age at 85, his back as straight as a ring post.

We shake hands on the patio by his driveway, and he invites me in. His hands are huge. "I'm a little cowed by this," I say to his back, walking inside. "It's awkward interviewing a good writer. You know all the tricks already."

"I was picking *their* brains for 50 years, so it's only fair."

"It's like stealing something. Taking people's stories. Sometimes I feel like a thief."

Without turning, he says, "I know."

Heinz has lived with his wife, Betty, in this modest house in Dorset, Vt., for 34 years. Betty isn't here yet. A neighbor has taken her down to Manchester to go shopping; Heinz didn't want to worry about her too much while we talked. Betty has Alzheimer's, and she's a handful lately, always walking off or trying to straighten up the house. They've been married 59 years.

Wilfred Charles Heinz was born on Jan. 11, 1915. Maybe he got the sports bug from dreaming that Dempsey fight or from the baseball cards he collected or from the few scrapes he had in the schoolyard. (He says boxing on the playground taught him to appreciate the value of a good left hand. He didn't have one.) When he was 10 years old, he saw Red Grange running right at him on a movie screen. Heinz was athletic, played hockey through high school, but he was light and knew he wasn't going to get much bigger: "I came to realize that I wasn't going to be a Dempsey or a Ruth when I found out that a punch in the nose hurt and didn't improve my appearance, and a baseball bounced off my head didn't clarify my thinking."

But Heinz was a reader too, and there were sets of Tennyson and Hugo and Balzac in the glass-front cabinet at home, Twain and Shakespeare and Poe. When he got the *Omnibus of Sport*, an anthology edited by Grantland Rice, for Christmas as a 17-year-old in 1932, he realized that sportswriting was literature of a sort and that a different kind of truth resided in it and that maybe it was a way into a world he loved.

He graduated from Middlebury College in Vermont in 1937 with a B.A. in political science. More important to history, he was the sports editor for the school newspaper. Most important of all, though, he met Betty there in his freshman year. Elizabeth Bailey was a junior, cochair of the 1934 winter carnival, and he saw her for the first time in the lecture hall of the science building. She was small and athletic, with luminous blue eyes set in a round face framed by short, light-brown hair. "She was absolutely beautiful," he says. "I was completely captivated." Bill and Betty started dating the following autumn.

When Heinz got out of school, a family friend helped him get a job as a messenger boy for the New York *Sun*. He earned $15 a week. In a megalopolis with nine daily papers, the media center for a nation during the worst depression in its history, hundreds of young men were scrambling for jobs at the papers, and an apprenticeship was a test of character. He hung on to become a copyboy for the same pay. For two years they yelled at him. "Boy? *Boy!* Where's that damned boy?"

He was writing now too, banging out short pieces on the black 1932 Remington portable his father had bought him. Frederick had been a typewriter repairman before he became a salesman, and he knew a good machine when he saw one. Keats Speed, the excellently named editor of the *Sun*, knew a good thing when he saw one too and gave Heinz a job on the city desk. There he covered a cub reporter's beat, the fires and the shootings and the school board meetings. He learned to report, to rewrite, to beat a hard deadline. He learned to listen to what people really said and how they said it.

Although he was doing well as an all-purpose reporter at the *Sun*, he had the itch to try more complicated forms of writing, and he wanted to write more about sports. He covered skiing and, occasionally, basketball at the *Sun* but was still writing too often for his taste about pushcart fires and corrupt borough presidents and roller-coaster trackwalkers. All that would change with the war.

"Let's eat some lunch."

He butters toast the way another man might perform a ritual tea ceremony, deliberate and contemplative—something worth doing right. We take our roast beef sandwiches on white toast out to the dining room. He points to my notebook and tape recorder and says gently, "Why don't you put those away for a while?"

We talk for a long time about writing, about the panic that creeps over you when you're sitting in the chair and nothing comes. About trying to find some music in the words and about the moment, when it's going well, that you look down at the page and the story comes to you in full, everyone and everything alive in your head and busy on the page, and when you look up again, eight hours are gone and you feel like Lindbergh landing in Paris.

> *They moved the curious back, the rain falling faster now, and they moved the colt over close to a pile of loose bricks. Gilman had the halter and Catlett had the gun, shaped like a bell with the handle at the top. This bell he placed, the crowd silent, on the colt's forehead, just between the eyes. The colt stood still and then Catlett, with the hammer in his other hand, struck the handle of the bell. There was a short, sharp sound and the colt toppled onto his left side, his eyes staring, his legs straight out, the free legs quivering.*
>
> *"Aw ----" someone said.*
>
> *That was all they said. They worked quickly, the two vets removing the broken bones as evidence for the insurance company, the crowd silently watching. Then the heavens opened, the rain pouring down, the lightning flashing, and they rushed for the cover of the stables, leaving alone on his side near the pile of bricks, the rain running off his hide, dead an hour and a quarter after his first start, Air Lift, son of Bold Venture, full brother of Assault.*
>
> —DEATH OF A RACEHORSE, 1949

Heinz became the *Sun*'s junior war correspondent in the fall of 1943. He spent a month and a half on the U.S.S. *Core*, an escort carrier on antisubmarine duty in the Atlantic. Seated now on the floor of his den, we go slowly through his many 11-by-14 scrapbooks. Pasted into one of the first are the transit chits and laundry tickets and clippings from his time aboard the *Core*. There are photos of Heinz on the flight deck in his Mae West, getting ready for a fly-along in a Grumman Avenger. Heinz in his wire-rim glasses, a sparse beginner's mustache on his upper lip, jaunty in his plain khaki uniform with the black and gold correspondent's patch.

The next scrapbook, though, chronicles what Heinz saw and what he did and what he wrote as he followed the ground war through Europe. It has a bad weight to it.

In April 1944 he packed that Remington portable and shipped out for London to cover the Allied invasion. The writer people talk about when they talk about W.C. Heinz was born during the Allied push across Europe. Everything he wrote after 1944 was informed by what he experienced as the fighting moved east toward Germany. Everything he came to understand about courage and cowardice and truth can be found, like seedlings, in his combat dispatches. He learned that men at war fight not for causes but for one another and that heroism is a kind of love. He learned to strip the artifice from his work. His style emerged, a refined transparency in which the *I* largely disappeared, and what the reader got was pure story.

Heinz is fond of saying that, for a young writer, the war was great training: "It was so dramatic, you couldn't write it badly." But plenty of writers did. Some covered the war from a briefing room at Army headquarters or, worse yet, filed thirdhand dispatches from behind a highball glass in hotel bars in Paris or Cherbourg. Heinz got as close to the fighting as the brass and good sense would let him. When the *Sun*'s senior correspondent was captured by the Nazis, Heinz replaced him.

Much of what he saw he couldn't write about; none of them could. It would never have made it past the censors. The infernal stink of infection and cordite and fear, the bodies of American teenagers sunk in the muddy roads beneath the weight of the tank tracks, the waste and the cruelty and the panic and the ineptitude. By September 1944 Heinz was on the verge of a nervous collapse, but he hung on through the fall and the winter, the Battle of the Bulge and the last push to Berlin. He came home in June, not long after V-E Day.

In the few pictures of Heinz in this dark scrapbook, from '44 and '45, he seems exhausted and cheerless, far older in the eyes than 29. There are the dispatches and cablegrams he sent back to New York, filed from Spa or Remagen or deep behind German lines. There are some of the little ends and bits he collected too, the Army manuals and business cards and train tickets. But maybe the one thing most revealing about W.C. Heinz, the writer and the man, is folded into the back of the scrapbook; a magazine piece about the war on which he's made a correction in the final paragraph: "After that there was just the muffled sound of the shelling, the sounds of the men breathing heavily and turning in their sleep, and the sound of the straw."

Between the words *the* and *sound* in the last clause he had, who knows how many years later, drawn a caret in soft lead pencil and inserted the word "taffeta." The taffeta sound of the straw. Even when it's done, it's never finished.

When Heinz got back to New York, the *Sun* gave him three months off and a $1,000 bonus. He asked to be moved over to sports, but the paper wanted him to go to the Washington bureau in the fall. His first morning back in the office, Keats Speed moved him to sports. To this day Heinz isn't sure why.

When Heinz's battered black Remington was shipped back from the war, the copyboy at the *Sun* who checked it in was a kid named David Anderson. He held it in his hands for a while before he put it up on the stockroom shelf. "I was in awe of him," says Anderson. "We all were." Anderson is now a Pulitzer Prize–winning sports columnist for *The New York Times*.

Indeed, by the end of the war Heinz's writing had earned him a wide following, especially among those who plied the same trade. When asked in 1946 by an editor from Hearst to recommend someone for a potential magazine article, Damon Runyon, silenced by throat cancer, wrote on a cocktail napkin, "W.C. Heinz very good." He underlined "very good" three times.

By the late '40s Frank Graham, the little giant of New York sportswriters, had mastered what was sometimes referred to as the "conversation piece," a fly-on-the-wall approach using long blocks of dialogue without writerly asides. Heinz took the device and refined it until, as he now puts it, "imitation and adaptation and conversion" had him walking comfortably in shoes of his own.

You don't see conversation pieces much anymore, those unbroken skeins of polished, colorful dialogue. One reason is that they weren't always word-for-word accurate. Graham worked without a notebook—what he reproduced so beautifully was what the people he was quoting wanted to say, and he said it in their voices. Heinz took notes but knew that the secret of this novelistic technique was to get the sound right. "Quoting like that is walking on thin ice," he tells me, sorcerer to apprentice. "You go gently so you don't break through."

By 1948 Heinz had earned the luxury and burden of his own column in the *Sun*, "The Sport Scene." In the picture next to it he looks urbane and sagacious, wearing a bow tie and an enigmatic half smile. He wrote about polo, about football, about hockey and basketball and baseball. He wrote about the six-day bicycle races at the 168th Street Armory. Mostly, though, he wrote about boxing.

When they came to the corner they stopped for just a moment under the streetlight. Then they turned left and started walking again.

"Who said being a fighter's wife is easy?" Lucille said.

"It's like being in the ring," Norma said.

"She fights right in the ring with him every fight," her mother said, talking to Lucille.

"That's the trouble," Norma said. "You can't get in the ring with him."
"What could you do?" her mother said.
"Well," she said, "if they put Fusari's wife in the ring."
"He just said Fusari's in trouble," Lucille said quickly.
"You heard it?" Norma said.
"Yes."
"I don't know," Norma said. "It's too much."
"That's the funny thing," Lucille said. "Everybody seems to wait for tonight but you."
"I wait for the night after tonight."

—THE FIGHTER'S WIFE, 1949

Betty and Bill had their first child, Barbara, in 1947 and had moved from Manhattan up to Old Greenwich, Conn., but Heinz spent his working days at places like Stillman's Gym at 919 Eighth Avenue, the alpha and omega of boxing in those days. It was a converted loft on the second floor that stunk of sweat and wintergreen, ambition and corruption. Everyone in the world of boxing came up those stairs at one time or another, and there was always a story to be found. By then, in addition to his five-day-a-week column, Heinz was writing magazine articles and fiction, and he had sold a handful of fine short stories.

He has two large scrapbooks full of his columns. Each has been neatly scissored from the newspaper and glued side by side, two per page. What is remarkable about them 50 years later is that none of them are bad. He wrote five of these things a week, 700 words a day, on deadline, for more than two years, and there isn't a clunker in the bunch. Some are better than others, certainly, but each is thoughtful and well-turned and tells a story. At the bottom of some of these yellowing clips, Heinz has become his own harshest critic and modestly written "good" on about every 14th column.

The postwar years were a boom time in New York sportswriting, and Heinz worked and socialized with the other famous names of his trade. He'd see A.J. Liebling, fat and round and pale as a snowman, making notes for a *New Yorker* piece at Stillman's in the afternoon; maybe give wisecracking Jimmy Cannon a lift to the Poughkeepsie regatta in his tiny Crosley. Seated shoulder to shoulder on the way there, Cannon deadpanned a look of genuine curiosity on his wide Irish mug. "Where's the other one?" Cannon asked, referring to his friend's subminiature automobile.

"The other what?" answered Heinz.

Cannon, milking it, looked around as though searching for something lost. "The other roller skate."

"Relax, Jimmy."

"Shhhh. Don't talk to me right now. . . . I'm trying to read this guy's hubcaps."

Some nights Heinz made it home in time for dinner with his best friend, *Herald Tribune* columnist Red Smith.

In the photos they wear camel-hair coats over their boxy double-breasted suits and striped suspenders and slender silk neckties, these kings of the city, these sportswriters, and fine, brushed fedoras and shoes polished brighter than the bar rails they were propped on. In those long, red banquettes at Toots Shor's or around a table at Dempsey's or ringside at Stillman's, their hats off and their sleeves rolled up, their elbows and their notebooks on that damp canvas, or in the swaying club car choked with cigarette smoke on the sleeper to Chicago to cover the second Tony Zale–Rocky Graziano bout, they were always together, working, talking, cracking wise.

The newspaper business was changing after the war. Undermined by television and declining circulation, the *Sun* was one of the first papers to fold in what would become a decades-long series of desperate press mergers and foreclosures. It disappeared from newsstands on Jan. 3, 1950. Heinz got the news from a friend as he walked through Grand Central Terminal. He was offered star columns in other papers, but he wanted to do longer pieces. No more would he say to Betty on New Year's Eve, "Well, I have to write 250 columns again before this time next year."

In 1951 the Heinzes had a second daughter, Gayl. Heinz was piecing together the kind of freelance income that most writers only dream of. Over the next few years he did some of his best work, including *Brownsville Bum* for *True* magazine. Most recently collected in *The Best American Sports Writing of the Century* (with two other Heinz pieces), it is the profile of Al (Bummy) Davis, a gifted, dirty fighter and chronic screwup who dies a hero. Its effect on other writers is legendary; the story is told and retold about the night in Manhattan when Jimmy Breslin shouted over a bar to his wife, Rosemary, "What's the best sports magazine piece of all time?" and she bellowed back immediately, "Bummy Davis by Bill Heinz."

It's a funny thing about people. People will hate a guy all his life for what he is, but the minute he dies for it they make him out a hero and they go around saying that maybe he wasn't such a bad guy after all because he sure was willing to go the distance for whatever he believed or whatever he was.

That's the way it was with Bummy Davis. The night Bummy fought Fritzie Zivic in the Garden and Zivic started giving him the business and Bummy hit Zivic low maybe thirty times and kicked the referee, they wanted to hang him for it. The night those four guys came into Dudy's bar and tried the same thing, only with rods, Bummy went nuts again. He flattened the first one and then they shot him, and when everybody read about it,

and how Bummy fought guns with only his left hook and died lying in the
rain in front of the place, they all said that was really something and you sure
had to give him credit for it.

—BROWNSVILLE BUM, 1951

Throughout the '50s Heinz wrote for *Collier's* and *Cosmopolitan*, *The Satur-day Evening Post* and *Sport*, for *Argosy* and *True* and *Esquire* and *Look*. He kept an office out in the converted garage after they moved to Stamford from Old Greenwich and wrote each day when he wasn't on the road reporting or doing research. He profiled every boxer from Carmen Basilio to Hurricane Jackson to Roy Harris, the Backwoods Battler from the Big Thicket. He wrote about Rocky Marciano and Ingemar Johansson, about Joe Louis and Archie Moore and Beau Jack and Floyd Patterson, Sugar Ray Robinson and Ezzard Charles.

In boxing he found the purest form of competition. He often compared it to painting or composing, an application of scientific principle to produce a work of art, and has said that when he watched Willie Pep fight—the best boxer he ever saw—he could almost hear the music. Prizefighting has always attracted a colorful crowd, too, which gives a writer great raw material. A sport full of gutter-poor kids bootstrapping their way up off the street, it appealed to Heinz as the proto-American success story.

Nineteen fifty-eight was probably the best year Heinz had as a writer. He published a much-anthologized article about Pete Reiser, the hard-luck Brooklyn Dodgers phenom who played with such exuberant abandon that he spent most of his injury-shortened career hobbled after running hell-bent into too many outfield walls.

In 1946, the Dodgers played an exhibition game in Springfield, Missouri.
When the players got off the train there was a young radio announcer there,
and he was grabbing them one at a time and asking them where they thought
they'd finish that year.

"In first place," Reese and Casey and Dixie Walker and the rest were
saying. "On top." "We'll win it."

"And here comes Pistol Pete Reiser!" the announcer said. "Where do you
think you'll finish this season, Pete?"

"In Peck Memorial Hospital," Pete said.

—THE ROCKY ROAD OF PISTOL PETE, 1958

Nineteen fifty-eight was also the year in which Heinz's first novel, *The Professional*, was published. He had earned enough from a two-part Eddie Arcaro profile in 1956 to take 11 months off to write a book he'd been taking notes on for years. He wrote through all of 1957. "It was like going from four-rounders to a 15-round title fight," he says.

It is the story of Eddie Brown, a middleweight contender, and his manager, Doc Carroll, told by a sportswriter named Frank Hughes. Brown is based on Billy Graham, a popular middleweight in the '40s and '50s with admirable skills and a missionary's work ethic, of whom Liebling said, "He's as good as a fighter can be without being a helluva fighter." Doc Carroll is drawn from Jack Hurley, boxing's last angry man, an on-the-level manager of the scrupulous old school. "There are two honest managers in boxing," said Damon Runyon. "One is Jack Hurley, and I can't remember the name of the other." The writer Frank Hughes is an alter ego for Heinz, who speaks to our fascination with prizefighting.

> *"[It's] the basic law of man. The truth of life. It's a fight, man against man, and if you're going to defeat another man, defeat him completely. Don't starve him to death, like they try to do in the fine, clean competitive world of commerce. Leave him lying there, senseless, on the floor."*
> *"I guess that's it," [Eddie said.] "I don't know."*
> —THE PROFESSIONAL, 1958

The book was generally well reviewed. It has everything Heinz knew and loved about boxing and everything he hated about the ascendancy of mendacity and mediocrity that was killing it. The novel is constructed in the manner of all Heinz's best work, in a series of interlocking, overlapping copy blocks that, once finished, become seamless and whole. "It's like building a stone wall without mortar," he tells me in the den. "You place the words one at a time, fit them, take them apart and refit them until they're balanced and solid."

Hemingway cabled congratulations from Cuba and called *The Professional* the "only good novel I've ever read about a fighter and an excellent first novel in its own right." Elmore Leonard sent Heinz a fan letter, "the only letter I've ever written to another writer," praising the book's honesty and clarity. Even Liebling wrote a note: "All praise in varying degrees from high to extra high."

All this is in the scrapbooks along with Heinz's original notes for the novel, sheets from a dime-store pocket notebook covered in his neat cursive, the blue ink long since faded to gray.

At the other end of this quiet house we hear the front door open and slowly close.

"Come meet Betty."

Heinz and I unfold ourselves from the floor and go out to the living room. Betty's eyes are as blue and clear and deep as a movie star's pool, but the

Alzheimer's has robbed her of most conversation and thus stolen from Bill as well. She'll sit in the chair by the window and look out across the valley to Bromley Mountain for hours, smiling, while he reads the paper, but her health is declining by the week. Bill's been unwell lately, too, and he nearly died in 1998 following a series of operations that cost him his left eye. Each of them takes a fistful of prescription drugs every day for an arm-long list of ailments.

Bill gets Betty settled into her chair by the big window. "We'll be in the office, Mom," he says, and leads me back down the hall to the other end of the house. In the office are shelves of the books he's written. On the wall he has an autographed copy of his friend Joe Rosenthal's famous photograph of the flag-raising at Iwo Jima. There's a painting of Stillman's Gym by combat artist John Groth. Beside the desk is a small statue of two boxers, one putting out a left jab, the other slipping it. On the desk is the same Remington portable he's used his entire working life.

After *The Professional*, Heinz continued to write magazine features, including profiles of quarterback Charlie Conerly and Paul Hornung and Stan Musial and bonus baby Joe Namath. He lived about two miles from Red Smith in Stamford, and the two families were close. ("He was the Willie Pep of the profession," Heinz says, "all solid skill and inventiveness.") There were lots of cocktail parties back and forth, the grownups dancing and the children watching from the top of the stairs, lots of dinners.

Heinz was skating on a backyard pond with Smith's son, Terry, during Christmas break in 1961 when Smith called to offer Heinz a book deal. Smith wanted him to cowrite a book with Vince Lombardi as part of a new series he was editing, a book that would take readers inside pro football. Heinz was already at work on a book, one that had grown out of his fascination with medicine. He had written a piece that year for LIFE magazine on J. Maxwell Chamberlain, a thoracic surgeon. He had watched three-dozen surgeries at Chamberlain's elbow and thought there was a novel in what he had seen. Heinz, being Heinz, wrote both.

The Lombardi book, which became *Run to Daylight!*, tested Heinz's patience as much as his skill. Lombardi was no storyteller and had a terrible memory for any kind of detail that wasn't an X or an O, so Heinz found himself filling his small Woolworth's notebooks with background from Marie, Lombardi's wife. He lived in their guest room for two weeks before the 1962 training camp, interviewing the coach every morning in his basement rec room to get the boilerplate epigrams about winning and losing and then talking to Marie in the afternoons for the color stuff, the psychology and personal history, while Vince played hurry-up, full-contact golf with Green Bay luminaries like Don Hutson and the local Pontiac dealer.

Heinz roomed with Lombardi through camp and preseason, a constant presence players dubbed "the shadow," those pale eyes behind the thick black glasses he wore then taking in everything while he filled those notebooks and Lombardi's office ashtrays. Over time they became guarded friends. Heinz has a sly sense of humor and to this day enjoys letting some air out of the pompous. Lombardi was, at times, as self-inflating as an expensive life raft. During the cocktail hour one night down in that rec room, Lombardi, in front of a large group of family and friends, barked, "Bill Heinz, wait'll you hear this! I got a letter the other day, and the only thing on the envelope was my picture and a stamp. But it came right here!"

Heinz didn't say anything. Bellows-chested and puffed full of himself, Lombardi needed an answer, an acknowledgment. "You're not impressed?"

Heinz paused. The room went quiet, just the sound of the ice in the glasses, everybody waiting for it.

"Coach," he said, "I'd be more impressed if your picture was on the stamp."

The Surgeon and *Run to Daylight!* were published in 1963. The former was a successful novel and sold well; the latter was a triumph and sold like no sports book before it. In it Heinz subsumed his own voice and gave the reader pure Lombardi. It chronicled a week inside Lombardi's head as he readied the Packers to play the Detroit Lions.

3:15 A.M.

I have been asleep for three hours and, suddenly, I am awake. I am wide awake, and that's the trouble with this game. Just twelve hours ago I walked off that field, and we had beaten the Bears 49 to 0. Now I should be sleeping the satisfied sleep of the contented but I am lying here awake, wide awake, seeing myself walking across that field, seeing myself searching in the crowd for George Halas but really hoping that I would not find him.

All week long there builds up inside of you a competitive animosity toward that other man, that counterpart across the field. All week long he is the symbol, the epitome, of what you must defeat and then, when it is over, when you have looked up to that man for as long as I have looked up to George Halas, you cannot help but be disturbed by a score like this. You know he brought a team in here hurt by key injuries and that this was just one of those days, but you can't apologize. You can't apologize for a score. It is up there on that board and nothing can change it now.

—RUN TO DAYLIGHT! 1963

The book went through 15 printings and was the first gospel, mythological and bronze-bound, of the legendary Lombardi. Heinz wrote an award-winning television adaptation of the Lombardi book (produced by his friend Howard Cosell), and by the end of 1963, at the top of his profession, he had the time and the money and the ease of mind, at 48, to consider carefully what he might do next.

Barbara Heinz, age 16, died on Feb. 27, 1964. It is quiet torture for him to tell this story, and he tells it carefully, as though these words were made of glass and might shatter in the telling. Might cut him.

On Feb. 25, the day of the first Clay-Liston fight, in Miami, Barbara told Betty she didn't feel well. She had a persistent fever, she couldn't eat, and she had a headache. Heinz had already left to cover the fight. Betty took Barbara to the doctor, who booked her into Stamford Hospital. On the way there, they dropped off Gayl, 13, who was going on a ski trip. A few minutes later, Barbara turned to Betty in the front seat of the car and said, "I'm going to die, Mom."

That night Cassius Clay beat Sonny Liston for the heavyweight championship. Heinz flew back to Manhattan a few hours after the fight to write a newsreel wrap-up that would play in movie theaters the next day. Betty called him early on the 27th, and told him to get to the hospital. All of Barbara's major organs were shutting down.

He arrived there at 11 a.m. At 7 p.m., Barbara died. Heinz remembers Betty standing in the hospital lobby saying, "She's gone." He remembers how tightly they held each other. Toxic shock or some virulent strep, they still don't know what it was. He can never forget "taking home Barbie's empty clothes" and being stricken for the next few days, in and out of a state like a horrible, waking sleep.

Forgoing a service, Bill and Betty took Barbara's ashes up to Vermont, where she'd been so happy the summer before at camp in Dorset Hollow, where she'd fallen in love for the first time. They spread the ashes beneath a tree, and Heinz, eyes shut tight against something he still can't stand to look at, tells me they "started on the road back, which never ends."

Bill and Betty lived apart for a time after that—they couldn't look at each other without crying. Each thought the other was thinking that they could have or should have done something more, anything, done the impossible somehow. Heinz returned to 919 Eighth Avenue, the old address where he'd spent so much time, Stillman's Gym. They'd torn it down and put up an apartment building.

He and Betty hung on, though, and in 1966 they bought the mountainside house in Dorset, reknit what they could of their hearts and started over.

It is getting dark, and snow is falling outside. Heinz is tired. He brought sportswriting across the century from Granny Rice and Ring Lardner and passed it like a gift to the writers we read today. Perhaps he'd have become as famous as Red Smith if he'd stayed in one place. He had bad luck with newspapers and magazines. *The Sun* and *The Saturday Evening Post, True* and *Argosy, Collier's* and *Look* have all gone under, and they pulled the memories down after them.

Heinz kept working, more pieces for the magazines, including *Great Day at Trickem Fork*, a breakthrough *Saturday Evening Post* piece on the Selma peace marches, and another successful book, *M*A*S*H*, which he cowrote in 1968 with Dr. H. Richard Hornberger under the pseudonym Richard Hooker. In 1974 there was another novel, *Emergency*, an episodic account of life in a city trauma unit. He updated and collected his earlier work in *Once They Heard the Cheers* in 1979 and in *American Mirror* in 1982. Last year he coedited the *Sports Illustrated Classics Book of Boxing*, typing the foreword and introduction on that ancient Remington. Gayl, who's 49, lives down in Boxford, Mass., with her husband and their daughter.

As I say good night, Bill's helping Betty out of that chair by the window. "You ready for dinner, Mom?" are the last words I hear.

What Bill Heinz knows and what Bill Heinz wrote is that life is the biggest fix of them all, and every one of us was bought the day we were born. Maybe you can pick the round you go down, or hold out for more money, or book yourself into the main event in a bigger room. But for all the training and the roadwork, for all the hours and weeks and years spent in patient, useless practice, for all the effort and hunger of it, the brutality and the sweetness of it too, the battering and the circling and the moments of perfect, silent pain or crazy, transcendent peace, on your feet or on your knees or on your ass, you know how this fight is going to end.

What Bill Heinz knows and what Bill Heinz wrote is that the dignity, the nobility of it all, lies in the fighting itself and in taking the thing as deep into the late rounds as you can. Bill and I talk about that fight on the phone these days, checking up on each other. A few weeks ago, dizzy, he fell and cracked his head on the mantel. Gashed like he'd been butted in a clinch. I ask if he's O.K.

"Oh sure," he says, "just another writer still beating his head against the wall."

Would You Let This Man Interview You?

BY MYRON COPE

There was a warning implicit in that title because the man in question was Howard Cosell, an abrasive, nasal-voiced ex-lawyer who was building a reputation as America's best sportscaster by interrogating athletes as if they were on trial.

O H, THIS HORIZONTAL LADDER OF MEDIOCRITY," SIGHS Howard Cosell, ruminating on the people who make up the radio-television industry, which pays him roughly $175,000 a year. "There's one thing about this business: there is no place in it for talent. That's why I don't belong. I lack sufficient mediocrity."

Cosell fondles a martini at a table in the Warwick bar, across the street from American Broadcasting Company headquarters. Anguish clouds his homely face. His long nose and pointed ears loom over his gin in the fashion of a dive bomber swooping in with fighter escort. "This is a terrible business," he says. It being the cocktail hour, the darkened room is packed with theatrical and Madison Avenue types. A big blonde, made up like Harlow the day after a bender, dominates a nearby table, encircled by spindly, effete little men. Gentlemen in blue suits, with vests, jam the bar. A stocky young network man pauses at Cosell's table and cheerfully asks if he might drop by Cosell's office some day soon. Cosell says certainly, whereupon the network man joins a jovial crowd at the bar. "He just got fired," Cosell whispers. "He doesn't know I already know." The man, he is positive, wants his help, but what is Cosell to do when there are men getting fired every week?

"This is the roughest, toughest, cruelest jungle in the world," Cosell grieves. A waiter brings him a phone, and he orders a limousine and chauffeur from a rental agency. He cannot wait to retreat to his rustic fireside in Pound Ridge up in Westchester County. It is Monday evening, barely the beginning of another long week in which he, Howard W. Cosell, middle-aged and tiring, must stand against the tidal wave of mediocrity, armed only with his brilliance and integrity.

It has been only 11 years since Cosell quit a New York law practice to become a sportscaster. Yet here he is, the most controversial figure in the business, an opinionated lone wolf in a profession populated by pretty-faced ex-athletes and fence-straddling play-by-play announcers who see angry sponsors under their beds. Teen-agers and adult athletes and men in neighborhood saloons do imitations of his nasally acerbic voice, which assaults millions on 30 radio and TV shows a week. His interviews with Muhammad Ali are the Hope Diamond in ABC's *Wide World of Sports*, television's most successful sports series. (To the disgust or titillation of viewers, Cosell meticulously addresses the heavyweight champion by his Muslim name. Privately he stridently defends the right to be known by the name of one's choice, however exotic, but after tossing off a few Muhammad Alis he lapses into Cassius Clays.)

Then there is Cosell the producer—the president of Legend Productions, Inc. His sports documentaries command prime network time, and the praise they attract from critics, Cosell hastens to point out, is "unbelievable." His intellect surpasses the boundaries of sports. Each Sunday night, 10 to 11 on New York radio, he may be heard grilling the likes of Governor Nelson A. Rockefeller and Mayor John V. Lindsay on affairs of the day, sometimes turning the interviews into Cosell-vs.-whomever debates, in which he acts as both contestant and judge. "I'm getting to you, Bill," he tells conservative William F. Buckley Jr. "Now, before we're done, you're going to be defeated. You *know* that."

Yet, most of all, Cosell's forward progress stems from the fact that, alone among sportscasters of national stature, he works at his trade. He goes out and looks for news and personalities, instead of waiting for gossip at Toots Shor's.

"If you say 'Manny Mota' to Howard Cosell, he knows something about Manny Mota," says Leonard Koppett of *The New York Times*. "If you say 'Manny Mota' to lots of the others in that field, you're going to get a blank stare or statistics they read on a file card."

Cosell is not the least bit reluctant to make it clear at every opportunity that he knows a lot of things about a lot of things. "I'm not the greatest man in the world," he says, careful to set the record straight, "but I've brought to this business the direct, honest and total reporting that previously has been the sole province of the press." Answering football commissioner Pete Rozelle's call for a major press conference, Cosell plunges into a folding chair in the first row of the press section, where he is within range of cameras and microphones. Rozelle sits on a sofa, flanked by Dallas general manager Tex Schramm and

Kansas City owner Lamar Hunt. The commissioner announces that the NFL and AFL are about to merge. Soon Cosell's voice clamors for Rozelle's attention like pots and pans falling off a shelf. He demands to know if the AFL has forced the merger by secretly making huge offers to NFL stars. "You *know* that it's true," he tells Rozelle.

"No, I do not know that it's true," Rozelle replies, evenly.

"*I* know that it's true," Cosell trumpets. He turns to Lamar Hunt, demanding a confession. Hunt equivocates. "You mean you're negotiating for your league without knowing what your league is doing?" Cosell persists.

"I've tried to answer your question," says Hunt. Painstakingly courteous, Hunt is a Wally Cox type, though he is worth hundreds of millions. "I don't mean to be abrupt," he apologizes.

"It's not a question of being abrupt, Lamar," Cosell breaks in, his voice threatening to shatter Hunt's spectacles. "It's a question of being evasive at a time when the American people are entitled to know the truth!"

The American people lose, but Howard Cosell wins another press conference. "You've got to treat Howard the way he treats you," says columnist Dick Young of the New York *Daily News.* "You've got to throw his flamboyant junk back in his face. He asks better questions than the other radio and TV interviewers, but he hokes up his questions so that actually they sound better than they are. 'Now, truthfully'—it's always 'truthfully,' as if it's a question the guy on the other end has been ducking—'people insist that you'—people don't say it, they insist it—'that you can not take a punch, Muhammad Ali. Now, truthfully, can you take a punch?' " The Cosell manner, observes Larry Merchant of the *New York Post,* manages "to make the world of fun and games sound like the Nuremberg trials."

Meanwhile, brimming with editorial comment, Cosell has gone after Casey Stengel and George Weiss, the New York Giants and NCAA football, Floyd Patterson and the sporting press, and all varieties of commissioners and leagues. Though ABC's New York radio outlet carries the Jets' games, he campaigned vigorously last fall against Jet coach Weeb Ewbank, whom he dismisses as "passé." In short, Cosell has traveled a course hardly calculated to take him to the goal that practically all sportscasters covet: a play-by-play assignment. He could not care less. "I'm a personality," he specifies. "With rare exceptions, they don't make them that way in the sports business anymore."

Play-by-play announcers, Cosell goes on, are nothing but shills for the ball clubs, and anybody who expects inquisitive journalism from them is a dunce. "Today the football games are a series of match-ups to see who leads in blimp shots," Cosell cries. Why would a man of his gifts want any part of such prosaic routine? "There is *no way* you will ever hear me saying"—and here he lowers his voice to a dulcet whisper—"This is Howard Cosell on the 16th green . . . 420 yards to the pin, with a dogleg to the left. . . . Up to this point, only four golfers have equaled par. . . . ' " With a shudder, Cosell pictures himself on the professional bowling circuit. "Can you imagine Howard Cosell saying, 'Wayne Zahn approaching the line . . . beautiful delivery!' " Does David Brinkley cover supermarket openings?

Anyhow, Cosell's forte is the interview. Years ago he decided that he would not go around asking athletes how they field ground balls or condition their hamstring tendons. They are intelligent, sensitive men, he argued; he would persuade them to bare their souls. "Look at Mantle!" Cosell says. "He did a half-hour show with me, and he felt like he had had a cathartic. He felt *cleansed.* Joe Namath! The kid poured his heart out to me. Colonel Red Blaik, who was supposed to be a martinet, an icicle, he opened up like a sieve. He said, 'Young man, this is the finest conversation I've ever had.' " Except when a natural comedian such as Cassius Clay appears on Cosell's show, the world of sports remains a lugubrious place, a bonanza of pathos that Cosell has barely begun to mine. "Someday," he promises, "I'm going to do a show on Roger Maris— *The American Tragedy.*"

The athlete who can fend off a Cosell interview has not been born. "Damn you, Koufax," he once said when, shortly before game time, Sandy balked at racing from the clubhouse to redo a film Cosell's technicians had fouled up. "You were a little nothing sitting in the corner of the Brooklyn dugout when I used to come around and talk to you." Koufax went along quietly.

Sonny Liston, having heard Cosell describe him on the air as a congenital thug, glared at him in his training camp and said, "You ain't my friend." "That's true," Cosell answered. He then launched into a speech, the gist of which was that, like Sonny and all the rest of the world's slobs, he had a living to earn. The next thing Liston knew, Cosell was walking him along a windswept beach where a bitter-gray sky supplied a backdrop for such questions as, *did* Liston throw the first Clay fight, and *was* he owned by gangsters?

Having elected to introduce journalism into sportscasting, Cosell has had to plow through a gantlet of carping sponsors, station executives and ad salesmen, all bent on convincing him that it is safer to read ball scores off a ticker tape. "It may be that my greatest accomplishment was my mere survival," he declares. There he was, putting the finishing touches on a one-hour documentary, *The Yankee from Texas,* the story of Johnny Keane, when a breathless ABC man staggered into his office, crying, "We gotta rewrite the opening!" The opening was a film clip of Budweiser baron Gussie Busch reading with great embarrassment Keane's letter of resignation from his post as manager of the St. Louis Cardinals. (The scene was opéra bouffe, for Busch earlier had decided to fire Keane but then changed his mind after Keane managed the

Cardinals to the 1964 pennant at the wire. Keane, however, considered himself fired and decided to stay fired.) The opening was a natural, except for the fact that Pabst was the principal sponsor of *The Yankee from Texas*. Now Pabst had phoned from Milwaukee and said, "Get Busch out of the opening."

"We are not rewriting any opening," Cosell informed the ABC man who had relayed the command to him. "Get me Milwaukee on the phone." Moments later Cosell's voice drilled into Milwaukee: "You gonna keep it a secret that Gussie Busch fired him? You gonna keep it a secret? You people have been talking about being stand-up guys. If you make us pull Busch out of the show, you're fakes!"

Busch stayed in the show.

Although every crisis plunges Cosell into a chasm of gloom, he requires only a reminder of his own genius to rebound strongly. The morning after Green Bay walloped Kansas City in the Super Bowl, Cosell sailed into his office at 10 a.m. crowing, "Just what I predicted! Just what I predicted on the air, right down to naming Willie Wood!" Cosell had known all along, he said, that Green Bay's pass coverage would be to the outside but that sooner or later safety man Wood would slip inside to intercept and turn the tide. "I said, 'The hero, the guy who will break the game open, will be Willie Wood.' " Cosell let his words fly into the corridor and fill every office on the sixth floor of the ABC Building, where he is called Coach, a title he revels in. "Of course," he added, "I've been wrong a million times in my predictions."

Cosell arose from behind his desk, launching into an explanation of why he knows so much. He demanded to know if any reporter in the world can match his connections with sports figures. Famous names—men who are, as he put it, his very, very dear friends—rolled from his tongue. He surged into his Big Story voice, biting off his phrases dramatically, as he often does in off duty monologues.

"*I'm* the guy . . . who gets to Lombardi! *I'm* the guy . . . who gets letters from Pancho Gonzalez! *I'm* the guy Champagne Tony Lema visited the very day he got back from the British Open, one week before his tragic death." Cosell's voice fell to a hush. "We sat on the veranda . . . and I said, 'Tony, when it's all over and done, how do you want to be remembered?' And he said, 'I guess I just want to be remembered as Tony Lema—nice guy.' I said, 'How about Tony Lema, glamour guy?' And he said, 'Yeah, I'd like that, if it doesn't carry the wrong implication.' " Cosell paused to let five seconds of silence grip the scene. He resumed in a whisper. "And then I got out a bottle of bubbly . . . and said, 'Shall we?' Tony Lema said, 'Why not? I'll open it.' He popped it open and said, 'Cheers.' And I said, 'Cheers.' Later I got a letter from him . . . the morning after he died. I read it . . . and I cried."

Now Cosell ticked off more famous names, pacing the floor of his office, although unable to take more than two steps in any direction. The room is little more than a cubicle—exactly like hundreds of other white-walled cubicles that line the stark-white corridors of the ABC skyscraper, a building that in Cosell's words has "a public-toilet whiteness about it that's frightening." He is the network's national sports director for radio and its New York sports director for television, but one wonders if his cramped quarters are the means by which the corporation's upper echelon reminds him he is still a sports reporter. When *Wide World* has a tough interview to cope with, Cosell is called in to handle it, but rumors persist that he gives the brass indigestion.

At 3:05 Cosell shoveled his ungainly frame into a cab and set off for ABC's West 66th Street studios to tape a two minute essay for the 11 o'clock news on WABC-TV, the network's New York station. In a pocket of his camel's hair overcoat he carried a hairpiece (which he keeps stored in a shoebox in his desk) that lengthens his receding hairline, though not to the extent of lying about his age. In his head, as the cab weaved through traffic, he created his essay. Cosell never works from a script and rarely knows exactly what he is going to say until he is on the air.

"You're wasting your love on me," he cried to a receptionist as he loped through the lobby of the 66th Street building. In another minute he was tearing past a second-floor newsroom, shouting at the staff, "Willie Wood! Willie Wood! You know where you first heard it!" He paused in a dressing room to have his face powdered, then emerged at the head of an iron staircase that descended into a huge studio cluttered with equipment and crew. "The coach is here!" Cosell announced. He planted himself at a lectern, awaiting his cue, and then rattled off an editorial censuring Lamar Hunt for putting bush-league football on the same field with the Green Bay Packers. His show completed, Cosell then censured his director for having put Lamar Hunt's picture on a screen that stood behind him and to his left. The cameras had had to divert from Cosell in order to film Hunt.

Cosell raced back to ABC headquarters and entered a glass-enclosed room on the eighth floor to do a 4½-minute radio show. "I can break the story now," he barked into a microphone. Charlie Finley, he said, was at it again, stealthily laying plans to move his Kansas City Athletics to Oakland. Having exposed Finley, Cosell turned from the mike and cried, "That, you see, is a sports show! Not an ounce of day-old wire copy about Max McGee retiring. I broke a story." The *Times* probably would have given the scoop two inches, but there was no holding Cosell. "Now, that show was a contribution journalistically." Cosell cantered to an elevator, calling over his shoulder to a secretary, "Oh, Shirley, if only I could have you one more time."

"One more time!" Shirley shrieked, careful to let the office know there hadn't been a first time. But Cosell was gone.

Arriving home that night, Cosell flung off his jacket, his tie, his shoes, his socks, and sprawled barefoot in a living-room chair. He accepted a martini from his wife, Emi, a pleasant woman with light-brown hair, and gazed happily into a roaring fire. The Cosells, with two attractive young daughters and an Irish setter named Kelly, live on 11 acres of woodland in a lodge-style house made of cedar and fieldstone and adjoined by a pool. Away from the radio-TV jungle, a curious change comes over Cosell. He speaks softly, with an occasional dash of humor that is missing in his broadcasts. "If you don't know Cosell well," says sportswriter Maury Allen of the *New York Post*, "the only side of him that comes out is this business of being on all the time. I've found him to be a man of great depth, honesty and knowledge."

In an industry rife with intrigue, not even Cosell's detractors accuse him of having backstabbed his way to the top. He praises colleagues exuberantly when impressed by a job they've done, but he has earned enmity by also telling them straight out—ABC's Chris Schenkel was one—that he caught their latest show and, by God, it was awful.

For all his suggestive sallies to secretaries (a form of false dash that serves to announce his presence), Cosell is considered the original square by an industry that is full of swingers. He is completely at ease only with his family and is dedicated to the proposition that in five more years he will have enough money to get out of the jungle and retire to Florida. When off on a major assignment—for example, a Clay fight via satellite from Europe—he practically trembles at the prospect that he will do a clumsy job and thereby play into the hands of a press that he is certain is lusting to rip him. Says Chet Forte, Cosell's producer on the satellite fight shows: "It's always Emi, Emi, Emi—'I gotta phone Emi. I oughta be home. I gotta see what Emi thinks of the way we're going to do this show.' I don't know if she builds him up or what, but after he phones her he seems to snap out of it."

A pillar of equanimity, Emi attends to her Pound Ridge house, unnerved only when she overhears townspeople mutter an epithet they apply to Cosell whenever he has done a show with draft dodger Clay. Pound Ridgers being a cultivated lot, they attack Cosell in the dialogue of the times. "Dove," they sneer.

Actually, Cosell himself served a brilliant, if not exactly action-packed, military career. Born Howard William Cohen, he grew up in Brooklyn, the son of a Jewish immigrant from Poland who worked as an accountant for a chain of credit clothing stores. Cosell aspired early to become a newspaper reporter, but Isidore and Nellie Cohen urged him into the law. At New York University he made Phi Beta Kappa, became an editor of the Law Review and upon his graduation in 1940 landed a job with a substantial firm. But when the Japanese bombed Pearl Harbor in '41 Cosell enlisted in the Army as a private, though he was destined for Officer Candidate School and lofty rank. He spent the war commuting by subway to his station at the New York Port of Embarkation on the Brooklyn docks, a situation the neighbors viewed with bitterness.

"Oh, I well remember the Minsky widow," he says. "Her husband was the burlesque king, remember? She couldn't stand the sight of me coming home every day, first with a gold bar, now with a silver bar, now two silver bars, now a gold leaf. I could understand this. She had a son serving in the Marines, on Guadalcanal." Cosell himself had become the boy wonder of the Port—a key brain who juggled a manpower pool of 50,000. Twice the Pentagon blocked his promotion to major on the ground that he was moving up too swiftly for a Stateside functionary, and he got the promotion only when Major General Homer M. Groninger, the Port commander, fired off a six-page letter that all but described him as the cornerstone of the war effort.

NEVER HAVING been keen on lawyer's work, Cosell emerged from the Army in 1946 bent on landing an executive position in personnel relations. He figured he had a useful connection, for he had married a WAC sergeant, Mary-Edith (Emi) Abrams, whose father, Norman Ross Abrams, was a prominent industrialist. The Abrams family, a Presbyterian mixture of Pennsylvania Dutch and Welsh, at that time had reservations about Emi's mixed marriage. Father-in-law told Cosell he had no opening. "I was looking for $25,000 to $30,000 a year," Cosell says. "I was a 24-year-old snot." (Perhaps he wasn't. The birth date on his Army records made him a 27-year-old snot. It also makes him 48 today, although the ABC publicity department says he is 46.) Undaunted, Cosell, confidently wrote to a former service comrade, an executive of Fisher Body, who coolly replied with a list of recommended college courses.

"I was in general discomfort," sighs Cosell. "Subliminally, I was sensitive about a Jew's place in industry. But I determined to rid myself of this crutch-type thinking." (It did not occur to him that he was a natural for sportscasting. His mother remembers him talking at nine months.) Cosell saw no choice but to resume the practice of law.

Eight years later, in 1954, the Little League catapulted Cosell to fame. Having drawn up a Little League charter for an American Legion post, he received a call from an ABC program manager asking if he would furnish a panel of kiddies to interview athletes on a weekly series of coast-to-coast radio shows. Radio was in a disheveled state, dying. Not surprisingly, the program manager suggested as an afterthought that Cosell be moderator—without pay. He leaped at the chance. Although an unknown, he corralled big-name guests by laying siege to hotel lobbies where baseball players congregated. He wooed them with free lunches—Wally Moon, Al Kaline, Fred Hutchinson. "We made news with that show," Cosell shouts. "Out of the mouths of babes came words of wisdom and depth!" Under Cosell's deft direction the brats conned Hank Bauer into putting the blast on Casey Stengel for platooning him.

When, in 1956, the network offered Cosell $250 to do 10 five-minute sports broadcasts each weekend, he immediately decided to abandon his legal work. It moved too slowly to suit him. "My disposition," he announced to his wife, "demands the immediacy of translation of effort into result!" So go translate, Emi told him.

Seeking exposure wherever he could find it, Cosell persuaded a men's adventure magazine to publish a monthly column called *Cosell's Clubhouse.* (The magazine dressed up the column with a cut that rather suggested a benign aardvark leaning against a doghouse.) His editor, Ray Robinson, who today is articles editor of *Good Housekeeping*, recalls the aplomb with which Cosell stepped up in class. "Well," Cosell greeted Robinson some years after the *Clubhouse* column had run its course, "are you still with that witless magazine?"

Seizing the attention of radio listeners, Cosell trampled the rules of sportscasting etiquette. Chet Forte, the producer, was a Columbia basketball star when he first met Cosell and consented to go on his radio show. "What sort of questions are you going to ask me, Howard?" Forte inquired.

"Don't worry, kid," Cosell reassured him. "It'll be a fine show."

Cosell then leaned into the mike and introduced Forte as the nation's leading scorer, a dazzling little man with an uncanny shooting touch. Then Cosell asked his first question. "Chet, is it true that some of your teammates hate to pass to you because you shoot so much?" The audience next heard the sound of Forte sucking in his breath.

Hustling to the scene wherever sports news was being made, Cosell sent chills up the spines of the working press as he trumpeted his way into press conferences and clubhouses. "He comes into a room as if nothing possibly could have happened before he got there," says one sportswriter. Cosell himself points out that when he walks into the Yankee clubhouse, for example, manager Ralph Houk at once turns his way, ignoring the newspapermen around him. "I'm sensitive to this situation and embarrassed by it," Cosell says. Somehow, his words translate to mean he's delighted by it.

Yet as he grew in prominence Cosell at times seemed like a man trying to scale the side of the ABC Building while people stood at the windows hurling buckets of water in his face. Gossip has it that Thomas W. Moore, who in 1958 became an ABC vice president in charge of programming en route to the presidency of ABC-TV, considered shoveling Cosell into an obscure bin and replacing him with Tom Harmon. Even if the rumor sprang from no basis in fact, it is likely that it raced through the company's power structure and created resistance to Cosell.

He pressed on, however. On the New York front he undertook to personally reshape the future of the Mets, and on a national level he hitched his wagon to a force that not even the U.S. government has been able to sidetrack—Muhammad Ali, of course. The bumbling Mets, adored by New Yorkers, caused Cosell to draw back in horror. "I'm suspicious of anything that causes kids to fall in love with futility," he says. WABC was broadcasting the Mets' games during their first two seasons, 1962 and 1963, and Cosell was assigned to do the pregame and postgame shows—a stint that normally consists of reassuring the audience that the home team will come back strong. Cosell, however, plunged into a campaign to drive manager Casey Stengel out of town. The outcome, instead, was that the Mets and WABC parted company, although Cosell insists it was the station, not the ball club, that asked for the divorce. "We didn't want to be identified with a loser," he explains. In any case, Cosell kept after Stengel on his various shows, and with a sense of accomplishment describes his role in the 1966 resignation of front-office boss George Weiss and the promotion of Weiss's successor, Bing Devine.

"I felt George had led me to believe he was going to unload Stengel," says Cosell, his tone that of a Senate majority leader whom the White House has double-crossed. "I only turned on George when I found out he had no intention of unloading Stengel." Casey's resignation in 1965 did not mollify Cosell. "Now here comes Bing Devine into the picture—Bing Devine joins the Mets' front office. One of my dearest friends. He stayed with me at Pound Ridge. So then I went to work on getting rid of Weiss so Bing could get the job. Well, I don't mean I got *rid* of George, but I poured it on. And I'm sure he stayed an extra year *because* I poured it on."

Meanwhile, legions of television viewers across the country were taking notice of Cosell, partly because they found it incredible that any white American male would throw his arm around Cassius Clay and with a straight face treat him to the Muhammads that even Clay's Negro opponents are reluctant to utter. A northern newspaper labeled Cosell a White Muslim. White supremacists and parents of servicemen wrote him a flood of strong letters, successfully ruining his mornings. (A single critical letter brings from him tortured cries that can be heard five doorways down the corridor. "I worry about the mass intelligence of this country," he says at such times. "I really do.") Actually, Cosell once attacked Clay's Muslim camp followers for their rudeness and on a satellite telecast neatly squelched the champion in one of his eulogies to the teacher Elijah. "Awright, we've been through that," Cosell broke in.

Whether or not he first catered to Clay because he foresaw the alliance would mean national attention, a genuine friendship seemed to develop between the two. At Cosell's urging, Clay delayed his fight with Henry Cooper 18 minutes, infuriating British boxing officials, so that ABC could finish telecasting its prefight show. "Howard worries about the kid," Chet Forte said shortly before Clay's February victory over Ernie Terrell. "I think he dreads the day when that kid loses. But if anything ever happens to the champ he'll turn around and look for Howard and Howard will be there." In the aftermath of the Terrell fight, however, a layer of frost settled over their relationship. On *Wide World* Clay demanded Cosell defend him against charges that he had taunted and fouled Terrell. Cosell refused, triggering a shouting match that in turn brought Cosell a barrage of letters accusing him of picking on Clay, to say nothing of being anti-Negro. Another morning ruined.

Although Clay may now be an exception, the people who work closely with Cosell usually enjoy the relationship. "Howard, you are not an insufferable egotist," one such man told him recently. "You are a sufferable egotist." Cosell was incredulous. "Do you really think I'm an egotist?" he said, wounded.

At any rate, he does not insist upon being the whole show. He has brought the television sports documentary to adulthood by hiring talented writers and then keeping his nose out of their work. "Documentary writing is lousy work," says Jerry Izenberg, who wrote Cosell's *Pro Football's Shotgun Marriage: $onny, Money and Merger*, a highly acclaimed study of the war between the football leagues, "because what happens is you get a producer-director who puts together a lot of film clips and then says, 'Write a script.' Cosell, on the other hand, puts the horse in front of the cart, and you don't end up writing bridge lines for guys catching passes."

Laying plans for *$onny, Money and Merger*, Cosell called his talent together. "What's your concept for the music?" he asked a short Middle European named Vladimir Selensky.

"First of all," said Selensky, "you do not want football music. You want something totally different."

Cosell glanced at an ad salesman in the room. The salesman's eyes carried an alarm that cried, "It'll never sell!"

"What do you have in mind?" Cosell patiently asked Selensky.

"I want storm clouds. I want tension. I want an all-is-not-well feeling." Silence blanketed the room. Selensky turned to Izenberg, searching for support. "What do you think?" he asked. "I like it," Izenberg said.

"You," Selensky informed him, "have a soul. You may call me Vlady."

Cosell, measuring the convictions of his talent against those of his ad salesman, instructed Selensky to put together the storm clouds and bring them in. When Selensky did so, Cosell listened to no more than five bars. "Perfect!"

he cried and walked away, knowing that the music (which was to endow the football war with all the intensity of a midwinter battle at the gates of Moscow) was in the hands of a professional.

If only the people on the industry's horizontal ladder of mediocrity would leave him alone, Cosell would remain at peace. As it is, he charged angrily from his office one recent morning, shouting over his shoulder at a nicely barbered blond man who trailed in his wake. (The man wanted Cosell to find no less than 24 sports events every weekend and assign network radio announcers to interview the stars of each event by phone.)

Cosell flung himself into an elevator. "Do you think," he bellowed as the doors slammed closed in the blond man's face, "that a mass audience is going to be interested in *barrel jumping*?"

The next day Cosell sat at his cocktail-hour post in the Warwick bar, his shoulders slumping, his face a mask of agony. "I am tired," he said, "morally, mentally, emotionally, physically, I am tired." The forces of ignorance had struck again this very day. A radio station in an AFL city—Cosell would not say which one— had disliked his latest critique on AFL football and had notified ABC that it was dropping all Cosell shows. (A couple of weeks later they were reinstated.)

"I have lived a lifetime with this kind of thing," Cosell said. "The impact of Howard Cosell on radio is enormous. People love him or hate him. Local yokels pressure the stations. The guy who runs the station in this AFL city said, 'You have destroyed the image of our city.' Our sales head was in a panic."

Cosell wondered what the world was coming to. "I'm in the toy department, sports!" he cried. "Are people so juvenile that you can't tell the truth in sports? This isn't Bill Manchester on Jackie Kennedy! This is Howard Cosell on sports! I don't take myself that seriously. Let's not make it Paul Revere on the horse. I'm no hero.

"The American Broadcasting Company has lived with me and permitted me," Cosell plowed on. "Tomorrow they may not. If so, there will be no sad songs for me. I'll go without a whimper. But ABC has been the only network to permit a Howard Cosell, and that's why Howard Cosell is important. *That's* why Howard Cosell is a story. If ever there was a trailblazer, if ever a broadcaster sought to bring sports out of the juvenile, out of the banal—this, you see, is my mission. I have been an electronic first," Cosell declared, "and I don't mean that egotistically."

The electronic first gazed at the ceiling, as if the magnificent trails that he had blazed were etched into the beams for him to see. "Yes," he at last decided. "When you get right down to it, I *am* a hero."

The Big Wind
In Chicago

BY RON FIMRITE

Long before he became a North Side deity, Harry Caray swept into the
Windy City as the White Sox announcer, a fan's fan who charmed the locals by
speaking the language of the paying customer.

I T WAS THE SHANK OF A SUMMER EVENING IN CHICAGO—AND Harry Caray, the inimitable White Sox broadcaster, was sauntering up State Street sipping a banana daiquiri. Harry's wee hours constitutionals, particularly those undertaken in the drinking quarter where State and Rush streets converge, have become the occasion for impromptu civic celebrations. Hordes of revelers trail him along the streets, shouting, "Hey, Harry," or chanting his name, "Har-ree . . . Har-ree." Cabdrivers stall traffic to hail him. Barflies press against dusty windows seeking a glimpse of him. "Hey, Harry" is a cry strangers to the Windy City hear about as often in the witching hours as they expect to hear "stick 'em up."

In the face of such adulation, Harry exhibits a generosity of spirit common only to those who know they deserve the best. He stops to chat and sign autographs. His manner is engaging, familiar: "Hiya, sweetheart. . . . Whaddya say, pal?" Earlier in the evening, Harry had hit a couple of spots, and in each he was accorded the sort of welcome John Travolta might receive should he appear in the girls' locker room of a small-town junior high school. "Hey, Harry!" "You're the greatest, Harry." "Hey, Harry, say hello to the people of the world." This had been a day like any other in his life, which is to say, utterly chaotic, a continuing test of his pluck and durability.

Harry had arisen brightly that morning after a revivifying four hours of sleep.

He placed a call to Jon Matlack, the Texas Ranger pitcher, identifying himself as Brad Corbett to the hotel operator when informed that Mr. Matlack was not in his room. It is Harry's conviction that even baseball players will return telephone calls if the caller is someone of recognizable financial clout, and Corbett is the principal owner of the Texas baseball team. Harry wanted to discuss with Matlack some intemperate remarks the pitcher had made to the press, to the effect that Harry should be "killed" or, at minimum, have "his lights punched out" for saying on the air that the tumultuous booing Matlack's teammate, Richie Zisk, had received from Chicago fans was richly merited.

Zisk, a White Sox player last year, had himself been critical of Chicago fans, a sin in Harry's eyes comparable to denouncing the game itself. Matlack returned the call and Harry said he would see him in the visitors' clubhouse at Comiskey Park that evening. There Harry found Matlack to be more contrite than murderous. Zisk was less conciliatory, but he concluded a protracted harangue ambiguously by insisting, "You say anything you want, Harry. O.K.?" Harry, ever unflappable, agreed he would do just that. When the crowd booed Zisk even more ferociously that night, Harry apologized, in a way. "There must be something wrong with your television sets," he advised his listeners.

After the game, Harry had a grand time recounting these infantile confrontations in the Bards Room, Comiskey Park's press lounge, but he had tired of the subject by the time he sat down to his midnight supper at the Cafe Bohemia with a party that included his third wife, Dutchie; Fred Brzozowski, a part owner of the Sox; and restaurateur Jimmy Gallios. Dutchie (real name, Delores) is a St. Louis girl who has known Harry long enough to be more amused by his indefatigable pub-crawling than intolerant of it. She can even stay with him on the shorter stretches. Harry is a stocky man of at least 59, with curly gray hair, a florid complexion and lips that, when still, are seen to be thick. He wears enormous spectacles, which give him the aspect of a gigantic guppy. And yet his is a pleasant face, one that scores of women seem to have found agreeable.

The party at the Cafe Bohemia moved right along, largely thanks to Harry, who urged Gallios, a dark, wry man, to recall his misadventures in pursuit of a striptease artist named Justa Dream. It was for love of the ravishing Justa, lamented Gallios, that he purchased the disreputable cocktail lounge in the old Hotel Majestic where she performed. It was not, he said, a prudent investment, particularly after the place nearly burned down when a customer threw a monkey into the light fixtures in back of the bar.

Later, Harry deposited a mildly protesting Dutchie—"Harry, don't you ever give up?"—in their apartment in the Ambassador East Hotel and set off on his rounds. His last stop was the Hotsie Totsie Club on Division near State, where he was literally served one for the road. Normally a Scotch, vodka or beer man, Harry favors a banana daiquiri as a nightcap, and since it was closing time at the Hotsie Totsie and he is, after all, Harry, he was allowed to transport the confection with him from the premises.

He was walking and sipping and talking with a companion when he was approached on State Street by two professional women, who embarked upon a familiar spiel. There were lamentations over the plight of the lonely middle-aged man and pointed suggestions as to how this deplorable state might, for one evening at least, be alleviated. The conversation had not gone far when one of the women stopped abruptly in mid-pitch. "Hey," she chirped, "you're Harry Caray, aren't you?" Harry cheerfully confirmed his identity. "How 'bout that," the woman said to her co-worker. "Harry Caray." A somewhat restructured conversation ensued, much of it pertaining to baseball. Harry complimented the women on their pleasing appearance and the eloquence of their presentation. He was a married man again, he said apologetically, so any association beyond the agreeable one they were now enjoying would be indiscreet. The women wanted no more of him, they protested, than an autograph. Harry signed an old dance bid or something, and the women continued on their appointed rounds.

"That was nothing," said Harry. "About seven years ago my car stalled outside the Chase-Park Plaza Hotel in St. Louis, where I used to spend a lot of time. I was sitting there, about four in the morning, cursing my bad luck, when these two guys came up to me. Each of them stuck a gun in my ribs. Hoo boy! Then one of them said, 'Hey, Harry. It's you, isn't it? What're you doing out this late? Are you one of us?' I'd been a broadcaster in St. Louis for 25 years, you know, so I was pretty well known there. Well, this guy put his gun away and we just stood there jawing about baseball. They forgot they were mugging me, and I forgot I was being mugged. We were all just fans. I signed a couple of autographs, and they took off without taking a nickel."

If nothing else, such escapes from the clutches of the lawless serve to dramatize Harry's extraordinary popularity in the communities where he broadcasts. But popularity is too pallid a word to describe Harry's relationship with his listeners. He seems to them not so much an announcer doing the old play-by-play as *one* of them who has somehow gained access to a microphone. His grievances, his prejudices, his obsessions are theirs. When the team is going badly, Harry howls with despair along with them; when it is going well, he exults as they do. The fact is, Harry *is* a fan. He is a survivor of a time when baseball announcers were neither retired athletes nor bewigged egomaniacs but somewhat truer voices of the people.

Howard Cosell, in a typical flash of false insight, once identified Harry as a "cheerleader." He is not that at all. Fans are not cheerleaders; they are *cheerers*—and booers. That is what Harry is. His is the language of the paying customer. This is not to say he is above show business. Catch phrases are part of his act—"You can't beat fun at the old ball park. . . . Well, that's baseball. . . . Listen to the crowd. . . . Hol-lee Cow!" But Harry is more than a disembodied voice to White Sox fans; he is a physical presence in the ballpark. He leans out of the broadcast booth to shout at friends or to join the crowd in cheers and song. He thrusts his butterfly net out in quest of foul balls. He strides through the stands before the game, shaking hands, signing autographs, slapping backs, embracing comely women. After the game, Harry is out among them, talking baseball in his favorite saloons. Four in the morning often arrives too soon for "the Mayor of Rush Street."

Harry was immensely successful as a Cardinal broadcaster from 1945 through 1969, but it is unlikely he ever had an audience more empathetic than the one he now enjoys. "Harry fits in with our group," says Sox president Bill Veeck. "He fits in with our philosophy and style, which is casual, even raucous. Our audience is not at all like the Cubs', which is mostly youngsters and people over 50. Ours comes from the 16-to-40 age bracket. They are as exuberant as any I've ever seen, and a great part of that is Harry. Can you envision Dodger fans standing up in the middle of a game to cheer Vin Scully the way they cheer Harry here? He says what he believes on the air, and the fans identify directly with him.

"Frankly, I hate to listen to him when we're losing because he can put the greatest degree of contempt in what he's saying. It's more than popularity. It's a matter of texture. Harry is basically one of the fans. He drinks beer with them or whatever else is available. He talks to them in saloons, which is good. But he's also a professional who does his homework. He's not merely flamboyant."

No one knows his audience better than Harry does. While interviewing *Chicago Tribune* sportswriter Bill Jauss recently, Harry took it upon himself to define the quintessential Sox fan: "He is a working-class guy, a guy who picks up a six-pack at a tavern before coming to the game. He's my kind of person." Comiskey Park itself has the look and feel of a neighborhood tavern. It is dark and wooden and musty and cozy. There is the aroma of beer and peanuts. It is noisy, and many nights there are fights in the stands. If the stadium is a saloon, Harry is the guy sitting down at the end of the bar telling funny stories.

"The announcer is the only liaison between the people and the ball club," says Harry. "The trouble with announcers today—and heck, I can't even think of most of their names—is that they're in it just for the money. Baseball has the advantage of having a lot of games. Because of the frequency of it, it pays better than the other sports. These guys would rather be out playing golf than doing play-by-play, and the boredom comes through in their voices. My enthusiasm is just me. I'm just expressing myself, and I do have opinions. I get in trouble with players and managers that way—like the Zisk thing. The trouble with the players is they feel the fan is so dumb he won't notice their shortcomings unless an announcer calls attention to them. Well, the fan isn't that stupid. The announcer doesn't create a player's weaknesses. The only thing I ask of a player is that he complain to me personally. I always ask, 'Did you hear it?' They rarely do, you know. They get it from a wife, a girlfriend, a groupie. All secondhand stuff."

Harry can become as quickly disenchanted with a player as a fan can, and the miscreant can be as easily restored to his affections with good deeds. These shifts in attitude do not always sit well with players, who prefer to think of the announcers as part of the team, not part of its following. Harry's relations with former White Sox manager Chuck Tanner also were frequently strained. Tanner not only disapproved of Harry's gibes on the air, but he also apparently chafed at the broadcaster's popularity, which far exceeded that of the manager or any of his players. In truth, a player or manager might be forgiven pangs of envy over Harry's special relationship with the fans. How often, after all, is the play-by-play announcer more popular than those whose play he is describing? In his business, Harry is an original.

He was born Harry Carabina in St. Louis and orphaned at nine. An aspiring athlete, he turned to broadcasting games instead of playing them after high school and survived for 25 years as the voice of the Cardinals. Then, after the 1969 season, his contract was not renewed by team owner August A. Busch Jr. It was a shocker, and unseemly rumor followed Harry's fall from grace. It was said he was playing fast and loose with a young woman who had married into the Busch clan, thereby imperiling the marriage. Rakehell Harry declined to comment on such tawdry allegations, except to say, "I'd rather have people believing the rumor and have my middle-aged ego inflated than deny it and keep my job."

Harry's popularity in St. Louis was scarcely diminished by the scandal. If anything, it achieved its apex that very year, in large part because of a comeback from a near-crippling injury as melodramatic as any ever made by a Cardinal player. On the rainy early morning of Nov. 3, 1968, Harry was struck down by a speeding auto as he crossed the street to his car, which was parked opposite the Chase-Park Plaza, site of so many of his adventures, amatory and otherwise. A woman friend was seated in the car, primping herself for the hours ahead, and Harry yet entertains himself with the thought of his companion watching him fly by the window, howling, "Holy Cow!"

There was, however, nothing amusing about the accident. Harry suffered broken legs, a broken shoulder and a broken nose. He nearly died in the street when rain and blood congested his lungs. And he almost lost one of his shattered limbs in the hospital. But after some months, he was as whole and hearty as ever.

His entrance into Busch Stadium on Opening Day of the 1969 season was terrific theater. Sensing the dramatic possibilities, Harry stepped out of the Cardinal dugout after his introduction, hobbling on two canes. As he crossed the foul line, he tossed one cane aside. Nearing the field microphone, he threw the other away and raised his arms over his head in triumph. As the crowd stood and cheered and chanted, "Har-ree. . . Harree," he limped unaided the rest of the way. "Well, it's all show business," Harry explained later. "I hadn't needed those canes in weeks."

Suspecting a Busch blacklisting, Harry departed St. Louis after 1969 and took up with an unlikely new employer—Charles O. Finley. The anticipated clash of monster egos never fully materialized; Harry and Charlie got on famously during Harry's brief stay in Oakland. Harry did, however, come a cropper against a more fragile personality. Monte Moore had been Finley's announcer since Kansas City days, and he was understandably piqued at being supplanted as the No. 1 man by the rogue from St. Louis. "I could feel the knife in my back every time I walked into the booth," says Harry of his single season in Oakland. "We couldn't go on like that." Besides, Moore was a teetotaler and something of a Bible thumper. The situation was clearly intolerable. So Harry left the A's and joined the then downtrodden White Sox in 1971.

The terms of his new contract were unusual in that they were geared to Harry's reputation for putting "fannies in the seats." Stu Holcomb, then the Sox' executive vice president, inserted an attendance clause that called for Harry to be paid a base annual salary of $50,000 with bonuses of $10,000 for every 100,000 spectators the Sox drew in excess of 600,000. In pre-Harry 1970 the Sox drew 495,355. In Harry's first year attendance climbed to 833,891. In 1972 it was 1,186,018, and in '73 it reached 1,316,527, the highest since 1960. Harry was by then making more in bonuses than he was in salary. The attendance provisions were discontinued after the '73 season.

Harry himself was nearly discontinued two years later by the team president, John Allyn. Harry had been feuding with Tanner, and Allyn made it abundantly clear whose side he was on during a television interview. Harry was watching another show when a newspaper friend called to suggest he catch his boss. Harry switched channels in time to see the end of an interview in which Allyn said that if he owned the team in 1976, Harry would not be back. It was Allyn, of course, who did not come back. The Sox were sold in '76 to a group headed by the redoubtable Veeck, and last year a team attendance record of 1,657,315 was established.

Even with Allyn and Tanner gone, Harry was not assured of a job. Veeck had been operating the perennially impoverished Browns in St. Louis at the same time that Harry was winning fans for the Cardinals. Harry sensed that the new White Sox president still held an old grudge against him, and at the outset of their interview nothing was said to disabuse him of this unpleasant notion. "Here I am talking to the man who ran me out of St. Louis," Harry recalls Veeck saying. "Yeah, me and Gussie Busch's millions," Harry retorted. Veeck laughed. Harry stayed. But the suspicion remains that Veeck might yet resent being upstaged in his own park. Would not the peg-legged entrepreneur prefer to be up there himself leading the cheers and songs?

"No, that's not Bill's style," says part owner Brzozowski. "Actually, his ego and Harry's go on like this." He moves his hands upward and parallel. "They don't cross." And Veeck does seem to appreciate Harry's antics, which, in Harry's view, is merely demonstrating good business sense. "I'm a walking advertisement for the White Sox," says Harry humbly. "That I relate to people is one heck of an asset to the team. And I don't make a nickel off the Sox anymore." Indeed, Harry is now paid by his radio and television stations, not by the White Sox; Veeck retains only the right to refuse his services.

Harry's current earnings for broadcasting Sox games—all of them on radio, 140 on television—are, by his accounting, as high as or higher than those of any announcer in baseball. He is probably worth it. "He's the most knowledgeable broadcaster in the game," says his color man, Jimmy Piersall, himself a personality of authenticated flamboyance. "A lot of play-by-play men have to pick your brains for information. Otherwise they're dead. Harry just knows the game."

IT IS SATURDAY, the day Harry does his broadcast from the centerfield bleachers in Comiskey Park. On this particular Saturday he is dressed in a powder-blue polo shirt and white shorts supported by a cloth belt emblazoned with the words HOLY COW. "When you got good wheels," says Harry, defending his apparel, "you show 'em."

Harry arrives at the ball park to the sounds of a familiar refrain: "Hey, Harry. . . Har-ree." He breezes through the crowd, signing programs and baseballs, commending a girl for looking smashing and advising her boyfriend that "with eyes like yours, pal, you could hit .300 in the big leagues." An elderly woman embraces him as he passes through the press gate. She is wearing a T-shirt on which is written BEAUTY IS SKIN DEEP. UGLY GOES RIGHT TO THE BONE. Harry hugs her back. He enters the Bards Room, pausing long enough to down a screwdriver and distribute recordings of a new disco version of *Take Me Out to the Ball Game*, on which his superimposed voice shouts, "Holy Cow!" "The record's great," Harry tells the newsmen. "You can hardly hear me." He rejoins the fans, passing through the stands to the playing field. Along the way there is more handshaking, backslapping and choruses of "Hey, Harry."

Harry's high good humor is threatened when he is told by one of his television people that Veeck has ordered the bleachers closed because of a threat of rain. Harry bounces into the dugout and telephones Veeck in the Bards Room. "Bill, what's this about the bleachers being closed? Yeah, yeah, I know, but there's bright sunshine out here now." This is almost true.

Harry bounds out of the dugout. "O.K., O.K., the bleachers are open. Gotta do some work now." He will do interviews with fans, one for radio, one for TV. For radio, he picks an elderly gent named Francis Cavanaugh, who says he first saw a White Sox game in 1922. Harry asks him how good Babe Ruth was. "Best I ever saw," says Mr. Cavanaugh, whom Harry is now calling "my good friend." Harry gives his guest a digital watch and a hearty handshake.

Spectators are filtering into the bleacher seats, so Harry rushes out to join them. He bustles down labyrinthine corridors underneath the stands, stocky legs pumping hard. It is nearly game time, but his crew is only now beginning to set up, and he still has a television interview to do. When he reaches the bleachers, he receives a tumultuous "Hey, Harry" welcome. He stands on the walkway below leading the cheering.

Harry's broadcasting table is situated on a platform to the left of the hitters' backdrop, a rope separating him from the fans. Near Harry's table is a barber's chair, where Lynn Gladowsky gives haircuts during the game at $4 a clip. Harry plugs her business on the air, interviews her customers and, naturally, has his own locks shorn by her. On the runway below there is a shower where overheated bleacherites douse themselves, Harry among them.

FOR HIS television interview, Harry selects from the crowd John Durkin, a 21-year-old Illinois State student. "I need a beer," Durkin says, steeling himself for the ordeal. "You want one, Harry?" Harry does. Durkin's college pals, who have quaffed many beers, cheer him noisily throughout the interview. They are encouraged by Harry, who cries out, "He's good, isn't he?" Harry waves his beer in a toast to Durkin, and there is a raucous demonstration in the bleachers.

Harry's attaché case and butterfly net arrive only moments before the national anthem. Conditions are seldom ideal for the bleacher broadcasts, but an increasingly capricious wind adds fresh complications. Harry's statistical sheets soar about him like kites, and strands of freshly trimmed hair from Gladowsky's barber chair drift into his beer. "You can't beat fun at the old ballpark," Harry shouts to no one in particular. The camera lights are on. "It's a hot, humid, windy. . . beeoootiful day for baseball," Harry begins in his hoarse baritone, "and here we are in the bleachers. These are baseball's true fans right here."

In the first inning of the game with Kansas City, Sox third baseman Eric Soderholm throws wildly to first on a routine ground ball. "Soderholm made a terrible throw," Harry moans. "He could've run the ball over in time to get that out and he threw it away. But that's baseball." One hitter later, the chastened Soderholm makes a diving catch of a hard ground ball between third and short and, from his knees, throws the runner out. "Hol-lee Cow!" Harry bellows. "What a sensational play! And after missing that easy one. That's baseball."

The wind, which is picking up, topples one of Harry's beers and drenches a stat sheet. Harry calls for a towel. The flying hair lends a gauzy effect to the already improbable scene, so that when seen head-on Harry appears to be a figure from a Renoir. Harry's television monitor is not functioning, and because a portion of rightfield is obscured by the black backdrop that rises to his left, he can only speculate on the ultimate destination of balls hit there. Inebriated bleacherites hover near him, demanding to be put on the air. The "Hey, Harry" cries grow more insistent, taking on a less friendly, more satirical tone. The loudest of these emanate from a man with a transistor radio affixed to his ear, someone obviously intent on hearing the sound of his own voice on the radio.

Harry revels in the chaos. Not even the most offensive drunk ruffles him. He poses for pictures between innings, flourishes his beer, shakes hands, kisses the ladies. His microphone becomes a baton as he conducts the bleacher chorus in a rendition of the White Sox fight song, *Na, Na, Hey, Hey, Kiss Him Goodbye*. And he dutifully reads the scribbled notes that find their way to him: "Aunt Carrie Gable from LaSalle is here celebrating her 85th birthday. . . . Now here's a bunch of guys who write, 'Please assure our wives we really did come to the game. . . .' "

Harry goes on to extol the virtues of bleacher dwelling. "We got a shower and we got a barber chair. I don't know what else we need." There is also the ball game. "Ooops, Joe Zdeb just singled for Kansas City. His name spelled backwards is. . . . "

The Sox win a laugher, and Harry leads the fans in a final cheer: "Sox win! Sox win! Sox win!" He is drenched with sweat, but he leaves the ballpark fulfilled, pleased with the show. He is a man who enjoys his work, his life. And the evening lies ahead.

Outside the park, Harry is approached by a well-dressed drunk. "How are you, my friend?" says affable Harry. The drunk says nothing. He just stares at Harry. Harry smiles uneasily. "I love you, Harry," the drunk says solemnly. Harry pats him on the arm. "I love you because. . . . " Harry pats him again and starts to walk away. "I love you," the drunk says, his voice trailing after the stocky man in the short pants. "I love you," he repeats, inspired now. "I love you because. . . you're Harry Caray."

Kentucky: May: Saturday

BY WILLIAM FAULKNER

In the spring of '55, SI sent a Nobel Prize winner to cover what loomed as the coronation of a once-in-a-lifetime colt named Nashua. Swaps upset the Big Horse in the Derby, but Faulkner delivered a unique piece of reportage, as expected.

THREE DAYS BEFORE. THIS SAW BOONE: THE BLUEGRASS, THE virgin land rolling westward wave by dense wave from the Allegheny gaps, unmarked then, teeming with deer and buffalo about the salt licks and the limestone springs whose water in time would make the fine bourbon whiskey; and the wild men too— the red men and the white ones too who had to be a little wild also to endure and survive and so mark the wilderness with the proofs of their tough survival—Boonesborough, Owenstown, Harrod's and Harbuck's Stations; Kentucky: the dark and bloody ground.

And knew Lincoln too, where the old weathered durable rail fences enclose the green and sacrosanct pace of rounded hills long healed now from the plow, and big old trees to shade the site of the ancient one-room cabin in which the babe first saw light; no sound there now but such wind and birds as when the child first faced the road which would lead to fame and martyrdom—unless perhaps you like to think that the man's voice is somewhere there too, speaking into the scene of his own nativity the simple and matchless prose with which he reminded us of our duties and responsibilities if we wished to continue as a nation.

And knew Stephen Foster and the brick mansion of his song; no longer the dark and bloody ground of memory now, but already my old Kentucky home.

TWO DAYS BEFORE. Even from just passing the stables, you carry with you the smell of liniment and ammonia and straw—the strong quiet aroma of horses. And even before we reach the track we can hear horses—the light hard rapid thud of hooves mounting into crescendo and already fading rapidly on. And now in the gray early light we can see them, in couples and groups at canter or hand-gallop under the exercise boys. Then one alone, at once furious and solitary, going full out, breezed, the rider hunched forward, excrescent and precarious, not of the horse but simply (for the instant) with it, in the conventional posture of speed—and who knows, perhaps the two of them, man and horse both: the animal dreaming, hoping that for that moment at least it looked like Whirlaway or Citation, the boy for that moment at least that he was indistinguishable from Arcaro or Earl Sande, perhaps feeling already across his knees the scented sweep of the victorious garland.

And we ourselves are on the track now, but carefully and discreetly back against the rail out of the way: now we are no longer a handful clotting in a murmur of furlongs and poles and tenths of a second, but there are a hundred of us now and more still coming, all craning to look in one direction into the mouth of the chute. Then it is as if the gray, overcast, slightly moist post-dawn air itself had spoken above our heads. This time the exercise boy is moving his mount at no schooled or calculated gait at all, just moving it rapidly, getting it off the track and out of the way, speaking not to us but to all circumambience: man and beast either within hearing: "Y'awl can git out of the way too now; here's the big horse coming."

And now we can all see him as he enters the chute on a lead in the hand of a groom. The groom unsnaps the lead and now the two horses come on down the now empty chute toward the now empty track, out of which the final end of the waiting and the expectation has risen almost like an audible sound, a suspiration, a sigh.

Now he passes us (there are two of them, two horses and two riders, but we see only one), not just the Big Horse of professional race argot because he does look big, bigger than we know him to be, so that most of the other horses we have watched this morning appear dwarfed by him, with the small, almost gentle head and the neat small feet and the trim and delicate pasterns which the ancient Arab blood has brought to him, the man who will ride him Saturday (it is Arcaro himself) hunched like a fly or a cricket on the big withers. He is not even walking. He is strolling. Because he is looking around. Not at us. He has seen people; the sycophant adulant human roar has faded behind his drumming feet too many times for us to hold his attention. And not at track either because he has seen track before and it usually looks like this one does from this point (just entering the back-stretch): empty. He is simply looking at this track, which is new to him, as the steeplechase rider walks on foot the new course which he will later ride.

He—they—go on, still walking, vanishing at last behind the bulk of the tote board on the other side on the infield; now the glasses are trained and the stopwatches appear, but nothing more until a voice says, "They took him in to let him look at the paddock." So we breathe again for a moment.

Because we have outposts now: a scattering of people in the stands them-selves who can see the gate, to warn us in time. And do, though when we see him, because of the bulk of the tote board, he is already in full stride, ap-pearing to skim along just above the top rail like a tremendous brown hawk in the flattened bottom of his stoop, into the clubhouse turn still driving; then something seems to happen; not a falter nor check though it is only after-ward that we realize that he has seen the gate back into the chute and for an instant thought, not "Does Arcaro want us to go back in there?" but "Do I want to turn off here?" deciding in the next second (one of them: horse or man) no, and now driving again, down to us and past us as if of his own in-tention he would make up the second or two or three which his own indeci-sion had cost him, a flow, rush, the motion at once long and deliberate and a little ungainly; a drive and power; something a little rawboned, not grace-less so much as too busy to bother with grace, like the motion of a big work-ing hunter, once again appearing to skim along just above the top rail like the big diminishing hawk, inflexible and undeviable, voracious not for meat but for speed and distance.

ONE DAY BEFORE. Old Abe's weathered and paintless rails are now the white panels of millionaires running in ruler-straight lines across the green and gentle swell of the Kentucky hills; among the ordered and parklike grove the mares with recorded lineages longer than most humans know or bother with stand with foals more valuable head for economic head than slum children. It rained last night; the gray air is still moist and filled with a kind of lumi-nousness, lambence, as if each droplet held in airy suspension still its mol-ecule of light, so that the statue which dominated the scene at all times any-way now seems to hold dominion over the air itself like a dim sun, until, looming and gigantic over us, it looks like gold—the golden effigy of the gold-en horse, "Big Red" to the groom who loved him and did not outlive him very long, Big Red's effigy of course, looking out with the calm pride of the old manly warrior kings, over the land where his get still gambol as infants, until the Saturday-afternoon moment when they too will wear the mat of roses in the flash and glare of magnesium; not just his own effigy, but symbol too of all the long recorded line from Aristides through the Whirlaways and Count Fleets and Gallant Foxes and Citations: epiphany and apotheosis of the horse.

THE DAY. Since daylight now we have moved, converged, toward, through the Georgian-Colonial sprawl of the entrance, the throne's anteroom, to bear our own acolytes' office in that ceremonial.

Once the horse moved man's physical body and his articles of commerce from one place to another. Nowadays all it moves is a part or the whole of his bank account, either through betting on it or trying to keep owning and feeding it.

So, in a way, unlike the other animals which he has domesticated—cows and sheep and hogs and chickens and dogs (I don't include cats; man has never tamed cats)—the horse is economically obsolete. Yet it still endures and probably will continue to endure as long as man himself does, long after the cows and sheep and hogs and chickens, and the dogs which control and protect them, are extinct. Because the other beasts and their guardians merely supply man with food, and someday science will feed him by means of synthetic gases and so eliminate the economic need which they fill. While what the horse supplies to man is something deep and profound in his emotional nature and need.

It will endure and survive until man's own nature changes. Because you can almost count on your thumbs the types and classes of human beings in whose lives and memories and experience and glandular discharge the horse has no place. These will be the ones who don't like to bet on anything which involves the element of chance or skill or the unforeseen. They will be the ones who don't like to watch something in motion, either big or going fast, no matter what it is. They will be the ones who don't like to watch something alive and bigger and stronger than man, under the control of puny man's will, doing something which man himself is too weak or too inferior in sight or hearing or speed to do.

These will have to exclude even the ones who don't like horses—the ones who would not touch a horse or go near it, who have never mounted one nor ever intend to; who can and do and will risk and lose their shirts on a horse they have never seen.

So some people can bet on a horse without ever seeing one outside a Central Park fiacre or a peddler's van. And perhaps nobody can watch horses running forever, with a mutuel window convenient, without making a bet. But it is possible that some people can and do do this.

So it is not just betting, the chance to prove with money your luck or what you call your judgment, that draws people to horse races. It is much deeper than that. It is a sublimation, a transference: man, with his admiration for speed and strength, physical power far beyond what he himself is capable of, projects his own desire for physical supremacy, victory, onto the agent—the baseball or football team, the prizefighter. Only the horse race is more universal because the brutality of the prizefight is absent, as well as the attenuation of football or baseball—the long time needed for the orgasm of victory to occur, where in the horse race it is a matter of minutes, never over two or three, repeated six or eight or 10 times in one afternoon.

4:29 P.M. And this too: the song, the brick mansion, matched to the apotheosis: Stephen Foster as handmaiden to the Horse as the band announces that it is now about to be the one 30 minutes past 4 o'clock out of all possible 4 o'clocks on one Saturday afternoon out of all possible Saturday afternoons. The brazen chords swell and hover and fade above the packed infield and the stands as the 10 horses parade to post—the 10 animals which for the next two minutes will not just symbolize but bear the burden and be the justification, not just of their individual own three years of life, but of the generations of selection and breeding and training and care which brought them to this one triumphant two minutes where one will be supreme and nine will be supreme failures—brought to this moment which will be supreme for him, the apex of his life which, even counted in lustra, is only 21 years old, the beginning of manhood. Such is the price that he will pay for the supremacy; such is the gamble he will take. But what human being would refuse that much loss, for that much gain, at 21?

Only a little over two minutes: one simultaneous metallic clash as the gates spring. Though you do not really know what it was you heard: whether it was that metallic crash, or the simultaneous thunder of the hooves in that first leap or the massed voices, the gasp, the exhalation—whatever it was, the clump of horses indistinguishable yet, like a brown wave dotted with the bright silks of the riders like chips flowing toward us along the rail until, approaching, we can begin to distinguish individuals, streaming past us now as individual horses—horses which (including the rider) once stood about eight feet tall and 10 feet long, now look like arrows twice that length and less than half that thickness, shooting past and bunching again as perspective diminishes, then becoming individual horses once more around the turn into the backstretch, streaming on, to bunch for the last time into the homestretch itself, then again individuals, individual horses, the individual horse, the Horse: 2:01⅘ minutes.

And now he stands beneath the rose escarpment above the flash and glare of the magnesium and the whirring film of celluloid immortality. This is the moment, the peak, the pinnacle; after this, all is ebb.

We who watched have seen too much; expectation, the glandular pressure, has been too high to long endure; it is evening, not only of the day but the emotional capacity too; Boots and Saddles will sound twice more and condensations of light and movement will go through the motions of horses and jockeys again. But they will run as though in dream, toward anticlimax; we must turn away now for a little time, even if only to assimilate, get used to living with, what we have seen and experienced. Though we have not yet escaped that moment. Indeed, this may be the way we will assimilate and endure it: the voices, the talk, at the airports and stations from which we scatter back to where our old lives wait for us, in the aircraft and trains and buses carrying us back toward the old comfortable familiar routine like the old comfortable hat or coat: porter, bus driver, pretty stenographer who has saved for a year, scanted Christmas probably, to be able to say "I saw the Derby," the sports editor who, having spent a week talking and eating and drinking horse and who now wants only to get home and have a double nightcap and go to bed, all talking, all with opinions, valid and enduring:

"That was an accident. Wait until next time."

"What next time? What horse will they use?"

"If I had been riding him, I would have rode him different."

"No, no, he was ridden just right. It was that little shower of rain made the track fast like California."

"Or maybe the rain scared him, since it don't rain in L.A.? Maybe when he felt wet on his feet he thought he was going to sink and he was just jumping for dry land, huh?"

And so on. So it is not the Day after all. It is only the 81st one.

IX

EXAMINED
LIVES

Farewell,
Teddy Ballgame

BY LEIGH MONTVILLE

When Ted Williams died at the age of 83, this SI writer—a New England native and longtime Boston columnist—recollected his encounters with the Splendid Splinter over the course of half a century.

I F YOU GREW UP WATCHING TED WILLIAMS HIT A BASEBALL, WELL, *you simply kept watching, even after he stopped hitting. That was the way it was. From the day he arrived at Fenway Park in Boston in 1939 as a slender 20-year-old outfielder with a swing for the ages* until last Friday, when he died of cardiac arrest in Inverness, Fla., at age 83, he was part of your life.

As years passed, he might have changed, and you might have changed, and times might have changed, but he always was a fascinating character. He was a superstar before the word was invented. He was a man's man, icon of all icons. Watch? You had to watch. At least I did. . . .

Ted I

The postcard from Ted Williams came to 80 Howe Street, New Haven, Conn., on a late summer day in 1953. That's the best I can figure. I tried, just now, to pull the card carefully from the lined, loose-leaf notebook page on which I had glued it apparently 49 years ago, but the postmark was lost in the process.

I say the late summer of 1953 because that was when I was an autograph demon. Most of the other cards in my old notebook—George Kell, Maurice (Mickey) McDermott, Jimmy Piersall, a bunch of forgotten Boston Red Sox names—have postmarks from the summer of 1953. I was on the case in 1953. I was 10 years old.

I lived in a six-story apartment house, an only child, and I somehow discovered, alone in my bedroom, that if you wrote to your athletic idols, they sometimes wrote back. I was a writing fool. My basic message on a penny postcard was "Dear So-and-So, I am your biggest fan! You are great! Please send me your autograph!" I finished with my name and address, sent out the card and waited with the anticipation and faith of a trout fisherman on the banks of a fast-running brook on a Sunday morn.

The arrival of the mail every day became true adventure. I would riffle through the bills and the circulars, the grown-up and the mundane, looking and looking until one magical day . . . a postcard from Ted Williams.

He was the biggest fish of all. I might not remember the exact date his postcard arrived, but I remember the feeling. Even now I can't think of another piece of mail that has made me feel happier, not college acceptances nor good reports from doctors, nothing. The Ted Williams postcard was unadulterated bliss, equivalent to a letter straight from heaven. Better. Straight from Fenway.

I had never seen a major league player in person, had never been to a major league stadium, had never seen a major league game. Television hadn't arrived at my house. Williams was a mythical figure, a creation of radio words and black-and-white newspaper pictures. He had the purity of Sir Lancelot, the strength of Paul Bunyan, the tenacity of, say, Mighty Mouse. Distance, to be sure, made heroes much more heroic than they ever can be today.

Williams had returned from the Korean War that July. He was almost 35 years old. He had been flying F-9 Panther jets for a year in Korea, fighting the Communists in their sneaky MiGs. He was back, and he was hitting as well as ever: a .407 average in the final 37 games of the season, 13 homers, a .901 slugging percentage. He could do anything, everything. He was number 9. He was the Kid, Teddy Ballgame, the Splendid Splinter. He hated to wear a tie! (I hated to wear a tie!) He was invincible.

I remember staring at the postcard for hours. Had he actually signed it? No doubt. The blue ink was a different color from the rest of the black-and-white card. On the front of the card was a black-and-white picture of Williams finishing a swing. His eyes seemed to be following a baseball he had just hit, probably into the bullpen in right. He seemed focused, serious, divine. I imagined him reading my own card by his locker, thinking about me. Should he reply? He could tell by my writing that I was an honest kid, a hard worker in school, obeyed my parents. Of course he should reply. I could see him pulling out this postcard from a special place, taking out his pen.

"Capital T," he wrote, with a big flourish, "e-d. Capital W," another flourish, "i-l-l-i-a-m-s." He dotted the *i*'s high.

"You know," an older sportswriter told me a number of years later, "he never signed any of that stuff. The clubhouse guy, Johnny Orlando, his buddy, signed everything. Johnny Orlando could sign Ted Williams's name better than Ted Williams could."

I look at the postcard now. I somehow have kept it through college, through marriage, divorce, changes of jobs, changes of residence. Forty-nine years.

I don't know. Johnny Orlando?

I think Ted might have made an exception. Just once.

Ted 2

The sound of his voice preceded him. Or at least that's what I remember.

The year must have been 1978. Or maybe '79. The Red Sox clubhouse at Chain O' Lakes Park in Winter Haven, Fla., was divided into two rooms. The smaller room was reserved for selected veterans and the coaching staff. They shared the space with a pair of enormous washing machines. The machines were at work, taking out the stains from another spring training day. I was a sportswriter now, working for a Boston newspaper.

"Tell me this," the new voice said, loud, very loud. "What detergent do you use to clean these uniforms?"

Everybody turned toward the noise because there was no alternative. There he was, Ted, himself, huge, instantly dominating his surroundings. He was wearing a Hawaiian shirt. He would have been 59 years old. Maybe 60. He was tanned and robust, looking as if he had just returned from the high seas or the deep woods. A pair of sunglasses hung from his neck on a piece of fishing line.

"Tide," an equipment man said. "We use Tide."

"Now why do you use Tide?" the voice boomed. "Is it better than all the other detergents? Is it cheaper? Is there some secret ingredient?"

The fun began. Somehow I had never been in the same room with Ted Williams, never talked to him, never been around him. Would he fill out the picture I'd had in my head for so long? Or would he—like so many famous figures encountered without their press agents and handlers—be a mean-spirited disappointment? What? At first glance I had to say he looked like John Wayne. He talked like John Wayne. He was John Wayne.

He was on the scene as a hitting instructor. For a number of years he had skipped the rituals of the baseball spring and gone off to fish for salmon or bonefish or do whatever he did, but for some reason he'd decided to return for this season. He would show up every morning in his old Ford station wagon, identifiable by the IF GUNS ARE OUTLAWED, ONLY OUTLAWS WILL HAVE GUNS sticker on the rusty bumper. He would change into his uniform and head to the minor league complex.

"What's your name?" he would ask some kid in a batting cage. "Get over here. Where are you from? Mississippi? Let's see what you're doing here."

He would jump from the cart, adjust the kid's stance. He would take the bat, squeeze it hard, swing with emphasis. See? *Pow!* He would talk baseball, baseball, more baseball, laying out hypothetical confrontations between pitcher and batter, each ball and strike forcing the pitcher to alter his strategy, so that at 3 and 2 he had to come in with a fastball, and, oh, brother, here it comes. *Pow!* The kid from Mississippi would return to work looking slightly dazed.

I stood with other members of the new generation of the Knights of the Keyboard, Williams's term for his longtime adversaries in the press box. I listened to his declarations. (If you were anywhere in the state of Florida, you couldn't avoid them.) I did the obligatory Ted-is-here column.

He was charming and frank. He actually listened to the questions, actually thought out the answers. He laughed easily in large sonic booms. The writers who had tormented him during his career, Colonel Dave Egan and Mel Webb and the rest, were dead. The torment also was dead. The uncomfortable star, sensitive to all criticism, spitting in the direction of the clacking typewriters, was long gone. Williams wore his advancing age as if it were a bathrobe and slippers. He couldn't care less what anyone wrote.

He would pose for pictures with a daily stream of worshipers, penitents, strangers. ("You gonna take that lens cap off before ya take the shot?" he would bellow. "Here, let me do it.") He would argue with anyone about politics, sports, detergents, anything. He would question. He would tell stories. He would interact, hour after hour. There was a liveliness about him that was different from the ordinary. He was larger than larger-than-life, if that makes any sense. He was Ted Williams, and he knew who he was. He played his own role. Himself.

The highlight of the spring came when he set up a public tennis match against Carl Yastrzemski, then the Red Sox' elder statesman. He didn't just challenge Yastrzemski to the match, he promoted it for an entire week. He told the world. Time, date, place, probable outcome (a huge Williams win). When the great day came—Yastrzemski, 21 years Williams's junior, won easily, making the big man move too much and lurch for shots—there must have been 1,000 people surrounding one of those apartment-complex courts, all to see an event that Williams simply invented.

"Is he always like this?" I asked Joe Lindia, a guy from Providence who was Williams's driver, old friend and roommate for the three weeks of spring training. "Is he always . . . Ted?"

"Always," Lindia said. "You go with Ted, anything can happen."

Lindia told a story: In one of Williams's last seasons as a player, the Red Sox trained in Scottsdale, Ariz. Lindia went out to visit. One day, an off day, Williams said they should take a ride. They drove to the far edge of the town and went to a seedy motel. Williams directed Lindia to a room at the back. Lindia had no idea what was happening. Williams knocked on the door. An old man, looking as seedy as the motel itself, answered. "Joe," Williams said. "Say hello to Ty Cobb."

They went into the room with Cobb. A bottle of whiskey was opened. Cobb and Williams talked baseball for a number of hours. Cobb, it seemed, had one theory about hitting. It was directly opposite to Williams's theory. The argument became intense. The two men were shouting at each other. They looked as if they might come to blows. "Look, I know how we can settle this," Williams finally said. "Ty, you say one thing. I say another. Joe, what do you say?"

"Funny, huh?" Lindia said. "The two greatest hitters in the history of baseball. I'm the one who's supposed to break the tie. I couldn't hit a baseball for a million dollars."

On one of the last days of training camp, I went to dinner with my young family at one of those steak houses with an all-you-can-eat salad bar. My son was five years old. Maybe six. I guided him to the salad bar to fill up his plate. On the way back to the table, I noticed Williams was in a booth with four or five people. Lindia was one of them. I was going to keep going, but Lindia waved and said hello. I waved back. Williams looked and saw my son.

"Hey," he said in that loud voice, "that's a great-looking kid."

My son had no idea who the man was. He smiled.

"I mean he's exceptional," Williams said, even louder now. "A great-looking kid." I could feel the eyes of everyone in the restaurant turning in my direction. People were looking at Williams, then staring at my son. People were nodding their heads in agreement. Yes, a great-looking kid. My son.

"Looks like he'd be a pretty good hitter," someone at the table suggested.

"I don't give a s--- about that," Williams said, loudest voice yet. "I'm just saying he's a great-looking kid. Look at him."

It was a moment. My son is 30 years old, and I still talk to him, maybe once a year, about what happened. He rolls his eyes.

Ted 3

The idea was that Ted was going to be dead pretty soon. That was what the producer said. Ted was going to hit his 80th birthday in a couple of weeks, he'd had the three strokes, he was half blind, and he didn't get around much, didn't submit to many interviews. Anything could happen, you know. This might be the last television interview he ever would do.

This was the summer of 1998. I was the interviewer. I showed up with two cameramen and the producer around noon on the appointed day at Williams's house in Hernando, Fla. The house was relatively new, part of the Citrus Hills development, which featured a bunch of streets named after former Red Sox players and officials. It wasn't the kind of house you would imagine for Williams. There was a commercial aspect here, a lack of dignity.

Buzz Hamon, then the director at the Ted Williams Museum and Hitters Hall of Fame, also located on the Citrus Hills property, briefed us on what to expect. There would be 30 minutes, no more than 45, with Williams. His attention would wander after that. He would be ready for his afternoon nap. He had a cook and an aide who helped him. Hamon said it had been a tough stretch for Williams. Not only had the strokes affected him, virtually all his friends had died. Joe Lindia had died. Williams's longtime companion, Louise Kaufman, had died. His dog had died. He pretty much had outlasted his generation.

I feared the worst. When Williams came into the den, where we had set up our lights, he was using a walker and was helped by the aide. He was shrunken, frail. The robust character of 20 years earlier was gone. The baseball god of 40, 50 years ago was long gone. He was helped into the easy chair and landed with a grateful thud. And he was wonderful.

I have a copy of the tape. From the core of that besieged and worn-out body, Ted Williams emerges. The voice is still loud, challenging, authoritative. It's him. His right hand might wander, almost out of control, and he might dab now and then at a little saliva coming from the side of his mouth, but he's funny and definitive and in charge.

I have my little list of questions, but they are mere starting points. He drives the conversation wherever he wants it to go. I'm only along for the ride. "Oh, brother. . . . Now here's something interesting! Glad you brought that up! . . . Oh, that's in all the books. Go read about it. . . . Where are you from? This is inside stuff you're getting, buddy."

He talks about fishing with Bobby Knight in Russia. He talks about how he thinks George Will knows a lot politically but not too much "baseballically." He talks about Joe Jackson and how he should be in the Hall of Fame, damn it! He talks about Mark McGwire, *loves* Mark McGwire, talks about Nomar Garciaparra, *loves* Nomar, talks about Joe DiMaggio and Willie Mays and Ken Griffey Jr., *loves* Ken Griffey Jr.

He takes a myth and deflates it. Remember the old story about the final doubleheader in 1941, when he could have finished with a .400 average simply by sitting out? The story is that manager Joe Cronin gave him the option, and Williams scoffed. Sit it out? He played the two games, went six for eight, finished at .406. He upheld the sanctity of the game, something no one would do in modern, stat-conscious times. Wasn't that how it went? Yes, but. . . .

"I never thought about sitting out," he says. "Not once. But I gotta say this. I didn't realize how much .400 would mean to my life. I mean it had happened only 11 years before I did it, and I thought someone else would do it pretty soon. I felt there certainly would be other .400 hitters. I said that. Always said that. Now here it is, 50, 60 years later."

He talks about hitting the slider, invented during the middle of his career. That new pitch. He talks about hitting against the Williams shift, stepping back an inch or two from the plate to be able to punch the inside pitch to left. He talks about flying in Korea in the squadron of future astronaut John Glenn. He talks . . . and then he stops. "You've got enough," he says. "Bye."

Just like that. Fifty-one minutes, 22 seconds. Exactly.

The tape doesn't show the conversation after the interview was finished. He talked informally for another 10 or 15 minutes. He was lively, friendly. He was funny. He took out the needle. "This isn't a paid interview, is it?" he said. "There's no money for this. Right?"

I said there wasn't. "Well, I enjoyed it, and I'd do it again," Williams said, "but the next time there should be a little remuneration. Do you know what I mean? Remuneration. Some compensation."

"Maybe we could send you a hat," I suggested.

"You know where you could put that hat," Williams said.

He asked me who my boss was. I said I had a lot of them. He asked who was the biggest boss, the boss of all the bosses. I said I guessed Ted Turner was the biggest boss. This was a CNN deal. "Well, you tell Ted Turner that Ted Ballgame would like some remuneration, O.K.?" Williams said. "Tell Ted that Ted would like something he could fold and put in his pocket. You know?"

I said that since this was an interview to celebrate his 80th birthday, maybe we could work something out, come back for his 100th. He laughed. He said, Ha, if we were back for that, he would do that interview for free. Ha. For sure.

The good news was that he didn't die soon after that day. The interview was far from his last. Within a year he seemed to be everywhere. He was the lead character in all celebrations for the Team of the Century. He was at the 1999 All-Star Game at Fenway. He was at Cooperstown. He was at the Yogi Berra Museum in Montclair, N.J. He was with Ted Koppel late at night, with the *Today* show in the morning. He talked cooking with Molly O'Neill in the pages of *The New York Times Sunday Magazine*. He had a last triumphant tour.

I remember him going to his bedroom with the walker for his afternoon nap at the end of the interview. Final picture. The big event at night was going to be a Red Sox game on television, off the satellite. He wanted to rest. The cameramen were breaking down the equipment. Suddenly chimes rang out from the bedroom. They played the tune, *Hail, Hail, the Gang's All Here*. They were a signal that Williams required assistance. The aide hurried to the room. A minute later he returned. He was laughing.

"Ted just wanted me to tell you one thing," he said. "Don't forget the part about the remuneration."

Not a disappointment. No. Never.

ॐ

The Ripples from Little Lake Nellie

BY GARY SMITH

Four months after a boating accident claimed the lives of two Cleveland Indians pitchers, SI ran this account of their families' and friends' struggle to come to grips with their grief. A decade later, the story's emotional impact is undiminished.

THE CHILDREN WERE PLAYING MARCO POLO OFF THE DOCK where the two ballplayers died. Their mother was sitting with her knees pulled up to her chest beneath a large pink umbrella on the end of the pier. She gazed across the soft green hills that cup Little Lake Nellie, across the cypress and orange trees and the reeds.

"Marco!"

"*Polo!*"

"Marco!"

"*Polo!*"

Everything was fine as long as her neighbor kept talking and her rottweiler kept snorting and churning those crazy zigzags in the water. Just fine as long as the sun was high and the children kept playing that silly game, one of them going under for a count of three and bursting up with his eyes closed, crying out, "Marco!" and waiting for the others to shout "Polo!" and then flailing toward the voices, groping through the darkness to touch them.

Because then Jetta Heinrich's eyes wouldn't be drawn to the new wood on her dock or to the big brown barn and the rise of land just across the tiny lake where one of the ballplayers' widows lived. And she might not get that sick feeling in her stomach and the echo of the thud again in her ears, the one she heard that night, standing on her back porch in her bathrobe. She wouldn't have to leave like she'd had to nearly every time she'd tried to come out on the dock since then.

"Marco!"

"*Polo!*"

The dock her husband had constructed with a ramp leading up to it instead of steps, so her aunt in a wheelchair and her shuffling grandfather could join them. A dock with a bench at the end so they could sit together and watch the children belly-flop into the water and play silly games. A place to build a family.

WERE THIS story a movie, it would open with a scene 20 years from today. Patti and Grover and Wick and Laurie and Bobby would be sitting around a fire near the cypress trees on the bank of the little lake in Clermont, Fla. They'd all be graying and wrinkled by then. They'd all have angle and distance on what occurred that night at the dock. In the campfire glow you would barely make out Bobby's scar, the one that loops across his forehead like the seams of a baseball. Laurie would be trying to explain what it was like sleeping for months in the same bed with three little bodies. Patti and Wick would be getting hopelessly tangled trying to remember the words to the song they each listened to a zillion times right after it happened, only you wouldn't quite know what it was, and you would have to wait two hours and two dozen flashbacks to make sense of it all.

But not even four months have gone by. There is no angle yet, no distance, no movie cliché. There are splinters of wood still flying, people still crying out a name, still groping through the darkness. The ripples haven't even begun to reach the edge of Little Lake Nellie.

So let us just reach into the swirl, choose a moment and begin: A Florida morning, a baseball clubhouse, a week after Tim Crews and Steve Olin died when their heads struck a dock during a family outing on a spring training off-day. Grover—that's what everyone around the clubhouse calls Cleveland Indian manager Mike Hargrove—is gazing out at the surviving members of his bullpen, wondering how in hell he is ever going to bring this team back from its grief. On Eric Plunk's chest is one of Steve Olin's T-shirts. On Ted Power's waist is the belt Oly wore when he broke into the major leagues. In Derek Lilliquist's hand are the two steel balls Oly squeezed to strengthen his wrist. On Kevin Wickander's feet are Oly's shower clogs. Thank god, they didn't know Tim Crews any better—another sweet human being, just like Oly. Thank god, Tim had just joined the team.

And now there's a ghost walking slowly toward Grover. Face white as bone, shoulders stooped, cheeks sunken, eyes dead as stones; a good breeze would blow him away. It's the third man who was in the boat that night, the 35-year-old whom the Indians had hired as a free agent three months earlier to be their No. 2 starter, a Los Angeles Dodger teammate of Crews's the previous two seasons. The one who pleaded, "Keep breathing, Crewser, *c'mon, keep breathing!*" barely aware that two quarts of his own blood were all over the boat, that his own scalp was ripped back like the top of a tennis ball can.

"I'D LIKE to talk to the team," Bobby Ojeda said softly.

Sure . . . of course, Bobby, fine, Grover heard himself say . . . but good lord. Grover glanced over the ghost's shoulder again at the team. He felt the lump, the goddam fist, rising in his own throat again. His whole life, a childhood amid the cattle ranches and oilfields of Texas, a manhood amid the cleats and tobacco-stained teeth of professional ball, he had been weaned on a truth, a way of surviving, that was being blown to bits here.

One day. That's what Grover's manager in Class A ball had offered him to get from Gastonia, N.C., to Perryton, Texas, and back when his grandfather, Papaw, died. You couldn't do that in one day, so Grover clenched his jaw and kept playing. A few years later his wife's dad died when Grover was a first base-man with the Texas Rangers. "That's not immediate family," said his manag-er, Billy Martin, when Grover asked for time off to attend the funeral. How many teammates even bothered to call him when he was traded in 1978 after five seasons with the Rangers? Two. *Two.* Baseball had too long a season, was too dependent upon mechanics, for spilling emotions; a high five now and then, an obscenity and a stream of brown goo, that's all a guy was supposed to let out. Even last year, when Grover risked a little kiss with his wife through the screen behind home plate after a spring training game, damned if that fan hadn't caught him and howled, "Get a room!"

If a man was around that long enough, he became it, even a good guy like Grover. When his wife's eyes welled up in front of a movie, he made the wise-crack. When his teammate Danny Thompson died of leukemia in the off-sea-son in 1976, Grover drove from Texas to the funeral in Oklahoma because that was the proper thing to do, but the agony, the enormity of what this did to Danny's family, never hit him, and he drove back home feeling as flat and arid inside as the land around him, wondering if something was wrong, if something was missing inside, but . . . crap, that speeding ticket he'd gotten on the way there . . . aw, screw it all. . . .

He wanted what Bert Campaneris got. He wanted, at the end of his career, for an umpire to walk over to him in the dugout the way he had seen Bill Haller do one day to Campy—his teammate, the Ranger shortstop who never whined, never cried, never even smiled—and offer a handshake and say, "You're a real professional." That was Grover's goal in life.

So what was happening to him now? The other day, for instance, when he was bawling like a baby, with his son in his lap. And the day after, head buried in his pillow and crying his eyes out on his bed at his spring training apartment, when his wife walked in, and right after her one of his relievers, Kevin Wickander, and Wick's wife, Kim. The four of them all ending up on the bed, talking and sobbing and wrapping their arms around each other. *That* was professional? Two things were warring inside Grover on the bed that day with the wives and Wick, the last player left on the roster whom he had managed in the minors, now that Oly was gone. "We've . . . we've got to get over this, Wick. . . . We've got to get *busy*. . . . You're my last *pup*."

For a year and a half, since Grover had become the Indians' manager, he and the front office had been telling the world how tight this young team was, how much like family. They had signed a core of 18 players to relatively modest multiyear contracts and planned to keep them together, use their closeness as a weapon against the big-market teams with the cash flow to keep famous free agents shuttling in and out. But lots of team managements yapped about family and waived you in a swing and a miss. Who could possibly trust that?

Now one of the family was in a box, and the other was ashes in an urn in the mountains of Oregon, and Grover had to look inside himself and discover if the sermons he had preached were true. If they were a *family*, how could he be a *professional*? He could only be a father who had lost two children. He sat on a chair in the middle of the locker room the morning after the accident and waved to his players to come sit close around him on the floor, like a kindergarten teacher and his kids. And now the emotions he had always wondered about were coming like a freight train, and the only choice was whether to stand in front of the train or leap out of its way. He stood there and let it happen in front of everyone, kept on talking about what the players meant to him even when the words were hitching and then turning to sobs, and then, one by one, they all did the same. God, it felt like family, the way they all kept drifting in and out of each other's apartments that week, the way Grover and his wife, Sharon, were always there for the players and their wives and the widows, ready to pack or cook or clean or hug or cry with anyone who needed it. It could never be the same after that morning in the clubhouse with Grover. Good or bad for a baseball team, nobody could be sure, but never the same.

Grover backed way off, let the players miss a cutoff man or a signal in those final exhibition games, but now Opening Day was just a week away, time to start sucking it up and setting the jaw . . . and here stood that ghost in front of the team.

It was not so much what Bobby Ojeda told the players that day—how it had happened that night on the boat, how the three of them had never even glimpsed that dock in the darkness, how he wanted them not to pity him or think about him at all. It was the way he said it, the utter deadness in his voice and eyes, the total absence of hope. Not a word of encouragement. Not a word about coming back.

And then he was gone. The players looked at one another. The clubhouse filled, again, with silence. How many million *attaboys* and *let's-pull-it-togethers* would it take to counteract that?

They would charge onto the field for Opening Day in Cleveland, the relievers lifting their thumbs to heaven to signal to Oly and Crewser that everything was going to be O.K., 73,290 people standing and crying and roaring for them and for the two widows clutching the empty jerseys at home plate . . . and would get crushed 9–1 by the Yankees. The Indians would lose 43 of their first 81 games, committing 71 errors, pressing to do what they couldn't and not even doing what they could. Injuries chopped down what remained of the staff—six pitchers, at one point, on the disabled list—as little pangs turned into deep pain; who could bring himself to mention a tendon or a tender lat in the wake of death? No one pointed a finger in the clubhouse. The team, fused by grief, remained one. But there was no resurrection. No clichés. No movies to be made in last place.

Grover would see a player making an idiot, an absolute idiot, out of himself on the field in May, open his mouth to tell him that . . . but then an image of that player from the day when they gathered around Grover's chair in the clubhouse would come to him, a memory of how much compassion that man had, and instead Grover would hear himself say, "You're *not* what you showed on the field today. I *know* you."

But he couldn't help wondering, as loss piled upon loss, as day after day passed without an offer of a contract extension from the front office that spoke so much about family, if he should've just chewed the guy's head off.

He came home after a loss one day in May and put his arms around Sharon. He had opened a letter before the game from a fan complaining that Grover had betrayed his responsibility to young people by downplaying Tim Crews's blood-alcohol level the night of the accident, and rage had rushed to Grover's face. He had grabbed the phone, tracked down the fan and screamed obscenities at him—how dare this moron judge him from a thousand miles away when there was so much pain, so many lives lying crumpled all around him. Now, for the first time in their lives together, his wife felt his body come unstrung, all his 215 pounds falling against her, and she felt as close to him as she ever had. "I don't know if I did the right or wrong thing about the alcohol," he sobbed. "I don't know anything. . . ."

Were there any standings, any stats, for good human beings? On a tired Sunday evening after a game, when his four-year-old, Shelly, wanted to read a book or his 11-year-old, Andy, wanted to play ball, Grover used to sink into his living room chair with the newspaper or a book and grunt, "Yeah . . . later. . . . " until it was their bedtime. Now he got up and did it. Now he swallowed hard and stared in wonder at the note tucked inside his bedroom mirror, written to him in May by his own father, a man who had never before come close to uttering such words to him: "I saw you on television the past few weeks and you seemed to have the weight of the world on your shoulders. You can only do so much with what you have. When you get down and everything keeps falling up tails, remember, He's with you. . . . With love, Pop."

FROM THE corner of her eye the old woman kept looking at the man seated next to her on the cross-country flight out of Los Angeles. Pulled low over his brow was a dark cap with a long bill. Under the cap, pulled tight over the crown of his head, nearly down to his eyebrows, was a blue bandanna. Zippering under and out from it, a terrible scar. On his nose was a pair of John Lennon glasses. She thought he might be a member of one of those gangs.

His finger was tracing a Delta route map, looking for the longest arc, the place farthest away from his home that he could go without a change of planes. He had refused to let doctors give him blood transfusions—he simply didn't believe in them. He might pass out if he tried to change planes. He might get lost. He might end up anywhere.

In his little carry-on bag was a book, a couple of pairs of underpants and socks, a few shirts, a plastic cylinder of sleeping pills and the passport he had sneaked out of his home in Upland, Calif., without his wife seeing. He had been so calm when he said goodbye to her and his little girl. They had never guessed.

He didn't want to talk. He just wanted to read. He just wanted to stare out the window and beat himself to death, thinking of six kids without fathers. But the old woman was so kind, and even though he often preferred to be alone, he had been the kind of guy who liked to pull out a chair when a stranger approached for an autograph or to ask a question and say, "C'mon, sit down."

"What do you do for a living?" the lady said now.

"Well . . . I used to play baseball . . . but then I had an accident."

"Oh." She looked at him again. *Ohhhhhhhh.*

She knew. The whole world knew. She started to tell a story. He didn't want to hear a story, but she was so kind. When she was two years old, her mother was eight months pregnant. And then . . . then her mother was dead. "A kid never loses the pain of that," the old woman said. "Never. But do you know what? When you grow up, it makes you stronger."

For just a second, his eyes flickered.

He got off the plane when it landed on the East Coast. He went to a bank. He cashed a check. A big check. Absurd. Still making $1.7 million a year. No credit card. No trace.

He met his brother-in-law. "Are you crazy?" his brother-in-law said. "They'll never let you in the country. They'll arrest you at customs. They'll give you a body-cavity search. Do you know what you look like now in the mirror?"

No. Two weeks straight without looking in a mirror. He bought the Delta ticket. He stuffed the wad of bills into the carry-on bag, next to the underwear, the socks, the shirts, the book, the passport, the plastic cylinder of sleeping pills. It was opening week in baseball.

YOU'RE NOT serious, Laurie. Not the dock. Not already. Not today. Christ, she's Clint Eastwood.

No, somebody said, she's tougher than Clint.

John Wayne, then.

No, tougher than John.

John Eastwood. That's who Laurie Crews is, they were kidding. She's John Eastwood.

The five men glanced at each other. Christ, she was serious. The lake. The dock. Just a few hours ago, they had buried her husband.

The uneasy teasing stopped. They started walking. Fernando Montes, the Indians' conditioning coach, and Perry Brigmond, a buddy of Tim's—the two men who waded in that night and dragged the boat with the ballplayers ashore. Kirk Gibson, a teammate of Tim's for three of his six years on the Dodgers, and Mark Ostreich, a workout pal, and Bobby Ojeda. Bobby took a few steps, and everything spun. Laurie took one of his arms. Kirk took the other. They walked that way to the edge of the water and stared across at the dock.

This was Laurie, pure Laurie. Don't put it off. Step right back up to it. Talk to Tim and Steve. Fix it, *now*. "You're comin' back, Bobby," she started saying that day. "You're *gonna* pitch again, hear me? Don't you worry about me. I got people comin' out of the woodwork supportin' me—worse 'n termites. You worry about you. I'll kick your butt if you don't come back. I *mean* it."

You looked at her body, tan and wiry, at her eyes, deep blue and honest, and you knew she did. People kept asking how she had the stomach to stay there, on the 45-acre ranch overlooking the lake and the dock. She kept asking, How could I not? You could smell Laurie and Tim's dream, just driving up the dirt road to their house. Fresh-painted horse fence. New cedar barn. New cedar house. Baby oaks. Runt magnolias. Lacy grass. Three little children. A dream all planted and spindly and ready to grow.

Every off-season Sunday morning for three years Laurie and Tim had done the same thing. Pulled the classified ads section out of the newspaper, circled every property that sounded faintly like their dream, eaten a big, greasy country breakfast and spent all day searching. It had to be a place where Laurie could raise horses and Tim could fish bass. Where two grown-up Florida country kids could walk dirt and raise kids. "A safe place," Tim kept saying. Not like Los Angeles, where he had pitched the last six years. Where kids drove Porsches, kids did crack, kids died. It had to be a place to build a family.

They found it one day. They worked on it for more than a year. They moved in in February. A month later Tim was dead. Now Laurie was going to live the dream for them both.

This is what you do with pain. You take it by the scruff of the neck, slap it around and put it to work. More horse fencing to go up. More tomatoes and cucumbers to be picked. More grass and shrubs to be planted. More quarter horses to be bought, sold, fed, hosed, trained. More pets to be taken to the vet. More homework to be done with the kids. More hugs to be given out. It's not healthy to be depressed, she would say, so I won't be depressed. A million people called her each day, but all they ever seemed to get was the answering machine: *Hi, it's Laurie. I'm doin' fine. Busy as ever. . . .*

She would come back to the house at the end of the day, exhausted, her eyes seeing Tim's maroon-and-silver Ramcharger in the driveway and shooting the words to her brain before she could stop them: *He's home!* She would lie in her bed at night, the three kids at crazy angles, lie there smelling their skin and their breath. Tricia, the nine-year-old, refusing to talk about it. Shawn, the five-year-old, saying, "Don't worry, Mommy. Don't cry. He'll never be away. He'll always be in your heart." Travis, the three-year-old, telling people, "My daddy's in church. He'll come out when he's done playing baseball with God."

Sometimes Laurie ached so bad to hold Tim that she would go to the closet and smell his clothes. Other times she went into the shower, let the warm water wash away her resolve, just let it all go, and go, and go. . . .

MIDNIGHT. PHONE ringing. "Bobby? You're not working out yet, are you? Look, I'm gonna hang up this telephone and get on a plane and come out there and train with you if you don't get goin'. You're gonna hate yourself one day if you don't come back. No more pity parties. I'll kick your butt. I *mean* it."

She couldn't quite put into words why it meant so much to her and Patti Olin, to Tim's parents, to everyone, that Bobby come back. It was almost too big, too *genetic.* Laurie was the daughter of Dutch parents born in Indonesia, both held for years by the Japanese in a prisoner-of-war camp, both hungry at the end of it all for America. Laurie's father had taken migrant farm work in

Florida, anything to survive, earned an engineering degree, carved out a good life. That's what everybody had come for, he figured, to a land full of the children and grandchildren of people who left their families and hometowns behind rather than surrender to circumstance, obey fate. A land full of people who kept turning to sports, to see Bo Jackson dragging his artificial hip back to the plate, Jimmy Valvano dragging his cancer-racked spine back to the microphone, to see men and women overcoming injuries, odds and setbacks, athletes reenacting the national allegory, reconfirming it, *taking charge.* So where was Bobby in April when Laurie flew to Los Angeles to see the Dodgers' home opener and to visit him at his house in nearby Upland? Bobby's wife, Ellen, shook her head. No Bobby. No trace. Gone.

Two a.m. Phone ringing. It was Patti. Thank god for Patti. Somebody Laurie could tell that she had dropped from a size 9 to a size 4, that her stomach was burning like a furnace, without feeling as if she were asking for a pity party. Somebody she had never even met before that afternoon. The only person on earth who understood. "What time is it, Patti?"

"It's late. . . . Sorry. . . . You said if I was going through a bad time to call you no matter what hour."

"That's right. Start talkin'. You gettin' out of that house yet? I tell you, you gotta move down here, and I'll build you a house across the lake, and we'll get you all fixed up. So tell me how you're doin', girl."

WHO DO you know here, sir?"

"No one."

"Why are you here?"

"Heard it was a nice place."

"How long will you stay?"

"I don't know."

The customs officer stared again at the photograph in the passport. Stared again at the man in front of him. Barely a resemblance. But this was Sweden. Go ahead.

The man took slow, small steps to the taxi. He checked into the best place he could find in Stockholm, the Grand Hotel. For a day and a night and a day, he put off what he was going to do. He was still so dizzy. He was still so weak. When the sun was setting on the second day, it was time.

He set two packs of cigarettes and two bottles of wine on the table in the alcove of the room. He stared out the window. Water everywhere. Boats. Docks.

All the adversity in his life, all those other brushes with death and pain, they didn't prepare him for this. They were nothing. The time in the early 1970s, when he was just a kid on a minibike, driving off a bridge. The time he and his dad hugged the floor of their fishing boat on a lake south of Fresno, listening to the bullets whine past, inches from their ears, because some lunatic, for the sheer hell of it, felt like squeezing off 10 or 15 rounds at two guys in a boat. The time when he was a teenager and had to heave away a can that had shot up in flames in his hand, because they were out of charcoal lighter for the grill and, well, why not use the gasoline? The time when he was in a Corvette and hit a telephone pole, the time an ambulance plowed clean through the trunk and backseat of a car he was riding in. The time, with the Mets in the thick of the '88 pennant race, when the hedge clippers slipped, turning the middle finger of his pitching hand into a stump dangling from another stump. He remembered coming home at 2 a.m. from road trips in '90, when the Mets had buried him in the bullpen, climbing onto his Harley Davidson in the suit he had to wear to comply with the team dress code, howling and roaring through the streets of his neighborhood until the sun came up. . . . All Little League stuff. Penny ante. No howling now.

If only . . . sure, Crewser had had a few beers, but he seemed fine. If only the Indians still trained in Arizona, like they always had till this spring, and hadn't chosen to move to Homestead, Fla., and if only the hurricane hadn't headed straight for Homestead and demolished the complex, and if only the team hadn't stumbled into Winter Haven—just an hour from Crewser's ranch—to train. If only it hadn't rained that afternoon, and they had gone fishing in daylight, as they'd planned. If only they hadn't already been past the dock when the truck headlights flashed on the shore, the signal that Tim's buddy, Perry, was ready to be picked up. If only Crewser and Steve had slouched when they sat, as he always did. If only he *hadn't* slouched—goddammit, what right did he have to be alive?

This is what you do with pain. You sit alone in a hotel room in a foreign country, and you start drinking wine and smoking cigarettes and staring out the window, talking out loud to the two dead men you were sitting with thigh-to-thigh, saying the most painful and horrific things you can possibly think of again and again, for six or seven hours, because if you can do that and get out of the chair at the end of it, you've put on another layer. And if you can do that the next day and the next, you can create a person who you're really not, but the person you need to be to go on. And it's worth it, worth everything you lose when you do that, because you don't lose everything. You don't reach for the plastic cylinder of pills you keep looking at, which would make your eyelids finally begin to sag, make all the *if onlys* drift away, and everything else too, forever and ever.

He lurched from the chair at 4 a.m., the room spun, he headed out the door. He walked for miles through the bitter cold and darkness—water everywhere, boats, docks—hanging by the thread, the thinnest, most ordinary thread, the old woman's words on the airplane: One day, because of it, the kids will be stronger. And when he came back, it was sunup, and he fell on the bed, his heart beating so hard and irregular that he thought it was coming right through his chest. Oh my god, he thought. I'm going to die in a hotel room 7,000 miles from home.

ON ONE shelf lies Steve Olin's folded game jersey. Next to it lie his hat, a ball he signed, and his baseball card in a frame. On another shelf lie his baseball pants and several of his T-shirts. On a third shelf lie his fishing-tackle box, his spinners, spent shells from his rifle, his fishing license, his photograph with a deer, and his locker nameplate. On a hook hangs his practice jersey. This is not the Olins' house. It's the Wickanders'.

Someday, when Wick has a little boy and the boy is four or five, Wick's going to start pointing at the shelves and telling him about a wonderful man who drove an hour to a ranch on a lake one day, his only off-day all spring, because he wanted to make sure that the newest member of the bullpen felt welcome. He'll tell the boy about a season that happens now and then, or maybe not even that often. The oldest member of the bullpen, Teddy Power, had already put in 16 years with 10 different teams in pro ball when it happened, and he said he had never seen anything like what they shared that summer. A summer in 1992 when five men who loved the same things—boats and tobacco and motorcycles and trout streams and hunting and silly pranks and four- wheeling in the mud—found a groove that made them the American League's best bullpen, and became best friends as well. A summer when they went on fishing trips together and threw pies in faces and sabotaged TV microphones and branded their names in bullpens with red-hot tarp stakes and shouted *Ch-ching! Ch-ching!* all the way to the mound in the middle of games whenever one of them had broken some screwy bullpen bylaw that would cost him five bucks in kangaroo court. The Pen, they called themselves. We poked our dirty little raccoon noses, Wick would say, into anything we could. Five men: Wickander, Olin, Lilliquist, Plunk, Power. Five boys: Wicky, Oly, Lilli, Plunky, Teddy. In the bubble-gum-chewing contest, Wicky and Oly tied, 71 pieces in each of their mouths.

And then, just like that, the little family was gone. Oly was dead, and Wick, who couldn't get over it, was traded, and Teddy, even though he was 38 and might've known better, kept throwing with pain to make up for it and strained his triceps muscle, and Lilli and Plunky were left to blink at all the names and faces checking in.

"You'll have the most excellent day ever." That was the fortune on the

Bazooka bubble-gum wrapper that Oly opened that day last summer. "Here, Wick," Oly said. "This is for you." And Wick believed him. He tucked it in the liner of his cap, won his first big league game that very day, framed the wrapper and put it on his wall.

That's how it was with Oly and Wick, the Pen's two best buddies. Oly wouldn't touch the third base line or flip the ball to the bullpen catcher when he entered a game, so Wick wouldn't either. Oly etched an arrow under his hat brim to direct the ball to the plate, so Wick had to have that too. They had been together since 1989, at the Indians' Triple A farm in Colorado Springs. Oly was a 16th-round pick, a devoted husband with skinny shoulders and a submarine delivery and ordinary stuff, who believed in himself deep down. Wick was a second-round pick, a classic bachelor with barroom radar and killer looks and wicked stuff, who, deep down, didn't. Wick leaned on Oly. Literally. They would both go down to one knee and take turns resting an arm on each other's back in the outfield during batting practice, head beside head. Like Siamese twins, Teddy would say. Like listening to two guys talk who'd been next-door neighbors all their lives, said Lilli.

Wick could almost feel not feeling that arm on his back, even weeks after Oly was dead. Could almost taste not tasting that cheesecake and milk they used to order as they watched a movie after games on the road. Could almost hear not hearing that wonderfully whiny little-boy voice Oly used to affect each day when Wick entered the clubhouse. "Wickyyyyyy. . . . Coooooome heeeeeere, Wickyyyyy. . . ." Which usually meant that Oly had thought of something wicked for Wick to do, and off they would go into a corner, whispering and giggling, and a few hours later the pitching coach would look down into his new pair of shoes and find the rat that the Pen had caught and cooked in the Angels' bullpen. Wick was happy to face the music. Happy as a puppy to chase the stick for Oly.

Who was there for Wick when he shattered his elbow in a cement runway at Anaheim Stadium in 1990 and then ran up $28,000 worth of bar and restaurant bills in one year, drinking himself all the way to the rehab center in Cleveland? It was Oly. Who was there for Oly in Triple A ball in '89 when Patti was pregnant and he wanted someone to move in with her while he went up to the big leagues? It was Wick. Finally, when Wick listened to Oly's advice, quit skirt-chasing and married his high school sweetheart, Kim, in May '92, Oly was there as Wick's best man. Oly was Wick's conscience, said Grover, who had managed Wick in A ball, Double A, Triple A, the majors.

You don't want to hear too much about Wick's first few days after Oly died. About waiting and calling and waiting for Oly to come home that night from the Crewses' so they could all go out to dinner. About Wick rolling over and over, screaming "No!" on the floor when Oly's name flashed on the TV screen that night, then helping Kim to the bathroom so she could throw up. About packing the things in Oly's locker into a box in an empty clubhouse six hours later, before dawn, and three straight nights when his eyes refused to close. "He was my family," Wick sobbed when it was his turn to speak at the funeral. "He taught me how to be a faithful husband, how to roll with life when things were going bad," he later said.

This is what you do with pain. You set up a locker for your dead best friend, with his nameplate and his glove and his uniform and his team jacket and his shoes and his framed photograph on a stool. Even when the team travels, you tape the nameplate over the locker next to you and set up the shrine, so no one ever forgets. You keep talking about him to the other players because they taught you in rehab never to repress your feelings. You keep walking around the clubhouse, even weeks later, with 5 X 7 photographs of Steve to send to the hundreds of well-wishers who have written, and offer them to players: "Thought you might like a picture of Oly." You get your brains beat out on the mound.

There was something almost heroic about it; Wicks's grief possessed him. Eyes started rolling in the Indian clubhouse. Guys were starting to get the creeps. Guys were trying to forget. Mourning is a private project in America, not a communal one . . . but then, wouldn't everyone in the world, whether he admitted it or not, want a Wick to keep him alive when he was gone? Grover called Wick into his office. He talked about counseling, about going on the disabled list.

"No," said Wick. "Oly wouldn't want that. He'd want me to pitch."

"But Wick," said Grover, "you can't work this out on the mound."

So what are you going to do about Wick? sportswriters began asking Indian management. Eight and two-thirds innings pitched, 15 hits allowed, three home runs. Can't send Oly's best buddy to the minors while he's in mourning, they said. It sure would look cruel.

Late afternoon, on May 7, Wick was waved into Grover's office at Chicago's Comiskey Park. Grover was brief. Barely blinked. There were others in the office. Wick had an hour and a half to catch a flight and join the Cincinnati Reds. He had been traded for a player to be named later. Best thing they could possibly do for him, Grover said.

Wick packed his bag in a stupor, said goodbye to the guys and walked out of the clubhouse. "Wick!" It was someone calling him from behind. Grover's eyes were welling, his arms lifting to hug. "If you ever need anything . . . you know . . . you know you're like a son to me."

A few things happened after Wick left the Indians. The clubhouse was so cramped for space, the deliveryman for the local dry cleaner began using Oly's memorial locker to hang pressed shirts and suits for the players to retrieve. By the end of May, Grover had the locker dismantled altogether. A reliever was acquired from the Chicago Cubs, a man named Heathcliff Slocumb, whose wife died of cancer in November. Another reliever was acquired from San Diego, Jeremy Hernandez. He got Wick's number, 53.

In Cincinnati, Wick started pitching better, feeling happy. Not ripping up records in either department, but he won a game, got some guys out, started smiling. He still wore Oly's shower clogs, sunglasses, wristwatch and T-shirts, but he sent the rest to keep in his off-season home in Phoenix. Someday he would let Oly's kids take from it whatever they wished.

He knew now that no baseball team, no bullpen, would ever again feel like a family, and he realized why Oly had kept urging him to get married and start one of his own. Kim was right beside him on virtually every road trip now. If she hadn't been there when Oly died, he knew he would've started drinking again.

God. He was remembering Oly's thousand-dollar bet at their wedding that Kim would be pregnant by their first anniversary. Easy money, Wick had thought, because they had no intention of having kids for at least a couple of years. When the anniversary came, six weeks ago, Kim and Wick held hands. Oly had lost—she wasn't pregnant—but when they thought about it, they actually grinned. In a few more months they were going to start trying. The baby's name, if it's a boy, will be Olin Wickander.

YES. THAT was it. Rip it right across the neck. Now straight down, from crown to chin. Now again, right through that smile. Now the eyes. Goodbye, jackass. Goodbye.

He used to love that charcoal portrait on his office wall. Himself when he was a big league pitcher. Himself when he was happy. He used to look at it and think with satisfaction about how far he had come. The man now making a million-seven a year, overlooked completely in the 1977 draft and signed the next year for $500. The man who used to live in Winter Haven, Fla., with a wife and two babies in a motel room wallpapered with drying diapers because they couldn't afford the Laundromat. The guy who used to grab handfuls of Sucrets from the jar in the Class A clubhouse and throw them in his mouth. Not for a sore throat. For dinner.

He put the frame back. He had made it home, somehow, from Sweden. He stared down at the confetti, then up at the wall. That was good. That was him. Exactly right. The empty frame.

Every day when he was home, it went like this. He would get out of bed, walk down the hall to the reclining chair in his office and sit there. Reading John Grisham novels. Staring out the window. Staring at the empty picture frame. Letting the phone ring. All day in one room, and then back to bed at night, to lie there turning. Another pill. Wake up sweating. Start all over again.

If only he could have it out in one showdown—one night, one week, one month—and then move on. But it didn't work that way. You could tear yourself to shreds in Sweden, tear yourself to shreds in your office at home . . . and it just went on and on and on.

He hadn't called his three children from his first marriage in weeks. He barely touched his 23-month-old daughter by his second wife. He and his wife barely saw each other. They hadn't separated. They just weren't together for a while, while he tried to figure things out.

His family kept begging him to open up, to share his pain. If he told them, if they knew. . . . No. All for him. Only for him. He was sorry about what it was doing to them, but do you want the truth? He felt so numb, so hard, it didn't really matter.

There were two people in the world he could let in. They talked on the phone every couple of days, he and the wives of his dead friends, sometimes for an hour or two. Anything they wanted, he kept telling them. Name it, he would do it. *Money?* No, the Players Association life insurance policy would take care of them well. A *nanny?* He knew a great woman, he would send her there next week. No, they already had help. *Him?* He would fly there in a minute, take the kids anywhere, let them be around a man.

No. They both wanted only one thing of him. The same thing Tim's mom had asked. The hardest thing. They wanted him to pitch again. To come back.

He flew to Cleveland, moved into a rented house and got the plastic surgery done on his head in late May. He still refused all interview requests, read no newspapers for a while. He waited until late in the afternoon, when nearly everyone in outpatient physical rehab at Lutheran Medical Center was gone. He would give it a try for a few days. He stretched the left shoulder that had undergone arthroscopy in April. He walked on the stair machine. His sweat dripped. He looked out the window. He had always read and heard that when you narrowly avoided death, you cherished the things you used to take for granted, you wanted to smell flowers. Why had they lied?

His physical therapist was ready to have a catch with him one day. She wanted to go outside. It was beautiful out there. He shook his head no. Not outside. They took the ball and the gloves and went down to the cellar. Down with the pipes and the bricks and the shadows. For the first time since March 21, he gripped a baseball and cocked it behind his ear. It felt so trivial.

Looking back on the memory of
The dance we shared 'neath the stars above
For a moment all the world was right
How could I have known that you'd ever say goodbye?

And now I'm glad I didn't know
The way it all would end, the way it all would go
Our lives are better left to chance I could've missed the pain
But I'd of had to miss the dance.

Holding you I held everything
For a moment, wasn't I a king?
But if I'd only known how the king would fall
Hey, who's to say, you know I might
Have chanced it all.

ALEXA MOVED. Patti woke. Oh god. Another day. She rose and went downstairs to the compact disc player. It was all set. Push a button and that Garth Brooks song *The Dance* played over and over. They had never really talked about death, but one day Steve had turned to her and said, "When I die, play that song at the funeral." She was still playing it, every morning. A hundred straight times, it played one day. This is what you do with pain.

Nearly everyone in Cleveland knew her face now. They asked her for autographs, they wanted to comfort her. She hated the helplessness, the thought that any moment she could be ambushed by grief in front of anyone. She hated crying in front of people. She hated anyone feeling sorry for her. She hated knowing that they were thinking, There goes poor Patti Olin—nine-month-old twins, three-year-old daughter, a 26-year-old widow.

The song, in a funny way, gave her power. She pushed the button. She listened. She cried. She turned it off. *She* decided when and where and how to grieve. Just a tiny bit, she took charge.

"I'm in intensive therapy," she would tell people who wanted her to see a psychologist, "all by myself."

Bobby wanted her to see a movie called *Indian Summer*. That would be therapy, he thought, but he wasn't in Cleveland, and he told her she couldn't go alone. "Why?" she asked. "Is the movie too close to home?"

"It is home," said Bobby. "Don't you go alone, Patti. You hear me?"

O.K., O.K. She longed to be as strong as Laurie, and without even knowing it, maybe she was. Four hours after the accident, with the police lights still glaring off the lake a few hundred yards outside Laurie's house, Patti ordered

Fernando Montes not to change the channel when the body bag came on the screen. She faced 77 reporters in Winter Haven three days after the accident. She kept that note on the refrigerator door that Steve had scribbled to her: WELCOME TO OUR NEW HOUSE! But Laurie was 33. Laurie knew who she was. Laurie had been a schoolteacher, a mother for nine years, and now a ranch owner—hell, a cowgirl! Patti was a . . . a baseball wife.

A great baseball wife. She loved being that. She was proud of it. A few days before Steve died, there she was, standing in the rain, watching Steve give his arm a workout in a minor league game. Pack up another apartment, haul the kids; she never complained. But who was she now? Where did she live?

She packed everything after the accident in Florida and went home, back to her family in Portland, Ore. But what was *home*? It wasn't just her, was it? A long time ago, when you left home to live in places like Colorado and Florida and Ohio, it was to prove you could make it on your own. Home was all right for a week or two, but after that, sometimes it almost felt like failure.

She put the kids and all their belongings in a plane and flew back to Cleveland. The house was brand-new, empty. She and Steve had bought it in the off-season but never lived there. She went back to the meetings of the Indian wives' organization, as she had before. Back to the wives' Bible-study classes. Back to the wives' section to watch ball games. That was her family, wasn't it? They were rootless, like her. Always looking for a new set of baby-sitters, grocery stores and doctors, like her. Always at the mercy of their husbands' last streak or slump, like her. It almost seemed unfair to lean on the neighbors who had nothing to do with baseball, because you could be gone tomorrow and not be able to pay back the loan. But among teammates and their wives, it was O.K., because it was all understood.

She went on a road trip to Chicago in May with the other wives. The only woman without a husband on the plane, and on the bus, and going back at night to the hotel rooms. She found herself, in the seventh inning of games, looking to the bullpen to see Steve warming up. Sometimes she had to stand and leave the stadium, barely able to keep her legs from running—all the same old tired goblins, all the *whys* and *what ifs* from that day at the lake roaring in her head. What in hell am I doing? she asked herself. I'm not a baseball wife. I don't belong here. Why am I pretending?

Laurie and her kids came to spend a week in June at Patti's house just outside Cleveland. Six little kids running and crawling everywhere. Two women chasing them. It was brutal. It was great. It was nuts. Laurie gave Patti pep talks: You're so smart, so tough, so pretty, all you need is a direction. Get a job, anything for a while, volunteer, go back to school, get out of the house.

Then Laurie broke down after they went to a ball game together, and she realized she needed Patti even more than she had thought.

They got a baby-sitter and went to Bobby's. He opened the door. He had said he was coming back, but those eyes. . . . Laurie walked right up to him, punched him in the arm and kicked him in the butt. Patti said it in a different way. "If you quit, Bobby," she said, "why can't we?"

She could say that to him. After all, she would say, they were family. One night Patti went to see *Indian Summer*. On the screen, staring out at a lake, was a woman—just about Patti's age, Patti's hair color—whose husband had died a year before. A man was telling the young widow about a lady who used to live on the shore whose husband had died too and been buried in the middle of the lake. "Poor woman," the man was saying to the young widow. "Spending the last 15 years of her life waiting to die, so she could go into the lake with her husband. Fifteen years of her life she wasted. We might as well have just thrown her in the lake the same day as her husband."

Patti blinked. She felt it coming, in her chest, in her throat, in her eyes, right there in a theater, in front of everybody. She glanced to one side. A hand had been waiting there beside her, she realized, even before the man had finished saying that. Bobby's hand. Bobby's Kleenex.

THERE ARE black and white pipes, bundles of wires, scabbed paint and fluorescent bulbs glaring on it all in the tunnel leading to the home dugout at Cleveland Stadium. On a gray, sweltering afternoon, five hours before a night game on June 25, Bobby Ojeda walked in a Cleveland Indian uniform down the tunnel, into the dugout, out of seclusion. The cameras snapped. The microphones leaned. The tape recorders clicked on. He said it had to be done.

The Best Years
Of His Life

BY JOHN ED BRADLEY

For the author, an All-SEC center at LSU in the late '70s, nothing would ever match the days he spent playing college football. So why did he hide from the team, and the teammates, who meant the world to him?

I T ENDS FOR EVERYBODY. IT ENDS FOR THE PRO WHO MAKES $5 million a year and has his face on magazine covers and his name in the record books. It ends for the kid on the high school team who never comes off the bench except to congratulate his teammates as they file past him on their way to the Gatorade bucket. In my case it ended on Dec. 22, 1979, at the Tangerine Bowl in Orlando. We beat Wake Forest that night 34–10, in a game I barely remember but for the fact that it was my last one. When it was over, a teammate and I grabbed our heroic old coach, hoisted him on our shoulders and carried him out to the midfield crest. It was ending that day for Charles McClendon, too, after 18 years as head coach at LSU and a superb 69% career winning percentage. The next day newspapers would run photos of Coach Mac's last victory ride, with Big Eddie Stanton and me, smeared with mud, serving as his chariot. Coach had a hand raised above his head as he waved goodbye, but it would strike me that his expression showed little joy at all. He looked tired and sad. More than anything, though, he looked like he didn't want it to end.

We were quiet on the flight back to Baton Rouge, and when the plane touched down at Ryan Field, no cheers went up and nobody said anything. A week or so later, done with the Christmas holidays, I went to Tiger Stadium to clean out my locker. I brought a big travel bag with me, and I stuffed it with pads, shoes, gym trunks, jockstraps, T-shirts and practice jerseys. I removed my nametag from the locker. Then I studied the purple stenciling against the gold matte. In one corner someone had scribbled the words TRAMPLE THE DEAD, HURDLE THE WEAK. The source of the legend eludes me now, but it had been a rallying cry for the team that year, especially for my mates on the offensive line.

The last thing I packed was my helmet. I'd been an offensive center, and the helmet's back and sides were covered with the little Tigers decals the coaches had given out as merit badges for big plays. I ran my fingertips over the surface, feeling the scars in the hard plastic crown. There were paint smudges and streaks from helmets I'd butted over the years. Was the gold Vanderbilt or Florida State? The red Alabama or Georgia, Indiana or USC?

When I finished packing, I walked down the chute that led to the playing field, pushed open the big metal door and squinted against the sudden blast of sunlight. I meant to have one last look at the old stadium where I'd played the last four years. Death Valley was quiet now under a blue winter sky. I could point to virtually any spot on the field and tell you about some incident that had happened there. I knew where teammates had blown out knees, dropped passes, made key blocks and tackles, thrown interceptions and recovered game-saving fumbles. I knew where we'd vomited in spring scrimmages under a brutal Louisiana sun and where we'd celebrated on autumn Saturday nights to the roar of maniacal Tigers fans and the roar of a real tiger, Mike IV, prowling in a cage on the sideline. We'd performed to a full house at most every home game, the crowds routinely in excess of 75,000, but today there was no one in sight, the bleachers running in silver ribbons around the gray cement bowl. It seemed the loneliest place on earth.

I was only 21 years old, yet I believed that nothing I did for the rest of my life would rise up to those days when I wore the Purple and Gold. I might go on to a satisfying career and make a lot of money, I might marry a beautiful woman and fill a house with perfect kids, I might make a mark that would be of some significance in other people's eyes. But I would never have it better than when I was playing football for LSU.

Despite this belief, I was determined to walk away from that place and that life and never look back. You wouldn't catch me 20 years later crowing about how it had been back in the day, when as a college kid I'd heard the cheers. I knew the type who couldn't give it up, and I didn't want to be him. He keeps going to the games and reminding anyone who'll listen of how things used to be. His wife and kids roll their eyes as he describes big plays, quotes from halftime speeches and embellishes a "career" that no one else seems to remember with any specificity. He stalks the memory until the memory reduces him to pathetic self-parody. To listen to him, he never screwed up a snap count or busted an assignment or had a coach berate him for dogging it or getting beat. In his mind he is forever young, forever strong, forever golden.

Standing there in Tiger Stadium, I squeezed my eyes closed and lowered my head. Then I wept.

Hell no, I said to myself. That wasn't going to be me.

I still remember their names and hometowns. And I can tell you, almost to a man, the high schools they went to. I remember how tall they were and how much they weighed. I remember their strengths and weaknesses, both as men and as football players. I remember the kinds of cars they drove, what religions they practiced, the music they favored, the hair color of their girlfriends, how many letters they earned, their injuries, their dreams, their times in the 40-yard dash. In many instances I remember their jersey numbers. On the day last August that I turned 43, I wondered what had happened to Robert DeLee. DeLee, a tight end from the small town of Clinton, La., wore number 43 on his jersey when I was a senior. During my freshman year a running back named Jack Clark had worn the number. Jack Clark, too, I thought to myself—where on earth has he slipped off to? I had seen neither of them in more than two decades.

That was the case with almost all of my teammates. Last summer I attended a wedding reception for Barry Rubin, a former fullback at LSU who is a strength coach with the Green Bay Packers. It had been about eight years since I'd last had a face-to-face conversation with a teammate, and even that meeting had come purely by chance. One day I was waiting in the checkout line at a store in suburban New Orleans when someone standing behind me called out my name. I wheeled around, and there stood Charlie McDuff, an ex-offensive tackle who'd arrived at LSU at the same time I did, as a member of the celebrated 1976 freshman class. A couple of shoppers separated Charlie and me, and I couldn't reach past them to shake his hand. "How are things going?" he said.

"Things are good," I said. "How 'bout with you?"

I felt uncomfortable seeing him again, even though we'd always gotten along well back in school. The media guide had listed him at 6' 6" and 263 pounds, but in actual fact he was a shade taller and closer to 275. Even after all these years away from the game he had a bull neck and arms thick with muscle. His hair was as sun-bleached as ever, his skin as darkly tanned.

I paid what I owed and started to leave. Then I turned back around and looked at him again. "You ever see anybody anymore, Charlie?" I said.

"Yeah. Sure, I see them. Some of them. You?"

"Not really."

He nodded as if he understood, and we parted without saying anything more, and two years later Charlie McDuff was dead. My sister called, crying with the news. Charlie had suffered a pulmonary embolism while vacationing with his family at a Gulf Coast resort. He left behind a wife and three young sons. I wanted to call someone and talk about him, and I knew it had to be a player, one of our teammates, and preferably an offensive lineman. But I couldn't do it, I couldn't make the call. Nobody wanted to remember anymore, I tried to convince myself. It was too long ago. So instead I pulled some cardboard boxes out of a closet and went through them. There were trophies and plaques wrapped in paper, letters tied with kite string, a short stack of souvenir programs and a couple of plastic-bound photo albums crowded with news clippings and yellowing images of boys who actually were capable of dying. If Charlie McDuff could die, it occurred to me, we all could.

At the bottom of the box I found a worn, gray T-shirt with purple lettering that said NOBODY WORKS HARDER THAN THE OFFENSIVE LINE. Charlie had had that shirt made, along with about a dozen others, and handed them out to the linemen on the '79 squad. The year before, we'd lost some outstanding players to graduation, and Charlie had hoped the shirts would inspire us to pull together as a unit. We wore the shirts at every opportunity, generally under our shoulder pads at practice and games. It seems crazy now, but there was a time when I considered stipulating in my will that I be buried in that ratty thing. I was never more proud than when I had it on.

I learned about Charlie's funeral arrangements, and I got dressed intending to go. I started down the road for Baton Rouge, rehearsing the lines I'd speak to his widow and children, and those I'd tell my old teammates to explain why I didn't come around anymore. I drove as far as the outskirts of Baton Rouge before turning around and heading back home.

Are there others out there like me? I've often wondered. Does the loss of a game they played in their youth haunt them as it's haunted me? Do others wake up from afternoon naps and bolt for the door, certain that they're late for practice even though their last practice was half a lifetime ago? My nightmares don't contain images of monsters or plane crashes or Boo Radley hiding behind the bedroom door. Mine have me jumping offside or muffing the center-quarterback exchange. They have me forgetting where I placed my helmet when the defense is coming off the field and it's time for me to go back in the game.

If it really ends, I wonder, then why doesn't it just end?

I suppose I was doomed from the start, having been sired by a Louisiana high school football coach. The year of my birth, 1958, was the same year LSU won its one and only national championship in football, and the month of my birth, August, was when two-a-day practices began for that season. Although my parents couldn't afford to take their five kids to the LSU games, we always listened to the radio broadcasts, usually while my father was outside barbecuing on the patio. He'd sit there in a lawn chair, lost in concentration, a purple-and-gold cap tipped back on his head. Not far away on the lawn I acted out big plays with friends from the neighborhood, some of us dressed in little Tigers uniforms. We played in the dark until someone ran into a tree or a clothesline and got hurt, then my dad would have me sit next to him and listen to the rest of the game, the real one. "Settle down now," I remember him saying. "LSU's on."

When I was a kid I always gave the same answer to adults who asked me what I wanted to be when I grew up. "I want to play football for LSU," I answered. Beyond that I had no clear picture of myself.

Nor could I fathom a future without the game when it ended for me 23 years ago. One day I was on the team, the next I was a guy with a pile of memories and a feeling in his gut that his best days were behind him. I shuffled around in my purple letter jacket wondering what to do with myself, and wondering who I was. Suddenly there were no afternoon workouts or meetings to attend. I didn't have to visit the training room for whirlpool or hot-wax baths or ultrasound treatments or massages or complicated ankle tapings or shots to kill the never-ending pain. If I wanted to, I could sit in a Tigerland bar and get drunk without fear of being booted from the team; I didn't have a team anymore. Every day for four years I'd stepped on a scale and recorded my weight on a chart for the coaches. But no one cared any longer how thin I got, or how fat.

That last year I served as captain of the offense, and either by some miracle or by a rigged ballot I was named to the second team All-Southeastern Conference squad. The first-team player, Alabama's Dwight Stephenson, went on to become a star with the Miami Dolphins and a member of the Pro Football Hall of Fame, and I'd seen enough film of the guy to know I was nowhere in his league. At the end of April, in the hours after the 1980 NFL draft, a scout for the Dallas Cowboys called and asked me to consider signing with the club as a free agent, but by then I'd already shed 30 pounds along with any notion of myself as an athlete. I gave some excuse and hung up. "You don't even want to try?" my father said.

I could've yelled at him for asking, but there was genuine compassion in his eyes. He and my mother were losing something, too. One of their sons had played football for LSU, and where I come from nothing topped that. "It's over," I said.

My father nodded and walked away.

Number 50 was Jay Whitley, the pride of Baton Rouge's Lee High. Fifty-one was Lou deLauney, then Albert Richardson; 52, Kevin Lair, then Leigh Shepard; 53, Steve Estes and Jim Holsombake; 54, Rocky Guillot. Fifty-five was linebacker S.J. Saia; then after my freshman year the number went to Marty Dufrene, probably the toughest offensive lineman ever to come out of Lafourche Parish. My number was 56. When we left the stadium after games, fans were waiting outside under the streetlamps, some of them with programs and slips of paper to sign. Even a lowly offensive lineman was asked for an autograph. "Number 56 in your program, Number 1 in your heart," I'd write, disgracing myself for all eternity but way too ignorant at the time to know it.

I don't recall how I first learned about what happened to Marty. Maybe it was from a news story about efforts to raise money to help pay his medical bills. Or maybe it was another tearful call from a relative. But one day I found myself punching numbers on a telephone keypad, desperate to talk to him again. Marty was living in LaRose, his hometown in the heart of Cajun country, or "down the bayou," as the natives like to say. His wife, Lynne, answered. "Lynne, do you remember me?" I said, after introducing myself.

"Yes, I remember you," she answered. "You want to talk to Marty? Hold on, John Ed. It's going to take a few minutes, because I have to put him on the speakerphone."

A speakerphone? When he finally came on he sounded as though he was trapped at the bottom of a well.

"Marty, is it true you got hurt?" I said.

"Yeah," he said.

"You're paralyzed, man?"

"Yeah," he said, raising his voice to make sure I could hear. "I broke my neck. Can you believe it?"

It had happened in July 1986, some five years before my call. While in his second year of studies at a chiropractic college then based in Irving, Texas, Marty was injured in a freak accident at a pool party to welcome the incoming freshman class. He and friends were horsing around when a pair of them decided to bring big, strong Marty down. One held him in a headlock, the other took a running start and plowed into him. Marty smashed through the water's surface of a shallow children's pool and struck his head on the bottom, shattering a vertebra. He floated in the water, unable to move or feel anything from his neck down, until his friends pulled him out.

As he told me about the accident I kept flashing back to the kid I'd known in school. Marty had been a lean, powerfully built 6' 2" and 235 pounds, small by today's standards but about average for a center in our era. On the field he'd played with a kind of swagger, as if certain that he could dominate his opponent. The swagger extended to his life off the field. Marty liked to have a good time. He spoke with a heavy Cajun accent, the kind of accent that made girls crazy and immediately identified him as a pure Louisiana thoroughbred. Football schools from the Midwest featured humongous linemen brought up on corn and prime beef. At LSU we had guys like Marty, raised on crawfish from the mud flats and seafood from the Gulf of Mexico.

The son of an offshore oil field worker, Marty was an all-state high school center in 1976. He was a highly recruited blue-chipper coming out of South Lafourche High, just as I had been at Opelousas High the year before. Marty had vacillated between committing to West Point and to LSU before he realized there really was only one choice for him. Air Force was the military academy that had tried to lure me before I snapped out of it and understood what my destiny was.

The only problem I'd ever had with Marty Dufrene was that we played the same position, and he wanted my job. Going into my senior year I was listed on the first team, Marty on the second. One day after practice he told me he was going to beat me out. I couldn't believe his gall. "I want to play pro ball," he said.

I shook my head and walked off, thinking, Pro ball? To hell with that, Dufrene. I'm going to see to it you don't even play in college.

Now, on the telephone, I was telling him, "I'd like to come see you, Marty."

"Yeah," he said. "It would be great to see you again."

"I'll do it. I promise. Just give me some time."

"Sure, whatever you need. I'd like to catch up."

But then 11 years passed, and I didn't visit Marty or follow up with another call. Nor did I write to him to explain my silence. How could I tell the man that I was afraid to see him again? Afraid to see him as a quadriplegic, afraid to have to acknowledge that, but for the grace of God, I could be the one confined to a chair, afraid to face the reality that what we once were was now ancient history.

I might've played football, in another life. But in my present one I had no doubt as to the depths of my cowardice.

At some point I decided to turn my back on it all, rather than endure the feeling of loss any longer. Marty Dufrene wasn't the only one I avoided. There were years when I tried to stay clear of the entire town of Baton Rouge. Travelers can see Tiger Stadium as they cross the Mississippi River Bridge and enter the city from the west, and whenever I journeyed across that elevated span I made sure to look at the downtown office buildings and the State Capitol to the north, rather than to the south where the old bowl sits nestled in the trees. I struggled to watch LSU games on TV and generally abandoned the set after less than a quarter. Same for radio broadcasts: I tuned most of them out by halftime. On two occasions the school's athletic department invited me to attend home games as an honorary captain, and while I showed both times, I was such a nervous wreck at being in the stadium again that I could barely walk out on the field before kickoff to receive my award and raise an arm in salute to the crowd.

Love ends, too, and when the girl invites you over to meet her new beau, you don't have to like it, do you?

I received invitations to participate in charity golf tournaments featuring former Tigers players; I never went to them. Teammates invited me to tailgate parties, suppers and other events; I never made it to them. The lettermen's club invited me to maintain a membership; except for one year, I always failed to pay my dues. Even Coach Mac tried to get in touch with me a few times. I was somehow too busy to call him back.

It wasn't until December of last year that I finally saw him again, and by then he was dying. In fact, in only three days he would be dead. Cancer had left him bedridden at his home in Baton Rouge, but even at the worst of it he was receiving guests, most of them former players who came by to tell him goodbye. One day I received a call from an old college friend, urging me to see Coach Mac again. She said it didn't look good; if I wanted to talk to him and make my peace, I'd better come right away.

So that was how I ended up at his doorstep one breezy weekday morning last winter, my hand shaking as I lifted a finger to punch the bell. I wondered if anyone in the house had seen me park on the drive in front, and I seriously considered walking back to my truck and leaving. But then the door swung open and there standing a few feet away was Coach Mac's wife, Dorothy Faye. I could feel my heart squeeze tight in my chest and my breath go shallow. My friend had called ahead and told her I might be coming; otherwise she surely would've been alarmed by the sight of a weeping middle-aged man at her front door. "Why, John Ed Bradley," she said. "Come in. Come in, John Ed."

She put her arms around me and kissed the side of my face. Dorothy Faye was as beautiful as ever, and as kind and gracious, not once asking why it had taken her husband's impending death to get me to come see him again. She led me down a hall to a bedroom, and I could see him before I walked in the door. He was lying supine on a hospital bed. His head was bald, the hair lost to past regimens of chemotherapy, and, at age 78, wrapped up in bedsheets, he seemed so much smaller than I remembered him. His eyes were large and haunted from the battle, but it was Coach Mac, all right. I snapped to attention when he spoke my name. "Come over here and talk to me, buddy," he said.

I sat next to the bed and we held hands and told stories, every one about football. He was still the aw-shucks country boy who'd played for Bear Bryant at Kentucky before going on to build his own legend in Louisiana, and the sound of his rich drawl made the past suddenly come alive for me. I named former teammates and asked him what had become of them, and in every case he had an answer. "Your old position coach was here yesterday," he said.

"Coach McCarty?"

"He sat right there." And we both looked at the place, an empty chair.

"And you're a writer now," he said.

"Yes sir, I'm a writer."

"I'm proud of you, John Ed."

I didn't stay long, maybe 20 minutes, and shortly before I got up to leave he asked me if I ever remembered back to 1979 and the night that the top-ranked USC Trojans came to Baton Rouge and the fans stood on their feet for four quarters and watched one of the most exciting games ever played in Tiger Stadium. "I remember it all the time," I said. "I don't always want to remember it, because we lost, Coach, but I remember it."

"I remember it too," he said in a wistful sort of way. The Trojans that year had one of the most talented teams in college football history, with standouts Ronnie Lott, Charles White, Marcus Allen, Brad Budde and Anthony Munoz. They would go on to an 11-0-1 season and finish ranked second nationally behind Alabama, and White would win the Heisman Trophy.

In his bed Coach Mac lifted a hand and ran it over the front of his face in a raking gesture. "They called face-masking against Benjy," he whispered.

"Sir?"

"That penalty. The one at the end."

"Yes, sir. They sure did call it. And it cost us the game."

He swallowed, and it seemed I could see that night being replayed in his eyes: the yellow flag going up, the 15 yards being marched off, the subsequent touchdown with less than a minute to play that gave USC the 17–12 win. "Benjy Thibodeaux didn't face-mask anybody," I said, the heat rising in my face as I started to argue against a referee's call that nothing would ever change.

Coach Mac was quiet now, and he eased his grip on my hand. I stood and started for the door, determined not to look back. His voice stopped me. "Hey, buddy?" he said. I managed to face him again. "Always remember I'm with you. I'm with all you boys." He lifted a hand off the bed and held it up high, just as he had so many years ago after his last game.

"I know you are, Coach."

"And buddy?" A smile came to his face. He pointed at me. "Next time don't wait so long before you come see your old coach again."

Now it is summer, the season before the season, and Major Marty Dufrene, Civil Department Head of the Lafourche Parish Sheriff's Department, motors his wheelchair to the end of a cement drive and nods in the direction of a horse barn at the rear of his 38-acre estate. Five horses stand along a fence and wait for him, just as they do every day when he rolls out to see them after work. "I'm going to be riding before the end of the year," he tells me. "I've got a saddle I'm making with the back beefed up for support, so I can strap myself in. Of course I'm going to have to use a lift to put me in the saddle. But I'm going to do it."

By now I have been with him for a couple of hours, and already the force of his personality has made the chair invisible. After the injury his muscles began to atrophy, and over time his midsection grew large and outsized, his face swollen. But the fire in his eyes hasn't changed. Marty is exactly as I remembered him. "One thing about him," says his wife, "Marty might've broken his neck, he might be paralyzed and in that chair, but he is still a football player."

Their large Acadian-style house stands only a stone's throw from Bayou Lafourche, the place where they met and fell in love as teenagers. Lynne and their 17-year-old daughter, Amy, are inside preparing dinner, and outside Marty is giving me a tour of the spread when we come to rest in the shade of a carport. I reach to touch the top of his shoulder, because he still has some feeling there, but then I stop myself. "Marty, you must've resented the hell out of me," I say.

He looks up, surprise registering on his face. He bucks forward and then back in his chair, and it isn't necessary for me to explain which of my failures might've led me to make such a statement. "No, never," he says. "I saw you as my competition, but I always have a lot of respect for my competition, and I did for you, too. You were standing in my way, standing in the way of where I wanted to be. But even then I knew my role and accepted it. I was going to push you as hard as I could. That was my duty to you and to the team. I looked up to you as a teacher, just as you looked up to Jay Whitley as a teacher when he was playing ahead of you. We were teammates, John Ed. That was the most important thing."

Lynne and Amy serve lasagna, green salad and blueberry cheesecake in the dining room, and afterward Marty and I move to the living room and sit together as dusk darkens the windows. He revisits the nightmare of his accident and the rough years that followed, but it isn't until he talks about his days as an LSU football player that he becomes emotional. "Nothing I've ever experienced compares to it," he says. "That first time I ran out with the team as a freshman—out into Tiger Stadium? God, I was 15 feet off the ground and covered with frissons. You know what frissons are? They're goose bumps. It's the French word for goose bumps." He lowers his head, and tears fill his eyes and run down his face. He weeps as I have wept, at the memory of how beautiful it all was. "It was the biggest high you could have," he says. "No drugs could match it. The way it felt to run out there with the crowd yelling for you. I wish every kid could experience that."

"If every kid could," I say, "then it wouldn't be what it is. It's because so few ever get there that it has such power."

We are quiet, and then he says, "Whenever I have a down time, or whenever I'm feeling sorry for myself, or whenever life is more than I can bear at the moment, I always do the same thing. I put the Tiger fight song on the stereo, and all the memories come back and somehow it makes everything O.K. All right, I say to myself. I can do it. I can do it. Let's go."

Marty and I talk deep into the night, oblivious to the time, and finally I get up to leave. He wheels his chair as far as the door, and as I'm driving away I look back and see him sitting there, a bolt of yellow light around him, arm raised in goodbye.

I could seek out each one of them and apologize for the vanishing act, but, like me, most of them eventually elected to vanish, too, moving into whatever roles the world had reserved for them. Last I heard, Jay Blass had become a commercial pilot. Greg Raymond returned to New Orleans and was running his family's jewelry store. Tom Tully became a veterinarian specializing in exotic birds, of all things. And Jay Whitley, somebody told me, is an orthodontist now, the father of four kids. If they're anything like their old man, they're stouthearted and fearless, and they eat linebackers for lunch.

When the pregame prayer and pep talks were done, we'd come out of the chute to the screams of people who were counting on us. The band would begin to play; up ahead the cheerleaders were waiting. Under the crossbar of the goalpost we huddled, seniors in front. I was always afraid to trip and fall and embarrass myself, and for the first few steps I ran with a hand on the teammate next to me. Arms pumping, knees lifted high. The heat felt like a dense, blistering weight in your lungs. If you looked up above the rim of the bowl you couldn't see the stars; the light from the standards had washed out the sky. Always in the back of your mind was the knowledge of your supreme good fortune. Everyone else would travel a similar course of human experience, but you were different.

And so, chin straps buckled tight, we filed out onto the field as one, the gold and the white a single elongated blur, neatly trimmed in purple.

He's Burning To Be a Success

BY JOHN UNDERWOOD

Eagles linebacker Tim Rossovich was a terror on the field and a teddy bear off it, an unusually thoughtful athlete who ate glass and set himself on fire. Everyone who met him had a Rossovich story—and the author collected them all.

H E HAD THE AEROSOL CAN IN HIS HAND, AND THE SHAVING lather billowed out, and when he began to apply it to his face, a familiar, fundamental impulse stirred within him—the possibilities seemed enormous—and he began to spray the lather around, sprsssshhh, over his forehead and across his chest, and then down his arms and over the length and breadth of his 6' 4", 245-pound naked body. And before the Earth had turned much farther, he had made of himself a pillar of white frosting, awesome to behold. And he looked in the mirror and saw that it was good. And because this was not something he would want to keep to himself, he ran outside the Sigma Chi house, at the University of Southern California, and down the street. And the cars on Figueroa Avenue bucked and jerked at the sight of him gliding among them. And as he turned and ran back, molting froth, Tim Rossovich chuckled inside, and he knew that he had done it again, and he was pleased.

The party was in an apartment at the Penn Towers in Philadelphia. The host's name was Steve Sabol. Not many seasons ago, when he was a fullback at Colorado College, Sabol called himself Sudden Death Sabol and sent out largely fanciful publicity releases on himself. Now he is executive vice president of NFL Films, Inc., where his imagination is paying off at last, and he has become latterly famous for his free-form parties. The doorbell rang, and when the door was opened a man with a Fu Manchu mustache and an immense hedge of curly hair the texture of pork rinds stood in the doorway, not in shaving cream this time but in flames. Ablaze. On fire. Guests cried out in horror. "Oh, God, he's...." " "Somebody do something!" The flaming man walked into the room, where Sabol and a guest knocked him to the floor and began beating him with blankets. The flames extinguished, Tim Rossovich got to his feet, looked casually around the room, said, "Sorry, I must have the wrong apartment," and walked out.

The lounge is on the Philadelphia Main Line, and he has become well-known there. On his first visit he wore a sleeveless shirt with a big decal of a rose on the front, crushed vinyl shoes and a pair of vinyl pants with a sash. When the man at the door asked to see his I.D. card, Tim Rossovich bent over and bit him on the head. This night he had a cast on his arm, and he explained that he had broken the arm at the Philadelphia Eagles' practice that afternoon. The regulars commiserated with him, and soon they were discussing some minor point of football. Apparently incensed by what was being said, Rossovich began shouting and pounding on the bar with the arm on which he wore the cast. He swung it wildly about, striking and breaking a chair. He pounded it on the bar again. The cast splintered and began to disintegrate. Pieces of plaster fluttered silently down like snowflakes. The lounge grew quiet. Everybody was looking, stunned, at the exposed arm. Rossovich held it up, his face expressive of an epiphany. "I'm cured!" he yelled.

The stories are told—in locker rooms, at bowling lanes, over long-distance phones—by almost anyone who knows or has ever met Tim Rossovich and by Rossovich himself. Only those who feel insecure around him, like coaches who think his life-style is a threat to the Republic, try to keep his wondrous light under a bushel. Tim Rossovich eats light bulbs. He wears tie-dyed shirts and shower-of-hail suits, Dracula capes and frontier buckskins and stands on his head in hotel lobbies. Sometimes when he stands on his head his head is in a bucket of water.

The stories are endless. Tim Rossovich had this motorbike. He drove it onto a pier. He drove it *off* the pier. Splash! Tim Rossovich had this car. It was one of many cars that suffered beyond repair at his hand. He drove the fellows in the car to a pub to get a beer. In order to stop the car, he drove it into the wall of the pub. Crash! Tim Rossovich was sitting at a table where the conversation lagged. He was smoking a cigarette. Suddenly he was not smoking the cigarette. He was eating it. Chomp! Tim Rossovich was opening a bottle of beer. He was opening it with his teeth. Actually, he was having a bottle-opening contest with Mike Ditka, the tight end. It was no contest. Tim Rossovich had opened 100 bottles to Ditka's three when he began to drink the beer. Then he began to eat the beer glass. Crackle! Crunch! Mike Ditka withdrew from the contest.

Tim Rossovich was at a birthday party. He was bored. Beneath the slack, soft-eyed countenance the drumbeat started, swelled, stirred him. *Do* something, Timmy. He began to pace. He excused himself. He went into the bathroom, took off his clothes and with a mighty croak came leaping into the living room like a great bronze frog, did a ponderous flip and landed bare, uh, back in the birthday cake. Slumpfh!

The chronology of these events is unimportant. The perils of Tim Rossovich have a way of repeating themselves anyway. (Was it at the fraternity meeting at USC that he stood up to make a speech, spread his arms, opened his mouth and the sparrow flew out? Or was it at a team meeting of the Philadelphia Eagles? Probably both.) It is enough to say, in introduction, that Tim Rossovich was an All-America defensive end at USC, where he was famous for falling off sorority house rooftops, and is now on his way to becoming an All-Pro middle linebacker for the Philadelphia Eagles, where he is known to have made death-defying leaps into the whirlpool tank in the training room. The whirlpool tank is roughly the size of a washing machine. Witnesses say it is a very hairy stunt indeed when the tank happens to be already occupied. Squish!

His friends in Southern California, where Rossovich lives in the off-season, told him there was no such place as Philadelphia when he went east as a rookie three years ago, but they were confident that if there were he would put it on the map. Ron Medved, the Eagles defensive back, says that once you have experienced Tim Rossovich you can never forget him, that his (Medved's) four-year-old son can pick him out of a program every time, squealing, "Rosso! Rosso!" Rossovich took the Medveds to Disneyland. He rode every ride. Three times he went through the haunted house, scaring people. "They thought he was part of the act," says Medved. "I've got a picture of him on the merry-go-round. What an expression! You never saw a guy having such a good time."

Medved recounts this conversation he had with Don Meredith, the TV announcer and reformed quarterback, in a shower: "Is it true," began Meredith, "that Rossovich—"

"It's true," said Medved, "and more."

"But listen," said Meredith, "did he really—"

"Whatever you've heard about Ross is true," said Medved.

"I'll be damned," said Meredith, and shook his wet head.

Rossovich is the first to admit that his reputation may have escalated in recent years. "Little things," he says modestly, "are built up to be greater than they are." But he does not deny any of it. Whenever the credibility of this episode or that is strained, it is usually a matter of mistaken locale. If it did not happen in one place, it probably did (or will eventually) in another. Rossovich says he is more subdued now than he used to be. As a star football player with responsibilities, including a wife and daughter, he says he is more mature. He sets fire to himself less frequently than you would think. "It is not something you do every day," he says.

On the other hand, Steve Sabol will tell you that Rossovich is actually expanding as a personality. Last spring Sabol tried to compress the essential Rossovich into a 25-minute film for national television. It so happens that Sabol has more than just a passing put-out-the-fire interest in him. He and Rossovich and Gary Pettigrew, the Eagles defensive tackle, have shared apartments in Philadelphia, charring the walls. Sabol has become Rosso's "second," always arriving in the nick of time to put out the fire. He found in Rossovich a kindred spirit and enjoys talking about Rossovich almost as much as he used to enjoy talking about himself. He liked the cut of Rosso's tie-dyed clothes, his Emperor Ming glasses, his Aladdin shoes with bells on the toes.

Sabol says he decided on Rossovich for the TV show because of these things and because he felt Dave Meggyesy, the pro football dropout, had taken a cheap shot at the game in his book *Out of Their League*, and he wanted to make a film about a "contemporary guy—a guy with long hair who did far-out things but who was a believer in football and didn't think like Meggyesy."

The show was called *The New Breed*, but what it depicted in Rossovich was a breed apart. Credit Sabol. The Rossovich he portrayed (discovered!) was more than just a pretty flake. He was actually three Tim Rossoviches residing cooperatively in the large, sculptured Rossovich superstructure, which is topped by that singular Slavic head. (It has been pointed out that Rossovich is three-quarters Italian, and Yugoslav from the neck up.) These things saw Sabol:

Rossovich the football player is at all times fearsome. When he hits the tackling sled he drives it into the ground, punches it, kicks it. He literally throws himself at running backs, and into pileups. ("Ferocious," says Sabol admiringly.) He gets into fights on the field because he will not let up. He fights not only the opposition but his own teammates. Medved says Rossovich always has the offensive players teed off because to him there is no such thing as a dummy scrimmage. He goes 30 yards out of his way to get a lick in. Rossovich himself says he has fought them all—all the Eagles offensive linemen at practice at one time or another—but is at peace with them afterward because they cannot stay mad long at someone so adorable, and they know down deep he really loves them.

And not only is he very fierce, Sabol showed, but he is also very good. Against the Atlanta Falcons last fall Rossovich made six tackles in a row, and the film showed him to be a leader who exhorted his teammates and called his virulent intentions across the line of scrimmage: "I love you, man, but I gotta wipe you out!" The film showed him wiping men out.

The second part of Rossovich is even dearer to Sabol's heart. "Some guys play with abandon," he says. "Rosso *lives* with abandon. People turn him on. When the organ grinder goes, he goes. He'll do anything. He puts things in his mouth I wouldn't put in my hand. He was going to have a footrace with this guy. To get ready he drank a quart of motor oil. I didn't see it, but it must have been awful. He likes to 'hang out.' We do that a lot around Philadelphia, hang out. We were hanging out at Rittenhouse Square, where they were having a concert. He saw this big box a guy had taken a tuba out of. He dragged it out into the middle of Walnut Street, crawled inside and curled up. People stopped and looked in. 'How are you?' he said. 'I'm Tim Rossovich.' 'What are you doing in there, Tim?' 'Well, we had a tough practice today and I'm relaxing.' "

Sabol warms to the subject. His memory races with figments of Tim Rossovich in action, doing brain-rattling things, exhibiting cosmic insight.

"His life-style is beautiful. He sleeps four hours a night. On the floor. You think of someone sleeping, you think of them on their side or on their back. He sleeps face down, like a man ready for artificial respiration. He always points his head north, he says, so the magnetic waves can run through and revitalize him. The maid came in and found him lying there one morning, naked, face down. She thought he was dead."

When the Rossovich-Sabol-Pettigrew triumvirate lived together, Rossovich played Christmas carols "so loud you could hear them on the 12th floor. We lived on the 24th floor. He loves Christmas carols. He plays them in September. He has this great look. He doesn't walk, he *slides*. He has this thing about fragrances. He covers himself with body lotions. He was hooked on patchouli oil for a while. It made him smell like a cedar closet."

Sabol admires the terrific diversity in Rossovich's wardrobe. They try to dress in periods—Frontier Period, Cosmic Period and so forth. When they were going through their Rain-Dance Period, Rossovich carried a wand around. Sabol went with him one night when he was invited to talk to a Sun Oil group. "What do I say?" he asked Sabol. "What do I wear?" Sabol told him these were business executives. Sabol wore a suit. Rossovich wore overalls that said "Unidentified Flying Object" on the front, an electric tie-dyed shirt and shades. But he communicated. "They loved him," says Sabol.

"His favorite book is the *Guinness Book of World Records*," says Sabol. "He says it's important to know what's biggest and best if you want to be the best. He wants to be the best middle linebacker in pro football. I ride him about it. I tell him he can't be as long as Dick Butkus is alive."

Sabol brought home a five-minute short that NFL Films made on Butkus, the one ministers and Boy Scout leaders objected to. Butkus tells in this film how he would like to knock somebody's head off and see it roll away. Rossovich loves it. He and Pettigrew look at it eight or nine times a week. "We put it on," said Sabol, "and some Rimsky Korsakov on the stereo or *Carmen*, the march of the toreadors, and have a little wine, and it's like a light show. Rosso had the defensive team in to watch it the day they played the Giants last year. Made 'em watch it three times. The Giants were fated. They lost 23–20."

But it is the third Rossovich that was Sabol's special discovery. The third Rossovich was revealed to be a serious, articulate, sensitive young man who could offer in a breath a reasonable defense for his generation's preoccupation with its hair and at the same time his own keen appreciation of disciplines and values of football. If the positions seem irreconcilable, Rossovich did not find them so. He said he would love to have had a football coach like General Patton. "Patton would have been the greatest football coach," he said. He recited verbatim from the opening monologue of the movie *Patton*. He said making a tackle was a creative thing, that each man did it in his own style. He likened Butkus's to that of an ape. His, he said, was more cobralike.

He said at the same time that at least some of his actions were attributable to his distaste for the stereotyped, slab-of-meat football player, and if he looked the way he did and impressed kids who identified with him that he was doing something positive, something meaningful, that would be worthwhile.

Sabol calls Rossovich a mind field which has lain fallow for years and is only now bursting into bloom. He cites a newly developed affinity for nature, Rossovich's "interest in organic foods, herbs and stuff," his vow to take up gardening. "He looks at the ocean and it's like taking vitamins," says Sabol. "Now he wants to study macrame, and he makes those candles. They're really beautiful." Off the field, says Sabol, Rossovich is so gentle you wouldn't believe it. "Everybody's scared of what he might do next, but he's never malicious. He's like a wildflower that wilts at the first breath of hot air. He'll turn from a fight like a little kid."

None of these characterizations came as a real surprise to the coaches who had Rossovich at Southern Cal. They often speak of him.

"Ah, old Timbo," said John McKay, the USC head coach, not long ago, shaking his head and smiling knowingly.

"A big puppy dog," said assistant coach Craig Fertig, shaking his head and smiling.

"A big boy, an intelligent boy, but above all, a mean boy," said McKay fondly.

"A very high threshold of pain," said assistant coach Marv Goux.

Goux said he had recruited Rossovich and had fallen in love with the Rossovich family, which lived a mile from the Stanford campus in Palo Alto. He said there were two other brothers and two sisters, and the parents were "the sweetest, straightest people you'd ever want to meet." Tim's grandfather on his mother's side had come over from Italy as a boy of 13 on the boat by himself. His father was a first-generation American success story: up from nothing to his own business, a fish and poultry market; he had also made profitable investments. His parents told Goux that Tim had been a very easy boy to raise, with only a few enlivening incidents, such as the time, at 10, he went through the windshield of a car and the day he rode his bicycle off the 12th row of the bleachers at the high school stadium. Goux said he became Tim's father confessor and kept the Rossoviches abreast of Tim's visits to the dean's office.

"Timbo actually was a very good student," said Goux. "He graduated with his class or a semester after. And he never, *never* cut corners on the football field. He was a leader. His senior year for us was a great year for him. Against Notre Dame he was fantastic. He blocked three passes at the line of scrimmage, forced a fumble on our three-yard line."

"But off the field, a big puppy dog," said Fertig. "You see a picture of a group up to something and there he is in the background, that great face gazing over the heads of the others."

Goux said he would never forget the scene in the Student Union Building when Tim had to appear before a student-faculty discipline committee to explain some of his actions. "There he sat, in the middle of this panel of guys in horn-rimmed glasses, them waving their fingers at him and him very contrite, very apologetic, promising to behave."

Fertig said they knew Rossovich was no ordinary anomaly when as a freshman he put dents in all the lockers by ramming them with his head.

"He was trying to prove a point," said Goux, as if to explain a natural chain of events. He said it began the summer before, when Rossovich was swinging on a rope over and into the Russian River near Palo Alto, competing with friends for a $40 pot. The object was to see who had the guts to land nearest a rock cliff. Rossovich assured himself of victory by crashing flush into the rocks. He said he knew he couldn't get any closer than that. But in triumph he sliced up his elbows, and a few days later when he dived into a contaminated fish pond at a USC fraternity party he developed an infection. He went into a coma. For four days he was incoherent. In the hospital he threw chairs and smashed a television set. The doctors told him to lay off football for eight weeks.

But when Rossovich got out of the hospital he pronounced himself ready to go. To prove it to Goux, he ran across the training room and banged head first into a locker. "See? I'm fine," he said. "*I* see, but the doctors say no," said Goux. The scene was repeated almost every day after that, Rossovich ramming home his point, Goux wincing but unyielding. No locker was safe.

Over the succeeding years, Goux said, he became especially fond of Rossovich. He used to drop by the house Rossovich and a friend rented their senior year. There was always a wrecked car out front, he said, and a keg of beer inside, and sawdust on the floor for the fake fights they staged. "They were really artistic," said Goux, "bodies hurtling around and bouncing off the walls."

Goux took a visitor on an automobile tour of Rossovich's former haunts: the Sigma Chi house where he had eaten many a glass, the various buildings he had fallen off of. Goux stopped when he came to a one-story frame house on University Avenue, just off fraternity row. The house appeared to be falling apart. The shingles hung like dead leaves. Grass and weeds grew all around. A piece of an automobile lay in the yard. There was a sign, scrawled in red, nailed to the front porch: CURE VIRGINITY.

"It's the same as when Timmy lived there," said Goux. "Exactly the same."

"Ah, that Timbo," said Craig Fertig. "He was a legend."

"HE WAS already a legend when I met him," said Mikey (for Michel) Rossovich, "and he was only a sophomore then. My girl friends were shocked when I told them we were engaged. They said, 'You must be crazy!' They said, 'Don't do it!' "

Smiling, she passed around glasses of iced tea in the living room of the Rossovich home in Manhattan Beach—a leggy, striking brunette in bare feet and short shorts and a T-shirt. Two-year-old Jamie Rossovich sat in the middle of the orange-on-orange rug, engaging in her own exclusive conversation. Tim Rossovich sat on the big billowy sofa, dressed only in green shorts with PHILADEL-PHIA EAGLES embroidered in an arc on the left leg. He said it was his California uniform. His hair, down to his shoulders, was parted in the middle, and he stroked it with both hands. Stephen Stills blared on the stereo and a parrot named Pancho made clicking noises as he chewed a newspaper in his cage.

"I think a lot of it was jealousy because he did things other people only dream of doing," said Mikey. "Some of the things he got blamed for weren't even his fault, but he had a reputation, and he was a little impulsive."

Impulsive?

"He jumped out the window of my sorority house one night. He wasn't supposed to be there, of course, and he heard the security guards were coming. Ran right through the room where my sorority mother, Clemmie, was playing cards and dived head first out the window. The room was on the second floor. I don't think Clemmie even looked up. She knew him pretty well. He'd done $200 worth of damage to a brick wall out front driving in to see me one night."

"I missed the turn," said Rossovich.

"I came running into Clemmie's room looking for him. 'Where's Timmy?' I said. Clemmie pointed to the window and kept on playing cards."

"I landed in a tree," said Rossovich. "Put a hole in my leg. Here." He pointed to a purple mound on his left leg.

There were other scars.

"It was a bad week for me," he added "I fell off two roofs and set fire to myself jumping over a car."

Jumping over a car?

"Well, we used to set fire to cars. We'd buy these old cars for $25, Mike Battle [who played for the Jets] and a few of us, and we'd set 'em on fire or we'd drive one to a big intersection and everybody would jump out and pound it with sledgehammers and saws and things. Sigma Chi was a crazy house. We used to collect bottles in a truck and go back to the house and have bottle fights in the halls. Always seemed to be about six inches of broken glass on the floor and two or three guys at the health center getting stitched up. We were like gunfighters. Every new guy comes to town has to make a challenge. We had a guy announce he was going to sleep for two weeks straight. He did it, too. He woke up just to eat and go to the bathroom."

What about falling off roofs?

"Somebody was always walking around somebody's roof. One guy used to dress up all in black with a clerical collar, and he'd take a bottle of Southern Comfort up on the roof and preach all night. I fell off the third story of the SAE house on my back on a concrete walk. I don't remember exactly why I was up there. My elbow dug into the ground next to the concrete and broke my fall. I was lucky."

Sigma Chi was eventually put on social probation for a number of reasons, Rossovich said, including filling the elevator of the Manix Hotel with water ("when the door opened, swoosh, into the lobby") and piling furniture in the living room of the Theta Chi house and for kissing a passing female motorist, a Mrs. LaFranch, against her wishes.

Rossovich said he had been a party to most, but not all, of these activities. He said the school authorities were aware of his tendencies. He had got to know the dean of men. He said they had been introduced his freshman year, when he walked out onto an eight-inch ledge at the dormitory and stood there. Naked. In broad daylight. He had just come out of the shower, he said.

Why did he do it? the dean asked.

"It was a windy day," said Rossovich. "It seemed like a good way to dry off."

Rossovich's house in Manhattan Beach is two blocks from the beach, where he sometimes runs with Adrian Young, an Irish-born Eagle linebacker who has been his close friend since their playing days at USC. The Rossoviches socialize with the Youngs and communicate on the same wavelength. Adrian's wife Pamela once meditated 13 hours straight in the basic yoga position. They also play volleyball on the beach, and Tim makes his candles there, and often, he says, he just goes there to think.

"The sea is just so big, so massive," he said, lounging on the sofa. "I can go there and feel so at peace. When I can't solve things I go there and when I've had a fight with my wife or something. I think, What am I going to do with my life? With myself? I haven't decided everything. I'd like to have $100,000 in the bank just like anybody else, but to have enough for the things I want is all I really care about. I'd like to contribute something. Adrian and I are going to open a boys' camp at my folks' ranch in Grass Valley. Give kids a chance to see nature, a place where they can throw a pass in the morning and milk a cow in the afternoon."

Rossovich drained his tea glass and jiggled the ice around.

"I have goals. I strive every day to achieve my goals. Some things are out of reach. I'll probably die first. One goal I have is to be completely at peace, to have the kind of peace—like in the movie about Shangri-la."

"*Lost Horizon?*"

"Yeah, with Ronald Colman. I saw that movie on the Late Show the other night. Wouldn't that be wonderful? To live 300 or 400 years and be completely at peace?"

Rossovich was up from the sofa, pacing, smoothing his hair with both hands.

"I live my life to enjoy myself. I can't explain things I do much beyond that. I have more energy than I know what to do with. I can't sit around. I get bored. A lot of what I do is silly, trying to cheer other people up, to cheer myself up. To be funny. To get attention. That's probably the best reason, to get attention."

His visitor said he had only heard of people eating glass, that he'd never seen it done. Rossovich took the empty tea glass and bit down through the lip. The glass shattered. Faint pulverizing noises could be heard as he chewed on it perfunctorily. Mikey screamed. "Timmy! I've been saving those glasses!"

"I'm willing to experience things," said Rossovich. "People should be willing to experience as much as they can. People should be able to do what they want without being concerned what others might think. I had a talk with Jerry Williams [the Eagles' head coach] about my hair. He listened. He didn't agree, but he listened.

"I respect authority. My objective is to be a good football player, not make waves. So I'll get my hair cut." He felt his hair. "Some of it. I'm subdued now, just thinking about it."

He sat down on the couch, subdued. "Everything about football can make you a better person. Teach you to react better to crises. Teach you responsibility. To be levelheaded. To make split-second decisions. It *is* brutal at times, of course, but that's part of it. I'm more physical than I should be, but it's a physical game. I like to hit people when I'm on the field. If I can't make the tackle, I turn around and knock somebody down. I see somebody loafing and I bring it to his attention by knocking him down. He's the enemy. Hit the enemy. That's what it's all about. Next time he'll be more alert.

"The harder I hit people the better I like it. When you hit a guy and he hits the ground hard, and his eyeballs roll, and you see it, and he looks up at you and knows you see it, then you've conquered him. It's a great feeling. I would love to do that, to put the quarterback, the halfback and the split end out of a game. Just the game, not the season. They have families, too. But I wouldn't feel guilty about that.

"But I don't go out there just to beat up a guy. I play to get respect. For me to hear a teammate say, 'Good job,' is more important than fans yelling or sportswriters writing about me. They don't realize what you do for a team. You break your fingers. You bleed. That's the thing about football, the thing about working together, being together."

Mikey brought in another round of iced tea and cautioned him to keep his teeth to himself. She said she was making beef Bourguignon for dinner, the Youngs were invited, and she needed money to get wine. She said her personal preference was that Tim cut it a *little* shorter, so that it stood out around his head rather than hanging like sausages.

Tim made a face and swore. When she had gone he was quiet for a while. Then he said, "We're thinking about adopting a child. You know, there are a lot of kids in this world without homes."

THE PHILADELPHIA EAGLES' training camp at Albright College in Reading, Pa., is like football training camps everywhere. The players live in a college dormitory (neat, cramped rooms), eat in a college cafeteria (nutritious food bereft of flavor), practice on an adequate small-college field and at night sample the inadequate small-town night life. The place the Eagles tend to go in Reading is a bowling alley called Heister Lanes, which has a lounge and, most evenings, a group of musicians.

Tim Rossovich is a regular at Heister's. He is, apart from the group, the only real attraction. He can usually be found hovering by the cigarette machine, a beer in his hand and a contemplative look on his face, watching, watching. One night a group of schoolteachers came in and took three tables. Rossovich, lingering nearby, watched as they had the tables shoved together. Then, when they were seated and conversing, he glided over and fell full-length across the tables, face up, and announced, "Do whatever you want to me, ladies."

Rossovich is the most popular Eagle. Photographers hound him. Kids with autograph books chase him. Grown-ups sit in the sun behind the ropes at Albright Field and scan the roster sheets looking for his number. "Which one is Rossovich?" "I gotta see Rossovich."

He is not hard to find. He is the one who seems always to do things out of tune, as though an ordinary push-up or a sit-up or a run through the ropes had undiscovered facets. Coaches do not object to this because he is not malingering. His enthusiasm, if unorthodox, is genuine. Jerry Williams believes Rossovich "would practice all day and night if I wanted him to." Williams converted him from defensive end to middle linebacker last fall. Rossovich said it was like a tonic, the change, "like an offensive guard being told he was going to play quarterback." He threw himself into the job. Literally, of course.

Otherwise, his coaches would just as soon not talk about Rossovich, as though to admit knowing too much would somehow discredit the game. They adopt a kind of "exactly which freak are you talking about?" tone. "No, I wouldn't know about that." "No, I never saw him do that, I don't really pay that much attention." "Well, yes, I suppose you would say he's a character, but you know how rumors are." They cannot always ignore him, though. At lunch in the dining hall the other day he leaped up from the table with a letter he had been reading, held it up and shouted, "Sexual distraction! Sexual distraction!" Then he grinned and disappeared. At those times there is nothing to do but laugh with everybody else.

And then there is the dream.

"I have this dream," Tim Rossovich says. "I've had it more than once. It's always the same."

Yes?

"It's the Super Bowl. We're in it, and the game is almost over. So far I've made every tackle. Every single tackle in the game! Everybody is going crazy. My teammates, the coaches, the fans. So excited. I'm excited."

Yes? Yes?

"We're ahead by a couple of points, but they're down near our goal, and their quarterback rolls out on the last play of the game. I don't know who he is. His face is empty in the helmet. But I get to him just as he nears the goal. We meet head on. The top of my helmet rams into his chin and *goes right through his head*. His head explodes and comes out the two earholes of his helmet. We both go down—"

He flops down on a couch. Flump!

"—the quarterback dead on the field, me mortally wounded. But I get up and begin to stagger off the field. Millions of people are cheering. 'Rossovich! Rossovich!' It's the greatest game and the greatest crowd ever. Millions of people. I'm reeling as I come off. I give them one last regal wave—"

He waves feebly but regally.

"—and collapse to the ground, dead. I feel myself floating, floating up to Heaven. Happy. Forever." Ahhh!

Laughing on The Outside

BY JOHN SCHULIAN

Josh Gibson, the greatest slugger never to play in the major leagues, was a genial teammate and an athletic marvel to his fellow Negro leaguers. But, in the end, he remained a tragic mystery to everyone who knew him.

PICTURE THIS: A BOY RACING TO THE BARBERSHOP, REVELING in his newfound freedom from his mother's hand, his pace accelerated by the thought that a black man's world is beckoning. There are no appointments at Scotty's, just three chairs and a wait that always eats up the clock. But the boy doesn't mind as long as the men are talking, and they always seem to be doing that, these cops, longshoremen and layabouts. Hour after hour they carry on as if there were no place they would rather be than here, where the only other sources of entertainment are a girlie calendar from *Jet* magazine and a transistor radio with a coat hanger for an antenna.

The men meander from topic to topic—politics, race, sex—and almost everything the boy hears is an education, especially about the action between the sheets. The one subject he feels fit to comment on is baseball. When the men ask him who his favorite players are, he has their names ready: Mays, Aaron, Clemente and, oh yeah, Richie Allen. Got to put Allen in there, because this is Philadelphia, and it's 1964, and he's hitting the ball so hard for the Phillies that he seems more an aspiring deity than a rookie.

Scotty gazes solemnly at the boy from behind the number 1 chair. He's the oracle of the shop, always has something certifiably intelligent to say, and when the boy looks back at him, Scotty seems as old as the blues, though he's probably only in his 40s. "You never heard of Josh Gibson?" the barber asks. The boy is puzzled. Why, no, he never has. And that is when the deluge begins. At first it's just Scotty, but pretty soon all the men are chiming in with stories. About Gibson hitting more homers than anybody—black, white or whatever. About the way Gibson and Satchel Paige tuned each other up for the greater glory of the Negro leagues. About Gibson dying of a broken heart because he never got a chance to take a swing in the Jim Crow major leagues. About Gibson still having the last laugh because he pounded a home run clean out of Yankee Stadium, and nobody else, not even Babe Ruth himself, ever did that.

As far as the men are concerned, you don't put any other hitter in the same sentence with Josh Gibson, least of all some damn rookie. When the boy finally leaves the barbershop, still trying to wrap his mind around everything he has heard, his one overriding thought is, Man, if this guy's better than Richie Allen. . . .

The boy will check for himself, for that is his nature long before he becomes known as Gerald Early, professor of English and African-American studies at Washington University in St. Louis and author of an award-winning collection of essays, *The Culture of Bruising*. He has a passion for books and a trust in the wisdom they hold. So he goes to the library and digs out every volume of baseball history he can find. In none of them is there so much as a word about Gibson. All the stories that the men at the barbershop offered up as gospel might as well be vapor.

WE KNOW just enough about Josh Gibson now to forget him. It's a perverse kind of progress, a strange step up from the days when the mention of his name drew blank looks. He has been a Hall of Fame catcher since 1972, so that's a start. And you can always remind people that he got the Ken Burns treatment on public television, or that he was a character in an HBO movie, or that he inspired Negro leagues memorabilia harking back to his old ball club, the Homestead Grays. Any of it will do to jog memories. *Josh Gibson, sure. Hit all those home runs, didn't he?* Then he's gone once more, gone as soon as he's remembered.

It happened again in the last two seasons as Mark McGwire and Sammy Sosa woke the long-ball ghosts with their history-making thunder. Suddenly the Babe and Roger Maris were leading a parade out of the mists of the past, counting cadence for Hank Greenberg, Jimmie Foxx and Mickey Mantle. Baseball grew misty over the musty, as only it can, and a grand time was had by all—except anyone who cared about Gibson.

He drew so few mentions that if you didn't know better, you would have wondered if he ever really picked up a bat. His obscurity recalled that of Jackie Robinson, a mystery to far too many African-American ballplayers three years ago, on the 50th anniversary of his shattering of baseball's color line.

But Robinson made it to the mountaintop, and in doing so he helped set the stage for Martin Luther King Jr. and Muhammad Ali, *Brown v. Board of Education* and the Civil Rights Act of 1964. For Gibson, there was none of that, only booze and dope and busted dreams.

Whatever pain he died with lives on in the Negro leaguers who played with him, against him and maybe even for him if they were fortunate enough to walk where he never could. "I almost hate to talk about Josh," says Hall of Famer Monte Irvin, who jumped from the Negro leagues to the New York Giants in 1949. "It makes me sad, for one thing, on account of he didn't get to play in the major leagues. Then, when you tell people how great he was, they think you're exaggerating."

But that's what greatness is: an exaggeration. Of talent, of charisma, of the acts that live long after the athletes we deem legendary have shuffled off this mortal coil. So it is with Gibson, who opened Irvin's eyes in 1937 by hitting a simple grounder so hard that it knocked the shortstop who caught it backward. Then there was the night in McKeesport, Pa., as Irvin's Newark Eagles played Gibson's Grays, when Gibson bashed a homer and the mayor stopped the game until the ball was found, because he'd never seen one hit that far. "I played with Willie Mays and against Hank Aaron," Irvin says. "They were tremendous players, but they were no Josh Gibson."

This is different from Roy Campanella telling one and all that he couldn't carry Gibson's mitt. Or Walter Johnson arguing that Gibson was better than Bill Dickey in the days when Dickey was the benchmark for catchers. Or Dizzy Dean, a true son of the South, wishing his St. Louis Cardinals would sign Gibson—and Satchel Paige—so they could wrap up the pennant by the Fourth of July and go fishing until World Series time. Irvin, with his proclamation, leaves himself no wiggle room. He doesn't just count Gibson among the game's greats; he ranks him first.

To help make his case, Irvin paints a picture of a ninth-grade dropout from Pittsburgh who grew up to become John Henry in baseball flannels: 210 pounds of muscle sculpted on a 6' 2" frame, with the speed of a sprinter and a throwing arm that cut down would-be base stealers with lightning bolts. There is no mention of the fact that Gibson was less than artistic behind the plate—"a boxer" for the way he jabbed at the ball, in the estimation of his otherwise admiring former teammate, Ted (Double Duty) Radcliffe. Likewise, Irvin remains silent on Gibson's struggles with pop-ups. Dwelling on shortcomings doesn't burnish a legend, and Irvin knows it. Better to concentrate on Gibson at the plate. "You saw him hit," Irvin says, "and you took your hat off."

You might even use that hat to fan yourself, so overheated are the statistics Gibson left behind: a .354 batting average for his 17 years in the Negro leagues, .373 for two summers in Mexico, .353 for two winters in Cuba. "Lifetime .300 and a whole lot," croons Buck O'Neil, the old Kansas City Monarch with a gift for euphonious phrasing. "He come up there righthanded, kind of a wide stance, didn't take much of a stride. But great shoulders, great wrists. Hit that ball a long way all over."

Gibson's statistical pinnacle was the .517 average he parked in the middle of the Grays' 1943 lineup. It looks like a typo, but *The Baseball Encyclopedia* says .517 is really what the man hit. He did it using bats and balls that were inferior to the ones big leaguers used. More significant, he did it with people arguing that his average wouldn't be so fat if he had to hit against white pitchers. These same doubters, however, never would have dreamed of belittling the Babe's 60 homers or Ted Williams's .406 season or Joe DiMaggio's 56-game hitting streak because they faced nary a pitcher of color. So maybe Gibson delivered his most important message by batting .412 against the big leaguers on autumn barnstorming tours that the black teams dominated. Says O'Neil: "He wanted to prove he wasn't inferior to anybody."

Gibson made his point with his batting average, then made it again by hitting so many home runs that only the blind and bigoted dared ignore him. If you embrace everything you hear, there were 962 homers—including 75 in 1931, 69 in 1934 and, brace yourself, 84 in 1936. But not even the greatest Gibson advocate will try to convince you that box scores are available to document all the homers with which Gibson is credited. Nor are you expected to believe that every pitcher to whom he laid waste was prime beef. There were too many games against semipros and independent teams, too many games played for the sole purpose of making enough money to get to the next backwater town and the next rocky diamond. That was life on the fringe, where black baseball existed.

Yet when Negro league teams went head-to-head, the competition matched that in the big leagues—and Gibson, predictably, was up to the challenge. Witness his 11 homers in 23 games in 1936, his seven in 12 games in '37 and his 17 in 29 games in '39. "If you factored in what he did in league games over the old 154-game schedule," says Negro leagues historian John B. Holway, "he would have broken Ruth's record at least three times."

It is doubtful that any of the old-timers at Scotty's barbershop knew that or would have put much stock in it if they had. Statistics were for kids and white people. The barbershop regulars wanted something more out of baseball, something they could feel the way they felt a Charlie Parker saxophone solo. "They were like African-Americans everywhere," Gerald Early says. "They connected to baseball in a different way from white Americans. They built stories, they built myths, and those tended to become the sole reality."

Thus the tale of how Gibson, alone among men, hit a home run out of Yankee Stadium. It would have been in September 1930, just months after he joined the Grays at age 18. They were playing the Lincoln Giants when he caught hold of a pitch thrown by the estimable Connie Rector and sent it soaring into never-never land. "I heard it bounced off the subway train," whispers Orlando Cepeda, sounding more like the awed child whose father played with Gibson in Puerto Rico than the slugger whose own plaque is in Cooperstown. Everybody has *heard* something about the homer—that's the problem. Nobody has ever found a shred of documentation, not even in a newspaper story about the game. The best guess is that the ball landed in the far reaches of the left-centerfield bullpen. Not that saying so will stop anyone from telling the story. Not that anyone will cease using it as a springboard to all the other home runs that fueled Gibson's mythology.

Some homers you can document, like the one he launched out of Forbes Field in Pittsburgh, a feat duplicated by only a select group that includes Ruth and Willie Stargell. Other shots are forever confined to folklore, like the one that supposedly knocked a public-address speaker off the grandstand roof in Washington's Griffith Stadium. "I didn't see it," confesses Don Newcombe, a workhorse righthander for the Newark Eagles and the Brooklyn Dodgers, "but that's what the other players said." Of course they did.

Ninety-seven-year-old Double Duty Radcliffe—nicknamed by Damon Runyon after he pitched one game of a doubleheader and caught the other—is still telling people about an old lady who thought she was safe watching Gibson from the rocking chair on her front porch. "Wasn't no fence in this particular park," Radcliffe recalls. "Someplace in Pennsylvania, I think it was. She's way out there in centerfield rockin' away when Josh hits one. And . . . and. . . . " Radcliffe erupts in laughter made raspy by a lifetime of cigars. "Josh made that old lady jump."

But of all the stories inspired by Gibson's homers, one resonates most memorably about his life and times. It comes from an article his son, Josh Jr., clipped out of the *Pittsburgh Press* years ago. In it the retiring mayor of suburban Dormont talked of the day in 1933 that he saw Josh hit a home run out of the local ballpark, over a flagpole and across a street, 470 feet if it was an inch. There were 500 people in the stands, but when they passed the hat, $66 was the best they could come up with in the heart of the Depression. The umpires and ball-chasers got paid first, and the two teams had to divvy up the $44 that remained. Josh's share was $1.67.

IT WAS a life on the run, and in the days when he could get away with ignoring real-world complications, he thrived on it. Didn't matter how many whistlestops he rolled into in the dead of night, or how many bug-infested hotels he slept in, or how many times he was turned away in restaurants by the same white people who cheered his slugging. Josh was going to be Josh: a muscle-stuffed scamp who teased opposing batters by throwing dirt on their shoes and who menaced pitchers by rolling up his sleeves to show off his biceps.

He never said much, but talking wasn't his game. Hitting was. When he had finished another day's work at the plate, he would climb back onto the bus that was his cocoon. It seemed as if nothing could touch him there. All he had to do to keep his teammates happy was lean out the window when they passed another ball club's bus and say what he always said: "Same team won today is gonna win tomorrow." Hell, it even kept the other ball club happy. This wasn't just anybody needling them. It was Josh Gibson.

They called him "the black Babe Ruth," but he was more than that. He was a 1,000-watt celebrity in the parallel universe that spawned him, and his star shone brightest whenever he rolled into one of the big cities on the Negro leagues' endless caravan: New York or D.C. or sweet home Pittsburgh. He would hit the jazz clubs then, places that were to black players what Toots Shor's was to the Yankees, and he would rub shoulders with Lena Horne, Duke Ellington and the Mills Brothers as if they were old friends. After a while maybe they were, because they let Gibson get up and sing with the band, sing something smoky or swinging in that rich voice of his.

Pittsburgh's hot club was the Crawford Grille, up on what the locals still know as the Hill. Gus Greenlee ran it with the money he made in the numbers racket, and when he branched out into the Negro National League, he bought Gibson. And Paige. And fearsome, hard-hitting Oscar Charleston. They were the engine that drove the Pittsburgh Crawfords in the '30s, and surely they would have lasted far longer if Greenlee hadn't run afoul of the IRS. Then, in 1937, Gibson went back to the Homestead Grays, back where he had started and where he would finish.

There was heartbreak at both ends of his journey, though the focus usually falls on his premature death, at 35. Overlooked too often is what he faced 17 years earlier, when he was just a kid with a big future in baseball and a pregnant girlfriend who became his wife. The former Helen Mason was 17 when she gave birth to twins, then died before she could hold them in her arms.

From that day forward Gibson didn't stop running until he, too, was in his grave. Fatherhood scarcely slowed him. Indeed, it might have done just the opposite. Says James A. Riley, director of research for the Negro Leagues Baseball Museum in Kansas City: "Every time he saw those kids, he thought of his wife." The thought, if you accept Riley's theory, was more than Gibson could bear.

His wife's family fought to change his rambling ways. They were strong Baptists who had been lured out of the South by the clang of Pittsburgh's steel mills, just the way Gibson's family had. The Masons weren't about to stand by while Gibson chose a mere game over the son who bore his name and the daughter who bore Helen's. "There was incredible bitterness," says Ken Solarz, the Hollywood screenwriter who sent a love letter to the Negro leagues with his 1979 documentary *Only the Ball Was White*. "Can you imagine what it was like when his wife's family told him he had to quit baseball and raise those children? It must have been devastating." It was also ineffective.

Josh Jr., 69 and twice the recipient of a kidney transplant, approaches the issue gingerly, conceding only that he was raised by his maternal grandmother and that growing up he didn't see much of his father. "They used to say the Negro leagues never dropped the ball," Josh Jr. says, "so my father, he was always off playing somewhere." Big Josh spent his summers Stateside, coming back to Pittsburgh every two weeks or so. In the winters he set sail for Latin America and the paydays to be had there. When he returned, it was always with gifts. "Good leather stuff for me and my sister," Josh Jr. says. An empty, groping moment passes. "And we were glad to see him."

The awkwardness of those words is amplified when the son recalls how he and his sister romped in a field across the street from the house where their father lived with his common-law wife. "We never knew her name," Josh Jr. says.

He thought things would change when he turned 11 and big Josh invited him to travel with the Grays as their batboy for two weeks. This was to be the bonding mechanism for father and son, a ritual that would continue for the next three summers. When Josh Jr. thinks back, however, his memories run mainly to his father's home runs, the art of living on $2 a day in meal money, and riding the team bus with the legend who begat him. They were supposed to sit together up front, Josh and Junior, but once the bus was on the road, the boy always found himself alone. His father had left him to play gin rummy in the back with the other Grays. It didn't matter where big Josh was; he couldn't stop running.

It's a different kind of crack of the bat. I'll tell you what, you listen to a .22 rifle, and then you listen to a .30-30. That's the difference right there.
—BUCK O'NEIL

IF YOU insist on calling the story that follows apocryphal, keep in mind that Buck O'Neil has been dining out on it for years, and he isn't about to stop. It begins sometime in the 1920s with Buck lurking behind the outfield fence in Sarasota, Fla., fresh out of the celery fields where he usually toiled, and surrounded by kids as hungry as he was. They were there to track down the balls that sailed over the fence and sell them to tourists eager for spring-training souvenirs. Never mind that the Yankees had rolled into town with their Murderers' Row. This was strictly business.

And then it wasn't. As the longest ball of the day soared into view and the take-no-prisoners race for it began, young Buck stood stock-still, mesmerized by the crack of the bat. "Oh, a beautiful sound," he says more than 70 years later, as rhapsodic as if he'd been the first to hear Heifetz or Hendrix. In an instant Buck was climbing the nearest pine tree, going up the wooden slats that kids had nailed into it as steps so they could watch games without paying. "When I got to the top," he says, "I saw this guy with a big barrel chest and skinny legs and a beautiful swing." Dramatic pause. "It was Babe Ruth."

A decade or so later, O'Neil was the Kansas City Monarchs' first baseman, and the first time he suited up in Griffith Stadium to face the Grays, he heard it again. That wondrous sound. "So I ran out of the clubhouse, through the dugout and onto the field," O'Neil says. "There was this beautiful black sucker. Big chest, broad shoulders, about 34 inches in the waist. That was Josh Gibson. Hitting the ball, making it sound just like Babe Ruth. I'm standing there taking it all in when I hear people laughing, people applauding. I look around, trying to find out what's the matter, and one of my teammates says, 'Buck, you got nothing on but your jockey strap.'"

O'Neil returned to the clubhouse embarrassed but wiser, for he knew he had the perfect standard for assessing sluggers. They had to match the Babe's sound, and Josh's. If you think it's easily done, be advised that when O'Neil traveled to St. Louis last year, McGwire flunked the test.

OH, THERE were some players back in the day—Cool Papa Bell and Mule Suttles, Ray Dandridge, Leon Day and Martin Dihigo. Legions of them when you get right down to it, men who make you want to weep for having missed out on seeing the Negro leagues. Yet the two names you always come back to in any discussion of that star-crossed age are the same ones that were on the billboards that shouted, SEE SATCHEL PAIGE STRIKE OUT THE 1ST NINE HITTERS. SEE JOSH GIBSON HIT TWO HOMERS!

Satch and Josh were as big as the type that promised these heroics, for both of them had moved beyond mere greatness into walking immortality. "Emblematic," Gerald Early calls them. "They represented the mythology of the Negro leagues." But when they played together on the Crawfords, everyone had five years to study how different they were as human beings.

"Josh rode the team bus; Satch drove his own car," James A. Riley says. "Josh showed up at the park when he was supposed to; Satch might not show up at all. Satch was a modern ballplayer before there were modern ballplayers." Gibson was a mystery, no matter how good-natured and playful he was.

He would win a game with a homer and have a beer with the guys afterward, but then, if there wasn't a bus to catch and another game waiting at the end of an all-night drive, he would be gone, off into a world all his own, a world he didn't share. Not that Satch ever noticed, as caught up as he was in his own magnitude. There were years when Satch won 70 games (by his count), and his singleness of purpose suggested that he was sizing Gibson up as an opposing hitter even when they were teammates. That was the only mystery Satch cared about.

He told Gibson as much, bless his heart, and both of them would sit there laughing, woofing, each promising to inflict unspeakable cruelty on the other. When these icons went head-to-head, in 1942, the showdown entered the mythos. It was mostly Satch's doing. That cunning rogue was pitching for Kansas City, and, according to legend, when he was one out from beating the Grays, he ignored the runner on third and walked the next two hitters for the express purpose of facing his old teammate. Gibson was so stunned that he watched three straight strikes, the last one on the fastball Satch called "a bee at your knee."

Satch acted as if that gave him bragging rights till the end of time. Josh never said much about it, but he did sidle up to Monte Irvin not long afterward and confide, "Satch is crazy." Publicly, that was all Gibson's pride would allow. Privately, it may have needed balm. Why else would one of the few newspaper clippings he kept be about the day that he went 4 for 4 against Satch at Wrigley Field? Gibson did the same against lots of pitchers, but this was special, this was the great Paige. While he was on base that day, Gibson might even have taunted his fellow legend by hooting, "If you could cook, I'd marry you." If he didn't say it that time, he said it later, or so the story goes. He always did enjoy beating Satch like a rented mule.

IT WAS strange having Josh around that winter. In the past he had headed south on the first thing smoking as soon as the Negro leagues' season was done, not to return until winter was melting. But after he had taken his last swing for the Grays in 1946 and gone to Latin America, illness made him retreat to the row house on Pittsburgh's Bedford Avenue, where his mother-in-law was raising his kids. Once he was there, nothing could get him to leave.

Sam Bankhead, his teammate, drinking buddy and best friend, thought it was just a matter of time before Gibson caved in to the old lures of Caribbean rum, dark-eyed women and December sunshine. "You ain't going back, Josh?" Bankhead kept asking, teasingly at first, then with more and more dismay as he realized that no, Josh wasn't going back. He was getting ready to die.

He had puffed up to 235 pounds, his knees were shot, and the rest of his once-proud body was sending distress signals. He had high blood pressure and a brain tumor that periodically leveled him with headaches. He drank too much, and there was talk that he had found another escape route in drugs. He had woman problems and psychiatric problems. It was no kind of shape for a legend to be in as he turned 35.

How odd—and unfortunate—that even today there are those who want to blame Gibson's demise on the ascension of Jackie Robinson. It's so easy, so poetic to say Gibson died of a broken heart when he realized that baseball's color line would be broken without him in the spring of '47. "That," Early insists, "has been romanticized way out of proportion."

Josh Jr. agrees, and so do most of the Negro leaguers who remember his father best. Talk to them for five minutes, and without prompting, they'll bring up their chagrin at the 1996 HBO movie *Soul of the Game*, which portrays Josh, Satch and Jackie as friends and rivals. "My father didn't even know Jackie Robinson," insists Josh Jr. The inaccuracy is compounded when the movie shows the elder Gibson belittling Robinson as a "house nigger."

"I asked the producers where they got their information," O'Neil says, "and they said, Ernie Banks's son. I said, 'Ernie Banks's son? He wasn't even born yet.'"

If Gibson was crushed by anything beyond his own demons, it wasn't bitterness but disappointment. For too many years his hopes had been raised by the praise of big league managers who coveted his talent, then dashed by the cowardice of team owners afraid to be the first to challenge the game's racist status quo. When Leo Durocher, the Dodgers' manager, dared muse in the early '40s about the joy of writing Gibson's name on his lineup card, commissioner Kenesaw Mountain Landis dressed him down. The Pittsburgh Pirates and Washington Senators also backed off when confronted by the bushy-browed Landis, who preached that there was white baseball and there was black baseball, and never would they meet. The teams got the message, and so did Gibson. "Finally," Riley says, "I think he just said, The hell with it."

Gibson's beverage of choice changed from beer to hard liquor. "Sometimes you could smell him from the night before," Don Newcombe remembers. "It was coming out his pores."

Radcliffe carries the same memory of Gibson. "He was smokin' that reefer too," Duty says.

Many old-timers trace Gibson's problems to a D.C. mobster's wife named Grace. Her husband was in the Army, and Gibson had drifted apart from the woman who shared his bed in Pittsburgh. Things just went from there, drugs and passion fueling Josh and Grace's relationship until the mobster came home and reclaimed his lady. Then Josh was back on his own, and it must have been a scary place to be. There were stays at St. Elizabeth's, a mental hospital in Washington that let him out only for games on weekends. And there were myr-

iad stories about his bizarre behavior, beginning with the one about the teammate who found him talking to a Joe DiMaggio who wasn't there.

Cepeda swears Gibson got arrested in Puerto Rico for running the streets
naked. Newcombe remembers how bad he and the other Newark Eagles felt
for laughing at a story imported from Latin America, about how Gibson slid
in with a double and started looking for the potatoes he said he had planted
under second base. "We wanted to be proud of Josh Gibson," says Newcombe.

By the mid-'40s, however, Gibson may not have even been proud of himself.
The knees that had kept him out of World War II were so bad that it hurt to
watch him trying to crouch behind home plate. Though he had won home
run championships in 1944 and '45 and hit .361 in '46, the power and menace
of old were gone. So he took refuge in the home where his children lived, and
he even shared a bed with Josh Jr. "I'd get up in the morning and go to school,"
his son recalls. "He'd get up and go wherever he wanted to."

On Jan. 20, 1947, almost a month to the day after his 35th birthday and
three months before Jackie Robinson played for the Dodgers, Josh went to
his mother's house, and it was there that he died. Some say a stroke killed
him, others a brain hemorrhage. Or maybe it was just life.

Death didn't treat him any better, letting him lie in an unmarked grave in
Allegheny Cemetery for nearly three decades. Finally, commissioner Bowie
Kuhn joined with one of Gibson's Crawfords teammates in 1975 to buy the
headstone his family couldn't afford. It hails him as a LEGENDARY BASE-
BALL PLAYER, but the words seem too spare, too perfunctory. How much
closer to the truth Newcombe comes when he says, "It's too bad Josh didn't get
a chance to live the life he should have lived."

THEY DON'T talk about Josh Gibson much in barbershops anymore. Too
many years have passed, too many other great players have come down the
pike, too many other shooting stars have flamed out. Even in Pittsburgh, the
launching pad for his greatness, he remains little more than an afterthought.
Mario Lemieux has a street named after him, and Roberto Clemente is honored by a park and a bridge. For years, all Gibson had was a blue-and-gold
plaque designating the site where he played at Greenlee Field, up on the Hill.
The plaque isn't much bigger than a NO PARKING sign, and the Historical
Society of Western Pennsylvania didn't get around to putting it up until 1996.

This year Gibson's likeness appeared on a downtown mural, but even so, all
he really has going for him is his son. "I got to keep my father's name ringing,"
Josh Jr. says. From his Pittsburgh home he travels anywhere he is invited:
minor league ball games, Negro leagues reunions, the Florida Marlins' Opening Day ceremonies last year and, most of all, baseball card shows. Alas, he

doesn't have much to offer in the way of memorabilia, no bats that big Josh used, no catcher's mitts, no spikes with their toes curling.

"The only thing I have of my father's are old newspaper articles he saved," Josh Jr. says. So he puts the articles in a display case, signs autographs for $25 a shot and tells stories about the father who died when he was 16 and left him with a name that has proved as much a burden as a blessing.

"It wasn't easy trying to be Josh Gibson," his son says. For Josh Jr. inherited his father's resonant voice and not much else in the way of gifts. He lacked size, power and a flair for the dramatic. The best thing he could do as a spindly third baseman was run, and that ended after he left the Homestead Grays in 1950 for Canada's Provincial League. He broke an ankle stealing a base and tried to keep playing by deadening the pain with novocaine. When he could run no more, he limped home to a city job slinging trash cans. The job lasted until one of his kidneys gave out 20 years ago, and his struggle intensified in 1985 when hypertension cut short his twin sister's life.

But keeping his father's name alive has given Josh Jr. a reason to soldier on. He travels with his grandson Sean, who, at 30, looks like big Josh: same heft, same round face, same easy smile. "He's learning the history," Josh Jr. says, "because he's going to take over when I die."

The two started a Josh Gibson League for kids in Pittsburgh last year, giving those youthful dreamers a place to learn about the Negro leagues and rack up their own hits, runs and errors. A place where they can hear Josh Jr. say, "The thing I don't like particularly is that people call my father the black Babe Ruth. I'd prefer it if they just called him Josh Gibson."

It is an understandable request, but the truth is, Gibson must be remembered before he can be called anything. In that regard, there is only so much reassurance Josh Jr. can offer himself. He can tell the story of how Johnny Bench stopped him at a card show and said he wished he'd seen big Josh play: one great catcher paying homage to another. Or he can pass along the tales told by the men who played with his father. Mainly it comes down to Josh Jr. sitting at the table in his cramped dining room, pulling something from an envelope and saying, "Here, I got to autograph this for you."

It is a picture of big Josh with the Grays in his prime, his arms thick, his smile shy, almost beguiling. Very carefully, Josh Jr. writes his name in blue ink across his father's shoulder. When a legend is on life support, you do what you have to.

The Best There Ever Was

BY FRANK DEFORD

*The death of Johnny Unitas moved the author, a Baltimore native, to
ponder the achievements of a man who was more than a boyhood hero: He was an
inspiration for the entire city.*

SOMETIMES, EVEN IF IT WAS ONLY YESTERDAY, OR EVEN IF IT just feels like it was only yesterday. . . .

Sometimes, no matter how detailed the historical accounts, no matter how many the eyewitnesses, no matter how complete the statistics, no matter how vivid the film. . . .

Sometimes, I'm sorry, but. . . .

Sometimes, you just had to be there.

That was the way it was with Johnny Unitas in the prime of his life, when he played for the Baltimore Colts and changed a team and a city and a league. Johnny U was an American original, a piece of work like none other, excepting maybe Paul Bunyan and Horatio Alger.

Part of it was that he came out of nowhere, like Athena springing forth full-grown from the brow of Zeus, or like Shoeless Joe Hardy from Hannibal, Mo., magically joining the Senators, compliments of the devil. But that was myth, and that was fiction. Johnny U was real, before our eyes.

Nowadays, of course, flesh peddlers and scouting services identify the best athletes when they are still in junior high. Prospects are not allowed to sneak up on us. But back then, 1956, was a quaint time when we still could be pleasantly surprised. Unitas just surfaced there on the roster, showing up one day after a tryout. The new number 19 was identified as YOU-ni-tass when he first appeared in an exhibition, and only later did we learn that he had played, somewhere between obscurity and anonymity, at Louisville and then, for six bucks a game, on the dusty Pittsburgh sandlots. His was a story out of legend, if not, indeed, out of religious tradition: the unlikely savior come out of nowhere.

The quarterback for the Colts then was George Shaw, the very first pick in the NFL draft the year before, the man ordained to lead a team that was coalescing into a contender. Didn't we wish, in Baltimore! Didn't we dream! The Colts had Alan (the Horse) Ameche and Lenny (Spats) Moore and L.G. (Long Gone) Dupre to carry the ball and Raymond Berry and Jim Mutscheller to catch it and Artie Donovan and Big Daddy Lipscomb and Gino Marchetti to manhandle the other fellows when they had the pigskin. Then one day, as it is written, Shaw got hurt in a game, and YOU-ni-tass came in, hunched of shoulder, trotting kind of funny. He looked *crooked*, is how I always thought of him. Jagged. Sort of a gridiron Abraham Lincoln.

And on the first play the rookie threw a pass that went for a long touchdown. Only it was an interception; the touchdown went the other way.

For those of us in Baltimore, this seemed like the cruelest fate (however likely). Finally Baltimore was going to amount to something, and then, wouldn't you know it, Shaw gets taken from us. It seemed so terribly unfair, if perhaps exactly what we could expect for our workingman's town, where the swells passed through, without stopping, on their way to Washington or New York.

But then, there couldn't have been a mother's son anywhere who knew exactly what Unitas had in store for us. Marchetti, apparently, was the first one to understand. It was a couple of weeks later, and he was lying on the training table when the equipment manager, Fred Schubach, wondered out loud when Shaw might come back. Marchetti raised up a bit and said, "It doesn't matter. Unitas is the quarterback now."

Evidently all the other Colts nodded; they'd just been waiting for someone to dare express what they were beginning to sense. Marchetti had fought in the Battle of the Bulge when he was a teenager and thus, apparently, had developed a keen appreciation for things larger than life.

OF COURSE, no matter who John Constantine Unitas had played football for, it would've been Katie-bar-the-door. But perhaps never has greatness found such a fitting address. It wasn't only that Baltimore had such an inferiority complex, an awareness that all that the stuck-up outlanders knew of our fair city was that we had crabs and white marble steps in profusion and a dandy red-light district, the Block. Since H.L. Mencken (he who had declared, "I

hate all sports as rabidly as a person who likes sports hates common sense")
had died, the most famous Baltimorean was a stripper, Blaze Starr. The city
hadn't had a winner since the Old Orioles of a century past. For that matter,
until very recently Baltimore hadn't even *had* a major league team in the
1900s. Before the Colts arrived in 1947, the best athlete in town was a woman
duckpin bowler named Toots Barger. Football? The biggest games in Baltimore had been when Johns Hopkins took on Susquehanna or Franklin &
Marshall at homecoming.

But no mother ever took her children to her breast as old Bawlmer, Merlin (as we pronounced it), embraced the Colts. It wasn't just that they played
on Sundays and thus finally made us "big league" in the eyes of the rest of a
republic that was rapidly becoming coaxial-cabled together. No, the Colts
were just folks, all around town, at crab feasts and bull roasts and what-have-
you. Why, I knew I could go a few blocks to Moses' Sunoco station on York
Road and see a bunch of Colts there, hanging out, kicking tires. Had I had a
good enough fake I.D., I could've even gotten into Sweeney's, up Greenmount
Avenue, and drunk beer with them. The Colts were real people, so we loved
them even more as they went on their merry way to becoming champions of
the world.

With each passing game, though, Unitas elevated above the others until,
on Dec. 28, 1958, he entered the pantheon of gods. 'Twas then, of course, in
Yankee Stadium itself, that he led us from behind to an overtime victory over
the despised New Yorkers in the Greatest Game Ever Played. Yet even as we
deified him, we still had it on the best authority that he remained one of the
boys. Just because he was quarterback, he wasn't some glamour-puss.

Certainly he didn't look the part of a hero. This is how his teammate Alex
Hawkins described Unitas when Hawkins first saw him in the locker room:
"Here was a total mystery. [Unitas] was from Pennsylvania, but he looked so
much like a Mississippi farmhand that I looked around for a mule. He had
stooped shoulders, a chicken breast, thin bowed legs and long, dangling arms
with crooked, mangled fingers."

Unitas didn't even have a quarterback's name. All by himself he redrew the
profile of the quarterback. Always, before, it had been men of Old Stock who
qualified to lead the pros. Baugh and Albert and Van Brocklin and Layne and
Graham. (All right, Luckman was a Jew, but he was schooled in the WASP-y
Ivy League.) Unitas was some hardscrabble Lithuanian, so what he did made
a difference, because even if we'd never met a Lithuanian before, we knew
that he was as smart a sonuvabitch as he was tough. Dammit, he was *our*
Lithuanian.

They didn't have coaches with headphones and Polaroids and fax machines then, sitting on high, telling quarterbacks what plays to call. In those halcyon days, quarterbacks were field generals, not field lieutenants. And there was Unitas after he called a play (and probably checked off and called another play when he saw what the ruffians across the line were up to), shuffling back into the pocket, unfazed by the violent turbulence all around him, standing there in his hightops, waiting, looking, poised. I never saw war, so that is still my vision of manhood: Unitas standing courageously in the pocket, his left arm flung out in a diagonal to the upper deck, his right cocked for the business of passing, down amidst the mortals. Lock and load.

There, to Berry at the sideline. Or Moore. Or Jimmy Orr real long. Lenny Lyles. John Mackey. Hawkins. Ameche out of the backfield. My boyhood memory tells me Johnny U never threw an incompletion, let alone an interception, after that single debut mistake. Spoilsports who keep the numbers dispute that recollection, but they also assure me that he threw touchdown passes in 47 straight games. That figure has been threatened less seriously than even DiMaggio's sacred 56. Yes, I know there've been wonderful quarterbacks since Unitas hung up his hightops. I admit I'm prejudiced. But the best quarterback ever? The best player? Let me put it this way: If there were one game scheduled, Earth versus the Klingons, with the fate of the universe on the line, any person with his wits about him would have Johnny U calling the signals in the huddle, up under the center, back in the pocket.

I'VE ALWAYS wondered how people in olden times connected back to their childhoods. After all, we have hooks with the past. When most of us from the 20th century reminisce about growing up, we right away remember the songs and the athletes of any particular moment. Right?

A few years ago I saw Danny and the Juniors performing at a club, and all anybody wanted them to sing was *At the Hop*, which was their No. 1 smash back in 1958, the year Unitas led the Colts to that first, fabled championship. About a year after I saw Danny, I read that he had committed suicide. I always assumed it was because no matter how many years had passed, nobody would let him escape from singing *At the Hop*, exactly as he did in 1958.

Unlike songs, athletes, inconveniently, get on. They grow old. Johnny U couldn't keep on throwing passes. He aged. He even let his crew cut grow out. Luckily for me, after I grew up (as it were) and became a sportswriter, I never covered him. Oh, I went to his restaurant, and I saw him on TV, and I surely never forgot him. Whenever Walter Iooss, the photographer, and I would get together, we would talk about Johnny U the way most men talk about caressing beautiful women. But I never had anything to do with Unitas professionally. That was good. I could keep my boy's memories unsullied.

Then, about five years ago, I finally met him for real, at a party. When we were introduced he said, "It's nice to meet you, Mr. Deford." That threw me into a tailspin. *No, no, no. Don't you understand? I'm not Mr. Deford. You're Mr. Unitas. You're Johnny U. You're my boyhood idol. I can't ever be Mr. Deford with you, because you have to always be number 19, so I can always be a kid.* But I didn't explain that to him. I was afraid he would think I was too sappy. I just said, "It's nice to meet you, too, Mr. Unitas," and shook his crippled hand.

A couple of years later I went down to Baltimore and gave a speech for a charity. What they gave me as a thank-you present was a football, autographed by Himself. When you're not a child anymore and you write about athletes, you tend to take 'em as run-of-the-mill human beings. Anyway, I do. I have only one other athlete's autograph, from Bill Russell, who, along with Unitas, is the other great star of the '50s who changed his sport all by himself.

After I got that autographed Unitas football, every now and then I'd pick it up and fondle it. I still do, too, even though Johnny Unitas is dead now, and I can't be a boy anymore. Ultimately, you see, what he conveyed to his teammates and to Baltimore and to a wider world was the utter faith that he could do it. He could make it work. Somehow, he could win. He *would* win. It almost didn't matter when he actually couldn't. The point was that with Johnny U, it always seemed possible. You so very seldom get that, even with the best of them. Johnny U's talents were his own. The belief he gave us was his gift.

Acknowledgments

HE STORIES COLLECTED HERE REPRESENT THE CUMULATIVE efforts of several generations of SPORTS ILLUSTRATED writers and editors. But this book would not have been possible without the contributions of many current members of the SI staff, who somehow found time, while putting out a weekly magazine, to work tirelessly on this project: Bob Roe, Kevin Kerr, Steve Hoffman, Jodi Napolitani, Chris Hercik, Craig Gartner, Linda Verigan, Peggy Terry, Natasha Simon, Barbara Fox and Gabe Miller. And special thanks to Peter Carry, who got the ball rolling.